JOHN CATT'S

Which School?

2019

Published in 2018 by
John Catt Educational Ltd,
15 Riduna Park,
Melton, Suffolk IP12 1QT UK
Tel: 01394 389850
Fax: 01394 386893
Email: enquiries@johncatt.com
Website: www.johncatt.com

A CIP catalogue record for this book is available from the British
Library.

ISBN: 978 1 911382911

Contacts

Editor
Jonathan Barnes
Email: jonathanbarnes@johncatt.com

Advertising & School Profiles
Tel: +44 (0) 1394 389850
Email: sales@johncatt.com

Distribution/Book Sales
Tel: +44 (0) 1394 389863
Email: booksales@johncatt.com

Website: www.schoolsearch.co.uk

Contents

How to use this guide

Which School? has been specifically designed with the reader in mind. There are clearly defined sections providing information for anyone looking at independent education in the UK today.

Are you looking for help and advice? Take a look at our editorial section (pages 5-42). Here you will find articles written by experts in their field covering a wide variety of issues you are likely to come across when choosing a school for your child. Each year we try to find a differing range of topics to interest and inform you about the uniqueness of independent education.

Perhaps you are looking for a school or college in a certain geographical region? Then you need to look first in the directories, which begin on page D293. Here you will find basic information about all the schools in each region complete with contact details. From this section you will be directed to more detailed information in the guide where this is available. An example of a typical directory entry is given below.

Are you looking for a certain type of school or college in your local area? Then you will need to look in the directories for your local area (see contents page for a list of all regions). Underneath each school you will find icons that denote the different types of schools or the qualifications that they offer.

Some of you may already be looking for a specific school or college. In which case, if you know the name of the school or college but are unsure of its location, simply go to the index at the back of the guide where you will find all the schools listed alphabetically. Page numbers prefixed with the letter D denote the directory section; those without, a detailed profile.

If, however, you need to find out more information on relevant educational organisations and examinations, then you can look in the appendices where you will find up-to-date information about the examinations and qualifications available (page 405). There is also a section giving basic details about the many varied and useful organisations in the education field (page 427).

The profile and directory information in this guide is also featured on **www.schoolsearch.co.uk**, which also includes social media links, and latest school news.

Key to directory

County ——————— **Wherefordshire**

Name of school or college ——————— **College Academy**

Indicates that this school has a profile ——————— *For further details see p. 12*

Address and contact number ———{ Which Street, Whosville, Wherefordshire AB12 3CD

Tel: 01000 000000

Head's name ——————— **Head Master:** Dr A Person

Age range ——————— **Age range:** 11–18

Number of pupils. ——————— **No. of pupils:** 660 B330 G330 VIth 200
B = boys G = girls VIth = sixth form

Fees per annum. ——————— **Fees:** Day £11,000 WB £16,000 FB £20,000
Day = fees for day pupils.
WB = fees for weekly boarders.
FB = fees for full boarders.

Key to directory icons

Key to symbols:
- ⊛ Boys' school
- ⊛ Girls' school
- ⊕ International school
- ⒃ Tutorial or sixth form college

Schools offering:
- Ⓐ A levels
- ⊛ Boarding accommodation
- ⓔ Bursaries
- ⒃ Entrance at 16+
- ⒾⒷ International Baccalaureate
- ⊘ Learning support
- ⊛ Vocational qualifications

The questions you should ask

However much a school may appeal on first sight, you still need sound information to form your judgement

Schools attract pupils by their reputations, so most go to considerable lengths to ensure that parents are presented with an attractive image.

Modern marketing techniques try to promote good points and play down (without totally obscuring) bad ones. But every Head knows that, however good the school prospectus is, it only serves to attract parents through the school gates. Thereafter the decision depends on what they see and hear.

When you choose a school for your son or daughter, the key factor is that it will suit them. Many children and their parents are instinctively attracted (or otherwise) to a school on first sight. But even if it passes this test, and 'conforms' to what you are looking for in terms of location and academic, pastoral and extracurricular aspects, you will need to satisfy yourself that the school does measure up to what your instincts tell you.

Research we have carried out over the years suggests that in many cases the most important factor in choosing a school is the impression given by the Head. As well as finding out what goes on in a school, parents need to be reassured by the aura of confidence which they expect from a Head. How they discover the former may help them form their opinion of the latter.

So how a Head answers your questions is important. Based on our research, we have drawn up a list of 24 points on which you may need to be satisfied. The order in which they appear below does not necessarily reflect their degree of importance to each parent, but how the Head answers them may help you draw your own conclusions:

- How accessible is the Head, whose personality is seen by most parents as setting the 'tone' of the school?
- Will your child fit in? What is the overall atmosphere?
- To which organisations does the school belong? How has it been accredited?
- What is the ratio of teachers to pupils?
- What are the qualifications of the teaching staff?
- How often does the school communicate with parents through reports, parent/teacher meetings or other visits?
- What is the school's retention rate? Do larger lower classes and smaller upper classes reflect a school's inability to hang on to pupils?
- What are the school's exam results? What are the criteria for presenting them? Are they consistent over the years?
- How does the school cope with pupils' problems?
- What sort of academic and pastoral advice is available?
- What is the school's attitude to discipline?
- Have there been problems with drugs or sex? How have they been dealt with?
- What positive steps are taken to encourage good manners, behaviour and sportsmanship?

- Is progress accelerated for the academically bright?
- How does the school cope with pupils who do not work?
- What is the attitude to religion?
- What is the attitude to physical fitness and games?
- What sports are offered and what are the facilities?
- What are the extracurricular activities? What cultural or other visits are arranged away from the school?
- What steps are taken to encourage specific talent in music, the arts or sport?
- Where do pupils go when they leave – are they channelled to a few selected destinations?
- What is the uniform? What steps are taken to ensure that pupils take pride in their personal appearance?
- What are the timetable and term dates?
- Is it possible to speak to parents with children at the school to ask them for an opinion?

Why our independent schools remain the envy of the world

Barnaby Lenon, chair of the Independent Schools Council, looks at the strength of the sector

This is a golden age for independent schools. At A-level, to take just one example, nearly half of independent school subjects were graded A* or A in 2018 compared to 22% for all other sixth form pupils in the UK. The Sunday Times Parent Power tables combined GCSE and A-level results for both state and independent schools: the top 10 schools were all independent schools and 42 out of the top 50 were independent schools. Research by the Centre for Evaluation and Monitoring at the University of Durham and the most recent OECD PISA test results both showed that pupils in independent schools were one to two years ahead of state school pupils of similar ability.

Independent schools are propping-up key subjects which have declined in state schools. This is especially true of Latin, Greek, music, French, German and Spanish as well as hard sciences. In maths and science independent school candidates comprise one fifth of all A-level entries but achieve nearly one third of all A* grades. Independent school pupils are five times more likely to apply to university for modern languages than those from other sectors.

The Gove reforms to the exams system implemented many changes that independent schools asked for: fewer exams, less resitting, the end of modules, the end of January exams, more stretching GCSE syllabuses, more differentiation at the top end of the GCSE grading scale, an end to grade inflation. Despite some moaning in the newspapers, these reforms were in fact all good developments.

A high proportion of students at the top universities are educated at our schools and many of these go on to very successful careers. Independent school actors, musicians, sportsmen, sportswomen and politicians, including in the Labour Party (!), are prominent.

Independently educated students get better degree results and earn higher salaries. HEFCE research found that of independent school pupils 82% got 1sts and 2:1s, compared to 73% for state school students. Research by the Social Market Foundation found that by the age of 42 a privately-educated person will have earned £194,000 more than a state-educated person.

Our research at the Independent Schools Council shows that parents want what our schools offer, including good behaviour, a focus on non-academic achievement and the explicit development of 'soft skills'. One reason for the pay difference described above is the possession of non-academic skills such as articulacy, assertiveness and imagination.

> A third of pupils at ISC schools are educated on a reduced fee and over £380 million is being spent this year on means-tested bursaries. The amount is rising every year, opening up our schools to pupils from a wider range of backgrounds.

The September 2016 Green Paper sent a shiver down the spines of our schools as it threatened us with loss of charitable benefits. But we now have good relationships with the government and in 2018 signed a memorandum of understanding which said that we would foster more partnerships with state schools in return for the government supporting private schools.

In 2019 ISC schools will be looking closely at the most effective strategies for improving mental health, reducing stress and dealing with the fallout from social networking. Meanwhile some issues are causing schools and pupils fewer problems that they were five years ago: illegal drug use, alcohol misuse, smoking, homophobic bullying and sexual health.

For the past four years fee increases have been low – amongst the lowest ever recorded. Meanwhile house prices have continued to rise in areas round all the best state schools, making access to these state schools more expensive than a good fee-charging school.

A third of pupils at ISC schools are educated on a reduced fee and over £380 million is being spent this year on means-tested bursaries. The amount is rising every year, opening up our schools to pupils from a wider range of backgrounds.

It is sometimes claimed that independent schools have 'survived' because of large numbers of foreign students. This is true of some boarding schools, but as boarding pupils only make up a small proportion of all those at independent schools it is not an argument which carries much weight. The number of pupils in ISC schools who are non-British and live abroad is 5.5% of all ISC pupils; many of these are at specialist colleges for overseas students, most of whom go on to UK universities.

There is also a group of non-British parents who live in London because they work there. Many send their children to ISC schools. Far from being 'a problem' we know that these highly-skilled parents would not have come to the UK had it not been for the attraction of good private schools. This is why, despite the good quality of many state schools in London, the proportion of London children going to independent schools is high.

British private schools are regarded throughout the world as being the best in the world. That is why our schools are being asked to set up branches abroad. It is a vote of confidence in our schools.

Character education and why it benefits businesses

Dr Eve Poole, Gordonstoun chairman, says that facing your fears encourages students to become successful leaders

When the University of Edinburgh research into Gordonstoun's out-of-classroom curriculum was launched in May 2018, it was greeted with predictable wails about public school privilege. "It's easy for them – they've got a YACHT!" But this is to misunderstand why we did it. We did it because being a charity is about more than sharing facilities or providing bursaries. It is also about being generous about anything we've been lucky enough to learn. Gordonstoun has already shared Outward Bound and the Duke of Edinburgh's Award with the world. We wanted to assist the public debate about it by providing real data. We're one of the only schools that can do that, because we have 80 years' worth of alumni to ask, all of whom were immersed in a carefully designed character-based curriculum, long before it became trendy. And character education cannot be tested at the time of acquisition, because the very point of it is its durability, and the fact that a good one will keep delivering for you throughout your life.

So let me summarise the essence of our findings, and why they are so transferable, not only through school populations, but for everyone involved in youth work, training and development.

Learning to try

Our research showed that a varied and repeated out-of-classroom curriculum that is compulsory for all students compels them to try things they would otherwise avoid. Our findings showed us that this 'have a go' mentality lasts well beyond the Gordonstoun years, and has inspired many alumni to keep trying new things for the rest of their lives. Schools who wish to emulate this need simply make more of their non-academic curriculum compulsory, so that young people gain a broader exposure to experience, and learn not be afraid of trying something new.

Learning to fail

Having to try everything means that failure is inevitable, given that it is unlikely that everyone will be good at everything. Students learn to fail, and they learn how others fail too. They learn that they may need other people to succeed, but also that they may be better than others at unexpected things. Again, schools wishing to help students learn to fail well could identify non-examined elements of the curriculum where there is opportunity for experimentation, and create a safe environment where failure is not considered socially terminal. This could be normalised by delaying specialisation, and by making elements of sporting, drama, musical and service to the community compulsory for all.

Learning to try again

Because the curriculum is regular and repeated, students inevitably have to have another go, even if they failed last time. So they learn resilience, and about conquering their fears, both about their own abilities, and about how their peers will react to them. Again, this teaches students how to pick themselves up, and many alumni told us that this ability to bounce back had been crucial in helping them to navigate subsequent career setbacks. Anyone working with young people, wishing to help them learn this important life skill, could design in opportunities for students both to identify their fears and to set about conquering them, whether it is public speaking, a fear of heights or water, or just plain social shyness.

Social levelling

We found that in the melting pot that is Gordonstoun, the out-of-classroom curriculum is a fantastic leveller. No-one cares who your parents are on a rainy expedition if you forgot to pack the hot chocolate. And because our students often find themselves being led or rescued by peers they would never have expected to thrive in these contexts, it engenders a humility and respect for other people based not on culture or background, but on ability and character. Any school delivers these lessons by exposing the same peer group to a range of contexts, where different people will have a chance to shine each time.

Gender

For the women in our sample, being pitted against men in so many different scenarios instils a particularly steady career confidence. Working together both in and out of the classroom, they were bound to have seen men be worse as well as better than them in such a wide variety of contexts. This means that their expectations in the workplace are very different, which has helped our female alumni to thrive. Again, any opportunity for mixed-gender groups to face challenges together can help with this, if the range of opportunities offered is sufficient to generate multiple data points.

I taught leadership for over a decade at Ashridge Business School, where I had the opportunity to meet thousands of senior leaders, and to learn about their challenges. What they told me was that they wanted to be more confident. What the Gordonstoun research shows is that confidence is a natural by-product of the experience of facing your fears, time after time, and surviving them. This robs them of their power to defeat you, because you know you have developed the power to prevail. The school motto is *plus est en vous* – there is more in you, and nowhere is this better taught and learned than through the out-of-classroom curriculum. If all schools and those who provided youth development activities took these findings to heart, and adapted them to use in their own contexts, we wouldn't have business leaders who are too scared to do the right thing. We'd have brave leaders of character, which is what the world so desperately needs today.

For more information about Gordonstoun, see page 274

Closing the gender gap in engineering

James Johns, Head of Physics at Dauntsey's, looks at changing attitudes towards careers in STEM

Engineering is all around you. From robotics and artificial intelligence, to mobile phones, medical technology and advanced sports equipment, to driverless cars and sending Sir Tim Peake into space. Engineering is shaping the future all around us.

All very exciting and interesting and yet it has long been acknowledged that STEM options from school through to post graduate and career paths have something of an image problem. EngineeringUK has said recently that the country needs 1.8 million new engineers and technicians by 2025. There is a particular issue in attracting women and girls to this industry. The gender gap is surprisingly wide with the UK having the lowest percentage of female engineering professionals in Europe, at less than ten per cent. According to the Institute of Physics, just 1.9% of girls chose A-level Physics in 2016, compared to 6.5% of boys. If we could shift the perception and encourage equal numbers of female STEM participants, the skills shortage would all but disappear.

A recent European study by Microsoft* is of particular interest to me. It found that the majority of girls became interested in STEM at around the time of starting secondary education, but that their interest had begun to wane prior to making A-level choices. This tells me that we have a key window where we as teachers can influence decisions that will set the trajectory of these students' academic life in the long-term.

When you look at GCSE, A-Level and University scores, girls tend to outperform boys in STEM subjects when they choose to do them. We must therefore increase their desire to pursue those options. Does a lack of female role models in the wider media make STEM less attractive? On Twitter, 92% of the most followed scientists are male and if asked to think of the current faces of Physics, I expect that Jim Al-Khalili, Brian Cox and perhaps even Morgan Freeman come to mind before the brilliant Dr Helen Czerski.

The key to inspiring future female engineers and scientists lies firmly in the everyday formative experiences of students at school. Here at Dauntsey's, we are lucky to have been able to appoint a second female Physics specialist. Three of the four previous schools that I have worked at didn't have any. We are also hopeful of securing a female Physicist, who is at the forefront of her field, as a guest speaker for our annual Physics society dinner and lecture next term. Practical engagement in lessons is vital

> Increasingly schools, and pupils, are recognising that University is not the only path to pursue.

and Physics at Dauntsey's is taught in way that engages with the current interests of our pupils, whether it is explicit in our specification or not. As a Head of Department, I would be astounded if the reason a pupil gave, boy or girl, for not continuing with Physics at a higher level, was because they found the subject boring.

Our efforts appear to be paying off. Nationwide, girls make up just over 20% of all A-Level Physics entrants. Here, more than 30% of our Upper Sixth Physics classes are girls and an equal percentage of boys and girls have attained University offers for STEM subjects this year.

As a Department, we work closely with the Careers Department to begin engagement with STEM during the critical pre A-level period. We help promote the EDT (Engineering Design Trust) residential courses for GCSE pupils. We are particularly keen to promote the female-only INSPIRE courses. Research has found that girls are more likely to engage in STEM and that they feel more confident when in female-only environments. This is proving to be successful; two of our Fifth Form girls were accepted on residential engineering courses at Durham University for this summer. Finally, the Careers Department recently ran a trip to the Sandhurst STEM showcase for girls. This was designed specifically to inform girls about career opportunities in STEM. Companies including Airbus, Dyson, Jaguar Land Rover and Network Rail were there, talking about what they do and the career opportunities available – all our girls came back truly inspired by what they learnt.

The message is starting to get through. We recently had a Sixth Form girl land a much sought-after degree apprenticeship in engineering, the competition was very tough, tougher than for many leading university places. Increasingly schools, and pupils, are recognising that University is not the only path to pursue. Degree Apprenticeships provide a great opportunity to continue education whilst contributing to a workforce and getting hands-on experience which is particularly valuable in the engineering industry.

Attitudes are slowly beginning to change but Microsoft's recent research found that 70% of British girls said they would feel more confident pursuing STEM careers if they knew men and women were equally employed in STEM disciplines. The lesson – for us all – starts at school.

* Why Europe's Girls Aren't Studying STEM, Microsoft Report March 2017

For more information about Dauntsey's, see page 52

Photograph right: Pupils from Dauntsey's attending a STEM showcase for girls at Sandhurst. This was designed specifically to inform girls about career opportunities in STEM.

Why an Olympic star told us that 'failing is good'

Liz Laybourn, Head of Burgess Hill Girls, explains how guest speakers have had an inspirational effect on pupils

'Failing is good'

Just one of the powerful mantras that girls should adapt as their own if they want to achieve their dreams.

A vital part of the curriculum at Burgess Hill Girls is our programme of guest speakers. We invite a wide variety of incredible women to visit our school, from Women's Equality Party Leader Sophie Walker to Antarctica Ice Maiden, Sophie Montagne. Their life stories inspire our girls to set their sights high as well as give them some invaluable and practical tips on how to get there.

Most recently Olympic champion Lizzy Yarnold was the guest of honour at our Junior School Sports Day.

Winning consecutive Olympic gold medals in 2014 and 2018, Lizzy is the most successful British Winter Olympian and the most successful Olympic Skeleton athlete of all time from any nation.

She stayed for the whole day at Burgess Hill Girls, chatting with girls, answering their questions and cheering them on.

She also gave a powerful motivational speech about the challenges she faced in her bid to be an Olympian, reducing several girls and staff to tears.

For one girl in particular, Lizzy's visit was particularly inspirational. As a teenage heptathlete and javelin thrower, Lizzy's sporting hero was Britain's Goldie Sayers. Sayers is also the idol of Burgess Hill Girls Year 10 pupil Peanut Meekings, aged 15, who throws javelin for Sussex.

But very few of us connect Lizzy with javelin. Lizzy revealed at the age of 18 she realised she wasn't going to make it and began to explore other events to succeed in her dream of becoming an Olympian.

Through UK Sport's Girls4Gold talent identification programme, she was identified as having potential in skeleton, in which a single rider on a small sled, known as a skeleton bobsled, hurtles down a frozen track while lying face down and head-first.

Seven years later she was World Champion, winning Gold at the 2014 Winter Olympic Games in Sochi and then again this year in Pyeongchang.

There are three lessons we can take from Lizzy's story. Firstly to aim high, secondly to be able to adapt. The third and perhaps most surprising lesson is that failing is good. In her own words: 'Succeed and celebrate; fail and you learn.' As she pointed out, 'you don't win much in life, so it is very important to deal with losing and to see it as a positive.'

'Failing is good' fits very closely with our philosophy at Burgess Hill Girls. Our nurturing and empowering community gives girls the complete freedom to take risks, to challenge themselves, to try new experiences and, most importantly, to make and learn from mistakes. A true driver in developing the necessary character and skills to succeed in the long term. And who knows, you might be seeing a Burgess Hill Girl on the podium some time soon.

For more information about Burgess Hill Girls, see page 170

'Succeed and celebrate; fail and you learn.' As Lizzy pointed out, 'you don't win much in life, so it is very important to deal with losing and to see it as a positive.'

Customisable educational care – a new concept in schooling

Su Smith, Director of Admissions at St. Helen's College Prep, thinks a new blueprint for educational care may be needed

More and more, parents ask us from their very first visit about extended care options. While their son or daughter is a babe in arms, they are keen to ensure that he or she will be not just educated by their school during traditional school hours, but cared for at a high level and with real integrity and intent during extended hours. Parents want to offer their children every opportunity to take part in the myriad of extra-curricular clubs, activities and sports now available and to ensure that homework is completed on time and to a good standard. However, today's savvy parents also want to avoid the terrible trio of traps of modern parenting: helicopter-parenting, over-scheduling children to the extent that dinner becomes a packed tea in the car between activities, and reducing parents' time with their children to stressful, snatched time rather than pre-planned quality time to share values, conversation and love away from the pressures of modern life.

However, modern parents don't necessarily want to pack their son or daughter off to board. Most prospective parents we meet are both working professionals who love their children dearly and want to spend as much time with them as they can; with busy working lives, they recognise their family's limitations and, as seasoned consumers, they are grateful to hear that we offer a customisable educational 'product' that works for them.

Here at St. Helen's College we offer a totally flexible package which could perhaps be seen as 'boarding without the boarding'. We have Breakfast Club from 7.30 each morning, extended care until 6pm each evening and care available also from 7.30am to 6pm throughout the school holidays, with the exception of bank holidays and a short break at Christmas. So we really do offer marvellous hours of care for busy working parents. But what is really special is that, while some other schools offer after school clubs either off site or on site but run by external companies, all of this care is provided here, at school, by the St. Helen's College staff. This means that the school's core values and expectations run through everything the children do, in both work and play, whether they are in a classroom of their immediate peers or taking part in after school club or holiday camps.

The core St. Helen's College values are family values: love, harmony and growth. We believe that children learn best when they feel loved, secure and happy. We want children to feel this way when they are eating breakfast, when they are in lessons (whether indoors or enjoying outdoor learning in our beautiful homely grounds), and after school either while taking part in exciting activities or enjoying 'down-time' with friends.

At our after school club, children may choose to play freely indoors or outdoors or to take part in adult-led activities. Older children have supervised prep where they can complete their homework, and (after a full two or three course hot lunch service) a light, healthy tea is served to all. This means that when busy parents pick their children up at the end of the day, each family really can have some quality time together talking about their days, eating, reading, watching TV or Facetiming friends and family abroad without the stresses of homework, playdates or endless ferrying to after school activities.

Indeed, St. Helen's College offers a quite remarkable co-curricular programme of 70+ clubs 'in house', including yoga, taekwondo, arts, crafts, drama, golf, rugby, musical ensembles, choirs and so much more. So parents do not need to source clubs and activities outside of school; they do not need to 'keep up with the Joneses', driving children from drama schools to language classes to football coaching. High quality provision in so many areas is available on the school site or nearby, run by school staff, and children can have a go at many things without any associated stress for parents. Parents and pupils make their selections from a co-curricular programme each term, knowing that all those providing clubs/education/care have gone through full school vetting checks and that the school 'quality assures' the provision it offers in all areas. In this way, pupils can discover and develop talents and interests during their extended hours, in familiar, friendly surroundings and without the need to drive from place to place polluting the environment!

The children's personal development, academic and co-curricular interests and talents are at the heart of everything the school does. Staff and children embody family values and the school really does provide a 'home from home' for the children. A unique and very special relationship of trust exists between school and home. Parents are grateful for the help the school gives them, and enjoy knowing that their children are safe, well-educated and exposed to the widest possible range of challenging and enjoyable activities. They also express thanks that, through extended care and co-curricular opportunities, children are able to develop friendships with other pupils from across the school and not just their own year group – which all adds to the happy, family atmosphere of the school. Inspectors called St. Helen's College a 'haven of harmony' and there is no doubt that the 'family care' aspect plays a big role in the harmonious atmosphere around the school.

Perhaps this really is a blueprint for the future: a prep school where before and after school care and year-round holiday care provision is quality-assured, fully flexible and available to all on a 'when needed' basis without the high cost of boarding.

For more information about St. Helen's College, see page 122

Every child deserves to be inspired

Michael Hodge, headmaster of Prospect House School in London, considers the impact of a great teacher

'If in 20 years from now one of my pupils says, "Mr Hodge, he made a difference", then I will have achieved my goal'.

Thinking back, most of us can name that one teacher who was inspirational (mine was called Mr Wessels). He listened to me and he made me feel my opinions mattered. As a result of his encouragement and contagious enthusiasm, my light-bulb moments came thick and fast. This resulted in my life-long love of learning and my desire to share knowledge with others. Mr Wessels's example taught me far more about being a good teacher than any other professional training I later undertook.

Teaching is so much more than imparting knowledge. To ignite a child's curiosity, teachers must first build relationships with their pupils, understanding what makes each child tick and developing a mutual level of trust.

Children are naturally inquisitive and it is through questioning that they gain a deeper understanding, which ultimately drives their desire to learn. But if a child lacks the self-confidence to speak up, many of their questions remain unanswered. What a wasted opportunity this represents.

It is our responsibility to create a learning environment where children feel free to raise their hand to ask a question or voice an opinion, safe in the knowledge this will lead to supportive discussion not derisive criticism.

The positive impact of recognising and rewarding success can never be underestimated. Regardless of a child's ability, every small success leads to greater self-belief, nurturing a confident 'can do' attitude.

Every child learns in a different way and we need to adapt our resources and teaching methods to respond to each individual's learning styles. It is the teacher's responsibility to identify where each individual pupil is in their learning and target their needs.

In today's environment where everything is immediate, and people are used to instant gratification, my staff and I believe in teaching children the value of perseverance and resilience and giving them the right skills to utilise these qualities when things feel difficult.

Children are naturally inquisitive and it is through questioning that they gain a deeper understanding, which ultimately drives their desire to learn.

We arm our pupils with the skills to navigate through this modern world; to teach them how to work both collaboratively and on their own, to solve problems and to communicate effectively. These are all essential life skills. This forms the backbone to our teaching, be it in computer coding lessons, constructing a go-kart or navigating a dinghy in the Isle of Wight.

As teachers we also need constantly to improve and update the way we educate. At Prospect House, we evaluate our own teaching methods continuously, investigating new educational thinking and initiatives. Classrooms should be alive with discussion and activities, not rooms where one person is speaking and the rest are quietly listening.

When walking around our school, I expect to see the children engaged, teachers working with groups or individuals, questions being asked, and interesting discussions taking place with everyone participating.

As the headmaster of Prospect House, in addition to the teaching of the children, I am tasked with the responsibility to develop and guide the next generation of teachers: the two go hand in hand. It is my aim to help each of our teachers to be brilliant practitioners. A great teacher makes a huge difference to a child's life and it is our responsibility to be great: it is what makes our profession so rewarding.

In the words of William Arthur Ward 'The mediocre teacher tells. The good teacher explains. The superior teacher demonstrates. The great teacher inspires.' Amen to that.

To see Prospect House's ethos in action, please ring Emily Porter on 020 8246 4897 to book a place at the next open morning.

For more information about Prospect House School, see page 126

Why does pupil wellbeing matter?

Chris Townsend, Headmaster of Felsted School, discusses why Felsted has taken an innovative approach to safeguard pupil happiness

Ten years ago the term 'wellbeing' was never used in schools; indeed it was not talked about at all. It was probably Anthony Seldon (former Master of Wellington College) who started the discussion, when he launched happiness lessons.

Personally, I am not a great advocate for happiness lessons, because I don't think wellbeing should be taught as a discreet part of what a school offers. I believe wellbeing should be a part of what a school is, at the heart of what the school is trying to deliver. Although I am proud to have just opened an in-school Wellbeing Centre (one of the first in a school in the UK) here at Felsted, it really is not the building, but the statement that is important, and what that means to members of our community, whether pupils, staff, or parents.

Why does wellbeing matter? It is a recognition of the challenges that young people face in society today. It is one of the hardest areas to come to terms with, the fact that there are increasing incidences of mental health challenges for young people. One question often asked is whether there are increasing incidents, or whether we just have greater awareness and are more prepared to talk about these issues. It is probably a combination of the two, but there's no doubt that the pace of life at which we live, the pressures which we apply and everything else that comes in around the life of young people, not least the ubiquitous social media, that combine to add to that pressure and anxiety.

So the purpose of our Wellbeing Centre is not just to provide a focus at the heart of the school for this particular area, but to show how important it is to us as a school that young people at Felsted are happy. It is an underrated value, an underrated quality, something that people either take for granted, or see as being a little bit 'airy-fairy'. Actually, it's absolutely the core of what we as a school want to deliver. We aim to create a culture of awareness of mental health needs, with no stigma or discrimination, providing high quality mental health training for staff, pupils and parents. And if a child is happy, they will be learning to their full potential and achieving the best that they can in all areas of school life.

> Why does wellbeing matter? It is a recognition of the challenges that young people face in society today. It is one of the hardest areas to come to terms with, the fact that there are increasing incidences of mental health challenges for young people.

We teach all our pupils, from the youngest years, the importance of mental health, through PSHE lessons, peer counselling, yoga sessions or mindfulness lessons. It forms an integral part of our pastoral care offering with all our staff equipped to understand and look out for the mental wellbeing of their pupils, whether in the boarding houses, classrooms, at lunch or in co-curricular activities.

A massive support network underpins our care for each child, which includes a house parent, tutor, teachers, matron, chaplain, peer counsellors, house and school prefects and now our in-house Wellbeing Centre and Counselling Service. The Centre provides a tranquil hub for pupils to drop in for some 'time-out', as well as providing a number of specialised services, such as paint, play and sand therapy, the latter being particularly popular with older students who may find it different to express themselves verbally.

My aim is to help to develop well-adjusted young people who are happy; happy in themselves, happy in their relationships with one another, and happy with who they are, ready to go out and make a difference in the world. That, for me, is why wellbeing matters at Felsted.

"The wellbeing centre is genius and ahead of the game in education. Wellbeing is core to personal success in many ways and will continue to be even more important in life after school. I am confident that my child is well looked after when they are not at home."

Parent of a weekly boarder

Felsted is a leading co-educational independent school, providing an all-round, holistic education for pupils aged 4 to 18, with day and contemporary boarding options to suit modern family life. Only 50 minutes north of London and south of Cambridge, find out why Felsted is becoming a popular choice for many families. www.felsted.org.

For more information on Felsted School see page 80

Educating for tomorrow

Jo MacKenzie, Headmistress, Bedford Girls' School, explains why her schools offers the IB alongside A Levels

I often speak about the role schools play in empowering young people to reach their full potential. We need to educate young people to understand their role as influential and meaningful members of society. The world is becoming increasingly volatile, uncertain, complex and ambiguous, and we must develop within our students the skills and attributes to help them navigate their brave new worlds.

The call from the professional world for graduates who can think creatively, solve problems, make decisions independently, communicate and collaborate are well known. As is the need for them to have the flexibility of thinking to exploit new technologies, and to be socially and emotionally aware so they can work together across boundaries.

I want to ensure that our students are not just highly employable but that they are thinking women who are confident to choose their own paths, who are willing to initiate positive change.

It is this ambition that underpins my commitment to the International Baccalaureate (IB) philosophy, an educational vision which does not define excellence by a narrow measure of examination grades but delivers a holistic approach to life-long learning and which, at its core, has the mission of creating a better, and more peaceful world though education.

I often feel that in the UK, the IB is misunderstood; it is not just a two-year Diploma Programme bolted onto the Sixth Form but a deeply rooted teaching pedagogy developed by educational experts over the last 50 years. The IB focuses on the development of a learner profile, centred around 10 clearly defined key attributes (being principled, communicators, thinkers, open-minded, caring, risk-takers, balanced, reflective, knowledge and inquirers). Each attribute provides the foundations of truly holistic, forward thinking education in which students are encouraged to work and think independently.

At Bedford Girls' School (BGS), we deliver an IB led approach to teaching and learning throughout the School. We are currently applying for candidacy of the Primary Year Programme (IBPYP) and offer the IB Diploma programme in the Sixth Form.

I am asked if the IB philosophy is at odds with preparation for GCSEs. GCSEs are a stepping-stone and I believe that the IB approach to learning enhances our girls' experiences at GCSE. The ability to think crucially, to research and work independently and to articulate their ideas helps them navigate the heavy content of the GSCEs more easily. They understand the inter-disciplinary nature of their subjects, making learning more rewarding, and it prepares them for the transition to Sixth Form studies.

At BGS, we offer a dual stream Sixth Form. A Levels suits students who have very clearly defined objectives, but I suggest that every student considers the IB Diploma Programme. It is the perfect platform for preparing for university and the wider world. The breath of subjects taken (six, including Maths, English, a Science, a Language, a Humanities and one other) keeps choices and interests wide, whilst allowing students to master attributes that they started to embed. Research shows that learning a language until the age of 18 enables you to maintain it for life – so why throw away all those years of studying Spanish until 16, for just another 18 months of study? The ability to communicate with fluency in another language is a life skill that sets graduates apart. Likewise, I cannot think of a day where I do not use Maths and English in my professional and personal life, the longer we practise the skills associated with these subjects such as critical thinking, looking at a question analytically and problem solving, the more fluent we become.

In addition, the wider core elements of the IB Diploma are equally as important; all students study the Theory of Knowledge (vital in the world of fake news), undertake compulsory Community and Service projects and write an independent 4,000 word essay. These elements help students gain a greater understanding of the world around them and, vitally, teach them how to reflect on their own strengths and weaknesses.

The IB Diploma still encourages young people to follow their passions but it provides them with a framework in which other subjects support those passions. The truly independent nature of the learning and the flexibility of the curriculums creates bespoke programmes of study in which students can really flourish. They are practising the skills they will need to be successful in life in a nurturing environment with teachers who understand them. The success of the IB Diploma programme is demonstrated in the competitive offers received from excellent universities and the shape of the career paths that IB Diploma graduates follow.

As we are once again are surrounded by headlines about shifting grade boundaries, harder exams and unemployable graduates I think it is important to reflect on the true purpose of education and to ensure that we are not defining students by quickly outdated grades and letters, but by the life-long contribution they can make to enrich their worlds.

Bedford Girls' School is an independent girls' school for students from age 7–18. *For more information see page 74*

Choosing an education fit for 2030+

David Harrow, Deputy Head (Academic), explains why Oakham School is introducing the IB's Middle Years Programme

That we live in changing times is not new: anyone from countless generations back through the ages, and across the globe, could have made a similar assertion. What is unprecedented is the rate of that change. There has been a great deal of speculation about the knowledge and skills that will be needed in the world of 2030 and, whilst no-one can predict the future with certainty, there is a remarkable degree of agreement on the broad sweep of qualities one is likely to require. Distilling the many conversations that have taken place, what is apparent is the importance of being able to think critically and creatively, to learn effectively and independently, to collaborate with others, and to manage copious information and 'big data'. We can reasonably suppose that people may need to switch fields several times during their working lives, and that professions will change in nature quite profoundly.

So: the education we need to offer to our young people today has a lot riding on it, and a traditional 'business as usual' knowledge-based curriculum is unlikely to do the job.

The challenge we at Oakham are facing, as well as all schools across the country, indeed the world, is how can we best equip our students with the knowledge, aptitude and skills to thrive in the world of 2030 and beyond?

Like many independent schools, philosophically, and in practice, there is a great deal in an Oakham education that already provides a brilliant preparation for the world that awaits them when they leave education. At Oakham, this includes our nationally acclaimed FOSIL framework for inquiry learning, our broad and balanced 'Total Curriculum', and our focus on Learning Habits. As an ambitious school that has always been at the forefront of educational developments (we were one of the first independent schools to move to co-education in the 1970s, and to introduce the IB Diploma over 15 years ago), we

have chosen to go even further to safeguard our students' future readiness.

The Govian revolution has meant that there is a danger of an education from ages 11 to 14 becoming a relatively bleak and utilitarian preparation for the core subjects to come. These are vital years, where habits are formed, and enthusiasms are readily nurtured, and therefore, we believe, should be used to better effect.

Our solution to the challenge of equipping pupils for the world of 2030+ is to ensure that these three years, relatively free from the constraints of studying for examinations, are put to the very best possible use. That is why, from this September, Oakham School is embarking on the phased development and implementation of the internationally celebrated IB Middle Years Programme (IB MYP) for our students aged 11 to 14.

The IB MYP is a holistic, concept-based framework that puts the student at the centre and makes understanding a real priority. In a traditional curriculum, knowledge and skills are taught, with the hope that deep understanding follows: sometimes it does, but there is nothing systematic about that. One can end up with rather a disparate appreciation of particular subjects, possibly in some depth, but without an awareness of the bigger picture, and limited experience in bringing a variety of ideas together to deal with the complex, and sometimes rather messy, interdisciplinary problems that arise all the time in real life. By way of contrast, IB MYP units start with the ideas and concepts that one wishes to convey, and the knowledge and skills needed to support understanding the concepts follow from that.

The IB MYP is a framework for learning rather than just a curriculum. It is more than a set of subjects: it addresses students' intellectual, social, emotional and physical well-being, and gives them the opportunities to develop the

knowledge, attitudes and skills they need to manage complexity and take responsible action for the future. It helps them to understand how their learning fits into the bigger picture, and in the wider world: subjects are linked with local and global perspectives, and across the disciplines, sometimes in surprising but revealing ways. Inquiry is fundamental: students learn how to ask and answer great questions, big and small. They are inspired and enabled to use their learning to make things happen: they think about how action or service can arise from what they learn, and how individually and together they can make a difference.

Taken as a whole, the IB MYP brings together everything Oakham believes about education in a way that will give our young people the best opportunity to thrive in the world to come, whether at school, at university or in the world of work. As we are now able to develop an IB MYP programme for just three years, we can also retain the currency of GCSEs.

Klaus Schwab, Executive Chairman of the World Economic Forum, said that 'there has never been a time of greater promise, or greater peril'. Whether one sees the future as scary, exciting, weird or just confusing, it is as well to be ready to actively take one's part in it as a responsible, prepared global citizen. At Oakham, we believe that the IB MYP is the best way we can give our young people the opportunity to do exactly this.

For more information about Oakham School, see page 104

10 steps to a successful mental health and wellbeing programme

Jonny Spowart, Deputy Head of Heath Mount School, outlines a strategy for a happier and healthier school

Heath Mount School was the winner of the Mental Health and Wellbeing Award at the Boarding School Association's 2018 Heads' Conference. Heath Mount is a co-educational Pre-Prep and Prep for children aged 3-13 set in 40 acres of the beautiful Woodhall Estate, near Hertford.

In this article, Jonny Spowart, Deputy Head (Pastoral), shares his '10 steps' to a successful programme:

1. The road ahead: know where you are going

How do you build upon strong pastoral foundations to create an effective wellbeing programme? It sounds obvious; we started at the beginning and drafted a four-year plan approved by the Senior Management Team and our Board of Governors. It was vital to get off to a flying start in 2017-18 after which our ideas would have a momentum of their own. Our plan covers our team and how we aim to achieve our goals, which can be summarised as: identifying and monitoring awareness; staff development and support; strengthening our ethos and environment and the curriculum, teaching and learning. Once you have a plan, be flexible. With input from staff, parents and the children, it can always be improved!

2. Assemble a great team

As those working in education like to remind children: Together Everyone Achieves More.

We recognised that, to be successful and sustainable, we needed to pull together the skills and experience we already had. Our first step was to appoint a Head of Wellbeing. With a detailed job description in place the successful applicant was appointed internally. Rebecca Post is passionate about wellbeing across the School and has been in the role for just over a year. Working alongside me, she has pushed forward many of the ideas in our plan.

Our team also draws upon the expertise of our nurses, school counsellor and Heads of Years. We strive to create an environment of 'mental wealth' where children are happy, ready to learn and can develop their own 'toolkit' to deal with the problems life may throw at them.

3. Get your procedures and policies in place

Once you have taken steps 1 and 2, establishing 'how' you want your wellbeing programme to work is easier. Map out a clear structure and referral framework. This should utilise both your internal and external wellbeing support network and allow pupils to progress through a 'wellbeing support pathway'. Brainstorm how this can work, refining the process so it can be easily communicated. It is not necessary to rush into a written policy. Instead, focus your energy on communicating goals that everyone can work towards. After your first year of a coordinated wellbeing programme, you will have a better idea of what should be captured by your mental health and wellbeing policy.

4. Training

Seek ways to knowledge share and increase the understanding of mental health and wellbeing amongst all staff. Look at the skills you can develop; for example, our Head of Art is now an ARTiculate facilitator.

5. Track pupil happiness

We have used 'Happiness Surveys' to track the happiness of our children for the past six years. Our quantitative data allows us to anticipate the shifting stressful times, identify any trends and respond proactively. For example, our transition process has been adapted to minimise the worry associated with moving year groups.

6. Know your Wellness Recovery Plan

A flow-chart support pathway means staff know the referral process depending on the nature of the concern. Concerns are 'triaged', with a Level 2 concern triggering the involvement of a network of external specialists. Individuals involved with a child are kept in the loop throughout interventions. The Head of Wellbeing is tasked with responsibility for checking progress, follow up intervention and parent liaison.

7. Parents are key

Parents want more than anything for their children to be happy. Work in partnership with them, offering them easy access to key members of the wellbeing team and provide a range of talks for them to attend.

8. Do not forget your staff

There is a growing body of evidence suggesting stressed, unhappy staff impact the happiness of children. Encourage your staff to stay active and look after their mental health. Engage with them to find ways to support them.

9. Get a nurture dog

Our nurture dog, Doodle, has been a welcome, calming addition during exams, learning support sessions and when listening to readers. He is available if a child feels sad, wants to talk whilst stroking him or if a member of staff would like to walk him around our grounds.

10. Keep improving

There is always room to grow and improve. Be proactive and stay ahead of the game. The issues impacting children's wellbeing change and schools should be quick to adapt and respond.

For more information about Heath Mount School, see page 84

Inspiring the person as well as educating the pupil

Jeremy Walker, Principal of King's Rochester, outlines the benefits of a strong co-curricular programme

At King's we believe that pupils should be introduced to a wide variety of opportunities and experiences alongside the academic curriculum to establish skills and interests that prepare them for a happy, successful and fulfilled life. We often say that 'exam results may get you job interviews but it is the whole person who gets the job'. While excellent academic results are crucial they do not develop the wider skills needed to be successful and with working lives becoming ever more extended it has never been more important to have a wide range of interests.

By expanding their education, often going outside their comfort zones, pupils add more depth to their existing knowledge as well as establishing skills and hobbies that could easily be overlooked. This is why a strong co-curricular programme is now as essential as academic classes. Time spent participating in such programmes introduce pupils to new experiences and grants them the opportunity to learn in new and intriguing ways. Often this can have the most unexpected rewards, from the quiet pupil who takes to the stage for an Open Mic Night, or the sporting star who gains personal satisfaction from taking part in Community Service. Trying new things certainly opens up opportunities for self-discovery.

This also encourages pupils to manage their time more effectively and this is essential for examination season when revision could seem overwhelming. Many pupils have found that these activities provide a welcome break from their academic studies, helping them to remain focused and relieve examination stress and pressure. Often putting new skills into practice can provide the clarity for an academic concept to make sense.

Some pupils struggle more than others in social situations. Starting a new co-curricular activity introduces pupils to like-minded peers and supports the development of their social skills. Working alongside a range of people helps to develop relationship and communication skills and, in many cases, lasting friendships.

Participation in activities requires pupils to make a longer-term commitment to something and see it through. Many pupils stay involved in the same activities year after year and eventually take on a leadership role with a good example being the Combined Cadet Force. Compulsory for the first two years of Senior School, many choose to continue through to the Sixth Form where they have amazing experiences with the regular Armed Forces.

At King's we also run a weekly Community Service programme which all Lower Sixth take part in and also includes taking Duke of Edinburgh Awards. Not only do pupils learn new skills such as gardening or cooking but they also put them into practice to help those in our local community including residential homes, charity shops and schools.

Charitable fundraising is strong part of life at King's with thousands of pounds raised each year with a focus on local charities. Being involved as part of a charity team opens pupils to the benefits of being selfless and experiencing the satisfaction of helping others while also developing organisational and communication skills alongside many others.

Inclusiveness is key for a successful programme. Not all pupils excel academically and experiencing success or being recognized for a contribution to an activity can greatly improve their self-esteem. Not every pupil enjoys being in the spotlight on stage but may wish to be involved in a drama performance, so they can join the Technical Theatre Crew. Those who enjoy physical education may not play to county standard but enjoy their sport enough to assist teaching the younger years.

King's co-curricular programme includes Citizenship and Personal, Social, Health and Economic Education (CPSHEE), Careers sessions, Combined Cadet Force, Duke of Edinburgh Award, the Enrichment Programme and Volunteering. Such activities can inspire pupils in the most rewarding way, a weekend of camping and hiking up Mount Snowdon can show even the most reluctant pupil that if they can reach the peak of such a mountain then they can grasp that tricky subject.

A Careers day where pupils are interviewed by the owners of local businesses for fictitious jobs, encourages confidence in real life situations and reviewing feedback alongside the interviewers allows pupils to develop foundation interview techniques onto which they can build as they grow. CPSHEE is vital for health, wealth, and happiness and prepares pupils for the complexities of life through dialogue with teachers who know them and their parents well as individuals.

At King's we complement our strong co-curricular programme with a wide range of clubs and clinics so that learning can blossom even after the last bell. After School sessions which cover areas as diverse as Mandarin, computer science, drone building, design and technology provide key skills ideal for the fast changing world. While activities such as debating, LAMDA lessons and drama improve confidence and mental stamina.

Enriching pupils in this way often sees their new external skills returned to the classroom. Our pupils are confident but also grounded and it is their enthusiasm that brings a great sense of fun to each school day. Knowing that they are being enabled to develop into balanced young men and women, equipped with the skills and interests they will need for a successful life after school makes the experience of being at King's hugely rewarding for staff, parents and pupils.

For more information about
King's Rochester, see page 194

Boarding in the 21st Century

Olivera Raraty, Headmistress of Malvern St James Girls' School, says innovation and modernity complement tradition

The modern boarding experience is a world away from that of previous generations. Gone are the days of letters written home on a Sunday afternoon, queuing for the only house phone with a stash of 10p pieces, dismal food, and long weekends stretching away with not much to do.

Pupils now enjoy accommodation with all modern conveniences, a raft of options for weekend and evening activities, excellent food to suit even the most fussy or jaded of palates (Vietnamese street food, anyone?) and the freedom, as they get older, to take the vital steps to independence which will be expected once they leave.

The gym is open till 9pm, the Library till 9.30pm, there is likely to be an in-house film night, an external subject lecture, a trip to the theatre or a social with a nearby school. Boarding houses also have kitchens for the older girls so they can cook for themselves if they want to, and entertaining spaces so that they can have friends around. It is a slice of freedom, but not so much as to overwhelm them. There is also the support and structure that young people need to feel secure. They have the chance to try new things and to take risks, but in a safe and supportive environment. They also have fun learning together in the House studies in the evening, and revision is so much easier and more fun when you have lots of friends to test you! Teachers are often available in the evenings as well as the House staff, so there are always people around to talk to and to get help from.

Anecdotally, from the feedback we get from parents, students, and employers, we know that as a sector we are getting this right. Former students who come back to talk at school, comment on how well prepared for university they were compared to their day pupil peer group. They had already worked out how to manage their time and work/life balance, they were more self-disciplined and self-motivated, and they were able to work a washing machine and cook themselves a decent meal! They have also learnt valuable life skills in knowing how to get on with and live with very different personalities and learning to see the funny side of things.

Boarding schools feel less of a 'bubble' and more real-world than they did in the past. In the last decade or so, change has really picked up pace and schools such as MSJ have been quick to respond to market trends and parents' feedback. Thus a generation ago, many schools would have only offered full boarding; some full or weekly boarding. Now, many offer flexi-boarding as well to fit in with family life. At MSJ, flexi means boarding 1, 2 or 3 nights per week; and girls can change their days with relatively short notice. This is really useful if they have an early morning or late night trip or sporting fixture; or if parents have work commitments.

Pastoral care has also stepped up enormously. All good boarding schools recognise how important it is to have caring, relatable and empathetic staff, available 24/7. Our boarders are aged from 8-18, and we know that wobbles, even from the most grounded of girls, are inevitable, whether they have been with us for five days or five years. We have a team of staff, at the House, in School, and at our Health and Wellbeing Centre, to ensure that we give the best possible advice and care.

Weekends are full of things to do with an emphasis on fun and adventure – canoeing in the Wye Valley, mountainboarding, heading to the beach in the Summer, punting in Oxford, or a virtual reality experience in Bath. If that sounds like too much after a hard week, then there is 'purposeful mooching' – reading, hanging out in the Houses, cooking, and walking up to Malvern to shop or see a film.

When boarders first enter school, we make that transition as gentle as possible. We link new girls and their families with those already at the school, so that they can meet before starting. We offer taster days and boarding nights before girls start, so that they will know the routine and what to expect. In the first term, new girls will share with an existing boarder, even in Sixth Form, before moving into a single room, once they have found their feet. As well as House activities specifically designed to get girls working and having fun together, there are induction trips and days for the whole school which focus on team building.

Thanks to Skype and Facetime, home life and school life feel far more connected, even if home is on the other side of the world. At MSJ, mobile phone use is banned during the day, but in the evening, girls can contact their family as much as they like. Social media is a great facilitator too – all the Houses have social media feeds so that parents can see what is going on and engage with activities. Communication between girls, parents, House staff and school is quick, easy and seamless via the many technologies in place.

Boarding schools are rightly associated with a sense of tradition, but even a fleeting glance will show you a huge measure of modernity and innovation. Anyone who has preconceptions about foreboding and stuffy places should reconsider – and come and visit these schools which pop with adventure, laughter and amazing opportunities.

For more information about Malvern St James Girls' School, see page 248

Excellence across all areas

Daniel Berry, Headmaster of Kirkham Grammar School, outlines the ethos of the school's seven-year vision

At Kirkham Grammar School we are convinced that in an environment that currently has a high reputation, we must continue to strive to offer the very best to all of our pupils. When one stands still, one is in effect going backwards. Kirkham Grammar is a remarkable school within the North-West educational landscape. In nurturing well-qualified, compassionate, self-assured members of the community, our vision sets out the opportunity to look forward and plan without losing sight of what has come before. Every child travels through our school only once and deserves the very best. The family ethos of the school is fundamental and should be a key factor in driving our future plans for growth and expansion. Our seven-year vision views the Foundation from 3–18 years as the key to our current and future ongoing success. The school has a particular niche within the marketplace and we must be careful to consider this in our planning. The expectation for any potential family joining Kirkham Grammar School is to join us for the journey from Pre-School through to Sixth Form. Therefore, all the facilities we provide and develop are of equal importance.

So what is it that makes such a school so special and unique? The range of opportunities given to our pupils is the main reason for such an envious reputation.

I firmly believe from my years as a Headmaster that it is the breadth and balance of the provision that helps pupils become the best they can possibly be. That must incorporate both the aspiration to succeed to the very highest levels and also an opportunity to find an activity within the school which gives all pupils the chance to excel. I have been overwhelmed at how many co-curricular opportunities are available in our school. The diversity and range of clubs and societies that take place weekly is outstanding and a true testament to the staff and pupils.

The virtue of a school does not depend entirely on its classrooms, the equipment in its laboratories, the number of its pupils, nor even the success of its exam results. There is an unseen influence that is exerted by buildings and surroundings that are beautiful and dignified. These are in keeping with fine honourable traditions and high ideals embedded at Kirkham Grammar School. We offer something that is intangible but very real, the atmosphere in which we dwell and the pervasive spirit which surrounds us, influences all of which we strive to achieve. Our most recent inspection confirmed what we all knew about Kirkham Grammar School; it is the best kept educational secret in Lancashire. However, we are delighted that it has been officially acknowledged against national criteria that we are working hard to ensure our pupils get the finest education. The inspection found that the quality of the pupils' academic and other achievements and the quality of the pupils' personal development is excellent. Pupils reflect the strong family ethos of the school and demonstrate excellent collaboration in and out of lessons.

Pupils develop excellent levels of confidence at all ages, supported by the strong PSHE (Personal, Social, Health and Educational) and enrichment programmes. Pupils show a clear respect for different faiths and diversity, demonstrating excellent levels of empathy and tolerance towards others. Pupils make informed choices, empowered and supported by their teachers.

The longer I spend at Kirkham Grammar School, the more I understand what clearly makes it such a unique school. We are about so much more than academic achievement and continue to thrive in a challenging market. The life of a school over a full academic year is a busy one. As Headmaster of Kirkham Grammar School this experience continues to be filled with wonderful opportunities.

As the school motto clearly states, 'Ingredere Ut Proficias'.

For more information about Kirkham Grammar School, see page 158

> I firmly believe from my years as a Headmaster that it is the breadth and balance of the provision that helps pupils become the best they can possibly be. That must incorporate both the aspiration to succeed to the very highest levels and also an opportunity to find an activity within the school which gives all pupils the chance to excel.

The role of technology in education

Graham Starkey, Assistant Head (Digital Learning) at Feltonfleet Preparatory School in Surrey, on finding the balance with 'traditional' teaching

In recent years, Feltonfleet has invested heavily in an IT infrastructure that enables fast, secure internet access through an enviable number and range of tablet and laptop computers, offering access to a strategically placed set of online tools geared to educational use. At the entrance to our Digital Learning suite, a "WHY?" poster clarifies our rationale, *"We are passionate about teaching pupils to become confident authors and creators of digital content"*, mirroring our vision to 'digitally empower' all our pupils to ensure that they are equipped with the skills and abilities required in the workplace of the future.

Technology in education is moving swiftly, with the latest offerings at this year's BETT (formerly British Educational Training and Technology show) including drones, artificial intelligence, robotics and augmented reality headsets. So, will your child be strapping on their augmented reality headset anytime soon, perhaps abandoning their trusty textbooks? With this in mind the central question for all schools is: 'What is the role of technology in education?'

As a Prep School we believe in blending the very best of traditional education with innovative new technologies. 'Digitally empowering' our pupils is about two very clear goals:

GOAL 1
Helping them to become discerning users of technology, confident in their ability to independently choose technologies to enhance and extend their learning outcomes where appropriate. As such, we strongly encourage critical thinking skills in order to question the role of technology by asking 'Will technology add any value to my learning process?'

With our 'Why?' already clear, our 'How?' is all about the process: nurturing confidence, building fluency, questioning, investigating and discovering creative workflows and outcomes, with assessment focusing on these qualities.

GOAL 2
Developing their knowledge and skills as authors and creators of their own digital content, as designers and computer programmers with knowledge of core computing concepts and acquisition of key skills to ready their access to developing technologies and future jobs.

With our 'Why?' already clear, our 'How?' is all about the process: nurturing confidence, building fluency, questioning, investigating and discovering creative workflows and outcomes, with assessment focusing on these qualities. With a pupil's ability to think and innovate often touted as the ideal outcome of education, the ingredients of 'coding', namely logical reasoning, the ability to structure an argument, problem solving, mathematical application, and buckets of creativity, make for a solid foundation in this regard.

Pupils at Feltonfleet confidently collaborate on shared documents online, compile multimedia digital portfolios to collate their learning processes in Art and Modern Foreign Languages, use video to analyse their performance in PE and program robots in Digital Learning using Swift, a new programing language designed by Apple quickly gaining prominence in the computing field.

Whilst these 'What?' elements will surely change over time the priority should surely always remain to question the added value of technology first, prior to its use for the sake of it. By doing so, the natural balance of when to use, and when to leave devices to one side, will surely prevail.

For more information about Feltonfleet Preparatory School, see page 184

Help in finding the fees

Chris Procter, joint managing director of SFIA, outlines a planned approach to funding your child's school fees

Average school fee increases in the last year, according to the ISC census, were 3.4% which is the lowest since 1994, however this is still significantly higher than inflation.

The latest Independent Schools Council (ISC) survey, completed by all 1,326 schools in UK membership indicate that there are now a record 529,164 pupils being educated privately, the highest number since records began in 1974. 86.8% of these were day school pupils, 13.2% were boarders. The share of girls and boys at ISC schools is very nearly equal, with boys representing 51% of all pupils.

The overall average boarding fee is £11,228 per term and the overall average day fee is £4,854 per term. However, fees charged by schools vary by region – for example the average boarding fee ranges from £9,159 per term in the North East to £13,080 per term in Greater London; the average day fee ranges from £3,572 per term in the North West to £5,751 per term in Greater London.

The overall cost (including university fees) might seem daunting: the cost of educating one child privately could well be very similar to that of buying a house but, as with house buying, the school fees commitment for the majority of parents can be made possible by spreading it over a long period rather than funding it all from current resources.

It is vital that parents do their financial homework, plan ahead, start to save early and regularly. Grandparents who have access to capital could help out; by contributing to school fees they could also help to reduce any potential future inheritance tax liability.

Parents would be well-advised to consult a specialist financial adviser as early as possible, since a longterm plan for the payment of fees – possibly university as well – can prove very advantageous from a financial point of view and offer greater peace of mind. Funding fees is neither science, nor magic, nor is there any panacea. It is quite simply a question of planning and using whatever resources are available, such as income, capital, or tax reduction opportunities.

The fundamental point to recognise is that you, your circumstances and your wishes or ambitions, for your children, or grandchildren are unique. They might well be similar to those of other people but they will still be uniquely different. There will be no single solution to your problem. In fact, after a review of all your circumstances, there might not be a problem at all.

So, what are the reasons for seeking advice about education expenses?

- To reduce the overall cost?

- To get some tax benefit?

- To reduce your cash outflow?

- To invest capital to ensure that future fees are paid?

- To set aside money now for future fees?

- To provide protection for school fees?

- Or just to make sure that, as well as educating your children, you can still have a life!

Any, some, or all of the above – or others not listed – could be on your agenda, the important thing is to develop a strategy.

At this stage, it really does not help to get hung up on which financial 'product' is the most suitable. The composition of a school fees plan will differ for each family depending on a number of factors. That is why there is no one school fees plan on offer.

The simplest strategy but in most cases, the most expensive option, is to write out a cheque for the whole bill when it arrives and post it back to the school. Like most simple plans, that can work well, if you have the money. Even if you do have the money, is that really the best way of doing things? Do you know that to fund £1,000 of school fees as a higher rate taxpayer paying 40% income tax, you currently need to earn £1,667, this rises to £1,818 if you are an additional rate taxpayer where the rate is 45%.

How then do you start to develop your strategy? As with most things in life, if you can define your objective, then you will know what you are aiming at. Your objective in this case will be to determine how much money is needed and when.

You need to draw up a school fees schedule or what others may term a cash flow forecast. So, you need to identify:

- How many children?

- Which schools and therefore what are the fees? (or you could use an average school fee)

- When are they due?

- Any special educational needs?

- Inflation estimate

- Include university costs?

With this basic information, the school fees schedule/cash flow forecast can be prepared and you will have defined what it is you are trying to achieve. Remember though, that senior school fees are typically more than prep school fees – this needs to be factored in. Also, be aware that the cost of university is not restricted to the fees alone;

there are a lot of maintenance and other costs involved: accommodation, books, food, to name a few. Don't forget to build in inflation, I refer you back to the data at the beginning of this article.

You now have one element of the equation, the relatively simple element. The other side is the resources you have available to achieve the objective. This also needs to be identified, but this is a much more difficult exercise. The reason that it is more difficult, of course, is that school fees are not the only drain on your resources. You probably have a mortgage, you want to have holidays, you need to buy food and clothes, you may be concerned that you should be funding a pension.

This is a key area of expertise, since your financial commitments are unique. A specialist in the area of school fees planning can help identify these commitments, to record them and help you to distribute your resources according to your priorities.

The options open to you as parents depend completely upon your adviser's knowledge of these complex personal financial issues. (Did I forget to mention your tax position, capital gains tax allowance, other tax allowances, including those of your children and a lower or zero rate tax paying spouse or partner? These could well be used to your advantage.)

A typical school fees plan can incorporate many elements to fund short, medium and long-term fees. Each plan is designed according to individual circumstances and usually there is a special emphasis on what parents are looking to achieve, for example, to maximise overall savings and to minimise the outflow of cash.

Additionally, it is possible to protect the payment of the fees in the event of unforeseen circumstances that could lead to a significant or total loss of earnings.

Short-term fees

Short-term fees are typically the termly amounts needed within five years: these are usually funded from such things as guaranteed investments, liquid capital, loan plans (if no savings are available) or maturing insurance policies, investments etc. Alternatively, they can be funded from disposable income.

Medium-term fees

Once the short-term plan expires, the medium-term funding is invoked to fund the education costs for a further five to ten years. Monthly amounts can be invested in a low-risk, regular premium investment ranging from a building society account to a friendly society savings plan to equity ISAs. It is important to understand the pattern of the future fees and to be aware of the timing of withdrawals.

Long-term fees

Longer term funding can incorporate a higher element of risk (as long as this is acceptable to the investor), which will offer higher potential returns. Investing in UK and overseas equities could be considered. Solutions may be the same as those for medium-term fees, but will have the flexibility to utilise investments that may have an increased 'equity based' content.

Finally, it is important to remember that most investments, or financial products either mature with a single payment, or provide for regular withdrawals; rarely do they provide timed termly payments.

Additionally, the overall risk profile of the portfolio should lean towards the side of caution (for obvious reasons).

There are any number of advisers in the country, but few who specialise in the area of planning to meet school and university fees. SFIA is the largest organisation specialising in school fees planning in the UK.

This article has been contributed by SFIA and edited by Chris Procter, Managing Director.
Chris can be contacted at: SFIA, 29 High Street, Marlow, Buckinghamshire, SL7 1AU
Tel: 01628 566777
Fax: 0333 444 1550
Email: enquiries@sfia.co.uk
Web: www.schoolfeesadvice.org

The Independent Schools Council

The Independent Schools Council (ISC) works with its members to promote and preserve the quality, diversity and excellence of UK independent education both at home and abroad

What is the ISC?

ISC brings together seven associations of independent schools, their heads, bursars and governors. Through our member associations we represent over 1,300 independent schools in the UK and overseas. These schools are ranked among the best in the world and educate more than half a million children each year.

The ISC's work is carried out by a small number of dedicated professionals in our offices in central London. We are assisted by the contributions from expert advisory groups in specialist areas. Our priorities are set by the board of directors led by our Chairman, Barnaby Lenon. We are tasked by our members to protect and promote the sector in everything we do.

ISC schools

ISC schools offer a high quality, rounded education. Whilst our schools are very academically successful, their strength also lies in the extra-curricular activities offered – helping to nurture pupils' soft skills and encourage them to be self-disciplined, ambitious and curious. There are independent schools to suit every need, whether you want a day or boarding school, single sex or co-education, a large or a small school, or schools offering specialisms, such as in the arts.

Our schools are very diverse: some of our schools are selective and highly academic, while others have very strong drama or music departments full of creative opportunities in plays, orchestras and choirs. For children with special needs such as dyslexia or autism there are many outstanding independent schools that offer some of the best provision in the country.

Many schools have very strong track records of high achievement at sport, offering a wide range of facilities and excellent coaches. Independent schools excel at the traditional sports like football and rugby, but also offer more unusual sports like rowing, fencing and even rock climbing.

There is also a wealth of co-curricular opportunity available. Whether your child is into debating, sailing, the Model United Nations or is interested in army training in the Combined Cadet Force, most schools offer numerous clubs and activities. It all adds up to an exciting, broad and stimulating all-round education.

Academic results

In 2018 47% of A-level subjects taken at independent schools were graded A*/A - this is almost double the national average of 26.4%. This year also saw nearly two thirds of independent school GCSE entries being awarded an A/7 or higher, three times the national average. This is especially impressive given the fact a third of ISC schools offering GCSEs are not academically selective. In 2018, figures demonstrated more students are following different pathways post-GCSE. There was an increase in candidates taking the Extended Project Qualification, Pre-U and BTEC qualifications compared to 2017. The average points score for pupils taking the IB Diploma was 36, roughly equivalent to 4.5 As at A-level. In the International Baccalaureate, 2% of pupils obtained 45 points, the highest mark, which is only achieved by 0.3% of candidates worldwide.

Fee Assistance

Independent schools are very mindful that hard working families can find it difficult to pay school fees. Affordability is of course a concern for schools and they work hard to remain competitive whilst facing pressures on salaries, pensions and maintenance and utility costs. Schools are strongly committed to widening access and have made strenuous efforts to increase the amount they can offer in bursaries. This year almost £400m was provided in means-tested fee assistance for pupils at ISC schools. Currently a third of pupils at our schools benefit from reduced fees.

ISC Associations

There are seven member associations of the ISC, each with a distinctive ethos in their respective entrance criteria and quality assurance:

Girls' Schools Association (GSA) – see page 38
Headmasters' and Headmistresses' Conference (HMC) – see page 39
Independent Association of Prep Schools (IAPS) – see page 40
Independent Schools Association (ISA) – see page 41
The Society of Heads – see page 42
Association of Governing Bodies of Independent Schools (AGBIS) – www.agbis.org
Independent Schools' Bursars Association (ISBA) – www.isba.org.uk

Further organisations who are affiliated to the ISC: Boarding Schools Association (BSA), Council of British International Schools (COBIS), Scottish Council of Independent Schools (SCIS) and Welsh Independent Schools Council (WISC).

The Independent Schools Council can be contacted at:
First Floor,
27 Queen Anne's Gate,
London,
SW1H 9BU
Telephone: 020 7766 7070
Website: www.isc.co.uk

independent schools council

Choosing a school initially

Educational institutions often belong to organisations that guarantee their standards. Here we give a brief alphabetical guide to what the initials mean

BSA

The Boarding Schools' Association

Since its foundation in 1966, the Boarding Schools' Association (BSA) has had the twin objectives of promoting boarding education and the development of quality boarding through high standards of pastoral care and boarding accommodation. Parents and prospective pupils choosing a boarding school can, therefore, be assured that the 560 schools in the UK and internationally that make up the membership of the BSA are committed to providing the best possible boarding environment for their pupils.

A UK boarding school can only be a full member of the BSA if it is also a member of one of the Independent Schools Council (ISC) constituent associations, or in membership of the State Boarding Forum (SBF). These two bodies require member schools to be regularly inspected by the Independent Schools' Inspectorate (ISI) or Ofsted. Other boarding schools who are not members of these organisations can apply to be affiliate members. Similar arrangements are in place for overseas members. Boarding inspection of ISC accredited independent schools has been conducted by ISI since September 2012. Ofsted retains responsibility for the inspection of boarding in state schools and non-association independent schools. Boarding inspections must be conducted every three years. Boarding is judged against the National Minimum Standards for Boarding Schools which were last revised in 2015 and is set to be updated again soon.

Relationship with government

The BSA is in regular communication with the Department for Education (DfE) on all boarding matters. The Children Act (1989) and the Care Standards Act (2001) require boarding schools to conform to national legislation and the promotion of this legislation and the training required to carry it out are matters on which the DfE and the BSA work closely.

Boarding training

The programme of training for boarding staff from BSA member schools has been supported and sponsored in the past by the DfE. The BSA maintains the high standards expected as a consequence of that support and from the BSA's Commitment to Care Charter – which all member schools must abide by.

The BSA organises five conferences and more than 90 seminars a year for governors, Heads, deputies, housemasters and housemistresses, and matrons and medical staff where further training takes place in formal sessions and in sharing good practice. The BSA provides the following range of training and information:

- Professional qualifications for both teaching and non-teaching staff in boarding schools. The BSA has been responsible for the development of a number of courses: Certificates of Professional Practice in Boarding Education, Certificate in International Boarding, Certificate in Professional Practice for Nurses and Matrons, and a Diploma for senior leaders. The certificates courses are the result of at least two years' study, and completion of the Diploma takes at least one year. Courses run across the UK.

- A rolling programme of day seminars on current boarding legislation and good practice.

- Bespoke training and consultancy on best boarding practice, particularly with regard to safeguarding.

- The Accredited Boarding Practitioner scheme, where individuals working in boarding can have their service and experience accredited by BSA.

- Centre for Boarding Education Research (CEBER) which brings together a wide variety of articles and research on all matters related to boarding.

State Boarding Forum (SBF)

The BSA issues information regards its 40 state boarding school members and the BSA should be contacted for details of these schools. In these schools, parents pay for boarding but not for education, so fees are substantially lower than in an independent boarding school.

BSA Leadership Team

National Director: Robin Fletcher
Direction of Operations: Aileen Kane
Director of Training and International: Andrew Lewin
Head of Safeguarding and Standards: Dale Wilkins

4th Floor
134-136 Buckingham Palace Road
London SWIW 9SA
Tel: 020 7798 1580
Email: bsa@boarding.org.uk
Website: www.boarding.org.uk

GSA

The Girls' Schools Association, to which Heads of independent girls' schools belong

The Girls' Schools Association represents the Heads of a diverse range of UK independent girls' schools, among which are some of the top-performing schools in the country. It is a member of the Independent Schools Council.

The GSA encourages high standards of education for girls and promotes the benefits of being taught in a largely girls-only environment. GSA schools are internationally respected and have a global reputation for excellence. Their innovative practice and academic rigour attract pupils from around the world. As a whole, students at GSA schools do well in 'difficult' modern foreign languages and STEM (science, technology, engineering, maths) subjects and a high percentage – 96% – progress to higher education. GSA schools share experience, specialisms, opportunities and facilities with state sector schools in a wide range of partnerships. Many also provide means-tested bursaries for families of limited financial means.

Twenty first century girls' schools come in many different shapes and sizes. Some cater for 100% girls, others provide a predominantly girls-only environment with boys in the nursery and/or sixth form. Some follow a diamond model, with equal numbers of boys but separate classrooms between the ages of 11 to 16. Educational provision across the Association offers a choice of day, boarding, weekly, and flexi-boarding education. Schools range in type from large urban schools of 1000 pupils to small rural schools of around 200. Many schools have junior and pre-prep departments, and can offer a complete education from 3/4 to 18. A significant proportion of schools also have religious affiliations. Heads of schools in the Girls' Day School Trust (GDST) are members of the GSA.

The Association aims to inform and influence national educational debate and is a powerful and well-respected voice within the educational establishment, advising and lobbying educational policy makers on core education issues as well as those relating to girls' schools and the education of girls. The Association liaises with the Department for Education, the Office for Standards in Education, the Qualifications and Curriculum Authority and other bodies.

The GSA also provides its members and their staff with professional development courses, conferences, advice and opportunities to debate and share best practice, ensuring that they have every opportunity to remain fully up-to-date with all aspects of their profession.

As the GSA is one of the constituent bodies of the Independent Schools' Council (ISC), its schools are required to undergo a regular cycle of inspections to ensure that these rigorous standards are being maintained. GSA schools must also belong to the Association of Governing Bodies of Independent Schools, and Heads must be in membership of the Association of School and College Leaders (ASCL). The Association's secretariat is based in Leicester.

Suite 105, 108 New Walk, Leicester LE1 7EA
Tel: 0116 254 1619
Email: office@gsa.uk.com
Website: www.gsa.uk.com
Twitter: @GSAUK

President 2019: Sue Hincks, Bolton School Girls' Division
Chief Executive: Vivienne Durham

HMC

The Headmasters' and Headmistresses' Conference, to which the Heads of leading independent schools belong

Founded in 1869 the HMC exists to enable members to discuss matters of common interest and to influence important developments in education. It looks after the professional interests of members, central to which is their wish to provide the best possible educational opportunities for their pupils.

The Heads of some 292 leading independent schools are members of The Headmasters' and Headmistresses' Conference, whose membership now includes Heads of boys', girls' and coeducational schools. International membership includes the Heads of around 56 schools throughout the world.

The great variety of these schools is one of the strengths of HMC but all must exhibit high quality in the education provided. While day schools are the largest group, about a quarter of HMC schools consist mainly of boarders and others have a smaller boarding element including weekly and flexible boarders.

All schools are noted for their academic excellence and achieve good results, including those with pupils from a broad ability band. Members believe that good education consists of more than academic results and schools provide pupils with a wide range of educational co-curricular activities and with strong pastoral support.

Only those schools that meet with the rigorous membership criteria are admitted and this helps ensure that HMC is synonymous with high quality in education. There is a set of membership requirements and a Code of Practice to which members must subscribe. Those who want the intimate atmosphere of a small school will find some with around 350 pupils. Others who want a wide range of facilities

and specialisations will find these offered in large day or boarding schools. Many have over 1000 pupils. 32 schools are for boys only, others are coeducational throughout or only in the sixth form. The first girls-only schools joined HMC in 2006. There are now 35 girls-only schools.

Within HMC there are schools with continuous histories as long as any in the world and many others trace their origins to Tudor times, but HMC continues to admit to membership recently-founded schools that have achieved great success. The facilities in all HMC schools will be good but some have magnificent buildings and grounds that are the result of the generosity of benefactors over many years. Some have attractive rural settings, others are sited in the centres of cities.

Pupils come from all sorts of backgrounds. Bursaries and scholarships provided by the schools give about a third of the 220,000 pupils in HMC schools help with their fees. These average about £34,500 per annum for boarding schools and £15,000 for day schools. About 190,000 are day pupils and 45,000 boarders.

Entry into some schools is highly selective but others are well-suited to a wide ability range. Senior boarding schools usually admit pupils after the Common Entrance examination taken when they are 13.

Most day schools select their pupils by 11+ examination. Many HMC schools have junior schools, some with nursery and pre-prep departments. The growing number of boarders from overseas is evidence of the high reputation of the schools worldwide.

The independent sector has always been fortunate in attracting very good teachers. Higher salary scales, excellent conditions of employment, exciting educational opportunities and good pupil/teacher ratios bring rewards commensurate with the demanding expectations. Schools expect teachers to have a good education culminating in a good honours degree and a professional qualification, though some do not insist on the latter especially if relevant experience is offered. Willingness to participate in the whole life of the school is essential.

Parents expect the school to provide not only good teaching that helps their children achieve the best possible examination results, but also the dedicated pastoral care and valuable educational experiences outside the classroom in music, drama, games, outdoor pursuits and community service. Over 95% of pupils go on to higher education, many of them winning places on the most highly-subscribed university courses.

All members attend the Annual Conference, usually held in a large conference centre in September/October. There are ten divisions covering England, Wales, Scotland and Ireland where members meet once a term on a regional basis, and a distinctive international division.

The chair and committee, with the advice of the general secretary and membership secretary, make decisions on matters referred by membership-led sub-committees, steering groups and working parties. Close links are maintained with other professional associations in membership of the Independent Schools Council and with the Association of School and College Leaders.

Membership Secretary: Ian Power
Tel: 01858 465260
General Secretary: Dr William Richardson
Tel: 01858 469059
12 The Point
Rockingham Road
Market Harborough
Leicestershire LE16 7QU
Email: gensec@hmc.org.uk
Website: www.hmc.org.uk

Leading
Independent
Schools

IAPS

The Independent Association of Prep Schools (IAPS) is a membership association representing leading headteachers and their prep schools in the UK and overseas

With more than 650 members, IAPS schools represent a multi-billion pound enterprise, educating more than 160,000 children and employing more than 20,000 staff.

Schools are spread throughout cities, towns and the countryside and offer pupils the choice of day, boarding, weekly and flexible boarding, in both single sex and coeducational settings. Sizes vary from 100 to more than 800 per school, with the majority between 150 and 400. Most schools are charitable trusts, some are limited companies and a few are proprietary. There are also junior schools attached to senior schools, choir schools, those with a particular religious affiliation and those that offer specialist provision as well as some schools with an age range extending to age 16 or above.

IAPS only accredits those schools that can demonstrate that they provide the highest standards of education and care. Member schools offer an all-round, values-led, broad education, which produces confident, adaptable, motivated children with a lifelong passion for learning. In order to be elected to membership, a Head must be suitably qualified and schools must be accredited through a satisfactory inspection. IAPS offers its members and their staff a comprehensive and up-to-date programme of professional development courses to ensure that high professional standards are maintained.

Pupils are offered a rich and varied school life. The targets of the National Curriculum are regarded as a basic foundation, which is greatly extended by the wider programmes of study offered. Specialist subject teaching begins at an early age and pupils are offered a range of cultural and sporting opportunities. Together with more than 30 recreational games, music, art and drama form part of curricular and extracurricular activities. In addition, IAPS organises holiday and term-time sporting competitions for pupils to take part in, including skiing, sailing, judo, swimming, golf, fencing and squash, amongst many others.

IAPS has well-established links with senior independent schools, and experience in methods of transfer and entry to them. As the voice of independent prep school education, it has national influence and actively defends and promotes the interests of its members. It lobbies the government on their behalf and promotes prep school issues on a national and international stage. IAPS works directly with ministers and national policy advisers to ensure that the needs of the prep school sector are met.

IAPS
11 Waterloo Place
Leamington Spa
Warwickshire CV32 5LA
Tel: 01926 887833
Email: iaps@iaps.uk
Website: iaps.uk

Excellence in Education
**The Independent Association
of Prep Schools**

ISA

The Independent Schools Association, with membership across all types of school

The Independent Schools Association (ISA), established in 1879, is one of the oldest of the Headteachers' associations of independent schools that make up the Independent Schools' Council (ISC). It began life as the Association of Principals of Private Schools, which was created to encourage high standards and foster friendliness and cooperation among Heads who had previously worked in isolation. In 1895 it was incorporated as The Private Schools Association and in 1927 the word 'private' was replaced by 'independent'. The recently published history of the association, *Pro Liberis*, demonstrates the strong links ISA has with proprietorial schools, which is still the case today, even though boards of governors now run the majority of schools.

Membership is open to any Head or Proprietor, provided they meet the necessary accreditation criteria, including inspection of their school by a government-approved inspectorate. ISA's Executive Council is elected by members and supports all developments of the Association through its committee structure and the strong regional network of co-ordinators and area committees. Each of ISA's seven areas in turn supports members through regular training events and meetings.

ISA celebrates a wide-ranging membership, not confined to any one type of school, but including all: nursery, pre-preparatory, junior and senior, all-through schools, coeducational, single-sex, boarding, day and performing arts and special schools.

Promoting best practice and fellowship remains at the core of the ISA, as it did when it began 140 years ago. The association is growing, and its 474 members and their schools enjoy high quality national conferences and courses that foster excellence in independent education. ISA's central office also supports members and provides advice, and represents the views of its membership at national and governmental levels. Pupils in ISA schools enjoy a wide variety of competitions, in particular the wealth of sporting, artistic and academic activities at area and national level.

President: Lord Lexden
Chief Executive: Neil Roskilly, BA PGCE NPQH FRSA FRGS

ISA House, 5-7 Great Chesterford Court, Great Chesterford, Essex CB10 1PF
Tel: 01799 523619
Email: isa@isaschools.org.uk
Website: www.isaschools.org.uk

ISA celebrates a wide-ranging membership, not confined to any one type of school, but including all: nursery, pre-preparatory, junior and senior, all-through schools, coeducational, single-sex, boarding, day and performing arts and special schools

The Society of Heads

The Society of Heads represents the interests of independent secondary schools

The Society of Heads represents the interests of independent, secondary schools. The Society celebrated its 50th Anniversary in 2011. The Society has as its members 118 Heads of well-established secondary schools, many with a boarding element, meeting a wide range of educational needs. All member schools provide education up to 18, with sixth forms offering both A and AS levels and/or the International Baccalaureate. Also some offer vocational courses. Many have junior schools attached to their foundation. A number cater for pupils with special educational needs, whilst others offer places to gifted dancers and musicians. All the schools provide education appropriate to their pupils' individual requirements together with the best in pastoral care.

The average size of the schools is about 350, and all aim to provide small classes ensuring favourable pupil:teacher ratios. The majority are coeducational and offer facilities for both boarding and day pupils. Many of the schools are non-denominational, whilst others have specific religious foundations.

The Society believes that independent schools are an important part of Britain's national education system. Given their independence, the schools can either introduce new developments ahead of the maintained sector or offer certain courses specifically appropriate to the pupils in their schools. They are able to respond quickly to the needs of parents and pupils alike.

Schools are admitted to membership of the Society only after a strict inspection procedure carried out by the Independent Schools Inspectorate. Regular inspection visits thereafter ensure that standards are maintained.

The Society is a constituent member of the Independent Schools Council and every full member in the Society has been accredited to it. All the Society's Heads belong to the Association of School and College Leaders (ASCL) (or another recognised union for school leaders) and their schools are members of AGBIS.

The Society's policy is: to maintain high standards of education, acting as a guarantee of quality to parents who choose a Society school for their children; to ensure the genuine independence of member schools; to provide an opportunity for Heads to share ideas and common concerns for the benefit of the children in their care; to provide training opportunities for Heads and staff in order to keep them abreast of new educational initiatives; to promote links with higher and further education and the professions, so that pupils leaving the Society's schools are given the best advice and opportunities for their future careers; and to help Heads strengthen relations with their local communities.

The Society of Heads Office,
12 The Point, Rockingham Road, Market Harborough,
Leicestershire LE16 7QU
Tel: 01858 433760
Email: gensec@thesocietyofheads.org.uk
Website: www.thesocietyofheads.org.uk

The average size of the schools is about 350, and all aim to provide small classes ensuring favourable pupil: teacher ratios. The majority are coeducational and offer facilities for both boarding and day pupils. Many of the schools are non-denominational, whilst others have specific religious foundations

School profiles

Channel Islands

St George's Preparatory School

Our School

St George's Prep and St George's Little Dragons Nursery boast some of the finest facilities in Jersey. The school is set in a stunning 35 acre site of woodland, grass playing fields, football pitches, adventure play, award winning sports hall, and an enviable swimming pool.

St George's is a non-selective school promoting a rich, varied and broad education. Our small class sizes and specialist teachers ensure our children are challenged and stimulated to strive for excellence in all they do. We assess all of our children before they join the school so that we are immediately able to offer whatever learning support they might need. We are quick to identify children with particular gifts and talents and set specific goals to challenge these children further. We also look to challenge children who excel at music, drama and sport.

Children are helped to understand themselves as individuals. We recognise that every child is an individual and aim to promote their happiness, self-confidence and well-being as members of a caring community.

Our idyllic walled garden for our younger children provides a secure and safe place for our children to play confidently with their friends. In the Manor house and stable block, there is a homely and safe environment where lessons take place in dedicated teaching rooms, by well-qualified specialist teachers.

The children enjoy freshly cooked healthy and nutritious lunches, prepared at school by our Chef, using locally grown produce. We are very fortunate to have an extremely active and well supported Parents Association. The GA organises a variety of events ranging from family quiz nights, film nights and the annual Family Bonfire Night. Although the main objective of the GA is to raise money for the school, we also ensure the events are very social, enabling parents throughout the school to feel part of the St George's family and many long term friendships are made here.

Curriculum

We choose to follow the Jersey Curriculum, which is based on the UK National Curriculum, to provide us with a comprehensive framework upon which to build. The freedom to augment, adapt and expand this curriculum, coupled with our small classes, use of specialist teachers and longer working days, helps to create the very best learning environment for our pupils and ensures they make the maximum progress, whether in the classroom, on the sports field or on the stage.

Such a tailor-made programme allows us to focus on each child as well as on the different expectations held by the many senior schools who welcome our pupils both at the Island colleges and mainland public schools.

Our excellent record of transfer testifies to the success of our unique set up. Importantly, we believe it is a set up that presents our pupils with a wider range of opportunities than those enjoyed by any other primary pupil in Jersey and promotes a balanced and well rounded outlook.

ST GEORGE'S
PREPARATORY SCHOOL

(Founded 1929)

La Hague Manor, Rue de la Hague, St Peter, Jersey JE3 7DB UK

Tel: 01534 481593

Fax: 01534 484304

Email: admin@stgeorgesprep.co.uk

Website: www.stgeorgesprep.co.uk

Headmaster: Mr Cormac Timothy

Appointed: April 2017

School type: Coeducational Day

Age range of pupils: 2–11

No. of pupils enrolled as at 01/09/2018: 210

Boys: 94 **Girls:** 116

Fees per annum as at 01/09/2018:

Day: £5,265–£14,460

Average class size: 15

Teacher/pupil ratio: 1:15

St Michael's Preparatory School

St. Michael's Preparatory School is situated in a unique educational setting on Jersey in the Channel Islands. A forward thinking IAPS prep school preparing pupils for the rigours of secondary school education both on and off island. We place great emphasis upon the traditional values of care, consideration and courtesy.

The staff and pupils are justifiably proud of the School, and work together to create and maintain a high-achieving, well-organised and friendly environment in which every child is encouraged to do 'a little bit better' than anyone thought possible.

The curriculum is designed to give all children a broad, balanced and relevant education, which enables them to develop as enthusiastic, active and competent learners acquiring the knowledge, skills and understanding to allow them to grow up in today's world leading a full and active life. The school's ethos places emphasis on the individual and aims to encourage development in academic, physical, spiritual, moral and cultural aspects of the 'whole child'.

The teaching is multi-sensory, allowing children of all abilities and learning styles to be able to make progress in their learning. Differentiation is integral to the curriculum and children with special needs are well supported, as are the gifted and talented, who go on to achieve scholarship success.

The schemes of work are based upon the National Curriculum, the Jersey Curriculum and the requirements of the ISEB Common Entrance and Scholarship syllabuses. The curriculum is enriched and enhanced by numerous trips and visits as Jersey has an array of museums, cultural sites of interest and environmental locations.

The school prepares children for Common Entrance and Scholarships to English boarding secondary schools as well as entry to local Jersey establishments. We also offer a shell year (Year 9) specifically to provide a bridging opportunity for Year 10 entry to our island state schools. Classes are small and there is a very low pupil to teacher ratio. All expected subjects are taught and there are flourishing and well-equipped Art, Music, Science, Design Technology and ICT departments as well as a custom built Sports Hall, Dance/Drama Studio, Gymnasium and indoor Swimming Pool.

As well as providing a wide range of academic subjects, the school seeks to introduce each child to a large variety of sports, performing arts, activities and challenges enabling him or her to discover, through experience, hidden talents and preferences with a view to future specialisation.

I hope St. Michael's pupils will leave us having achieved the very best they are capable of, having found out what it is that they love and are good at, having learned to challenge themselves and to value other people.

"St Michael's makes ordinary children special, and special children extra-ordinary." A parent quote.

ST MICHAEL'S
PREPARATORY SCHOOL

(Founded 1949)

La Rue de la Houguette, St Saviour, Jersey JE2 7UG UK

Tel: 01534 856904

Email: office@stmichaels.je

Website: www.stmichaels.je

Head of School: Mr Mike Rees

Appointed: 2014

School type: Coeducational Day

Age range of pupils: 3–14

No. of pupils enrolled as at 01/09/2018: 328

Boys: 176 **Girls:** 152

Fees per annum as at 01/09/2018:

Day: £9,750–£15,060

Average class size: 18 max

Teacher/pupil ratio: 1:9

Central & West

Dauntsey's School

Dauntsey's is a leading co-educational boarding and day school for 11-18 year olds. The school sits in an estate of one hundred and fifty acres of idyllic countryside in Wiltshire and offers some 800 pupils challenge and inspiration both inside and outside the classroom.

The Dauntsey's Experience

Academic excellence is at the heart of all that we do. However, education is much more than grades on a piece of paper. It's about developing the skills and characteristics, such as resilience, flexibility and a willingness to have a go, which we all need to have a successful, happy life. That's where our adventure, enrichment and extra-curricular activities have a crucial role to play. From drama, dance, music, sport and a huge range of clubs and societies, to our lecture series, adventure programmes and volunteering initiatives – there are opportunities to suit everyone.

The Dauntsey's Community

Community and collaboration underpin many aspects of Dauntsey's; it is a happy place with a strong family atmosphere, where friendship matters and where courteous informality between staff and pupils is highly valued.

Our pupils are expected to give of their best and to have a spirit of adventure. We aim to push them out of their comfort zone, both inside and outside the classroom, and we want them to arrive at the end of their time in the School saying: 'I did not think that I could do that, but I did.'

Our pupils, both boarding and day, come from many different schools and so arrive at Dauntsey's eager to make new friends. Both communities are fully integrated and boarding houses rapidly become home-from-home and fellow boarders become extended family. All pupils attend School six days a week with Saturday school compulsory for day and boarders alike, with a full academic programme for all year groups and sports matches every Saturday afternoon. A range of activities on Saturday evening and Sunday encourage friendship and a sense of community.

Houses in the Upper School (for pupils aged 14-18 years) are single sex. Lower School pupils (aged 11-14 years) board at the co-educational Manor, a fabulous Victorian mansion in extensive grounds, a short walk away from the main School campus.

"Coming back to the Manor at the end of the day feels like coming home. There is so much to do and so many people I like – I've certainly never felt lonely!" – Richard, Second Form Boarder at The Manor

Entry Requirements

At all stages, admission to Dauntsey's is via examination and interview. Pupils can join Dauntsey's aged 11, 13 or 16. We recommend that potential applicants and their families attend one of our open mornings, which offer an opportunity to see the School on a normal working day, to meet current pupils and talk to both teaching and admissions staff. We hold two open mornings a year in May and October. Individual appointments can be organised by contacting the Admissions Office at admissions@dauntseys.org.

For more information please visit our website which gives a real flavour of life at Dauntsey's – www.dauntseys.org

"We ask our pupils and staff to be ambitious and to pursue excellence in all areas of school life." – Head Master, Mark Lascelles

(Founded 1542)

High Street, West Lavington, Devizes, Wiltshire SN10 4HE UK

Tel: 01380 814500

Fax: 01380 814501

Email: admissions@dauntseys.org

Website: www.dauntseys.org

Head Master: Mr Mark Lascelles

Appointed: September 2012

School type: Coeducational Boarding & Day

Age range of pupils: 11–18

No. of pupils enrolled as at 01/09/2018: 820

Boys: 416 *Girls:* 404 *Sixth Form:* 270

No. of boarders: 300

Fees per annum as at 01/09/2018:

Day: £18,990

Full Boarding: £31,440

Average class size: 18; 12 in Sixth Form

Teacher/pupil ratio: 1:8

EF Academy Oxford

EF Academy International Boarding Schools prepares students for a global future with a superior secondary school education in the U.S. or UK. At EF Academy, we believe in every student's ability to succeed. We empower them to do so through our renowned curricula, as well as quality one-on-one relationships with teachers and mentors alike. With a student body made up of 75 different nationalities, multilingualism and intercultural exchange are built into every course, which helps distinguish our students' academic credentials to both university admissions officers and future employers.

The School

Our private boarding school is situated in the city of Oxford, renowned for its scholastic tradition and rich cultural and architectural heritage. EF Academy students join Oxford's vibrant academic community, which attracts leading scholars from around the world. Ten minutes from Oxford's center, the campus has spacious classrooms, modern science labs and inviting lounges. Students have access to the library and sports center of nearby Oxford Brookes University. In the international environment at EF Academy Oxford, students aged 16 to 19 live and learn together.

Students live in on-campus residences with their classmates and house parents. House parents look after the students and ensure that they are safe and comfortable when they are not in class.

Academics

Education at EF Academy Oxford is highly individualized. Students follow the IB Diploma or A-Level program and take intensive English language courses. They benefit from an enrichment program that includes visits to University of Oxford and they regularly attend lectures in a variety of subjects. Our teachers with links to the university often arrange visits to its math department and science laboratories, ensuring students at EF Academy receive the ultimate pre-university experience.

University Placement

EF Academy Oxford graduates have gone on to attend universities such as Imperial, St. Andrews and Durham. All of our students receive acceptance to university degree programs, many for highly competitive courses such as Economics, Engineering or Medicine. Dedicated university advisors work together with students to help them prepare the best applications possible. This involves giving them feedback on their personal statements, holding mock interviews and exploring program options with them. Our university advisors can also support students who are interested in applying to universities in the US or in their home country.

Pastoral Care

At EF Academy Oxford, each student is assigned a personal tutor whose role is to monitor the student's academic progress and general welfare. They can turn to their tutor whenever they need support with homework and courses, or when they are experiencing homesickness.

Co-curricular Activities

Universities look for well-rounded students who get involved and extend their learning beyond the classroom. Students at EF Academy Oxford have access to a wide range of co-curricular activities. From subject-specific academic groups and competitions to sports and arts, there is an option for every student. The school's activities coordinator also arranges excursions for students on the weekends so they have the opportunity to experience the culture in and around Oxford.

INTERNATIONAL BOARDING SCHOOLS

Pullens Lane, Headington, Oxfordshire OX3 0DT UK

Tel: +41 (0) 43 430 4095

Email: iaeurope@ef.com

Website: www.ef.com/academy

Head of School: Dr. Paul Ellis

School type: Coeducational Boarding

Age range of pupils: 16–19

No. of pupils enrolled as at 01/09/2018: 175

Fees per annum as at 01/09/2018:

IB Diploma/A-Levels: £30,750

Headington School

Headington is a highly successful day and boarding school in Oxford for 820 girls aged 11-18 with a Preparatory School for 260 girls aged 3-11 occupying its own site just across the road. The School offers girls an unrivalled opportunity to pursue academic, sporting and artistic excellence in a caring and nurturing environment.

Founded in 1915 and set in 23 acres of playing fields and gardens, our superb facilities provide the perfect backdrop for teaching and learning that extends way beyond the classroom and curriculum. We encourage participation in all aspects of sport and culture, teamwork and leadership, challenging girls to discover and explore their own potential and achieve more than they thought possible.

Consistently in the premier league of academic schools in the UK, life at Headington is about much more than exam results. Through the sheer breadth of subjects and activities at Headington – and the option to study for the International Baccalaureate or A Levels – we aim to educate the complete individual, giving girls the confidence and self-awareness to compete, contribute and succeed at school, university and in their adult lives.

Facilities

Headington offers a superb range of facilities to day girls and boarders to support and enhance their learning.

These include a state-of-the-art Music School complete with recording studio, 240-seat professional theatre, light and airy Art School, Dance and Fitness Centre, Swimming Pool and award-winning Library.

Outside the classroom

More than 100 extra-curricular activities take place every week during lunchtime, before and after school. A wide choice of subjects, sports, interests and hobbies ranges from the Duke of Edinburgh's Award and Drama to Astronomy and Young Enterprise and includes such diverse pastimes as Debating and Robotics, Cheerleading and CCF.

From Olympic rowers to recreational dancers, Headington offers a genuinely inclusive approach to PE and extra-curricular sport and encourages each girl to enjoy sport at the level that suits her. Girls can choose from more than 30 different sporting activities, from Dance and Fencing to Equestrian and Trampolining. More than 70 girls currently compete at county level and beyond and the School enjoys national success in a wide range of sports including Rowing, Athletics, Swimming and Equestrian.

Around 450 individual music lessons take place each week and 29 visiting teachers offer girls the opportunity to learn a wide range of instruments. The Senior School has four orchestras and three choirs and numerous ensembles.

There is a busy programme of productions in our Theatre each year and girls become involed in all aspects of theatre, from writing and producing their own plays, to lighting, costume and make up.

The Dance Department was established in 2015 and there is a huge range of dance options, from Ballet to Street Dance and Contemporary. As well as annual Dance Shows, the Headington Dance Company competes in local and national competitions.

Boarding

Headington has always been a boarding school and just over a quarter of the School board with us today. The five boarding houses provide the girls with a 'home from home' where, supported by a team of highly experienced staff, they learn to develop into mature and independent young people. Many of our boarders come from the UK and we are also very proud of our international boarding community, made up of more than 30 nationalities from all over the world. Girls can choose between full boarding or weekly boarding or half-weekly boarding.

(Founded 1915)

London Road, Oxford, Oxfordshire OX3 7TD UK

Tel: +44 (0)1865 759100

Fax: +44 (0)1865 760268

Email: admissions@headington.org

Website: www.headington.org

Headmistress: Mrs Caroline Jordan MA(Oxon)

School type: Girls' Day & Boarding

Age range of girls: 11–18

No. of pupils enrolled as at 01/09/2018:

Senior School: 800

Fees per term as at 01/09/2018:

Senior Day: £5,884 – £6,417

Senior Boarding: £8,005 – £12,762

Prep: £3,105 – £4,694

Average class size: Depends on age

Teacher/pupil ratio: 1:8

Kingham Hill School

Kingham Hill School, surrounded by idyllic rural Cotswold beauty, offers a secondary school experience to girls and boys marked by nurturing pastoral care and academic rigour. The clear Christian foundation is central to its ethos in the 21st century, and it welcomes pupils of all backgrounds into family-style boarding and day houses. Although inclusive in intake, GCSE and A Level results are well above the national average, with a high proportion of Upper Sixth leavers taking up places at Russell Group and other elite universities in the US and Europe. KHS is also unique in being a traditional British school with a US accreditation, through the Middle States Association (MSA). Around one in six pupils are American, who graduate with both A Level and AP qualifications, and the bespoke US college guidance programme is available to all pupils alongside UCAS. A similar proportion of pupils come from a diverse range of international backgrounds, and the 30 or so nationalities represented makes for a globally-minded and mature community.

The unofficial motto of KHS is, "Work hard, play hard, and serve well." Outside of the classroom, the daily extra-curricular programme is compulsory, and includes a huge range of opportunities including sport, music, drama, CCF, Duke of Edinburgh's Award and a School Farm. Sports teams punch above their weight with full fixture lists at all levels, and the School is rightly proud of its Performing Arts Academy, which offers an annual series of concerts, plays, and musical theatre. A STEM programme gives pupils from Year 7 a hands-on experience of engineering, robotics, electronics, and aeromodelling, including a kart team which participates in the National Schools Karting Association (NatSKA) and the British Schools Karting Championship (BSKC). Service and leadership activities form an essential part of the weekly routine from Year 9, and in the Sixth Form, pupils are encouraged to spend time during the summer holidays at an orphanage in Zambia which has been supported by KHS for many years.

The School has a clear 15-year vision for its future, centred around seeking excellence in 10 strategic themes. This articulates the way KHS intends to remain faithful to its foundation, and to a small-school family home, whilst offering state-of-the-art facilities and a rounded education which prepares personable and engaging young men and women to face the challenges of higher education and a career. Most recently, the School has opened a new Maths and Science building and a new Library; a new Sports Hall is also currently under construction. True to its Founder's desire to see children with boarding need benefit from a KHS education, a recently launched Founder's Pupils initiative seeks to widen access to the opportunities and excellence on offer.

Transport links are excellent, and the School operates an extensive bus network for day pupils. For boarders, a mainline train station in Kingham allows a journey time of 25 minutes to Oxford, and 80 minutes to London Paddington. London Heathrow is just over an hour away, and the School arranges transport to the airport at the beginning and end of terms and half-terms.

The essence of a Kingham Hill education is rounded and servant-hearted personal development. The School prizes academic curiosity and a love of learning in the context of a classical liberal education, and promotes conservative family values. Above all is the belief that character is what really counts in life; the importance of resilience, courtesy, good manners, respect, hard work, adaptability, a sense of humour, and a willingness to make the best of every opportunity. To meet current pupils and see the ethos of KHS at first hand, please contact our Registrar, Miss Helen McRae, at h.mcrae@kinghamhill.org, to arrange a personal visit.

KINGHAM HILL SCHOOL

(Founded 1886)

Kingham, Chipping Norton, Oxfordshire OX7 6TH UK

Tel: 01608 658999

Fax: 01608 658658

Email: secretary@kinghamhill.org

Website: www.kinghamhill.org.uk

Head of School: Mr Nick Seward

Appointed: 2008

School type: Coeducational Boarding & Day

Religious Denomination: Christian

Age range of pupils: 11–18

No. of pupils enrolled as at 01/09/2018: 340

Boys: 209 *Girls:* 131

No. of boarders: 200

Fees per annum as at 01/09/2018:

Day: £17,220–£19,620

Weekly Boarding: £24,390–£30,120

Full Boarding: £25,170–£33,045

Average class size: 15

Teacher/pupil ratio: 1:7

Monkton Combe School

Setting standards for life

Monkton Combe School, just a mile from the World Heritage City of Bath, is an independent, co-educational boarding and day school for pupils aged 2-18. We pride ourselves on our lively Christian ethos, excellent exam results and our strong pastoral care. At Monkton, we are setting standards for life; giving young people the qualities of character they need to become trusted employees, inspiring leaders and valued friends. Boarding is at the very heart of Monkton, and the unique atmosphere of the School is enjoyed by boarders and day pupils alike. All the houses reflect the spirit and ethos of the School, but each exudes its own personality generated by its pupils, houseparents and staff.

A broad and varied curriculum

As shown by Monkton's outstanding exam results over the last five years fulfilling academic potential is one of our key priorities. However Monkton thinks differently, we start with a proactive pastoral environment to develop academically strong enthusiastic learners within a living Christian ethos. Our students work hard and are well motivated, being supported and encouraged through the care and enthusiasm of our gifted teachers, who are committed to delivering lessons that are lively and enjoyable, as well as being rigorous and demanding. Strategies for supporting gifted and talented students are well established and are continually updated and extended.

Busy days and full weekends

One of Monkton's strengths is the breadth of activities available to pupils at weekends – in fact, many of our day pupils will spend all weekend at school just so they can join in the Monkton social life. Every Saturday afternoon there is a full programme of sporting activities which follow on after morning lessons. There are some brilliant social events hosted by the houses throughout the year – a bonfire party, a summer fete, a barbecue, to name but a few – and these, together with the music, drama and sporting competitions, keep the students extremely busy. They can also enjoy the School productions, DVD nights, sixth form centre parties, junior discos and informal concerts – there is almost too much to choose from!

Transforming lives

Our outstanding pastoral care, strong moral framework and culture of service to others make us an ideal choice for parents looking for a school that will nurture and challenge their child spiritually, emotionally and socially as well as developing their academic potential to the full. We aim to instil our values of confidence, integrity, humility and service in all of our pupils.

Come and visit

To find out more, visit www.monktoncombeschool.com or to arrange a visit, please contact the Head of Admissions, on +44 (0)1225 721133 or e-mail: admissions@monkton.org.uk.

(Founded 1868)

Monkton Combe, Bath,
Bath & North-East Somerset BA2 7HG UK

Tel: 01225 721133

Email: admissions@monkton.org.uk

Website: www.monktoncombeschool.com

Principal: Mr Chris Wheeler

Appointed: January 2016

School type: Coeducational Day & Boarding

Age range of pupils: 2–18

Average class size: 22

Teacher/pupil ratio: 1:9

Oxford Tutorial College

Oxford Tutorial College is a highly successful independent college specialising in A-level, BTEC and GCSE courses for students 15-19 in the heart of Oxford.

Established in 1988, the college has gained an excellent reputation for providing effective preparation for public examinations and university entry, achieved by thorough, exam-specific teaching and close attention to the needs of each individual student. We strongly believe that one size really does not fit all. We have a fantastic track record in helping students achieve their best, with many of our students being offered places at Russell Group and top 20 universities.

The OTC Experience

The college offers an environment quite different from that of a traditional school. The teaching approach is refreshingly interactive and informal. The emphasis on small group work enables a clear focus on individual needs and learning styles and a variation of pace and emphasis, which helps students to approach their work calmly and objectively. This 'tutorial method' is an extremely flexible teaching approach, which provides a dialogue between tutor and students and thus enables reinforcement of understanding and careful attention to areas of weakness.

The support provided by both subject tutors and each student's Senior Tutor is thoughtful and creative and students are encouraged at every stage to take an active part in the learning process through self-motivation, involvement, personal study and research. This is an important preparation for higher education. Various extra-curricular activities are offered enabling students to explore and develop the skills they will need in later life.

"I have found the quality of the teaching to be great and the enthusiasm teachers have tfor the subject inspiring."
– Lisha, A Level Student

Preparing students for University Life

The college has an inclusive ethos and a culture which encourages industry and a growing sense of responsibility. Students are encouraged at every stage to take an active part in the learning process.

There are no restrictions as to the choice of subjects or subject combinations, although students are helped to make choices appropriate to their degree course or vocational aim and directed towards subjects which engage their interest and fit in with their abilities and aptitudes.

The College

Our campus is a friendly, welcoming place and a home away from home for young people of many different cultures. There are plenty of social events throughout the year to let you get to know your fellow students better. We are very proud of what our students accomplish every year.

Our graduates go on to study at some of the UK's most prestigious universities and have stellar careers ahead of them thanks to the skills they learnt and choices they made while studying with us. They leave us equipped with essential qualifications, valuable life experience and English language skills that help them communicate confidently. But more than that, they also take away happy memories and lasting friendships.

Academic scholarships are available, please ask the College for further details.

To align itself with its increased focus on 2-year A-Level and BTEC programmes and the significant investment being made in improving its teaching buildings,

The college will, on 1st January 2019, be renamed Oxford Sixth Form College.

OXFORD
TUTORIALCOLLEGE
INDEPENDENT SIXTH FORM

(Founded 1988)

12-13 King Edward Street, Oxford, Oxfordshire OX1 4HT UK

Tel: +44 (0)1865 793333

Email: admissions@oxfordtutorialcollege.com

Website: www.oxfordtutorialcollege.com

Principal: Mr Mark Love

Appointed: 2017

School type: Co-educational Day & Boarding

Age range of pupils: 15–19

No. of pupils enrolled as at 01/09/2018: 207

Average class size: Av 4-8, Max 6-10

Shiplake College

Shiplake College is a thriving boarding and day school for boys aged 11-18, with girls joining in the Sixth Form. The College starts its 60th anniversary year in September 2018 with a record 485 pupils on roll, including 200 girls and boys in the Sixth Form. Overlooking the River Thames, two miles upstream of the famous Henley Royal Regatta stretch, students enjoy an inspirational 45-acre rural site. Flexi, weekly and full boarding is available from Year 7 (age 11).

Shiplake provides a friendly, supportive and structured environment to bring out the best in each and every pupil and aims to equip them with the skills they need to enter the next stage of their lives as confident, personable and talented young adults. Increasingly academically ambitious and renowned for outstanding pastoral care and personal development, the College welcomes pupils with wide-ranging skills and talents, who will make the most of the many opportunities we offer them.

Every pupil is placed at the heart of Shiplake life and the College's ethos is underpinned by the three Is – Inclusive, Individual and Inspirational. All pupils are valued regardless of academic prowess, artistic flair or sporting ability, with opportunities for all to join in and try new things.

We are a small community where every pupil becomes well-known to their House's pastoral team, especially the Housemaster, personal tutor and matron. Each pupil's best method of learning is identified and catered for by their teachers, with high-achieving pupils continually stretched while those requiring additional support can access it in a variety of ways. Interpersonal skills, confidence and talents are also discovered outside the classroom. Two afternoons are reserved for an array of clubs and activities, including a comprehensive outdoor education programme, with pupils encouraged to extend their horizons and experience new challenges and responsibilities.

We recruit highly motivated teaching staff with an ability and passion to inspire future generations and we ensure pupils have the best possible learning resources and facilities at their disposal. The environment we provide encourages pupils to take inspiration from their teachers, their surroundings, and each other.

2019 should see the College open a Sixth Form Centre, with a café where Year 12 and 13 girls and boys can socialise and work independently and some additional classrooms, and also a Boathouse and Multi-Activity Centre. This exciting facility will not only include storage for rowing boats and other watersports, mountain biking and outdoor education, CCF and DofE equipment, but will also incorporate an indoor archery/rifle range, a climbing wall, weights room and an ergo room, which transforms into a function room with a balcony overlooking the river.

There are evening boarding games and activities and full boarders take part in a vibrant weekend programme of trips and events on Saturday afternoons and Sundays.

Academic, Art, Music, Drama and Sport Scholarships, and means-tested bursaries, are available. The College is also offering one 100% All-Rounder scholarship to an exceptional boy currently at a state-maintained primary school looking to join Year 7 in September 2019, who would not be able to attend Shiplake without substantial financial support.

Entry points are normally at Year 7 (11+), Year 9 (13+) and Year 12 (16+). Prospective families are encouraged to arrange an individual visit or attend an open morning, which take place in September and March each year. Please go to www.shiplake.org.uk to book your attendance, complete a registration form and explore the whole site, which includes details of admissions processes, fees, bus routes and answers to most academic, co-curricular and pastoral questions that prospective parents may have.

SHIPLAKE COLLEGE
HENLEY-ON-THAMES

(Founded 1959)

Henley-on-Thames, Oxfordshire RG9 4BW UK

Tel: +44 (0)1189 402455

Fax: +44 (0)1189 405204

Email: registrar@shiplake.org.uk

Website: www.shiplake.org.uk

Headmaster: Mr A G S Davies BSc(St Andrews)

Appointed: 2004

School type: Boys' Boarding & Day

Religious Denomination: Church of England

Age range of boys: 11–18

Age range of girls: 16–18

No. of pupils enrolled as at 01/09/2018: 485

Boys: 433 **Girls:** 52 **Sixth Form:** 200

No. of boarders: 135

Fees per annum as at 01/09/2018:

Day: £17,700–£22,230

Weekly Boarding: £24,810–£31,020

Full Boarding: £33,075

Flexi Boarding (2 nights per week): £20,895 – £25,425

Average class size: 16

Teacher/pupil ratio: 1:6

St Mary's Calne

St Mary's (founded in 1873) is an independent boarding and day school for girls aged 11-18, a happy, purposeful and flourishing community of around 365 pupils with an 80% to 20% boarding-to-day ratio. St Mary's welcomes cultural diversity and around 15% of the students come from overseas.

The school is located in the market town of Calne and amidst the Wiltshire Downs, an area of stunning natural beauty and historical significance. The school is within easy reach of the university towns of Bath, Bristol and Oxford and just over an hour by train from London. This ideal location means that the girls benefit from a huge range of curriculum-enhancing opportunities as well as extra-curricular ones.

Focus on the individual

Small by design, St Mary's provides exceptional all-round education in a warm, nurturing environment. It is the individualised approach to every aspect of school life that makes St Mary's Calne special.

The pastoral care is outstanding. Every girl has a Tutor to support her through aspects of school life, from organisational skills and subject choices through to university application.

High Achievers

St Mary's Calne has a well-deserved reputation for academic excellence. The school was the top achieving independent school in the South West, (The Sunday Times Schools Guide 2018) and is also the first independent school in the UK to be given the prestigious Platinum Science Mark Award. In 2018, St Mary's Calne students went on to study at a range of leading Russell Group universities including: Oxford, Cambridge, Durham, Edinburgh, Exeter, Imperial, LSE, Newcastle, UCL and Warwick. The girls will be studying a diverse range of subjects, ranging from Architecture, Chemistry, Civil Engineering to Fine Art, Politics & Modern Languages, Law and Medicine.

Outside the Classroom

Opportunities in sport, music, art and drama abound and the facilities are superb, including a new £2.55 million sports complex and full-size astro, theatre, and a Sixth Form Centre with 120+ girls.

80% of girls play musical instruments and take part in a wide variety of ensembles. The girls perform at many events, both in the locally community and further afield.

Drama productions in the purpose-built theatre are of the highest standard and have transferred to the London stage. The Drama Department has a unique relationship with RADA, offering a course in advanced communication skills and girls also perform annually at the Edinburgh Fringe.

The girls do exceptionally well in the Young Enterprise Programme, progressing to the National Final in 2017. Many pupils are talented artists and 2018 saw a student win the Digital Prize in Saatchi's National LOVE ART Competition and two girls had their works longlisted by The Arts Society to become Royal Society of British Artists (RBA) Scholars. The girls excel at sport, and the school is represented at county level in several major sports, nationally in athletics and lacrosse, and internationally in horse riding, with all girls taking advantage of the superb sports facilities. The girls also enjoy many other sports, including tennis, hockey, fencing and ski racing.

Trips abound and in 2017-18 included a Classics Trip to Rome, a French Trip to Samoens and a Music Tour to Poland.

For further information, or to book onto one of our Open Days, please visit: www.stmaryscalne.org

ST MARY'S CALNE

(Founded 1873)

Curzon Street, Calne, Wiltshire SN11 0DF UK

Tel: 01249 857200

Fax: 01249 857207

Email: office@stmaryscalne.org

Website: www.stmaryscalne.org

Headmistress: Dr Felicia Kirk BA(University of Maryland), MA, PhD(Brown University)

Appointed: January 2013

School type: Girls' Boarding & Day

Religious Denomination: Church of England

Age range of girls: 11–18

No. of pupils enrolled as at 01/09/2018: 365

Sixth Form: 120

No. of boarders: 290

Fees per annum as at 01/09/2018:

Day: £29,025

Full Boarding: £38,925

Average class size: Max 17, smaller in the Sixth Form

Teacher/pupil ratio: 1:5

Wycombe Abbey

Wycombe Abbey is a global leader in outstanding education and modern boarding. The School is committed to creating tomorrow's women leaders and has a long tradition of academic excellence, it is consistently one of the country's top performing schools.

Our learning environment is supportive, yet challenging, with a sense that pupils and their teachers are on an educational journey together. We pride ourselves on the outstanding teaching provided by our specialists who communicate a genuine love of their subject and serve to inspire the girls they teach.

We believe that education should not simply be about delivering a curriculum and examination syllabus, but that real learning stems from stimulating intellectual curiosity and nurturing a love for the subjects being taught, which will stay with our girls throughout their lives.

In all we do, boarding is the key to our continued success. The School has a culture that inspires throughout the day, seven days a week, empowering girls to achieve their best, academically and socially. In our happy and close community, each girl is known, and cherished, as an individual. Consequently, every girl's potential, whatever that might be, is explored and fulfilled.

Girls learn to be independent, to value and support others, and to develop the skills needed for future challenges in a global workplace. Given the nature of boarding life, girls are able to enjoy a wealth of co-curricular opportunities. Each and every girl carves out a unique learning path according to her interests and has the space to thrive within our magnificent grounds. Our approach to boarding is also sympathetic to the needs of today's families and pupils have the opportunity to go home regularly and parents are actively involved in the numerous School events and activities.

The School is an oasis of calm, set in 170 acres of magnificent, conservation-listed grounds and woodland. Modern, state-of-the-art facilities include the Sports Centre, with a 25-metre indoor pool, the Performing Arts Centre with a theatre and recital hall, an atrium café, dance and fitness studios, and extensive sports pitches. Two brand new Boarding Houses opened in September 2017 and a refurbishment of all the boarding accommodation will follow.

Wycombe Abbey is easily accessible with excellent transport links. It is about 35 miles west of London and 30 miles east of Oxford. It is a 30-minute journey from Heathrow Airport and a 90-minute journey from Gatwick Airport by road.

To find out more about gaining a place at Wycombe Abbey, please visit our website at www.wycombeabbey.com or contact our Admissions Team on (+44) (0) 1494 897008 or by emailing registrar@wycombeabbey.com.

WYCOMBE ABBEY

(Founded 1896)

High Wycombe, Buckinghamshire HP11 1PE UK

Tel: +44 (0)1494 897008

Email: registrar@wycombeabbey.com

Website: www.wycombeabbey.com

Headmistress:
Mrs Rhiannon J Wilkinson MA (Oxon) MEd

Appointed: September 2013

School type: Girls' Day & Boarding

Religious Denomination: Church of England

Age range of girls: 11–18

No. of pupils enrolled as at 01/09/2018: 631

Fees per annum as at 01/09/2018:

Day: £29,205

Full Boarding: £38,940

East

Abbot's Hill School

Abbot's Hill School is a happy and thriving community in which pupils are encouraged to aim high, to grasp opportunities, enjoy learning and make lasting friendships.

The school offers an all-round education for girls aged 4-16 years, and the Day Nursery & Pre-School caters for girls and boys from 6 months. Our happy and united community gives each pupil the opportunity to shine.

The school is set within 76 acres of parkland on the outskirts of Hemel Hempstead, where our first-rate facilities provide space for outdoor sport and extra-curricular activities. Our Abbot's Hill's historic campus offers modern and extensive facilities in a magnificent country setting.

Abbot's Hill has a strong record of academic success. Throughout the school, pupils are taught in genuinely small classes. Excellent teaching and personalised support ensure that everyone is inspired to exceed their potential and to thrive.

The broad curriculum is enhanced by a wide range of trips and activities to stimulate learning. Extra-curricular clubs offer a lively balance of music, sports, languages, debating, drama and more. In short, there is something for everyone!

At Abbot's Hill, we pride ourselves on our pastoral care. We give individual attention to each girl so that she will develop as a person, but also to ensure she succeeds. The sense of being part of an extended family is frequently commented on by pupils, parents and staff alike.

The school's ethos is one which places the well-being and success of the individual child at its centre, and this is reflected in many aspects of school life.

In such a nurturing environment, pupils grow naturally in confidence, are happy to embrace new challenges and eagerly take on increasing responsibilities. Pupils leave Abbot's Hill fully equipped to take on the challenges and opportunities life has to offer.

Abbot's Hill girls progress seamlessly from one stage of education to the next. They become fully equipped to take on the challenges and opportunities life has to offer.

Our consistently excellent results at GCSE are testament to our ethos – that at Abbot's Hill, your daughter will achieve her very best because she is happy.

"I feel happy sending my daughter to school knowing that she is being given every opportunity to develop into a confident, well-rounded individual." – Prep School Parent

"There is a huge variety of things to do here and so many options. It really inspires you and helps you to spread your wings." – Senior School Pupil

Abbot's Hill

(Founded 1912)

Bunkers Lane, Hemel Hempstead, Hertfordshire HP3 8RP UK

Tel: 01442 240333

Email: registrar@abbotshill.herts.sch.uk

Website: www.abbotshill.herts.sch.uk

Headmistress: Mrs E Thomas BA (Hons), PGCE, NPQH

Appointed: January 2013

School type: Girls' Day

Age range of girls: 4–16

No. of pupils enrolled as at 01/09/2018: 510

Boys: 20 *Girls:* 490

Prep School: 240

Senior School: 270

Fees per annum as at 01/09/2018:

Prep School: £10,764 – £13,521

Years 7–11: £18,516

Average class size: 12–18

Bedford Girls' School

As parents, we often ask ourselves how we can help our children become happy and successful.

As educators, we are asking the same question, and Bedford Girls' School believes the answers lie in preparing students not for the world of today but for the world of tomorrow. We believe in developing lifelong learners who are able to communicate, collaborate, question, work independently and engage in an ever changing world.

Employers often tell us that graduates are unable to think for themselves, articulate clearly or work cross-functionally. It is the role of educators to make sure students are prepared to enter a global world with confidence and knowledge.

Underpinned by the International Baccalaureate philosophy, Bedford Girls' School focuses on providing a truly holistic education for girls aged 7 to 18. Central to the School's ethos is delivering a forward thinking education, which is not solely determined by academic success, but by the development of wider learner attributes, ensuring students are equipped with the skills and self-assurance to face the challenges and opportunities ahead.

Our education puts equal emphasis on the co-curricular and the academic, engaging students in drama, music and sport where they learn vital wider life skills. We help our students recognise the responsibility they have to create a better world through extensive community service programmes.

Girls join us from the age of 7 (into Year 3) and our Junior School offers an exciting and innovative International Baccalaureate led curriculum developing inquiring minds, where the girls think independently and embrace creativity. As they move into the Senior School in Year 7, we embed deeper learning skills so the demands of the GCSE years can be easily achieved. Students continue to flourish as they enter the Sixth Form where they can choose to study either the International Baccalaureate Diploma Programme or A Levels. Our wide academic curriculum allows them to follow their interests free from gender stereotyping, with two thirds of Sixth Formers taking at least one STEM subject and balancing their options with a mix of Humanities, Languages and Arts.

We are a top five UK girls' sports school, excelling across a wide range of sports including lacrosse, hockey, netball, rowing, tennis and athletics. We offer outstanding art, textiles, music and drama facilities, including a dedicated Music House and a state of the art Drama Studio, enabling the girls to grow as both performers and artists, but also develop skills behind the scenes in technical, and production roles. With over 100 co-curriculum clubs running each year and endless trips and excursions, the choices are vast and our students are always expanding their horizons, taking risks and exploring new opportunities.

Our results speak for themselves. In Summer 2018 we averaged 37.5 points at IB Diploma, 75% of entries attained an A*–B grade at A Level and IB Combined; and over 71% of all GCSE papers were graded A*–A, with 29% of papers awarded a Level 9. Each year over 90% of Sixth Form leavers achieve their first or second place offers and go on to study at top universities both in the UK and overseas. However, more importantly, our girls leave Bedford Girls' School as confident young women ready to make a positive difference to the world around them.

(Founded 1882)

Cardington Road, Bedford, Bedfordshire MK42 0BX UK

Tel: 01234 361900

Fax: 01234 353 552

Email: admissions@bedfordgirlsschool.co.uk

Website: www.bedfordgirlsschool.co.uk

Headmistress: Miss Jo MacKenzie BSc, MSc

Appointed: 2010

School type: Girls' Day

Religious Denomination:
Christian, open to all faiths or none

Age range of girls: 7–18

No. of pupils enrolled as at 01/09/2018: 903

Fees per term as at 01/09/2018:

Junior School: £3,146

Senior School: £4,421

Sixth Form: £4,421

Average class size: 20-24

Bedford School

Bedford School is an independent boarding and day school that offers boys aged 7-18 a complete and balanced education. We aim to teach boys to think intelligently, act wisely and be fully engaged in a challenging and changing world.

Situated on an extensive parkland estate of 50 acres in the heart of Bedford, the school is a lively community of day boys, weekly and full boarders.

Our highly qualified teaching staff are selected on their ability to communicate and inspire. The result is a vibrant, stimulating environment, were boys can be happy, grow in self-confidence, thrive academically and make the most of the wide range of opportunities on offer. Our broad curriculum offers boys a varied choice of subjects, and our academic success is demonstrated by a long history of impressive examination results at GCSE, A level, and in the International Baccalaureate Diploma, and university entrances: in 2017 78% of boys went on to Russell Group universities, including Oxford and Cambridge.

In addition to our established reputation for academic excellence, we are renowned for our strengths in sport, music and the arts.

Throughout each boy's time at the school, we aim to inspire a lifelong interest in sport, promoting teamwork, wellbeing, fitness and, most of all, enjoyment. The School's sporting resources are outstanding – a floodlit twin Astroturf complex, indoor swimming pool, tennis and squash courts, playing fields, fitness centre and recreation centre combine to provide first-class facilities from which many international players have emerged.

With our state-of-the-art music school, Bedford has one of the largest music departments in the country and a high proportion of students learn to play one or more instruments. In fact many parents choose Bedford School in preference to a specialist music school to provide excellent music tuition within a strong academic environment.

Drama and theatre studies continue to thrive, and our commitment to the arts is demonstrated through our stunning 290-seat theatre, The Quarry Theatre at St Luke's, which officially opened in July 2015. Our first-rate art studios are available to everyone to explore sculpture, photography, fine art and design.

We offer an extensive and diverse programme of extracurricular activities to all boys; including the CCF (Combined Cadet Force), Duke of Edinburgh's Award Scheme, community service, fundraising charity groups, and more than 50 other clubs and societies from astronomy to young enterprise.

Whilst committed to the benefits of single sex teaching, we also work closely with our sister school Bedford Girls' School to provide a wide ranging programme of co-educational extracurricular and social activities.

Scholarships worth up to 35% of annual school fees are available to boys who excel academically, or show outstanding talent in art, drama, music or sport. Families can also apply for additional funding through our means-tested bursary scheme.

We warmly invite you to join us at one of our open mornings or for a private visit to see the school in action, meet the boys and staff, and get a flavour of life here at Bedford School. Please contact Anna Steiger, Director of Admissions, for further information on 01234 362216 or email admissions@bedfordschool.org.uk.

Bedford School is part of The Harpur Trust. Company No. 3475202/Charity no. 1066861.

(Founded 1552)

De Parys Avenue, Bedford, Bedfordshire MK40 2TU UK

Tel: +44 (0)1234 362216

Email: admissions@bedfordschool.org.uk

Website: www.bedfordschool.org.uk

Head Master: Mr James Hodgson BA

Appointed: 2014

School type: Boys' Day & Boarding

Religious Denomination: Anglican

Age range of boys: 7–18 years

No. of pupils enrolled as at 01/09/2018: 1124

Fees per annum as at 01/09/2018:

Day: £12,333–£19,032

Weekly Boarding: £20,919–£31,125

Full Boarding: £21,948–£32,190

Average class size: 15-20

Teacher/pupil ratio: 1:10

Brentwood School

Brentwood School shines out as a beacon of excellence. Academically, we sit comfortably alongside the best day and boarding schools in the country, and we enjoy an unparalleled local reputation.

Our students are happy individuals who thrive on the high standards which are expected of them. They benefit from state-of-the-art facilities, set in the heart of Brentwood in Essex, and surrounded by 75 acres of green playing fields and gardens.

We celebrate a 462-year history and take our heritage seriously. We are a Christian School with a chapel and a chaplain, and our School values, encapsulated in our motto "Virtue, Learning and Manners", have as much resonance today as they did when written by English poet John Donne in 1622. Our pupils are expected to have self-respect, to exhibit pride in their appearance and embrace values such as courtesy, consideration for others, kindness, looking after each other, honour, courage, sportsmanship, duty and selflessness.

Brentwood School pupils achieve excellent academic standards that rank among some of the best in the country. Our track record of exam results shows consistent high grades are achieved by all our pupils. They work exceptionally hard and are supported by highly professional and inspiring teachers to achieve excellent results at both GCSE level and in Sixth Form, whether studying A levels or the IB Diploma. An average of eight students per year are offered places at Oxford or Cambridge and over 80% of offers are from Russell Group universities.

We use the freedom of independence wisely to innovate and develop a truly creative curriculum – one that really is best for our pupils.

We offer both GCSEs and IGCSEs; A levels and the IB Diploma. More recent curriculum developments include the introduction of a Human Universe course in the Fourth and Fifth Year, which examines critical thinking and global issues.

Brentwood was the first school in Essex, and one of the first in the country, to adopt the Diamond Model: single-sex classes from the age of 11-16 within an overall mixed gender environment. We believe this model helps our teachers to tailor their teaching to the different learning styles of boys and girls and provides the best of single gender teaching within a coeducational environment.

From an early age, we encourage pupils to aim high, think creatively and develop independence, so by the time they leave Sixth Form, they are well prepared for the expected, but can also tackle the unknowns. A flourishing Old Brentwoods community keeps thousands of alumni connected across the globe.

Our vast and exciting co-curricular programme enjoys national prominence, and we focus on providing opportunities for all to participate, as well as the pursuit of excellence for the most able.

Our Combined Cadet Force is one of the oldest and largest in the country, we offer The Duke of Edinburgh's Award to pupils who want to satisfy their taste for adventure, and a Community Service Unit which raises tens of thousands of pounds every year to help specific charitable organisations.

Our sports centre houses a 25-metre swimming pool, glass-backed squash courts, fencing salle and dance studio and pupils achieve top sporting honours both nationally and internationally.

Our musicians have played in the National Youth Orchestra, and our actors have gained places in the National Youth Theatre, RADA and other top Drama schools.

The lessons pupils learn at Brentwood will last for a lifetime. Integrity, initiative, a spirit of enterprise and an international mind-set help our pupils to thrive in the twenty-first century.

Brentwood School

(Founded 1557)

Middleton Hall Lane, Brentwood, Essex CM15 8EE UK

Tel: 01277 243243

Fax: 01277 243299

Email: headmaster@brentwood.essex.sch.uk

Website: www.brentwoodschool.co.uk

Headmaster: Mr Ian Davies

Appointed: September 2004

School type: Coeducational Day & Boarding

Religious Denomination: Church of England

Age range of pupils: 3–18

No. of pupils enrolled as at 01/09/2018: 1600

Boys: 880 **Girls:** 720

Fees per annum as at 01/09/2018:

Day: £18,945

Full Boarding: £37,128

Average class size: 18 in Prep & Senior; 8 in Sixth Form

Teacher/pupil ratio: 1:9

Felsted School

Felsted offers boys and girls aged four to eighteen a first class all round education, based on a safe, rural village campus in stunning North Essex, only one hour from London and Cambridge. We welcome students from all over the world to appreciate a British boarding school education. For our more local families we also offer day and a variety of boarding options, with daily bus routes from across the region.

A rounded, holistic approach

At Felsted, we value emotional and social development as much as academic and intellectual development. From the moment that your son or daughter joins Felsted's supportive and close knit community, he or she will be nurtured and challenged. We take pride in knowing and valuing every child as an individual, stretching them, encouraging them, and appreciating them for every contribution that they make to the community. Characteristics such as compassion towards one's peers or resilience through adversity are developed just as much as creative, academic or sporting prowess.

Pupils instantly become part of the Felsted family and quickly make new friends. They thrive in a School which cares for the individual and gives so many opportunities to excel both academically and in a wide range of activities. Away from the classroom, your child will become a valuable member of sporting teams (hockey, tennis, netball, cricket, rugby, squash, polo etc), involved in drama and music or many of the other clubs and activities available. The welcoming Boarding and Day Houses ensure that strong friendships are made, with an active weekend programme to ensure your child is happy and stimulated.

We believe that our rounded and holistic approach, supported by the global Round Square network to which we belong, is what will make a difference to your child's path through life. In return, we hope that your child will also develop into someone who seeks to make a difference to the lives of others at school and in the wider world. Leadership, Service, Charity and Internationalism are core values here at Felsted.

Felsted Highlights
- Leading British all round education for boys & girls aged 4 to 18, established in 1564
- Small class sizes, modern and dedicated facilities
- Top degree apprenticeships and university entry, including Oxbridge
- GCSEs, International Baccalaureate Diploma & A Levels
- Superb International induction course and Summer School
- Established international links and work education programme
- Outstanding co-curricular opportunities on site
- Excellence in sport: top quality coaches, facilities and fixtures
- West End quality drama and outstanding art facilities
- Unique partnership with the Junior Guildhall School of Music
- Scholarships, Awards and Bursaries available
- Rated 'Excellent' in every aspect, ISI Inspection
- A stunning village campus only one hour from London & Cambridge

"Felsted produces self-starting, entrepreneurial and independent spirits...a school that brings out the best in everyone."
The Good Schools Guide

Felsted

(Founded 1564)

Felsted, Great Dunmow, Essex CM6 3LL UK

Tel: 01371 822605

Email: internationaladmissions@felsted.org

Website: www.felsted.org

Headmaster: Mr Chris Townsend

Appointed: 2015

School type: Coeducational Day & Boarding

Age range of pupils: 13–18

No. of pupils enrolled as at 01/09/2018: 522

Boys: 307 **Girls:** 215 **Sixth Form:** 426

Fees per annum as at 01/09/2018:

Day: £23,550

Weekly Boarding: £33,390

Full Boarding: £35,985

Average class size: 18

Haileybury

Haileybury is an independent co-educational boarding school, located between London and Cambridge, in 500 acres of beautiful Hertfordshire countryside. Our spectacular grounds are home to outstanding facilities, excellent teaching and superb pastoral care for our community of boarding and day pupils.

Founded in 1862, Haileybury is proud of its history, tradition and values, taking the best from the past whilst also looking to the future. Academic rigour and outstanding co-curricular provision are at the heart of the college, providing exceptional opportunities and a truly all-round education, which enables our pupils to discover enduring passions and talents. Haileyburians leave as confident, tolerant and ambitious individuals, who are leaders and life-long learners and who can make a difference in the world beyond school.

Academic opportunity

We offer a dedicated Lower School for Years 7 and 8, a wide range of GCSEs and IGCSEs and the choice of the IB Diploma or A Levels in the Sixth Form. Haileybury is one of the leading IB schools in the UK as ranked by The Times' IB League Table and in the Top 100 Independent Schools for A Levels.

Boarding and day

More than two thirds of pupils are boarders and school life is centred around the 12 different boarding houses and Lower School. Children may join at 11+, 13+ or 16+. Flexi-boarding is available in Lower School (Years 7 and 8), allowing families this option without committing to full boarding early in a child's senior school career. From Year 9 onwards, full boarding is offered with the additional flexibility of pupils being able (if they so wish) to return home after sports commitments on Saturday afternoons.

Exceptional opportunities

A key part of our philosophy is about empowering each child to follow their passions and to build their self-confidence.

We therefore provide an enormous range of co-curricular opportunities, spanning everything from music and drama to sport and physical activities. There are a huge number of clubs and societies to cater for all interests including sailing, rowing, rugby, lacrosse, netball, swimming, Combined Cadet Force, Duke of Edinburgh Award, Model United Nations, charity and community action and much more.

Pupils benefit from professional sports coaches and the college regularly hosts speakers and performers from the arts, sporting and academic worlds. Music at Haileybury is exceptional, with an abundance of concerts, recitals and public performances each year and more than 30 visiting specialists teaching hundreds of instrumental lessons every week.

Supportive environment

A caring environment is crucial to happiness and fulfilment. For those who join us, Haileybury is like a home-from-home. Warm and friendly, we give each and every child the confidence to find their identity, embracing failings as much as successes in their personal journey of discovery.

A warm welcome

We have a busy programme of Open Days and taster events which take place throughout the year. We warmly invite you to visit to discover what life at Haileybury has to offer and why your child will flourish here. For further information, please contact the Head of Admissions, Mrs Michele Metcalfe, at admissions@haileybury.com.

(Founded 1862)

Haileybury, Hertford, Hertfordshire SG13 7NU UK

Tel: +44 (0)1992 706200

Email: admissions@haileybury.com

Website: www.haileybury.com

The Master: Mr Martin Collier MA BA PGCE

Appointed: September 2017

School type: Coeducational Boarding & Day

Age range of pupils: 11–18

(entry at 11+, 13+ and 16+)

No. of pupils enrolled as at 01/09/2018: 833

Boys: 482 **Girls:** 351 **Sixth Form:** 317

No. of boarders: 541

Fees per annum as at 01/09/2018:

Day: £17,031–£25,620

Full Boarding: £21,837–£34,422

Teacher/pupil ratio: 1:7

Heath Mount School

Description: Heath Mount is a thriving independent, co-educational Pre-prep and Prep school for children aged 3-13. It is set in 40 acres on the idyllic Woodhall Park Estate, near Ware and Hertford.

We promote an ethos underpinned by strong values. These are acceptance, respect, integrity, industry and achievement. Whilst academic achievement and exam success are important, it is equally vital that the school nourishes, prepares, stimulates, supports and channels pupils physically, emotionally, socially and mentally and provides them with drive and resilience for the years ahead.

Facilities: We benefit from our own Forest School and an all-weather Astroturf. A spacious central plateau houses rugby, football and cricket pitches, as well as our netball courts.

We have a well-equipped gymnasium, and our swimming pool offers the best of both worlds, with a retractable roof giving shelter in the winter and outdoor swimming in the warmer summer months, so our children really do have the opportunity to enjoy sport all year round.

Inside, all classrooms are equipped with the very latest in interactive technology. We have a dedicated ICT suite in the Pre-prep school and a newly refurbished ICT facility in the Prep school.

Our purpose-built Pre-prep is in the same grounds as the Prep school but separate from it. It has its own library, computer room, music room, dining room and hall in addition to a beautiful outdoor playground.

Pre-prep children also use many of the Prep school's facilities such as the Sports Hall, Astroturf, Swimming Pool, Pottery Room and Chapel.

In September 2015 we opened our new classroom block for Year 3 and 4 pupils and in summer 2017 we opened our magnificent new Performing Arts Centre.

Feeder Schools: We feed to a wide range of senior schools including Eton, Harrow, Westminster, Radley, Oundle, Uppingham, Benenden, St Albans Boys, St Albans Girls, Haileybury, Bishop's Stortford College, Felsted, The Leys and Brighton College.

Exam results: In the academic year 2017-18, we gained 48 scholarships to senior schools.

Entrance procedure: Prospective pupils may be registered with us from any time after birth and we welcome the majority of our children to our Nursery in the September following their third birthday. We are not a selective school and do not assess children starting at this stage though we do encourage early registration as places are limited and our Pre-prep is often oversubscribed.

We usually have a smaller number of spaces available as our children enter Reception and do not formally assess at this age, but will invite your child in to spend time with us to ensure that they have the social and developmental skills to access the Early Years Curriculum.

For entry into the Prep school for Year 3 and above, assessments in Maths, reading, writing and non-verbal reasoning will usually take place in addition to an observational assessment to ensure that your child is able to access our broad curriculum. References will also be sought from your child's current school. Provided we have space in our school we do accept children at any stage from Year 3 up to Year 8 entry.

Heath Mount School

(Founded 1796)

Woodhall Park, Watton-at-Stone, Hertford, Hertfordshire SG14 3NG UK

Tel: 01920 830230

Email: registrar@heathmount.org

Website: www.heathmount.org

Headmaster: Mr Chris Gillam BEd(Hons)

Appointed: September 2014

School type: Coeducational Day & Flexi-boarding

Age range of pupils: 3–13

No. of pupils enrolled as at 01/09/2018: 480

Boys: 254 **Girls:** 226

Fees per annum as at 01/09/2018:

Day: £11,550–£17,805

Average class size: 10-18

King's Ely

We know that if we could bottle the spirit of King's Ely we would be onto a real winner, but we would like you to come and experience it for yourself.

Nestled in the heart of the beautiful cathedral city of Ely, King's Ely is an inspiringly visionary independent co-educational day and boarding school, yet one that is built on a fascinating history stretching back over 1,000 years.

We serve the academic and pastoral needs of around 1,000 boys and girls from the age of one right the way through to 18, with boarders from seven years old. King's Ely is located just 15 minutes north of Cambridge and a short walk from Ely train station, with school buses stopping at key locations around the area.

The adventure of a King's Ely education enables pupils of all ages to flourish, from the toddlers in King's Ely Acremont and Nursery to the young men and women in our Sixth Form; and whether a student shines in a classroom or lab, on a stage, on a pitch or on a mountainside, our school promises an abundance of opportunity for personal development, both academically and socially.

We empower our young people to challenge themselves, to push beyond the boundaries of their own expectations and to achieve more than they ever believed possible. King's Ely students achieve excellent GCSE and A Level results, with 98% gaining places in their first or insurance choice university. But our school is about much more than league tables.

Innovative approaches to teaching and learning are the hallmark of every section of King's Ely. Through a broad and balanced curriculum, pupils develop the self-knowledge and inner resilience that will enable them to face the challenges of an ever-changing world.

Music, drama, art and textiles are each embedded in the culture of King's Ely, with vast opportunities for pupils of all abilities and aspirations.

All major sports are offered, along with an impressive array of other activities, helping every pupil to realise their sporting potential. Rowing, athletics, golf, cricket, hockey, tennis, rugby, netball, equestrian and football – the choices are endless. The working week, which no longer includes formal lessons on Saturdays, also enables pupils to participate fully in regional and national events.

King's Ely boasts some of the region's most historic buildings yet teaching facilities are modern and purpose-built. Our close links with Ely Cathedral make the perfect setting for concerts and performances, a daily extension to the school's workspace, the school chapel, and a place of outstanding beauty and spirituality.

Boarders, including the Ely Cathedral Boy and Girl Choristers, live in picturesque boarding houses, well led by caring housemasters and housemistresses. A strong pastoral structure where childhood is respected and cherished is a key feature.

From the high peaks of the Himalayas to the gushing torrents of the rivers in the Alps, our unique Ely Scheme also offers boundless opportunities for pupils to learn through outdoor education. We also give students the chance to undertake their Duke of Edinburgh Award at all three levels.

King's Ely is a family – a community that is vibrant, nurturing and inclusive. We are a school that can take each child on a seamless journey, travelling from one section to the next, whilst welcoming newcomers at key transition stages. Only by visiting King's Ely can you feel the energy and warmth of our community.

(Founded 973)

Ely, Cambridgeshire CB7 4DB UK

Tel: 01353 660557

Fax: 01353 667485

Email: admissions@kingsely.org

Website: www.kingsely.org

Principal:
Mrs Susan Freestone MEd, GRSM, LRAM, ARCM, FRSA

Appointed: 2004

School type: Coeducational Boarding & Day

Age range of pupils: 1–18

No. of pupils enrolled as at 01/09/2018: 1048

Fees per annum as at 01/09/2018:

Day: £10,077–£21,459

Full Boarding: £22,692–£31,065

Average class size: Max 20

Teacher/pupil ratio: 1:9

Mander Portman Woodward – Cambridge

Cambridge is where the MPW success story began. Some 44 years ago, three Cambridge graduates – Messieurs Mander, Portman and Woodward came together with an ambition to create a unique secondary education experience. They focused on several elements, based on their great Alma Mater, which they considered significant to the overall learning experience. Amongst these were the following: small class sizes, a strong tutorial system and superb teaching – and all of these within an informal atmosphere, which would allow creative minds to flourish.

Move the clock forward to the present day and these elements are still very much the hallmark of an MPW education. With fewer than 10 students per class for GCSE and A level, (though in fact the college average is closer to 6 in a class), the learning experience is truly personalised. As well as simulating the small class size at Oxbridge our students experience the privilege of being treated as an individual and not a number. Small classes mean our students know their questions will be answered and that they will have genuine contact time with their tutors in every lesson. With more than 30 A level subjects on offer and no restrictions on combinations, our students can choose subjects that suit them. Whilst Maths, Business, Economics and of course the Sciences remain popular choices, less well known subjects such as Ancient History and Classical Civilisation are also -available.

With a current cohort of 60% British and 40% International, MPW Cambridge offers a world-class education to all. Education, however, is much more than what happens in the classroom. The preparation for life after secondary education is important too. Students need to be especially well-informed when they begin their UCAS application. The daily help by the personal tutors to each tutee is immense. From initial, informal discussion on determining the most suitable university course, through several drafts of the personal statement, often through BMAT or other entrance tests, for some even through daunting interview prospects, the MPW Personal Tutor is there. Their mandate is to 'hold the student's hand' throughout, providing encouragement and support.

We're also proud to assist those who might not have done so well the first time around. Our weekly assessments provide diagnostics where we can see which elements require further support. They also ensure that all of our students are fully prepared for the actual exam and properly understand critical success factors such as timing and weighting.

Last but not least, what others say. *'The college provides an outstanding quality of education. An outstanding curriculum supported by very well informed teaching enables students to reach standards of work that are well above average. The provision for the students' spiritual, moral, social and cultural development and their welfare, health and safety are outstanding. By the time the students leave they have developed into mature, thoughtful and responsible young people.'* Ofsted 2016.

Mander Portman Woodward

(Founded 1987)

3-4 Brookside, Cambridge, Cambridgeshire CB2 1JE UK

Tel: 01223 350158

Fax: 01223 366429

Email: cambridge@mpw.ac.uk

Website: www.mpw.ac.uk

Principal: Dr Markus Bernhardt

Appointed: September 2017

School type: Coeducational Day & Boarding

Age range of pupils: 15–19

Average class size: 6

Teacher/pupil ratio: 1:5

Orwell Park School

Developing a life-long love of learning in a magical setting...

Orwell Park, established in 1868, is a co-educational prep school for day pupils and boarders from 2½ to 13. The outstanding beauty of the grounds and the historic 18th century buildings contribute to an inspiring experience which combines the legacy and the traditions of the past with the dynamism and energy of the present and future. Outstanding facilities include a working Victorian observatory, a walled garden with outdoor pool, a nine-hole golf course, floodlit sports facilities, a library in the mansion house, as well as a new, state of the art outstanding Pre-Prep facility, which was opened in 2013, set in the shadow of the main building among woods full of opportunities for outdoor learning.

Boys and girls are given every opportunity to be the best they can be, both in and outside the classroom. High expectations, and learning strategies tailored to the individual child, lead to high levels of attainment. Pupils progress to a wide range of senior schools both local and national and our leaving year group in 2018 achieved 31 scholarships in art, academic, music, DT, sport and all-rounder.

Whilst we value greatly the past, we also embrace technology and, as such, every child in Years 3-8 has their own ipad in order to enhance learning in the classroom and beyond. The ipads allow pupils to learn in a way that they are used to, fostering collaboration between pupils, whilst providing portability.

In addition to the traditional curricular subjects, Orwell Park pupils are involved in a comprehensive activity programme, including: orchestra and various ensembles, chess, community service, skiing, equestrianism, climbing on the bouldering wall, OPS Challenge (a two-year mini D of E course), camping and campfire fun in the School's woodlands, Art and DT clubs, Goldies and Blueys (boys' and girls' clubs), as well as numerous large scale theatrical productions. The school achieves success in all the major sports and recently introduced cricket for all girls as the summer sport. In addition, Orwell Park is linked with Mayo College in Rajasthan, India and Year 7 pupils have the opportunity to visit India and sample the Taj Mahal, Jaipur and spend time at one of India's most famous boarding schools.

Boarding is extremely popular at Orwell Park and takes the form of flexible boarding, weekly boarding and full boarding, which incorporates a comprehensive programme of weekend activities. Pupils choose to board, driven by a desire to enjoy the company of friends once the normal school day is over. Dormitories are bright, spacious and clean and a dedicated team of boarding staff and school matrons are totally committed to the health and welfare of the boys and girls in their care.

Join us at an Open Morning to see for yourself what makes Orwell Park such a special and inspirational place to be.

Open Mornings:
1 February 2019
11 May 2019
For more information contact our Registrar on 01473 653224 or email admissions@orwellpark.org.

ORWELL PARK SCHOOL | Celebrating 150 YEARS

(Founded 1867)
Nacton, Ipswich, Suffolk IP10 0ER UK
Tel: 01473 659225
Fax: 01473 659822
Email: admissions@orwellpark.org
Website: www.orwellpark.co.uk
Headmaster: Mr Adrian Brown MA(Cantab)
Appointed: September 2011
School type: Coeducational Boarding & Day
Religious Denomination: Interdenominational
Age range of pupils: 2–13
No. of pupils enrolled as at 01/09/2018: 289
Boys: 166 *Girls:* 123
No. of boarders: 125
Fees per term as at 01/09/2018:
Pre-Prep Day: £2,700 – £3,840
Prep Day: £5,621 – £6,230
Prep Boarding: £7,207 – £8,667
Average class size: 12-14
Teacher/pupil ratio: 1:12

St Cedd's School

St Cedd's School is a co-educational 3-11 IAPS Charitable Trust School offering pupils the opportunity to aspire and achieve in a caring environment that nurtures talent and supports individual endeavour. This is a school in which every child matters. We value and celebrate their many diverse talents and qualities and the grounded confidence the pupils develop results in great personal achievement.

Individual Pupil Progress

The progress of pupils, of all abilities, throughout the school is rapid. Our internal SATs assessment results and 11+ scores far exceed national averages and annually we celebrate an unrivalled success rate to selective grammar and independent senior schools with an impressive track record of scholarship awards. This level of achievement is significant given that we are academically non-selective. Assessments on entry are designed to capture the strengths, weaknesses and areas for development of each child so that the education is tailored to the needs of the individual.

Centre of Excellence

The Independent Schools Inspectorate (ISI) placed St Cedd's School at the top level in every category of inspection in February 2013 which places the school amongst the very best 3-11 preparatory schools in the country. The accolade confirms what we witness every day; high academic achievement, outstanding records of attainment in music, an inclusive sporting ethos and successes at national tournaments, a sense of purpose and ambition that shows itself in the attitude and actions of the pupils and staff, and a very effective pastoral care system.

Broad and Balanced Curriculum

With over 70 after-school activities to choose from, extra study opportunities are balanced with a firm focus on academic work. This synergy supports the development of confident self-assured pupils ready for the challenges ahead. PE, music, art, French and science are taught by specialists with the teaching of PE, music and French starting in the Pre-School. Acknowledging the breadth of talents of pupils is an important aspect of life at St Cedd's School. To this end, our baccalaureate-style Year 6 curriculum, HOLDFAST, leads to awards in recognition of 'Holistic Opportunities to Learn and Develop, Furthering Achievement, Service and Talent'.

As a member of the Choir Schools Association our Choristers sing in the Cathedral Choir and the Junior and Senior Chamber Choirs sing at Evensong in Chelmsford Cathedral.

Nurturing the Future

For more than 85 years, boys and girls at St Cedd's School have been enjoying a quality of education that is among the very best you will find. We provide the best start in our recently refurbished Pre-School where the boys and girls thrive in a colourful and nurturing environment that widens their horizons and instils in them a love of learning.

Breakfast Club operates from 7:30am-8:00am and a wrap-around care programme is open until 6:00pm. Fees include curriculum-linked extra-curricular activities, 1-1 learning support, lunch and the majority of after-school clubs.

To attend an open day, request a prospectus or to arrange an individual tour, please contact Mrs Abbott on 01245 392810 or email admissions@stcedds.org.uk.

St Cedd's School

(Founded 1931)

178a New London Road, Chelmsford, Essex CM2 0AR UK

Tel: 01245 392810

Email: info@stcedds.org.uk

Website: www.stcedds.org.uk

Head: Mr Matthew Clarke

Appointed: September 2018

School type: Co-educational Day

Age range of pupils: 3–11

No. of pupils enrolled as at 01/09/2018: 400

Boys: 200 **Girls:** 200

Fees per annum as at 01/09/2018:

Day: £8,550–£10,515

Average class size: 24

St Faith's

Bright Beginnings – Exciting Futures

A world of future-thinking academic teaching, personal and social development, competitive sport and artistic appreciation is opened up to children as they enter St Faith's. Donning our iconic striped blazer and stepping into our school, rich in heritage and ambitious for the future, instils a sense of pride and eagerness in every child. Opportunities to learn, explore, create and think abound in every classroom from English to Engineering, Computing to Classics.

At St Faith's each child is taught, developed and nurtured, to equip them well for life, whatever path they choose to take. Our teachers are passionate about sharing their knowledge, exploring new ideas, challenging the status quo and instilling a life-long passion for learning. Teaching styles are tailored to meet each individual child's needs. Lessons are accessible, engaging and challenging for all pupils. Top-down excellence in all lessons ensures we continually stretch our pupils to achieve more than they thought possible.

Our academic curriculum is ground-breaking in its innovative content and has been commended by institutions including the Royal Society, Cambridge University, the James Dyson Foundation and the Spanish Embassy. In 2018 The Times awarded us 'Strategic Education Initiative of the Year' for our introduction of Engineering to the curriculum for all children aged seven upwards. Furthermore The Week Independent Schools Guide named us 'The Best of the Best' for STEM education.

Innovative and forward-facing academic subjects such as computing and engineering are interspersed each day with sporting endeavours, musical experiences, artistic creations and dramatic performances. Our curriculum covers all National Curriculum subjects and more. Owing to small class sizes, exceptional teachers and the above average ability of our children all subjects follow an accelerated curriculum and the vast majority of pupils work at a higher level commensurate with their age.

Our green and spacious 9-acre site, located in the heart of Cambridge, together with extensive playing fields a two-minute walk away, provide some of the best facilities of any prep school in the UK. Every classroom is equipped with modern teaching technology. Crucially, teachers are trained how and when to use this technology to enhance learning. The shelves in our library are crowded with over 11,000 works of fiction and non-fiction with relevance to our youngest and most mature of pupils. Engineering suites provide access to tools and equipment beyond many inventor's wildest dreams. Fully-equipped science laboratories and computer suites are used by all year groups. Our new Hub provides state-of-the-art flexible large indoor spaces for interdisciplinary projects, a roof-top greenhouse and a night sky viewing platform.

Sport is a conduit for developing mental and physical fitness, team spirit and resilience. Twenty different individual and team sports are taught at St Faith's. Our 'Sport for All' culture ensures that all pupils, irrespective of ability, receive specialist sports teaching from the age of 5. Drama, Music and Art are tools not only for teaching children a life-long love of the arts but for promoting self-belief and confidence.

St Faith's pupils stand out as confident, articulate, grounded and courteous, attributes which will stand them in good stead for their futures. On average 28 scholarships are awarded to our Year 8 pupils as they move to senior schools, with over 90% of leavers gaining a place at their first choice school.

St Faith's

CAMBRIDGE

(Founded 1884)

Trumpington Road, Cambridge, Cambridgeshire CB2 8AG UK

Tel: 01223 352073

Fax: 01223 314757

Email: admissions@stfaiths.co.uk

Website: www.stfaiths.co.uk

Headmaster: Mr N L Helliwell

Appointed: September 2011

School type: Coeducational Day

Age range of pupils: 4–13

No. of pupils enrolled as at 01/09/2018: 545

Boys: 310 **Girls:** 235

Fees per annum as at 01/09/2018:

Day: £12,660–£15,945

Average class size: 16-18

The Leys School

The School – to inspire
Located in the heart of the historic university city of Cambridge, The Leys' leafy 50 acre campus offers pupils the very best of both worlds; a traditional Cambridge education making the most of the School's links with the University, balanced with some of the most envied facilities in the country. The School's ethos centres around its aim to give every child a rounded and holistic education.

Academic life – to learn
Through the provision of a broad and balanced curriculum, pupils at The Leys develop into articulate, creative and culturally-aware individuals. Whether at GCSE or A Level stage the School's reputation for academic success is well-earned with high-ranking results and almost all pupils going to their first choice university. The School frequently calls upon its Cambridge University connections, bringing in a range of distinguished guest speakers such as Professor Stephen Hawking (who's own son is indeed an Old Leysian), running alongside The Leys' own Lecture Series. Each pupil's timetable is tailored to suit their needs, interests and aptitudes while encouraging them to succeed and develop their own, individual talents.

Outstanding facilities – to motivate
The School is not all about academia; the opportunities for broadening horizons are endless. Recent developments at The Leys include: Great Hall – a world-class, state-of-the-art theatre, dance studio and drama centre combining contemporary performance spaces with brand new science facilities. The Boathouse – situated along the banks of the River Cam and shared with Kings, Selwyn and Churchill Colleges, this £4M redeveloped facility offers pupils an unrivalled opportunity to become involved in a true 'Cambridge' sport. In addition to this there are over 40 acres of dedicated sports fields and astro-turf allowing every pupil, irrespective of ability, to enjoy a huge range of sporting activities.

Extra-curricular activities – to achieve
All pupils at The Leys take part in either Duke of Edinburgh awards or CCF (Combined Cadet Force) and this plays a valuable part in their wider education. There are also endless opportunities for debating, community service, leadership, fundraising, music and numerous clubs and societies to join.

Pastoral care – to support
The Leys is, primarily, a boarding school and places much importance on providing a caring, friendly and secure environment for all its pupils. Each child, whether a full boarder, home boarder or day pupil, is attached to one of 11 houses. Housemasters, Housemistresses and Matrons with support from a number of assistant staff are on hand 24/7 to ensure each child is given a real home from home. The feeling of 'Community' lies at the heart of the School, so while they may live in one House, they mix with their peers across the whole campus.

Scholarships – to encourage
While it is true that all children are in some way gifted, The Leys is keen to encourage those with sporting, academic, artistic or musical talents and offers a range of scholarships across all year groups.

Visiting The Leys
The School's prospectus and website will give a good overview of the opportunities available but prospective parents and pupils are encouraged to visit the School. To arrange this please contact the Admissions Team on 01223 508904 or email admissions@theleys.net

THE Leys
CAMBRIDGE

(Founded 1875)

Trumpington Road, Cambridge, Cambridgeshire CB2 7AD UK

Tel: 01223 508900

Fax: 01223 505303

Email: admissions@theleys.net

Website: www.theleys.net

Headmaster: Mr Martin Priestley

Appointed: September 2014

School type: Coeducational Boarding & Day

Age range of pupils: 11–18

No. of pupils enrolled as at 01/09/2018: 569

Fees per annum as at 01/09/2018:

Day: £15,900–£22,035

Full Boarding: £24,000–£32,925

Average class size: 15-20

Teacher/pupil ratio: 1:8

The Peterborough School

The Peterborough School is the city's only independent day school for boys and girls from Nursery to Sixth Form.

Situated on one beautiful, leafy campus in the heart of Peterborough, the Nursery, Prep and Senior Schools enjoy excellent transport links and shared facilities.

The combined campus means the School is a vibrant place with small classes providing boys and girls with the individual attention, opportunities, confidence and ability to exploit fully their natural potential within a happy, caring and friendly community.

The 56-place Nursery has been rated Outstanding in its last two ISI Inspections. It enjoys an excellent location in a separate building on the School site, with ample gardens and outside spaces, and is close enough to Peterborough station, with its high-speed train services to London, to make it highly attractive for working families.

In the Preparatory School (4 to 11 years), the children are encouraged to be independent and inquisitive learners and develop many important skills through the extended curriculum and many extra curricular clubs and activities available.

In the Senior School and Sixth Form, students' unique talents are identified and developed, whether they are in the classroom, in the creative arts or on the sports field. Closely monitored academic performance means students usually achieve levels higher than those originally expected.

The Sixth Form is going from strength to strength with consistently impressive A Level results and is an area of focus for development, with a bespoke Sixth Form block being created for September 2018. This facility will have a large, wi-fi enabled Study Room, including a student meeting space, offices and a large, well-facilitated Common Room with kitchen. This development will also create a new state-of-the art Senior Library.

Our pastoral support is extremely strong and we passionately believe that children cannot learn well unless they are happy.

Headmaster, Adrian Meadows, is proud that the long-standing traditions of the school, which was founded in 1895, remain but at the same time it is a forward-looking, progressive place where children continually surprise and delight him. *"I have seen students winning a national STEM award on the same day that the Reception Classes and Pre-schoolers enjoyed a Teddy Bear's Picnic. Being amongst children of such a wide are range is fascinating, entertaining and always interesting but overall it is incredibly rewarding and humbling to be part of such an amazing school and community."*

Visitors to the School and Nursery are very welcome. We have Open Days on Saturdays in September and May each year when appointments are not necessary. There is also a Sixth Form Open Evening in October. Alternatively, visits can be booked by calling the School on 01733 343357 or completing the Request A Visit form on our website www.thepeterboroughschool.co.uk.

The Peterborough School

(Founded 1895)

Thorpe Road, Peterborough, Cambridgeshire PE3 6AP UK

Tel: 01733 343357

Fax: 01733 355710

Email: office@tpsch.co.uk

Website: www.thepeterboroughschool.co.uk

Headmaster: Mr A D Meadows BSc(Hons)

Appointed: September 2007

School type: Coeducational Day

Age range of pupils: 6 weeks–18 years

No. of pupils enrolled as at 01/09/2018: 440

Fees per annum as at 01/09/2018:

Day: £9,942–£14,868

Average class size: 15

Tring Park School for the Performing Arts

Tring Park School for the Performing Arts is unique amongst specialist schools in the UK. At Tring Park talented young people from 8–19 specialise in Dance, Acting, Musical Theatre or Commercial Music, while also having the opportunity to study for GCSEs and up to 23 A Level subjects. Entrance is via audition and scholarships are available for Dance via the Government's Music and Dance Scheme. School scholarships and bursaries are available for Drama and Musical Theatre.

Pupils perform regularly both in Tring Park's Markova Theatre as well as in London, throughout the UK and Europe. Our graduating dance students perform in 'Encore Dance', Tring Park's touring company which, this year, performed 11 shows in England and Wales culminating in a London performance at the Sadler's Wells Lilian Baylis Studio. Musical Theatre students have a regular season at the Pizza Express Pheasantry in Chelsea. Tring Park provides ballet dancers annually to perform in the Christmas production of *Nutcracker* with English National Ballet at the London Coliseum. Six pupils have played the part of Billy in *Billy Elliot* in the West End and on tour, The Tring Park choir "The Sixteen" won the BBC Songs of Praise Senior School Choir of the Year and recently came third in the highly competitive International Eisteddfod.

During the Summer Tring Park runs highly sought-after boarding and day courses in Dance, Musical Theatre and Acting.

Work has started on the first stage of a multi-million pound development project, which includes a four-storey building that will contain a state-of-the-art boarding house, six academic and vocational teaching spaces, a theatre workshop and other valuable pupil facilities due to open in September 2019. Stage two will include an art department and 6th Form Study Centre and the final phase will create a 450 seat theatre.

Alumni success

Daisy Ridley – Rey in *Star Wars* and *Murder on the Orient Express*
Lily James – *Mamma Mia! Here we go again*
Nafisa Baba – winner BBC Young Dancer of the Year 2017
Kit Esuruoso – played Tina Turner's son in the West End show *Tina*. Soon to star in Australian film *Akoni*.
Drew McOnie – Director of the Musical *King Kong* on Broadway
Max Westwell & Will Bozier – 'lead Swan' in Matthew Bourne's New Adventures new production of *Swan Lake*.

Testament to Tring Park's academic provision, students have left to read Medicine, Law, Physics and Engineering whilst others have careers in stage management and other performance-related industries.

Please check the website for upcoming Open Days.
To apply online: www.tringpark.com/opendays
Registrar: Adélia Wood-Smith
registrar@tringpark.com
Registered charity No. 1040330

(Founded 1919)
Tring Park, Tring, Hertfordshire HP23 5LX UK
Tel: 01442 824255
Fax: 01442 891069
Email: info@tringpark.com
Website: www.tringpark.com
Principal: Mr Stefan Anderson MA, ARCM, ARCT
Appointed: September 2002
School type: Co-educational Boarding & Day
Religious Denomination: Non-denominational
Age range of pupils: 8–19
No. of pupils enrolled as at 01/09/2018: 374
Boys: 108 *Girls:* 243 *Sixth Form:* 266
No. of boarders: 229
Fees per annum as at 01/09/2018:
Day: £14,865–£23,655
Full Boarding: £25,275–£35,760

East Midlands

Oakham School

The possibilities for learning really are limitless at Oakham. As a large co-educational boarding and day school we are proud to be able to offer a truly staggering range of experiences, activities and opportunities.

Whilst academic excellence lies at the heart of everything we do, our focus goes far beyond just encouraging our students to achieve outstanding results in their examinations. Our genuinely holistic approach to education means that students leave Oakham as intellectually ambitious thinkers, who are effective and independent learners, well equipped with the skills and habits of mind to thrive in tomorrow's world.

At Oakham, learning is never just confined to the four walls of a classroom. Hundreds of students take part in the Arts – there are five major drama productions every year, we teach over 500 individual music lessons each week, and our award-winning Art & Design Department is a hive of creative activity. Oakham also has a national reputation for Sport, offering 30 different sports to students of all levels – from enthusiasts to elite athletes. Activities are also an integral part of life beyond the classroom, with students able to choose from over 125 activities to take part in each week, to discover and develop their interests and talents, and provide service to others. In addition to Duke of Edinburgh, CCF, and Voluntary Action, options range from dance to robotics, e-textiles to sailing – there really is something for everyone!

Oakham is an exceptionally caring community and we nurture all aspects of our pupils' well-being during every stage of their Oakham journey. Our unique House structure ensures students have an age-appropriate space to develop and grow, surrounded by staff who are expertly trained to both support their needs and to challenge them to become independent, thoughtful, and responsible young adults.

Students also benefit from the School's location close to Rutland Water, in the heart of rural England. They are able to enjoy the safety of living and working in a beautifully green campus just a few minutes' walk from Oakham's historic town centre and amenities, yet at the same time Oakham's excellent road and rail links mean that London, Birmingham and Cambridge are all within easy reach.

Oakham is well known and loved for being a friendly and unpretentious school. Whilst we are proud of our 400-year heritage, our priority is always to be at the forefront of educational developments: in short, to be educational innovators. We were one of the first independent schools to move to co-education in 1971 and we were also one of the first schools to introduce the IB Diploma, alongside A-levels. We continue to look to the future and our focus now, in today's digital world, is on effectively teaching students Information Literacy.

By the time they leave us, Oakhamians are well rounded and confident young adults, equipped to ask the right questions, to know how to find the answers for themselves, and in doing so, to be able to make a difference in the world.

"Oakham School is an inspirational place, where opportunities abound, talent is nurtured and characters are formed." Nigel Lashbrook, Headmaster

"This is a clear-eyed, energetic, forward-thinking school." The Good Schools Guide

(Founded 1584)

Chapel Close, Oakham, Rutland LE15 6DT UK

Tel: 01572 758758

Fax: 08714 299263

Email: admissions@oakham.rutland.sch.uk

Website: www.oakham.rutland.sch.uk

Headmaster: Mr Nigel M Lashbrook BA

Appointed: September 2009

School type: Coeducational Boarding & Day

Religious Denomination: Church of England

Age range of pupils: 10–18

No. of pupils enrolled as at 01/09/2018:

Boys: 539 **Girls:** 526 **Sixth Form:** 405

No. of boarders: 584

Fees per annum as at 01/09/2018:

Day: £16,905–£20,535

Full Boarding: £25,605–£33,660

Flexi Boarding (2-5 nights): £20,145 – £31,980

Average class size: 18 (10-16); 10 (16-18)

Teacher/pupil ratio: 1:7

Greater London

Avon House Preparatory School

"Avon House is a family, concerned for the happiness and general well-being of all. Celebrating and supporting every pupil begins with self-esteem, honesty, fairness, integrity, respect for oneself and respect for others. In our happy, secure environment the emphasis is placed on each child being recognised as a valued individual. We hope our pupils will develop their full potential in both academic and non-academic fields, with a strong moral understanding of truth, equality and humanity. We aim to give our pupils life-enhancing strategies to build on as they progress towards the adult world."

Avon House is an independent, co-educational prep school in Essex offering a happy, stable and disciplined environment for children aged from three to eleven.

Our preparatory school aims to provide a happy, supportive and disciplined environment where emphasis is placed on the development of each child as an individual, allowing each one to realise their potential and to thrive in other areas such as sport, music, dance and drama.

Avon House School offers a broad and balanced curriculum delivered by a highly capable team of professional staff.

Situated on the High Road in Woodford Green, Essex, our convenient location and caring environment offer all children a secure start to an educational life that will be rich in opportunity and experience.

We aim to provide our children with an appetite for learning, a thirst for knowledge and a curiosity for the wider world.

We strive to achieve academic excellence beginning with firm foundations and to present children with occasions to create memorable experiences during these important years.

Avon House is a school community where children are valued as individuals and encouraged to demonstrate their own unique personalities both in class and beyond.

The energy and imagination of the staff provide children with the enthusiasm to go the extra mile creating opportunities within our unique learning environment.

We welcome visits from prospective parents during the school day.

AVON HOUSE PREPARATORY SCHOOL

490 High Road, Woodford Green, Essex IG8 0PN UK

Tel: 020 8504 1749

Email: office@ahsprep.co.uk

Website: www.avonhouseschool.co.uk

Headteacher: Mrs Amanda Campbell

Appointed: September 2011

School type: Coeducational Day

Religious Denomination: Christian

Age range of pupils: 3–11

No. of pupils enrolled as at 01/09/2018: 230

Fees per annum as at 01/09/2018:

Day: £9,375–£10,290

Breaside Preparatory School

Breaside Preparatory School, located in Bromley, Kent, prepares pupils from 2½ to 11 years for both Grammar and Independent Senior Schools in a caring and nurturing environment.

Breaside work closely with NACE (National Association for Able Children in Education) which nationally recognises and celebrates those schools which provide the very highest level of challenge for its pupils. NACE helps teachers provide excellent teaching and learning for able, gifted and talented pupils. As of June 2018, NACE has named Breaside the first school in Bromley to be accredited with the NACE Challenge Award meaning that we are now placed in a select group of just 1.6% of schools across the UK who have achieved this prestigious Challenge Award.

We are also pleased to share with you that we have been placed 16th in the Sunday Times Top 100 Independent Schools list 2018 – an absolutely fantastic achievement of which we are incredibly proud!

"It is wonderful to be recognised for all of the hard work that the staff and children put into Breaside to make it the very special place that it is." Mrs Karen Nicholson, Executive Principal.

Once again, SATs and 11+ entry results for 2018 were outstanding, with 100% of Year 6 pupils gaining their first choice at Senior School.

Parents are given guidance on the schools that we recommend for their children throughout their time at Breaside and we pride ourselves on getting the children into the right school for them as individuals.

Should I choose Breaside Preparatory School for my child?
Do they really offer more than a local primary school? The answer to both of these questions is a resounding 'Yes'.

As their name suggests, the role of preparatory schools is to prepare your child for their entrance into senior education, so don't be surprised to see a plethora of subjects on the curriculum. Your child will experience a well rounded education albeit in a nurturing environment. Classes are significantly smaller, allowing all pupils to progress. At the same time, this allows all staff to know their pupils and therefore offer a bespoke curriculum. Preparatory schools provide a wealth of opportunity for your child both academically and pastorally. Self confidence is encouraged and children are constantly motivated to enjoy and embrace all the opportunities that arise within this positive learning environment.

If the above isn't enough to tempt you, consider the other aspects of a stimulating, all-round education. Your child will have the opportunity to experience a wide range of music, playing in an orchestra or participating in the choir. Peripatetic teachers within a preparatory school can introduce your child to a wealth of instruments, regardless of ability. Drama is also extensive with children as young as 3 taking part in plays. Within the encouraging atmosphere of a preparatory school, this can only help to aid your child's confidence. Let's not forget the range of sporting events that your child can take part in. Children in a preparatory school experience a range of sports, including rugby, hockey, swimming and cricket.

Should you choose a preparatory school for your child? Well, if you want to give them the best possible start in life, then the answer has to be yes. The investment will pay off as you see your child blossom into a well rounded, self confident, individual, ready to face the world!

For more information or a personal tour of the School and Kindergarten please call 020 8460 0916, info@breaside.co.uk, www.breaside.co.uk

(Founded 1950)

41-43 Orchard Road, Bromley, Kent BR1 2PR UK

Tel: 020 8460 0916

Fax: 020 8466 5664

Email: info@breaside.co.uk

Website: www.breaside.co.uk

Executive Principal:
Mrs Karen A Nicholson B.Ed, NPQH, Dip EYs

Appointed: 2008

School type: Coeducational Day

Age range of pupils: 2½–11

No. of pupils enrolled as at 01/09/2018: 360

Boys: 178 **Girls:** 182

Fees per annum as at 01/09/2018:

Day: £11,070–£12,900

Farringtons School

Aims

Our aims are numerous, but very clear: to provide the best in education for every child in our care within a happy, safe, supportive Christian environment; to offer a wide variety of extracurricular pursuits to all age groups in order to promote the healthy development of the whole child; and to produce confident, self-reliant, compassionate and responsible young men and women, who, when they leave us at 18, will be equipped to take up the challenges of the 21st century.

Location

Farringtons occupies 25 acres of parkland in picturesque Kent, yet it is only 12 miles from central London. Chislehurst is five minutes from the M25, 45 minutes from Gatwick Airport, 1.5 hours from Heathrow International Airport and 20 minutes by train from Charing Cross and Waterloo stations.

Academic Achievement

With most pupils proceeding to higher education, academic standards are high; each pupil is encouraged to strive to reach his or her full potential. Our academic success is due to small classes, dedicated staff and supportive teaching, which ensures each pupil receives the individual attention needed. Academic achievement, as well as the all-round development of the individual, is of prime importance at Farringtons.

Sixth Form

The Sixth Form should be a bridge between school and university, and our Sixth Form leavers regularly go on to degree courses in their chosen subjects, including medicine, law and engineering, as well as courses at prestigious universities.

There is a wide choice of A Level subjects on offer, and staff are always on hand to offer advice on the correct combination of subjects to suit the aspirations and abilities of each student.

Sixth Formers are given a greater degree of freedom than pupils in other years and are encouraged to take a responsible and independent approach to their studies, albeit with the guidance and help of their tutor.

Boarding

At Farringtons we provide happy, warm and friendly surroundings for our boarders, and different living areas for each age group.

When parents are unable to be nearby, we know we must create and maintain a homely and secure living environment in which the pupils feel safe, confident and cared for, whatever their age. Boarders are cared for by house staff, who liaise with parents, guardians, form tutors and other staff to ensure the wellbeing of each student.

Weekly boarding provides a happy solution for those parents who wish to prioritise schoolwork and activities during the week. It also enables attendance for those whose daily travel is difficult and ad hoc. Boarding is also available for pupils who need to board for short periods when parents are away.

A debating society, football club, tae kwon do, a maths club and maths clinic, The Duke of Edinburgh's Award, a textiles club, drama club, jazz dance, fencing, Business Enterprise, ballet, trampolining, a choir, concert band and an orchestra are just some of the many interests available to pupils at lunch times and after school.

At weekends there are regular sporting fixtures and also supervised outings to the theatre, cinema, ice rink, shopping centre, museums, roller skating rink, waxworks and local places of interest, as well as to London, of course, which remains a firm favourite.

(Founded 1911)

Perry Street, Chislehurst, Kent BR7 6LR UK

Tel: 020 8467 0256

Email: admissions@farringtons.kent.sch.uk

Website: www.farringtons.org.uk

Head: Mrs Dorothy Nancekievill

Appointed: January 2015

School type: Co-educational Day & Boarding

Religious Denomination: Methodist

Age range of pupils: 3–18

No. of pupils enrolled as at 01/09/2018: 700

Boys: 366 **Girls:** 334 **Sixth Form:** 100

No. of boarders: 60

Fees per annum as at 01/09/2018:

Day: £15,120

Weekly Boarding: £29,850

Full Boarding: £31,680

Average class size: 15-20

Halliford School

At Halliford School we strongly believe that every young person should be seen as an individual with their own personality, talents and skills and that it is this individuality that we seek to encourage and develop at all stages of their education. Our aim is to enable each of our students to become the very best version of themselves that they can possibly be.

As young Hallifordians we recognise that a child's potential could lie anywhere – so we ensure that every student is exposed to a vast array of opportunities and experiences. We then pride ourselves on identifying and honing their strengths to make the most of their natural abilities, while assisting in every way to develop any areas that might need further improvement. We are able to offer small class sizes which enable personalised teaching and suitable learning strategies.

We recognise that the environment in which a child learns is just as important as what they learn. Renowned for our outstanding pastoral care, we work hard to create a community where our students can come together, where they are encouraged to flourish, where they can feel safe and comfortable, confident and proud, stimulated and inspired and, most of all, happy. We are extremely fortunate as a small school to have many outstanding facilities on our beautiful site nestled alongside the River Thames.

The administrative centre of the school is a fine Georgian house set in six acres beside the River Thames. Behind the house are modern buildings housing light and airy classrooms, science laboratories, a state-of-the-art information technology centre, design & technology workshop, large and well equipped sports hall, well-stocked library and study centre, school dining room and kitchen, and 320 seat theatre equipped as a multimedia lecture theatre and over four acres of playing fields. Only 400 yards away are another 6 acres of sports fields. There is a separate Sixth Form Centre which has a newly refurbished common room with study pods and the latest computer technology as well as a seminar room and cafeteria. The building also houses the Art and Music Schools.

At Halliford School we seek to be both academically ambitious as well as academically sensitive. We challenge and support our students to make the most of their abilities and show them how to take responsibility for their progress. Students who need additional support are identified and nurtured to achieve their very best in our well-established learning support unit.

We also give our students every opportunity to immerse themselves in a wide variety of co-curricular activities from Creative Writing and Jazz Band, and Basketball to Debating.

We have a wide range of coach services covering Kew, Richmond, Esher, Cobham, Hampton Court, Woking, Staines and Wraysbury. We also run minibus shuttle services from Walton on Thames and Staines Stations.

There is no better way to experience the distinctive culture and ethos of our Halliford School than by visiting us. We look forward to welcoming you to see for yourself if it is the right school for your child's future education. For details on all of our Open Days please visit our website. Personal visits are also available throughout the year. Please book a visit at www.hallifordschool.co.uk or call the Registrar, Mrs Fran Clatworthy, on 01932 223593 for more information.

Halliford School SHEPPERTON

(Founded 1921)

Russell Road, Shepperton, Middlesex TW17 9HX UK

Tel: 01932 223593

Fax: 01932 229781

Email: registrar@hallifordschool.co.uk

Website: www.hallifordschool.co.uk

Head: Mr James Davies BMus (Hons) LGSM FASC ACertCM PGCE

School type: Independent Day School for Boys Coeducational Sixth Form

Religious Denomination: Non-denominational

Age range of boys: 11–18

Age range of girls: 16–18

No. of pupils enrolled as at 01/09/2018: 402

Fees per annum as at 01/09/2018:

Day: £15,960

Average class size: 20

Teacher/pupil ratio: 1:8

Kew College

Set in leafy South-West London, Kew College is a gem of a school. In terms of education, it is a centre of excellence providing a rich, relevant and varied curriculum, but it is much more than that.

The minute you walk through the door, the ethos of the school is apparent; it is a friendly and caring environment which is relaxed but purposeful. The relationship between staff and pupils is warm and open and there is a tangible buzz of creativity in the air. The children are respectful, responsible, hard-working, and fun-loving individuals who thrive given opportunities to take risks in their learning and set challenges for themselves.

The results of entrance exams to secondary schools at Year 6 are excellent year on year, with numerous scholarships attained. Set this against the school's non-selective background and it is testimony to the quality of education that it provides. The children display an overwhelming desire to achieve and are inspired by staff who work with boundless energy, dedication and determination. No stone is left unturned as they strive to support and nurture every child to achieve to their full potential.

Education at Kew College is also about helping the pupils to develop their intellectual character. The children have a concrete sense of their own strengths and a confidence that goes hand in hand with that self-belief. This is coupled with a gracious sense of humility and open-mindedness, the realisation that the way forward in tomorrow's world is through co-operation and team work. This strong moral value system is embedded from an early age so that, by the time the pupils leave Kew College, they are able to think independently and critically. They are inquisitive, reflective and well-rounded; true individuals who are prepared for the rigours of secondary school and for the changing world in which they live.

"Both of our boys joined the school in the Nursery and have flourished in the nurturing and caring environment the school provides. The children are all confident, articulate, well-mannered, and thoroughly nice kids who are comfortable in the company of adults. Our boys have thrived at Kew College and always raced enthusiastically into school each day. The teaching and school philosophy is very much focused on helping each child to achieve their best in a happy environment. As parents, we really couldn't ask for more."
The Stewart family

"We chose Kew College for our four daughters for its warm atmosphere and its happy, friendly, and well-mannered pupils. We feel fortunate to have also found a school which fulfils its promise of educating our children to their highest potential. We have children with differing abilities and personalities but Kew College has provided support and education for all of them. Every child at this school is unique, but one thing that every child here has in common is that they will leave strengthened by their experience."
The Ahmed Family

Registrar: Mwarburton@kewcollege.com

(Founded 1953)

24-26 Cumberland Road, Kew, Surrey TW9 3HQ UK

Tel: 020 8940 2039

Fax: 020 8332 9945

Email: enquiries@kewcollege.com

Website: www.kewcollege.com

Head:
Mrs Marianne Austin BSc(Hons), MA(Hons), ACA, PGCE

School type: Coeducational Day

Age range of pupils: 3–11

No. of pupils enrolled as at 01/09/2018: 296

Boys: 148 **Girls:** 148

Fees per annum as at 01/09/2018:

Nursery: £7,050

Kindergarten – Year 6: £12,150

Average class size: 20

King's House School

'An excellent, all-round, happy prep school that brings out the best in all its children.' King's House Parent

King's House is a lively, busy, happy School and one where we feel that the boys (and girls in our wonderful nursery) thrive. Our aim is to offer a broad education to all our pupils, enabling them to develop their academic, social, sporting and artistic attributes. This breadth and balance on offer is we believe one of the strengths of the School.

King's House is a friendly, caring and supportive School. We have a strong sense of community both within the School and with our parents but we are also keen to play a role in the local and global community and to develop our pupils' sense of awareness of the world around them.

King's House is non-selective at our two main entry points, Nursery and Reception. We believe that boys benefit from staying in the prep environment until they are 13 years old before moving on. Their final two years here allow them to flourish, grow up and develop their sense of responsibility, taking on roles around the School. The boys are well-prepared for the transition to senior schools and we are justifiably proud of our 100% pass rate at Common Entrance into some of the most academic schools in the country. The emphasis though is always on finding the right school for the right child.

King's House believes in the importance of developing its pupils physically through PE and Games taught from Nursery upwards. From Year 1, the boys take advantage of our 35-acre sports ground in Chiswick for games with plenty of teams enabling as many boys as possible the opportunity to experience competitive fixtures. The main sports are football, rugby and cricket but athletics, swimming and tennis also feature. In recent years the School has enjoyed considerable sporting success particularly with its rugby teams and successful sports tours. At the School we have a fully equipped gym and AstroTurf which offers variety for weekly PE sessions.

King's House prides itself in a strong tradition of excellence in the Arts recognising that by giving our children the opportunity to express themselves we are helping them to develop self-confidence and awareness. With a large, fully equipped theatre we can be ambitious in our choice of productions.

Art and Design Technology are central to the creative arts teaching and the boys are encouraged to express themselves using a variety of media with work being displayed all around the School.

Computing and programming are playing an increasingly important role in the children's education from Nursery upwards. The Junior and Senior departments have computer suites and all classrooms have interactive whiteboards. There is also a Mac suite.

The School takes advantage of the opportunity our proximity to London affords us with regular trips to museums, galleries and theatres as well as Richmond Park and Kew Gardens. There are annual and bi-annual trips such as the Classics trip to Italy, French trip to Brittany and ski trip as well as sports tours.

King's House is proud of its 70 year history. Its principles and standards are founded on Christian values although the School is not aligned to any particular religion, and welcomes pupils of all religions and backgrounds.

(Founded 1946)

68 King's Road, Richmond, Surrey TW10 6ES UK

Tel: 020 8940 1878

Fax: 020 8939 2501

Email: schooloffice@kingshouseschool.org

Website: www.kingshouseschool.org

Head: Mr Mark Turner BA, PGCE, NPQH

Appointed: September 2012

School type: Boys' Day

Age range of boys: 3–13

Age range of girls: 3–4

No. of pupils enrolled as at 01/09/2018: 460

Fees per term as at 01/09/2018:

Day: £2,370–£5,560

Average class size: 24

St Catherine's School

St. Catherine's combines over 100 years' experience of Independent education with a modern curriculum that prepares girls for success in the 21st Century. It is a Catholic school with pupils from many different faith and ethnic backgrounds. Everyone is a member of a vibrant, caring and supportive community in which pupils are happy, confident and inspired to meet challenges. Inspectors from the Diocese of Westminster reported that 'pupils flourish because of the secure, caring ethos of the School.' 'Teaching at St. Catherine's is more than the sum of its classroom parts. Pupils have a wrap-around experience that leads them to learn exceptionally well.' A recent inspection by the Independent Schools Inspectorate endorsed this, giving St. Catherine's the highest accolade possible, judging the pupils' academic and other achievements as well as their personal development to be excellent.

It is in the Prep Department, which takes girls from 3 to 11 years of age, that the firm foundations are laid to prepare pupils for the challenges and opportunities available in the Senior School.

The girls certainly rise to the challenges posed by public examinations. The school is proud of the value that is added to their achievements as they progress through the school and that their academic predictions are consistently exceeded. This is borne out in their excellent GCSE and A level results.

With the present A level system it is important for pupils to have continuity and stability from GCSE into A level. The teaching staff are passionate about giving the girls at St. Catherine's the opportunity to build on their outstanding GCSE results in the environment where they feel confident that their teachers know them and will both support and challenge them. This gives them the optimum chance of obtaining the best possible results in order to achieve a place at the University of their choice.

In partnership with parents, the Headmistress and her staff strive to produce well educated, confident, balanced young people who are outward looking and are able to meet the challenges of adult life with common sense, integrity and resilience.

Those who visit St. Catherine's often remark on the warm, caring and friendly atmosphere and the self-confidence and enthusiasm of its pupils.

A school can never stand still and St. Catherine's is no exception. In the last ten years major building projects have enhanced the facilities at the school, added new subjects to the curriculum and changed syllabi and schemes of work to make them even more challenging and interesting. The Sixth Form offers further opportunities to the girls in both curricular and extra-curricular programmes, as well as supporting them and helping them to prepare for university and beyond.

Information about public examination results, extra-curricular opportunities, wrap-around care facilities can all be found on the school website: www.stcatherineschool.co.uk

With recent changes to the National Curriculum and public examinations at both GCSE and A level, the Senior Management Team and Governors remain ever vigilant and will ensure all staff are fully prepared to continue to provide the best education possible for the pupils they teach.

(Founded 1914)

Cross Deep, Twickenham, Middlesex TW1 4QJ UK

Tel: 020 8891 2898

Fax: 020 8744 9629

Email: info@stcatherineschool.co.uk

Website: www.stcatherineschool.co.uk

Headmistress: Mrs Johneen McPherson MA

Appointed: September 2018

School type: Girls' Day

Age range of girls: 3–18

No. of pupils enrolled as at 01/09/2018: 430

Fees per annum as at 01/09/2018:

Day: £10,795–£14,910

Average class size: 15-20

Teacher/pupil ratio: 1:11

St Helen's College

Nestled on the edge of Court Park in a quiet corner of Hillingdon, St. Helen's College is a family-run independent school for boys and girls aged 3 to 11, with a super, new Kindergarten for boys and girls aged 2-3.

The school has a real family feel and has been described by inspectors as a 'haven of harmony'. Indeed, the most recent ISI quality inspection judged St. Helen's College outstanding, the quality of teaching excellent, the pupils' personal development outstanding and pupils' achievements, both academic and extra-curricular, excellent.

The report said: *'Pupils achieve high standards in academic work and a wide range of other activities. They are extremely successful in all aspects of learning...this is reflected in their success in entrance examinations both to maintained grammar and independent schools'.*

The school's values and ethos set it apart. Led by the Head, Shirley Drummond, staff create a harmonious, loving environment, nurture the individual qualities of every pupil and ensure that children develop a lifelong love of learning, find out where their talents and interests lie, and leave school with traditional values and strength of character, ready to face the challenges of adult life with confidence, resilience and joy!

The children enjoy lessons taught by highly qualified specialist teachers right from the start, allowing them to study at a high level led by teachers with a real passion for their subject. There is also an extremely wide-ranging and quite unique range of 70+ co-curricular activities available, with superb music, drama and sports provision and clubs including cookery, gardening, yoga, taekwondo, ceramics, dance and many, many more.

The school benefits from specialist modern facilities and is strongly rooted in its local community, enjoying links with local churches, Brunel University and local theatres.

The safe, loving, encouraging environment at St. Helen's College fosters excellent academic achievement and well-rounded, confident pupils. Inspectors noted, *'Pupils' personal development is outstanding, well supported by excellent pastoral care. The overall feeling is of a warm, friendly community where everyone knows each other and feels safe and secure'.*

St. Helen's College operates a flexible year-round extended care provision, with Breakfast Club from 7.30 a.m. and after school care until 6 p.m. daily during term time, and Holiday Club running during school holidays to assist working parents.

Parents may register children for entry to the school at 2+ (Kindergarten) or 3+ (Nursery). This is an extremely popular school and early registration is advisable. Prospective parents may register online using the online registration form or by contacting the school using the details below.

'School at work' open mornings are held in October and April each year, at which current pupils conduct tours of the school and answer questions for prospective parents. The Head, Head of Lower School and Director of Admissions are available to answer questions and take registrations at these events.

Alternatively, prospective parents may book an individual tour one morning during term time by telephoning 01895 234371 or emailing info@sthelenscollege.com.

(Founded 1924)

Parkway, Hillingdon, Uxbridge, Middlesex UB10 9JX

Tel: 01895 234371

Email: info@sthelenscollege.com

Website: www.sthelenscollege.com

Head: Mrs. Shirley Drummond BA, PGCert, MLDP

Appointed: 2016

School type: Coeducational Day

Age range of pupils: 2–11

No. of pupils enrolled as at 01/09/2018: 383

Boys: 193 *Girls:* 190

Fees per annum as at 01/09/2018:

Day: £9,600–£11,850

Average class size: 22

Teacher/pupil ratio: varies

London

Bassett House School

At Bassett House, we believe that all children deserve to learn to fly and achieve their very best. The school was founded in 1947 by Sylvia Rentoul who recognised children as individuals, and encouraged them to express themselves, helping to grow their achievements and self-confidence. Our teaching techniques and apparatus are continually updated but our ethos remains constant.

Our children's energy, exuberance and curiosity for learning stand out. These have been engendered by our whole school commitment to adopting a growth mindset. Mention you cannot do something at Bassett House and any child will roar back at you "I can't do it YET!"

Focused attention remains our hallmark. We believe tailor-made teaching opens up young minds to endless possibilities, encouraging them to think creatively. We start by ensuring high staff-to-pupil ratios and many specialist teaching staff. Our teachers know every child in their care inside out and use great teaching supported by our excellent equipment (including cutting-edge technology) to bring lessons to life for each child.

Our 'sport for all' ethos encourages all our children to think of themselves as athletes, while allowing our sporting stars to shine. We offer football, netball, tag rugby, hockey, tennis, rounders, athletics, gymnastics and eurhythmics as part of the core curriculum and clubs in swimming, fencing, volleyball, yoga and dance.

We don't stop there. Vibrant music and drama give our children a passion for participation and performance, fostering a sense of achievement and boosting self-confidence. Our children first take to the stage from age 3 and have many opportunities to shine throughout life at Bassett House, whether in whole-school assemblies, stage shows or concerts. We have choirs, musical ensembles and an orchestra and provide individual instrumental music lessons from specialist music teachers.

Our extra-curricular clubs, together with our weekly enrichment hour, expand our children's horizons beyond the core curriculum. Each term children can choose to add a variety of activities to the school day, be it Lego modelling, computer coding, Scottish dancing, origami, chess, geography, cookery, arts and crafts or debating.

Residential trips from year 3 onwards create a sense of adventure and build self-reliance. The glow of a 7-year-old's face recounting a night-time bug-hunting expedition, a 9-year-old's thrill at working with a friend to sail a dinghy, a 10-year-old embracing the challenge of sleeping out under a self-made shelter: we create these memorable moments, knowing that their positive effects will last a lifetime.

All of this makes not only for well-rounded individuals, it translates into excellent academic results. When they leave aged 11, Bassett House children are ready to thrive at London's best senior schools. And they do: our children win places to the cream of London's senior schools. For those who want to board, Bassett House prepares them well for life at leading boarding schools.

We collaborate closely with our sister schools, Orchard House and Prospect House, sparking off new ideas to promote ever more successful teaching practices. The three schools share a common ethos but each retains its unique personality.

The schools (brought together under the umbrella of House Schools Group) are proudly non-selective. True to our belief, children are not tested and judged at the tender age of 3 or 4 years. Our outstanding results repeatedly show all children can fulfil their potential, regardless of early learning ability. We encourage our high-flyers to skyrocket, whilst children who need a little extra help are given the support they need to reach their fullest potential.

Our last full ISI inspection awarded us 'excellent' and 'outstanding' in all areas and we flew through our 2016 compliance inspection.

BASSETT
HOUSE SCHOOL

(Founded 1947)

60 Bassett Road, London, W10 6JP UK

Tel: 020 8969 0313

Email: info@bassetths.org.uk

Website: www.bassetths.org.uk

Headmistress:
Mrs Philippa Cawthorne MA (Soton) PGCE Mont Cert

Appointed: January 2014

School type: Co-educational Day

Age range of pupils: 3–11

No. of pupils enrolled as at 01/09/2018: 190

Fees per annum as at 01/09/2018:

Day: £8,850–£18,450

Average class size: 20

Teacher/pupil ratio: 1:7

Cameron House

The curriculum

'An excellent curriculum provides all pupils... with opportunities to achieve high standards in a wide range of subjects and activities... within a creative, stimulating environment where all pupils are treated as individuals and encouraged to do their best. The quality of the pupils' achievements and learning is excellent.' (ISI Inspection 2016) Pupils of all abilities are prepared broadly and deeply for the full gamut of 11+ examinations within a rich and dynamic academic curriculum, using high quality resources and a broad range of ICT. We encourage children to research, reflect, ask questions, listen well and problem-solve – and to develop positive learning habits for life around the 'Five Cs of Cameron House': curiosity, collaboration, creativity, critical thinking and courage.

Setup and atmosphere

'Across the school the quality of the pupils' personal development is excellent... All pupils display excellent moral development, have a firm sense of right and wrong, and are extremely courteous.' (ISI Inspection 2016) We aim to be a vibrant, warm and high-energy school, to which pupils are proud to belong and to which they contribute by growing their own skills, character and personal relationships. Our dedicated and highly qualified teachers know every pupil and every family, aiming to care for each with wisdom, professionalism and kindness.

Games and the arts

'Pupils develop excellent physical skills at all ages through the busy and demanding range of activities and... achieve significant success in competitive sports in relation to the size of the school.' (ISI Inspection 2016) Sport is integral to the rhythm of school life both within the timetable, and within the extra-curricular programme, with our team sports including touch rugby, netball, football and hockey, and individual sports such as fencing and karate offered as well. We are passionate about the arts, and provide a wealth of creative activities in art, design and technology, music and drama – through timetabled specialist teaching, after-school clubs, themed days, cultural visits and opportunities to train and perform in the school's arts programme, as well as local and national events.

Pastoral care

'Pastoral care makes an excellent contribution to pupils' personal development. Strong personal relationships reflect the friendly, family atmosphere. Staff know their pupils very well and... the school maintains very close links with parents.' (ISI Inspection 2016) We are a relaxed but respectful community, working together for the common good within a culture of praise and mutual respect, aiming to develop self-respect, self-discipline and empathy in our relationships, strong spiritual awareness and a deep appreciation of the beauty of the natural world. We want to embody our motto – 'Da Mihi Sapientiam' (Give Me Wisdom) – by growing wisdom in our pupils in thought, word and deed.

Outstanding characteristics

Cameron House has been led by the same Director-Principal for 37 years, providing seamless, detailed and passionate oversight and care. 'The quality of governance is excellent. Dynamic and energetic leadership across the school is highly effective in enabling the school to successfully fulfil its aim to create a happy and warm family atmosphere in which pupils are treated as individuals and are motivated to work and play to the best of their ability. Senior and middle managers provide clear educational direction and this is demonstrated in the excellent quality of pupils' achievements and in their outstanding personal development' (ISI Inspection 2016)

(Founded 1980)

4 The Vale, Chelsea, London, SW3 6AH UK

Tel: 020 7352 4040

Fax: 020 7352 2349

Email: laura@cameronhouseschool.org

Website: www.cameronhouseschool.org

Headmistress: Mrs Dina Mallett

Principal:
Miss Josie Cameron Ashcroft BSc(Hons), DipEd, CertT

School type: Coeducational Day

Religious Denomination:
Church of England, all denominations welcome

Age range of pupils: 4–11

Fees per annum as at 01/09/2018:

Day: £18,465

City of London School
A rounded education in the Square Mile

'There is no such thing as a typical City boy. What characterises the education offered is a true preparation for life.'

City of London is a truly unique independent school, not least because of its unrivalled location on the banks of the Thames, between St. Paul's Cathedral and the Tate Modern. We are at the heart of the capital and our pupils benefit enormously from all that is on offer on our doorstep. Our location allows us to attract the very best outside speakers, offer top-class work shadowing placements and visit the many places of interest in this world-class city.

We are a modern and forward-looking institution drawing on clever boys from all social, economic and ethnic backgrounds and, in so doing, truly reflect the diversity of the capital in the 21st century. Boys come from a huge number of both state primary and independent preparatory schools and, once here, receive an academic yet liberal education. Our central location allows boys to travel to City from all over London, encouraging resourcefulness and self-reliance in their journey to school, and in their wider life.

Our examination results are excellent, but, more importantly, boys leave us with a sense of identity and an independence of thought and action which are rare among leavers from private schools; it is significant that the vast majority of boys go on to their first choice of university, with a large number attending Oxford and Cambridge universities, and various medical schools.

Facilities are outstanding (the school moved downstream to its new buildings in 1986) and are continually updated. The state-of-the-art Winterflood Theatre and refurbished Science laboratories provide a first-rate environment in which our pupils learn and thrive. A new Creative Learning Centre and Library opened to pupils in September 2016, further enhancing our facilities.

We are generously endowed with academic, music and sports scholarships and, in addition, the bursary campaign has raised significant funding for a number of full-fee places to be awarded each year to those who could not otherwise afford even a proportion of fees. In this way, the school seeks to maintain the socio-economic mix which has always been its tradition and strength.

Admission at 10+, 11+ and 13+ is by entrance examinations, followed by interviews for those candidates who complete their examination papers to a satisfactory standard.

To book onto one of our open days please contact the Admissions Department
Tel: 020 3680 6300
Email: admissions@cityoflondonschool.org.uk

CITY OF LONDON SCHOOL

(Founded 1442)

Queen Victoria Street, London, EC4V 3AL UK

Tel: 020 3680 6300

Fax: 020 3680 6328

Email: admissions@cityoflondonschool.org.uk

Website: www.cityoflondonschool.org.uk

Head: Mr A R Bird MSc

Appointed: January 2018

School type: Boys' Day

Age range of boys: 10–18

No. of pupils enrolled as at 01/09/2018: 930

Sixth Form: 250

Fees per annum as at 01/09/2018:

Day: £17,901

Devonshire House Preparatory School

Academic and leisure facilities

The school is situated in fine premises in the heart of Hampstead with its own walled grounds. The aim is to achieve high academic standards whilst developing enthusiasm and initiative throughout a wide range of interests. It is considered essential to encourage pupils to develop their own individual interests and a good sense of personal responsibility.

Curriculum

Early literacy and numeracy are very important and the traditional academic subjects form the core curriculum. The younger children all have a class teacher and classroom assistant and their day consists of a mixture of formal lessons and learning through play. Whilst children of all ages continue to have a form teacher, as they grow older an increasing part of the curriculum is delivered by subject specialists. The combined sciences form an increasingly important part of the timetable as the children mature. The use of computers is introduced from an early stage, both as its own skill and as an integrated part of the pupils' education.

Expression in all forms of communication is encouraged, with classes having lessons in art, music and drama, and French. Physical exercise and games also play a key part of the curriculum. Much encouragement is given to pupils to help widen their horizons and broaden their interests. The school fosters a sense of responsibility amongst the pupils, and individuality and personal attention for each pupil is considered essential to make progress in the modern world.

The principal areas of the National Curriculum are covered, though subjects may be taken at a higher level, or at a quicker pace. For the girls approaching the 11+ senior schools' entry examinations, special emphasis is given to the requirements for these, and in the top two years for the boys, Common Entrance curriculum is taught. The pupils achieve great success in these examinations and a number also sit successfully for senior school scholarships.

The school has its own nursery, The Oak Tree Nursery, which takes children from two-and-a-half years of age.

Entry requirements

The Oak Tree Nursery: For children entering the Oak Tree Nursery, places are offered on the basis on an informal assessment made at the nursery. Children in The Oak Tree Nursery transfer directly to the Junior School.

The Junior School: For children entering the junior school from the ages of three to five, places are offered on the basis of assessment made at the school. From the age of six, places are usually subject to a written test taken at school. At eight, children transfer directly into the upper school. Parents and their children are welcome to visit for interview and to see around the school.

The Upper School: Entry to the upper school is principally from the junior school. For pupils seeking to join the school from elsewhere places are normally subject to a written entrance test.

(Founded 1989)

2 Arkwright Road, Hampstead, London, NW3 6AE UK

Tel: 020 7435 1916

Email: enquiries@devonshirehouseprepschool.co.uk

Website: www.devonshirehouseschool.co.uk

Headmistress: Mrs S. Piper BA(Hons)

School type:
Preparatory, Pre-preparatory & Nursery Day School

Religious Denomination: Non-denominational

Age range of boys: 2½–13

Age range of girls: 2½–11

No. of pupils enrolled as at 01/09/2018: 650

Boys: 350 **Girls:** 300

Fees per annum as at 01/09/2018:

Day: £10,125–£18,600

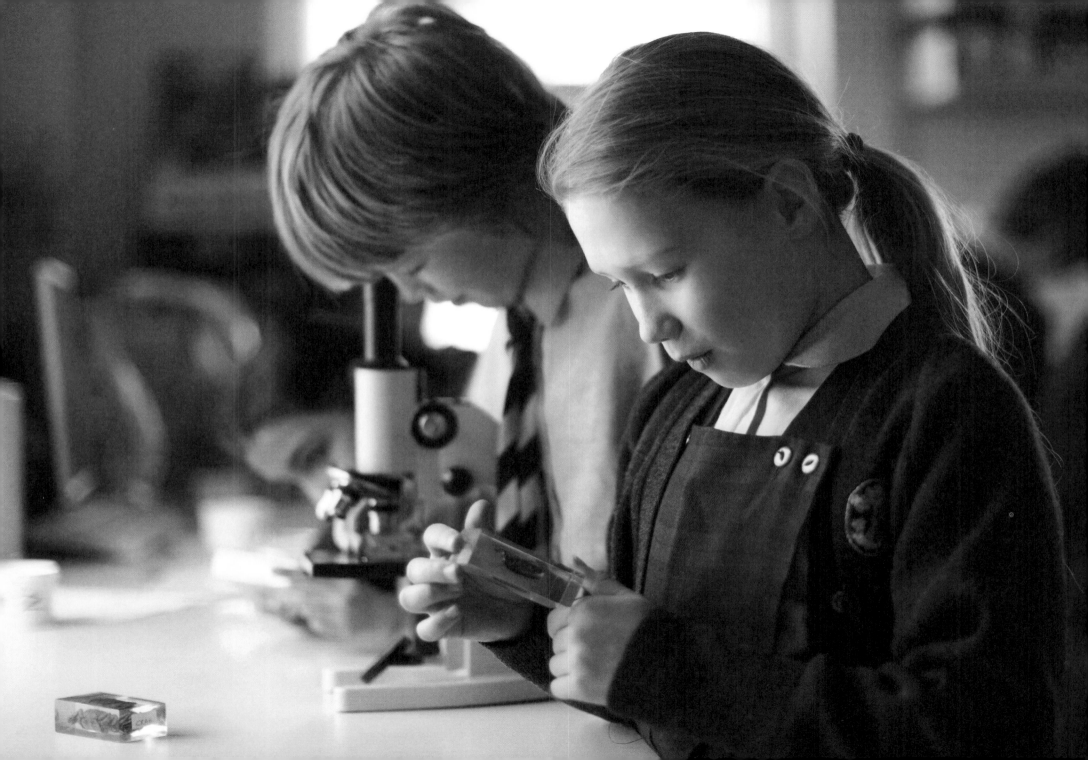

Heathside School

Heathside is a friendly day and boarding school housed in historic buildings a few minutes' walk from Hampstead Heath where Heathside children play every day.

The school is a unique and highly successful learning environment rated 'Outstanding' by Ofsted in September 2017. With talented and inspirational teachers and a strong focus on individual learning and pastoral care, our students flourish.

The 2017 Ofsted report states, *"Excellent teaching is underpinned by exemplary working relationships and strong mutual respect between staff and pupils. This, together with high-quality pastoral care, motivates pupils to do their very best. Senior leaders and staff have created an exceptional learning ethos across the school. Pupils are highly motivated and keen to excel in all aspects of school life."*

We encourage the development of the whole person and, as a result, Heathside is a relaxed and happy place and academic standards are high. We have a proud tradition of tailoring our teaching so that every child gets the best from a lesson – a high staff-to-student ratio, a focus on small-group work and individual attention allow us to offer challenge and support as appropriate.

"The head teacher is an inspirational and highly effective leader who is relentless in her drive to bring about improvements. She instils both staff and pupils with high expectations of themselves and each other. These high expectations are the foundation of all aspects of school life and enable pupils to thrive, both academically and in their personal development."

Our curriculum builds on strong foundations in literacy and numeracy, scientific understanding and creative thinking. *"The curriculum is exceptional and inspires pupils to flourish. The wide range of extra-curricular activities ensure that pupils acquire very strong knowledge, understanding and skills in all aspects of their education."*

We produce highly able mathematicians and lifelong readers and writers. We playfully bring out the artist in everyone. Every child in school learns French from a native speaker and we offer lessons in Spanish, Mandarin, German, Italian, Latin, Ancient Greek and Russian. Music and drama are particular strengths, and everyone performs several times a year. We play a wide range of sports to high standards and we have been national chess champions many times. Extra-curricular activities range from capoeira and Chinese to fencing and philosophy clubs.

In January 2018 we opened our doors for boarders at the High School. Our boarders benefit from a warm, highly supportive and safe environment and have more access to more of everything that makes Heathside life special. 'Amazing', 'special' and 'unique' are just some of the words parents used to describe Heathside.

We continue to prepare children for 11+ and 13+ examinations and have an outstanding track record of gaining scholarships and entry into many highly respected independent schools. Many Heathside children decide to continue their learning at our High School, and we are now equipped to progress to GCSE.

Most children join us in the Nursery, which can take children from two years of age. We do have occasional places in other years. It is never too early to register for a place which you can do from our website. At the right time, your child will be invited to spend a morning with us. We do have waiting lists and we give priority to Heathside siblings.

(Founded 1993)

84-86 West Heath Road, London, NW3 7UN UK

Tel: +44 (0)20 3058 4011

Email: admissions@heathside.net

Website: www.heathside.net

Headteacher: Ms Melissa Remus MSc

School type: Coeducational Day & Boarding

Age range of pupils: 2–14

No. of pupils enrolled as at 01/09/2018: 550

Fees per annum as at 01/09/2018:

Day: £15,000–£18,300

James Allen's Girls' School
Including James Allen's Preparatory School

'When you begin your life as a JAGS girl you join a community which combines extraordinary tradition with a forward-looking approach. The oldest girls' school in London, we strive for excellence in all we do, developing scholarly young women who gain top academic results and places at top institutions. But there is nothing pompous or old fashioned about a JAGS education. Come and visit us and you will meet future doctors and engineers in our labs, Oxbridge scholars in our library and the next generation of politicians and diplomats in our lecture theatre. But these same girls will also be volunteers in charity placements at the weekends, will sing loudly in the gospel choir or tap dance across our stage.

The portrait of our founder, James Allen, hangs on the main school corridor. The same man who had the vision to educate young women back in 1741, proudly declares beneath the painting that he was 'Six feet high, skilful as a Skaiter, a Jumper, athletic and humane'. We love the fact that James could skate – a true advocate of a full extra-curricular programme. But it's his humanity we most admire and most seek to uphold.

Celebrating a grounded approach and founded on a long standing tradition of diversity and access, JAGS is a genuine reflection of modern, south London life.'

Sally-Anne Huang, Headmistress

James Allen's Girls' School provides first class education to girls aged 4-18 in South London with a strong focus on developing personal and professional skills to prepare them for adulthood.

Key to our success is the ability attract a diverse mix of intellectually curious and dynamic pupils, with a means tested bursary scheme making the school accessible to girls from all economic backgrounds. Academic scholarships are also available alongside scholarships in music, sport and art.

JAGS is consistently ranked highly in national A-level results tables and students go on to study the top institutions in the UK and abroad.

Every girl is encouraged to explore a wide range of subjects when the join, covering all key areas and including several language options and creative disciplines. As they mature and choose to focus on subject specialisms, our teachers will help them gain qualifications at the highest level as well as develop research skills and become independent learners.

Our facilities include 22 acres of playing fields and a sports complex that includes a swimming pool, climbing wall and astro pitches. A professionally designed theatre gives girls a chance to learn about performing arts whilst a vibrant music department holds performances throughout the year which from next year will be in our new Community Music Centre with its 500 seat auditorium and 15 practice rooms.

School trips in the UK and around the world provide further opportunities to enhance academic learning and broaden life skills. Recent trips include volunteering at a school in Uganda and performing concerts during a music tour of Italy.

At JAGS we care that your daughter is happy and have a strong pastoral care team to give them support if they need it. The school has two School Nurses who are available to deal with medical and personal problems. Students can also talk to CAMHS counsellor and our School Chaplain.

For more information, visit our website www.jags.org.uk and follow us on Twitter and Facebook (@JAGSSchool).

James Allen's Girls' School 4–18

jags

(Founded 1741)

144 East Dulwich Grove, Dulwich, London, SE22 8TE UK

Tel: 020 8693 1181

Email: enquiries@jags.org.uk

Website: www.jags.org.uk

Head of School: Mrs Sally-Anne Huang MA, MSc

Appointed: September 2015

School type: Girls' Day

Religious Denomination: Church of England

Age range of girls: 4–18

No. of pupils enrolled as at 01/09/2018: 1075

Fees per term as at 01/09/2018:

Pre-Prep & Prep: £5,215

Senior School: £5,997

Average class size: 18-28

Teacher/pupil ratio: 1:9

Kensington Park School

Academic Excellence in the Heart of London

Kensington Park School is a new independent day and boarding school for boys and girls aged 11-18. It boasts some of the country's most experienced teachers and offers excellent cultural and sporting opportunities, all in the heart of London.

The school operates from two buildings either side of Kensington Gardens:

- KPS Lower School, in Bark Place, opened in September 2018 for pupils aged 11-16
- KPS Sixth Form, opposite the Natural History Museum, opened in September 2017 for pupils aged 16-18

This configuration enables the school to have a dedicated Sixth Form Centre where A-levels and preparation for university entrance can be taught in a specialist environment. KPS also has excellent boarding facilities in South Kensington, welcoming pupils from all over the UK and from around the world.

Although a new school, pupils benefit from some of the best teachers in the country. The core team has been drawn from the UK's top schools including St Paul's School, Dulwich College and Winchester College. They are led by Headmaster Paul Vanni, previously Deputy Head of St Paul's Girls' School, who brings a proven track record of academic excellence and comprehensive pastoral care to KPS.

Modern and Dynamic Outlook on Education

The school prides itself on its forward-thinking approach; its ethos, curriculum and co-curricular provision are geared towards preparing pupils for the challenges of the 21st century. The school places emphasis on creativity, on developing its pupils' interpersonal skills, and encouraging a sense of global understanding. This is supported through a modern curriculum with subjects such as Computer Science and Mandarin on offer; hands-on, experiential learning; and an array of exciting sports and activities.

Superb Cultural and Sporting Opportunities

Activities on offer range from technical theatre and dance to fencing and swimming, making use of both the school's own facilities and those in the surrounding area. The school has partnered with local sports organisations such as Imperial College's Ethos Sports Centre with its state-of-the-art gym, pool and climbing wall; expert coaches, including former Olympians, in fencing and riding; and Fulham Reach Boat Club, a superbly equipped new rowing facility on the Thames. There is an exciting outdoor education programme, including the Duke of Edinburgh award scheme. Similar partnerships are in place for music and drama.

How to Apply

Regular open evenings are held throughout the term, details of which can be found on the school website – www.kps.co.uk. Individual visits can also be arranged for those unable to attend an open event. Please contact the Director of Admissions, Jane Lovell – j.lovell@kps.co.uk – for more information.

Kensington Park
S C H O O L

Kensington Park School (Years 7-11)
40-44 Bark Place, London, W2 4AT

Tel: +44 (0)20 7616 4400

Kensington Park School Sixth Form
59 Queen's Gate, South Kensington, London SW7 5JP UK

Tel: +44 (0)20 7225 0577

Email: admissions@kps.co.uk

Website: www.kps.co.uk

Headmaster: Mr Paul Vanni MA

School type: Co-educational Boarding & Day

Age range of pupils: 11–18

Fees per term as at 01/09/2018:

Day (UK): £8,000

Boarding (UK): £13,300

Day (International): £8,167

Boarding (International): £13,467

Lloyd Williamson Schools

Introduction

The Lloyd Williamson Schools have grown in both size and reputation to become the established schools they are today. The main departments are: three Nurseries, a Transition School for 5-7 year olds, a Senior School for 7-11 year olds and an Upper School for 11-14 year olds. We plan to expand age range to 18 taking one extra year group per year from 2019.

The names *Lloyd* and *Williamson* are family names that belong to the proprietor. We believe they convey one of the main points of ethos at the school: that we are a *family* – and a strong one at that!

We have built an excellent reputation for strong academic standards and personalised, holistic learning for individual children.

We are based in W10 and W8 in the Borough of Kensington and Chelsea, with small classes to a maximum of sixteen. The schools have extended opening hours, competitive, realistic fees and all-year-round provision, including Holiday Clubs.

Mission Statement and Ethos:

- We celebrate childhood and nurture each child to be the best they can be in a challenging and inspiring environment that ignites a passion for life and learning – we are not a one-size-fits-all school
- Teachers build positive relationships, working with each child to be curious, intellectual and creative – we all like to think outside the box – fear of failure is banished!
- Equality and diversity permeate the fabric of our school – we are a family where everyone belongs, based on empathy and respect
- We encourage partnership and dialogue with parents and children thrive academically without losing their childhood – we cherish each child's self-esteem
- A blend of traditional and forward thinking teaching prepares our children for their next school and for life

Admissions

Parents are invited to meet the Co-Principals for personal and individual tours of the school during school hours in order to gain a real flavour of how the school operates on a daily basis.

The school supports requests for places from families with a diverse range of backgrounds; the binding quality is motivation! We do not compare children with one another; we challenge them against their own goals and next steps. This allows children to feel safe, be creative and curious instead of managing anxiety about 'not keeping up'! Our children are happy, confident students available to learn – they develop a rich and positive sense of who they are and can be.

The school is open from 7:30am-6:00pm (main school hours from 8:30am-3:30pm). This means that working parents can drop off their children and get to work knowing their children are safe and without the additional cost of nannies.

As a small school, everyone knows everyone from the babies up to our oldest member of staff!

We cherish individuality and self-confidence and our aim is that every child will develop an organic and strong positive sense of self. We enable this through the development of positive relationships so that all our children can learn to be strong and independent.

Contact Information

www.lws.org.uk
Admissions: admin@lws.org.uk
Main School and W10 Nursery: 020 8962 0345
W8 Nurseries: 020 7243 3331

LLOYD WILLIAMSON
—— S C H O O L S ——

(Founded 1999)

Nursery and Lower School
12 Telford Road, London, W10 5SH UK

Additional Nurseries
104 and 112 Palace Gardens Terrace, London, W8 4RT

Upper School
77 St Charles Square, London, W10 6EB

Tel: 020 8962 0345

Fax: 020 8962 0345

Email: admin@lws.org.uk

Website: www.lloydwilliamson.co.uk

Co-Principals: Ms Lucy Meyer & Mr Aaron Williams

Appointed: December 1999

School type: Coeducational Day

Age range of pupils:
4 months–14 years (15 in 2019, 16 in 2020)

Fees per annum as at 01/09/2018:

Day: £14,085

Average class size: 12-16

Teacher/pupil ratio: 1:12

Newton Prep

In a London landscape crowded with prep schools, Newton Prep stands out for its unbeatable combination of vibrant size and eclecticism, its extraordinary facilities and outside spaces and its position at the heart of Central London's most burgeoning community: the rapidly growing Battersea Power Station development, the new US embassy and the massive regeneration of Nine Elms.

There's an electricity in the air and it's important that we are a part of that buzz. It is also key to our ethos: to ensure that Newton children are well-educated, curious, kind and articulate but, above all, in this modern world (and equipped with the best of British values), to encourage them to think for, and be, themselves.

At Newton Prep, we provide a liberal environment in which children are equipped with a sense of self, resilience and hopefulness, beyond the obvious need to excel academically. We encourage children to think beyond the curriculum and they hoover it up. Whether it's piano lessons, judo or Boggle, children need ways of engaging. We aim for our Newton Prep children to enter adolescence feeling that they already have more to contribute than just academic achievements. Yes, we need to get them into the right schools but not at the expense of their well-being and character.

We encourage all our children to reflect on school life, not just power through it. Delegates from Year 3 upwards take part in the Pupil Parliament, which meets regularly. Through this means, children can express their views and make suggestions about how we might improve the school. Each child is therefore encouraged to embrace the notion of using their voice to influence things for the good of the many.

Despite the excellence of their education, Newton Prep children are notable for their lack of arrogance and entitlement. The kindness and generosity shown by the pupils towards their peers is remarkable and we are particularly proud of the engagement between the older children and the little ones. This spirit of community is also built into the Newton Diploma, our new humanities curriculum for our Years 7 and 8. This is a cross-curricular, rigorous and exciting programme that scraps the creaky arts syllabi of Common Entrance and allows pupils to exploit links between subjects, extend initiatives for service and leadership and breathe real fire into their intellectual curiosity.

Luckily, our extensive resources enable such growth. With a huge all-weather pitch capable of supporting four fixtures at a time, a state-of-the-art, 120-seat recital hall, a music technology suite, recording studio, 300 seat auditorium, three gymnasiums, bustling art studios, dance studios, a library and collegiate-style science labs, children are encouraged to "do" as well as "learn". We even have an oasis of a garden: where our children practise circus skills, hunt for mini-beasts and conduct scientific experiments: like when Year 8 students lit up the London skies with their own explosion.

We are not a blazers-and-boaters kind of school. We don't have to look to the past and can focus all our present energies on ensuring a bright future for our children. One parent who, after sending her five children through Newton, is now serving on our Bursary Fund board to ensure access for bright children who may not be able to access a Newton education otherwise, commented, *"Newton combines a quirky nature and knowledge of families with great space and facilities… All the teachers understood my (very different) children, the management is open to fresh ideas and the school is large enough to accommodate variety."*

Above all, we want Newton Prep children to enjoy their precious childhood years.

Admission to the Nursery is by registration; to the Lower School (Reception to Y2) by registration, with a gentle and informal assessment; to the Upper School (Y3-8) by registration and competitive testing.

Newton PREP

(Founded 1991)

149 Battersea Park Road, London, SW8 4BX UK

Tel: 020 7720 4091

Fax: 020 7498 9052

Email: enquiries@newtonprep.co.uk

Website: www.newtonprepschool.co.uk

Headmistress: Mrs Alison Fleming BA, MA Ed, PGCE

Appointed: September 2013

School type:
Coeducational Pre-Preparatory & Preparatory Day

Age range of pupils: 3–13

No. of pupils enrolled as at 01/09/2018: 632

Boys: 311 **Girls:** 321

Fees per annum as at 01/09/2018:

Day: £9,300–£19,695

Average class size: 20 (smaller in Years 7 & 8)

North Bridge House

North Bridge House prides itself on providing an individually tailored education for boys and girls, aged from 2 years 9 months to 18 years. We know, support and inspire every pupil to achieve their full potential and provide a solid foundation for a successful academic career and adult life.

Pupils can join us from Nursery and stay until Sixth Form or benefit from first-class preparation for other top senior schools. We work closely with parents to choose the right educational environment for their child, ensuring that every individual thrives and helping them to gain many sought after scholarship places.

Our high-achieving Senior Schools and Sixth Form prepare pupils for university life and the world of work with careers events, industry speakers and UCAS support, and celebrate top GCSE results. 2018 saw NBH Senior Hampstead and NBH Senior Canonbury achieve 61% 7-9 grades, with NBH Canonbury accumulating 27% grade 9s.

At the heart of each school is a highly qualified and inspirational team of teachers who deliver a rich and varied range of academic and extra-curricular activities, tailor-made to challenge, stimulate and reward our pupils. This, together with our outstanding pastoral support, allows them to grow in confidence and independence. At our Senior and Sixth Form, the progressive teaching team also refer to research into teen development to further understand and maximize the potential of their pupils. For example, Sixth Formers start their lessons later in the day as studies have shown that their sleeping patterns make them less likely to absorb teaching early in the morning.

Through PE and games we develop the individual's physical and emotional wellbeing, as well as essential team working skills. The latter are then further enhanced in the senior years through the Duke of Edinburgh Awards, civic engagements and leadership programmes.

At North Bridge House we nurture each individual to exceed their expectations – and pave the way to success and the top universities. To find out more, please do join us at an open day or book a guided tour at northbridgehouse. com/open.

School locations:
North Bridge House Nursery School
33 Fitzjohn's Avenue, Hampstead, London NW3 5JY
North Bridge House Pre-Prep School
8 Netherhall Gardens, Hampstead, London NW3 5RR
North Bridge House Prep School
1 Gloucester Avenue, Regent's Park, London NW1 7AB
North Bridge House Senior Hampstead
65 Rosslyn Hill, Hampstead, London NW3 5UD
North Bridge House Senior School & Sixth Form Canonbury
6-9 Canonbury Place, Islington, London N1 2NQ

North Bridge House

(Founded 1939)

65 Rosslyn Hill, London, NW3 5UD UK

Tel: 020 7428 1520

Email: admissionsenquiries@northbridgehouse.com

Website: www.northbridgehouse.com

Head of Nursery & Pre-Prep Schools:
Mrs. Christine McLelland

Head of Prep School: Mr. Brodie Bibby
(Mr James Stenning will take over in Jan 19)

Head of Senior Canonbury: Mr. Jonathan Taylor

Head of Senior Hampstead: Mr Brendan Pavey

School type: Co-educational Day

Age range of pupils: 2 years, 9 months–18 years

No. of pupils enrolled as at 01/09/2018: 1375

Fees per annum as at 01/09/2018:

Day: £7,200 – £19,335

Average class size: 20

Orchard House School

At Orchard House School, children are loved first and taught second. Our Pupil Pastoral Plan monitors the well-being of each child and was recently shortlisted for a TES (Times Educational Supplement) national award for educational innovation. This emphasis on a nurturing environment is not, however, at the cost of academic excellence. In fact, our outstanding results show how creating the right environment enables every child to thrive academically and emotionally. We believe learning should be exciting and fun, and the children should positively want to come to Orchard House every day. And they do: we harness the exuberance and energy of every child in our care, and instil within them a lifelong love of learning.

Orchard House's diverse curriculum creates a sense of adventure, developing the children's appetite for risk. This feeds into greater academic and creative achievements. Whether it's a whole-school skipping day, a project with Jaguar to enable our 10- and 11-year-old mathematicians to engineer performance cars or learning archery in Normandy (taught solely in French), Orchard House children embrace novel tasks throughout their time with us. By the time they sit 11+ exams, they are past masters at tackling new challenges with verve: this shows in our stellar results.

Sport at Orchard House encourages a respectful, competitive attitude, teaching children the value of camaraderie and the buzz of going for gold, or goal. We offer football, netball, rugby, hockey, lacrosse, cross country, tennis, athletics, triathlon, cricket, rounders, swimming and gymnastics and arrange regular team-sport fixtures against other schools, often lifting the trophy but always relishing the match.

Similarly, music and drama build confidence and self-esteem, as well as many opportunities for every child to perform. Visiting music teachers offer individual instrumental tuition on a variety of instruments. We have a school orchestra, Pippin choir, chamber choir, senior and junior choir and a parent and staff choir. There are many other instrumental groups including a pupil-led rock band.

We collaborate closely with our sister schools, Bassett House and Prospect House, sparking off new ideas to promote ever more successful teaching practices. The three schools share a common ethos but each retains its unique personality. The schools (brought together under the umbrella of House Schools Group) are proudly non-selective. True to our belief, children are not tested and judged at the tender age of 3 or 4 years. Our educational success shows all children can fulfil their potential, regardless of early learning ability.

The Independent Schools Inspectorate awarded Orchard House the highest accolades of 'excellent' in all areas and 'exceptional' in achievements and learning in its last full inspection and we flew through our 2018 compliance inspection. The top-notch education we provide leads to our first-class academic results and the scholarships our pupils win to their next schools.

ORCHARD
HOUSE SCHOOL

(Founded 1993)

16 Newton Grove, Bedford Park, London, W4 1LB UK

Tel: 020 8742 8544

Email: info@orchardhs.org.uk

Website: www.orchardhs.org.uk

Headmistress: Mrs Maria Edwards BEd(Beds) PGCE(Man) Mont Cert

Appointed: September 2015

School type: Co-educational Day

Age range of pupils: 3–11

No. of pupils enrolled as at 01/09/2018: 290

Fees per annum as at 01/09/2018:

Day: £8,850–£18,450

Average class size: 20

Teacher/pupil ratio: 1:7

Prospect House School

At Prospect House School, we focus on making each child feel valued and secure and on making their educational experience both challenging and fun. This allows us to develop every child to their fullest potential, as our outstanding results demonstrate. Our most recent full Independent Schools Inspectorate inspection, in 2013, rated us 'excellent' against all the inspectors' criteria and we flew through our 2017 regulatory compliance inspection.

Prospect House's superb teachers provide a supportive and encouraging academic environment in which children excel. The sound of laughter is never far away, as Prospect House children discover their aptitude for sport, music, art, computing, drama or a whole host of other opportunities both within the curriculum or before or after school. Whether taking up the trombone, building a go-cart or orienteering on Putney Heath, our children relish each new challenge and emerge better able to face the next challenge that comes their way.

Music is an important part of life at Prospect House. We have over 200 individual music lessons taking place each week and a school orchestra, chamber choir and senior and junior choirs, as well as a number of ensembles. All children act in assemblies, school plays, musical productions and concerts throughout the year. Children in Years 1 to 6 enjoy drama lessons and our high-quality staging, lighting, sound and props give every production a professional feel.

Physical activity promotes wellbeing, so we offer a busy sports programme. This includes football, netball, hockey, running, cross country, tennis, athletics, cricket, rounders, swimming, dance and gymnastics. Our approach to fixtures and tournaments successfully balances participation for everyone with letting our sports stars shine.

Residential trips thrill the children with the sense of adventure, encouraging risk-taking and building self-reliance, whether on a history expedition, a bushcraft adventure or a week in Normandy immersed in the French language and culture.

We encourage our children to think for themselves, to be confident and to develop a sense of responsibility for the world in which they live. By the time they leave us aged 11, Prospect House children are ready to thrive at London's best senior schools. This is reflected in our impressive 11+ results. Every year, a notable proportion of our children win scholarships to leading senior schools.

We collaborate closely with our sister schools, Bassett House and Orchard House, sparking off new ideas to promote ever more successful teaching practices. The three schools share a common ethos but each retains its unique personality.

The schools (brought together under the umbrella of House Schools Group) are proudly non-selective. True to our belief, children are not tested and judged at the tender age of 3 or 4 years. Our stellar results repeatedly show all children can fulfil their potential, regardless of early learning ability. We encourage our high-flyers to soar, whilst children who need a little extra help are given the support they need to reach their fullest potential. At Prospect House, every child is helped to achieve a personal best.

PROSPECT
HOUSE SCHOOL

(Founded 1991)

75 Putney Hill, London, SW15 3NT UK

Tel: 020 8246 4897

Email: info@prospecths.org.uk

Website: www.prospecths.org.uk

Headmaster: Mr Michael Hodge BPED(Rhodes) QTS

Appointed: September 2017

School type: Co-educational Day

Age range of pupils: 3–11

No. of pupils enrolled as at 01/09/2018: 300

Fees per annum as at 01/09/2018:

Day: £8,850–£18,450

Average class size: 20

Teacher/pupil ratio: 1:7

Queen's Gate School

Queen's Gate School is an independent day school for girls between the ages of 4 and 18 years. Established in 1891, the school is an Educational Trust situated in five large Victorian Houses within easy walking distance of Kensington Gardens, Hyde Park, and many of the main London museums.

The School offers an education for life in a challenging environment where sound values and individuality are nurtured within a supportive atmosphere. Our aim is to create a secure and happy environment in which the girls can realise their academic potential and make full use of individual interests and talents. We encourage the development of self-discipline and create an atmosphere where freedom of thought and ideas can flourish.

Girls follow as wide a curriculum as possible and generally take GCSEs in ten subjects that must include English, Mathematics, a science and a modern language. A full range of A level subjects is offered. In the Lower Sixth girls normally take four subjects, reducing to three in the Upper Sixth.

Sport is highly valued at Queen's Gate with two compulsory sessions for all girls each week. We have many sports available at other times during the school day including netball, athletics, basketball, hockey, fencing, swimming, rowing, horse riding, cross-country, biathlon and dance.

The Principal, Mrs Rosalynd Kamaryc, has been in post since 2006 and has built on the existing strengths of the school, whilst enabling girls to enjoy new opportunities in and out of the classroom.

In September 2007, the School entered an exciting new period in our long history when the Junior School moved into splendid new buildings at 125 and 126 Queen's Gate, just a few yards down the road from the Senior School. The new buildings, beautifully restored, boast spacious form rooms, three fully equipped laboratories, a state of the art ICT Room, a separate Art and DT studio and an elegant Assembly Hall. Junior pupils also use some of the Senior School facilities and benefit from specialist subject teaching from Senior School staff. Senior girls often visit the Junior School to assist with activities, thus reinforcing the continuity of education from 4-18 available at Queen's Gate.

Admission is by test and interview in the Junior School. Entrance to the Senior School is by the London 11+ Consortium entrance examination. Applicants for the Sixth Form must achieve six GCSEs at Grade 7 or above with Grade 8 or 9 (or their equivalent) required in those subjects they wish to pursue at A level.

In addition to the Open Events that are run by the Senior and Junior Schools throughout the year, parents are always welcome to make a private visit to see the schools at work. Appointments can be made by contacting the Registrar on 0207 594 4982 or by email registrar@queensgate.org.uk.

Queen's Gate

(Founded 1891)
133 Queen's Gate, London, SW7 5LE UK
Tel: 020 7589 3587
Fax: 020 7584 7691
Email: registrar@queensgate.org.uk
Website: www.queensgate.org.uk
Principal: Mrs R M Kamaryc BA, MSc, PGCE
Appointed: January 2006
School type: Girls' Day
Age range of girls: 4–18
No. of pupils enrolled as at 01/09/2018: 542
Sixth Form: 97
Junior School: 145
Senior School: 397
Fees per annum as at 01/09/2018:
Junior School: £18,510
Senior School: £20,550
Average class size: 23
Teacher/pupil ratio: 1:10

St Paul's Cathedral School

Governed by the Dean and Chapter and seven lay governors, the original residential choir school, which can date its history back to the 12th century, has, since the 1980s, included non-chorister day boys and girls aged 4-13. The number of pupils is currently 250.

In its 2017 inspection, the ISI awarded the School its highest accolade of 'Excellent' in both educational attainment and pupil progress.

A broad curriculum prepares all pupils for 11+ and 13+ examinations including scholarship and Common Entrance examinations. The school has an excellent record in placing pupils in outstanding senior schools, many with scholarships. With its unique and central location, the school is able to make the most of what London can offer culturally and artistically in particular. A wide variety of sports and musical instrument tuition is offered: the school has an exceptional record in preparing pupils for ABRSM exams. Choristers receive an outstanding choral training as members of the renowned St Paul's Cathedral Choir.

The life of the school is based on the following aims and principles:

St Paul's Cathedral School is a Christian, co-educational community which holds to the values of love, justice, tolerance, respect, honesty, service and trust in its life and practice, to promote positive relationships throughout the school community and where the safety, welfare and emotional well-being of each child is of the utmost importance.

The school aims to instil a love of learning through a broad curriculum. It aims to give each pupil the opportunity to develop intellectually, socially, personally, physically, culturally and spiritually. All pupils are encouraged to work to the best of their ability and to achieve standards of excellence in all of their endeavours.

Through the corporate life of the school, and through good pastoral care, the school encourages the independence of the individual as well as mutual responsibility. It aims to make its pupils aware of the wider community, espouses the democratic process and encourages a close working relationship with parents and guardians.

Facilities: the school is situated on one site to the east of St Paul's Cathedral. It has a separate Pre-Prep department, excellent Science lab and ICT room. It has two outside play areas and a hall. There are plans to provide new boarding facilities for the choristers.

Entry is at 4+ and 7+ years. 4+ entry is held in the November preceding the September a child will enter the school and 7+ entry is held in the January preceding the September a child will enter the school. At 7+, pupils are given a short test and spend a day in school. Chorister voice trials are held throughout the year for boys between 6 and 8 years old. Occasional places in other year groups sometimes become available and, at 11+, the school now offers scholarship awards in music, the arts, sport and academics. Further information can be found on the school's website www.spcslondon.com

St Paul's Cathedral School is a registered charity (No. 312718), which exists to provide education for the choristers of St Paul's Cathedral and for children living in the local area.

ST PAUL'S CATHEDRAL SCHOOL

(Founded 12th Century or earlier)

2 New Change, London, EC4M 9AD UK

Tel: 020 7248 5156

Fax: 020 7329 6568

Email: admissions@spcs.london.sch.uk

Website: www.spcslondon.com

Headmaster: Simon Larter-Evans BA (Hons), PGCE, FRSA

Appointed: September 2016

School type: Coeducational Pre-Prep, Day Prep & Boarding Choir School

Religious Denomination:
Church of England, admits pupils of all faiths

Age range of pupils: 4–13

No. of pupils enrolled as at 01/09/2018: 252

Boys: 146 **Girls:** 106

Fees per term as at 01/09/2018:

Day: £4,677–£5,035

Full Boarding: £2,912

Average class size: 15-20

Teacher/pupil ratio: 1:10

North-West

Chetham's School of Music

The thriving creative community at Chetham's includes around 300 students aged 8-18, whose common passion is music. Entry to the School is based solely on musical ability and potential, never on background or ability to pay; 90% of students receive bursaries up to full fees through the Government's Music and Dance Scheme. This common bond of musical passion makes for a truly inspirational place which transforms the lives of all who are part of it.

There are many different qualities that permeate the fabric of Chetham's: the warm and welcoming atmosphere, the constant creative buzz, admirable academic standards, Chetham's history and heritage, superb teaching and performance spaces, the cosmopolitan city of Manchester, diverse backgrounds and personalities – and of course, the music. Chetham's is the largest specialist Music School in the UK and the only one based in the north of England. The School is also a national and international resource for music education – welcoming teachers, professional players, composers and conductors, community groups, school children and other young musicians, both experienced and novices, to come together and make music. Launching in 2018, Chetham's Fit to Perform programme takes an innovative new approach to wellbeing, promoting mental and physical fitness designed specifically with young musicians in mind.

Based in the heart of Manchester, Chetham's is housed in a state-of-the-art new School building, with its onsite concert hall, The Stoller Hall, offering a world-class acoustic for student performances and visiting artists from around the world. Excellent academic results are achieved through small class sizes, a dedicated teaching team, and a community which values success. Ongoing investment into boarding accommodation, and a cross-departmental team helping students to balance music and academic study with time to socialise, explore and grow, ensure that students finish school as well-developed, ambitious and curious young people. Our network of partnerships with professional orchestras and organisations extends across the music industry, encompassing performance, outreach and leadership, and creating vital connections for students' professional futures.

In 2016, Chetham's was the highest achieving non academically-selective school in Manchester, and every year students progress to leading music conservatoires and universities across the world. We take as much pride in those who move on to careers in engineering, medicine or law as in those playing leading roles on the concert platform; in DJs, jazz pianists and folk singers as in classical conductors and soloists. What unites every member of the Chetham's community is their passion for music; a passion that, whatever their future direction, will forever enrich their lives.

Admissions to Chetham's
Open Days:
Saturday 6 October 2018
Saturday 19 January 2019
Summer Open Days in May and June

Chetham's holds regular whole-school Open Days in October and January each year, when prospective students can meet staff and students, hear ensembles in rehearsals, and discover more about a specialist music education. Further Open sessions in May and June support students planning entry in 2020 onwards, and specifically target Juniors, Secondary Phase, and Sixth Form applicants.

Admission is by musical audition only. There are no academic requirements, and means-tested Government funding provides up to full support with school fees. Many students benefit from Advice Auditions, a chance to receive guidance on your musical progression before making a full application to the School.

Auditions and Advice Auditions run throughout the year.

Chetham's
School of Music

(Founded 1969)

Long Millgate, Manchester,
Greater Manchester M3 1SB UK

Tel: 0161 834 9644

Fax: 0161 839 3609

Email: hello@chethams.com

Website: www.chethams.com

Head of School: Mr Alun Jones

Appointed: September 2016

Chair of Governors: Mr Malcolm Edge

School type: Coeducational Boarding & Day

Age range of pupils: 8–18

No. of pupils enrolled as at 01/09/2018: 306

Fees per annum as at 01/09/2018:

Day: £25,068 (overseas £26,001)

Full Boarding: £32,352 (overseas £33,999)

Average class size: 20

Teacher/pupil ratio: 1:10

Kirkham Grammar School

At Kirkham Grammar School, we believe in the values of a traditional education alongside a drive towards modern ambition. It is our intention to continue to build upon our history as a recognised centre of excellence for academic attainment and the holistic development of the learner. We believe everyone has a place in our community including our parents, pupils, staff, governors and alumni alike; we all have a part to play in the drive for continued excellence.

Kirkham Grammar School is an Independent Co-educational Day and Boarding School for pupils aged 3-18. The school prides itself on its warm family atmosphere. Academic success remains at the heart of the school's aims.

The Senior School has undergone a transformation over the last decade and boasts a host of magnificent new facilities. In addition, this summer saw phase one of a planned four phase development programme commence. This included the refurbishment of the Summerlee Hall, a multi-purpose space available for use by the whole foundation; a new psychology classroom; a new conference room and an upgrade to the rugby pitches and sports facilities. The teaching provision includes twelve interactive classrooms and a science block designed to meet the needs of the large number of pupils who pursue studies in this area. Sporting facilities are outstanding with a floodlit all weather surface and Lawrence House Pavilion. Drama provision has been enhanced by the fine studio dedicated to Theatre Studies.

The Junior School is situated opposite the Senior School and has a roll of 250 pupils aged from 3-11 years. As well as enjoying its own on-site state of the art facilities, it also has access to the Senior School facilities, including an Astroturf pitch and multi-purpose hall.

Our newly designed Pre-School opened in September 2018, perfectly timed for the start of the new academic year. The setting has been thoughtfully designed to meet the needs and requirements of children from rising threes to 4 years old. The Pre-School offers a wide range of exciting activities and resources, which promote each child's learning across all areas of the Early Years Foundation Stage framework. The setting is a welcoming 'home-from-home' where children feel relaxed and happy, while being guided and nurtured by our dedicated Pre-School team. As always at Kirkham Grammar Junior School, our fundamental aim is to offer the best possible environment in which children can flourish and naturally love learning forever.

Our most recent inspection, recognised the school as, 'excellent across all areas', the highest grading possible within the independent sector. During the inspection, over 60 lessons were observed, meetings undertaken and every aspect of the school's infrastructure and life inspected. The inspection found that the quality of the pupils' academic and other achievements is excellent, saying: "Pupils are articulate and display excellent verbal and communication skills." The report added: "Pupils are ambitious learners, eager to respond to challenging opportunities in lessons and clear target setting in marking." The quality of the pupils' personal development was also deemed excellent: "Pupils reflect the strong family ethos of the school and demonstrate excellent collaboration in and out of lessons." Following the inspection, Headmaster Mr Berry said: "The inspection confirmed what was already known; Kirkham Grammar School is the best kept educational secret in Lancashire. However, it was pleasing for everyone that it has been officially acknowledged against national criteria that we are working hard to ensure our pupils receive the finest education."

We believe Kirkham Grammar School exists for our children and therefore they must have the best!

KIRKHAM
GRAMMAR SCHOOL

(Founded 1549)

Ribby Road, Kirkham, Preston, Lancashire PR4 2BH UK

Tel: 01772 684264

Fax: 01772 672747

Email: info@kirkhamgrammar.co.uk

Website: www.kirkhamgrammar.co.uk

Headmaster: Mr. Daniel Berry

Appointed: 2016

Head of Junior School: Mrs. Annette Roberts

School type: Co-educational Boarding & Day

Age range of pupils: 3–18 years

No. of pupils enrolled as at 01/09/2018: 870

Boys: 455 **Girls:** 415 **Sixth Form:** 180

No. of boarders: 70

Fees per term as at 01/09/2018:

Junior School (4–11 years) Day: £2,895

Senior School (11-18 years) Day: £3,875

Senior School (11-18 years) Boarding:
£3,480 (in addition to the Day fee)

Pre-School (3-4 years): £250 (Full week)– £51 (Full day)

Average class size: 15

Teacher/pupil ratio: 1:9

Rossall School

For many, a childhood by the sea is a dream; at Rossall, that dream becomes a reality. Rossall is an exceptional school, rooted in its heritage yet innately dynamic, brimming with personality and excited about the future.

We are shaped by our coastal location and somehow infused with the sense of anticipation, curiosity and adventure that early explorers must have felt – where can we go? What will we find? How can we get there?

We are shaped by the wonderful architecture which creates a safe haven within its Cambridge-like quads, by the vast dining hall, atmospheric Chapel and beautiful rooms.

We are shaped by our expansive site and make full use of our 160 acres, particularly for outdoor activities and sport, from cross country running and CCF field exercises to golf practice and Ross-hockey on the beach. Our ponds, trees, marsh, grassland and dunes also provide unending scope for outdoor learning and discovery.

But above all, we are shaped by the great people, both staff and students, who live and work at Rossall. There is an indelible Rossall spirit that is cultivated here – warmth, courage, humour, empathy, resilience, curiosity and the ability to talk to anyone are some of its most prominent features! It is a compelling mix.

Our teachers provide a brilliant balance of inspiration, care and deep subject knowledge to fire the imagination and ensure that our students have all the building blocks they need for success, not only at school and not only in the classroom, but also later on in life. We are proud of our students' academic achievements and delighted that they achieve consistently above national and world averages in their examinations.

We deliver a broad and balanced curriculum with the principles of the International Baccalaureate learner profile at its heart. In the Nursery, we follow the Early Years Foundation Stage (EYFS) learning goals. From the age of 2 to 11, we offer the IB Primary Years Programme (PYP). At age 16, students sit GCSE and iGCSE examinations, then students choose between the IB or A Level route in the Sixth Form. The IB principles run through our teaching and learning in every phase of the school and underpin a dynamic and enjoyable yet rigorous learning experience.

With nearly fifty different nationalities living and learning together at Rossall, we truly are a global village. The combination of UK day students and students from right across the world creates an exciting international dimension and an appreciation of diverse culture, religions and politics.

Whether joining Rossall as a day or boarding pupil, you will be coming to a vibrant and happy community. All the basic needs are catered for, but in a most generous way – food is plentiful and delicious, we have an on-site Medical Centre, our houses are beautifully appointed and our houseparents and tutors are amazing – adept, knowledgeable and attuned to the needs of the young people in their care.

To come and experience the School first hand, you can arrange a private tour to fit in with your commitments.

Scholarships: To enable a wide range of children to join Rossall, we offer a number of scholarships each year. We offer academic, music, drama and sports scholarships to children in Years 7, 9 and 12.

EXPANDING HORIZONS

(Founded 1844)

Broadway, Fleetwood, Lancashire FY7 8JW UK

Tel: +44 (0)1253 774201

Email: admissions@rossall.org.uk

Website: www.rossall.org.uk

Head: Mr Jeremy Quartermain

Appointed: August 2018

School type: Co-educational Boarding & Day

Religious Denomination:
Church of England but accept all religions

Age range of pupils: 2–18

No. of pupils enrolled as at 01/09/2018: 640

Boys: 350 **Girls:** 290 **Sixth Form:** 180

No. of boarders: 260

Fees per annum as at 01/09/2018:

Day: £8,040–£13,080

Full Boarding: £20,610–£37,350

Average class size: 16

Teacher/pupil ratio: 1:11

Stonyhurst College

Stonyhurst is Britain's leading Catholic boarding and day school, with over 400 years of history, set in a magnificent Grade I listed building in a beautiful setting. The oldest Jesuit school in the world, Stonyhurst is part of a well-proven educational tradition, with global links to other Jesuit schools and colleges in every continent. We achieve high academic results, have exceptional pastoral care, and offer an enormous range of extra-curricular opportunities.

The pupils in our care are given the individual attention, resources and space in which to grow intellectually, spiritually and emotionally. Stonyhurst has an outstanding academic record, with many pupils going on to top universities in the UK, Europe and around the world; Stonyhurst pupils will attend Oxbridge in September 2017, with others attending the Russell Group and International universities of their choice.

Teaching at Stonyhurst centres on the individual and encourages pupils to study independently, and to think for themselves. Small classes and exceptionally good teacher-pupil relationships enable pupils to achieve their full academic potential. All pupils have a personal tutor. A strong learning support department enables those with special educational needs to achieve their best. In the sixth form we offer the International Baccalaureate alongside A levels. Pupils have a wealth of support to guide them through their chosen courses and to assist them with their application to university.

The creative life of the College is rich and varied, offering many opportunities in music, art, drama and dance. Standards are high, with prestigious choral and organ scholarships frequently awarded to Stonyhurst pupils, as well as places on National Youth Theatre courses. Sport plays an important part in the life of Stonyhurst; we are represented in local and national fixtures, and international tours take our pupils all over the world. The main team games are rugby, hockey, cricket, netball, athletics and football. Additional sports include cross-country running, squash, tennis, gymnastics, basketball, fencing and swimming. Facilities include a heated swimming pool, state-of-the-art tennis dome, a 9 hole golf course, all weather pitch, squash and tennis court.

Ethos

As a Jesuit school, Stonyhurst seeks to enable each individual pupil to thrive, by enabling them to find, develop and use their unique talents. We believe the distinctive nature of Stonyhurst, informed also by an extensive volunteering programme, helps to ensure that the strong leadership qualities many pupils develop are tempered with a thoughtful compassion and awareness of others.

Each year group (known as a Playroom) has its own Head of Playroom, who has an overview of each student's complete experience at Stonyhurst. Boarding at Stonyhurst is centred upon excellent pastoral care in a happy, well-ordered environment, in high quality accommodation. Boys board in year-groups (called playrooms) and are cared for by their pastoral head and his team. For girls, there are two boarding houses: one for Lower Line (years 9 to 11) and another for Higher Line (the sixth form). Each is run by a pastoral head and her team.

Everyone attends Whole School Mass in St Peter's Church on Sunday morning. About 65% of our pupils are Catholic, we also have young people who belong to other Christian traditions, and other faiths; all are encouraged to play a full part in the spiritual life of the school. Special celebrations are held to mark the major feast days of the year.

STONYHURST

(Founded 1593)

Stonyhurst, Clitheroe, Lancashire BB7 9PZ UK

Tel: 01254 827073

Fax: 01254 827131

Email: admissions@stonyhurst.ac.uk

Website: www.stonyhurst.ac.uk

Headmaster: Mr John Browne BA LLB MBA

Appointed: 2016

School type: Coeducational Boarding & Day

Age range of pupils: 13–18

No. of pupils enrolled as at 01/09/2018: 727

Fees per annum as at 01/09/2018:

Day: £19,950

Weekly Boarding: £29,850

Full boarding (UK & EU): £34,800

Full boarding (iGCSE/IB): £36,300

Full boarding (non-EU): £36,300

Average class size: 15

Teacher/pupil ratio: 1:8

Windermere School

Windermere School is situated in the heart of the Lake District National Park. The rugged beauty of this UNESCO World Heritage Site not only makes for an inspiring educational setting but enables students to make use of what surrounds them.

The curriculum offered at Windermere School reflects the belief that students should be exposed to as many opportunities as possible and leave the School as well-rounded individuals. We have offered the International Baccalaureate Diploma programme (DP) since 2009.

Windermere School is not academically selective and we aim to help each student find the pathway most suitable for their ambitions. We believe that it is essential that students have access to high quality careers advice and are given the opportunity to explore an extensive range of career options. We are committed to finding what is right for each student, whether it be the DP or Certificate programme. The latest inspection report by the ISI recognised the quality of education provided as 'Excellent'.

Over the past few years, leavers have gone onto a variety of universities, including Oxford, Cambridge, Imperial College and Durham.

We are a Round Square School and this blends perfectly with the IB philosophy and the two intersect with Service at their cores and we support many Service initiatives. Each year a group of students travel to South Africa to support the Thussanang Service project. We also support worldwide humanitarian appeals and, locally, provide support in residential care homes and with conservation projects.

There is a vast array of academic and extra-curricular opportunities available to students: School musical, sports and adventurous expeditions. The School boasts its very own RYA accredited watersports centre and in 2018 it was chosen to become a British Youth Sailing Recognised Club for its race training.

The Sixth Form boarding house is designed to promote the successful transition between School and Higher Education. It is laid out in apartments with twin and single bedrooms, a bathroom, common room and kitchen. There is also a large communal space for socialising and numerous socials events are held throughout the year.

We offer a challenging and enriching education from the age of three at Elleray and up to the age of 18 at Browhead. Windermere School has a modern and innovative approach that encourages young people to strive for excellence in all things.

WINDERMERE SCHOOL

(Founded 1863)

Patterdale Road, Windermere, Cumbria LA23 1NW UK

Tel: 015394 46164

Fax: 015394 88414

Email: admissions@windermereschool.co.uk

Website: www.windermereschool.co.uk

Head of School: Ian Lavender

School type: Coeducational Boarding & Day

Age range of pupils: 3–18

No. of pupils enrolled as at 01/09/2018: 340

Fees per annum as at 01/09/2018:

Day: £17,775

Weekly Boarding: £30,150

Full Boarding: £31,335

South-East

Bethany School

Set on a 60 acre rural campus in the beautiful Kent countryside, Bethany School is a flourishing co-educational day and boarding school that provides a welcoming and caring environment for pupils between the ages of 11 and 18.

Bethany enjoys a reputation as a particularly friendly and happy community. It is a strong, thriving school with an enviable building programme, including recent and regular upgrading of boarding school facilities; a fantastic new six lane 25m indoor swimming pool, state-of-the-art fitness suite and a new Sixth Form centre with excellent facilities.

Location
Situated in Kent's 'Garden of England', Bethany has an idyllic location with easy accessibility. London is less than an hour by train, Gatwick Airport one hour by taxi and Heathrow an hour and a half. The Eurostar terminal at Ashford International is just 30 minutes away.

The curriculum and information technology
As a mainstream school, Bethany prides itself on nurturing academic excellence while catering for pupils with a broad range of abilities. The School offers a wide variety of subjects in modern classrooms with specialist facilities, including our Science Centre with modern laboratories.

The entire campus is served by a wireless network and all pupils have their own laptop. Much of the curriculum is delivered through ICT and pupils gain important digital skills. Almost all of our Sixth Formers progress on to university courses, leaving Bethany with a mature self-confidence and clear direction.

CReSTeD registered since 1994, Bethany's Learning Support department enjoys an international reputation for its success in giving specialist help to dyslexic pupils within the mainstream curriculum. In addition, for those pupils who require it, we offer support for English as an Additional Language.

Boarding life and overseas pupils
We offer boarding in full, weekly and flexi arrangements across five boarding houses, and our boarding community brings great diversity to Bethany. We are a small school and yet we have boarders coming from 22 different countries, enriching our education with a variety of experiences and backgrounds.

We aim to inspire individual excellence in every pupil and this approach underlies everything we do at Bethany. Its success is evidenced by the excellent transition from School to university made by our pupils each year. Sixth Form boarders benefit from single bedrooms with en suite bathrooms, all with easy access to kitchens and laundry rooms. This experience, combined with our Body for Life programme, is designed to be a stepping stone to life at university, all within the supportive environment of the School.

Outside the classroom
At Bethany, we believe that pursuits outside the classroom are very important in developing pupils' personalities. Everyone takes part in sport at least three times a week, and chooses from a huge array of extra-curricular activities including horse riding, chef school, golf, fishing, clay pigeon shooting, archery, orchestra and country pursuits. The Duke of Edinburgh's Award is hugely popular and very successful at Bethany.

Throughout the School there are opportunities to perform in drama, music and dance. Our Art department is particularly strong and many pupils join us to take advantage of our 'mini art college'.

The Headmaster firmly believes that school should be enjoyed rather than endured and it is the atmosphere of positive nurturing and encouragement, focused on the potential of each individual, that helps makes Bethany 'refreshingly different'.

Bethany since 1866

(Founded 1866)

Curtisden Green, Goudhurst, Cranbrook, Kent TN17 1LB UK

Tel: 01580 211273

Fax: 01580 211151

Email: admissions@bethanyschool.org.uk

Website: www.bethanyschool.org.uk

Headmaster: Mr Francie Healy BSc, HDipEd, NPQH

Appointed: 2010

School type: Co-educational Boarding & Day

Age range of pupils: 11–18 years

No. of pupils enrolled as at 01/09/2018: 313

Boys: 203 **Girls:** 110 **Sixth Form:** 98

No. of boarders: 106

Fees per annum as at 01/09/2018:

Day: £16,725–£18,465

Weekly Boarding: £25,950–£28,655

Full Boarding: £27,990–£31,500

Average class size: 15-17

Teacher/pupil ratio: 1:8

Burgess Hill Girls

"A fantastic school with a beating heart for every pupil. Burgess Hill Girls has an atmosphere that facilitates and creates confident, able and independent girls – ready for whatever the world has to throw at them."
Millie McQuillin, Burgess Hill Girl 2008–2013

A transformative education
Burgess Hill Girls is an Excellent rated independent school in Sussex for girls aged 2 to 18 years of age.

Whatever the stage at which your daughter joins Burgess Hill Girls you can be confident of two things: that she will be known for who she is as an individual and she will be provided with an outstanding, transformative education of the whole person.

I am, I can, I should, I will
Our school motto, 'I am, I can, I should, I will', conveys and underpins our whole approach, identifying and releasing the potential of your daughter as she proceeds, giving her the very best possible opportunities to become a successful women of the future.

As parents, success will be having a happy and healthy daughter who loves going to school, loves to learn, loves participating, and is able to make friends for life. For the girls, success may be doing well in lessons and tests, being part of a team, playing a musical instrument and having fun with friends. At Burgess Hill Girls we pride ourselves on unlocking the academic talent that is found within our girls and strongly believe each individual will thrive in our high-achieving environment. Whilst Burgess Hill Girls aims to provide the very best opportunities for everyone to excel, we believe that success is more than obtaining the highest marks and grades. We recognise just as much all those fantastic qualities that are not materialistic or target driven. Success at our school is when we produce bright, confident and independent young women who have and will continue to achieve great things.

Perfectly located
Burgess Hill Girls stands in 14 acres of beautiful grounds within a conservation area close to Burgess Hill's town centre in the centre of Sussex. All aspects of the school are located on this one campus; Nursery, Junior, Senior, Sixth Form and Boarding Houses. The school is only a five minute walk from the railway station (on the London to Brighton line) and close to excellent road networks (10 miles from Brighton and only 20 miles from Gatwick); the school is easily accessible for local and international students. A flexible, daily minibus service is provided for girls across Sussex and beyond.

Visit Burgess Hill Girls
We would be very pleased to meet you, put a name to a face and show you round our school. Please get in touch to arrange a visit.

BURGESS HILL
— GIRLS —
Tomorrow's Women

(Founded 1906)

Keymer Road, Burgess Hill, West Sussex RH15 0EG UK

Tel: 01444 241050

Email: registrar@burgesshillgirls.com

Website: www.burgesshillgirls.com

Head of School: Liz Laybourn

Appointed: 2017

School type: Girls' Day & Boarding

Religious Denomination: Interdenominational

Age range of boys: 2½–4

Age range of girls: 2½–18

No. of pupils enrolled as at 01/09/2018: 505

Boys: 29 **Girls:** 476 **Sixth Form:** 70

No. of boarders: 50

Fees per annum as at 01/09/2018:

Day: £7,800–£19,200

Full Boarding: £28,050–£34,200

Average class size: Max 20

Teacher/pupil ratio: 1:11

Churcher's College

Churcher's College is an Independent day school for boys and girls from 3-18 years of age offering Nursery, Junior, Senior and Sixth Form education. With around 865 pupils in the Senior School and 225 pupils in the Junior School (not including the Nursery) of approximately equal numbers of boys and girls, Churcher's College enjoys recognition as one of the most accomplished independent, co-educational day schools in the country.

The school is hosted on two sites in Hampshire which enables the Junior School and Nursery pupils to flourish in their own beautiful grounds in Liphook, whilst maintaining close links to the Senior School and Sixth Form located in nearby Petersfield. Both sites offer extensive on-site playing fields and unrivalled facilities, providing the comfort and opportunities of an open, healthy environment.

Churcher's College offers the widest range of experiences and the opportunity to be the best. The school has received independent acknowledgement for its academic success, creative and performing arts, adventurous activities and sporting achievements. Churcher's is an inclusive school where parents, children, staff and friends all contribute to the rich and broad education provided. We aim to nurture children into educated informed, socially responsible and respectful citizens ready to succeed in life.

"I am hugely impressed with the number of opportunities that have been made available to me throughout my time at Churcher's. I have taken part in the Biology, Chemistry, and Physics Olympiads and completed an EPQ on human evolution. I have also been very fortunate to receive an offer to study Natural Sciences at Cambridge where I hope to continue my education in Chemistry, Cell Biology and Maths. As for extra-curricular opportunities I have thoroughly enjoyed the adventurous activities available. These have included the 2016 Devizes to Westminster kayak marathon and completions of the Ten Tors and the Welsh 3000's events. However, my highlight has been going on expedition to the Galapagos for 5 weeks. The last seven years have been incredibly busy and even more enjoyable due to the huge array of opportunities available in all areas of school life."
Pupil

"Thank you ... we are very proud of her ... she is absolutely over the moon to be going to her first choice of university. We wanted to say what a wonderful two years she has had at Churcher's – she has never been so happy at school and has done amazingly well in all areas as well as creating a great friendship group – we couldn't have asked for more!"
Sixth form parent

"Our family feel hugely privileged to have discovered Churcher's and its team."
Senior school parent

"By the time the pupils leave the school they are well balanced, thoughtful and considerate individuals with an excellent standard of personal development."
"Teachers have strong knowledge which they present enthusiastically to their pupils; this acts as a stimulus for increasingly sophisticated thinking."
"The extra-curricular provision is excellent."
ISI Inspection 2015

"Value added is impressive: one whole grade at A level higher than ALIS value added expectation."
"The school achieves balance very well ... those happy keeping busy in a lively environment will enjoy life at Churcher's College."
The Good Schools Guide Inspection 2017

CHURCHER'S COLLEGE
NURSERY • JUNIOR • SENIOR • SIXTH FORM

(Founded 1722)
Petersfield, Hampshire GU31 4AS UK
Tel: 01730 263033
Email: admissions@churcherscollege.com
Website: www.churcherscollege.com
Headmaster: Mr Simon Williams MA, BSc
Appointed: September 2004
School type: Coeducational Independent Day
Age range of pupils: 3–18 years
No. of pupils enrolled as at 01/09/2018:
Senior School: 865
Junior School: 225
Fees per annum as at 01/09/2018:
Day: £9,915–£15,420
Average class size: 24
Teacher/pupil ratio: 1:12

Cranleigh School

Cranleigh is Surrey's leading co-educational independent school offering both day and boarding education for children aged 7-18, enabling siblings to be educated together.

Set on adjacent hills, the Preparatory School and the Senior School enjoy a spectacular 280-acre rural setting on the Surrey/West Sussex border, by the Surrey Hills, an Area of Outstanding Natural Beauty; yet they are conveniently situated close to the mainline city of Guildford, roughly equidistant between Gatwick and Heathrow, and only an hour's drive from London, where Cranleigh pupils regularly visit professional exhibitions and performances.

Both the Prep and the Senior Schools are proud of their excellent academic track records, culminating in outstanding performances at Common Entrance, GCSE and A-level. 99% of pupils go on to Higher Education, and Cranleigh also has a consistently strong Oxbridge contingent.

Such academic excellence does not come at the expense of co-curricular success at Cranleigh and the Schools currently boast national and county level representatives in a wide range of sports, including kayaking, cricket, riding, hockey, rugby and swimming. The School is currently rated third best school in the country for sports.

Pupil participation in sport, music and drama is actively encouraged at all levels; most Saturdays see every pupil playing sport for the school. More than 10 dramatic productions each academic year provide acting opportunities for all and the hugely popular Technical Theatre encourages the development of backstage skills.

Around 40 per cent of pupils play at least one musical instrument. Many take the opportunity to perform in more than 30 concerts a year, with over 10 musical groups, including symphony orchestra, wind band, chapel choir, big band, strings, trios, quartets and several other choirs.

The Schools offer outstanding facilities alongside new academic blocks. Sports facilities enjoyed by both the Prep and the Senior School include a double-sized indoor sports centre, four artificial playing surfaces, full equestrian centre, two expansive hard court areas for netball and tennis, a generous array of rugby and cricket pitches, a three-par, nine-hole golf course and an indoor pool. Equally outstanding sports staff includes former England players, a former Davis Cup player, an England national coach and an Olympic Gold Medallist (Hockey).

The Schools also boast professional-standard theatre facilities, rehearsal rooms, beautiful art studio spaces and a modern design centre fully equipped with 3D printers. The students have the opportunity to showcase their work in professional exhibitions several times a year.

Most importantly, Cranleigh prides itself on providing a happy, nurturing environment, founded upon an extremely supportive pastoral system (every pupil has their own tutor) and a high staff to pupil ratio, underscored by an invariably passionate House spirit. In such an environment, pupils can flourish into the well-rounded, self-motivated and confident individuals Cranleighans are famed for becoming, well prepared for life after school and invariably blessed with a circle of lifelong friends.

Pupils enter Cranleigh following a process of holistic review, at the main entry points of 13 and 16, and in other years where places are available. Regular small groups open mornings are held and a wide range of academic and non-academic Scholarships are available.

CRANLEIGH
EX CULTU ROBUR

(Founded 1865)

Horseshoe Lane, Cranleigh, Surrey GU6 8QQ UK

Tel: +44 (0) 1483 273666

Fax: +44 (0) 1483 267398

Email: admissions@cranleigh.org

Website: www.cranleigh.org

Headmaster: Mr Martin Reader MA, MPhil, MBA

Appointed: September 2014

School type: Co-educational Boarding & Day

Age range of pupils: 7–18 (including Prep School)

No. of pupils enrolled as at 01/09/2018: 654

Boys: 402 *Girls:* 252 *Sixth Form:* 240

No. of boarders: 467

Fees per annum as at 01/09/2018:

Day: £31,170

Full Boarding: £37,905

Average class size: 20 (9 in Sixth Form)

Teacher/pupil ratio: 1:6

Cranmore School

Cranmore is a leading independent prep school in Surrey, situated in West Horsley between Guildford and Leatherhead. Its Christian ethos is central to supporting every child's development and pupils come from a variety of backgrounds with about one-third from Roman Catholic families. The majority live locally, although some come from a wider geographical area. The overall ability profile on entry is above average, and the majority of pupils start in the Cranmore Nursery and Reception with a few joining later in Year 3 or if spaces occur in other year groups. Having established a strong co-educational Nursery several years ago, Cranmore is committed to becoming fully co-educational throughout the school in planned phases.

Prior to joining Cranmore as Headmaster in 2006, Michael Connolly enjoyed twelve years of successful experience as Headmaster at his previous school and, before that, had a rich and varied journey in education within several senior schools and a short spell working overseas.

He is a highly experienced School Inspector and has served on the Board of several national and local educational bodies and often writes articles for leading publications. He is passionate about ongoing education and is currently studying for his 5th University Degree by research in Philosophy.

Q & A with the Head:

Who/what inspired you to become a teacher?
I very much enjoyed my own time as a pupil as I had inspiring teachers who gave me a love for learning. Therefore, I decided that this would be a wonderful career.

What achievement are you most proud of as Head?
No single achievement but a satisfaction in seeing many pupils develop their talents in various aspects of school life.

What does a successful school look like to you?
Children are happy, confident, feel secure and have developed a love for learning.

What is the most important quality you want every child to have when they leave your school? And why?
Respect for others.
It is in through our relationships with others that we define who we really are as a person.

Please give 5 words to describe the ethos of your school.
Nurturing, Supportive, Encouraging, Aspirational, Resilient

(Founded 1968)
Epsom Road, West Horsley, Surrey KT24 6AT UK
Tel: 01483 280340
Fax: 01483 280341
Email: office@cranmoreprep.co.uk
Website: www.cranmoreprep.co.uk
Headmaster: Mr Michael Connolly BSc, BA, MA, MEd
Appointed: September 2006
School type: Coeducational Day
Religious Denomination: Roman Catholic
Age range of pupils: 2½–13
No. of pupils enrolled as at 01/09/2018: 430
Fees per annum as at 01/09/2018:
Day: £12,375–£14,775

Ditcham Park School

Ditcham Park School is situated in the uplifting and inspirational surroundings of the South Downs National Park, near Petersfield, Hampshire, and provides school transport from the surrounding area. The grounds are extensive and they include 16 acres of playing fields as well as woodland, play areas and lawns. The impressive views over Hampshire and West Sussex to the Isle of Wight provide a beautiful and spacious natural environment. The school is unique in the area, having an age range of pupils from 2½ to 16 years on the same site. The setting, buildings and staffing all help to promote a very friendly, supportive and inclusive family atmosphere.

As a co-educational school, all housed on one spectacular site, we believe Ditcham Park School makes a most significant impact and difference to children's confidence, happiness, achievement and success, through a broad range of curricular and extra-curricular learning opportunities and experiences. Wrapped firmly within our aims and ethos are robust academic goals for each pupil; from learning to read and write in our youngest age groups to the challenge and rewards of GCSE, we have a very strong and consistent pattern of academic success. Our most recent school inspection report completed by The Independent Schools' Inspectorate graded the school excellent in 11 of the 12 inspection aspects and good in the remaining one.

One of our School Aims is to 'Prepare our pupils for the Future'. We do this by providing our pupils with the best possible exam qualifications, excellent pastoral support and opportunities and challenges outside the classroom which help build self confidence and self esteem. Our whole School Science Technology Engineering and Maths or STEM Programme has been introduced this year specifically to provide our pupils with the technological skills that are increasingly needed in a fast changing world. The School

is investing in the Future. Four new Junior Classrooms have been built this academic year and a new Nursery will open in September. Plans are being advanced for an exciting Centre for the Creative Arts.

From those first days of school for new Nursery age pupils, right through to the GCSE challenges for our eldest students, the special ethos of our caring family school challenges and supports each student in their progression towards personal academic success, as well as very impressive achievements in a wide range of music and drama exams. Most of our pupils also achieve Bronze and Silver Duke of Edinburgh Awards and many perform at the highest level in sports as well as raising funds for charities. Our pupils leave Ditcham as happy, confident and enthusiastic students, eager to take on the challenge of their 'A' level studies at a Sixth Form College or School.

(Founded 1976)

Ditcham Park, Petersfield, Hampshire GU31 5RN UK

Tel: 01730 825659

Fax: 01730 825070

Email: admissions@ditchampark.com

Website: www.ditchampark.com

Headmaster: Mr Graham Spawforth MA, MEd

Appointed: April 2017

School type: Co-educational Day

Age range of pupils: 2½–16

No. of pupils enrolled as at 01/09/2018: 379

Boys: 212 **Girls:** 167

Fees per term as at 01/09/2018:

Day: £2,835–£4,753

Average class size: 18

Durlston Court

"Pupils develop high levels of self-understanding, growing into confident, resilient young people who are prepared to take risks, and have huge determination to succeed." ISI, May 2017

Durlston Court Prep School is known for happy pupils, exceptional pastoral care, the breadth of opportunities and our excellent teaching and learning. We are a friendly, family school where the children and parents enjoy being part of a secure and happy community – the Durlston family.

Our Pre-Prep department (including Kindergarten) provides an outstanding foundation for learning within a nurturing and caring environment. Dedicated Pre-Prep facilities offer bright, spacious, indoor and outdoor learning areas. Our younger pupils also regularly visit other areas of the school to use specialist facilities and to be taught by our specialist teachers. Pre-Prep can often be found in 'The Den' – our Forest School, where the mud kitchen, art area and activities such as den building and stick whittling enhance our children's learning.

"The excellent outdoor facilities for learning…, allow many opportunities for quiet reflection and immersion in the natural world whilst learning." ISI, May 2017

Pupils at Durlston make full use of all of our impressive facilities and specialist teaching including our fully equipped Design and Technology Centre complete with 3D printers and laser cutter. We also offer various STEM related clubs from Engineering to Programming and we have 2 fully equipped IT suites. All pupils learn to play at least one musical instrument and are given regular opportunities to perform, helping them to develop their confidence. Our drama productions showcase talent but also provide opportunities

for all pupils to be involved in a spectacular show including being part of the back stage technical team. Pupils also develop their creativity in the Art Room, Ceramics Studio and outdoors in our Art Terrace as well as further afield around our spacious grounds. From Year 3 all pupils have at least one hour of sport with daily lessons and weekly opportunities to compete in fixtures. Specialist coaching and teaching takes place across our extensive facilities. Additionally, we have over 50 activities and clubs on offer for pupils. There is something to suit everyone from our Tennis Academy to fencing, from construction to mindfulness.

"Pupils demonstrate high levels of success… in an extremely wide variety of activities including in the creative and performing arts and sport." ISI, May 2017

We are committed to promoting an all-round education and fully preparing our pupils for Senior School. Our academic achievements in terms of scholarships, entrance examinations and CE results speak for themselves. We are extremely proud of our pupils' academic success including 100% pass rate in Year 8 Common Entrance Examinations and we have a strong record of scholarship awards to senior schools in all areas including academics, sport, art and music demonstrating the all-round nature of a Durlston Education.

High expectations, both inside and outside the classroom, ensure pupils leave Durlston as well-rounded, independent and confident young people, equipped and prepared to engage and to succeed in the world of today and tomorrow.

◆

DURLSTON COURT
Preparatory School

(Founded 1903)

Becton Lane, Barton-on-Sea, New Milton, Hampshire BH25 7AQ UK

Tel: 01425 610010

Fax: 01425 622731

Email: secretary@durlstoncourt.co.uk

Website: www.durlstoncourt.co.uk

Head of School: Mr Richard May

Appointed: September 2015

School type: Coeducational Day

Age range of pupils: 2–13

No. of pupils enrolled as at 01/09/2018: 296

Boys: 165 **Girls:** 131

Fees per annum as at 01/09/2018:

Day: £3,540–£15,390

Average class size: 12-15

Teacher/pupil ratio: 1:4-1:15

Eagle House School

Eagle House is a coeducational, boarding and day Prep, Pre-Prep and Nursery located in Berkshire. The school's superb grounds and excellent facilities are the background to an experience where success, confidence and happiness are paramount. The school is proud of its academic record, preparing children for a host of top independent schools and boasting a diverse and robust curriculum. In December 2017 Eagle House received an 'excellent' rating in all areas from the ISI inspection team.

Younger pupils follow the International Primary Curriculum and our older children have embarked on a new Humanities curriculum that links subjects through topics and themes. Great teaching, new technology and a focus on the basics mean that children make good progress and love to be in the classroom. Independent learning is a focus for all children and our Extended Project programme helps drive inquisitive minds.

Eagle House was recently recognised by The Week Magazine as having the best Prep School extra-curricular programme and we unashamedly offer lots as part of our Golden Eagle activities experience. Children benefit from a huge range of opportunities in sport, music, drama, art, outward bound and community programmes. Busy children are happy and fulfilled children and we like to think that all pupils are Learning for Life.

Learning for Life means that children benefit from the best all-round education. They can feel confident in the classroom, on the games field, on stage, in the concert hall and in the community. Everyone is given the chance to stretch themselves in every area. Challenge is an important part of growing up and at Eagle House we learn that success and failure are both positive experiences.

Bright learning environments, outdoor learning areas and wonderful sporting facilities are important but it is the community that shapes a young person. Through the excellent pastoral care and tutor system, coupled with a buddy structure, ensuring children have an older pupil to support them, Eagle House seeks to develop wellbeing from the youngest to the oldest.

Recognising how to be a positive influence within a community is also part of the Eagle House journey. Through our wonderful Learning for Life programme that teaches children about themselves and the wider community, we aim to make all our pupils responsible and independent as well as able to show empathy and understanding towards others. Time for reflection in chapel and assemblies also improves the way we look at the world and mindfulness sessions help us all take stock.

Boarding is a popular option and allows children to experience a varied evening programme of activities as well as being part of a vibrant and caring community. Boarding encourages independence but it is also great fun and whether full, weekly or flexi, boarders have the most wonderful time.

We often say that Eagle House children have the time of their lives and we firmly believe this. Learning for Life at Eagle House opens the doors to all sorts of opportunities and this results in children who are highly motivated and enthusiastic in all they do.

Eagle House buzzes with achievement and laughter – not a bad way to grow up!

Eagle House is a registered charity (No 309093) for the furtherance of education.

(Founded 1820)

Sandhurst, Berkshire GU47 8PH UK

Tel: 01344 772134

Email: info@eaglehouseschool.com

Website: www.eaglehouseschool.com

Headmaster: Mr A P N Barnard BA(Hons), PGCE

Appointed: September 2006

School type: Coeducational Day & Boarding

Age range of pupils: 3–13

No. of pupils enrolled as at 01/09/2018: 380

Boys: 208 *Girls:* 172

No. of boarders: 50

Fees per annum as at 01/09/2018:

Day: £11,580–£18,105

Full Boarding: £24,330

Average class size: 16

Teacher/pupil ratio: 1:8

Feltonfleet School

Feltonfleet is a community where 'individuals really matter' – a core belief which shapes all we say and do.

We know the most enjoyable personal growth comes from developing a child's natural talents and skills. In nurturing this potential within a sharing community, with a strong sense of family, children are able to discover their gifts and grow in self-confidence, independence and compassion.

Our ethos is based upon positive learning, living and leading, alongside core values of kindness, honesty, respect and responsibility. The overriding sense of happiness and laughter is palpable in the classrooms, on the playing fields and in the Boarding House. Our unique blend of day and boarding pupils creates a real buzz around school. Feltonfleet children are optimistic and inquisitive, with a thirst for life and learning. They thrive here.

The combination of talented and dedicated staff, an inspiring curriculum and 25 acres of beautiful grounds with exceptional facilities, encourages children to use their imagination, to think creatively, to explore the world around them and to strive to excel.

In 2015 a brand new Performing Arts Centre opened to complement the Drama, Music and Dance departments. The new, award nominated space, which includes the Ashbee Theatre and Dance Studio, is linked to the original building via an impressive glass corridor which houses the Main Reception. The theatre has retractable seating for up to 400 and advanced sound and light systems, providing a wonderful performance space and event venue.

In addition to a well-equipped sports hall, extensive playing fields and hard surface tennis courts, Feltonfleet boasts a 15m indoor swimming pool, floodlit all-weather Astroturf pitch and climbing wall. The school has its own rifle ranges for both air-rifle and .22 shooting. Beyond the playing fields a band of woodland is home to the eco-pond and a wilderness area for play and Science study.

High standards and expectations are grounded in the conviction that academic excellence and enjoyment of childhood go hand in hand. Unusually for a prep school, we have 'time to stop & think' lessons to nourish emotional wellbeing and to develop resilience and strategies for lasting mental health.

The Feltonfleet journey falls into four stages and reflects our belief that success and achievement happen in a happy, optimistic environment where children travel at different speeds along their bespoke academic and personal pathway.

Throughout the curriculum we seek to equip each child with the core academic skills and learning attributes so that they can take pride and responsibility for their own learning. Children gradually progress from being dependent learners to inter-dependent learners, developing the self-esteem and the confidence in themselves to 'risk' learning and acquiring new skills. Each stage in the journey is linked by our core values and strong sense of community.

As our pupils complete the four stages of their Feltonfleet journey, graduating after Common Entrance, they secure places and scholarships to leading independent senior schools in a range of academic, sporting, musical and all-round disciplines. They are well prepared for the next stage of their journey.

Come and see what makes Feltonfleet a wonderful school for your child's preparatory education. We would be delighted to show you around.

Feltonfleet
PREPARATORY SCHOOL

(Founded 1903)

Cobham, Surrey KT11 1DR UK

Tel: 01932 862264

Email: office@feltonfleet.co.uk

Website: www.feltonfleet.co.uk

Head of School: Mrs S Lance

Appointed: January 2018

School type: Coeducational Day & Weekly Boarding

Age range of pupils: 3–13

No. of pupils enrolled as at 01/09/2018: 398

Fees per annum as at 01/09/2018:

Day: £11,799–£17,325

Weekly Boarding: £21,051

Nursery: £6,318

Average class size: 17

Teacher/pupil ratio: 1:7

Gordon's School

Gordon's – The Most Unique School in England

Built by public subscription over a century ago at the insistence of Queen Victoria, Gordon's School is the national monument to General Charles Gordon of Khartoum and is listed as one of Britain's outstanding schools by Her Majesty's Chief Inspector.

A non-selective, co-educational residential and day boarding school, the School's academic record outstrips many selective schools. The progress made by students over the past three years has put Gordon's in the top one per cent of schools in England and Wales at GCSE and A2.

But while Gordon's School embraces modern ideas, General Gordon's legacy of traditional values remains. The School's ethos is that high performance without good character is not true success.

To this end, it's not just in the classrooms where students excel. Successes are achieved in drama and the arts; debating and public speaking; dance and sport. The School also boasts an enviable record in attaining Duke of Edinburgh awards.

While the individual is celebrated, the whole School unites for parades. Since its inception, students have marched and there has always been a Pipes and Drums band. Dressed in their Blues uniform, the students parade around eight times a year and the school is the only one permitted to march along Whitehall – an annual tradition in remembrance of General Gordon.

Set in over 50 acres of beautiful Surrey countryside within easy access of major airports and roads, the School is home to some 800 students and offers Day and Residential (weekly and termly) Boarding from only £5,378 per term.

Each Student is assigned to one of the ten Houses – four residential boarding and six day boarding – (named after places and people associated with General Gordon)

and Inter-House competitions involving the majority of the students in all years are fiercely contested.

Spiritual guidance and support is given through chapel services and informal worship. And House Parents provide a 'home from home', lending special atmosphere to each Boarding House and ensuring that free time off for students is fun, with numerous activities.

There are three main admission points – at 11 years old; 13 years old and for Sixth Form.

Scholarships in sport and the creative arts are offered for those coming into the Sixth Form. As well as reduced fees, the scholarships enable those awarded to benefit from a programme to enhance their development and give them wider opportunities to progress in their field. Bursaries are also available.

The real judgement of Gordon's is the students. All who visit are struck by the friendliness, discipline and vibrancy throughout the school and by the family atmosphere, exemplified by the special rapport between staff and students. This is borne from a community that strives to live with integrity, to be courteous, enthusiastic and diligent, even in adversity.

Gordon's School is unique. Please book a visit and find out why.

(Founded 1885)

West End, Woking, Surrey GU24 9PT UK

Tel: 01276 858084

Fax: 01276 855335

Email: registrar@gordons.school

Website: www.gordons.school

Head Teacher: Andrew Moss MEd

Appointed: September 2010

School type: Co-educational Day & Boarding

Age range of pupils: 11–18

No. of pupils enrolled as at 01/09/2018: 850

Boys: 448 **Girls:** 402 **Sixth Form:** 250

Fees per annum as at 01/09/2018:

Day: £5,790

Weekly Boarding: £16,134

Full Boarding: £17,235

Average class size: 22

Teacher/pupil ratio: 1:12

Hoe Bridge School

Hoe Bridge School is set in a perfect location on the outskirts of Woking surrounded by 22 acres of beautiful grounds and is only 25 minutes from London. In the latest inspection, the School achieved a grade of 'excellent', something that both the girls & boys and staff are extremely proud of.

At the heart of Hoe Bridge stands the stunning 17th century mansion, Hoe Place. Around this mansion, the School has recently undertaken several major building projects to further enhance the facilities. The Pre-Prep department has been completely rebuilt to create more space and light for the younger children and the Nursery offers busy parents the option of five full days. Further projects in the Prep department will also create more space for the older girls and boys.

In the Pre-Prep department, the creative curriculum enables the children from Nursery to Year 2 to learn through play, adventure, discovery and experience. Transition to the Prep Department is seamless and as children mature they become increasingly independent learners in preparation for the move to some of the country's leading senior schools.

Alongside the academics sport, music, art and drama play a major part throughout the school and the girls and boys excel in many areas; end of year productions; sporting excellence achieving national success in netball and hockey, county success in cricket, football and hockey; individual musical success in national youth orchestras and choirs and a spectacular annual art exhibition. Scholarships in all these areas are won every year to a variety of schools across the country.

Senior pupils in Years 7 and 8 take part in regular extra-curricular activities and it is at this stage of their time at Hoe Bridge that they take on extra responsibility becoming prefects and role models to the younger children.

The atmosphere of every school is unique and we consider the strength and attraction of Hoe Bridge to lie in the atmosphere here. Standards and targets are realistic, though set as high as possible, the bright are challenged and the less able supported; we endeavour to instil confidence in all our children. Visitors are amazed how happy the children are, how determined they are to succeed and how much they care about each other.

The School has an extremely good reputation and is constantly striving to preserve the family atmosphere, improve results and explore all possibilities for enriching both the School and the lives of the children.

HOE BRIDGE SCHOOL

(Founded 1987)

Hoe Place, Old Woking Road, Woking, Surrey GU22 8JE UK

Tel: 01483 760018 & 01483 772194

Fax: 01483 757560

Email: enquiriesprep@hoebridgeschool.co.uk

Website: www.hoebridgeschool.co.uk

Head: Mr C Webster MA BSc (Hons) PGCE

Appointed: September 2018

School type: Coeducational Day

Age range of pupils: 3–13

No. of pupils enrolled as at 01/09/2018: 460

Boys: 330 *Girls:* 130

Fees per annum as at 01/09/2018:

Day: £5,940–£15,345

Average class size: 20

Teacher/pupil ratio: 1:10

Kent College

Kent College is an outstanding day and boarding school that celebrates both its 130 years of history and tradition, and its forward-looking, innovative approach to education. It has a reputation as a friendly school, and is most definitely a place where teachers really get to know the pupils, with the time and space to give individual attention, both academically and pastorally. Music, drama and sport all play central roles in the life of the school, and many pupils also enjoy the opportunities provided by the school's Farm and Riding Centre.

Part of the Methodist Schools group, Kent College is deeply rooted in the Methodist tradition that welcomes all pupils of every faith and none. *'Do all the good you can do'* is a guiding principle, and one that allows pupils to develop into confident young adults, aware of their responsibilities and their place in the world.

Location
The school's location, on the outskirts of the historic city of Canterbury, provides a safe, healthy and beautiful environment for pupils to grow up. The school sits in 80 acres (32 hectares) of land with extensive sports fields, as well as the Farm and Riding Centre. Yet the centre of Canterbury, with its wide selection of shops, restaurants, theatres, cinemas and world-heritage site, within which sits Canterbury Cathedral, is only a 5-minute journey by car. A high-speed train service links Canterbury to London, and the school is within 100 minutes of Gatwick, Heathrow, Stansted and City of London airports.

Academic profile
Kent College prides itself on offering personalised academic programmes, small class sizes and an exceptionally well-qualified and experienced teaching staff. All students are provided with a MacBook laptop when they start at the school. Pupils achieve excellent academic results at GCSE, A level, and in the International Baccalaureate (IB), with 100% pass rates for GCSE and A level. An average point score of 37 in the IB consistently places Kent College in the top 10 IB schools in the UK. The school also offers a wide range of additional support for pupils, including access to a dyslexia unit and specialist English language teaching for overseas students in the International Study Centre.

Boarding
Kent College has a long history of welcoming boarding pupils from abroad, as well as from British families resident in the UK or working overseas. Boarders make up around one third of pupils, and there are over 40 countries represented in the boarding community. The five friendly and comfortable Senior boarding houses truly become a 'home away from home'. The school also offers weekly and occasional boarding.

Beyond the classroom
The performing arts are a particular strength at Kent College, with an impressive line-up of vocal and instrumental ensembles, and many opportunities to perform for all ages and abilities. An exciting new development is the construction of the Great Hall, a state-of-the-art 600-seat auditorium, due to open in Summer 2019. In sport, the aim is to provide something for every pupil, from recreational sport and promoting fitness to top-level coaching for our elite players. Hockey and cricket are particular strengths, with regular representation by Kent College pupils in county and national squads. There is also a wide-ranging list of activities and clubs, on offer for all pupils, including a full Duke of Edinburgh programme, and the opportunity to work on the school Farm.

(Founded 1885)

Whitstable Road, Canterbury, Kent CT2 9DT UK

Tel: 01227 763231

Email: enquiries@kentcollege.co.uk

Website: www.kentcollege.com

Executive Head Master: Dr D J Lamper

Appointed: September 2007

Senior School Head: Mr Julian Waltho

School type: Coeducational Day & Boarding

Religious Denomination: Methodist

Age range of pupils: 0–18 years

No. of pupils enrolled as at 01/09/2018: 760

Fees per annum as at 01/09/2018:

Day: £16,464–£18,315

Full Boarding: £25,236–£34,491

Average class size: 15, max 20

Teacher/pupil ratio: 1:8

King Edward VI School

King Edward VI School, Southampton, has been at the heart of the city for over 460 years and is one of the UK's leading independent 11-18 co-educational day schools.

With a reputation for academic excellence, the School boasts a thriving Sixth Form that produces consistently excellent A Level examination results ensuring students continue on to a range of competitive institutions, most to one of the UK's top 25 universities and, on average, approximately 10% of students proceed to Oxford or Cambridge. Results at GCSE and IGCSE level are also excellent, further consolidating King Edward's reputation for outstanding academic achievement.

Not only does King Edward's promote academic excellence, it also aims to foster in every pupil a sense of personal worth through a wide range of co-curricular activities, particularly with an active engagement in community work, so that every individual emerges as a fully responsible member of society. In the last year alone the student Charities Commission has raised over £27,000 for local and national charitable causes.

Each year students can be found taking part in excursions to worldwide destinations. A yearly charitable trip to South Africa allows Sixth Formers to work with disadvantaged children living in rural poverty, whilst other recent destinations have included Maine, USA for the annual ski trip, kayaking in the Swedish archipelagos, a Biology field trip in Ecuador and the Galapagos Islands, a cultural excursion to Morocco and a trekking expedition in the Himalayas. Language students regularly participate in the exchange programmes on offer to Germany, France and Spain as well as in cultural visits to schools in the USA and Prague. Closer to home the School also organises an annual summer camp to Swanage for local young carers, run by our Sixth Formers.

Sport and the arts are an integral part of school life. Students are given the opportunity to represent the School across the major team games as well as individual sports. Overseas tours, regular fixtures, tournaments and school events offer a competitive sporting environment and King Edward's boasts 33 acres of sports ground, a fully equipped gym and multiple all weather pitches. The Creative Arts Faculty offers an amazing array of facilities from recital rooms, a recording studio and music technology suite to a custom-built dance studio. A wonderful new theatre has just been built that has a capacity for 400 seats and provides a superb venue for our talented dramatists and musicians. An array of public performances throughout the year allow King Edward's performers to showcase their talents, whatever their ability level.

Students are actively encouraged to become involved in fund-raising and community work and take part in some of the 150 clubs and societies that are available outside of lesson time. King Edward's also runs a well-established Duke of Edinburgh Award Scheme that makes use of the school's Rural Studies Centre in Dartmoor.

King Edward's strives to ensure that all pupils reach and fulfil their full potential. A happy atmosphere amongst first-class teaching facilities provide exceptional academic stimulus alongside an extraordinary breadth of co-curricular opportunities. Seventeen bus routes extend throughout south Hampshire, allowing students from the New Forest, Salisbury, Winchester and east of Southampton easy and direct access to the School.

Founded 1553

(Founded 1553)

Wilton Road, Southampton, Hampshire SO15 5UQ UK

Tel: 023 8070 4561

Fax: 023 8070 5937

Email: registrar@kes.hants.sch.uk

Website: www.kes.hants.sch.uk

Head Master: Mr A J Thould MA(Oxon)

Appointed: April 2002

School type: Coeducational Day

Age range of pupils: 11–18

No. of pupils enrolled as at 01/09/2018: 960

Fees per annum as at 01/09/2018:

Day: £16,050

Average class size: 22

Teacher/pupil ratio: 1:10

King's Rochester

The overwhelming characteristic of King's Rochester is its warmth and friendliness, nestled in in the beautiful cathedral precinct of historic Rochester. As the Good Schools Guide says: "A *tangible sense of community where everyone knows each other well...*"

Founded in 604AD, King's is the second oldest school in the UK and the world's oldest Cathedral Choir School. It has evolved into an outstanding 21st century day and boarding co-educational School for ages 3 to 18. Located in North Kent, just 38 minutes by train from London, it benefits from high-speed services from St Pancras and direct services from Victoria and Charing Cross.

King's Rochester has a strong reputation for maximising the potential of pupils. A wide ranging curriculum, and extensive co-curricular programme, allows greater choice for GCSE and A level options. In 2017, pupils achieved record results at GCSE and a fifth of students achieved straight A*/A grades at A Level, securing them places at top universities, and scholarships to prestigious colleges.

King's prides itself on knowing all students very well: pastoral care and links with parents and guardians have been graded as 'Excellent' in all inspections and it is this strength that makes King's such a distinctive place to be.

We believe that independent thinking and a love of learning are just as important as great grades. To achieve this, we keep our class sizes small so that teachers know their pupils as individuals and can help each of them flourish. We encourage pupils to establish interests that stay with them for life, as well as learning the skills that will make them stand out in a fast-changing world.

Music is a huge strength and we are privileged to use Rochester Cathedral as our chapel. We hold seasonal concerts throughout the year in the Nave and the Cathedral Choristers are educated in our Preparatory School. Music Scholars go on to leading international conservatoires.

Recent pupil success includes the BBC Young Chorister of the Year and an Oliver Award, and our brass section was commended by Julian Lloyd Webber.

Under the refurbished Vines Church is our Drama studio, equipped with digital sound and lighting. We are a proud RSC Associate School and our pupils have staged productions of Julius Caesar at the Marlowe Theatre and Macbeth at Dover Castle. King's has a strong reputation for exceptional drama performances and recent productions of "*Into the Woods*" and "*Les Miserable*" have been in comparison with the West End.

Our coaches and many of our pupils play at County, National and International level. The King's Rochester Sports Centre provides pupils with extensive facilities to train, in addition to playing fields, a heated indoor swimming pool and boat house, while the Paddock is regarded as one of the finest cricket fields in the country. All pupils play for a variety of games teams and fixtures are held throughout the year.

The boarding community at King's reflects the personal approach of the school. Boarding starts from age 11 and we have 65 beds across our two Boarding Houses, "St Margaret's House" for girls and "School House" for boys. The small boarding community ensures a real family feel to both Houses which are comprised of British and international students.

King's Rochester is truly a community which enables individuals to flourish.

(Founded 604 AD)

Satis House, Boley Hill, Rochester, Kent ME1 1TE UK

Tel: 01634 888555

Fax: 01634 888505

Email: admissions@kings-rochester.co.uk

Website: www.kings-rochester.co.uk

Principal: Mr J Walker

Appointed: 2012

School type: Coeducational Day & Boarding

Age range of pupils: 13–18

No. of pupils enrolled as at 01/09/2018: 625

Sixth Form: 92

No. of boarders: 49

Fees per annum as at 01/09/2018:

Day: £7,125–£19,320

Full Boarding: £21,960–£31,590

Average class size: 16

Teacher/pupil ratio: 1:16

Lanesborough

Lanesborough Prep School for boys is located in the centre of Guildford, and offers a superb range of facilities. A fabulous new Sports Hall has just been completed extending the range of sports available to the boys, it has a viewing gallery and extensive changing rooms. A dedicated performance space provides outstanding facilities for both drama and music.

The academic success of Lanesborough is renowned, with boys regularly achieving academic, music and sports scholarships to their chosen senior school.

The superb music tradition is enhanced with the cathedral boy choristers all attending the school. Over 50 different clubs from Astronomy to Warhammer are on offer enabling the boys to develop a wide range of interests. However, the most important aspect for all staff is ensuring that the boys thrive, are happy and reach their full potential in a stimulating, fun and caring environment.

Lanesborough is about learning how to learn, not just what to learn, developing a range of interests and preparing the young men so that they are interesting and interested citizens, resilient and ready to take their place in our ever evolving world.

To fully appreciate Lanesborough you will need to visit and experience first-hand, all that is on offer. We have bursaries and choral scholarships available from Year 3.

Open Mornings are held in October and March – check the website for full details. Alternatively, parents can arrange an individual tour with the Head. Please call Mrs Francis, Admissions Secretary, on 01483 880489, admissions@lanesborough.surrey.sch.uk.

Lanesborough *Preparatory School*

(Founded 1930)

Maori Road, Guildford, Surrey GU1 2EL UK

Tel: 01483 880489

Fax: 01483 880651

Email: admissions@lanesborough.surrey.sch.uk

Website: www.lanesborough.surrey.sch.uk

Head: Mrs Clare Turnbull BA(Hons) MEd

Appointed: September 2007

School type: Boys' Day

Age range of boys: 3–13

No. of pupils enrolled as at 01/09/2018: 350

Fees per annum as at 01/09/2018:

Day: £10,890–£15,270

Average class size: 16

Lord Wandsworth College

Lord Wandsworth College (LWC) is a highly successful, well-respected boarding and day school for children aged 11-18 on the north Hampshire/Surrey border. It offers a broad, well-balanced curriculum and an incredible range of sports, activities and co-curricular opportunities. The heart of the school sits within an idyllic 1200 acre site of leafy woodlands, rolling hills and beautiful landscapes. It is an extremely happy and strong community where pupils are challenged, cheered-on and supported by classmates, houseparents and teachers.

At LWC, there are five key pillars that inspire our pupils, leaving them with an inner self-confidence, but an outward modesty and resilience to make a positive difference in the world. We believe in character education, in championing the pupil voice, in good mental health and wellbeing, in challenging pupils and creating opportunities to make a difference to others.

Lord Wandsworth College is named after a wealthy London banker who, in 1912, left a generous bequest to educate orphaned children. This charitable spirit lives on today as the Lord Wandsworth Foundation offers a number of assisted places to children who have lost the support of one or both parents and who would benefit from an outstanding education in a caring, nurturing environment. All pupils are conscious of this, and a sense of inclusion and collective responsibility for the happiness of others is strong here. In fact, it is paramount.

Lord Wandsworth College offers full, weekly and flexi boarding (three nights a week). There are eight boarding houses, all run by caring houseparents who provide the main point of contact between school and home, organise house activities and social events and are supported by a team of compassionate tutors and matrons. Day pupils are fully integrated into the boarding house system.

Pupils find a wide range of subjects to challenge, engage and inspire them. The curriculum is taught by experienced teachers who create 'high challenge – low threat' learning environments and use a variety of techniques to bring learning to life. The school's goal is to develop a life-long love of learning. Pupils are encouraged to stretch themselves to an academic level two years ahead and urged to ask that extra question, discover new inter-relationships and share their knowledge.

The sporting facilities are outstanding and include two floodlit astroturfs, a 25 metre indoor swimming pool, tennis courts, 2 sports halls, squash courts, a climbing wall, netball courts, indoor and outdoor cricket nets, numerous cricket, rugby, hockey and football pitches, a grass athletics track and a cross-country course. Many pupils take advantage of the adventure training and leadership opportunities provided by the Combined Cadet Force and the Duke of Edinburgh Award scheme is also immensely popular.

Renowned for the high standard of its productions, the Music and Drama Centre provides opportunities for personal instruction, performance and exhibition in the 120 seat bespoke auditorium. Students are encouraged to get involved in all aspects of theatre production including acting, directing, set design, costume, make-up, lighting and sound. LWC also offers ballet, street dance and modern dance lessons and there are many vocal and instrumental groups including Concert Band, Chamber Orchestra, Senior Choir, Barbershop, Flautissimo, Classical Guitar and Sax Group.

Further information, including forthcoming Open Days, can be found at www.lordwandsworth.org.

LORD WANDSWORTH COLLEGE

A GREAT FOUNDATION

(Founded 1922)

Long Sutton, Hook, Hampshire RG29 1TB UK

Tel: 01256 862201

Fax: 01256 860363

Email: admissions@lordwandsworth.org

Website: www.lordwandsworth.org

Head of School: Mr Adam Williams

Appointed: September 2015

School type: Coeducational Boarding & Day

Religious Denomination: Non-denominational

Age range of pupils: 11–18 years

No. of pupils enrolled as at 01/09/2018: 615

Fees per annum as at 01/09/2018:

Day: £20,430–£23,460

Weekly Boarding: £28,290–£31,800

Full Boarding: £29,250–£33,300

Flexi Boarding (3 nights): £24,780 – £27,600

Average class size: Approx 19

Teacher/pupil ratio: 1:9

Maltman's Green School

Our Approach

At Maltman's Green we believe in the pursuit of excellence whilst maintaining a sense of enjoyment. Girls are inspired to do their best inside and outside of the classroom through an exceptional academic curriculum and extensive extra-curricular opportunities. We prepare girls for the modern world through a relevant, adaptable and innovative approach that is supported by a foundation of traditional values. Our girls are given every opportunity to succeed across multiple disciplines, fostering confidence and self-belief, and empowering them for whatever future awaits.

We believe that the emotional, social and physical wellbeing of our girls is paramount. By providing a personalised learning experience in an encouraging and nurturing environment, we ensure our girls feel happy, confident and valued – a perfect foundation from which children can flourish. This ethos has been recognised by the ISI who applauded our "outstanding" pastoral care.

Games and The Arts

Our sports provision is an outstanding feature of the School, with dedicated facilities and daily lessons. All girls enjoy friendly tournaments between houses and within year groups where those with the talent and inclination can progress to squad level to compete locally, regionally or nationally with exceptional results.

Music is a very important part of life at Maltman's Green. Specialist teaching and excellent facilities and lots of choice give our girls plenty of opportunity to explore and showcase their musical talents. Over 100 girls participate in our various choirs and we have nine different musical instrument lessons available as well as a variety of instrumental ensemble groups to join. Drama too has a big part to play in school life where regular performances and workshops give girls a strong sense of confidence and creative expression. Our dedicated performance space with high-quality staging, lighting, costumes and props give our shows a professional feel.

Achievements

Our girls are encouraged to be independent thinkers, to challenge themselves and to always try their best. Maltman's Green provides a firm foundation, preparing girls to face senior school and beyond with confidence, determination and a lifelong love of learning. This is reflected in our impressive 11+ results – an 80% pass rate in 2018 – and a record number of scholarships being awarded to Independent Senior Schools. This, combined with our girls' impressive achievements across sport, music and drama affirm our position as one of the foremost prep schools in the country.

Outstanding Characteristics

2018 marks our 100th Anniversary and, since the School was founded in 1918, we have seen numerous developments and upgrades to our facilities, including dedicated subject classrooms, a 6-lane, 25-metre indoor swimming pool, a multi-use gymnasium, a state-of-the art theatre space and a dedicated 2-3yr olds day-care centre. This excellent suite of facilities is complemented by our highly committed, well-qualified and experienced body of staff who enable us to provide an outstanding and unique breadth of challenging opportunities for our girls. Maltman's Green has only ever seen seven headmistresses. The current headmistress, Mrs Pardon, has been in post since 2005 and is the 3rd longest serving head. Such seamless and passionate leadership means that we can look confidently to the next hundred years with every expectation for the continued success, development and happiness of our girls.

MALTMAN'S GREEN
SCHOOL

(Founded 1918)

Maltman's Lane, Gerrards Cross, Buckinghamshire SL9 8RR UK

Tel: 01753 883022

Fax: 01753 891237

Email: registrar@maltmansgreen.com

Website: www.maltmansgreen.com

Headmistress: Mrs J Pardon MA, BSc(Hons), PGCE

Appointed: 2005

School type: Girls' Day

Age range of girls: 2–11

No. of pupils enrolled as at 01/09/2018: 394

Fees per term as at 01/09/2018:

Day: £1,860–£5,090

Day Care:
£45 – £75 per daily session depending on duration

Manor House School, Bookham

Founded in 1920 and soon to be celebrating its Centenary Year, Manor House School can be found nestled amidst seventeen acres of gardens, woodland and sports fields in Bookham, Surrey. The School provides an excellent all-rounded approach to education in a happy, friendly and caring school environment. An individual approach to teaching and learning enables each pupil at the School to achieve their personal best, both academically and personally. The aim is to develop happy young women who love coming to school and believe in their abilities to learn and succeed.

There is an extensive co-curricular enrichment programme with up to 50 extra-curricular clubs and activities operating across the school each term. Girls are encouraged to seek out new experiences and try something new.

In 2018, Manor House reported excellent Key Stage 2 results and GCSE results, despite a year of uncertainty and increased challenge under the new grading system. For more information on their results, visit: www.manorhouseschool.org/academic-results/gcse-results.

Seven school values form the foundations of school life and the school motto 'To Love is to Live' was chosen in 1921 by the Bishop of Plymouth. Dr. Masterman, who was a close friend of one of the school's original founders.

The School has recently appointed a new Head of PE and Manor House girls are increasingly enjoying high levels of success in all areas of Sport boasting some future world class soccer players, cyclists, triathletes and tennis stars in its midst.

There is a new and popular Senior Scholarships Programme from Year 7 (application in Year 6) offering Major and Minor Academic Scholarships at 50% and 40% of the basic annual tuition fee and up to 30% for an Art, Drama or Music award.

The school has been voted in the top ten most beautiful schools in the country in recent years. Facilities include an award-winning Nursery, new Well-Being Centre, Forest School, indoor sports hall which transforms into a seated theatre space for professional productions, outdoor swimming pool, a Tennis Academy, tennis and netball courts and purpose-built science blocks. Girls enjoy many opportunities in the creative and expressive arts, with additional music, singing and drama lessons a popular choice.

The day operates from 7.45am to 6pm to accommodate working and/or busy parents. Fees include a daily hot lunch and afternoon tea is available as an optional extra each day at 4pm.

The School operates a minibus service in the mornings and afternoons and a late bus to the local train station which is serviced by good rail connections. The School bus routes service Ashtead, Dorking, Claygate, Cobham, Epsom, Esher, Fetcham, Hinchley Wood, Guildford, Kingswood, Walton-on-Thames, Weybridge, Wimbledon/Kingston, West Byfleet and surrounding areas.

For more information visit www.manorhouseschool.org.

There are three main Open Morning events per year in October, February and May. For more information, contact: admissions@manorhouseschool.org.

(Founded 1920)

Manor House Lane, Little Bookham, Leatherhead, Surrey KT23 4EN UK

Tel: 01372 457077

Email: admin@manorhouseschool.org

Website: www.manorhouseschool.org

Headteacher: Ms Tracey Fantham

School type:
Girls' Day School with Co-educational Nursery

Age range of boys: 2–4

Age range of girls: 2–16

No. of pupils enrolled as at 01/09/2018: 300

Fees per annum as at 01/09/2018:

Day: £9,255–£17,403

Average class size: 14-20

ENGLAND: South-East

Northbourne Park School

Northbourne Park School is a co-educational independent day and boarding school for children between the ages of Nursery and 13. Set in over 100 acres of beautiful park and woodland in rural Kent, the school is within easy reach from central London, Eurostar and Gatwick Airport. Northbourne Park School provides children with a first-class education focussing on the individual needs of every child, inspiring them to succeed across a wide range of learning experiences. We are a school that offers each child freedom and space, together with countless opportunities to grow in confidence and succeed.

Academic

From the Nursery and Pre-Prep right through to the Prep School, Northbourne Park School is an environment where each and every child can flourish. Pupils gain confidence in their learning and through inspirational teaching from dedicated staff, and adapt well to an engaging and stimulating curriculum with a real sense of achievement. We focus on individual needs and consistently achieve academic excellence, with many of our pupils gaining scholarships to prestigious Senior Schools. The school's unique Language Programme helps every child develop foreign languages in an integrated learning environment. The result is a clear advantage when they move on to Senior Schools.

Sport

We are passionate about sport and through an excellent sports programme the pupils develop key skills and learn the importance of teamwork and leadership. There are many opportunities to try a variety of sports from traditional sports to the more diverse such as archery and trampolining.

Creative Arts

We nurture a love for all the Arts. Many pupils learn one or more instruments in our purpose-built Music suite. They have the opportunity to take part in the choir, band, orchestra, string and brass groups performing regularly within the school and in the local area. Other opportunities include LAMDA lessons, regular drama productions and Public Speaking that ensure the pupils are articulate and confident in their performances. Artistic talents are encouraged through a range of media including sculpture, costume design, film-making on iMacs and pottery.

Community

Pupils are provided with a first-class level of pastoral care in a safe and nurturing environment with a real family atmosphere. Our welcoming boarding community provides a home-from-home environment and a continuous boarding service at weekends throughout the term. Boarders enjoy regular excursions and activities, and the accompanied services to London and Paris provide opportunities for weekends at home. Northbourne Park School holds Tier 4 Status for non-European pupils requiring visas under the UK Visa and Immigration Service scheme.

Extra Curricular

We provide the pupils with a fun and extensive programme of afternoon clubs that help develop their interests and skills in hobbies that can endure long into adult life. Love of the outdoors and respect for the environment begins in the Pre-Prep and develops through into the Prep School with fun physical adventures. Whether they are playing in the woods, camping out overnight or following our pioneering Outdoor Education Programme, children love Northbourne Park life.

The children are at the heart of everything we do and it is important to us that they learn with confidence and enjoy each and every day at school. All prospective pupils are welcome and we offer a wide range of scholarships.

Every day is an Open Day at Northbourne Park School, come and visit us!

(Founded 1936)
Betteshanger, Deal, Kent CT14 0NW UK
Tel: 01304 611215/218
Fax: 01304 619020
Email: admissions@northbournepark.com
Website: www.northbournepark.com
Headmaster: Mr Sebastian Rees BA(Hons), PGCE, NPQH
Appointed: September 2015
School type: Coeducational Day & Boarding
Age range of pupils: 3–13
No. of pupils enrolled as at 01/09/2018: 175
Boys: 90 **Girls:** 85
No. of boarders: 56
Fees per annum as at 01/09/2018:
Day: £7,632–£16,755
Weekly Boarding: £20,985
Full Boarding: £24,300
Average class size: 15
Teacher/pupil ratio: 1:9

204

Prince's Mead School

About Us

Prince's Mead is a co-educational independent prep school in Winchester, Hampshire for 4-11 year olds. We have worked hard to create a culture which actively celebrates and acknowledges individual achievements. We recognise the need to give the children in our care the very best start in life and we are mindful of our responsibility to educate them academically, spiritually, morally, socially and culturally.

Academic

Children need an excellent all round education that provides the foundation for future learning and life in general. Our educational approach is designed to shape our pupils' ability to think in ways that will enhance their future and give greater meaning and enjoyment to their lives right now.

At Prince's Mead our teaching programme offers pupils the opportunity to participate in lessons which serve both as a model of rigorous thinking and as a celebration of wonder and open-mindedness. All children, no matter what their academic profile can gain much from the curriculum they are offered.

As a school, we will find something that ensures every pupil will succeed and thrive. Everything we offer shapes the development of our pupils and better prepares them for their life ahead; it is by looking at pupils as unique individuals that we are able to give them the confidence to move successfully on to their chosen senior schools.

Pastoral Care

The school has a strong leadership team, well supported by a cohesive management team, which has a clear vision for the development of the school. This vision, shared by the whole school community working together, has at its core the well-being of each pupil.

The history of our wonderful building as a family home sets the tone for the family atmosphere that permeates through the school and while the whole staff care for the children we have a full time Matron on site to give them professional care if they are poorly or injured.

Prince's Mead has a Christian Foundation while recognising and valuing other world faiths and cultural differences. It is a harmonious community in which the values of tolerance, loyalty and understanding go hand-in-hand with an emphasis on the value of individual talents and resilience to give the children a positive attitude, confidence and respect for each other.

Family Life

Prince's Mead is a school with a great family appeal with the full educational programme during the week meaning weekends are free for family time. We encourage a strong sense of community within the school; 'Drop in Mornings', 'Grandparents Tea Parties' and weekly 'Friday Prayers' are just some of the opportunities for parents and relatives to participate in the life of the school.

We recognise the pressures of daily life and to this end we provide a unique, personalised minibus service that is included in the fees and managed by our in-house transport team to ensure our excellent pastoral care extends to the children's journey to and from school.

We also provide an extensive range of extra-curricular activities and wraparound care, including a before school Breakfast Club. These are managed to ensure the children get places on their first choice clubs and parents get certainty of routines. The minibus service is dovetailed with the clubs to provide an efficient and flexible service.

PRINCE'S — MEAD —

(Founded 1949)

Worthy Park House, Kings Worthy, Winchester, Hampshire SO21 1AN UK

Tel: 01962 888000

Fax: 01962 886888

Email: admin@princesmeadschool.org.uk

Website: www.princesmeadschool.org.uk

Headmistress: Ms Penelope Kirk

Appointed: 2002

School type: Co-educational Day

Age range of pupils: 4–11

Average class size: 20

Teacher/pupil ratio: 1:12

Reddam House Berkshire

The Reddam House philosophy is unlike any other and with a worldwide reputation for academic, cultural and sporting excellence. Reddam House Berkshire is a majestic school, in a beautiful, secure setting at the heart of the 125-acre estate – a truly inspirational environment.

Our philosophy is designed around the individual, giving students a large amount of freedom in how their schooling is organised, with personalised supervision and guidance from Reddam House committed teachers. Because we cater for children from just three months old to 18 years, we can offer a unique, seamless education to all and lasting friendships. Our co-educational, non-denominational formula is designed to inspire students to attain their maximum potential in a nurturing, progressive and academic environment.

We carefully select our teachers, who are specialists in their field, to ensure students get the very best guidance and advice throughout their schooling: we create happy, well-rounded children who love school and the school experience. In addition to an extensive range of subjects at GCSE and A-level, the EPQ (Extended Project Qualification) course in the Sixth Form allows our young people to further develop their research and communication skills. Light and airy classrooms, equipped with the latest in technology, provide an enhanced learning environment.

Public speaking is a timetabled lesson in Middle School and students can take part in local competitions. Both Dance and Music are an integral part of the Reddam House experience, giving students the chance to work their way through graded examinations, further increasing their confidence. Our magnificent theatre, with seating for up to 350, puts students centre stage in a wide range of productions, from plays and musicals, to dance shows and debates. We have a large dance studio, two smaller studios and a music school with numerous practice rooms.

All students are encouraged to learn at least one musical instrument, and we have a wide range of music and instrumental groups, from jazz and rock to string ensembles and a chamber choir.

While students are encouraged and pushed to reach their full potential, the primary aim is for students to enjoy their sport and to participate. Regular fixtures take place in Rugby, Hockey, Football, Cricket, Netball, Rounders, Swimming, Tennis, Basketball, Golf, Cross Country and Judo.

Our dedicated Gymnasium Centre, with its sprung floor, encourages our award-winning gymnasts, who are already recognised at national and international level. The Duke of Edinburgh award and the Combined Cadet Force (CCF) are also both popular options. Further investments in our sporting facilities have continued with our new Astroturf pitches and an extensive upgrade to our swimming pool completed for September 2018.

Class tutors are fine-tuned to respond to students' individual emotional needs while our senior students act as mentors to the younger students and lead by example. Our Student Voice reports to the Sixth Form Judiciary – elected by a whole school vote – which meets regularly with the Principal to convey students' comments and feedback.

Alongside our Extended Day Options, which offer supervision and meals from 7.30am – 8.30pm, we offer the full range of boarding options – flexi, weekly and full. We currently have two boarding houses with separate accommodation for boys and girls aged 11-18, with resident house-parents, tutors and a matron. All rooms have recently been refurbished to a high standard and single rooms are en-suite. There is a full programme of activities for students who stay with us at weekends, with cinema and theatre trips, visits to places of interest and, of course, shopping!

(Founded 2015)

Bearwood Road, Sindlesham, Wokingham, Berkshire RG41 5BG UK

Tel: 0118 974 8300

Fax: 0118 977 3186

Email: registrar@reddamhouse.org.uk

Website: reddamhouse.org.uk

Principal: Mrs Tammy Howard

School type: Co-educational Boarding & Day

Religious Denomination: Non-denominational

Age range of pupils: 3 months–18 years

No. of pupils enrolled as at 01/09/2018: 570

Fees per annum as at 01/09/2018:

Day: £10,200–£17,280

Weekly Boarding: £27,075–£31,215

Full Boarding: £28,665–£32,805

THREE
MONTHS
TO **18**
YEARS

REDDAM
House
WE SHALL GIVE BACK

Seaford College

Seaford College is a coeducational independent day and boarding school for pupils aged 7 to 18, situated amid 400 acres of picturesque parkland in West Sussex. The College, with its excellent amenities and outstanding panoramic views, offers an inspirational environment that nurtures academic excellence, sporting success and creative talent.

The college uses its resources to provide and enhance educational, cultural, spiritual and social opportunities so that students leave school as confident, articulate and well-rounded individuals.

Pupils in the Preparatory School at Seaford College share the superb facilities with the Senior School and enjoy a seamless education from 7 to 18. The Prep School prides itself on its friendly atmosphere.

Boarding is offered to students from the age of 10 and many pupils elect to board in order to take full advantage of the social, sporting and extracurricular activities on offer. The College offers full boarding, weekly and flexible boarding in order to meet the needs of pupils and their parents.

A new boys' boarding house, has individual and twin bedrooms opened in 2011. Girls board in the historic Mansion house.

Recent developments include a new music suite, which consists of individual teaching and practice rooms, a computer and keyboard room, a sound-proofed band practice room and outdoor concert arena.

A state-of-the-art maths and science block offers the latest technologies and facilities, while the College has long been recognised as a centre of excellence for art and design. A large exhibition gallery is incorporated into the purpose-built arts faculty.

Seaford College offers outstanding sports facilities, including an all-weather water-based Astroturf hockey pitch, golf course and driving range. Students regularly play at county level.

All the usual academic subjects are taught, with 24 subjects available at GCSE and 28 at A level. The college also offers preparation for the Cambridge Pre-U.

Overseas students are expected to study English as a foreign language and study for the International Language Testing System, which is a requirement for UK university entrance.

Seaford sees its Sixth Form very much as a transitional stage. They have their own social centre, which has facilities for individual study, a lounge area and several classrooms where subjects such as Economics, Business Studies and Media Studies are taught.

Sixth Form boarders have individual study bedrooms, as well as their own common room. Students are divided into small tutor groups, but most commonly meet on a 1-to-1 basis with their tutors to discuss aspects of their work and progress.

Many of Seaford's Sixth Formers go on to university or higher education – all are equipped with self-confidence, as well as a passion for life and a willingness to succeed.

Entry to the College is by test and Trial Day and, although intake is non-selective, expectations are high. If your child is talented and enthusiastic, the College offers a range of scholarships at 11+, 13+ and Sixth Form, including Academic Studies, Music, Art and Sport.

The college has its own dedicated learning support unit, catering for pupils with dyslexia, dyscalculia and dyspraxia.

Whatever their chosen path, Seaford College seeks to prepare young people for adult life so that they have the personal skills and confidence to make it a success. The school allows its pupils to achieve their potential and beyond, inspiring personal ambition and success so that personal ambitions are achieved inside and outside the classroom.

(Founded 1884)

Lavington Park, Petworth, West Sussex GU28 0NB UK

Tel: 01798 867392

Fax: 01798 867606

Email: headmasterpa@seaford.org

Website: www.seaford.org

Headmaster: J P Green MA BA

School type: Coeducational Boarding & Day

Age range of pupils: 7–18

No. of pupils enrolled as at 01/09/2018: 732

Boys: 508 **Girls:** 224 **Sixth Form:** 194

No. of boarders: 194

Fees per annum as at 01/09/2018:

Day: £10,320–£21,390

Weekly Boarding: £21,510–£28,980

Full Boarding: £33,090

Average class size: 15-20

Teacher/pupil ratio: 1:9

St Catherine's, Bramley

Welcome to St Catherine's, Bramley. Founded as both a boarding and day school for girls in 1885, we believe that the successful blending of these two aspects of school life into one happily integrated community is part of what makes St Catherine's. Everyone, boarder or day girl, feels part of the whole. Boarding fosters a strong respect and care for others and gives girls the confidence to develop their independence and their own sense of style.

Academic results place us comfortably in the top 5 girls' independent boarding schools in the country. The curriculum is designed to ensure it has breadth and variety. Our very impressive Destinations of Leavers' data is testament to the excellent outcomes at A Level, enabling our Sixth Formers to go to their chosen universities, in the UK and worldwide, and feel well prepared to take on new challenges.

Our location is perfect for families based both in the UK and overseas. Bramley village is set in the heart of attractive Surrey countryside with acres of opportunity for outside activities. Being under an hour from Heathrow and Gatwick means no long journeys at the start and end of terms. Regular trains to London from nearby Guildford, make a day in the capital city very easy to organise. On Fridays/Sundays a return bus service into SW London runs for weekly boarders.

St Catherine's weekend boarding programme has been singled out on a number of occasions for particular praise; from cultural excursions to theatres, museums and galleries to theme parks, the seaside, Christmas Markets and culturally interesting cities: Bath, Winchester, Windsor, Portsmouth etc. London's cultural and entertainment attractions are just an hour away, whilst the historic county town of Guildford is on our doorstep which offers theatres, a multiplex cinema and shopping opportunities.

The Anniversary Halls sports and performing arts complex houses a multi-function sports hall and professional dance studio as well as a superb auditorium for concerts and theatrical productions. Musicians benefit from the auditorium's impressive acoustics and full orchestra pit. Numerous choirs, Wind Band, String Orchestra, Symphony Orchestra, Concert Band, Jazz Band, and Brass Ensemble represent some of the musical groups girls can enjoy. Music, Sport, Dance, Drama, Art, Chess, Debating, Sailing, Equestrianism, Young Enterprise, community projects, Charity fund-raising and The Duke of Edinburgh's Award Scheme feature in a long list of extra-curricular activities. Girls can master skills in stage design, lighting and sound under the guidance of our Technical Director. They enjoy learning ballet, jazz, tap and modern dance in St Catherine's own professional dance school. Sport for all and Sport to national team standard are possible and girls are encouraged to commit and enjoy some 15 sports at their own level.

St Catherine's is unequivocally for girls. It is a school where girls grow and develop at their own pace, not one dictated by others. The advantages of girls' schools are legion – not only do girls achieve better examination results, they also have more opportunities for leadership. Girls do particularly well in STEM subjects – Science, Technology, Engineering and Mathematics and are more likely to continue with these at A Level and into university. We educate girls to see themselves as future leaders in society, movers and shakers, politicians, thinkers, creators and industrialists. The St Catherine's Association, comprising thousands of alumnae, parents, and friends of the School gives the girls access to invaluable careers' advice, global networks and opportunities for work experience/internships and sponsorships.

St Catherine's offers an unforgettable education for every girl. Visit our website and visit us in person. A warm welcome awaits.

(Founded 1885)

Bramley, Guildford, Surrey GU5 0DF UK

Tel: 01483 899609

Fax: 01483 899608

Email: admissions@stcatherines.info

Website: www.stcatherines.info

Headmistress: Mrs A M Phillips MA(Cantab)

Appointed: April 2000

School type: Girls' Day & Boarding

Religious Denomination: Church of England

Age range of girls: 4–18

No. of pupils enrolled as at 01/09/2018: 900

No. of boarders: 125

Fees per annum as at 01/09/2018:

Day: £8,985–£18,375

Full Boarding: £30,285

Average class size: Lower School 20, Sixth Form 8

Teacher/pupil ratio: 1:8

St Neot's School

St Neot's, founded in 1888 is a happy, vibrant community for boys and girls from 2 to 13 years. The school is situated on the border of Hampshire and Berkshire and is set in 70 acres of beautiful grounds and woodland.

The school's educational philosophy is to inspire children to develop a love of learning in a supportive and happy environment, where each individual is encouraged to achieve their full academic potential and beyond. Children are motivated to discover their full range of talents and to develop the passion to pursue them. They are given the opportunity to embrace challenge, think creatively, develop self-confidence and foster empathy towards others, preparing them both intellectually and emotionally for success in the 21st Century.

We aim to provide the highest standards in teaching and learning within a well rounded educational experience and St Neot's has a very strong record of success in achieving Scholarships and Awards to numerous Senior Schools.

St Neot's is committed to providing a World of Opportunity in every aspect of school life. Stimulating learning environments ensure that engaged pupils work towards the highest academic standards whilst also enjoying a breadth of experience in sport, music, art, drama and dance.

Emphasis is placed on developing independence, self confidence, curiosity and collaboration. Forest School and Outdoor Education programmes encourage children of all ages to develop these attributes, which are so vital in the modern world. The St Neot's journey culminates in the Years 7 and 8 leadership programme, which draws together a mix of skills through the core elements of the Prep Schools Baccalaureate (PSB).

Physical Education is a strength of the school and our sports complex, comprising sports hall, 25m indoor swimming pool, all-weather astro, cricket nets, hard tennis and netball courts, significantly supplement our extensive playing fields. There is also an on-site mountain bike track and a traversing wall. Judo, dance, tennis and swimming are taught by specialist coaches and there are many after school clubs and activities covering a wide range of interests. Holiday Clubs run in all school breaks and offer a wealth of opportunities, both sporting and creative.

St Neot's holds a Gold Artsmark award, giving recognition to our achievements in art, music, drama and dance. A number of plays, concerts and recitals take place throughout the school year for all age groups, either in the school grounds or the Performing Arts Centre.

Open Mornings take place termly and details of these can be found on the school website – www.stneotsprep.co.uk. We would also be delighted to arrange an individual tour and a meeting with the Head. Please contact Admissions on 0118 9739650 – e-mail – admissions@stneotsprep.co.uk

ST NEOT'S
PREPARATORY SCHOOL

(Founded 1888)

St Neot's Road, Eversley, Hampshire RG27 0PN UK

Tel: 0118 9739650

Email: admissions@stneotsprep.co.uk

Website: www.stneotsprep.co.uk

Head of School: Deborah Henderson

Appointed: September 2015

School type: Co-educational Day, Preparatory

Age range of pupils: 2–13 years

No. of pupils enrolled as at 01/09/2018: 330

Boys: 184 *Girls:* 146

Fees per annum as at 01/09/2018:

Day: £3,655–£15,600

Average class size: 18

Teacher/pupil ratio: 1:8

St Swithun's School

Compassion, integrity, and a quiet sense of self-confidence
St Swithun's School is a renowned independent day, weekly and full-boarding school for girls set in 45 acres overlooking the Hampshire Downs on the outskirts of Winchester, yet only 50 minutes by train from central London. It offers excellent teaching, sporting and recreational facilities.

The school has a long-standing reputation for academic rigour and success. Girls are prepared for public examinations and higher education in a stimulating environment in which they develop intellectual curiosity, independence of mind and the ability to take responsibility for their own learning. They achieve almost one grade higher at GCSE than their already significant baseline ability would suggest, and approximately half a grade higher at A level. St Swithun's offers a comprehensive careers and higher education support service throughout the school years. Its Oxbridge preparation is part of a whole-school academic enrichment programme providing additional challenge and stimulation.

St Swithun's describes itself as an 'appropriately academic' school, celebrating intellectual curiosity and the life of the mind, but not to the exclusion of all else. They expect their pupils to develop individual passions and through them to acquire a range of skills and characteristics. These characteristics will include a willingness to take risks, to question and to debate, and to persevere in the face of difficulty. In the words of Samuel Beckett: *"Ever tried. Ever failed. No matter. Try again. Fail again. Fail better."*

Whilst achieving academic excellence, girls also have the opportunity to do 'something else'. There is an extensive co-curricular programme of over 100 weekly and 50 weekend activities to choose from.

As well as academic classrooms and science laboratories, there is a magnificent performing arts centre with a 600-seat auditorium, a music school, an art and technology block, a sports hall and a full-size indoor swimming pool. There is an impressive library and ICT facility. The grounds are spacious and encompass sports fields, tennis courts and gardens.

With kindness and tolerance at the heart of its community, St Swithun's provides a civilised and caring environment in which all girls are valued for their individual gifts. By the time a girl leaves she will be courageous, compassionate, committed and self-confident with a love of learning, a moral compass and a sense of humour.

Open days provide an excellent introduction to the school and include a student-led tour, an opportunity to meet the staff and a presentation from the head giving an overview of the unique atmosphere and opportunities at St Swithun's. To book a place on an open day, or to arrange an individual visit at a more convenient time, please contact Kate Cairns on 01962 835703 or email registrar@stswithuns.com. Keep up to date with latest news by visiting www.stswithuns.com, or on Twitter @StSwithunsGirls.

St Swithun's
WINCHESTER

(Founded 1884)

Alresford Road, Winchester, Hampshire, SO21 1HA, UK

Tel: 01962 835700

Fax: 01962 835779

Email: office@stswithuns.com

Website: www.stswithuns.com

Head of School: Jane Gandee MA(Cantab)

Appointed: 2010

School type: Girls' Boarding & Day

Age range of girls: 11–18

No. of pupils enrolled as at 01/09/2018: 509

Sixth Form: 136

No. of boarders: 214

Fees per annum as at 01/09/2018:

Day: £20,565

Full Boarding: £33,600

St. Andrew's School

St. Andrew's School was founded in 1937 and is a respected and thriving coeducational prep school, of around 300 children. Set in 11 acres of grounds approximately half a mile from Woking town centre, the School seeks to create a nurturing and happy environment of trust and support in which all pupils are encouraged and enabled to develop their skills, talents, interests and potential to the full – intellectually, physically and spiritually.

At St. Andrew's children feel secure and confident and are highly motivated to perform to the best of their ability in all aspects of school life. They are competitive without losing sight of their responsibility to share and they are justifiably proud of their school and their own personal achievements. We also place great emphasis on consideration for others. Courtesy and mutual respect underpins the behaviour policy at St. Andrew's and we aim to teach children about patience, empathy and unselfishness, whilst encouraging them to use their time wisely in an independent and self-reliant manner.

St. Andrew's School prides itself in providing a broad based curriculum that focuses on enabling our children to enjoy a full range of subjects. Educating the whole child is central to our ethos and, whilst academic standards are high, there are also real opportunities to develop their skills in art, music and sport together with a fantastic programme of after school activities. This is supported by specialist teaching facilities for all subjects including science, ICT, music and art. In our latest ISI inspection (Jan 2016) the school was rated 'excellent' in all areas and, with the benefit of individual attention and specialist teachers in all areas of the curriculum, the children are able to reach their full potential in a happy, caring and supportive environment.

When it is time to move on to senior schools at the end of Year 8, the children are prepared for entrance and scholarship exams to a wide range of independent senior schools and the school provides guidance and advice to parents on the senior school choices that best suit each individual child.

St. Andrew's is very proud of its excellent on-site facilities including sports pitches, all weather sports surface, tennis courts, cricket nets and a swimming pool. We are very fortunate to enjoy the benefits of carefully designed school grounds that meet the needs of the children's physical and social development. Main school games are football, hockey, cricket, netball and rounders. Other activities include cross-country running, swimming, tennis and athletics.

Children can be supervised at school from 8am and, through our extensive after-school activities programme for Year 3 and above, until 6-6.30 pm most evenings during the week. An after-school club is available from 4pm to 6pm (chargeable) for Pre-Prep, Year 3 and Year 4 children.

Children are assessed for entry into Year 2 and above. The school has a number of scholarships and bursaries available.

Don't just take our word for it, come and visit the school to see for yourself! We have three open days, one per term, but you are also welcome to visit the school at other times. Please contact the Headmaster's PA (Registrar) for more information and to arrange a visit. We look forward to welcoming you.

ST. ANDREW'S

SCHOOL · WOKING

(Founded 1937)

Church Hill House, Horsell, Woking, Surrey GU21 4QW UK

Tel: 01483 760943

Email: admin@st-andrews.woking.sch.uk

Website: www.st-andrews.woking.sch.uk

Headmaster: Mr A Perks

Appointed: 2008

School type: Coeducational Day Preparatory

Age range of pupils: 3–13

No. of pupils enrolled as at 01/09/2018: 300

Fees per annum as at 01/09/2018:

Day: £3,789–£14,925

Teacher/pupil ratio: 1:10

Sutton Valence School

Although steeped in more than 440 years of history and tradition, Sutton Valence School is innovative and passionate about developing its curriculum to extend the learning of every child. It is something we do very well, being one of the top schools nationally for the academic value we add to all our students. In recent years, the School has gone from strength-to-strength. Examination grades are consistently improving and our value added score is superb. We are seeing students flourish within their passions and being stretched as they take on new challenges. Parental feedback is overwhelmingly positive, as one parent put it: 'All schools promise the earth, Sutton Valence delivers'.

None of this is by chance; the School leadership team is focused on continuous improvement and innovation. Our four journeys (Academic, Enrichment, Community and Leadership and Service) create bespoke challenges for each child that grow strengths and address weaknesses. We stretch our students to surpass their expectations, not just in exams, but their whole education.

Sutton Valence firmly believes in the strength of its four Journeys, where academic pursuits are supported by exciting and challenging enrichment opportunities, transferable leadership skills and positive character traits are developed and the School community supports and encourages all to achieve their potential. No child is the same as another and, through our Journeys, we enable our students to find their niche; this not only helps individual self-confidence but also inspires the pupils to apply their passion and self-discipline to other areas of School life. As they mature, they will grow in their determination and self-esteem, leaving the School as confident, charming and capable, but not arrogant, young adults.

(Founded 1576)

North Street, Sutton Valence, Kent ME17 3HL UK

Tel: 01622 845200 **Fax:** 01622 844103

Email: enquiries@svs.org.uk

Website: www.svs.org.uk

Headmaster:
Bruce Grindlay MA Cantab, MusB, FRCO, CHM

Appointed: September 2009

Head of Prep: Claire Corkran MEd, BEd(Hons) Cantab

School type: Coeducational Day & Boarding

Religious Denomination: Church of England

Age range of pupils: 3–18

No. of pupils enrolled as at 01/09/2018: 870

Fees per term as at 01/09/2018:

Junior Tuition: £5,465 (First Form) – £6,210 (Second Form)

Senior Tuition: £7,135

Full Boarding (plus tuition): £3,170 (Junior) – £3,980 (Senior)

Weekly Boarding (plus tuition):
£2,765 (Junior) – £3,200 (Senior)

Prep Fees: £3,000 (Nursery) – £4,610 (Year 6)

Average class size: 17

Teacher/pupil ratio: 1:9

Wellington College

Wellington College, founded in 1853, is arguably the UK's leading coeducational boarding and day school. Its pupils develop a unique identity inspired by intellectual curiosity, true independence, a generous and far-reaching inclusivity and the courage to be properly and unselfishly individual.

The College is celebrated for its achievements both in and out of the classroom and its sporting, artistic and dramatic provision are second to none. Stellar examination results, outstanding provision across all co-curricular areas, and a raft of national accolades contribute to the College's national and international reputation.

Wellingtonians study GCSEs, followed by the IB Diploma or A-levels and, whichever route they take, results are superb: in 2018, the average A-level outcome was AAA, and the College's IB average of 39.3 yet again made Wellington one of the UK's highest achieving boarding schools to offer the IB Diploma. Over the past five years, half of IB pupils have secured scores of above 40 and 20 have achieved a perfect 45. Close to 100 Wellingtonians have been offered places at Oxford or Cambridge over the past four years and over 20 pupils move on to US universities each year, many to Ivy League institutions.

The College has an outstanding reputation in sport and 31 different activities are offered. National team and individual success this year came in Athletics, Basketball, Cricket, Hockey, Equestrian, Golf, Gymnastics, Kickboxing, Modern Pentathlon, Rackets, Real Tennis, Shooting, Rugby, Skiing, Swimming and Triathlon: a staggering number of individuals gained National or International honours across 16 different sports. A relay team swam the English Channel for the sixth year in a row.

Performing Arts are equally strong. Music and Drama are stunning, with nearly two-thirds of pupils taking lessons in musical instruments or LAMDA. Recent activities have included a trip to Geneva for the Yehudi Menuhin International Violin Competition, a Choir tour to Spain, an annual musical (this year was Cats), contemporary Shakespeare productions and imaginative and inclusive junior plays. Dance enjoys a purpose-designed studio and two spectacular shows each year play to packed houses. The G.W. Annenberg Performing Arts Centre, Wellington's new 900-seater performing arts venue, opened in September. It was no surprise that Wellington was awarded Artsmark Gold by the Arts Council.

Leadership and service to others are central to the College's core values: co-curricular activities include CCF, Duke of Edinburgh, and its outward-facing Global Social Leaders programme, in which pupils learn to create and run innovative social action projects, tackling local and global issues. Over 70 clubs and societies provide some unique opportunities, from WTV (Wellington's own television company) to the pupil-run Radio Station, DukeBox, which broadcasts 24 hours a day, seven days a week, reaching listeners in 41 countries across the globe. Wellington's family of schools includes its prep school, Eagle House, six schools in China, one in Thailand and sponsored Primary and Secondary Academies in Wiltshire. Wellington was the first HMC school to be accredited as a Teaching School and now partners 18 local state schools. All of this provides pupils and staff with meaningful opportunities for partnership and service within the national and international communities.

Further information including details about Visitors' Days can be found on the website and the Admissions Office can be contacted on +44 (0)1344 444013.

WELLINGTON COLLEGE

(Founded 1853)

Duke's Ride, Crowthorne, Berkshire RG45 7PU UK

Tel: +44 (0)1344 444000

Fax: +44 (0)1344 444002

Email: admissions@wellingtoncollege.org.uk

Website: www.wellingtoncollege.org.uk

Master: Mr Julian Thomas

Appointed: September 2015

Director of IB: Mr Richard Atherton

School type: Coeducational Boarding & Day

Religious Denomination: Church of England

Age range of pupils: 13–18

No. of pupils enrolled as at 01/09/2018: 1040

Boys: 640 **Girls:** 400 **Sixth Form:** 455

No. of boarders: 850

Fees per annum as at 01/09/2018:

Day: £29,040–£33,360

Full Boarding: £39,750

Average class size:
Lower + Middle = 20 Upper School = 12

Teacher/pupil ratio: 1:7

South-West

EF Academy Torbay

EF Academy International Boarding Schools prepares students for a global future with a superior secondary school education in the US or UK. At EF Academy, we believe in every student's ability to succeed. We empower them to do so through our renowned curricula, as well as quality one-on-one relationships with teachers and mentors alike. With a student body made up of 75 different nationalities, multilingualism and intercultural exchange are built into every course, which helps distinguish our students' academic credentials to both university admissions officers and future employers.

The School
Our private high school is situated in a modern-day castle on a hill overlooking the sea and Torquay, a quiet town on England's sunny south coast. The art studio has large windows that face the sea – perfect for landscape study – and the state-of-the-art science labs are ideal for conducting experiments and research in class and with study groups. The community, made up of students, school staff and locals, has often been described as a family and our students feel very much at home in this encouraging, international learning environment.

Students live in on-campus residences with their classmates and house parents. House parents look after the students and ensure that they are safe and comfortable when they are not in class.

Academics
At EF Academy Torbay, students follow the IGCSE program in their first two years of secondary school and can choose from the IB Diploma or A-Level program in their last two years. They benefit from our small class sizes and the interactive learning styles our experienced teachers employ in their lessons.

Personal tutors provide one-on-one individualized support and guidance. Each student is assigned a personal tutor whose role is to monitor the student's academic progress and general welfare. Students are encouraged to nurture their talents and develop new skills and confidence. The guidance counselors support students in everything from managing homework and selecting the right courses, to helping them overcome homesickness or culture shock.

University Placement
EF Academy Torbay students have been accepted to universities such as Durham, Warwick and Exeter. They have also gone on to study Business at the University of Bath, ranked number one for Business in the UK, and Accounting and Finance at the University of Leeds, also ranked number one for that subject in the UK. Our dedicated university advisor works together with our students to help them explore program and career options, research universities in the UK, US and their home country, and prepare for entrance exams and interviews.

Co-curricular Activities
Students at EF Academy Torbay have access to a wide range of co-curricular activities. From subject-specific academic groups and competitions to sports and arts, there is an option for every student. On weekends, students often enjoy exploring nearby Babbacombe Beach, sailing in the harbor or rock climbing with a guide. The school's enrichment coordinator also arranges teacher-led excursions for students on the weekends so they have the opportunity to experience the culture of the community and the country in which they are studying.

INTERNATIONAL
BOARDING SCHOOLS

Castle Road, Torquay, Devon TQ1 3BG UK

Tel: +41 (0) 43 430 4095

Email: iaeurope@ef.com

Website: www.ef.com/academy

Head of School: Mr. Mark Howe

School type: Coeducational Boarding

Age range of pupils: 14–19

No. of pupils enrolled as at 01/09/2018: 300

Fees per annum as at 01/09/2018:

IB Diploma/A-Levels: £26,250

IGCSE: £26,250

Exeter Cathedral School

Exeter Cathedral School is a leading independent day and boarding Prep School for girls and boys aged 2½ – 13.

Founded in the 12th century as a choir school, ECS now educates approximately 260 pupils. 36 of these are the boy and girl Choristers of Exeter Cathedral, who continue the centuries-old pattern of leading the daily sung worship in the Cathedral. Nowadays, we offer a fully-rounded Prep School education to pupils from a variety of backgrounds and with a range of talents and interests, whether they be sporting, academic, artistic or musical.

We have an enviable location (right in the heart of the city and yet nestled safely in the lee of the Cathedral); small class sizes, allowing us to really know each and every pupil as an individual; a proven track record of securing places and scholarships (academic, art, music, performing arts, sport) to a range of leading senior schools; and a firm commitment to being a forward-thinking Prep School with traditional values. We aim to offer an outstanding Prep School experience and are proud of our commitment to educating the 'whole child': we seek to do this by providing a nurturing, purposeful, exciting and gently-Christian environment in which each child is known as an individual, and in which each child is mindful of, and grateful for, those around them, and aware of the part that they and others play in building their community.

Our purpose-built Nursery building was opened in 2015 and is housed in our Pre-Prep Department in the Cathedral Close. Run by our specialist Head of Nursery and a team of Key Workers, the ECS Nursery offers a first-rate Nursery Education which encourages children to explore, to question, to discover and to build confidence. Children spend 2 years in our Nursery before moving across the playground into our Reception classes.

Our Pre-Prep is housed in a former Canonry in the Cathedral Close, nestled safely between the ancient city wall and the Bishop's Garden. Children transfer across the playground into Reception, before moving up to Year 1 and then Year 2. Our dedicated and highly-qualified staff, led by our Head of Pre-Prep, work with the children (c15 per class) and families to build independence, enquiry, curiosity and a genuine love of learning.

Our Prep School is located right next to the Cathedral: our main site is on Palace Gate and other departments are clustered together in the corner of the Cathedral Green. In the younger years, the core subjects are taught by Form Teachers and our creative curriculum is delivered by in-house specialists. Our senior pupils receive Common Entrance preparation from experienced subject specialists. At 13, pupils move on to a range of leading Senior Schools, many with scholarships and awards: in 2017, 73% of Year 8 pupils secured a scholarship at their first-choice senior school.

We expect high standards from our pupils and our staff, and we share a commitment to rigorous academic endeavour; outstanding pastoral care and individualized attention; an exciting range of extra-curricular opportunities; a world-class musical heritage; and to working with families to help each child flourish and thrive.

Above all, we are a school where people matter, and where staff and families work in partnership to help children acquire the right habits for life.

UT VOCE ITA VITA

EXETER CATHEDRAL SCHOOL

Nursery | Pre-Prep | Prep

(Founded 1179)

The Chantry, Palace Gate, Exeter, Devon EX1 1HX UK

Tel: 01392 255298

Email: admissions@exetercs.org

Website: www.exetercs.org

Headmaster: James Featherstone

Appointed: January 2016

School type: Co-educational Day & Boarding

Age range of pupils: 2½–13

No. of pupils enrolled as at 01/09/2018: 256

Boys: 131 **Girls:** 125

No. of boarders: 23

Fees per annum as at 01/09/2018:

Day: £7,125–£11,877

Full Boarding: £18,222–£19,287

Average class size: 15

Hazlegrove Prep School

Whether you are thinking of making the big move to the country or looking for a prep school where your children can experience a genuine childhood away from the hothouse pressures so prevalent in London and the South East, do come and visit us at Hazlegrove. Located in 200 acres of parkland just off the A303 in Somerset, we are committed to providing the very best all-round education to the boys and girls in our care.

In our rapidly changing and demanding world, it is vital that our children experience a breadth of opportunity that encourages them to be independent thinkers and confident problem-solvers so that they are ready to embrace whatever challenges lie ahead. At Hazlegrove we do this right from the start where even the very youngest pupils in the Nursery and Pre-Prep will enjoy specialist teaching for Forest School, Music, Drama, Tennis and Games whilst establishing the building blocks of English and Maths with experienced classroom teachers. As the children move up through the school, French, Latin and Mandarin are introduced as is Design Technology (including digital design and realisation), Food Technology and Outdoor Education which covers a myriad of activities from archery and kayaking to putting up tents and looking after animals on the mini-farm. Sport, Music and Drama all play a significant part with countless matches (from local to national level), concerts nearly every week and every child being involved in a major dramatic production every year. We want the stage to hold no fears whether they are presenting to peers or performing to a wider audience.

This wealth of opportunity does not come at the expense of academic endeavour and all pupils work towards the 13+ Common Entrance or Academic Scholarship so they move on, appropriately equipped, to a wide range of destinations from local schools to prestigious national institutions. The foundations of learning are firmly laid in the pre-prep. On joining the prep school (progression to which is automatic), the children will start moving around the school for subjects such as science and by the time they reach Year 6 (aged 10) they can expect to have specialist teaching for every subject. Setting and streaming ensure that all pupils are working at the appropriate level and a highly accredited learning support department is on hand to help those children who would benefit from a little extra help.

Fundamental to success is providing a caring, structured and secure environment where the children can focus their energy on being the best that they can be – not looking over their shoulders and worrying about what others think. The secret is not just in having very-well qualified staff who are inspirational teachers but them being the sort of people who can be excellent role-models and who can build strong relationships with your children. This applies not just to the classroom, but throughout all aspects of life from the thriving boarding houses via the tutoring system to the extensive extra-curricular program.

We want all our children to leave Hazlegrove having enjoyed a proper childhood as confident (not arrogant) individuals who are ready to make the most of the opportunities at their next schools – the fabulous feedback we get suggests we certainly achieve this. Do please come and meet us either by appointment or at one of our many open mornings – we would be delighted to meet you.

(Founded 1947)

Hazlegrove House, Sparkford, Somerset BA22 7JA UK

Tel: +44 (0)1963 442606

Email: admissions@hazlegrove.co.uk

Website: www.hazlegrove.co.uk

Headmaster: Mr Mark White MA (Hons)

Appointed: September 2017

School type: Coeducational Boarding & Day

Age range of pupils: 2½–13

No. of pupils enrolled as at 01/09/2018: 364

Boys: 187 *Girls:* 177

No. of boarders: 97

Fees per term as at 01/09/2018:

Day: £2,928–£5,937

Full Boarding: £6,886–£8,787

Average class size: 14.5

Teacher/pupil ratio: 1:11

Kingsley School

Welcome to Kingsley School

There are many reasons students could fall in love with Kingsley School, an independent co-educational boarding and day school located in Bideford on the banks of the River Torridge in North Devon.

One reason could be location – Kingsley is set in 25 acres of playfields and woodland, surrounded by stunning countryside, and just five minutes from popular surfing beaches. And another reason could be the school's strong academic tradition – at Kingsley every sixth form student typically goes on to university, including top-tier higher education institutes like Oxford and Cambridge.

But ultimately our students rate the opportunity to find their place, the exceptional support they receive and the welcome as the prime reasons they just can't see themselves going anywhere else but Kingsley.

Kingsley School is an inclusive day and boarding school where every child is important and is treated with dignity and respect. As a relatively small school of around 400 boys and girls, Kingsley's atmosphere is like that of a large family where everybody knows each other well.

The school's philosophy encourages personal qualities such as courage, generosity, honesty, imagination, tolerance and kindness. In addition, we develop the students' wider interests and skills in sport, music, art, and drama. Kingsley also has a national reputation for its Learning Development Centre which provides additional support for students with moderate learning needs. Overall, a Kingsley education develops the individual character and talents of each and every student both inside and outside the classroom.

Becoming part of the family: The boarding houses at Kingsley help form part of the family atmosphere at the school. Students live in three comfortable and well-equipped houses in the school's grounds; two for boys and one for girls. Each house has 30-40 students who are supervised by two teachers and their families who live in the houses as well.

Sport and Clubs: Sport includes traditional sports plus judo, handball and gymnastics squads competing at a National level. As part of the National Theatre Connections programme, the school drama cast performed at the Theatre Royal, Plymouth and the National Theatre, London this year. Popular extra-curricular clubs include the Duke of Edinburgh's Award Scheme, orchestra, computing, art, film making, choir and surfing.

Transport: we run an accompanied coach service to and from Heathrow Airport and Bristol Airport at the beginning and end of each term. Weekly boarding options with transport to London and the South East.

Headmaster Pete Last said: "As a parent, I know that choosing the right school can be daunting, but Kingsley is a place which really does recognise that each child has individual needs, with their own set of skills and talents that deserve to be developed. Smaller, more attentive classes with caring and supportive teachers gives the school a familial feel. I am proud of each and every student, their progress, support of one another and their outstanding personal achievements."

Do follow us on social media

Facebook: Kingsley School Bideford
Instagram: Kingsley School
Twitter: @KSBideford
Pinterest: Kingsley School
YouTube: Kingsley School Bideford
www.kingsleyschoolbideford.co.uk

KINGSLEY SCHOOL
BIDEFORD

(Founded 2009)

Northdown Road, Bideford, Devon EX39 3LY UK

Tel: 01237 426200

Fax: 01237 425981

Email: admissions@kingsleyschoolbideford.co.uk

Website: www.kingsleyschoolbideford.co.uk

Headmaster: Mr Pete Last

Appointed: January 2017

Head of the Prep School: Mr Andrew Trythall

School type: Coeducational Day & Boarding

Age range of pupils: 0–18

No. of pupils enrolled as at 01/09/2018: 395

No. of boarders: 100

Fees per term as at 01/09/2018:

Day: From £1,950

Weekly Boarding: From £5,495

Full Boarding: From £7,095

Average class size: 14

Teacher/pupil ratio: 1:9

Sands School

Sands School is an Independent day school for students aged 11-16, situated on the edge of Dartmoor National Park in Ashburton. We have direct access to the rugged coastlines and wild moorland of Devon, both of which we make frequent use of to extend our educational horizons beyond the limitations of a classroom.

The heart of Sands is the School Meeting. Once a week every member of the school is invited to discuss any day-to-day issues that affect our community. If decisions need to be made – which might be anything from painting the Common Room to employing new staff members, or offering a place to a new student – a discussion will be had and a vote will be taken. Every member of Sands has an equal vote, regardless of age, experience or perceived status.

Of course, democracy has its disadvantages: it is often inefficient, and we sometimes make mistakes. But we strongly believe that humanity is yet to find a better, fairer system of government, which is why we put it at the centre of our educational life. If children are to grow to become responsible citizens, how better to learn than by practising democratic engagement in real terms?

We offer a full and varied curriculum of both academic and practical subjects, and students are able to gain qualifications and experience in all of the usual traditional subjects, as well as some more unusual ones. We build as much flexibility as possible into everything we do, enabling students to create their own individual pathways through their educational journey.

Personal, individual well-being is essential to the success of any community. Each student at Sands chooses their own personal academic tutor whose job it is to help guide and advise them through the vagaries of adolescence. Our staff are committed to supporting each other, and encouraged to look after their own needs. When we care for ourselves we are able to care for each other. When we care for each other, we flourish.

At Sands School we do things differently: we have no bells, we have no uniform, we have no head teacher. When students 'forget' to do their homework, they will not be given a detention; rather, we will encourage them to understand how independent study might benefit them. When students break a rule, they will not be automatically punished; instead, they will work with a small group of their peers and/or tutors to understand where they have gone wrong and work out how they can put it right. When students challenge a teacher's authority, they will not be silenced; they will be encouraged to do so in a respectful manner so that everybody feels that their opinions are valued, and that everybody has the opportunity to gain new perspectives.

If you are still reading, Sands might well be the place for your child. We understand that education is not just about exam results, although for many they are, of course, of the utmost importance. Education is about learning how to carve out your own unique niche in life and to contribute positively and actively to your environment, your local community and your wider society. Only when a person is happy in their own skin are they able to seek to extend their potential. Education is not something that is done to you; it is something each of us can do for ourselves. And it doesn't stop at the classroom door.

To find out more, visit our website, or call to arrange a visit. It is impossible to describe exactly what we do at Sands, or how this kind of education can work for your child: you have to see it to believe it.

(Founded 1987)

Greylands, 48 East Street, Ashburton, Devon TQ13 7AX UK

Tel: 01364 653666

Fax: 01364 653666

Email: enquiry@sands-school.co.uk

Website: www.sands-school.co.uk

Administrator: Sean Bellamy MA(Cantab), PGCE

Appointed: 1987

School type: Coeducational Day

Age range of pupils: 11–16

Boys: 36 *Girls:* 29

Fees per annum as at 01/09/2018:

Day: £10,710

Average class size: 15 max

Teacher/pupil ratio: 1:10

Talbot Heath

Talbot Heath is blazing a trail with its ground-breaking educational model that aims to prepare its students, from the age of 3 to 18, for the exciting future that awaits them. Its ten year 'Think Big' vision will see the establishment of a new whole school curriculum that will provide every student with an education in design-thinking, digital proficiency, material science, problem-solving and ethics.

We are determined to offer our pupils an education fit for the exciting future that awaits them – one of nanotechnology, artificial intelligence and global solutions to global problems. Instead of regressing back to the 1950s with a curriculum that focuses on rote learning, as so many schools are being forced to do, Talbot Heath will prepare pupils for 2050. The career pathways that 50% of our young people will follow currently do not exist, that much is sure, such is the speed of change within our world. The skill sets that they will require, however, are known. School leavers will need to be creative, adaptable, resilient, digitally proficient, able to work independently and collaboratively. We cannot afford for our young people to be data rich and skills poor.

This is why, at Talbot Heath, while retaining the high academic standards and intellectual rigour for which we are known, we launched an innovative new curriculum model in September 2018. Many believe that the future will be powered by STEAM (Science, Technology, Engineering, the Arts and Mathematics). Our new programme will ensure that all of our pupils leave school confident in these areas, regardless of the pathway that they choose. We will be working with experts from universities and industry to deliver dynamic, cutting-edge projects and opportunities. We are delighted to be working with BU, AUB, Southampton University and UCL, as well as Siemens, Atlas Elektronik , Pavilion Dance and RMP Filmmakers, among many others

In addition, our pupils will be taught in an interdisciplinary way for a number of lessons each term, seeing the links between subjects-a model that high-performing companies and universities are adopting globally. Physicists have to be able to think like artists, students of literature need to have an appreciation of History, Politics and Art. Our pupils will look at the Maths and Physics of the ancient temples in their Classics lessons, learning how to model both digitally and practically, understanding the importance of design, structure, purpose, sustainability and production. In History, they will look at the combustion engine in detail and consider how a development in Science changed the nature of society for ever.

In order to facilitate our new vision, Talbot Heath is building a state of the art interdisciplinary and STEAM learning Hub which will incorporate augmented reality and holographic studios, a 600 seater auditorium, a gallery space, a green screen studio, art, design, textiles, robotics, electronics, drama and food studios. In addition the complex will include an indoor pool which shall be home to our new Swimming Academy. This iconic building will open in Spring 2019, providing a wonderful facility for the School and local community.

Talbot Heath is thriving and pioneering innovative education, inspiring others to follow where it is leading. These are exciting times at Talbot Heath. We are determined to educate our children for their future and not our past.

Angharad Holloway, Head.

Talbot Heath is the No. 1 performing school in Dorset based on 2018 A level and EPQ results and the No. 1 tennis school for girls in the UK.

Talbot Heath
Independent School for Girls aged 3-18

HONOUR BEFORE HONOURS

(Founded 1886)

Rothesay Road, Bournemouth, Dorset BH4 9NJ UK

Tel: 01202 761881

Fax: 01202 768155

Email: office@talbotheath.org

Website: www.talbotheath.org

Head: Mrs A Holloway MA, PGCE

Appointed: September 2010

School type: Girls' Day & Boarding

Age range of girls: 3–18

No. of pupils enrolled as at 01/09/2018: 582

Fees per term as at 01/09/2018:

Day: £2,201–£4,801

Weekly Boarding: £3,305

Full Boarding: £3,704

Flexi Boarding: £50 per night/£120 for a 3-day package

Average class size: Max 20

West Midlands

Denstone College

Achievement, confidence and happiness are central to the College philosophy, with pupils always encouraged to aim high and reach their full potential.

We offer a rounded education, where proper emphasis is placed on academic achievement, but where a wide range of other opportunities ensures that every individual finds and develops his or her own talents. Denstonians emerge with a degree of self-esteem and confidence that is only possible after years of opportunity and challenge, both academic and extracurricular. The College site of over 100 acres is located in magnificent countryside, yet is well served by road, rail and air. We welcome parents and their children to visit us and experience a taste of the Denstone education.

Three-school structure

At the heart of our approach to educating young people is the 'three-school structure'. Unusual in traditional independent schools, this is a structure that allows our three different age groups to live, work and socialise in their own unique areas. It is based on the fact that 18-year-olds and the under-13s have very different needs. The traditional house system runs happily alongside this structure, and all its best features remain. House loyalty and spirit are as strong as ever in competitions, sport, music and drama.

Facilities

In recent years the College has benefited from a £10m development programme, with a new Music School and additional classrooms opened in September 2010. Further extensive classroom facilities and the Adamson's sports complex were completed and opened in June 2012. Then in September 2013 the doors opened to a beautiful library which is at the heart of teaching and learning at Denstone.

In addition a brand new classroom block, housing Maths and Modern Foreign Languages was completed in June 2017.

The day and boarding accommodation undergoes regular improvement and redecoration, and impressive language and IT teaching facilities have been developed, along with general classroom refurbishments to a high standard.

A large sports hall allows for a wide range of minority and unusual sports. Other recent improvements include a second Astroturf, and all weather cricket facilities.

Academic focus

Pupils are given every support and opportunity to realise their full academic potential, with progress being monitored closely through a highly developed system of tutors, reports and grade sheets. We provide a purposeful environment with skilled teachers, where high standards are expected and pupil/teacher ratios are very favourable.

Opportunities

A Denstone education gives students more choices and greater opportunities to expand their horizons. Frequent trips are a feature of our calendar, and a programme of more than 40 activities and an excellent record in the Duke of Edinburgh's Award Scheme also help to ensure that Denstonians are always busy. Our sporting history is outstanding with College teams county champions and national finalists many times over. We have a modern sports hall, swimming pool, two all-weather AstroTurfs, fives courts and an English Golf Union (EGU)-affiliated golf course.

"Being a Denstonian gives you more chances in life... there's no limit to what you can do." Sixth-former

(Founded 1868)

Uttoxeter, Staffordshire ST14 5HN UK

Tel: 01889 590484

Fax: 01889 590744

Email: admissions@denstonecollege.net

Website: www.denstonecollege.org

Headmaster: Mr Miles Norris MA (Oxon)

Appointed: September 2018

School type: Coeducational Boarding & Day

Age range of pupils: 11–18

No. of pupils enrolled as at 01/09/2018: 616

Boys: 366 **Girls:** 250 **Sixth Form:** 198

No. of boarders: 197

Fees per annum as at 01/09/2018:

Day: £13,137–£15,879

Weekly Boarding: £19,032–£27,648

Full Boarding: £18,387–£26,712

Average class size: Less than 20

Teacher/pupil ratio: 1:11

Ellesmere College

Founded in 1884, Ellesmere is a co-educational boarding and day school which offers students between the ages of seven and 18 a platform for academic success and personal development. A wide ranging academic curriculum and extensive activities programme allows each student the opportunity to advance in a range of disciplines, whether in the Arts, Music, Drama, Sport, or to develop leadership and entrepreneurial skills. Ellesmere College treats every pupil as an individual and where success is *'doing the very best you can'*; a philosophy that all parents, pupils and staff recognise and support wholeheartedly.

The Lower School (7-13) provides an environment which focuses on individual needs, and helps children grow into happy, secure young people, with the confidence to tackle new challenges and understand the world around them.

Students joining the Middle School (13-16) enjoy a stimulating environment with an extensive academic programme and an even wider range of curricular and co-curricular opportunities. Ellesmere students consistently celebrate excellent GCSE results – where over a third of all grades were in the top A*/A, and more than half of all grades awarded were in the A*/B.

Music is a key element of Ellesmere life and there is something for everyone – from the Chapel Choir to National Finalists in the Barnardo's Choir of the Year Competition and Songs of Praise Young Choir of the Year 2018. The standard of drama is also very high and Ellesmere is the only UK independent school to hold the Arts Council's Arts Mark Platinum Award.

For sports enthusiasts, Ellesmere is one of only nine schools in the world to be an accredited Athlete Friendly Education Centre (AFEC) by the World Academy of Sport (WAoS), which provides greater flexibility to students allowing them to balance their studies with heavy training and competition schedules. With the nationally renowned Titans Swimming team, 7 sporting academies, and incredible state of the art facilities, pupils can train in every Olympic discipline.

Following GCSEs, students have a choice of A-levels, BTEC or the International Baccalaureate Diploma. The College takes the preparation of students for Oxbridge and the USA very seriously and the academic enrichment programme offers extension activities in all subjects. With 82 per cent of applications gaining offers from the top 50 Universities in the world and an exclusive careers partnership programme which finds opportunities for sixth form pupils to experience the real world; preparation for life is central to the development of the individual.

What makes a successful school? A committed leadership team, an excellent set of professional teachers, a globally recognised set of qualifications and a broad approach to pupil development via an expansive academic and co-curricular programme.

At Ellesmere we believe that developing the whole pupil is much more than just passing examinations; a philosophy which is paramount to the continued success of nurturing our students.

Come and experience this unique environment for yourself by booking a visit or join us on one of our Open Days throughout the year – visit our website for more details: www.ellesmere.com

Ellesmere

(Founded 1878)

Ellesmere, Shropshire, SY12 9AB, UK

Tel: 01691 622321

Fax: 01691 623286

Email: hmsecretary@ellesmere.com

Website: www.ellesmere.com

Head: Mr B J Wignall MA, FRSA, MCMI

Appointed: 1996

School type: Coeducational Day & Boarding

Age range of pupils: 7–18

Teacher/pupil ratio: 1:8

King Edward VI High School for Girls

Founded in 1883, King Edward VI High School for Girls is one of the country's premier day schools, achieving GCSE and A Levels which rank it consistently amongst the highest-performing day schools in the country. KEHS offers girls a richly varied and exciting education in a friendly, nurturing environment and has the capacity to transform the lives of the bright, multi-talented girls who come here from an extraordinary range of backgrounds.

As a close-knit, caring community, KEHS is able to offer individual attention and support – whether a girl is a gifted mathematician, a talented linguist or a scientist enjoying the extra stimulation of university level extended projects. As one parent put it: *"KEHS does difference well"*, and our liberal, tolerant ethos and respect for diversity, allows students to flourish.

KEHS aims to support girls to become resilient, confident young women, prepared for the challenges of modern life in further education and employment. We believe KEHS offers the best possible preparation for university life and beyond, thanks to the academic rigour expected and the intellectual confidence instilled in our girls through the outstanding teaching and the wide range of experiences on offer.

Last year saw one of our most successful set of results ever.

GCSE results 2017
- 98% of grades were at A*/ A
- 83% A*
- 64% of girls achieved 9 or more A*
- Ranked Third Nationally

A Level results 2017
- 89% A*/B
- 77% ABB or better
- 73% of girls completed the EPQ

The School was voted as the Midlands School of the Year 2018 by *The Sunday Times Parent Power*.

The majority of girls join King Edward VI High School for Girls in Thirds (Year 7). Each year around 96 girls join us from a wide variety of backgrounds and schools.

Entrance examinations for Thirds (Year 7) take place at the beginning of October the year before entry. Registration opens the prior Easter and closes two weeks before the entrance examination takes place.

Girls wishing to join the Sixth Form are required to attend an academic interview before conditional offers are considered and applications are received between September and January, the year before entry.

Our Governors' Assisted Places Scheme aims to ensure girls who would benefit from an education at KEHS can come to the school irrespective of parental income. The scheme is means-tested and parents wishing to apply for fee remission must complete and return a statement of income annually.

We also offer academic scholarships to recognise girls who excel in our 11+ entrance examinations and 16+ applications. These scholarships are independent of parental income and can be combined with Assisted Places for exceptional candidates.

To understand what makes us so distinctive – the intellectual curiosity, the inspirational teaching and the excitement of so many bright creative people working together – you need to experience it first-hand; meet our amazing girls and staff and see for themselves the unique blend of tradition and innovative thinking which lie at the heart of KEHS.

Further information is available at www.kehs.org.uk/.

KING EDWARD VI
HIGH SCHOOL FOR GIRLS

(Founded 1883)

Edgbaston Park Road, Birmingham, West Midlands B15 2UB UK

Tel: 0121 472 1834

Fax: 0121 471 3808

Email: admissions@kehs.co.uk

Website: www.kehs.org.uk

Principal: Ms Ann Clark

Appointed: 2013

School type: Girls' Day

Age range of girls: 11–18

No. of pupils enrolled as at 01/09/2018: 591

Fees per annum as at 01/09/2018:

Day: £12,888

Average class size: 20

Teacher/pupil ratio: 1:12

Lucton School

Small classes, talented and committed teachers, a friendly atmosphere and a wonderful rural location combine to provide an outstanding, all-round educational experience at Lucton.

An Oxford University admissions tutor commented that the typical thing about Lucton students is that there is no typical student – they are very much individuals! What they do have in common is that they leave us confident in their abilities and strengths, ready to embrace opportunities and play their part.

They also achieve excellent results at A-level and GCSE and secure an impressive range of university places. The School is justly proud of its remarkable added-value scores and its ability to draw out the full potential of every individual.

A safe and secure location

Founded in 1708, the School is set in a safe, healthy location in 55 acres of beautiful Herefordshire countryside. There is a good mix of day pupils, weekly boarders and full boarders. Many team and individual sports are offered and boarders enjoy a wealth of weekend activities – sporting, cultural, social and just good fun – all included in the fees.

Senior boarders have individual rooms – although some younger ones prefer to share – and pastoral care at Lucton is second to none. Overseas students may use the School's free airport buses at the beginning and end of term.

Strong academic record

Offering a wide range of GCSE and A-level subjects, Lucton has a strong academic record and an established tradition of getting the best possible results from each pupil. We accept mixed ability students, yet over the last two years A-level results have averaged 80% A–C. In 2017 the A-level results were over 30% A* to A grades and all leavers have gained places at their first choice universities.

A unique feature is Lucton's 'Access to A-level' course, which also serves as a Pre-IB course, designed to provide overseas students with a grounding in a range of subjects and incorporating accelerated learning of English – ultimately preparing them for entry to the best courses at the best universities.

Excellent facilities

Facilities include junior and senior libraries, science laboratories, ICT rooms, a design and technology workshop, sports hall, tennis courts, indoor swimming pool, many games fields and Equestrian Centre. Senior students enjoy their own sixth-form centre, including library, IT suite, comfortable common room and quiet study area.

Admission can take place at any time of year by interview and assessment. The School offers discounts to Forces families.

In a previous boarding inspection, Lucton School was awarded 'Outstanding' for Equality and Diversity, an excellent reflection of how well boarders from all backgrounds are made welcome at Lucton. In the latest whole school inspection, along with many other categories, boarding was rated as 'Excellent'.

(Founded 1708)

Lucton, Herefordshire HR6 9PN UK

Tel: 01568 782000

Fax: 01568 782001

Email: admissions@luctonschool.org

Website: www.luctonschool.org

Headmistress: Mrs Gill Thorne MA

Appointed: 2003

School type: Coeducational Day & Boarding

Religious Denomination: Christian

Age range of pupils: 1–18

No. of pupils enrolled as at 01/09/2018: 330

No. of boarders: 90

Fees per term as at 01/09/2018:

Day: £3,300–£4,575

Weekly Boarding: £7,500–£8,825

Full Boarding: £9,295–£10,625

Teacher/pupil ratio: 1:8

Malvern St James

"…full of girls who are going to change the world". Good Schools Guide 2017

MSJ is a leading independent school for girls set at the foot of the majestic Malvern Hills. What helps to make us distinct and refreshing, is our recognition and active support for the individual talents, interests and passions of girls, and the liberating and inclusive ethos the school embraces.

We nurture a freedom of spirit, respect for others and support of every member of our school community. Our staff are innovative and passionate about their work and constantly evolve new ways to inspire learning and exploration of their subjects, often beyond the curriculum. We actively encourage debate and open discussion. We explore the world around us, at home and across the globe. We believe in maintaining truth and transparency as a school community.

The Prep Department, Senior School and dedicated Sixth Form Centre sit together on the main school site, whilst Boarding houses are a stone's throw away, and a short walk from the town of Malvern where girls can go to shop, have coffee, or to see a film or play as they grow older and more independent. As well as full or weekly boarding, girls can flexi-board one, two or three nights per week.

MSJ is a refreshing and inspiring school for girls. A school that helps girls to truly develop their thinking skills, to explore who they are and to develop the courage and self-belief to go out into the world and be true to who they are.

Curriculum

MSJ doesn't produce a 'type' of girl. We achieve excellent academic results but we are not an exam factory. Our ethos is one of inclusion and respect. Girls can pursue their passions and interests in the field of their choice – all routes are equal. It may be horse riding, engineering, politics, the environment or climbing. We recognise the importance of allowing each individual to grow and flourish. We find ways to support girls to achieve their passions.

The curriculum also supports pupils who need special provision including very able pupils, and those for whom English is an additional language. Those who have specific areas of expertise have adapted timetables to allow them to focus on their specialism, giving time to practise and train, with personalised coaching and mentoring sessions.

Our 'Russell Up' provides preparation for the most competitive UK and international universities and career pathways.

Scholarships

Academic, Drama, Music, Art, Riding, Technology and Sport Scholarships are available and our Founders' Awards bursary programme enables outstanding girls applying for Sixth Form to access the excellent educational opportunities offered at MSJ. We also offer generous bursaries.

Entrance examinations

- Prep: informal assessment.
- Senior School: cognitive ability tests (CAT 4) and an English comprehension examination.
- Sixth Form: three subject entrance papers and general essay. Girls will also have an interview, face-to-face or on Skype, and there will be an additional EAL paper for non-native English speakers.

Location

The School benefits from being positioned in the small but culturally lively town of Malvern, on a direct rail route from London Paddington. The M5 and M50 are nearby and London, Birmingham, Bristol and Manchester airports are within easy reach.

MALVERN ST JAMES
Girls' School

(Founded 1893)

15 Avenue Road, Great Malvern, Worcestershire WR14 3BA UK

Tel: 01684 892288

Fax: 01684 566204

Email: admissions@malvernstjames.co.uk

Website: www.malvernstjames.co.uk

Headteacher: Mrs Olivera Raraty BA PGCE

Appointed: 2016

School type: Girls' Boarding & Day

Age range of girls: 4–18

No. of pupils enrolled as at 01/09/2018: 400

No. of boarders: 200

Fees per annum as at 01/09/2018:

Day: £8,445–£19,380

Weekly Boarding: £19,725–£33,285

Full Boarding: £21,915–£36,720

Teacher/pupil ratio: 1:8

Mander Portman Woodward – Birmingham

MPW Birmingham was founded in 1980 with the goal of ensuring that students experience an education based on the Oxford and Cambridge tutorial system. This means that lessons are more relaxed and informal than a typical school, but are also academically stimulating and demanding. With fewer than ten students in any class, lessons are intensive but rewarding with plenty of opportunity for individual attention and personalised teaching.

MPW Birmingham guides students in their learning by encouraging them to focus on our model of success: aspiration, attitude, attendance, application and achievement. We help students obtain results that all too often they never thought were possible. With almost 30 subjects to choose from at A level and many at GCSE, MPW Birmingham provides a breadth of study opportunity that is unique for a small college. MPW helps students demystify the examination process and develop both the technical skills and academic knowledge needed to perform well under timed conditions. We offer all of our students the opportunity to sit weekly assessments enabling students to perfect examination technique.

We run a university support programme that values every student in equal measure regardless of aspiration; we treat all students as though they are elite. We prepare students for a range of courses including medicine, dentistry and Oxbridge and ensure that they are well equipped to cope with the demands of university life.

Students benefit from outstanding pastoral care with each student being allocated a Personal Tutor. This builds upon our core values of diligence, respect, tolerance and care. We expect our students to work hard but we also expect to provide more support to our students than they would receive at other schools. Our culture is one based on high expectations but one that is both nurturing and unpretentious. We run a non-compulsory enrichment programme in which many students participate, developing both sporting and cultural interests. There is no glass ceiling in MPW Birmingham and we strive to enable all students to reach their potential and use their talents without inhibition.

Our mission is to be one of the leading colleges of its type within the country, enabling students to develop confidence, maturity, knowledge and skills, turning academic aspirations into reality. MPW helps build the character of students enabling them to develop good self-discipline regarding work, intellectual curiosity and a sense of duty regarding community. Our best ambassadors are our students and we are rightly proud of what they achieve with us and what they go on to achieve afterwards. We change lives for the better and help bring about progress and success. Irrespective of where a student is starting from, MPW helps young people achieve special things.

Mander Portman Woodward

(Founded 1980)

17-18 Greenfield Crescent, Edgbaston, Birmingham, West Midlands B15 3AU UK

Tel: 0121 454 9637

Fax: 0121 454 6433

Email: birmingham@mpw.ac.uk

Website: www.mpw.ac.uk

Principal: Mr Mark Shingleton

School type: Coeducational Day

Age range of pupils: 14–19

Average class size: 8

Packwood Haugh School

Founded in 1892, Packwood Haugh is a co-educational, independent day and boarding prep school, which over its long and illustrious history has earned a reputation for excellence in all areas – academic, sporting and in the arts. Success is reflected on the school's Honours Boards (including more than 90 scholarship awards in the last five years alone), and by its proud record of 100% pass rate in Common Entrance every year in living memory. This year's scholarships include top academic awards to St Edward's, Shrewsbury and Rugby as well as awards for music, sport, art and drama to many of the best independent senior schools across the country.

With a focus on educating the whole child, the ethos at Packwood is to develop characteristics of grit, determination and resourcefulness that prepare pupils for future challenges at senior school and beyond. Pupils are encouraged to aim high and to work hard to fulfil their potential in everything they do.

Set in 65 acres of glorious Shropshire countryside in the heart of the country, the school's outstanding facilities and grounds enable the provision of a truly all-round education. Outdoor learning features on the curriculum as much as possible with teachers of every subject finding ways to use the school's wonderful environment to bring learning to life.

There is a strong sporting tradition and Packwood enjoys great success in a variety of team and individual sports at county, regional and national level. Furthermore, the Independent Schools Inspectorate reported on 'particularly high standards in Music, Art and Drama' with many pupils enjoying extra clubs and one-to-one tuition, in addition to class lessons.

Alongside the wide-ranging, academically rigorous curriculum, Packwood offers countless opportunities and experiences to enrich and broaden the children's development. An excellent programme of extra-curricular activities, and regular workshops and speakers at school as well as educational visits and trips both at home and overseas. In recent years, pupils have visited Bavaria, France and The Netherlands with a trip to Italy planned for autumn 2018.

Boarding at Packwood remains an enduringly popular option and was greatly praised by the ISI inspectors who reported that 'the quality of boarding provision and care is excellent'. Boarders thrive in the happy, supportive environment of their boarding houses where they 'develop key qualities such as tolerance, confidence and independence'. The boarders' weekends are full and busy with activities ranging from clay pigeon shooting and gymnastics to drama workshops and cupcake baking, and camping out in the grounds is a perennial favourite. The children themselves are unfailingly enthusiastic about everything available to them, and most importantly of all, about building friendships for life.

Headmaster, Clive Smith-Langridge, says, "Packwood is thriving and continues to go from strength to strength. We are committed to providing the best possible education for our pupils in every way we can. The success we enjoy every year is testament to not only the dedication and professionalism of members of staff, but above all to the diligence and enthusiasm of the children. They flourish in the happy and positive environment at Packwood and invariably meet – and exceed – the high expectations we have of them."

(Founded 1892)
Ruyton XI Towns, Shrewsbury, Shropshire SY4 1HX UK
Tel: 01939 260217
Fax: 01939 262077
Email: hm@packwood-haugh.co.uk
Website: www.packwood-haugh.co.uk
Headmaster: Clive Smith-Langridge BA(Hons), PGCE
Appointed: September 2012
Headmaster (From April 2019): Robert Fox BSc (Hons), PGCE
School type: Coeducational Day & Boarding
Age range of pupils: 4–13
No. of pupils enrolled as at 01/09/2018: 212
Boys: 149 **Girls:** 63
No. of boarders: 89
Fees per annum as at 01/09/2018:
Day: £8,805–£18,330
Full Boarding: £23,430 (UK)–£26,430 (Overseas)
Average class size: 13
Teacher/pupil ratio: 1:7

Shrewsbury School

Set in the heart of England Shrewsbury is a unique school in many ways. We are committed to strong academic standards and we believe in a vision of holistic education, as demonstrated through an incredible range of different activities and societies.

We are passionate about boarding not just being for convenience, but in providing the best opportunity for young men and women to develop real confidence and belief in themselves. We are fortunate to have one of the best locations of any school in the country, a most beautiful campus-style site on the edge of one of the most historic county towns in England.

Life at Shrewsbury is founded on a close partnership between staff, parents and pupils to promote the strength of family life, foster responsibility, and balance the claims of developing individuality with the needs of a vibrant community.

We believe our traditional values and time-honoured reputation is enhanced by a dynamic development plan designed to fully embrace the advantages of co-education. We are committed to providing an environment where young men and women can learn together on foundations of trust and mutual respect. We are confident that the future will be a more equal one and we support that historical evolution.

The celebration of individuals and individual talent is central to education at Shrewsbury – both in and beyond the classroom. In whatever sphere, a pupil will find a member of staff to support and encourage, enthuse and inspire him or her to exceed their expectations and meet the challenges that lie ahead with confidence and good judgement.

The results speak for themselves. Our 2017 leavers achieved another excellent year for A Level results with 79% of the exams awarded the top A*, A or B grades and 20% of all exams gaining the top A* grade.

We celebrated a strong set of GCSE results, with 66% of the exams awarded an A* or A grade and 40% of results achieving the top A* grade.

We want all our pupils, whatever their ability, to enjoy their life beyond the classroom, and Shrewsbury has a well-earned reputation for academic, musical and sporting excellence. We compete internationally in cricket and rowing, and we are one of the strongest schools in the country for football, cross-country running and fives; facilities and coaching for these and a host of other sports including tennis, fencing, lacrosse, hockey, rugby, and netball are excellent.

Our school plays and musicals have drawn praise at the Edinburgh Fringe Festival and in London. As one would expect from one of the strongest music departments in the country, the breadth and quality of music-making is remarkable, and a number of students win places at some of the top music colleges each year.

We also offer our pupils an extraordinary array of clubs, societies and other extra-curricular activities, many of which take place on a dedicated weekly activity afternoon. The majority are led by members of school staff. Shrewsbury is surrounded by glorious unspoilt countryside and the School makes the most of its easy access to the Shropshire Hills, the Welsh Marches and Snowdonia.

Above all, in the words of the motto of our youth club, based in inner-city Liverpool, 'People matter more than things'. You will find at Shrewsbury a community which is aiming for the stars in every respect. Come and visit our beautiful school and meet some of the people who make it such an inspirational place.

Shrewsbury School

(Founded 1552)

The Schools, Shrewsbury, Shropshire SY3 7BA UK

Tel: 01743 280552

Fax: 01743 243107

Email: admissions@shrewsbury.org.uk

Website: www.shrewsbury.org.uk

Headmaster: Mr. Leo Winkley

Appointed: 2018

School type: Coeducational Day & Boarding

Religious Denomination: Anglican

Age range of pupils: 13–18

No. of pupils enrolled as at 01/09/2018: 792

Boys: 545 **Girls:** 247 **Sixth Form:** 386

No. of boarders: 617

Fees per annum as at 01/09/2018:

Day: £24,885

Full Boarding: £36,270

Average class size: GCSE: 18; A level: 8

Teacher/pupil ratio: 1:9

The Royal School Wolverhampton

The extensive work begins in earnest! Following the ambitious and successful growth programme in pupil numbers over the past three years, The Royal School's exciting building programme is now well under way to develop first class teaching facilities for pupils from four to 19. Phase one of the school's development plan will see a new Sixth Form Centre and refurbished classrooms and is expected to be completed by the start of term, ready for phase two.

At the centre of all that we do is our inclusive community where students study, play and live together harmoniously. After the first Wolverhampton City Secondary Sports Award Presentation evening Mark Heywood, Principal, said *"we are delighted to have been awarded the 'Inclusive School of the Year 2017/18' which reflects that nearly 90% of our pupils have played competitive sport for the school and been engaged in teams that have also won many of the local tournaments in different age groups and in a range of different sports."* This is a huge achievement brought about by a fantastic team effort from the School's sports' department.

This excellent contribution, combined with more than 95% of Year 13 pupils achieving their first choice university place last summer, indicates that in developing the 'whole person' in sport, drama, music and adventurous activity, young people at The Royal are also better placed to make the best of their opportunities to become well-rounded individuals with confidence and empathy for those around them.

The Royal School
Wolverhampton

Penn Road, Wolverhampton,
West Midlands WV3 0EG UK

Tel: +44 (0)1902 341230

Email: info@theroyal.school

Website: www.theroyalschool.co.uk

Head of School: Mark Heywood

School type: Co-educational Day & Boarding

Age range of pupils: 4–19

Boarding: 11–19

No. of pupils enrolled as at 01/09/2018: 1285

Fees per annum as at 01/09/2018:

Full Boarding: £11,900

Average class size: 25

West House School

Situated in the leafy oasis of the Calthorpe Estate, West House School has occupied the same site since its foundation in 1895. Since that time, the school has evolved significantly to become an independent preparatory school for boys aged 4-11 years, with a co-educational Early Years Department offering care and education for children aged from 12 months. West House is a member of The Independent Association of Preparatory Schools and, as such, upholds the requirement to provide a 'world class education'.

Set within five acres of beautiful grounds, less than two miles from Birmingham city centre, the school lies at the heart of a thriving community. Pupils of all ages benefit from two all-weather playing surfaces, a nature reserve and the multi-functional Duce Hall, providing indoor sporting and theatrical facilities. The school is also surrounded by many outstanding cultural and recreational amenities which enrich the lives of all pupils and allow them to explore and extend their talents in numerous curricular and extra-curricular pursuits.

West House is a non-denominational school, guided by Christian principles. It is divided into three departments – Prep (Years 3-6), Pre-Prep (Years 1 & 2) and the Early Years Foundation Stage (Nursery – Reception). From their earliest years, children are encouraged to adopt the core values of the school which are actively promoted throughout the working day and frequently form the focus of assemblies and PSHE lessons.

The school continues to boast a unique family atmosphere of which founding Headmaster, Arthur Perrott Cary Field, would have been proud. In the spirit of combining the best of its traditions with an education that prepares pupils for life in the middle part of the twenty first century, it remains determined to be at the forefront of innovation. This is reflected in the delivery of an ambitious curriculum which complements academic rigour with significant opportunities for pupils to explore personal interests in sport, art, music and drama.

Employing 45 full-time and part-time academic staff, many of whom are subject specialists, West House has grown considerably during the last five years to accommodate approximately 330 pupils, with 130 attending the EYFS Department.

Pupils are prepared for a wide range of senior schools, and standards at 11+ are consistently high, with most Year 6 boys transferring to local grammar schools, King Edward's School, Birmingham and Solihull School. A number of pupils are awarded academic and sporting scholarships and the school also enjoys outstanding success in academic challenges, quizzes and competitions at regional and national level.

Further details about the school can be found at www.westhouseprep.com

(Founded 1895)

24 St James's Road, Edgbaston, Birmingham, West Midlands B15 2NX UK

Tel: 0121 440 4097

Fax: 0121 440 5839

Email: secretary@westhouseprep.com

Website: www.westhouseprep.com

Headmaster:
Mr Alistair M J Lyttle BA(Hons), PGCE, NPQH

School type: Boys' Day

Age range of boys: 1–11

Age range of girls: 1–4

No. of pupils enrolled as at 01/09/2018: 350

Fees per term as at 01/09/2018:

Day: £1,466–£3,908

Average class size: 17 (two form entry)

Teacher/pupil ratio: 1:12

Wolverhampton Grammar School

Wolverhampton Grammar School is a selective, independent school, located to the west of Wolverhampton. Families from across the West Midlands, Staffordshire and Shropshire choose the school because of its excellent reputation and mission to deliver education that transforms lives as well as minds.

Founded in 1512, the school is an iconic local landmark and remains the top independent school in Wolverhampton. With over 500 years of exceptional education history, the school is still the first choice for parents who want approachability and a human dimension to education. Large enough to be able to offer an experience like no other and yet personal enough to adapt to suit the ambitions and interests of every child.

The school provides education with a personalised curriculum full of academic and extra-curricular opportunities. Providing this experience to boys and girls from Year 3 through to Year 13 (ages 7–18) with students coming from all kinds of backgrounds and cultures. Their knowledge and skills are diverse, and are a source of strength and richness to the school that partners with a range of local, national and international organisations.

The 23-acre school site blends stunning original architecture with creative, innovative learning spaces. Walk through the school and you will see how the Senior and Sixth Form buildings wrap around the Junior School; how superb grounds, a sports centre and pavilion provide the perfect showcase for sport and how the use of green and open spaces offer the ideal setting for the development of creative and critical thinkers.

The school accepts applications to the Junior, Senior School and Sixth Form throughout the year and there are a number of Scholarships and means-tested Bursaries available. As a selective, independent school all applicants (for Years 3–11) are asked to sit an assessment/entrance test relevant to their year of entry. Applicants to the Sixth Form are also invited to meet with the Head of Sixth Form. Students go on to achieve great things and have their pick of the best Russell Group and International Universities. The school also has a thriving worldwide alumni community of thousands in over 30 countries.

As the leading independent school in the area, demand for the school is high, it's therefore recommended that you contact the school as soon as possible to ensure you receive regular updates about open days and key application and assessment/entrance test dates.

The school actively encourages all applicants to visit and experience their approach to learning and it's famously welcoming atmosphere. To arrange a visit, taster or discover day or to register for an Open Day contact:

Jane Morris, Admissions Registrar, Wolverhampton Grammar School, Compton Road, Wolverhampton WV3 9RB tel: 01902 422939, email: jam@wgs-sch.net or visit the website www.wgs.org.uk for more details.

WOLVERHAMPTON
GRAMMAR SCHOOL

(Founded 1512)

Compton Road, Wolverhampton,
West Midlands WV3 9RB UK

Tel: 01902 421326

Email: wgs@wgs-sch.net

Website: www.wgs.org.uk

Head: Kathy Crewe-Read BSc

School type: Coeducational Selective Day

Age range of pupils: 7–18

No. of pupils enrolled as at 01/09/2018: 738

Boys: 433 **Girls:** 305 **Sixth Form:** 156

Fees per term as at 01/09/2018:

Day: £3,457–£4,554

Average class size: 24 Max

Yorkshire & Humberside

Pocklington School

Young people flourish in the supportive environment of Pocklington School, where specialist and innovative teaching from the ages of 3-18 helps each pupil achieve their full potential.

We are renowned for our emphasis on pastoral care as part of an excellent all-round education, with a focus on the individual, which produces confident, resourceful and capable young adults.

Pocklington School lies 12 miles east of York in a safe, rural setting on the edge of a small, friendly market town, on a 50-acre campus with good public transport links and its own minibus pick-up service.

The day and boarding school's extensive facilities include a 300-seat theatre, an indoor sports hall, conditioning room and swimming pool, plus 21 acres of grass sports pitches and two full-sized synthetic pitches.

Numerous co-curricular activities take place every day until 5pm, and each pupil is encouraged to pursue their own interests to help develop the depth of character and self-awareness to tackle life's challenges on their own terms.

Pocklington School was founded in 1514 and has remained true to its strong tradition of encouraging pupils to have the courage to take chances with learning and always remain true to themselves. Our motto Virtute et Veritate: With Courage and With Truth, reflects this.

Right through from Prep School, with its emphasis on nurturing children's natural curiosity, imagination and enthusiasm for learning, to the Sixth Form where independent thought is prized, our pupils are encouraged to be resilient, resourceful learners.

Lessons are planned around giving pupils the opportunity to evaluate and apply a solid foundation of learning, rather than simply acquiring and retaining facts.

We employ the best educational tools and appropriate new technology facilities to ensure youngsters are enthused and inspired by the world of knowledge available to them. The flexibility of learning platforms and the individual approach allows each pupil to progress at his or her pace, boosting their confidence and self-esteem so they often exceed their expectations.

Our new £3m Art and Design Technology Centre, which opened in Autumn 2017, has every facility to encourage the pursuit of traditional arts and crafts, as well as provide cutting-edge equipment for digital and computer design, and manufacturing technology. The innovation and cross fertilisation of ideas the Centre promotes are increasingly valued in society today.

Sixth Form facilities include spacious communal areas, a study centre, and comprehensive library. Students are encouraged to work both collaboratively and independently as they begin to make the transition to university study and/or workplace success.

Full, flexible and casual boarding options are available, in boarding houses which create a home from home for both domestic and international students. A flexible range of opportunities allows them to create a balanced programme which not only fulfils their academic objectives, but also leaves time to explore new sporting, cultural and vocational activities to develop individual skills and strengths.

Recent former pupils who retain links with the school include Davis Cup winner Kyle Edmund, England rugby star Rob Webber and world-renowned concert pianist Alexandra Dariescu.

We aim to inspire our pupils for life, helping develop an inquiring mind and the self-respect they need to emerge as capable, adaptable and resilient young people ready to make a real contribution to society.

POCKLINGTON SCHOOL

Ages 3 to 18

(Founded 1514)

West Green, Pocklington, York, North Yorkshire YO42 2NJ UK

Tel: 01759 321200

Fax: 01759 306366

Email: enquiry@pocklingtonschool.com

Website: www.pocklingtonschool.com

Headmaster: Mr Mark Ronan MA (Cantab)

Appointed: January 2008

School type: Coeducational Day & Boarding

Religious Denomination:
Christian ethos welcoming all faiths and none

Age range of pupils: 3–18

No. of pupils enrolled as at 01/09/2018: 750

Boys: 403 **Girls:** 347 **Sixth Form:** 162

No. of boarders: 100

Fees per annum as at 01/09/2018:

Day: £14,619

Weekly Boarding: £26,205

Full Boarding: £28,491

Queen Ethelburga's Collegiate Foundation

Students and staff at Queen Ethelburga's College and Faculty are celebrating another successful year, following the publishing of the 2018 A level and BTEC examination results. Students in the academically focused College achieved 96% A*-B at A level and 97% D*/D in the small number of BTECs taken to enrich the A level programmes (equivalent in university points to A* and A grades at A Level). The Faculty, which offers a wider range of academic, creative and vocational courses, achieved 91% A* – B at A level and 64% D*/D in BTECs. *"This is a great achievement across the board and I am sure our students are as delighted with their efforts as we are."* said Steven Jandrell, Collegiate Principal. As seen in national league tables, the A level results for both the College and the Faculty have been in the top 20 schools in the country over last few years.

QE also places great emphasis on our students growing into resilient, caring, compassionate and confident adults, who develop independence and initiative, and who can take responsibility for their own learning and futures. We provide opportunities for students to take part in a range of wider enrichment and extra-curricular activities to help them to gain skills in leadership, teamwork and collaboration, and decision making.

Students at QE have access to an impressive 150 sports and activities each week, including popular sports such as rugby, hockey, football, netball, cricket, swimming, basketball, rounders, tennis, dance, gymnastics, trampolining, climbing, athletics, badminton, and volleyball. Our team of sports staff cater for all abilities and encourage each student to make the most of all the fantastic opportunities on offer during their time here. We have a well-honed mix of physical education teachers and specialist sports coaches, many of whom are ex-professional sportspeople themselves. This means there really is no limit to the level our students can train to. Health

and fitness is so central to school life for students that many continue with sport and exercise, either recreationally or as a route of study, that it continues to be a key part of their lives long after they have left us for the next step in their education or career.

What enables us to deliver all of this sporting activity so successfully of course is the outstanding range of high quality facilities on campus. We're pretty unique in that we have a dedicated Sports Village, completed in 2016, to which all students have access to inside and outside of formal school hours. The Village is home to a 25-metre swimming pool, triple court sports hall, 100 station fitness suite and free weights centre. Outside we have a four-lane synthetic cushioned running track and over 30 acres of both grass and artificial 3G pitches. We also have a number of specialist studios used for; martial arts, wrestling, dance, gymnastics, table tennis, cycling, archery, fencing and boxing.

In addition to all this, the students can make use of an eight-metre climbing wall at the campus activity centre, which also houses an assault course, BMX track and additional tennis courts.

There really is something for everyone and for all abilities.

All of Queen Ethelburga's students follow a sports programme with the values of fair play, honesty and determination at its heart. Our motto of 'be the best that I can, with the gifts that I have' is never more evident than through the work we do as TEAM QE.

(Founded 1912)

Thorpe Underwood Hall, Ouseburn, York, North Yorkshire YO26 9SS UK

Tel: 01423 33 33 30

Email: info@qe.org

Website: www.qe.org

Principal: Steven Jandrell BA

Appointed: September 2006

School type: Coeducational Day & Boarding

Religious Denomination: Multi-Denominational

Age range of pupils: 3–19

No. of pupils enrolled as at 01/09/2018: 1550

Boys: 780 *Girls:* 770 *Sixth Form:* 595

No. of boarders: 1128

Average class size: 18

Teacher/pupil ratio: 1:10

The Froebelian School

The Froebelian School in Horsforth is a thriving and dynamic independent prep school, which places children at the very heart of all it strives to achieve. From the age of three, we seek to equip our boys and girls with a lifelong thirst for and love of learning and the school continually achieves impressive levels of academic success; preparing our children for the next stage in their educational journey.

The children and staff work harmoniously together creating a special place, with a uniquely happy atmosphere.

Our aim is to provide a first class all-round education and committed pastoral care in which the unique needs, abilities, interests and aspirations of our bright, inquisitive children are met and their talents can flourish in a caring, structured and secure environment. This enables us to develop the whole child and we work hard to build solid foundations, which balance both the co-curricular and academic spheres of school life and honour our school motto – 'Giving a flying start to the citizens of tomorrow.' As a result, our children regularly secure a place at their first choice senior school and we enjoy an excellent scholarship success rate.

We are delighted that Froebelian children are happy and want to come to school every day and are passionate that all children enjoy a positive experience. Throughout the year extensive learning opportunities are balanced by a wide range of co-curricular activities in sport, music, art and technology and events. We foster our children's curiosity and imagination at every stage of school life and the children are nurtured and supported by an excellent staff:pupil ratio of 1:10.

Welcoming over 180 pupils between the ages of 3 and 11, we set the highest standards and expectations and The Froebelian School is acknowledged as one of the North's leading Independent prep schools. We have been placed consistently as the highest ranked school in the area in the prestigious Sunday Times Parent Power Survey.

The latest Independent Schools Inspectorate report judged The Froebelian School as 'excellent' for the quality of the pupils' achievements and the quality of pupils' personal development – this is the highest judgement available from the Independent Schools Inspectorate.

"The pupils' attitudes to learning are exceptional" **ISI Inspectorate 2017**

Awarded 'Outstanding' by Ofsted, our private day nursery, First-Steps at Froebelian, follows the school's ethos closely and offers younger children the opportunity to start realising their full potential at an earlier age.

"The leadership and management are inspirational" **Ofsted**

Situated in Horsforth, a pleasant and vibrant suburb of Leeds near to the ring road, the school is easily accessible from most areas of Leeds, Bradford and Harrogate. Our site is very secure with a wooded area offering delightful views over the Aire valley.

The school is an educational charity where ultimate responsibility rests with a School Council (governors). The day-to-day running of the school is delegated to the Headteacher, supported by a Senior Leadership Team.

Our children adore their school and are justly proud of all they do. They love learning and there is a true sense of fun. We would love you to experience the warmth and politeness of our children for yourselves – please do come and meet them!

Visit www.froebelian.com to find out more.

THE FROEBELIAN SCHOOL
GIVING A FLYING START TO THE CITIZENS OF TOMORROW

(Founded 1913)

Clarence Road, Horsforth, Leeds, West Yorkshire LS18 4LB UK

Tel: 0113 2583047

Fax: 0113 2580173

Email: office@froebelian.co.uk

Website: www.froebelian.com

Head Teacher: Mrs Catherine Dodds BEd (Hons), PGCE

Appointed: 2015

School type: Coeducational Day

Age range of pupils: 3–11

No. of pupils enrolled as at 01/09/2018: 189

Boys: 96 **Girls:** 93

Fees per annum as at 01/09/2018:

Day: £5,220–£7,785

Teacher/pupil ratio: 1:10

Woodhouse Grove School

Woodhouse Grove was founded in 1812 and is a co-educational day and boarding school with 1060 pupils aged from 3 to 18 years.

An Independent Schools Inspectorate (ISI) inspection in March 2017 rated all aspects of Woodhouse Grove School as excellent. The Inspectors came away with very clear evidence of the attributes that we seek to promote, namely: Inspiration, Challenge and Grovian Values. Our outstanding academic and co-curricular programme was recognised and our aim to ensure that all our pupils reach their full potential was substantiated.

At Woodhouse Grove, we appreciate that every child is a unique individual and this is at the heart of everything we do. We aim to motivate pupils academically and beyond the classroom and to provide an educational environment designed to allow students to fully participate in school life.

We offer a rich, challenging and dynamic curriculum and want our students to ask questions of the world around them with an open mind; to have the character to listen to others, but also to stand up for their beliefs. We encourage our pupils to 'give back' to their community and we believe that this well-rounded, diverse approach is the key to building academic and personal confidence. Ultimately, our objective is to provide our students with the drive and aspiration to become the very best version of themselves that they can be.

Set in idyllic grounds near Leeds, the school is opposite Apperley Bridge train station and within four miles of Leeds Bradford Airport. We have high standards and an all-encompassing approach to education and our outstanding facilities reflect this. A recording studio, 230 seater theatre, sports halls, swimming pool and climbing wall are all within our 70 acre campus.

Our junior school, Brontë House enjoys its own facilities on a superb site situated half a mile from the Senior School, and includes our purpose built Early Years centre, Ashdown Lodge. Brontë is a busy and friendly place with the happiness and wellbeing of its pupils firmly at its heart. Our excellent academic curriculum is supported by enriching experiences in music, drama, art, outdoor education and sport. Our small class sizes allow us to focus on individuals and to instil a love of learning in each and every pupil. Children automatically transfer through to Woodhouse Grove at age 11.

Woodhouse Grove's holistic approach to education means that we offer a comprehensive range of co-curricular activities to run alongside our academic curriculum. Woodhouse Grove has a proud sporting heritage and we aim to nurture a love of sport in all of our students regardless of ability. Significant numbers of Grovians gain district, county, regional and international honours and pursue sporting careers at leading universities, professional sports clubs and scholarship opportunities in the USA.

We also have an extensive music and drama programme involving 30% of all pupils at the school, across a wide variety of clubs. School productions are held in our fully equipped theatre, offering both on stage and technical backstage opportunities to students from all age groups.

The diversity and richness of boarding at Woodhouse Grove School, coupled with our strong academic standards, attracts students from all over the world. Boarding is a thriving and integral part of our school life where students are enveloped in a caring family environment and are provided with stimulating and challenging experiences throughout the week and at weekends. They have access to all the school facilities as well as the chance to participate in specific boarding events, such as camping trips.

We welcome parents to visit Woodhouse Grove and Brontë House on our open days or at any time by prior arrangement. Dates and details are publicised on the school website or telephone for further information.

(Founded 1812)

Apperley Bridge, Bradford, West Yorkshire BD10 0NR UK

Tel: 0113 250 2477

Fax: 0113 250 5290

Email: amos.jl@woodhousegrove.co.uk

Website: www.woodhousegrove.co.uk

Headmaster: Mr James Lockwood MA

Appointed: 2016

School type: Coeducational Day & Boarding

Age range of pupils: 2–18

No. of pupils enrolled as at 01/09/2018: 1080

Fees per annum as at 01/09/2018:

Day: £9,000–£13,575

Full Boarding: £27,900–£28,020

Average class size: 20

Teacher/pupil ratio: 1:10

Scotland

Gordonstoun

As well as preparing students for exams, Gordonstoun prepares them for life.

The school's uniquely broad curriculum encourages every individual to fulfil their potential academically, but it does more than that. It encourages students to fulfil their potential as human beings. The school motto is 'Plus est en vous' – There is more in you. At Gordonstoun, this sense of possibility is presented to its students, every single day.

"It wasn't until we saw the curriculum and the schedule of what they would be doing each day that we truly understood the difference between Gordonstoun and other schools." Current parent.

Although Gordonstoun is within striking distance of two international airports, the school's remarkable location on a 200 acre woodland estate by the Moray Coast in the North of Scotland provides the background for its world beating outdoor education programme. Gordonstoun was the birth place of both the Outward Bound Movement and the Duke of Edinburgh's Award, and expeditions to the Scottish Highlands or sail training on the School's 80ft Sailboat are an integral part of the school's day to day life. Students gain invaluable experience in being both leaders and team players and in having compassion and understanding for their fellows – and of themselves. Their outlook is broadened, their ability to consider the needs of others developed, and they gain resilience – life skills which can only complement the school's commitment to, and realisation of, academic excellence.

Active engagement in service to the local community also comprises a core part of Gordonstoun's 'working week', further expanding the students' sense of personal and social responsibility and building self-esteem. From Year 11 each student commits to one of the school's twelve services. These range from the Fire Service and Coastguards to Community Service and Technical support.

Gordonstoun follows the English GCSE and A level curriculum. With a staff/pupil ratio of 1:7 and every student's progress carefully overseen by their tutor, they go on Universities, Colleges and Art Schools all over the world – from Oxford and Cambridge, to Central St Martins, MIT or the Northern School of Music – to study a diverse range of subjects, from Latin to aeronautical engineering, from physics to drama and performance.

The students at Gordonstoun inhabit a community which is both balanced and internationally dynamic. Pupils aged 7-18 live and learn alongside fellow students from across the social, cultural and geographical board. And because Gordonstoun is one of the few remaining full boarding schools, it has a seven day programme which ensures that students are happily integrated and engaged. It also affords the opportunity to make full use of the comprehensive facilities on offer – which include an expansive sports centre, a drama and dance centre and music studios.

The uniquely all-round education on offer at Gordonstoun provides its students with the chance to develop intellectually, emotionally, physically and spiritually because Gordonstoun understands that the broader the experience the broader the mind.

In the words of a current parent:
"I send my children to Gordonstoun because I want them to have an excellent academic education. But I want them to have more than that. I want them to enter the ever changing world with a sense of possibility and optimism about themselves and their options. Gordonstoun's uniquely broad curriculum gives them the best possible chance of achieving that."

(Founded 1934)

Elgin, Moray IV30 5RF UK

Tel: 01343 837829

Fax: 01343 837808

Email: admissions@gordonstoun.org.uk

Website: www.gordonstoun.org.uk

Principal: Ms Lisa Kerr BA

Appointed: 2017

School type: Coeducational Boarding & Day

Age range of pupils: 6–18

No. of pupils enrolled as at 01/09/2018: 530

Boys: 310 **Girls:** 220 **Sixth Form:** 210

Senior: 420

No. of boarders: 390

Fees per annum as at 01/09/2018:

Day: £14,361 (Junior School)–£28,365 (Sixth Form direct entry)

Weekly Boarding: £23,358 (Junior School only)

Full Boarding: £23,358 (Junior School)–£38,295 (Sixth Form direct entry)

Average class size: 12

Teacher/pupil ratio: 1:7

Lomond School

Lomond School is a co-educational independent school, for children aged 3 to 18 years. Positioned in the elegant suburb of Helensburgh, only 10 minutes from Loch Lomond and the Trossachs National Park, our location delivers the perfect mix of town and country with Glasgow International Airport only 30 minutes away and cities steeped in culture and history on our doorstep.

We make the most of our unique location by providing and encouraging participation in a wide range of opportunities for outdoor learning, sports, trips and activities.

At Lomond School we believe passionately that education should be about supporting our pupils to develop and grow, both academically and personally. Our young people leave school as rounded individuals with strong values, prepared to embark confidently and successfully on their life beyond Lomond. We uphold this commitment with six Guiding Principles which are delivered throughout our curriculum and co-curriculum. These include: Internationalism; Environmentalism; Adventure; Leadership; Lifelong Learning and Service.

Living at Lomond
Our boarding house, Burnbrae, adds a distinctive dimension to the school; the mix of cultures and backgrounds enriches our curriculum and co-curriculum, supporting all of our pupils to develop their global awareness. Our experienced pastoral care team ensures the welfare and onward progression of all of our pupils. Our young people are well known by staff and teachers, and we see ourselves as a large family where any issues or problems are identified and dealt with promptly and effectively.

For our boarders, home is a short walk from the main school building, in a quiet residential area of Helensburgh. This is key to the formation of friendships outwith boarding, as it means that day pupils can visit their friends at Burnbrae and boarders, with parental permission, can visit their friends who are day pupils at the school with ease. The co-educational aspect allows siblings to live together under the same roof and further engenders a family atmosphere in the house. Boarders at Lomond live a full and exciting life in a safe and supportive environment.

Extra-curricular and Outdoor Learning
The Duke of Edinburgh Award is, without doubt, a significant feature and we have enjoyed great success carrying out expeditions both locally and abroad.

Many of our school trips and excursions revolve around our passion for the outdoors and have included trekking in Morocco, canoeing in Norway and skiing in Austria. We also build many cultural and educational trips into the school year with visits to Paris, Berlin, Brussels and Iceland, as well as Hockey and Rugby tours to South Africa or more locally. We support and encourage our young people to make the most of the opportunities available, recognising both the immediate and long-term benefits of the personal development these experiences and activities can offer.

A great place to live and learn
At Lomond, our pupils enjoy a fantastic lifestyle where a culture of hard work exists and is complimented by a sense of fun and adventure. Whether pupils stay for one term or complete their whole education at Lomond, our young people leave with a strong sense of achievement and an appetite for lifelong learning.

(Founded 1977)
10 Stafford Street, Helensburgh,
Argyll & Bute G84 9JX UK
Tel: +44 (0)1436 672476
Fax: +44 (0)1436 678320
Email: admissions@lomondschool.com
Website: www.lomondschool.com
Principal: Mrs Johanna Urquhart
School type: Co-educational Day & Boarding
Age range of pupils: 3–18
No. of pupils enrolled as at 01/09/2018: 360
No. of boarders: 40
Fees per annum as at 01/09/2018:
Day: £8,640–£11,970
Full Boarding: £27,750
Weekly and Flexi-Boarding available on request

Strathallan School

Harry Riley founded Strathallan in 1913 with the ambition of creating a school where there would be opportunities for every pupil to excel and perform to the very best of their abilities, and that vision is one we hold true today.

No matter what a pupil's passion or interest, they are supported and inspired to shine during their time at Strathallan. Consequently, our pupils achieve brilliant things. They excel academically, compete in sports at national and international levels, succeed in scholastic championships, perform on national stages and play as part of nationwide orchestras and ensembles.

Core to our ethos, however, is inclusion. All pupils represent the School in team sports under the age of 15 and participation in sports right through to Sixth Form is extremely high. There are opportunities for everyone to get involved with music and drama, whether it be performing on stage or working as backstage crew on our School productions. Other pupils take on responsibilities such as becoming a Peer Mentor or Head of House, volunteering in the local community or teaching younger children in the Junior School, Riley House.

Any parent choosing Strathallan will quickly realise that their child will be known here – for who they are, for their individual abilities and for their potential.

Academic excellence

Our flexible curriculum and innovative teaching means we can support every pupil, whatever their ambitions and style of learning. Strathallan offer's GCSE's, Scottish Higher's and A Levels giving our students the flexibility to ensure they leave Strathallan with the academic qualifications required to propel them into their chosen career.

As the top Scottish co-ed boarding school for A Level results in 2017, we constantly achieve superb academic results. Our pupils perform exceptionally well across many different disciplines, achieving excellent results in public examinations.

Our pupils go on to Oxbridge and Russell Group universities, international study, work placements, professional sporting careers or even start their own business.

Pastoral Care

We believe that the supportive nature of the whole Strathallan community and house system provide a pastoral care programme which gives pupils the confidence to pursue their academic studies with vigour and enthusiasm, leading them to achieve the highest results

An all round education

One of the things that sets Strathallan apart is the scale of what's on offer outside the classroom. We offer over 80 different activity options – some are linked to academic departments, some are sports, while others are purely recreational. Our extensive onsite facilities also help to foster a sense of community and mutual ambition. There's something for everyone and we're always looking for initiatives to give our pupils new experiences.

Global outlook

Although we enjoy the advantages of a self-contained, rural location, we're an international community and welcome young people from around the globe. This diversity of experience gives our pupils the maturity and cultural intelligence to go out into the world and succeed, as well as enjoying a worldwide network of friends.

(Founded 1913)

Forgandenny, Perth, Perth & Kinross PH2 9EG UK

Tel: 01738 812546

Fax: 01738 812549

Email: admissions@strathallan.co.uk

Website: www.strathallan.co.uk

Headmaster: Mr Mark Lauder MA Hons

Appointed: 2017

School type: Coeducational Boarding & Day

Age range of pupils: 9–18

Average class size: 14

Teacher/pupil ratio: 1:7

Wales

Llandovery College

MAKING A DIFFERENCE TO YOUR CHILD'S FUTURE

What Makes Llandovery College Special?

Llandovery College offers excellent facilities, first class teaching in small class sizes and a wide range of opportunities for intellectual, social and physical development. Our broad ability and inclusive school ensures that the learning needs of each pupil are catered for enabling them to reach and exceed their individual potential.

A Llandovery College education stands apart in the values and attitudes it engenders in its young men and women. Compassion, tolerance, kindness, integrity, generosity of spirit and good citizenship underpin a dedication to academic excellence.

Stunning Setting and Strong Sense of Community

Set within 45 acres of beautiful grounds in the picturesque Towy Valley there is a tangible sense of community and common purpose within the College. The House system brings boarders and day pupils together, promoting a strong sense of belonging and loyalty whilst forging deep bonds of friendship. Our pupils are well known by teachers and staff and we consider ourselves one large family.

Academic Success

The College boasts an enviable university entrance record with Oxbridge successes and a high proportion of pupils moving on to Russell Group universities. In addition, our pupils achieve an exceptionally high rate of acceptance to their first choice university.

Outstanding Opportunities

The College is renowned for its outstanding rugby heritage and achievements, producing world class rugby players such as Internationals and British & Irish Lions George North and Alun Wyn Jones.

The College's passion for sport is unrivalled and pupils have competed at regional, national and international levels in no less than 17 sports. Facilities include a 9 hole golf course, fully equipped gym and extensive pitches.

Music and the performing arts also have an enviable reputation with the orchestra and choir performing to an exceptionally high standard both at home and overseas.

Co-Curricular Activities

An extensive co-curricular programme offers pupils the opportunity to explore new interests as well as develop expertise in existing passions. The College has a thriving Combined Cadet Force and one of the highest Duke of Edinburgh's Award Scheme achievement rates with almost every pupil working towards bronze, silver or gold awards.

Scholarships

Academic and special talent scholarships are available from Year 7 onwards.

"The pupils achieve excellent levels of personal development, feeling secure, safe and valued in the friendly, mutually trusting ethos which prevails throughout the school" – **ISI Report**

Contact

For more information or to visit Llandovery College please contact the Admissions Registrar Mrs Vicky Douch on 01550 723005 or admissions@llandoverycollege.com

Llandovery College

(Founded 1847)

Queensway, Llandovery, Carmarthenshire SA20 0EE UK

Tel: +44 (0)1550 723005

Email: admissions@llandoverycollege.com

Website: www.llandoverycollege.com

Warden: Guy Ayling MA

Appointed: April 2012

School type: Co-educational Boarding & Day

Religious Denomination: Church in Wales

Age range of pupils: 4–18 years

No. of pupils enrolled as at 01/09/2018: 280

No. of boarders: 120

Fees per annum as at 01/09/2018:

Day: £5,985–£17,520

Full Boarding: £17,880–£26,460

Average class size: 10

Teacher/pupil ratio: 1:8

Overseas

École Jeannine Manuel – Lille

École Jeannine Manuel Lille is a non-profit pre-K-12 coeducational school founded in 1992. As the sister school of École Jeannine Manuel Paris, they have the same educational project and the same mission: develop international understanding through bilingual (French/English) education. An associated UNESCO school, École Jeannine Manuel Lille is the only non-denominational independent school in Nord-Pas-de-Calais, with over 800 pupils representing 40 nationalities and every major cultural tradition. The school's academic excellence matches its diversity: École Jeannine Manuel Lille achieves excellent performances, both at the French Baccalaureate and the International Baccalaureate. The school is accredited by the French Ministry of Education, the International Baccalaureate Organization (IBO), the Council of International Schools (CIS) and the New England Association of Schools and Colleges (NEASC).

The campus of school extends over 3.5 hectares and includes a boarding house, a restaurant, two football fields, a multi-sport room, and high standard sports facilities and equipment. The boarding house welcomes this year 111 pupils from 6th to 12th grades.

Each year, École Jeannine Manuel Lille welcomes non-French speaking students. Over the years École Jeannine Manuel has developed a program to suit the needs of these students, for whom the emotional challenge of relocation is often as great than its academic challenge. Thanks to their French teachers and their methods, the students will be fluent in French in a few months.

The lower and middle school follow the French national curriculum with several exceptions: English is taught every day and, in middle school, experimental sciences, history and geography are taught in English. The curriculum is enriched at all levels, not only with a more advanced English language and literature curriculum, but also, for example,

with Chinese language instruction (compulsory in grades 3-4-5), an integrated science programme in lower school, and independent research projects in middle school.

In upper school, 10th graders follow the French national curriculum, albeit taught 50% in French and 50% in English. In 11th grade, pupils choose between the French track (international option of the French baccalaureate (OIB)) and the International Baccalaureate Diploma Programme (IBDP). Approximately 25% of our pupils opt for the IBDP. (Please note that, since the IBDP does not receive any government subsidies, its tuition is three times the French track tuition.)

Admission

Although admission is competitive, every effort is made to reserve space for international applicants, including children of families who expect to remain in France for a limited period of time and wish to combine a cultural immersion in French education with the ability to re-enter their own school systems and excel.

International understanding through a bilingual education

(Founded 1954)

418 bis rue Albert Bailly, Marcq-en-Baroeul, 59700 France

Tel: +33 3 20 65 90 50

Fax: +33 3 20 98 06 41

Email: admissions-lille@ejm.net

Website: www.ecolejeanninemanuel.org

Head of School: Jérôme Giovendo

School type: Coeducational Day & Boarding

Age range of pupils: 4–18 years

No. of pupils enrolled as at 01/09/2018: 870

Fees per annum as at 01/09/2018:

Day: €4,977

Full Boarding: €13,695–€20,795

IB Classes: €17,485

Average class size: 25 (15 in IBDP)

École Jeannine Manuel – Paris

École Jeannine Manuel is a non-profit pre-K-12 coeducational school founded in 1954 with the mission to develop international understanding through bilingual (French/English) education. An associated UNESCO school, École Jeannine Manuel welcomes pupils representing 80 nationalities and every major cultural tradition. The school's academic excellence matches its diversity: École Jeannine Manuel is regularly ranked among the top French high schools (state and independent) for its overall academic performance (ranked first for six consecutive years). The school is accredited by the French Ministry of Education, the International Baccalaureate Organization (IBO), the Council of International Schools (CIS) and the New England Association of Schools and Colleges (NEASC).

Each year, École Jeannine Manuel welcomes more than one hundred new non-French speaking pupils who enroll in 'adaptation' classes where they follow a French immersion programme. A senior advisor follows them closely and, the following year, they join the mainstream where they continue to be supported with a special French programme involving three additional weekly hours of special French classes.

The lower and middle school follow the French national curriculum with several exceptions: English is taught every day and, in middle school, experimental sciences, history and geography are taught in English. The curriculum is enriched at all levels, not only with a more advanced English language and literature curriculum, but also, for example, with Chinese language instruction (compulsory in grades 3-4-5), an integrated science programme in lower school, and independent research projects in middle school.

In upper school, 10th graders follow the French national curriculum, albeit taught 50% in French and 50% in English. In 11th grade, pupils choose between the French track (international option of the French baccalaureate (OIB))

and the International Baccalaureate Diploma Programme (IBDP). Approximately 25% of our pupils opt for the IBDP. (Please note that, since the IBDP does not receive any government subsidies, its tuition is three times the French track tuition.)

Over the past three years, approximately 20% of our graduating class have gone to US colleges or universities, 48% chose the UK or Canada, 37% entered the French higher education system, and the balance pursued their education all over the world.

Admission

Although admission is competitive and applications typically exceed available spaces by a ratio of 7:1, every effort is made to reserve space for international applicants, including children of families who expect to remain in France for a limited period of time and wish to combine a cultural immersion in French education with the ability to re-enter their own school systems and excel.

(Founded 1954)

70 rue du Théâtre, Paris, 75015 France

Tel: +33 1 44 37 00 80

Fax: +33 1 45 79 06 66

Email: admissions@ejm.net

Website: www.ecolejeanninemanuel.org

Principal: Elisabeth Zéboulon

School type: Coeducational Day

Age range of pupils: 4–18 years

No. of pupils enrolled as at 01/09/2018: 2380

Fees per annum as at 01/09/2018:

Day: €6,117–€6,447

IB Classes: €20,385

Average class size:
25 (15 in adaptation classes and IBDP)

EF Academy New York

EF Academy International Boarding Schools prepares students for a global future with a superior secondary school education in the US or UK. At EF Academy, we believe in every student's ability to succeed. We empower them to do so through our renowned curricula, as well as quality one-on-one relationships with teachers and mentors alike. Built into every course is an emphasis on multilingualism and intercultural exchange, which helps distinguish our students' academic credentials to both university admissions officers and future employers.

The School

Our private boarding school, which attracts students from 75 countries around the world, is located in upper New York State, approximately 40 minutes away from Manhattan. EF Academy's secure campus offers 100 acres of landscaped grounds, running trails and playing fields in the quiet suburban town of Thornwood. Theater students step into the spotlight in our beautiful auditorium where full-length plays are staged twice a year. Science labs equipped with state-of-the-art equipment and welcoming art studios not only enrich classwork, they also host science and art clubs after school and are available for students to use for independent study. Our students often complete their school day with physical activity in our fully equipped gym, dance studio, basketball court or off-road biking trails.

Students live in comfortable and secure on-campus dormitory accommodation. House parents and teachers provide support and mentorship around the clock, and ensure a safe "home away from home."

Academics

EF Academy New York is a four-year high school. Students can follow the IGCSE program in their first two years and the IB Diploma program in the last two years. Alternatively, students can enroll in the US High School Diploma at any point in grades 9 through 10. Those who successfully complete their high school studies at EF Academy New York are awarded a nationally recognized New York State High School Diploma in addition to the other qualifications they earn.

Instruction and guidance at EF Academy New York is highly personal. Students engage in interactive lessons in small classes led by inspiring teachers and they benefit from the individualized support they receive from dedicated counselors and university advisors who help them achieve their goals.

University Placement

EF Academy New York graduates have been accepted to top-ranked universities such as Harvard, Columbia University, University of Pennsylvania, High Point University and Rochester Institute of Technology, and other premiere business and engineering schools as well. Dedicated university guidance counselors work with students on a one-on-one basis to help them with everything from researching universities and writing college essays, to selecting a major that falls in line with their career goals. Students at EF Academy New York apply to universities in the US as well as in the UK and in their home countries.

Co-curricular Activities

Universities look for well-rounded students who extend their learning beyond the classroom. Students at EF Academy New York have access to a wide range of co-curricular activities. From subject-specific academic groups and competitions to club and varsity sports, there is an option for every student. The school's activities coordinator also arranges teacher-led excursions for students on the weekends so they have many opportunities to explore Manhattan and the museums, musicals and sights the city is known for.

INTERNATIONAL
BOARDING SCHOOLS

582 Columbus Avenue, Thornwood, NY 10594 USA

Tel: +1 914 495 6028

Email: iaadmissionsny@ef.com

Website: www.ef.edu/academy

Head of School: Mr. George Stewart

School type: Coeducational Day & Boarding

Age range of pupils: 13–19

No. of pupils enrolled as at 01/09/2018: 800

Fees per annum as at 01/09/2018:

Grades 9 & 10 (IGCSE, US High School Diploma): US$35,250

Grades 11 & 12: (IB, US High School Diploma): US$41,000

Geographical directory of schools

Channel Islands

Jersey D296

Guernsey

Elizabeth College
The Grange, St Peter Port,
Guernsey GY1 2PY
Tel: 01481 726544
Principal: Elizabeth Palmer
Age range: B11–18
No. of pupils: 500
Fees: Day £11,995
Ⓐ £ ✎ 16•

Elizabeth College Junior School
Beechwood, Queen's Road, St
Peter Port, Guernsey GY1 1PU
Tel: 01481 722123
Headteacher: Richard Fyfe
Age range: 2½–11
No. of pupils: 270
Fees: Day £10,350–£11,370
✎

The Ladies' College
Les Gravees, St Peter Port,
Guernsey GY1 1RW
Tel: 01481 721602
Principal: Ashley Clancy
Age range: G2½–18
No. of pupils: 600 VIth100
Fees: Day £10,560–£11,175
Ⓐ 16•

Jersey

Beaulieu Convent School
Wellington Road, St Helier,
Jersey JE2 4RJ
Tel: 01534 731280
Headmaster: Mr C Beirne
Age range: G4–18
No. of pupils: 762 VIth127
Fees: Day £5,835
Ⓐ £ ✎ 16•

De La Salle College
Wellington Road, St Saviour,
Jersey JE2 7TH
Tel: 01534 754100
Head of College: Mr Jason Turner
Age range: 3–18
No. of pupils: 762
Fees: Day £5,805
Ⓐ 16•

FCJ Primary School
Deloraine Road, St Saviour,
Jersey JE2 7XB
Tel: 01534 723063
Headmistress: Ms Donna Lenzi
Age range: 4–11
No. of pupils: 290
Fees: Day £4,440
✎

Helvetia House School
14 Elizabeth Place, St
Helier, Jersey JE2 3PN
Tel: 01534 724928
Headmistress: Mrs Lindsey
Woodward BA, DipEd
Age range: G4–11
No. of pupils: 82
Fees: Day £4,725

Jersey College For Girls
Le Mont Millais, St Saviour,
Jersey JE2 7YB
Tel: 01534 516200

ST GEORGE'S PREPARATORY SCHOOL
For further details see p. 46
La Hague Manor, Rue de la
Hague, St Peter, Jersey JE3 7DB
Tel: 01534 481593
Email: admin@stgeorgesprep.co.uk
Website: www.stgeorgesprep.co.uk
Headmaster: Mr Cormac Timothy
Age range: 2–11
No. of pupils: 210
Fees: Day £5,265–£14,460
£ ✎

ST MICHAEL'S PREPARATORY SCHOOL
For further details see p. 48
La Rue de la Houguette, St
Saviour, Jersey JE2 7UG
Tel: 01534 856904
Email: office@stmichaels.je
Website: www.stmichaels.je
Age range: 3–14
No. of pupils: 328
Fees: Day £9,750–£15,060
£ ✎

Victoria College
Le Mont Millais, St Helier, Jersey JE1 4HT
Tel: 01534 638200
Headmaster: Mr Alun Watkins
Age range: B11–18
No. of pupils: 720 VIth200
Fees: Day £5,310
Ⓐ £ ✎ 16•

Victoria College Preparatory School
Pleasant Street, St Helier, Jersey JE2 4RR
Tel: 01534 723468
Headmaster: Dan Pateman BA (Hons)
Age range: B7–11
No. of pupils: 300
Fees: Day £5,268
✎

Central & West

KEY TO SYMBOLS

- ♂ *Boys' school*
- ♀ *Girls' school*
- 🌐 *International school*
- 16 *Tutorial or sixth form college*
- Ⓐ *A levels*
- ⚓ *Boarding accommodation*
- £ *Bursaries*
- IB *International Baccalaureate*
- ✎ *Learning support*
- 16 *Entrance at 16+*
- *Vocational qualifications*
- (IAPS) *Independent Association of Preparatory Schools*
- (HMC) *The Headmasters' & Headmistresses' Conference*
- (ISA) *Independent Schools Association*
- (GSA) *Girls' School Association*
- (BSA) *Boarding Schools' Association*
- Ⓢ *Society of Heads*

Unless otherwise indicated, all schools are coeducational day schools. Single-sex and boarding schools will be indicated by the relevant icon.

Bath & North-East Somerset

Bath Academy
27 Queen Square, Bath, Bath &
North-East Somerset BA1 2HX
Tel: 01225 334577
Principal: Tim Naylor
BA(Hons), MSc, PGCE
Age range: 14–19+
No. of pupils: 120
Fees: Day £23,700 FB £35,000
🏉 16• Ⓐ 🏛 16•

Downside School
Stratton-on-the-Fosse, Radstock, Bath,
Bath & North-East Somerset BA3 4RJ
Tel: 01761 235103
Head Master: Andrew Hobbs
Age range: 11–18
No. of pupils: 350 VIth135
Fees: Day £16,242–£19,251
FB £25,236–£33,861
🏉 Ⓐ 🏛 £ 🖉 16•

King Edward's Junior School
North Road, Bath, Bath & North-
East Somerset BA2 6JA
Tel: 01225 464218
Head: Mr Greg Taylor
Age range: 7–11
No. of pupils: 182
Fees: Day £11,250
🖉

**King Edward's Pre-Prep
& Nursery School**
Weston Lane, Bath, Bath & North-
East Somerset BA1 4AQ
Tel: 01225 421681
Head: Ms. Jayne Gilbert
Age range: 3–7
No. of pupils: 107
Fees: Day £8,370–£10,155

King Edward's Senior School
North Road, Bath, Bath & North-
East Somerset BA2 6HU
Tel: 01225 464313
Head: Mr MJ Boden MA
Age range: 11–18
No. of pupils: 1085
Ⓐ £ 🖉 16•

Kingswood Preparatory School
College Road, Lansdown, Bath, Bath
& North-East Somerset BA1 5SD
Tel: 01225 734460
Headmaster: Mr Mark Breary
Age range: 9 months–11
No. of pupils: 335
Fees: Day £10,002–£11,973 WB
£19,809 FB £23,583–£24,720

Kingswood School
Lansdown Lane, Bath, Bath &
North-East Somerset BA1 5RG
Tel: 01225 734200
Age range: 9 months–11
(Prep)–11–18 (Senior)
No. of pupils: 642 VIth189
Fees: Day £15,183 WB £23,868–
£29,568 FB £28,459–£32,727
🏉 Ⓐ 🏛 £ 🖉 16•

MONKTON PREP SCHOOL
For further details see p. 60
Church Road, Combe Down, Bath,
Bath & North-East Somerset BA2 7ET
Tel: +44 (0)1225 837912
Headmaster: Mr M Davis
Age range: 7–13 (boarding from 8)
No. of pupils: 220
🏛 £ 🖉

MONKTON SENIOR SCHOOL
For further details see p. 60
Monkton Combe, Bath, Bath &
North-East Somerset BA2 7HG
Tel: 01225 721133
Email: admissions@monkton.org.uk
Website:
www.monktoncombeschool.com
Principal: Mr Chris Wheeler
Age range: 11–18
🏉 Ⓐ 🏛 £ 🖉 16•

Prior Park College
Ralph Allen Drive, Bath, Bath &
North-East Somerset BA2 5AH
Tel: 01225 831000
Head: Mr James Murphy-O'Connor
Age range: 11–18
No. of pupils: 580 VIth180
Fees: Day £15,000–£16,995 WB
£20,745–£25,500 FB £23,505–£32,100
🏉 Ⓐ 🏛 £ 🖉 16•

The Paragon School
Lyncombe House, Lyncombe
Vale, Bath, Bath & North-
East Somerset BA2 4LT
Tel: 01225 310837
Headmaster: Mr Andrew Harvey
Age range: 3–11
No. of pupils: 252
Fees: Day £8,745–£10,245
£ 🖉

The Royal High School, Bath GDST
Lansdown Road, Bath, Bath &
North-East Somerset BA1 5SZ
Tel: +44 (0)1225 313877
Head: Mrs Jo Duncan BA, MA
Age range: G3–18
No. of pupils: 640
Fees: Day £3,315–£4,700 WB
£8,760–£9,257 FB £9,797–£10,298
🏃 🏉 Ⓐ 🏛 £ ⒾⒷ 🖉 16•

Bristol

Badminton Junior School
Westbury-on-Trym, Bristol BS9 3BA
Tel: 0117 905 5200
Head of the Junior School: Mrs E Davies
Age range: G3–11
No. of pupils: 130
Fees: Day £9,750–£11,235
FB £21,840–£24,945
🏃 Ⓐ 🏛 £ 🖉

Badminton School
Westbury-on-Trym, Bristol BS9 3BA
Tel: 0117 905 5271
Headmistress: Mrs Rebecca
Tear BSc, MA, PGCE
Age range: G3–18
No. of pupils: 450
Fees: Day £9,750–£16,425
FB £21,840–£37,575
🏃 🏉 Ⓐ 🏛 £ 🖉 16•

Bristol Grammar School
University Road, Bristol BS8 1SR
Tel: 0117 973 6006
Headmaster: R I Mackinnon
Age range: 4–18
🏉 Ⓐ 🏛 ⒾⒷ 🖉 16•

Bristol Steiner School
Redland Hill House, Redland,
Bristol BS6 6UX
Tel: 0117 933 9990
Age range: 3–11
No. of pupils: 213
Fees: Day £7,977

Carmel Christian School
817A Bath Road, Brislington,
Bristol BS4 5NL
Tel: 0117 977 5533
Headteacher: Jaap Van Wyk
Age range: 3–16
No. of pupils: 28
Fees: Day £1,440–£2,580

Cleve House School
254 Wells Road, Knowle, Bristol BS4 2PN
Tel: 0117 9777218
Headmaster: Mr Craig Wardle
Age range: 2–11
No. of pupils: 90
Fees: Day £6,525
🖉

Clifton College
32 College Road, Clifton, Bristol BS8 3JH
Tel: 0117 315 7000
Headmaster: Dr Tim Greene
Age range: 3–18
No. of pupils: 1330 VIth280
Fees: Day £10,020–£25,590 WB
£16,305–£34,200 FB £24,180–£39,405
🏉 Ⓐ 🏛 £ 🖉 16•

**Clifton College
Preparatory School**
The Avenue, Clifton, Bristol BS8 3HE
Tel: +44 (0)117 405 8396
**Head of Preparatory
School:** Mr Jim Walton
Age range: 2–13
No. of pupils: 495
Fees: Day £10,020–£17,460 WB
£16,305–£20,565 FB £24,180–£28,650
🏛 £ 🖉

Clifton High School
College Road, Clifton, Bristol BS8 3JD
Tel: 0117 973 0201
Head: Dr Alison M Neill BSc, PhD, PGCE
Age range: 3–18
No. of pupils: 527
Fees: Day £8,895–£14,985 FB £19,605
Ⓐ 🏛 £ 🖉 16•

Clifton Tutors Limited
31 Pembroke Road, Clifton,
Bristol BS8 3BE
Tel: 0117 973 8376
Director of Studies: Sue Morgan
Age range: 7–19
16• Ⓐ

Colston's School
Stapleton, Bristol BS16 1BJ
Tel: 0117 965 5207
Headmaster: Jeremy McCullough
Age range: 3–18
No. of pupils: 581 VIth138
Fees: Day £7,680–£13,950
🌐Ⓐ🏛️£🖋️16️⃣

Ecole Française de Bristol
Fonthill Centre, Stanton Road,
Southmead, Bristol BS10 5SJ
Tel: +44 (0) 117 9692410
Headmistress: Mathilde Monnet
Age range: 2–11
🌐

Fairfield School
Fairfield Way, Backwell, Bristol BS48 3PD
Tel: 01275 462743
Headmistress: Mrs Lesley Barton
Age range: 2–11
No. of pupils: 136
Fees: Day £7,650–£8,445
£🖋️

Gracefield Preparatory School
266 Overndale Road,
Fishponds, Bristol BS16 2RG
Tel: 0117 956 7977
Headmistress: Mrs E Morgan
Age range: 4–11
No. of pupils: 90
Fees: Day £5,382
🖋️

Queen Elizabeth's Hospital
Berkeley Place, Clifton, Bristol BS8 1JX
Tel: 0117 930 3040
Head: Mr Stephen Holliday
MA (Cantab)
Age range: B7–18 G16–18
No. of pupils: 688
Fees: Day £9,654–£14,406
🧍Ⓐ£🖋️16️⃣

Silverhill School
Swan Lane, Winterbourne,
Bristol BS36 1RL
Tel: 01454 772156
Principal: Mr Julian Capper
Age range: 2–11
No. of pupils: 185
Fees: Day £5,130–£9,150
🖋️

The Downs School
Wraxall, Bristol BS48 1PF
Tel: 01275 852008
Head: M A Gunn MA(Ed), BA, PGCE
Age range: 4–13
No. of pupils: 262
£

The Red Maids' Junior School
Grange Court Road, Westbury-
on-Trym, Bristol BS9 4DP
Tel: 0117 962 9451
Headteacher: Mrs Lisa
Brown BSc (Hons)
Age range: B3–7 G3–11
Fees: Day £3,135
🧍🖋️

The Red Maids' Senior School
Westbury Road, Westbury-
on-Trym, Bristol BS9 3AW
Tel: +44 (0)117 962 2641
Headmistress: Mrs Isabel
Tobias BA (Hons)
Age range: G11–18
🧍🌐Ⓐ£🆔16️⃣

Tockington Manor School
Washingpool Hill Road,
Tockington, Bristol BS32 4NY
Tel: 01454 613229
Headmaster: Mr Stephen Symonds
Age range: 2–14
No. of pupils: 250
Fees: Day £9,333–£14,553 FB £21,045
🏛️£🖋️

Torwood House School
8, 27-29 Durdham Park,
Redland, Bristol BS6 6XE
Tel: 0117 9735620
Headmistress: Mrs D Seagrove
Age range: 0–11
No. of pupils: 70
Fees: Day £7,500–£7,800
£🖋️

Buckinghamshire

Akeley Wood School
Akeley Wood, Buckingham,
Buckinghamshire MK18 5AE
Tel: 01280 814110
Headmaster: Dr Jerry Grundy BA, PhD
Age range: 12 months–18 years
No. of pupils: 833 VIth119
Fees: Day £7,185–£10,575
Ⓐ£🖋️16️⃣

Ashfold School
Dorton House, Dorton, Aylesbury,
Buckinghamshire HP18 9NG
Tel: 01844 238237
Headmaster: Mr Michael Chitty BSc
Age range: 3–13
No. of pupils: 280 VIth28
Fees: Day £9,525–£16,845 WB £20,190
🏛️£🖋️

**Broughton Manor
Preparatory School**
Newport Road, Broughton, Milton
Keynes, Buckinghamshire MK10 9AA
Tel: 01908 665234
Headmaster: Mr James Canwell
Age range: 2 months–11 years
No. of pupils: 250
Fees: Day £13,980
£

Caldicott
Crown Lane, Farnham Royal,
Buckinghamshire SL2 3SL
Tel: 01753 649301
Headmaster: Mr Jeremy Banks MEd
Age range: B7–13
No. of pupils: 275
Fees: Day £16,833–£18,780
FB £24,918–£27,687
🧍🌐£🖋️

Chesham Preparatory School
Two Dells Lane, Chesham,
Buckinghamshire HP5 3QF
Tel: 01494 782619
Headteacher: Hilary Rudol
Age range: 3–13
No. of pupils: 392
Fees: Day £9,270–£14,400
🖋️

Childfirst Day Nursery Aylesbury
Green End, off Rickford's Hill, Aylesbury,
Buckinghamshire HP20 2SA
Tel: 01296 392516
Registrar: Mrs Carole Angood
Age range: 2 months–7 years
No. of pupils: 80
Fees: Day £6,276

Childfirst Pre School Aylesbury
35 Rickfords Hill, Aylesbury,
Buckinghamshire HP20 2RT
Tel: 01296 433224

Crown House School
19 London Road, High Wycombe,
Buckinghamshire HP11 1BJ
Tel: 01494 529927
Headmaster: Ben Kenyon
Age range: 3–11
No. of pupils: 120
Fees: Day £9,005–£10,185
🖋️

Dair House School
Bishops Blake, Beaconsfield
Road, Farnham Royal,
Buckinghamshire SL2 3BY
Tel: 01753 643964
Headmaster: Mr Terry Wintle BEd(Hons)
Age range: 3–11
No. of pupils: 125
Fees: Day £3,425–£4,345
£🖋️

Davenies School
Station Road, Beaconsfield,
Buckinghamshire HP9 1AA
Tel: 01494 685400
Headmaster: Mr Carl
Rycroft BEd (Hons)
Age range: B4–13
No. of pupils: 335
Fees: Day £11,985–£16,800

Filgrave School
Filgrave Village, Newport
Pagnell, Milton Keynes,
Buckinghamshire MK16 9ET
Tel: 01234 711534
Headteacher: Mrs H Schofield
BA(Hons), MA, PGCE
Age range: 2–7
No. of pupils: 27
Fees: Day £5,160

**Focus School – Stoke
Poges Campus**
School Lane, Stoke Poges,
Buckinghamshire SL2 4QA
Tel: 01753 662167
Headteacher: Mr Connery Wiltshire
Age range: 11–16
No. of pupils: 120

Gateway School
1 High Street, Great Missenden,
Buckinghamshire HP16 9AA
Tel: 01494 862407
Headteacher: Mrs Sue
LaFarge BA(Hons), PGCE
Age range: 2–11
No. of pupils: 355
Fees: Day £2,235–£11,175

Godstowe Preparatory School
Shrubbery Road, High Wycombe,
Buckinghamshire HP13 6PR
Tel: 01494 529273
Headmistress: Sophie Green
Age range: B3–7 G3–13
No. of pupils: 409
Fees: Day £10,800–£16,620 FB £24,645

Griffin House School
Little Kimble, Aylesbury,
Buckinghamshire HP17 0XP
Tel: 01844 346154
Headmaster: Mr Tim Walford
Age range: 3–11
No. of pupils: 100
Fees: Day £8,238–£8,580

Heatherton House School
Copperkins Lane, Chesham Bois,
Amersham, Buckinghamshire HP6 5QB
Tel: 01494 726433
Headteacher: Mrs Debbie Isaachsen
Age range: B3–4 G3–11
Fees: Day £1,140–£13,335

High March School
23 Ledborough Lane, Beaconsfield,
Buckinghamshire HP9 2PZ
Tel: 01494 675186
Headmistress: Mrs S J Clifford
BEd (Oxon), MA (London)
Age range: B3–4 G3–11
No. of pupils: 307
Fees: Day £5,730–£14,805

Milton Keynes Preparatory School
Tattenhoe Lane, Milton Keynes,
Buckinghamshire MK3 7EG
Tel: 01908 642111
Heads of School: Mr C
Bates & Mr S Driver
Age range: 2 months–11 years
No. of pupils: 500
Fees: Day £4,560–£15,120

Pipers Corner School
Pipers Lane, Great Kingshill, High
Wycombe, Buckinghamshire HP15 6LP
Tel: 01494 718 255
Headmistress: Mrs H J Ness-
Gifford BA(Hons), PGCE
Age range: G4–18
No. of pupils: VIth72
Fees: Day £8,880–£18,390

**St Teresa's Catholic
School & Nursery**
Aylesbury Road, Princes Risborough,
Buckinghamshire HP27 0JW
Tel: 01844 345005
Joint Heads: Mrs Jane Draper
& Mrs Yasmin Roberts
Age range: 3–11
No. of pupils: 130
Fees: Day £8,985–£9,165

Stowe School
Buckingham, Buckinghamshire
MK18 5EH
Tel: 01280 818000
Headmaster: Dr Anthony Wallersteiner
Age range: 13–18
No. of pupils: 769 VIth318
Fees: Day £26,355 FB £36,660

Swanbourne House School
Swanbourne, Milton Keynes,
Buckinghamshire MK17 0HZ
Tel: 01296 720264
Head of School: Mrs Jane Thorpe
Age range: 3–13
No. of pupils: 323
Fees: Day £1,410–£18,360 FB £23,520

The Beacon School
Chesham Bois, Amersham,
Buckinghamshire HP6 5PF
Tel: 01494 433654
Headmaster: William Phelps
Age range: B3–13
No. of pupils: 470
Fees: Day £11,850–£17,250

**The Chalfonts Independent
Grammar School**
Newland Park, Gorelands
Lane, Chalfont St Giles,
Buckinghamshire HP8 4AD
Tel: +44 (0)1494 875502
Head of School: David Shandley
Age range: 11–18

The Grove Independent School
Redland Drive, Loughton, Milton
Keynes, Buckinghamshire MK5 8HD
Tel: 01908 690590
Principal: Mrs Deborah Berkin
Age range: 3 months–13 years
No. of pupils: 210

The Webber Independent School
Soskin Drive, Stantonbury Fields, Milton
Keynes, Buckinghamshire MK14 6DP
Tel: 01908 574740
Principal: Mrs Hilary Marsden
Age range: 3–18
No. of pupils: 300 VIth15
Fees: Day £9,030–£12,705

Thornton College
Thornton, Milton Keynes,
Buckinghamshire MK17 0HJ
Tel: 01280 812610
Headmistress: Mrs Jo Storey
Age range: B2–4 G2–16
No. of pupils: 370
Fees: Day £9,555–£15,240 WB
£16,320–£20,655 FB £20,295–£25,185

**Walton Pre-Preparatory
School & Nursery**
The Old Rectory, Walton Drive, Milton
Keynes, Buckinghamshire MK7 6BB
Tel: 01908 678403
Headmistress: Mrs Chantelle
McLaughlan
Age range: 2 months–5 years
No. of pupils: 120
Fees: Day £7,200–£14,280

Gloucestershire

Airthrie School
29 Christchurch Road, Cheltenham,
Gloucestershire GL50 2NY
Tel: 01242 512837
Headteacher: Mrs Sara Jackson
Age range: 3–11
No. of pupils: 168
Fees: Day £6,770–£9,930

**Al-Ashraf Secondary
School for Girls**
Sinope Street, off Widden Street,
Gloucester, Gloucestershire GL1 4AW
Tel: 01452 300465
Head: Mufti Abdullah Patel
Age range: G11–16
No. of pupils: 67
Fees: Day £1,325–£2,000

Beaudesert Park School
Minchinhampton, Stroud,
Gloucestershire GL6 9AF
Tel: 01453 832072
Headmaster: Mr J P R
Womersley BA, PGCE
Age range: 3–13
No. of pupils: 450
Fees: Day £5,745–£17,661 FB £22,677

Berkhampstead School
Pittville Circus Road, Cheltenham,
Gloucestershire GL52 2QA
Tel: 01242 523263
Head: R P Cross BSc(Hons)
Age range: 3–11
No. of pupils: 215
Fees: Day £2,397–£10,380

Bredon School
Pull Court, Bushley, Tewkesbury,
Gloucestershire GL20 6AH
Tel: 01684 293156
Head Teacher: Mr Koen Claeys
Age range: 7–18
No. of pupils: 215
Fees: Day £11,040–£21,945 WB
£15,440–£26,345 FB £15,440–£26,345

Cheltenham College
Bath Road, Cheltenham,
Gloucestershire GL53 7LD
Tel: 01242 265600
Headmaster: Nicola Huggett
Age range: 13–18
No. of pupils: 650 VIth270
Fees: Day £27,585–£28,575
FB £36,780–£37,770

Cheltenham College Preparatory School
Thirlestaine Road, Cheltenham,
Gloucestershire GL53 7AB
Tel: 01242 522697
Headmaster: Mr Tom O'Sullivan
Age range: 7–13
No. of pupils: 420
Fees: Day £11,985–£18,315
FB £18,255–£23,790

Cheltenham Ladies' College
Bayshill Road, Cheltenham,
Gloucestershire GL50 3EP
Tel: +44 (0)1242 520691
Principal: Eve Jardine-Young MA
Age range: G11–18
No. of pupils: 850 VIth305
Fees: Day £24,810–£28,230
FB £36,945–£41,610

Dean Close Pre-Preparatory & Preparatory School
Lansdown Road, Cheltenham,
Gloucestershire GL51 6QS
Tel: 01242 512217
Age range: 2+–13
No. of pupils: 292
Fees: Day £7,959–£18,750
FB £19,260–£25,365

Dean Close School
Shelburne Road, Cheltenham,
Gloucestershire GL51 6HE
Tel: 01242 258044
Headmaster: Mr Bradley
Salisbury MEd, PGCE
Age range: 13–18
No. of pupils: 490 VIth220
Fees: Day £23,316–£24,600
FB £34,455–£35,817

Dormer House School
High Street, Moreton-in-Marsh,
Gloucestershire GL56 0AD
Tel: 01608 650758
Headmistress: Mrs Alison Thomas
Age range: 2–11
Fees: Day £8,586

Eastbrook College
7a Eastbrook Education Trust,
Gloucester, Gloucestershire GL4 3DB
Tel: 01452 417722
Age range: 11–16
No. of pupils: 59

Focus School – Berkeley Campus
Wanswell, Berkeley,
Gloucestershire GL13 9RS
Tel: 01453 511282
Headteacher: Mrs Lucy Sherrin
Age range: 7–18
No. of pupils: 100

Gloucestershire International School
Wotton House, Horton Road,
Gloucester, Gloucestershire GL1 3PR
Tel: +44 (0) 1452 764248
Age range: 11–16
No. of pupils: 25

Hatherop Castle School
Hatherop, Cirencester,
Gloucestershire GL7 3NB
Tel: 01285 750206
Headmaster: Mr Nigel Reed
M.Ed, B.Sc (Hons), PGCE
Age range: 2–13
No. of pupils: 210
Fees: Day £6,285–£10,455
FB £15,270–£16,110

Hopelands Preparatory School
38 Regent Street, Stonehouse,
Gloucestershire GL10 2AD
Tel: 01453 822164
Headmistress: Mrs S Bradburn
Age range: 3–11
No. of pupils: 59
Fees: Day £6,288–£9,123

Kitebrook Preparatory School
Kitebrook House, Moreton-in-Marsh, Gloucestershire GL56 0RP
Tel: 01608 674350
Headmistress: Mrs Susan McLean
Age range: 3–13
No. of pupils: 180

Rendcomb College
Rendcomb, Cirencester,
Gloucestershire GL7 7HA
Tel: 01285 831213
Headmaster: Mr R Jones BA(Hons), MEd
Age range: 3–18
No. of pupils: 371 VIth54
Fees: Day £2,010–£7,775 WB
£7,470–£9,785 FB £8,190–£10,815

St Edward's Preparatory School
London Road, Charlton
Kings, Cheltenham,
Gloucestershire GL52 6NR
Tel: 01242 538900
Headmaster: Mr Stephen
McKernan BA(Hons) MEd NPQH
Age range: 1–11
No. of pupils: 295
Fees: Day £7,770–£12,975

St Edward's School
Cirencester Road, Cheltenham,
Gloucestershire GL53 8EY
Tel: 01242 538600
Head: Mrs P Clayfield BSc
Age range: 11–18
No. of pupils: 344 VIth105
Fees: Day £14,550–£17,760

The Acorn School
Church Street, Nailsworth,
Gloucestershire GL6 0BP
Tel: 01453 836508
Headmaster: Mr Graeme E B Whiting
Age range: 7–18
No. of pupils: VIth30
Fees: Day £6,675–£12,045

The King's School
Gloucester, Gloucestershire GL1 2BG
Tel: 01452 337337
Headmaster: David Morton
Age range: 3–18
No. of pupils: VIth80
Fees: Day £7,350–£19,185

The Richard Pate School
Southern Road, Cheltenham,
Gloucestershire GL53 9RP
Tel: 01242 522086
Headmaster: Mr Robert MacDonald
Age range: 3–11 years
No. of pupils: 300
Fees: Day £3,330–£10,410

Westonbirt Prep School
Westonbirt, Tetbury,
Gloucestershire GL8 8QG
Tel: 01666 881400
Headmaster: Mr Sean Price
Age range: 3–11
Fees: Day £2,680–£3,865

Westonbirt School
Westonbirt, Tetbury,
Gloucestershire GL8 8QG
Tel: 01666 881333
Headmistress: Mrs Natasha
Dangerfield
Age range: G11–18 years
Fees: Day £4,995 FB £9,750

Wycliffe Preparatory & Senior School
Bath Road, Stonehouse,
Gloucestershire GL10 2JQ
Tel: 01453 822432
Senior School Head: Mr
Nick Gregory BA, MEd
Age range: 2–18
No. of pupils: VIth178
Fees: Day £9,675–£20,985
FB £20,625–£38,115

Wynstones School
Whaddon Green, Gloucester,
Gloucestershire GL4 0UF
Tel: 01452 429220
Chair of the College of Teachers: Marianna Law-Lindberg
Age range: 3–18
No. of pupils: VIth9
Fees: Day £2,820–£9,540 FB £8,160

North Somerset

Ashbrooke House School
9 Ellenborough Park North, Weston-Super-Mare, North Somerset BS23 1XH
Tel: 01934 629515
Headteacher: Karen Wallington
Age range: 3–11
Fees: Day £5,535–£6,411
£ ✐

Sidcot School
Oakridge Lane, Winscombe,
North Somerset BS25 1PD
Tel: 01934 843102
Head: Iain Kilpatrick
Age range: 3–18
No. of pupils: 515 VIth170
Fees: Day £7,860–£17,640
FB £26,610–£31,830
🌐 A 🏛 £ IB ✐ 16⁺

Oxfordshire

Abacus College & Oxford Language Centre
Victory House, 116-120 London Road,
Headington, Oxfordshire OX3 9AX
Tel: +44 (0)1865 240111
Principal: Dr Paul Quinn
Age range: 13–19+
No. of pupils: VIth90
Fees: Day £12,500–£14,500
16⁺ A

Abingdon Preparatory School
Josca's House, Frilford, Abingdon,
Oxfordshire OX13 5NX
Tel: 01865 391570
Headmaster: Mr Craig Williams
Age range: B4–13
No. of pupils: B250
Fees: Day £12,090–£16,620
👤 🏛 ✐

Abingdon School
Park Road, Abingdon,
Oxfordshire OX14 1DE
Tel: 01235 521563
Head: Michael Windsor
Age range: B11–18
No. of pupils: 1000
Fees: Day £19,950 WB £33,210 FB £39,750
👤 🌐 A 🏛 £ 16⁺

Bloxham School
Bloxham, Banbury,
Oxfordshire OX15 4PE
Tel: 01295 720222 or 724301
Headmaster: Mr Paul Sanderson
Age range: 11–18
No. of pupils: 431
Fees: Day £17,985–£25,785 WB
£25,785 FB £33,675–£35,175
🌐 A 🏛 £ ✐ 16⁺

Burford School
Cheltenham Road, Burford,
Oxfordshire OX18 4PL
Tel: 01993 823303/823283
Headteacher: Mrs K Haig BA, MEd
Age range: 11–18
No. of pupils: 1156 VIth200
Fees: FB £9,900
A 🏛 £ ✐ 16⁺

Carfax College
25 Beaumont Street, Oxford,
Oxfordshire OX1 2NP
Tel: +44 1865 200 676
Principal: Dr Victoria Jefferson
🌐 A 🏛

Carrdus School
Overthorpe Hall, Banbury,
Oxfordshire OX17 2BS
Tel: 01295 263733
Head: Mr Edward Way
Age range: B3–8 G3–11
No. of pupils: 122
Fees: Day £735–£11,625
£ ✐

Chandlings
Bagley Wood, Kennington,
Oxford, Oxfordshire OX1 5ND
Tel: 01865 730771
Head: Christine Cook
Age range: 2–11
Fees: Day £10,110–£15,870
✐

Cherwell College
Cantay House, Park End Street,
Oxford, Oxfordshire OX1 1JD
Tel: 01865 242670
Principal: Stephen Clarke
Age range: 15+
No. of pupils: 100
Fees: Day £26,520 FB £13,600
16⁺ A 🏛 £ ✐

Childfirst Day Nursery Banbury
The Old Museum, 8 Horsefair,
Banbury, Oxfordshire OX16 0AA
Tel: 01295 273743

Childfirst Day Nursery Bicester
32 Launton Road, Bicester,
Oxfordshire OX26 6PY
Tel: 01869 323730
Headmistress: Miss J
Fowler BA(Hons), QTS
Age range: 2 months–7 years
Fees: Day £7,500

Christ Church Cathedral School
3 Brewer Street, Oxford,
Oxfordshire OX1 1QW
Tel: 01865 242561
Headmaster: Richard Murray
Age range: B3–13 G3–4
No. of pupils: 159
Fees: Day £5,667–£16,569 FB £7,560
👤 ✐

Cokethorpe School
Witney, Oxfordshire OX29 7PU
Tel: 01993 703921
Headmaster: Mr D Ettinger
BA, MA, PGCE
Age range: 4–18
No. of pupils: 666 VIth133
Fees: Day £12,600–£19,200
A £ ✐ 16⁺

Cothill House
Abingdon, Oxfordshire OX13 6JL
Tel: 01865 390800
Headmaster: Mr D M Bailey
Age range: B8–13
No. of pupils: 250
Fees: FB £27,660
👤 🏛 £ ✐

Cranford House School
Moulsford, Wallingford,
Oxfordshire OX10 9HT
Tel: 01491 651218
Age range: B3–11 G3–16
No. of pupils: 380
Fees: Day £10,500–£16,530
£ ✐

d'Overbroeck's
333 Banbury Road, Oxford,
Oxfordshire OX2 7PL
Tel: 01865 310000
Principal: Mrs Emma-Kate Henry
Age range: 11–18
No. of pupils: 475 VIth263
Fees: Day £16,725–£23,025
FB £30,225–£36,225
🌐 16⁺ A 🏛 £ ✐

Dragon School
Bardwell Road, Oxford,
Oxfordshire OX2 6SS
Tel: 01865 315400
Head: Mr Crispin Hyde-Dunn
Age range: 4–13
No. of pupils: 844
Fees: Day £11,988–£21,135 FB £30,615
🏛 £ ✐

EF ACADEMY OXFORD
For further details see p. 54
Pullens Lane, Headington,
Oxfordshire OX3 0DT
Tel: +41 (0) 43 430 4095
Email: iaeurope@ef.com
Website: www.ef.com/academy
Head of School: Dr. Paul Ellis
Age range: 16–19
No. of pupils: 175
🌐 16⁺ A 🏛 IB

Emmanuel Christian School
Sandford Road, Littlemore,
Oxford, Oxfordshire OX4 4PU
Tel: 01865 395236
Principal: Mrs Elizabeth Nesbitt
Age range: 3–11
No. of pupils: 43
Fees: Day £5,550
£ ✐

Greene's Tutorial College
45 Pembroke Street, Oxford,
Oxfordshire OX1 1BP
Tel: 01865 248308
Senior Tutor: Matthew
Uffindell MA, DipEd
No. of pupils: 213 VIth160

Headington Preparatory School
26 London Road, Oxford,
Oxfordshire OX3 7PB
Tel: +44 (0)1865 759116
Head: Mrs Jane Crouch BA (Hons), MA
Age range: G3–11
No. of pupils: 280

HEADINGTON SCHOOL
For further details see p. 56
London Road, Oxford,
Oxfordshire OX3 7TD
Tel: +44 (0)1865 759100
Email: admissions@headington.org
Website: www.headington.org
Headmistress: Mrs Caroline
Jordan MA(Oxon)
Age range: G11–18

KINGHAM HILL SCHOOL
For further details see p. 58
Kingham, Chipping Norton,
Oxfordshire OX7 6TH
Tel: 01608 658999
Email: secretary@kinghamhill.org
Website: www.kinghamhill.org.uk
Age range: 11–18
No. of pupils: 340
Fees: Day £17,220–£19,620 WB
£24,390–£30,120 FB £25,170–£33,045

Magdalen College School
Cowley Place, Oxford,
Oxfordshire OX4 1DZ
Tel: 01865 242191
Master: Helen Pike
Age range: B7–18
No. of pupils: 669 VIth161
Fees: Day £17,799–£18,477

Moulsford Preparatory School
Moulsford, Wallingford,
Oxfordshire OX10 9HR
Tel: 01491 651438
Headmaster: Mr B Beardmore-Gray
Age range: B4–13
Fees: Day £11,415–£17,055 WB £21,360

New College School
2 Savile Road, Oxford,
Oxfordshire OX1 3UA
Tel: 01865 285 560
Headmaster: Mr N R Gullifer MA, FRSA
Age range: B4–13
No. of pupils: 160
Fees: Day £9,870–£15,951

Our Lady's Abingdon School
Radley Road, Abingdon,
Oxfordshire OX14 3PS
Tel: 01235 524658
Principal: Mr Stephen Oliver
Age range: 3–18
No. of pupils: 499 VIth81
Fees: Day £9,033–£15,300

Oxford High School GDST
Belbroughton Road, Oxford,
Oxfordshire OX2 6XA
Tel: 01865 559888
Head: Dr Phillip Hills
Age range: G4–18
No. of pupils: 900
Fees: Day £9,000–£15,546

Oxford Montessori School
Forest Farm, Elsfield, Oxford,
Oxfordshire OX3 9UW
Tel: 01865 358210
Principal: Judith Walker Mont Dip, NNEB
Age range: 5–10
No. of pupils: 169

OXFORD TUTORIAL COLLEGE
For further details see p. 62
12-13 King Edward Street,
Oxford, Oxfordshire OX1 4HT
Tel: +44 (0)1865 793333
Email: admissions@
oxfordtutorialcollege.com
Website:
www.oxfordtutorialcollege.com
Principal: Mr Mark Love
Age range: 15–19
No. of pupils: 207

Radley College
Radley, Abingdon,
Oxfordshire OX14 2HR
Tel: 01235 543000
The Warden: Mr J S Moule
Age range: B13–18
No. of pupils: 688
Fees: FB £38,325

Rupert House School
90 Bell Street, Henley-on-Thames,
Oxfordshire RG9 2BN
Tel: 01491 574263
Headmistress: Mrs C Lynas
Age range: B4–7 G4–11
No. of pupils: 214
Fees: Day £5,640–£13,785

Rye St Antony
Pullens Lane, Oxford,
Oxfordshire OX3 0BY
Tel: 01865 762802
Headmistress: Miss A M Jones BA, PGCE
Age range: B3–11 G3–18
No. of pupils: 400 VIth70
Fees: Day £9,870–£15,330 WB
£21,000–£24,690 FB £22,230–£25,935

SHIPLAKE COLLEGE
For further details see p. 64
Henley-on-Thames,
Oxfordshire RG9 4BW
Tel: +44 (0)1189 402455
Email: registrar@shiplake.org.uk
Website: www.shiplake.org.uk
Headmaster: Mr A G S
Davies BSc(St Andrews)
Age range: B11–18 G16–18
No. of pupils: 485 VIth200
Fees: Day £17,700–£22,230 WB
£24,810–£31,020 FB £33,075

Sibford School
Sibford Ferris, Banbury,
Oxfordshire OX15 5QL
Tel: 01295 781200
Head of School: Toby Spence
No. of pupils: VIth840
Fees: Day £9,180–£14,739 WB
£26,154–£26,670 FB £28,077–£28,644

St Clare's, Oxford
139 Banbury Road, Oxford,
Oxfordshire OX2 7AL
Tel: +44 (0)1865 552031
Principal: Mr Andrew Rattue
Age range: 15–19
No. of pupils: 270
Fees: Day £16,707 FB £34,990

St Edward's, Oxford
Woodstock Road, Oxford,
Oxfordshire OX2 7NN
Tel: +44 (0)1865 319200
Warden: Stephen Jones
Age range: 13–18
No. of pupils: 700
Fees: Day £10,095 FB £12,615

St Helen and St Katharine
Faringdon Road, Abingdon,
Oxfordshire OX14 1BE
Tel: 01235 520173
Headmistress: Mrs R Dougall BA MA
Age range: G9–18
No. of pupils: VIth189
Fees: Day £15,990

St Hugh's School
Carswell Manor, Faringdon,
Oxfordshire SN7 8PT
Tel: 01367 870700
Headmaster: Mr A J P Nott
BA(Hons), PGCE
Age range: 3–13
Fees: Day £11,655–£20,085
WB £21,600–£23,100

St John's Priory School
St John's Road, Banbury,
Oxfordshire OX16 5HX
Tel: 01295 259607
Headmistress: Tracey Wilson
Age range: 3–11
Fees: Day £6,715–£9,450

St Mary's School
13 St Andrew's Road, Henley-on-
Thames, Oxfordshire RG9 1HS
Tel: 01491 573118
Headmaster: Mr Rob Harmer (BA)Hons
Age range: 2–11
No. of pupils: 118
Fees: Day £3,825

Summer Fields
Mayfield Road, Oxford,
Oxfordshire OX2 7EN
Tel: 01865 454433
Headmaster: Mr David
Faber MA(Oxon)
Age range: B4–13
No. of pupils: 256
Fees: Day £12,000–£21,159 FB £30,360

The King's School, Witney
New Yatt Road, Witney,
Oxfordshire OX29 6TA
Tel: 01993 778463
Principal: Mr Steve Beegoo
Age range: 3–16
No. of pupils: 200
Fees: Day £5,244

The Manor Preparatory School
Faringdon Road, Abingdon,
Oxfordshire OX13 6LN
Tel: 01235 858458
Headmaster: Mr Alastair Thomas
Age range: 2–11 years
No. of pupils: 390
Fees: Day £9,270–£15,570

The Unicorn School
20 Marcham Road, Abingdon,
Oxfordshire OX14 1AA
Tel: 01235 530222
Headteacher: Mr. Andrew Day BEd
(Hons)University of Wales (Cardiff)
Age range: 6–16 years
No. of pupils: 74
Fees: Day £19,500

Tudor Hall School
Wykham Park, Banbury,
Oxfordshire OX16 9UR
Tel: 01295 263434
Headmistress: Miss Wendy Griffiths BSc
Age range: G11–18
No. of pupils: 332 VIth81
Fees: Day £7,115 FB £11,370

Windrush Valley School
The Green, London Lane,
Ascott-under-Wychwood,
Oxfordshire OX7 6AN
Tel: 01993 831793
Headmaster: Mr Alan Wood MEd,
TCert, DipSpEd, ACP, FCollP
Age range: 3–11
No. of pupils: 125
Fees: Day £6,801

Wychwood School
74 Banbury Road, Oxford,
Oxfordshire OX2 6JR
Tel: 01865 557976
Headmistress: Mrs A K
Johnson BSc (Dunelm)
Age range: G11–18
No. of pupils: 120 VIth40
Fees: Day £15,900 WB
£24,300 FB £27,900

West Berkshire

**Brockhurst & Marlston
House Schools**
Hermitage, Newbury, West
Berkshire RG18 9UL
Tel: 01635 200293
Joint Heads: Mr David Fleming
& Mrs Caroline Riley
Age range: 3–13
No. of pupils: 275
Fees: Day £10,650–£17,850 FB £23,925

Cheam School
Headley, Newbury, West
Berkshire RG19 8LD
Tel: +44 (0)1635 268242
Headmaster: Mr Martin Harris
Age range: 3–13
No. of pupils: 407
Fees: Day £11,940–£21,285
FB £26,055–£27,630

Downe House School
Hermitage Road, Cold Ash,
Thatcham, West Berkshire RG18 9JJ
Tel: 01635 200286
Headmistress: Mrs E
McKendrick BA(Liverpool)
Age range: G11–18
No. of pupils: VIth174
Fees: Day £27,495 FB £37,530

Horris Hill
Newtown, Newbury, West
Berkshire RG20 9DJ
Tel: 01635 40594
Headmaster: Mr G F Tollit B.A.(Hons)
Age range: B7–13
No. of pupils: 120
Fees: Day £5,600 FB £8,900

**Marlston House
Preparatory School**
Hermitage, Newbury, West
Berkshire RG18 9UL
Tel: 01635 200293
Headmistress: Mrs Caroline
Riley MA, BEd
Age range: G3–13
No. of pupils: 110
Fees: Day £10,650–£17,850 FB £23,925

Newbury Hall
Enborne Road, (corner of
Rockingham Road), Newbury,
West Berkshire RG14 6AD
Tel: +44 (0)1635 36879

St Gabriel's
Sandleford Priory, Newbury,
West Berkshire RG20 9BD
Tel: 01635 555680
Principal: Mr Richard Smith
MA (Hons), MEd, PGCE
Age range: B6 months–11
G6 months–18
No. of pupils: 469 VIth40
Fees: Day £10,668–£17,418

St Michael's School
Harts Lane, Burghclere, Newbury,
West Berkshire RG20 9JW
Tel: 01635 278137
Headmaster: Rev. Fr. Patrick Summers
Age range: 5–18
No. of pupils: VIth5

The Cedars School
Church Road, Aldermaston,
West Berkshire RG7 4LR
Tel: 0118 971 4251
Headteacher: Mrs Jane O'Halloran
Age range: 4–11
No. of pupils: 50
Fees: Day £8,910

Thorngrove School
The Mount, Highclere, Newbury,
West Berkshire RG20 9PS
Tel: 01635 253172
Headmaster: Mr Adam King
Age range: 2 –13
Fees: Day £14,070–£17,595

Wiltshire

Ashwicke Hall School
Ashwicke Hall, Marshfield,
Chippenham, Wiltshire SN14 8AG
Tel: +44 (0) 1225 891841
School Director: Mr J Nicholson
Age range: 10–18
No. of pupils: 150

Avondale School
High Street, Bulford, Salisbury,
Wiltshire SP4 9DR
Tel: 01980 632387
Headmaster: Mr Stuart Watson
Age range: 2–11
Fees: Day £8,097

Bishopstrow College
Bishopstrow, Warminster,
Wiltshire BA12 9HU
Tel: +44 (0)1985 219210
Principal: Ms Lorraine Atkins
Age range: 7–17 years

Chafyn Grove School
33 Bourne Avenue, Salisbury,
Wiltshire SP1 1LR
Tel: 01722 333423
Headmaster: Mr Simon Head
Age range: 3–13
No. of pupils: 265

DAUNTSEY'S SCHOOL
For further details see p. 52
High Street, West Lavington,
Devizes, Wiltshire SN10 4HE
Tel: 01380 814500
Email: admissions@dauntseys.org
Website: www.dauntseys.org
Head Master: Mr Mark Lascelles
Age range: 11–18
No. of pupils: 820 VIth270
Fees: Day £18,990 FB £31,440

Emmaus School
School Lane, Staverton,
Trowbridge, Wiltshire BA14 6NZ
Tel: 01225 782684
Head: Mrs M Wiltshire
Age range: 5–16
No. of pupils: 75
Fees: Day £3,500–£4,400

Focus School – Wilton Campus
The Hollows, Wilton, Salisbury,
Wiltshire SP2 0JE
Tel: 01722 741910
Age range: 11–18
No. of pupils: 100

Godolphin Preparatory School
Laverstock Road, Salisbury,
Wiltshire SP1 2RB
Tel: 01722 430 652
Headmistress: Emma Hattersley
Age range: G3–11
No. of pupils: 100
Fees: Day £7,125–£13,935
WB £21,540 FB £25,230

Heywood Prep
The Priory, Corsham, Wiltshire SN13 0AP
Tel: 01249 713379
Headmistress: Rebecca Mitchell
Age range: 2–11
No. of pupils: 140
Fees: Day £5,760–£8,985

Leehurst Swan School
Campbell Road, Salisbury,
Wiltshire SP1 3BQ
Tel: 01722 333094
Headmaster: Mr Stuart Morgan-Nash B
Age range: Reception–16 years
Fees: Day £8,400–£10,800

Maranatha Christian School
Queenlaines Farm, Sevenhampton,
Swindon, Wiltshire SN6 7SQ
Tel: 01793 762075
Headteacher: Mr Paul Medlock
Age range: 3–18
No. of pupils: 68

Marlborough College
Marlborough, Wiltshire SN8 1PA
Tel: 01672 892300
the Master: Mr Jonathan Leigh MA
Age range: 13–18
No. of pupils: 940 VIth408
Fees: FB £36,525

Meadowpark Nursery & Pre-Preparatory
Calcutt Street, Cricklade,
Wiltshire SN6 6BA
Tel: 01793 752600
Headteacher: Mrs R Kular
Age range: 0–11
Fees: Day £6,585–£8,550

Pinewood School
Bourton, Swindon, Wiltshire SN6 8HZ
Tel: 01793 782205
Headmaster: Mr P J Hoyland
Age range: 3–13
No. of pupils: 313
Fees: Day £8,790–£17,895 WB £22,260

Prior Park Preparatory School
Calcutt Street, Cricklade,
Wiltshire SN6 6BB
Tel: 01793 750275
Headteacher: Guy Barrett
Age range: 2–13
No. of pupils: 240
Fees: Day £6,900–£14,460

Salisbury Cathedral School
The Old Palace, 1 The Close,
Salisbury, Wiltshire SP1 2EQ
Tel: 01722 555300
Head Master: Mr Clive Marriott BEd MA
Age range: 3–13
No. of pupils: 220
Fees: Day £8,700–£15,690
FB £16,065–£23,053

Sandroyd School
Rushmore, Tollard Royal,
Salisbury, Wiltshire SP5 5QD
Tel: 01725 516264
Headmaster: Mr Alastair Speers
Age range: 5–13
No. of pupils: 225
Fees: Day £8,760–£25,410
FB £20,100–£25,410

St Francis School
Marlborough Road, Pewsey,
Wiltshire SN9 5NT
Tel: 01672 563228
Headmaster: Mr David Sibson
Age range: 0–13
Fees: Day £4,821–£12,571

St Margaret's Preparatory School
Curzon Street, Calne, Wiltshire SN11 0DF
Tel: 01249 857220
Headmistress: Mrs Karen Cordon
GLCM LLCM (TD) ALCM
Age range: 3–11
No. of pupils: 200
Fees: Day £9,900–£13,500

ST MARY'S CALNE
For further details see p. 66
Curzon Street, Calne,
Wiltshire SN11 0DF
Tel: 01249 857200
Email: office@stmaryscalne.org
Website: www.stmaryscalne.org
Headmistress: Dr Felicia Kirk
BA(University of MD), MA,
PhD(Brown University)
Age range: G11–18
No. of pupils: 365 VIth120
Fees: Day £29,025 FB £38,925

Stonar School
Cottles Park, Atworth, Melksham,
Wiltshire SN12 8NT
Tel: 01225 701740
Head of School: Dr Sally Divall
Age range: 2–18
No. of pupils: 330
Fees: Day £8,496–£16,500
FB £21,954–£33,195

The Godolphin School
Milford Hill, Salisbury, Wiltshire SP1 2RA
Tel: 01722 430509
Headmistress: Mrs Emma Hattersley
BA (Dunelm) Postgrad RAM
Age range: G11–18
No. of pupils: 380 VIth100

Warminster School
Church Street, Warminster,
Wiltshire BA12 8PJ
Tel: +44 (0)1985 210160
Headmaster: Mr Mark
Mortimer MBA BA
Age range: 3–18
No. of pupils: 550
Fees: Day £7,650–£15,330
FB £21,615–£32,640

East

KEY TO SYMBOLS

- ⚘ *Boys' school*
- ⚘ *Girls' school*
- 🌐 *International school*
- 16 *Tutorial or sixth form college*
- Ⓐ *A levels*
- ♨ *Boarding accommodation*
- £ *Bursaries*
- ⒾⒷ *International Baccalaureate*
- ✐ *Learning support*
- 16 *Entrance at 16+*
- ⚒ *Vocational qualifications*
- Ⓘ *Independent Association of Preparatory Schools*
- Ⓗ *The Headmasters' & Headmistresses' Conference*
- Ⓘ *Independent Schools Association*
- Ⓖ *Girls' School Association*
- Ⓑ *Boarding Schools' Association*
- Ⓢ *Society of Heads*

Unless otherwise indicated, all schools are coeducational day schools. Single-sex and boarding schools will be indicated by the relevant icon.

Bedfordshire

Bedford Modern School
Manton Lane, Bedford,
Bedfordshire MK41 7NT
Tel: 01234 332500
Headmaster: Mr Alex Tate
Age range: 7–18
No. of pupils: 1226
Fees: Day £9,771–£13,404

Bedford Preparatory School
De Parys Avenue, Bedford,
Bedfordshire MK40 2TU
Tel: 01234 362271/362274
Headmaster: Ian Silk
Age range: B7–13
No. of pupils: 438
Fees: Day £12,333–£16,161 WB
£20,919–£25,038 FB £21,948–£26,067

**Focus School –
Biggleswade Campus**
The Oaks, Potton Road, Biggleswade,
Bedfordshire SG18 0EP
Tel: 01767 602800
Age range: 7–18 years
No. of pupils: 75

Focus School – Dunstable Campus
Ridgeway Avenue, Dunstable,
Bedfordshire LU5 4QL
Tel: 01582 665676
Age range: 11–16
No. of pupils: 77

**Luton Pentecostal Church
Christian Academy**
15 Church Street, Luton,
Bedfordshire LU1 3JE
Tel: 01582 412276
Principal: Pastor Chris Oakey
Age range: 3–13
No. of pupils: 56
Fees: Day £2,280–£3,360

Orchard School & Nursery
High Gobion Road, Barton-le-Clay,
Bedford, Bedfordshire MK45 4LT
Tel: 01582 882054
Headteacher: Mrs A Burton
Age range: 0–6
No. of pupils: 127

Pilgrims Pre-Preparatory School
Brickhill Drive, Bedford,
Bedfordshire MK41 7QZ
Tel: 01234 369555
Head: Mrs J Webster BEd(Hons), EYPS
Age range: 3 months–7 years
No. of pupils: 385
Fees: Day £9,771–£13,980

Polam School
43-45 Lansdowne Road, Bedford,
Bedfordshire MK40 2BU
Tel: 01234 261864
Head: Mrs Jessica Harris
Age range: 1–9
No. of pupils: 100
Fees: Day £8,145

Rabia Girls School
12-16 Portland Road, Luton,
Bedfordshire LU4 8AX
Tel: 01582 493239
Headteacher: Mrs F Shaikh
Age range: G4–16
No. of pupils: 265

Rushmoor School
58-60 Shakespeare Road, Bedford,
Bedfordshire MK40 2DL
Tel: 01234 352031
Headteacher: Ian Daniel BA, NPQH
Age range: B3–16 G3–11
Fees: Day £6,429–£11,022

St Andrew's School
78 Kimbolton Road, Bedford,
Bedfordshire MK40 2PA
Tel: 01234 267272
Headmaster: Mr Ian Daniel
Age range: B3–9 G3–16
No. of pupils: 385
Fees: Day £5,598–£11,022

St George's School
28 Priory Road, Dunstable,
Bedfordshire LU5 4HR
Tel: 01582 661471
Headmistress: Mrs Plater
Age range: 3–11
No. of pupils: 120
Fees: Day £6,852–£7,119

Cambridgeshire

Abbey College Cambridge
Homerton Gardens, Purbeck Road,
Cambridge, Cambridgeshire CB2 8EB
Tel: 01223 578280
Principal: Dr Julian Davies
Age range: 13–21
No. of pupils: VIth370
Fees: Day £22,000 FB £39,000–£43,000

Bellerbys College Cambridge
Queens Campus, Bateman Street,
Cambridge, Cambridgeshire CB2 1LU
Tel: +44 (0)1223 652 800
Principal: Mr Nicholas Waite
Age range: 14–25

Cambridge International School
Cherry Hinton Hall, Cherry Hinton Road,
Cambridge, Cambridgeshire CB1 8DW
Tel: +44 (0)1223 416938
Principal: Mrs Phillippa Mills
Age range: 3–18 years

**Cambridge Seminars
Tutorial College**
Logic House, 143-147 Newmarket Road,
Cambridge, Cambridgeshire CB5 8HA
Tel: 01223 313464
Principal: M R Minhas BSc, CEng
Age range: 16–20
Fees: Day £1,800–£24,000

Cambridge Steiner School
Hinton Road, Fulbourn, Cambridge,
Cambridgeshire CB21 5DZ
Tel: 01223 882727
Age range: 2–14
No. of pupils: 125
Fees: Day £7,665

CATS College Cambridge
1 High Street, Chesterton, Cambridge,
Cambridgeshire CB4 1NQ
Tel: 01223 314431
Principal: Dr Craig Wilson
Age range: 14–19+

**CCSS (Cambridge Centre
for Sixth-form Studies)**
4-5 Bene't Place, Lensfield Road,
Cambridge, Cambridgeshire CB2 1EL
Tel: 01223 716890
Principal: Mr Stuart Nicholson
MA(Oxon), MBA, PGCE, NPQH, CPhys
Age range: 15–21
Fees: Day £18,750–£23,655
FB £25,050–£37,200

Kimbolton School
Kimbolton, Huntingdon,
Cambridgeshire PE28 0EA
Tel: 01480 860505
Headmaster: Jonathan Belbin BA
Age range: 4–18
No. of pupils: VIth170
Fees: Day £9,870–£15,795 FB £26,280

**King's Acremont, King's
Ely Nursery & Pre-Prep**
30 Egremont Street, Ely,
Cambridgeshire CB6 1AE
Tel: 01353 660702
Head: Sue Freestone
Age range: 3–7
Fees: Day £10,077

King's College School
West Road, Cambridge,
Cambridgeshire CB3 9DN
Tel: 01223 365814
Head: Mrs Yvette Day
BMus, MMus, GDL
Age range: 4–13
No. of pupils: 404
Fees: Day £12,240–£15,555 FB £24,210

KING'S ELY
For further details see p. 86
Ely, Cambridgeshire CB7 4DB
Tel: 01353 660557
Email: admissions@kingsely.org
Website: www.kingsely.org
Principal: Mrs Susan Freestone
MEd, GRSM, LRAM, ARCM, FRSA
Age range: 1–18
No. of pupils: 1048
Fees: Day £10,077–£21,459
FB £22,692–£31,065

King's Ely Junior
Ely, Cambridgeshire CB7 4DB
Tel: 01353 660707
Head: Mr Richard Whymark
Age range: 7–13
No. of pupils: 345
Fees: Day £13,180–£14,382
FB £21,013–£22,181

**Magdalene House
Preparatory School**
North Brink, Wisbech,
Cambridgeshire PE13 1JX
Tel: 01945 586 780
Head: Mr Chris Staley
Age range: 3–11
No. of pupils: 180
Fees: Day £9,297–£9,597

**MANDER PORTMAN
WOODWARD – CAMBRIDGE**
For further details see p. 88
3-4 Brookside, Cambridge,
Cambridgeshire CB2 1JE
Tel: 01223 350158
Email: cambridge@mpw.ac.uk
Website: www.mpw.ac.uk
Principal: Dr Markus Bernhardt
Age range: 15–19

Sancton Wood School
2 St Paul's Road, Cambridge,
Cambridgeshire CB1 2EZ
Tel: 01223 471703
Head Teacher: Mr Richard Settle
Age range: 1–16
No. of pupils: 193
Fees: Day £11,775–£13,470

St Andrew's Cambridge
2A Free School Lane, Cambridge,
Cambridgeshire CB2 3QA
Tel: 01223 360040
Principal: Wayne Marshall
Age range: 14–20
No. of pupils: VIth130
Fees: FB £15,000–£17,000

ST FAITH'S
For further details see p. 94
Trumpington Road, Cambridge,
Cambridgeshire CB2 8AG
Tel: 01223 352073
Email: admissions@stfaiths.co.uk
Website: www.stfaiths.co.uk
Headmaster: Mr N L Helliwell
Age range: 4–13
No. of pupils: 545
Fees: Day £12,660–£15,945

St John's College School
73 Grange Road, Cambridge,
Cambridgeshire CB3 9AB
Tel: 01223 353532
Headmaster: Mr N. Chippington
MA(Cantab), FRCO
Age range: 4–13
No. of pupils: 453
Fees: Day £12,210–£15,330 FB £24,210

St Mary's School
Bateman Street, Cambridge,
Cambridgeshire CB2 1LY
Tel: 01223 353253
Headmistress: Ms Charlotte Avery
Age range: G4–18
No. of pupils: 619 VIth90
Fees: Day £9,909–£15,861 WB
£26,286–£28,032 FB £30,819–£32,562

**Stephen Perse Foundation
Junior School**
St Eligius Street, Cambridge,
Cambridgeshire CB2 1HX
Tel: 01223 346 140
Head: Miss K Milne
Age range: 7–11
No. of pupils: 135
Fees: Day £15,150

**Stephen Perse Foundation
Senior School**
Union Road, Cambridge,
Cambridgeshire CB2 1HF
Tel: 01223 454700
Principal: David Walker
Age range: 11–16 years
No. of pupils: VIth150
Fees: Day £17,550

**Stephen Perse Pre-
prep, Madingley**
Cambridge Road,
Madingley, Cambridge,
Cambridgeshire CB23 8AH
Tel: 01954 210309
Head of Pre-prep: Mrs Sarah Holyoake
Age range: 3–7
No. of pupils: 60
Fees: Day £12,000

THE LEYS SCHOOL
For further details see p. 96
Trumpington Road, Cambridge,
Cambridgeshire CB2 7AD
Tel: 01223 508900
Email: admissions@theleys.net
Website: www.theleys.net
Headmaster: Mr Martin Priestley
Age range: 11–18
No. of pupils: 569
Fees: Day £15,900–£22,035
FB £24,000–£32,925

**The Perse Pelican Nursery and
Pre-Preparatory School**
Northwold House, 92 Glebe Road,
Cambridge, Cambridgeshire CB1 7TD
Tel: 01223 403940
Headmistress: Mrs S C Waddington MA
Age range: 3–7
No. of pupils: 154
Fees: Day £13,530

The Perse Preparatory School
Trumpington Road, Cambridge,
Cambridgeshire CB2 8EX
Tel: 01223 403920
Head: Mr James Piper
Age range: 7–11
No. of pupils: 283
Fees: Day £15,705

The Perse School
Hills Road, Cambridge,
Cambridgeshire CB2 8QF
Tel: 01223 403800
Head: Mr Ed Elliott
Age range: 11–18
No. of pupils: 851 VIth250
Fees: Day £17,322

THE PETERBOROUGH SCHOOL
For further details see p. 98
Thorpe Road, Peterborough,
Cambridgeshire PE3 6AP
Tel: 01733 343357
Email: office@tpsch.co.uk
Website:
www.thepeterboroughschool.co.uk
Headmaster: Mr A D
Meadows BSc(Hons)
Age range: 6 weeks–18 years
No. of pupils: 440
Fees: Day £9,942–£14,868
(A) (£) (✐) (16)

Whitehall School
117 High Street, Somersham,
Cambridgeshire PE28 3EH
Tel: 01487 840966
Principal: Rebecca Hutley
Age range: 3–11
No. of pupils: 109
Fees: Day £6,975–£7,980

Wisbech Grammar School
North Brink, Wisbech,
Cambridgeshire PE13 1JX
Tel: 01945 583 631
Head: Mr Chris Staley BA, MBA
Age range: 11–18
No. of pupils: 410
Fees: Day £13,347
(A) (£) (✐) (16)

Essex

Alleyn Court Preparatory School
Wakering Road, Southend-
on-Sea, Essex SS3 0PW
Tel: 01702 582553
Headmaster: Mr Rupert Snow
Age range: 2–11
Fees: Day £3,258–£12,729
(£) (✐)

Brentwood Preparatory School
Middleton Hall Lane, Brentwood,
Essex CM15 8EQ
Tel: 01277 243333
Headmaster: Mr Jason Whiskerd
Age range: 3–11
No. of pupils: 415
Fees: Day £7,236–£14,472
(✐)

BRENTWOOD SCHOOL
For further details see p. 78
Middleton Hall Lane,
Brentwood, Essex CM15 8EE
Tel: 01277 243243
Email: headmaster@
brentwood.essex.sch.uk
Website:
www.brentwoodschool.co.uk
Headmaster: Mr Ian Davies
Age range: 3–18
No. of pupils: 1600
Fees: Day £18,945 FB £37,128
(🌐) (A) (🏅) (£) (IB) (✐) (16)

Colchester High School
Wellesley Road, Colchester,
Essex CO3 3HD
Tel: 01206 573389
Principal: David Young BA(Hons), PGCE
Age range: 2–16
No. of pupils: 486
Fees: Day £3,300–£10,000
(£) (✐)

Coopersale Hall School
Flux's Lane, off Stewards Green
Road, Epping, Essex CM16 7PE
Tel: 01992 577133
Headmistress: Miss Kaye Lovejoy
Age range: 2–11
No. of pupils: 275
Fees: Day £10,350–£10,575

Dame Bradbury's School
Ashdon Road, Saffron
Walden, Essex CB10 2AL
Tel: 01799 522348
Headmistress: Ms Tracy Handford
Age range: 3–11
No. of pupils: 254
Fees: Day £4,350–£13,800
(£) (✐)

Elm Green Preparatory School
Parsonage Lane, Little Baddow,
Chelmsford, Essex CM3 4SU
Tel: 01245 225230
Principal: Ms Ann Milner
Age range: 4–11
No. of pupils: 220
Fees: Day £8,844
(✐)

Felsted Preparatory School
Felsted, Great Dunmow, Essex CM6 3JL
Tel: 01371 822610
Headmaster: Mr Simon James
Age range: 4–13
No. of pupils: 460
Fees: Day £9,285–£17,820
FB £23,250–£24,465
(🏅) (£) (✐)

FELSTED SCHOOL
For further details see p. 80
Felsted, Great Dunmow,
Essex CM6 3LL
Tel: 01371 822605
Email: internationaladmissions@
felsted.org
Website: www.felsted.org
Headmaster: Mr Chris Townsend
Age range: 13–18
No. of pupils: 522 VIth426
Fees: Day £23,550 WB
£33,390 FB £35,985
(🌐) (A) (🏅) (£) (IB) (✐) (16)

Gosfield School
Cut Hedge Park, Halstead Road,
Gosfield, Halstead, Essex CO9 1PF
Tel: 01787 474040
Headteacher: Mr Guy Martyn
Age range: 4–18
No. of pupils: VIth21
Fees: Day £6,690–£15,525
(🌐) (A) (🏅) (£) (✐) (16)

Great Warley School
Warley Street, Great Warley,
Brentwood, Essex CM13 3LA
Tel: 01277 233288
Head: Mr David Bell
Age range: 3–11

Heathcote School
Eves Corner, Danbury,
Chelmsford, Essex CM3 4QB
Tel: 01245 223131
Headmistress: Caroline Forgeron
Age range: 2–11
Fees: Day £4,830–£7,245
(£) (✐)

Herington House School
1 Mount Avenue, Hutton,
Brentwood, Essex CM13 2NS
Tel: 01277 211595
Principal: Mr R. Dudley-Cooke
Age range: 3–11
No. of pupils: 130
Fees: Day £1,955–£3,865
(£) (✐)

**Holmwood House
Preparatory School**
Chitts Hill, Lexden, Colchester,
Essex CO3 9ST
Tel: 01206 574305
Headmaster: Alexander Mitchell
Age range: 4–13
No. of pupils: 302
Fees: Day £10,140–£17,895 FB £35
(🏅) (✐)

Hutton Manor School
428 Rayleigh Road, Hutton,
Brentwood, Essex CM13 1SD
Tel: 01277 245585
Head: Paula Hobbs
Age range: 3–11

Littlegarth School
Horkesley Park, Nayland,
Colchester, Essex CO6 4JR
Tel: 01206 262332
Headmaster: Mr Peter H Jones
Age range: 2–11 years
No. of pupils: 318
Fees: Day £3,205–£3,723
(£) (✐)

Maldon Court Preparatory School
Silver Street, Maldon, Essex CM9 4QE
Tel: 01621 853529
Headteacher: Elaine Mason
Age range: 3–11
Fees: Day £8,236.80
(✐)

New Hall School
The Avenue, Boreham,
Chelmsford, Essex CM3 3HS
Tel: 01245 467588
Principal: Mrs Katherine Jeffrey MA,
BA, PGCE, MA(Ed Mg), NPQH
Age range: Coed 3-11, Single
11-16, Coed 16–18
No. of pupils: 1180 VIth217
Fees: Day £9,801–£19,878 WB
£19,761–£28,569 FB £21,531–£30,681
(🌐) (A) (🏅) (£) (✐) (16)

Oxford House School
2-4 Lexden Road, Colchester,
Essex CO3 3NE
Tel: 01206 576686
Head Teacher: Mrs Sarah Leyshon
Age range: 2–11
No. of pupils: 158

Saint Nicholas School
Hillingdon House, Hobbs Cross
Road, Harlow, Essex CM17 0NJ
Tel: 01279 429910
Headmaster: Mr D Bown
Age range: 4–16
No. of pupils: 400
Fees: Day £9,960–£12,660
(£)

Saint Pierre School
16 Leigh Road, Leigh-on-Sea,
Southend-on-Sea, Essex SS9 1LE
Tel: 01702 474164
Headmaster: Mr Chris Perkins
Age range: 2–11+
Fees: Day £7,218–£8,181
£

St Anne's Preparatory School
New London Road, Chelmsford,
Essex CM2 0AW
Tel: 01245 353488
Head: Mrs Fiona Pirrie
Age range: 3–11
No. of pupils: 160
Fees: Day £3,450–£8,100

ST CEDD'S SCHOOL
For further details see p. 92
178a New London Road,
Chelmsford, Essex CM2 0AR
Tel: 01245 392810
Email: info@stcedds.org.uk
Website: www.stcedds.org.uk
Head: Mr Matthew Clarke
Age range: 3–11
No. of pupils: 400
Fees: Day £8,550–£10,515

St John's School
Stock Road, Billericay, Essex CM12 0AR
Tel: 01277 623070
Head Teacher: Mrs F Armour BEd(Hons)
Age range: 2–16 years
No. of pupils: 392
Fees: Day £5,328–£13,500

St Margaret's Preparatory School
Gosfield Hall Park, Gosfield,
Halstead, Essex CO9 1SE
Tel: 01787 472134
Headmaster: Mr. Callum Douglas
Age range: 2–11
Fees: Day £9,315–£11,280

St Mary's School
Lexden Road, Colchester,
Essex CO3 3RB
Tel: 01206 572544
Admissions: 01206 216420
Principal: Mrs H K Vipond
MEd, BSc(Hons), NPQH
Age range: B3–4 G3–16
No. of pupils: 430
Fees: Day £6,855–£14,985

**St Michael's Church Of
England Preparatory School**
198 Hadleigh Road, Leigh-on-Sea,
Southend-on-Sea, Essex SS9 2LP
Tel: 01702 478719
Head: Steve Tompkins BSc(Hons),
PGCE, MA, NPQH
Age range: 3–11
No. of pupils: 271
Fees: Day £4,104–£9,600

St Philomena's Catholic School
Hadleigh Road, Frinton-on-
Sea, Essex CO13 9HQ
Tel: 01255 674492
Headmistress: Mrs B McKeown DipEd
Age range: 4–11
Fees: Day £6,240–£7,500

Thorpe Hall School
Wakering Road, Southend-
on-Sea, Essex SS1 3RD
Tel: 01702 582340
Headmaster: Mr Andrew Hampton
Age range: 2–16 years
No. of pupils: 359
Fees: Day £9,000–£12,600

Ursuline Preparatory School
Old Great Ropers, Great Ropers Lane,
Warley, Brentwood, Essex CM13 3HR
Tel: 01277 227152
Headmistress: Mrs Pauline Wilson MSc
Age range: 3–11
Fees: Day £6,450–£12,015

Widford Lodge School
Widford Road, Chelmsford,
Essex CM2 9AN
Tel: 01245 352581
Headmaster: Mr Simon Trowell
Age range: 2–11
Fees: Day £7,365–£9,330

Hertfordshire

ABBOT'S HILL SCHOOL
For further details see p. 72
Bunkers Lane, Hemel Hempstead,
Hertfordshire HP3 8RP
Tel: 01442 240333
Email:
registrar@abbotshill.herts.sch.uk
Website:
www.abbotshill.herts.sch.uk
Headmistress: Mrs E Thomas
BA (Hons), PGCE, NPQH
Age range: G4–16
No. of pupils: 510

Aldenham School
Elstree, Hertfordshire WD6 3AJ
Tel: 01923 858122
Headmaster: Mr James C Fowler MA
Age range: 3–18
No. of pupils: 700
Fees: Day £16,491–£22,614
FB £22,791–£33,234

Aldwickbury School
Wheathampstead Road,
Harpenden, Hertfordshire AL5 1AD
Tel: 01582 713022
Headmaster: Mr V W Hales
Age range: B4–13
No. of pupils: 330
Fees: Day £13,110–£16,215

Beechwood Park School
Markyate, St Albans,
Hertfordshire AL3 8AW
Tel: 01582 840333
Headmaster: Mr E Balfour
BA (Hons), PGCE
Age range: 3–13
No. of pupils: 532
Fees: Day £11,025–£16,530 WB £20,460

Berkhamsted School
Overton House, 131 High Street,
Berkhamsted, Hertfordshire HP4 2DJ
Tel: 01442 358001
Principal: Mr Richard
Backhouse MA(Cantab)
Age range: 3–18
No. of pupils: 1772 VIth402
Fees: Day £10,365–£20,250
WB £27,115 FB £32,255

Bhaktivedanta Manor School
Hilfield Lane, Aldenham, Watford,
Hertfordshire WD25 8EZ
Tel: 01923 851000 Ext:241
Headteacher: Guru
Carana Padma dasi
Age range: 4–12
No. of pupils: 45
Fees: Day £1,860

Bishop's Stortford College
10 Maze Green Road, Bishop's
Stortford, Hertfordshire CM23 2PJ
Tel: 01279 838575
Headmaster: Mr Jeremy Gladwin
Age range: 13–18
No. of pupils: VIth249
Fees: Day £19,662–£19,839 WB
£30,228–£30,411 FB £30,528–£30,711

**Bishop's Stortford College
Prep School**
Maze Green Road, Bishop's
Stortford, Hertfordshire CM23 2PH
Tel: 01279 838607
Head of the Prep School: Mr
Bill Toleman
Age range: 4–13
No. of pupils: 590
Fees: Day £9,090–£15,729 WB
£21,102–£22,911 FB £21,327–£23,142

East: ENGLAND

D311

Charlotte House Preparatory School
88 The Drive, Rickmansworth, Hertfordshire WD3 4DU
Tel: 01923 772101
Head: Miss P Woodcock
Age range: G3–11
No. of pupils: 140
Fees: Day £3,432–£12,102

Duncombe School
4 Warren Park Road, Bengeo, Hertford, Hertfordshire SG14 3JA
Tel: 01992 414100
Headmaster: Mr Jeremy Phelan M.A. (Ed)
Age range: 2–11
No. of pupils: 301
Fees: Day £10,380–£14,565

Edge Grove School
Aldenham Village, Hertfordshire WD25 8NL
Tel: 01923 855724
Headmaster: Mr Ben Evans BA (Hons), PGCE
Age range: 3–13
No. of pupils: 494
Fees: Day £6,930–£16,935
WB £20,756–£23,150

Egerton Rothesay School
Durrants Lane, Berkhamsted, Hertfordshire HP4 3UJ
Tel: 01442 865275
Headteacher: Mr Colin Parker BSc(Hons), Dip.Ed (Oxon), PGCE, C.Math MIMA
Age range: 5–19
No. of pupils: 179
Fees: Day £16,020–£22,800

Haberdashers' Aske's School
Butterfly Lane, Elstree, Borehamwood, Hertfordshire WD6 3AF
Tel: 020 8266 1700
Headmaster: Mr P B Hamilton MA
Age range: B5–18
No. of pupils: 1402 VIth310
Fees: Day £15,339–£20,346

Haberdashers' Aske's School for Girls
Aldenham Road, Elstree, Borehamwood, Hertfordshire WD6 3BT
Tel: 020 8266 2300
Headmistress: Miss Biddie A O'Connor MA (Oxon)
Age range: G4–18
No. of pupils: 1190
Fees: Day £16,980–£18,393

HAILEYBURY
For further details see p. 82
Haileybury, Hertford, Hertfordshire SG13 7NU
Tel: +44 (0)1992 706200
Email: admissions@haileybury.com
Website: www.haileybury.com
The Master: Mr Martin Collier MA BA PGCE
Age range: 11–18
No. of pupils: 833 VIth317
Fees: Day £17,031–£25,620
FB £21,837–£34,422

Haresfoot School
Chesham Road, Berkhamsted, Hertfordshire HP4 2SZ
Tel: 01442 872742
Principal: Karen O'Connor BA PGCE NPQH
Age range: 3–7
Fees: Day £1,845–£7,770

HEATH MOUNT SCHOOL
For further details see p. 84
Woodhall Park, Watton-at-Stone, Hertford, Hertfordshire SG14 3NG
Tel: 01920 830230
Email: registrar@heathmount.org
Website: www.heathmount.org
Headmaster: Mr Chris Gillam BEd(Hons)
Age range: 3–13
No. of pupils: 480
Fees: Day £11,550–£17,805

High Elms Manor School
High Elms Lane, Watford, Hertfordshire WD25 0JX
Tel: 01923 681 103
Headmistress: Ms Liadain O'Neill BA (Hons), AMI 0-3, AMI 3-6, Early Years FdA Dist.+
Age range: 2–12
No. of pupils: 100
Fees: Day £10,500–£12,675

Howe Green House School
Great Hallingbury, Bishop's Stortford, Hertfordshire CM22 7UF
Tel: 01279 657706
Age range: 2–11
Fees: Day £8,235–£11,793

Immanuel College
87/91 Elstree Road, Bushey, Hertfordshire WD23 4EB
Tel: 020 8950 0604
Headmaster: Mr Gary Griffin
Age range: 4–18
No. of pupils: 520 VIth127
Fees: Day £10,995

Kingshott
St Ippolyts, Hitchin, Hertfordshire SG4 7JX
Tel: 01462 432009
Headmaster: Mr Mark Seymour
Age range: 3–13
No. of pupils: 372
Fees: Day £5,835–£12,540

Little Acorns Montessori School
Lincolnsfield Centre, Bushey Hall Drive, Bushey, Hertfordshire WD23 2ER
Tel: 01923 230705
Age range: 12 months–6
No. of pupils: 28
Fees: Day £2,120

Lochinver House School
Heath Road, Little Heath, Potters Bar, Hertfordshire EN6 1LW
Tel: 01707 653064
Headmaster: Ben Walker BA(Hons), PGCE, CELTA
Age range: B4–13
No. of pupils: 349
Fees: Day £11,175–£14,685

Lockers Park
Lockers Park Lane, Hemel Hempstead, Hertfordshire HP1 1TL
Tel: 01442 251712
Headmaster: Mr C R Wilson
Age range: B4–13 G4–7
No. of pupils: 170
Fees: Day £10,050–£16,530 FB £23,160

Longwood School
Bushey Hall Drive, Bushey, Hertfordshire WD23 2QG
Tel: 01923 253715
Head Teacher: Claire May
Age range: 3 months–11
Fees: Day £3,705–£7,800

Manor Lodge School
Rectory Lane, Ridge Hill, Shenley, Hertfordshire WD7 9BG
Tel: 01707 642424
Headmaster: Mr G Dunn CertEd
Age range: 3–11
No. of pupils: 430
Fees: Day £10,650–£11,910

Merchant Taylors' Prep
Moor Farm, Sandy Lodge Road, Rickmansworth, Hertfordshire WD3 1LW
Tel: 01923 825648
Headmaster: Dr Karen McNerney BSc (Hons), PGCE, MSc, EdD
Age range: B4–13
No. of pupils: 300
Fees: Day £5,148–£16,000

Princess Helena College
Preston, Hitchin, Hertfordshire SG4 7RT
Tel: 01462 443888
Headmistress: Mrs Sue Wallace-Woodroffe
Age range: G11–18
No. of pupils: 194 VIth35
Fees: Day £16,125–£19,635
FB £22,965–£28,545

Queenswood
Shepherd's Way, Brookmans Park, Hatfield, Hertfordshire AL9 6NS
Tel: 01707 602500
Principal: Mrs Jo Cameron
Age range: G11–18
No. of pupils: 400 VIth120
Fees: Day £20,925–£24,825 WB £23,355–£31,035 FB £23,985–£33,750

Radlett Preparatory School
Kendal Hall, Watling Street, Radlett, Hertfordshire WD7 7LY
Tel: 01923 856812
Principal: Mr G White BEd (Hons)
Age range: 4–11
Fees: Day £9,735

Sherrardswood School
Lockleys, Welwyn, Hertfordshire AL6 0BJ
Tel: 01438 714282
Headmistress: Mrs Anna Wright
Age range: 2–18
No. of pupils: 357
Fees: Day £10,383–£16,113

St Albans High School for Girls
Townsend Avenue, St Albans,
Hertfordshire AL1 3SJ
Tel: 01727 853800
Headmistress: Mrs Jenny
Brown MA (Oxon)
Age range: G4–18
No. of pupils: 940 VIth170

St Albans School
Abbey Gateway, St Albans,
Hertfordshire AL3 4HB
Tel: 01727 855521
Headmaster: Mr JWJ Gillespie
MA(Cantab), FRSA
Age range: B11–18 G16–18
No. of pupils: 870
Fees: Day £18,600

St Albans Tutors
69 London Road, St Albans,
Hertfordshire AL1 1LN
Tel: 01727 842348
Principals: Mr. A N Jemal
& Mr Elvis Cotena
Age range: 15+
Fees: Day £2,700–£5,900

St Christopher School
Barrington Road, Letchworth,
Hertfordshire SG6 3JZ
Tel: 01462 650 850
Head: Richard Palmer
Age range: 3–18
No. of pupils: 511 VIth78
Fees: Day £4,590–£18,075 WB
£19,950–£24,675 FB £31,650

St Columba's College
King Harry Lane, St Albans,
Hertfordshire AL3 4AW
Tel: 01727 855185
Headmaster: David R Buxton
Age range: B4–18
No. of pupils: 860 VIth150
Fees: Day £10,482–£15,699

St Columba's College Prep School
King Harry Lane, St Albans,
Hertfordshire AL3 4AW
Tel: 01727 862616
Head of Prep: Mrs Ruth Loveman
Age range: B4–11
No. of pupils: 250
Fees: Day £10,482–£13,557

St Edmund's College & Prep School
Old Hall Green, Nr Ware,
Hertfordshire SG11 1DS
Tel: 01920 824247
Head: Paulo Durán BA MA
Age range: 3–18
No. of pupils: 799 VIth135
Fees: Day £10,650–£17,205 WB
£22,665–£25,905 FB £26,040–£29,865

St Edmund's Prep
Old Hall Green, Ware,
Hertfordshire SG11 1DS
Tel: 01920 824239
Head: Mr Steven Cartwright
BSc (Surrey)
Age range: 3–11
No. of pupils: 185
Fees: Day £10,650–£13,365

St Francis' College
Broadway, Letchworth Garden
City, Hertfordshire SG6 3PJ
Tel: 01462 670511
Headmistress: Mrs B Goulding
Age range: G3–18
No. of pupils: 460 VIth75
Fees: Day £9,990–£16,980 WB
£22,350–£26,475 FB £27,990–£31,995

St Hilda's
High Street, Bushey,
Hertfordshire WD23 3DA
Tel: 020 8950 1751
Headmistress: Miss Sarah-
Jane Styles MA
Age range: B2–4 G2–11
No. of pupils: 144
Fees: Day £12,012–£12,843

St Hilda's School
28 Douglas Road, Harpenden,
Hertfordshire AL5 2ES
Tel: 01582 712307
Headmaster: Mr Dan Sayers
Age range: G3–11 years
No. of pupils: 144
Fees: Day £6,615–£11,535

St John's Preparatory School
The Ridgeway, Potters Bar,
Hertfordshire EN6 5QT
Tel: 01707 657294
Headmistress: Mrs C Tardios BA(Hons)
Age range: 4–11
No. of pupils: 184
Fees: Day £10,350–£10,980

St Joseph's In The Park
St Mary's Lane, Hertingfordbury,
Hertford, Hertfordshire SG14 2LX
Tel: 01992 513810
Age range: 3–11
No. of pupils: 150
Fees: Day £5,718–£16,899

St Margaret's School, Bushey
Merry Hill Road, Bushey,
Hertfordshire WD23 1DT
Tel: 020 8416 4400
Head: Mrs Rose Hardy
MA(Oxon), MEd, FRSA
Age range: G4–18 years
No. of pupils: 450 VIth100
Fees: Day £11,286–£16,902 WB
£23,220–£27,279 FB £31,770

Stanborough School
Stanborough Park, Garston,
Watford, Hertfordshire WD25 9JT
Tel: 01923 673268
Head Teacher: Ms Lorraine Dixon
Age range: 3–17
No. of pupils: 300
Fees: Day £6,630–£10,224
WB £10,350–£13,995

Stormont
The Causeway, Potters Bar,
Hertfordshire EN6 5HA
Tel: 01707 654037
Age range: G4–11
Fees: Day £12,300–£13,050

The Christian School (Takeley)
Dunmow Road, Brewers End,
Takeley, Bishop's Stortford,
Hertfordshire CM22 6QH
Tel: 01279 871182
Headmaster: M E Humphries
Age range: 3–16
Fees: Day £6,012–£8,436

The King's School
Elmfield, Ambrose Lane, Harpenden,
Hertfordshire AL5 4DU
Tel: 01582 767566
Principal: Mr Clive John Case BA, HDE
Age range: 4–16
Fees: Day £7,680

The Purcell School, London
Aldenham Road, Bushey,
Hertfordshire WD23 2TS
Tel: 01923 331100
Headteacher: Dr Bernard Trafford
Age range: 10–18
No. of pupils: 180
Fees: Day £25,707 FB £32,826

Westbrook Hay Prep School
London Road, Hemel Hempstead,
Hertfordshire HP1 2RF
Tel: 01442 256143
Headmaster: Keith D Young BEd(Hons)
Age range: 3–13
No. of pupils: 300
Fees: Day £10,125–£14,580

York House School
Redheath, Sarratt Road,
Croxley Green, Rickmansworth,
Hertfordshire WD3 4LW
Tel: 01923 772395
Headmaster: Jon Gray BA(Ed)
Age range: 3–13
No. of pupils: 240
Fees: Day £10,440–£13,905

Norfolk

All Saints School
School Road, Lessingham,
Norwich, Norfolk NR12 0DJ
Tel: 01692 582083
Head teacher: P Wright
Age range: 7–16
Fees: Day £3,600–£5,400
🏫🎓

Aurora Eccles School
Quidenham, Quidenham,
Norfolk NR16 2NZ
Tel: 01953 887217
Acting Headteacher: Chris Brown
Age range: 5–19
No. of pupils: 150
Fees: Day £6,945–£11,370
FB £16,740–£19,785
🏫🏠£🎓🎓

Beeston Hall School
Beeston Regis, West Runton,
Cromer, Norfolk NR27 9NQ
Tel: 01263 837324
Headmaster: Mr Fred de
Falbe BA(Hons) PGCE
Age range: 4–13
Fees: Day £8,550–£17,730
FB £18,360–£23,820
🏠£🎓

Downham Preparatory School & Montessori Nursery
The Old Rectory, Stow Bardolph,
Kings Lynn, Norfolk PE34 3HT
Tel: 01366 388066
Headmistress: Mrs E Laffeaty-
Sharpe MontDip
Age range: 3 months–11
No. of pupils: 170
Fees: Day £6,426–£8,721
🎓

Focus School – Swaffham Campus
Turbine Way, Swaffham,
Norfolk PE37 7XD
Tel: 01760 336939
Headteacher: Mr John Shanahan
Age range: 7–18
No. of pupils: 161 VIth29
Ⓐ🎓

Glebe House School
2 Cromer Road, Hunstanton,
Norfolk PE36 6HW
Tel: 01485 532809
Headmaster: Mr Crofts
Age range: 0–13
No. of pupils: 110
Fees: Day £8,316–£13,290
🏠£🎓

Gresham's Nursery and Pre-Prep School
Market Place, Holt, Norfolk NR25 6BB
Tel: 01263 714575
Headmistress: Mrs Sarah Hollingsworth
Age range: 2–7
No. of pupils: 90
Fees: Day £10,050–£10,770
🏫🎓

Gresham's Prep School
Cromer Road, Holt, Norfolk NR25 6EY
Tel: 01263 714600
Headmaster: Mr J H W Quick BA, PGCE
Age range: 7–13
No. of pupils: 263
Fees: Day £14,670–£18,090 FB £25,350
🏫🏠£🎓

Gresham's Senior School
Cromer Road, Holt, Norfolk NR25 6EA
Tel: 01263 714 614
Headmaster: Mr Douglas
Robb MA, MEd
Age range: 13–18
No. of pupils: 480 VIth195
Fees: Day £24,420 FB £34,980
🏫Ⓐ🏠£Ⓑ🎓16+

Hethersett Old Hall School
Hethersett, Norwich, Norfolk NR9 3DW
Tel: 01603 810390
Headmaster: Mr S Crump
Age range: B3–11 G3–18
No. of pupils: 200
Fees: Day £10,032–£15,630 WB
£18,000–£24,060 FB £20,550–£29,280
🏫Ⓐ🏠£🎓16+

Langley Preparatory School at Taverham Hall
Taverham, Norwich, Norfolk NR8 6HU
Tel: 01603 868206
Headmaster: Mr Mike A
Crossley NPQH, BEd(Hons)
Age range: 2–13
Fees: Day £10,275–£14,175 WB £18,315
🏠£🎓

Langley School
Langley Park, Loddon,
Norwich, Norfolk NR14 6BJ
Tel: 01508 520210
Headmaster: Dominic Findlay
Age range: 10–18
No. of pupils: 461 VIth97
Fees: Day £15,720 WB £26,649 FB £31,941
🏫Ⓐ🏠£🎓16+

Norwich High School for Girls GDST
95 Newmarket Road, Norwich,
Norfolk NR2 2HU
Tel: 01603 453265
Headmistress: Mrs Kirsty von Malaise
Age range: G3–18
No. of pupils: VIth120
Fees: Day £9,198–£14,562
Ⓐ£🎓16+

Norwich School
70 The Close, Norwich, Norfolk NR1 4DD
Tel: 01603 728430
Head Master: Steffan D A Griffiths
Age range: 4–18
No. of pupils: 1065
Fees: Day £10,998–£16,212
Ⓐ£16+

Norwich Steiner School
Hospital Lane, Norwich,
Norfolk NR1 2HW
Tel: 01603 611175
Headteacher: Mr Andrew Vestrini
Age range: 3–18
No. of pupils: 91
Fees: Day £3,830–£7,010
🎓

Notre Dame Preparatory School
147 Dereham Road, Norwich,
Norfolk NR2 3TA
Tel: 01603 625593
Headmaster: Mr K O'Herlihy
Age range: 2–11
No. of pupils: 140
Fees: Day £2,985–£6,465
£🎓

Riddlesworth Hall Preparatory School
Garboldisham, Diss, Norfolk IP22 2TA
Tel: 01953 681 246
Principal: Mrs Sally Judd
Age range: 2–13
No. of pupils: 137
Fees: Day £10,470 WB £16,500 FB £17,535
🏠£🎓

Sacred Heart School
17 Mangate Street, Swaffham,
Norfolk PE37 7QW
Tel: 01760 721330/724577
Headmistress: Sr Francis Ridler
FDC, BEd(Hons), EYPS
Age range: 3–16 years
No. of pupils: 156
🏫🏠£🎓

St Nicholas House Prep School & Nursery
46 Yarmouth Road, North
Walsham, Norfolk NR28 9AT
Tel: 01692 403143
Headteacher: Mr Philip Oldroyd
Age range: 2–11
No. of pupils: 95
Fees: Day £5,847
£🎓

Thetford Grammar School
Bridge Street, Thetford, Norfolk IP24 3AF
Tel: 01842 752840
Headmaster: Mr Mark Bedford
Age range: 4–18
No. of pupils: 298 VIth20
Fees: Day £8,250–£13,665
Ⓐ£🎓16+

Thorpe House Langley Preparatory School
7 Yarmouth Road, Norwich,
Norfolk NR7 0EA
Tel: 01603 433055
Headmaster: Simon Marfleet
Age range: 2–11
No. of pupils: 144
Fees: Day £2,100–£2,540
£🎓

Town Close House Preparatory School
14 Ipswich Road, Norwich,
Norfolk NR2 2LR
Tel: 01603 620180
Headmaster: Mr Nicholas Bevington
Age range: 3–13
No. of pupils: 455
Fees: Day £8,670–£13,152
£🎓

Suffolk

Barnardiston Hall Preparatory School
Barnardiston, Nr Haverhill, Suffolk CB9 7TG
Tel: 01440 786316
Headmaster: Lt Col K A
Boulter MA(Cantab)
Age range: 6 months–13 years
No. of pupils: 220
Fees: Day £8,040–£13,395
WB £18,510 FB £20,085
ⓐ ⓔ ✐

Brookes Cambridge
Flempton Road, Risby, Bury St
Edmunds, Suffolk IP28 6QJ
Tel: 01284 760531
Headteacher: Mrs C Beedham
Age range: 2–18
No. of pupils: 240
Fees: Day £3,050–£4,760
FB £6,530–£9,390
ⓐ ✐

Culford Preparatory School
Culford, Bury St Edmunds, Suffolk IP28 6TX
Tel: 01284 385383
Headmaster: Mr Mike Schofield
Age range: 7–13
No. of pupils: 214
Fees: Day £11,625–£15,225
FB £22,485–£23,985
ⓐ

Culford Pre-Preparatory School
Fieldgate House, Bury St
Edmunds, Suffolk IP28 6TX
Tel: 01284 385412
Headmistress: Mrs Sarah Preston BA
Age range: 1–7
Fees: Day £8,940–£9,645

Culford School
Culford, Bury St Edmunds, Suffolk IP28 6TX
Tel: 01284 728615
Headmaster: Mr J F Johnson-
Munday MA, MBA
Age range: 1–18
No. of pupils: 650 VIth150
Fees: Day £8,940–£19,500
FB £22,485–£29,985
ⓖ Ⓐ ⓐ ⓔ ✐ ⑯

Fairstead House School
Fordham Road, Newmarket,
Suffolk CB8 7AA
Tel: 01638 662318
Head: Lynda Brereton
Age range: 9 months–11 years
No. of pupils: 118
Fees: Day £9,747–£10,611
ⓔ ✐

Felixstowe International College
Maybush Lane, Felixstowe,
Suffolk IP11 7NA
Tel: 01394 282388
Principal: Rev Seungjin Peter Kim
Age range: 10–17
No. of pupils: 20
Fees: FB £24,000
ⓐ ⓔ ⑯

Finborough School
The Hall, Great Finborough,
Stowmarket, Suffolk IP14 3EF
Tel: 01449 773600
Principal: Mr Steven Clark
Age range: 2–18
No. of pupils: 226 VIth20
Fees: Day £8,775–£13,590 WB
£16,455–£22,020 FB £20,475–£27,450
ⓖ Ⓐ ⓐ ⓔ ✐ ⑯ ⓦ

Framlingham College
College Road, Framlingham,
Suffolk IP13 9EY
Tel: 01728 723789
Headmaster: Mr Paul Taylor BA(Hons)
Age range: 2–18
No. of pupils: 700
Fees: Day £8,409–£19,176 FB £29,823
ⓖ Ⓐ ⓐ ⓔ ✐ ⑯

Ipswich High School
Woolverstone, Ipswich, Suffolk IP9 1AZ
Tel: 01473 780201
Head of School: Ms Oona Carlin
Age range: 3–18
No. of pupils: 500 VIth40
Fees: Day £8,769–£14,322
Ⓐ ⓔ ✐ ⑯

Ipswich Preparatory School
3 Ivry Street, Ipswich, Suffolk IP1 3QW
Tel: 01473 282800
Headteacher: Mrs A H Childs
Age range: 2–11
No. of pupils: 311
Fees: Day £11,850–£12,984
✐

Ipswich School
Henley Road, Ipswich, Suffolk IP1 3SG
Tel: 01473 408300
Headmaster: Mr Nicholas Weaver MA
Age range: 2–18
No. of pupils: 739 VIth218
Fees: Day £11,850–£15,579 WB
£24,402–£27,381 FB £26,376–£30,171
ⓖ Ⓐ ⓐ ⓔ ✐ ⑯

Moreton Hall Preparatory School
Mount Road, Bury St Edmunds,
Suffolk IP32 7BJ
Tel: 01284 753532
Headmaster: Mr Chris Moxon BA PGCE
Age range: 4–13
No. of pupils: 100
Fees: Day £8,700–£14,325
WB £19,425 FB £22,500
ⓐ ⓔ ✐

Old Buckenham Hall School
Brettenham, Ipswich, Suffolk IP7 7PH
Tel: 01449 740252
Headmaster: Mr David Griffiths
Age range: 3–13
No. of pupils: 228
Fees: Day £9,501–£19,272 WB
£16,521–£24,294 FB £22,056–£25,110
ⓐ ⓔ ✐

ORWELL PARK SCHOOL
For further details see p. 90
Nacton, Ipswich, Suffolk IP10 0ER
Tel: 01473 659225
Email: admissions@orwellpark.org
Website: www.orwellpark.co.uk
Headmaster: Mr Adrian
Brown MA(Cantab)
Age range: 2–13
No. of pupils: 289
ⓐ ⓔ ✐ ⑯

Queen's House School
Bredfield Street, Woodbridge,
Suffolk IP12 4NH
Tel: 01394 615070
Headteacher: Nicola Mitchell
Age range: 4–7

Saint Felix School
Halesworth Road, Southwold,
Suffolk IP18 6SD
Tel: 01502 722175
Headmaster: Mr. James Harrison
Age range: 2–18
No. of pupils: 312 VIth65
Fees: Day £7,485–£16,185 WB
£17,670–£22,470 FB £23,370–£28,170
ⓖ Ⓐ ⓐ ⓔ ✐ ⑯

South Lee Preparatory School
Nowton Road, Bury St
Edmunds, Suffolk IP33 2BT
Tel: 01284 754654
Headmaster: Mr Mervyn
Watch BEd (Hons)
Age range: 2–13
Fees: Day £9,645–£11,820
✐

St Joseph's College
Birkfield, Belstead Road,
Ipswich, Suffolk IP2 9DR
Tel: 01473 690281
Principal: Mrs Danielle Clarke
Age range: 3–18
No. of pupils: 564
Fees: Day £6,045–£15,150 WB
£24,990–£27,315 FB £26,145–£33,795
ⓖ Ⓐ ⓐ ⓔ ✐ ⑯

Stoke College
Stoke-by-Clare, Sudbury,
Suffolk CO10 8JE
Tel: 01787 278141
Head: Mr Frank Thompson
Age range: 3–18
Fees: Day £6,132–£14,979 WB
£20,829–£24,231 FB £27,096–£31,518
ⓖ ⓐ ⓔ ✐

Summerhill School
Leiston, Suffolk IP16 4HY
Tel: 01728 830540
Principal: Mrs Zoe Readhead
Age range: 5–17
No. of pupils: 69
Fees: Day £5,475–£11,205
FB £12,069–£19,041
ⓐ ✐

The Abbey School
Church Street, Woodbridge,
Suffolk IP12 1DS
Tel: 01394 382673
Headteacher: Nicola Mitchell
Age range: 7–11

The Meadows Montessori School
32 Larchcroft Road, Ipswich,
Suffolk IP1 6AR
Tel: 01473 233782
Headteacher: Ms Samantha Sims
Age range: 4–11
No. of pupils: 54

The Old School Henstead
Toad Row, Beccles, Suffolk NR34 7LG
Tel: 01502 741150
Head: Mr W J McKinney
Age range: 2–11
No. of pupils: 123
Fees: Day £6,990–£10,077

The Royal Hospital School
Holbrook, Ipswich, Suffolk IP9 2RX
Tel: +44 (0) 1473 326200
Headmaster: Mr Simon Lockyer
Age range: 11–18
No. of pupils: 700 VIth220
Fees: Day £15,690–£17,490 WB
£24,090–£29,910 FB £25,290–£32,595
ⓖ Ⓐ ⓐ ⓔ ✐ ⑯

Woodbridge School
Marryott House, Burkitt Road,
Woodbridge, Suffolk IP12 4JH
Tel: 01394 615000
Headmaster: Dr Richard Robson
Age range: 4–18
No. of pupils: 900 VIth104
Fees: Day £9,741–£16,500 FB £30,885
ⓖ Ⓐ ⓐ ⓔ ✐ ⑯

East Midlands

KEY TO SYMBOLS

- ⚲ *Boys' school*
- ⚲ *Girls' school*
- 🌐 *International school*
- 16 *Tutorial or sixth form college*
- Ⓐ *A levels*
- ⚱ *Boarding accommodation*
- £ *Bursaries*
- IB *International Baccalaureate*
- ✐ *Learning support*
- 16 *Entrance at 16+*
- ✥ *Vocational qualifications*
- (IAPS) *Independent Association of Preparatory Schools*
- (HMC) *The Headmasters' & Headmistresses' Conference*
- (ISA) *Independent Schools Association*
- (GSA) *Girls' School Association*
- (BSA) *Boarding Schools' Association*
- Ⓢ *Society of Heads*

Unless otherwise indicated, all schools are coeducational day schools. Single-sex and boarding schools will be indicated by the relevant icon.

Derbyshire

Barlborough Hall School
Barlborough, Chesterfield,
Derbyshire S43 4TJ
Tel: 01246 810511
Headteacher: Mrs Karen Keeton
Age range: 3–11
No. of pupils: 210
Fees: Day £7,741–£10,318
£ ✎

Dame Catherine Harpur's School
Rose Lane, Ticknall, Derby,
Derbyshire DE73 7JW
Tel: 01332 862792
Head: Ms Whyte
Age range: 3–11
No. of pupils: 28
Fees: Day £4,794

Derby Grammar School
Rykneld Hall, Rykneld Road, Littleover,
Derby, Derbyshire DE23 4BX
Tel: 01332 523027
Head: Dr Ruth Norris
Age range: B7–18 G16–18
No. of pupils: 255
Fees: Day £8,823–£13,449
✦ Ⓐ £ ✎ 16+

Derby High School
Hillsway, Littleover, Derby,
Derbyshire DE23 3DT
Tel: 01332 514267
Headteacher: Mrs Denise Gould
Age range: B3–11 G3–18
No. of pupils: 576 VIth74
Fees: Day £8,820–£12,870
Ⓐ £ ✎ 16+

Emmanuel School
Juniper Lodge, 43 Kedleston Road,
Derby, Derbyshire DE22 1FP
Tel: 01332 340505
Headteacher: Mr Ian Birkin
Age range: 3–16
No. of pupils: 65
Fees: Day £3,519
✎

Foremarke Hall
Milton, Derby, Derbyshire DE65 6EJ
Tel: 01283 707100
Headmaster: Mr R Merriman
MA, BSc(Hons), FCollP
Age range: 3–13
✦ £ ✎

Gateway Christian School
Moor Lane, Dale Abbey,
Ilkeston, Derbyshire DE7 4PP
Tel: 0115 9440609
Head Teacher: Mrs Corinna Walters
Age range: 3–11
No. of pupils: 31
Fees: Day £2,400
✎

Michael House Steiner School
The Field, Shipley, Heanor,
Derbyshire DE75 7JH
Tel: 01773 718050
Age range: 3–16
No. of pupils: 150
Fees: Day £2,212.15–£6,088.50

Mount St Mary's College
College Road, Spinkhill,
Derbyshire S21 3YL
Tel: 01246 433388
Headmaster: Dr Nicholas Cuddihy
Age range: 11–18
No. of pupils: 360
Fees: Day £11,669–£13,406 WB
£18,202–£23,431 FB £22,128–£29,046
✦ Ⓐ ✦ £ ✎ 16+

Normanton House Primary School
Normanton House, Village Street,
Derby, Derbyshire DE23 8DF
Tel: 01332 769333
Headteacher: Mr Nighat Sultana Khan
Age range: 5–10
No. of pupils: 97

Ockbrook School
The Settlement, Ockbrook,
Derby, Derbyshire DE72 3RJ
Tel: 01332 673532
Head: Mr Tom Brooksby
Age range: 2–18
No. of pupils: 409 VIth55
Fees: Day £8,955–£13,170
✦ Ⓐ ✦ £ ✎ 16+

Old Vicarage School
11 Church Lane, Darley Abbey,
Derby, Derbyshire DE22 1EW
Tel: 01332 557130
Headmaster: Mr M J Adshead
Age range: 3–13
No. of pupils: 95
Fees: Day £7,650–£8,124
£ ✎

Repton School
The Hall, Repton, Derbyshire DE65 6FH
Tel: 01283 559222
Head: Mr W M A Land MA
Age range: 13–18
No. of pupils: 653 VIth299
Fees: Day £26,493 FB £35,712
✦ Ⓐ ✦ £ ✎ 16+

S. Anselm's School
Stanedge Road, Bakewell,
Derbyshire DE45 1DP
Tel: 01629 812734
Headmaster: Peter Phillips BA
(Hons), MA, PGCE (SPLD), NPQH
Age range: 3–13
No. of pupils: 215
Fees: Day £10,950–£20,700 FB £26,100
✦ £ ✎

St Peter & St Paul School
Brambling House, Hady Hill,
Chesterfield, Derbyshire S41 0EF
Tel: 01246 278522
Headteacher: Mrs Jill Phinn
Age range: 3 months–11 years
No. of pupils: 120
Fees: Day £8,658–£9,159
£ ✎

St Wystan's School
High Street, Repton,
Derbyshire DE65 6GE
Tel: 01283 703258
Head Teacher: Karan Hopkinson
Age range: 3–11
Fees: Day £4,500–£8,655
£ ✎

Leicestershire

Al-Aqsa Schools Trust
The Wayne Way, Leicester,
Leicestershire LE5 4PP
Tel: 0116 2760953
Headteacher: Mrs Amina Patel
Age range: 5–16
No. of pupils: 231
✎

Ashby School
School House, Leicester Road, Ashby-
de-la-Zouch, Leicestershire LE65 1DH
Tel: +44 (0) 1530 413748
Headteacher: Mr Geoff Staniforth
Age range: B11–19
No. of pupils: 1643
✦ Ⓐ ✦ ✎ 16+ ✦

Brooke House College
Leicester Road, Market Harborough,
Leicestershire LE16 7AU
Tel: 01858 462452
Principal: Mr Mike Oliver
Age range: 14–20
No. of pupils: VIth73
Fees: Day £19,650–£21,525
FB £33,000–£36,000
✦ 16+ Ⓐ ✦

Brooke House Day School
Croft Road, Cosby, Leicester,
Leicestershire LE9 1SE
Tel: 0116 286 7372
Head: Mrs Joy Parker
Age range: 3–14

Darul Arqam Educational Institute
2 Overton Road, Leicester,
Leicestershire LE5 0JA
Tel: 0116 2741626
Headteacher: Mr Ahmed
Abdul Dadipatel
Age range: B5–16
No. of pupils: 75
✦

Darul Uloom Leicester
119 Loughborough Road,
Leicester, Leicestershire LE4 5LN
Tel: 0116 2668922
Headteacher: Moulana Ishaq Boodi
Age range: B11–25
Fees: Day £1,800 FB £2,700

Fairfield Preparatory School
Leicester Road, Loughborough,
Leicestershire LE11 2AE
Tel: 01509 215172
Headmaster: Mr A Earnshaw
BA Lancaster NPQH
Age range: 3–11
No. of pupils: 498

Grace Dieu Manor School
Grace Dieu, Thringstone,
Leicestershire LE67 5UG
Tel: 01530 222276
Head of School: Mrs Margaret Kewell
Age range: 12 weeks–11
No. of pupils: 315
Fees: Day £10,280–£10,821

Jameah Girls Academy
49 Rolleston Street, Leicester,
Leicestershire LE5 3SD
Tel: 0116 262 7745
Headteacher: Ms Erfana Bora
Age range: G6–16
No. of pupils: 142

Leicester Grammar Junior School
London Road, Grea Glen,
Leicester, Leicestershire LE8 9FL
Tel: 0116 259 1950
Age range: 3–11
No. of pupils: 391

Leicester Grammar School
London Road, Great Glen,
Leicester, Leicestershire LE8 9FL
Tel: 0116 259 1900
Head & Chief Executive: C P M King MA
Age range: 11–18
No. of pupils: 704 VIth188
Fees: Day £13,029

Leicester High School for Girls
454 London Road, Leicester,
Leicestershire LE2 2PP
Tel: 0116 2705338
Headmaster: Mr Alan Whelpdale
Age range: G3–18
No. of pupils: 435 VIth60
Fees: Day £2,995–£4,065

Leicester International School
16-20 Beal Street, Leicester,
Leicestershire LE2 0AA
Tel: 0116 2515345
Principal: Mr N Hussein
Age range: 5–11
No. of pupils: 146

Leicester Islamic Academy
320 London Road, Leicester,
Leicestershire LE2 2PP
Tel: 0116 2705343
Headteacher: Mrs S Khan
Age range: 3–11
Fees: Day £1,980

Leicester Prep School
2 Albert Road, Leicester,
Leicestershire LE2 2AA
Tel: 0116 2707414
Headmaster: Paul Hitchcock
Age range: 3–11
No. of pupils: 130
Fees: Day £7,800

Loughborough Amherst School
Gray Street, Loughborough,
Leicestershire LE11 2DZ
Tel: 01509 263901
Headmaster: Dr Julian Murphy
Age range: B4–11 G4–18
No. of pupils: 224
Fees: Day £9,816–£12,189

Loughborough Grammar School
6 Burton Walks, Loughborough,
Leicestershire LE11 2DU
Tel: 01509 233233
Headmaster: Mr Duncan Byrne
Age range: B10–18
No. of pupils: 1010
Fees: Day £12,549 WB £12,966
FB £16,203–£16,983

Loughborough High School
Burton Walks, Loughborough,
Leicestershire LE11 2DU
Tel: 01509 212348
Headmistress: Mrs G Byrom
Age range: G11–18
No. of pupils: VIth170
Fees: Day £12,549

Manor House School
South Street, Ashby-de-la-Zouch,
Leicestershire LE65 1BR
Tel: 01530 412932
Headteacher: Mr Andrew Messent
Age range: 3–16
Fees: Day £7,545–£11,621

Ratcliffe College
Fosse Way, Ratcliffe on the Wreake,
Leicester, Leicestershire LE7 4SG
Tel: 01509 817000
Headmaster: Mr J Reddin
BSc, MSc, NPQH
Age range: 3–18
No. of pupils: 831 VIth142
Fees: Day £9,345–£16,287 WB
£20,676–£23,959 FB £25,959

St Crispin's School
6 St Mary's Road, Stoneygate,
Leicester, Leicestershire LE2 1XA
Tel: 0116 2707648
Head Master: Andrew Atkin
Age range: 2–16

Stoneygate School
6 London Road, Great Glen,
Leicester, Leicestershire LE8 9DJ
Tel: 0116 259 2282
Headmaster: Mr J F Dobson
Age range: 3–16
Fees: Day £11,082–£14,028

The Dixie Grammar School
Station Road, Market Bosworth,
Leicestershire CV13 0LE
Tel: 01455 292244
Headmaster: Richard Lynn MA
Age range: 3–18
No. of pupils: 474 VIth71
Fees: Day £8,835–£12,015

Tiny Tots Pre-School & Primary
16-20 Beal Street, Leicester,
Leicestershire LE2 0AA
Tel: 0116 2515345
Principal: Mr N Hussein
Age range: 2–11
No. of pupils: 104

Lincolnshire

Ayscoughfee Hall School
Welland Hall, London Road,
Spalding, Lincolnshire PE11 2TE
Tel: 01775 724733
Headmistress: Mrs Clare
Ogden BA(Hons), PGCE
Age range: 3–11
No. of pupils: 146
Fees: Day £4,560–£6,720

**Bicker Preparatory
School & Early Years**
School Lane, Bicker, Boston,
Lincolnshire PE20 3DW
Tel: 01775 821786
Head Teacher: Mrs J Miles BA.PGCE
Age range: 3–11
No. of pupils: 74

Copthill Independent Day School
Barnack Road, Uffington,
Stamford, Lincolnshire PE9 3AD
Tel: 01780 757506
Headmaster: Mr J A Teesdale
BA(Hons), PGCE
Age range: 2–11
No. of pupils: 300
Fees: Day £9,255–£10,350

Dudley House School
1 Dudley Road, Grantham,
Lincolnshire NG31 9AA
Tel: 01476 400184
Headmistress: Mrs Jenny Johnson
Age range: 3–11
No. of pupils: 50
Fees: Day £5,220

Grantham Preparatory International School
Gorse Lane, Grantham,
Lincolnshire NG31 7UF
Tel: +44 (0)1476 593293
Headmistress: Mrs K A Korcz
Age range: 3–11
No. of pupils: 142
Fees: Day £7,950–£9,690

Greenwich House School
106 High Holme Road, Louth,
Lincolnshire LN11 0HE
Tel: 01507 609252
Headmistress: Mrs J Brindle
Age range: 9 months–11 years
No. of pupils: 50

Handel House Preparatory School
Northolme Road, Gainsborough,
Lincolnshire DN21 2JB
Tel: 01427 612426
Headmistress: Mrs Victoria Haigh
Age range: 2–11
Fees: Day £3,585–£4,320

Kirkstone House School
Main Street, Baston, Peterborough,
Lincolnshire PE6 9PA
Tel: 01778 560350
Head: Mrs C Jones BSocSc
Age range: 3–18
No. of pupils: 234
Fees: Day £9,498–£11,640

Lincoln Minster School
Upper Lindum Street, Lincoln,
Lincolnshire LN2 5RW
Tel: 01522 551300
Headmaster: Mr J M Wallace
Age range: 2–18
No. of pupils: 840 VIth144
Fees: Day £9,276–£13,632 WB
£23,013–£26,715 FB £20,901–£24,186

St Hugh's School
Cromwell Avenue, Woodhall
Spa, Lincolnshire LN10 6TQ
Tel: 01526 352169
Head: C Ward BEd(Hons)
Age range: 2–13
No. of pupils: 195
Fees: Day £8,880–£14,928 FB £18,750

Stamford Endowed Schools
Brazenose House, St Paul's Street,
Stamford, Lincolnshire PE9 2BE
Tel: 01780 750310
Principal: Mrs Vicky Buckman
Age range: 2–18
No. of pupils: 1634 VIth400
Fees: Day £9,414–£15,318 WB
£19,821–£24,801 FB £21,864–£28,446

Stamford High School
St Martin's, Stamford,
Lincolnshire PE9 2LL
Tel: 01780 428200
Principal: Mrs Vicky Buckman
Age range: G11–18
No. of pupils: 633 VIth201
Fees: Day £15,318 WB £21,552–
£24,801 FB £28,446

Stamford Junior School
Kettering Road, Stamford,
Lincolnshire PE9 2LR
Tel: 01780 484400
Headteacher: Mrs Emma Maria Smith
Age range: 2–11
No. of pupils: 344
Fees: Day £9,414–£12,102 WB
£17,415–£19,821 FB £21,864

Viking School
140 Church Road North, Skegness,
Lincolnshire PE25 2QJ
Tel: 01754 765749
Principal: Mrs S J Barker
Age range: 3–11
No. of pupils: 100
Fees: Day £4,050–£4,350

Witham Hall Preparatory School
Witham-on-the-Hill, Bourne,
Lincolnshire PE10 0JJ
Tel: +44(0)1778 590222
Headmaster: Mr Charles
Welch B.Ed (Hons)
Age range: 4–13
No. of pupils: 250
Fees: Day £9,555–£16,080 FB £21,690

Northamptonshire

Beachborough School
Westbury, Brackley,
Northamptonshire NN13 5LB
Tel: 01280 700071
Interim Head: Elizabeth Hill
Age range: 2–13
No. of pupils: 260
Fees: Day £10,728–£16,845

Bosworth Independent College
Nazareth House, Barrack
Road, Northampton,
Northamptonshire NN2 6AF
Tel: 01604 235090
Principal: Fiona Pocock MA PGCE
Age range: 13–University
No. of pupils: VIth250
Fees: Day £12,600 WB £20,030–
£21,230 FB £21,900–£23,100

Childfirst Day Nursery Northampton
Moulton Lodge, Moulton Way
North, Moulton, Northampton,
Northamptonshire NN3 7RW
Tel: 01604 790440
Headmistress: Mrs Mary
Heal BA(Hons)Ed
Age range: 2 months–7 years
Fees: Day £6,255

Laxton Junior School
East Road, Oundle, Peterborough,
Northamptonshire PE8 4BX
Tel: 01832 277275
Head of School: Mr Sam Robertson
Age range: 4–11
No. of pupils: 260
Fees: Day £10,185–£11,925

Maidwell Hall
Maidwell, Northampton,
Northamptonshire NN6 9JG
Tel: 01604 686234
Headmaster: Mr R A
Lankester MA, PGCE
Age range: 7–13
No. of pupils: 124
Fees: Day £17,505 WB
£26,880 FB £26,880

Northampton High School GDST
Newport Pagnell Road,
Hardingstone, Northampton,
Northamptonshire NN4 6UU
Tel: 01604 765765
Headmistress: Dr Helen
Stringer DPhil, MA, PGCE
Age range: G3–18
No. of pupils: 649 VIth128
Fees: Day £10,551–£14,511

Oundle School
Oundle, Peterborough,
Northamptonshire PE8 4GH
Tel: 01832 277 122
Head of School: Mrs Sarah Kerr-Dineen
Age range: 11–18
No. of pupils: 1107
Fees: Day £17,880–£23,505
FB £27,885–£36,690

Overstone Park School
Overstone Park,
Overstone, Northampton,
Northamptonshire NN6 0DT
Tel: 01604 643787
Principal: Mrs M F Brown
BA(Hons), PGCE
Age range: 0–18
No. of pupils: 85

Pitsford School
Pitsford Hall, Pitsford, Northampton,
Northamptonshire NN6 9AX
Tel: 01604 880306
Headmaster: N R Toone BSc, MInstP
Age range: 4–18
No. of pupils: VIth49
Fees: Day £8,223–£14,277
Ⓐ £ ⏩ 16+

Quinton House School
Upton Hall, Upton, Northampton,
Northamptonshire NN5 4UX
Tel: 01604 752050
Headteacher: Mr Tim Hoyle
Age range: 2–18
No. of pupils: 390
Fees: Day £8,040–£11,985
Ⓐ £ ⏩ 16+

Spratton Hall
Smith Street, Spratton,
Northamptonshire NN6 8HP
Tel: 01604 847292
Head Master: Mr Simon Clarke
Age range: 4–13
No. of pupils: 376
Fees: Day £10,050–£15,060
£ ⏩

St Peter's Independent School
Lingswood Park,
Blackthorn, Northampton,
Northamptonshire NN3 8TA
Tel: 01604 411745
Acting Head: Julie Fenlon
Age range: 4–18
No. of pupils: 130
Fees: Day £6,825–£9,150
Ⓐ 16+

St Peter's School
52 Headlands, Kettering,
Northamptonshire NN15 6DJ
Tel: 01536 512066
Headmistress: Mrs Maria Chapman
Age range: 2–11
No. of pupils: 161
£ ⏩

Wellingborough School
Wellingborough,
Northamptonshire NN8 2BX
Tel: 01933 222427
Headmaster: Mr A N Holman
Age range: 3–18
No. of pupils: VIth145
Fees: Day £9,420–£15,990
Ⓐ £ ⏩ 16+

Winchester House School
High Street, Brackley,
Northamptonshire NN13 7AZ
Tel: 01280 702483
Head: Mrs Emma Goldsmith
Age range: 3–13
No. of pupils: 307
Fees: Day £10,905–£19,230 WB £24,330
🏠 £ ⏩

Nottinghamshire

Colston Bassett Preparatory School
School Lane, Colston
bassett, Nottingham,
Nottinghamshire NG12 3FD
Tel: 01949 81118
Headteacher: Mrs Ruth O'Dell
Age range: 4–11
Fees: Day £7,098

Coteswood House School
19 Thackeray's Lane, Woodthorpe,
Nottingham, Nottinghamshire NG5 4HT
Tel: 0115 9676551
Head: Mrs S M Fernley
Age range: 3–11
No. of pupils: 40
Fees: Day £4,200

Highfields School
London Road, Newark,
Nottinghamshire NG24 3AL
Tel: 01636 704103
Headmaster: Mr R C R Thomson
BEd (Hons) NPQH
Age range: 2–11
No. of pupils: 140
Fees: Day £9,195
£ ⏩

Hollygirt School
Elm Avenue, Nottingham,
Nottinghamshire NG3 4GF
Tel: 0115 958 0596
Headmistress: Mrs Pam Hutley
BA(Hons), PGCE, MSc
Age range: 3–16
No. of pupils: 200
Fees: Day £9,300–£12,234
£ ⏩

Iona School
310 Sneinton Dale, Nottingham,
Nottinghamshire NG3 7DN
Tel: 01159 415295
Chair of College: Richard Moore
Age range: 3–11
Fees: Day £6,373.52

Jamia Al-Hudaa Residential College
Forest House, Berkeley Avenue,
Mapperley Park, Nottingham,
Nottinghamshire NG3 5TT
Tel: 0115 9690800
Principal: Raza ul-Haq Siakhvy
Age range: 11–19
No. of pupils: 224
🏃 🏠

Jubilee House Christian School
226 Nottingham Road, Eastwood,
Nottinghamshire NG16 3GR
Tel: 01773 688100
Headteacher: Mrs J Marks
Age range: 3–16
No. of pupils: 70
£

Lammas School
Lammas Road, Sutton-in-Ashfield,
Nottinghamshire NG17 2AD
Tel: 0208 424 8475
Head: Mrs Sara Baldry
Age range: 4–19
No. of pupils: 57
Fees: Day £6,544–£8,489
Ⓐ ⏩

Nottingham Girls' High School GDST
9 Arboretum Street, Nottingham,
Nottinghamshire NG1 4JB
Tel: 0115 9417663
Head: Miss Julie Keller
Age range: G4–18
No. of pupils: 786 VIth155
Fees: Day £9,873–£13,581
🏃 Ⓐ £ 16+

Nottingham High Infant and Junior School
Waverley Mount, Nottingham,
Nottinghamshire NG7 4ED
Tel: 0115 845 2214
Headteacher: Mrs Clare Bruce
Age range: 4–11
No. of pupils: 180
Fees: Day £3,393–£4,955
⏩

Nottingham High School
Waverley Mount, Nottingham,
Nottinghamshire NG7 4ED
Tel: 0115 9786056
Headmaster: Mr Kevin Fear BA
Age range: 4–18
No. of pupils: 1023 VIth229
Fees: Day £10,179–£14,865
🏃 Ⓐ £ ⏩ 16+

Nottingham Islamia School
30 Bentinck Road, Hyson Green,
Nottingham, Nottinghamshire NG7 4AF
Tel: 0115 970 5858
Head: Dr Musharraf Hussain
Age range: 5–11

Plumtree School
Church Hill, Plumtree, Nottingham,
Nottinghamshire NG12 5ND
Tel: 0115 937 5859
Head Teacher: Phil Simpson
Age range: 3–11
Fees: Day £6,540

Salterford House School
Salterford Lane, Calverton,
Nottingham, Nottinghamshire
NG14 6NZ
Tel: 0115 9652127
Headmistress: Mrs Marlene
Venables CertEd
Age range: 3–11
No. of pupils: 124
Fees: Day £7,800–£7,890
⏩

Saville House School
11 Church Street, Mansfield
Woodhouse, Mansfield,
Nottinghamshire NG19 8AH
Tel: 01623 625068
Joint Head: Mrs See & Mrs Hill
Age range: 3–11
No. of pupils: 89
Fees: Day £5,475
⏩

St Joseph's School
33 Derby Road, Nottingham,
Nottinghamshire NG1 5AW
Tel: 0115 9418356
Head Teacher: Mr Ashley Crawshaw
Age range: 1–11
Fees: Day £7,728
🖉

The Orchard School
South Leverton, Retford,
Nottinghamshire DN22 0DJ
Tel: 01427 880395
Principal: Mrs S M Fox BA, PGCE
Age range: 5–16
No. of pupils: 150
Fees: Day £4,770–£7,575

Trent College
Derby Road, Long Eaton, Nottingham,
Nottinghamshire NG10 4AD
Tel: 0115 8494949
Head: Mr Bill Penty
Age range: 11–18
No. of pupils: 1117 VIth200
Fees: Day £13,890–£17,442 WB
£21,945–£23,568 FB £31,644–£32,517
🌐 Ⓐ 🏫 £ 🖉 16+

Wellow House School
Wellow, Newark,
Nottinghamshire NG22 0EA
Tel: 01623 861054
Headmaster: Nicola Matthews
Age range: 3–13
No. of pupils: 152
Fees: Day £7,485–£11,985
🏫 £ 🖉

Worksop College
Worksop, Nottinghamshire S80 3AP
Tel: 01909 537100
Headmaster: G W Horgan MA (Oxon)
Age range: 3–18
No. of pupils: 614 VIth141
Fees: Day £8,385–£17,985
FB £19,485–£29,085
🌐 Ⓐ 🏫 £ 🖉 16+

Worksop College Preparatory School, Ranby House
Retford, Nottinghamshire DN22 8HX
Tel: 01777 714387 (Admissions)
Headmaster: C S J Pritchard
MA, BA(Hons), QTS
Age range: 3–11 years
No. of pupils: 190
Fees: Day £8,385–£13,485
FB £19,485–£20,085
🏫 £ 🖉

Rutland

Brooke Priory School
Station Approach, Oakham,
Rutland LE15 6QW
Tel: 01572 724778
Headmaster: Mr R Outwin-
Flinders BEd (Hons)
Age range: 2–11
No. of pupils: 193
Fees: Day £7,395–£9,195
£ 🖉

OAKHAM SCHOOL
For further details see p. 104
Chapel Close, Oakham,
Rutland LE15 6DT
Tel: 01572 758758
Email:
admissions@oakham.rutland.sch.uk
Website:
www.oakham.rutland.sch.uk
Headmaster: Mr Nigel
M Lashbrook BA
Age range: 10–18
No. of pupils: VIth405
Fees: Day £16,905–£20,535
FB £25,605–£33,660
🌐 Ⓐ 🏫 £ IB 🖉 16+

Uppingham School
Uppingham, Rutland LE15 9QE
Tel: 01572 822216 Admissions:
01572 820611
Headmaster: Dr Richard Maloney
Age range: 13–18
No. of pupils: 798 VIth344
Fees: Day £8,771 FB £12,530
🌐 Ⓐ 🏫 £ 🖉 16+

Greater London

KEY TO SYMBOLS

- Boys' school
- Girls' school
- International school
- Tutorial or sixth form college
- A levels
- Boarding accommodation
- £ Bursaries
- IB International Baccalaureate
- Learning support
- Entrance at 16+
- Vocational qualifications
- IAPS Independent Association of Preparatory Schools
- HMC The Headmasters' & Headmistresses' Conference
- ISA Independent Schools Association
- GSA Girls' School Association
- BSA Boarding Schools' Association
- S Society of Heads

Unless otherwise indicated, all schools are coeducational day schools. Single-sex and boarding schools will be indicated by the relevant icon.

Essex

Al-Noor Primary School
Newton Industrial Estate, Eastern
Avenue, Chadwell Heath,
Romford, Essex RM6 5SD
Tel: 020 8597 7576
Head: Mrs Someera Butt
Age range: 4–10
No. of pupils: 175
Fees: Day £3,600

**AVON HOUSE
PREPARATORY SCHOOL**
For further details see p. 108
490 High Road, Woodford
Green, Essex IG8 0PN
Tel: 020 8504 1749
Email: office@ahsprep.co.uk
Website:
www.avonhouseschool.co.uk
Headteacher:
Mrs Amanda Campbell
Age range: 3–11
No. of pupils: 230
Fees: Day £9,375–£10,290

Bancroft's School
High Road, Woodford
Green, Essex IG8 0RF
Tel: 020 8505 4821
Head: Mr Simon Marshall MA, PGCE
(Cantab), MA, MPhil (Oxon)
Age range: 7–18
No. of pupils: 1143 VIth245

Beehive Preparatory School
233 Beehive Lane, Redbridge,
Ilford, Essex IG4 5ED
Tel: 020 8550 3224
Headteacher: Miss Richards
Age range: 4–11
Fees: Day £5,685

Braeside School for Girls
130 High Road, Buckhurst
Hill, Essex IG9 5SD
Tel: 020 8504 1133
Headmistress: Claire Osborn
Age range: G3–16
No. of pupils: 199
Fees: Day £8,700–£12,750

Chigwell School
High Road, Chigwell, Essex IG7 6QF
Tel: 020 8501 5700
Headmaster: Mr M E Punt MA, MSc
Age range: 4–18
No. of pupils: 915 VIth185
Fees: Day £11,985–£17,985 FB £30,885

Eastcourt Independent School
1 Eastwood Road, Goodmayes,
Ilford, Essex IG3 8UW
Tel: 020 8590 5472
Headmistress: Mrs Christine
Redgrave BSc(Hons), DipEd, MEd
Age range: 3–11
Fees: Day £7,200

Gidea Park College
2 Balgores Lane, Gidea Park,
Romford, Essex RM2 5JR
Tel: 01708 740381
Headmistress: Mrs Katherine Whiskerd
Age range: 3–11
No. of pupils: 177
Fees: Day £9,675

Goodrington School
17 Walden Road, Hornchurch,
Essex RM11 2JT
Tel: 01708 448349
Head Teacher: Mrs J R Ellenby
Age range: 3–11
Fees: Day £6,915

**Guru Gobind Singh
Khalsa College**
Roding Lane, Chigwell, Essex IG7 6BQ
Tel: 020 8559 9160
Principal: Mr Amarjit Singh
Toor BSc(Hons), BSc, BT
Age range: 3–19
Fees: Day £5,892–£6,720

Immanuel School
Havering Grange Centre, Havering
Road North, Romford, Essex RM1 4HR
Tel: 01708 764449
Principal: Simon Reeves
Age range: 3–16

Loyola Preparatory School
103 Palmerston Road, Buckhurst
Hill, Essex IG9 5NH
Tel: 020 8504 7372
Headteacher: Mrs Kirsty Anthony
Age range: B3–11
No. of pupils: 183
Fees: Day £9,330

**Maytime Montessori Nursery
– Cranbrook Road**
341 Cranbrook Road,
Ilford, Essex IG1 4UF
Tel: 020 8554 3079

**Maytime Montessori
Nursery – Eastwood Road**
2 Eastwood Road, Goodmayes,
Essex IG3 8XB
Tel: 020 8599 3744

**Maytime Montessori
Nursery – York Road**
87 York Road, Ilford, Essex IG1 3AF
Tel: 020 8553 1524
Age range: 0–6

Oakfields Montessori School
Harwood Hall, Harwood Hall Lane,
Corbets Tey, Essex RM14 2YG
Tel: 01708 220117
Headmistress: Katrina Carroll
Age range: 2–11
Fees: Day £9,720–£10,500

Oaklands School
8 Albion Hill, Loughton, Essex IG10 4RA
Tel: 020 8508 3517
**Group Managing
Principal:** Mr M Hagger
Age range: 2–16
No. of pupils: 243
Fees: Day £10,350–£10,575

Park School for Girls
20-22 Park Avenue, Ilford, Essex IG1 4RS
Tel: 020 8554 2466
Headmistress: Mrs Androulla Nicholas
Age range: G4–16
No. of pupils: 230 VIth19
Fees: Day £6,795–£10,260

Raphael Independent School
Park Lane, Hornchurch, Essex RM11 1XY
Tel: 01708 744735
Head of School: Mrs C Salmon
Age range: 4–16
No. of pupils: 135
Fees: Day £6,285–£9,045

St Aubyn's School
Bunces Lane, Woodford
Green, Essex IG8 9DU
Tel: 020 8504 1577
Headmaster: Mr Leonard
Blom BEd(Hons) BA NPQH
Age range: 3–13
No. of pupils: 525
Fees: Day £5,370–£12,195

**St Mary's Hare Park
School & Nursery**
South Drive, Gidea Park,
Romford, Essex RM2 6HH
Tel: 01708 761220
Head Teacher: Mrs K Karwacinski
Age range: 2–11
No. of pupils: 180
Fees: Day £8,775

The Daiglen School
68 Palmerston Road, Buckhurst
Hill, Essex IG9 5LG
Tel: 020 8504 7108
Headteacher: Mrs P Dear
Age range: 3–11
No. of pupils: 130
Fees: Day £9,300–£9,450

**The Ursuline Preparatory
School Ilford**
2-8 Coventry Road, Ilford,
Essex IG1 4QR
Tel: 020 8518 4050
Headteacher: Mrs Victoria
McNaughton
Age range: G3–11
No. of pupils: 159
Fees: Day £7,320–£9,828

**Woodford Green
Preparatory School**
Glengall Road, Woodford
Green, Essex IG8 0BZ
Tel: 020 8504 5045
Headmaster: Mr J P Wadge
Age range: 3–11
No. of pupils: 383
Fees: Day £3,270

Hertfordshire

Lyonsdown School
3 Richmond Road, New Barnet,
Barnet, Hertfordshire EN5 1SA
Tel: 020 8449 0225
Head: Mr C Hammond BA (Hons) PGCE
Age range: B3–7 G3–11
No. of pupils: 185
Fees: Day £4,080–£10,200

Mount House School
Camlet Way, Hadley Wood,
Barnet, Hertfordshire EN4 0NJ
Tel: 020 8449 6889
Headmaster: Mr Matthew Burke
Age range: 11–18
No. of pupils: 180
Fees: Day £14,820

**Norfolk Lodge Montessori
Nursery & Pre-Prep School**
Dancers Hill Road, Barnet,
Hertfordshire EN5 4RP
Tel: 020 8447 1565
Nursery Manager: Suzanne Clarke
Age range: 6 months–7 years
No. of pupils: 140

Susi Earnshaw Theatre School
68 High Street, Barnet,
Hertfordshire EN5 5SJ
Tel: 020 8441 5010
Age range: 9–16
No. of pupils: 60
Fees: Day £9,000–£12,000

The Royal Masonic School for Girls
Rickmansworth Park, Rickmansworth,
Hertfordshire WD3 4HF
Tel: 01923 773168
Headmaster: Mr Kevin Carson
M.Phil (Cambridge)
Age range: G4–18
No. of pupils: 930 VIth165
Fees: Day £11,475–£17,475 WB
£20,115–£27,495 FB £21,225–£29,835

Kent

Ashgrove School
116 Widmore Road,
Bromley, Kent BR1 3BE
Tel: 020 8460 4143
Principal: Patricia Ash CertEd,
BSc(Hons), PhD, CMath, FIMA
Age range: 4–11
No. of pupils: 106
Fees: Day £8,730

Babington House School
Grange Drive, Chislehurst, Kent BR7 5ES
Tel: 020 8467 5537
Headmaster: Mr Tim Lello
MA, FRSA, NPQH
Age range: B3-11 & 16–18 G3–18
No. of pupils: 364

**Benedict House
Preparatory School**
1-5 Victoria Road, Sidcup,
Kent DA15 7HD
Tel: 020 8300 7206
Headteacher: Mr Malcolm Gough
Age range: 3–11
Fees: Day £3,807–£7,929

Bickley Park School
24 Page Heath Lane, Bickley,
Bromley, Kent BR1 2DS
Tel: 020 8467 2195
Headmaster: Mr Patrick Wenham
Age range: B3–13 G3–4
No. of pupils: 370
Fees: Day £6,990–£14,940

Bishop Challoner School
228 Bromley Road, Shortlands,
Bromley, Kent BR2 0BS
Tel: 020 8460 3546
Headteacher: Ms Paula Anderson
Age range: 3–18
No. of pupils: 363
Fees: Day £8,331–£11,547

**BREASIDE PREPARATORY
SCHOOL**
For further details see p. 110
41-43 Orchard Road,
Bromley, Kent BR1 2PR
Tel: 020 8460 0916
Email: info@breaside.co.uk
Website: www.breaside.co.uk
Executive Principal: Mrs Karen A
Nicholson B.Ed, NPQH, Dip EYs
Age range: 2 ½–11
No. of pupils: 360
Fees: Day £11,070–£12,900

Bromley High School GDST
Blackbrook Lane, Bickley,
Bromley, Kent BR1 2TW
Tel: 020 8781 7000/1
Head: Mrs A M Drew
BA(Hons), MBA (Dunelm)
Age range: G4–18
No. of pupils: 912 VIth120
Fees: Day £13,356–£16,563

Darul Uloom London
Foxbury Avenue, Perry Street,
Chislehurst, Kent BR7 6SD
Tel: 020 8295 0637
Principal: Mufti Mustafa
Age range: B11–18
No. of pupils: 160
Fees: FB £2,400

FARRINGTONS SCHOOL
For further details see p. 112
Perry Street, Chislehurst, Kent BR7 6LR
Tel: 020 8467 0256
Email:
admissions@farringtons.kent.sch.uk
Website: www.farringtons.org.uk
Head: Mrs Dorothy Nancekievill
Age range: 3–18
No. of pupils: 700 VIth100
Fees: Day £15,120 WB
£29,850 FB £31,680

Merton Court Preparatory School
38 Knoll Road, Sidcup, Kent DA14 4QU
Tel: 020 8300 2112
Headmaster: Mr Dominic
Price BEd, MBA
Age range: 3–11
Fees: Day £8,670–£12,765

St Christopher's The Hall School
49 Bromley Road, Beckenham,
Kent BR3 5PA
Tel: 020 8650 2200
Headmaster: Mr A Velasco
MEd, BH(Hons), PGCE
Age range: 3–11
No. of pupils: 305
Fees: Day £3,750–£9,165

St. David's Prep
Justin Hall,, Beckenham Road,
West Wickham, Kent BR4 0QS
Tel: 020 8777 5852
Principal: Mrs J Foulger
Age range: 4–11
No. of pupils: 155
Fees: Day £5,850–£8,550

West Lodge School
36 Station Road, Sidcup, Kent DA15 7DU
Tel: 020 8300 2489
Head Teacher: Mr Robert Francis
Age range: 3–11
No. of pupils: 163
Fees: Day £5,475–£9,150

Wickham Court School
Schiller International, Layhams Road,
West Wickham, Kent BR4 9HW
Tel: 020 8777 2942
Head: Mrs Lisa Harries
Age range: 2–16
No. of pupils: 121
Fees: Day £6,983.40–£12,344.55

Middlesex

Acorn House College
39-47 High Street, Southall,
Middlesex UB1 3HF
Tel: 020 8571 9900
Principal: Dr Francis Choi
Age range: 13–19
No. of pupils: 121 VIth85
Fees: Day £4,100–£15,525

**ACS Hillingdon
International School**
Hillingdon Court, 108 Vine
Lane, Hillingdon, Uxbridge,
Middlesex UB10 0BE
Tel: +44 (0) 1895 259 771
Head: Martin Hall
Age range: 4–18
No. of pupils: 520
Fees: Day £10,640–£24,400

Alpha Preparatory School
21 Hindes Road, Harrow,
Middlesex HA1 1SH
Tel: 020 8427 1471
Head: C.J.W Trinidad BSc(Hons), PGCE
Age range: 3–11
No. of pupils: 154
Fees: Day £3,400–£3,750

Ashton House School
50-52 Eversley Crescent,
Isleworth, Middlesex TW7 4LW
Tel: 020 8560 3902
Headteacher: Mrs Angela Stewart
Age range: 3–11
Fees: Day £7,986–£11,586

Buckingham Preparatory School
458 Rayners Lane, Pinner,
Harrow, Middlesex HA5 5DT
Tel: 020 8866 2737
Head of School: Mrs Sarah Hollis
Age range: B3–11 G3–4
Fees: Day £9,600–£12,300

Buxlow Preparatory School
5/6 Castleton Gardens, Wembley,
Middlesex HA9 7QJ
Tel: 020 8904 3615
Headteacher: Mr Ralf Furse
Age range: 2–11
Fees: Day £8,970–£9,330

**Edgware Jewish Girls
– Beis Chinuch**
Yeshurun Synagogue, Fernhurst
Gardens, Edgware, Middlesex HA8 7PH
Tel: 020 8951 0239
Headteacher: Mr M Cohen
Age range: G3–7

HALLIFORD SCHOOL
For further details see p. 114
Russell Road, Shepperton,
Middlesex TW17 9HX
Tel: 01932 223593
Email:
registrar@hallifordschool.co.uk
Website: www.hallifordschool.co.uk
Head: Mr James Davies BMus (Hons)
LGSM FASC ACertCM PGCE
Age range: B11–18 G16–18
No. of pupils: 402
Fees: Day £15,960

**Hampton Prep and
Pre-Prep School**
Gloucester Road, Hampton,
Middlesex TW12 2UQ
Tel: 020 8979 1844
Headmaster: Mr Tim Smith
Age range: 3–11
Fees: Day £6,030–£13,935

Hampton School
Hanworth Road, Hampton,
Middlesex TW12 3HD
Tel: 020 8979 9273
Headmaster: Mr Kevin
Knibbs MA (Oxon)
Age range: B11–18
No. of pupils: 1200
Fees: Day £6,390

Harrow School
5 High Street, Harrow on the
Hill, Middlesex HA1 3HT
Tel: 020 8872 8000
Head Master: Mr Jim Hawkins
Age range: B13–18
No. of pupils: 830 VIth320
Fees: FB £40,050

Holland House School
1 Broadhurst Avenue, Edgware,
Middlesex HA8 8TP
Tel: 020 8958 6979
Headmistress: Mrs H Stanton-
Tonner BEd(Hons) PGCE
Age range: 4–11
Fees: Day £7,827

Jack and Jill School
30 Nightingale Road, Hampton,
Middlesex TW12 3HX
Tel: 020 8979 3195
Principal: Miss K Papirnik BEd(Hons)
Age range: B2–5 G2–7
No. of pupils: 155
Fees: Day £4,608–£13,143

Kew House School
Kew House, 6 Capital Interchange
Way, London, Middlesex TW8 0EX
Tel: 0208 742 2038
Headmaster: Mr Mark Hudson
Age range: 11–18
No. of pupils: 450
Fees: Day £6,849

**Lady Nafisa Independent
Secondary School for Girls**
83A Sunbury Road, Feltham,
Middlesex TW13 4PH
Tel: 020 8751 5610
Headteacher: Ms Fouzia Butt
Age range: G11–16

Menorah Grammar School
Abbots Road, Edgware,
Middlesex HA8 0QS
Tel: 020 8906 9756
Headteacher: Rabbi A M Goldblatt
Age range: B11–17
No. of pupils: 203

Merchant Taylors' School
Sandy Lodge, Northwood,
Middlesex HA6 2HT
Tel: 01923 820644
Head: Mr S J Everson MA (Cantab)
Age range: B11–18
No. of pupils: 865 VIth282
Fees: Day £19,998

Newland House School
Waldegrave Park, Twickenham,
Middlesex TW1 4TQ
Tel: 020 8865 1305
Headmaster: Mr D A Alexander
Age range: B3–13 G3–11
No. of pupils: 425
Fees: Day £3,848–£4,306

North London Collegiate School
Canons, Canons Drive, Edgware,
Middlesex HA8 7RJ
Tel: +44 (0)20 8952 0912
Headmistress: Mrs Sarah Clark
Age range: G4–18
No. of pupils: 1080
Fees: Day £16,923–£20,028

Northwood College for Girls GDST
Maxwell Road, Northwood,
Middlesex HA6 2YE
Tel: 01923 825446
Head Mistress: Miss Jacqualyn
Pain MA, MA, MBA
Age range: G3–18
No. of pupils: 840 VIth100

Oak Heights
3 Red Lion Court, Alexandra Road,
Hounslow, Middlesex TW3 1JS
Tel: 020 8577 1827
Head: Mr S Dhillon
Age range: 11–16
No. of pupils: 48
Fees: Day £6,000

Orley Farm School
South Hill Avenue, Harrow,
Middlesex HA1 3NU
Tel: 020 8869 7600
Headmaster: Mr Tim Calvey
Age range: 4–13
No. of pupils: 497
Fees: Day £14,160–£16,335

Quainton Hall School & Nursery
91 Hindes Road, Harrow,
Middlesex HA1 1RX
Tel: 020 8861 8861
Headmaster: S Ford BEd
(Hons), UWE Bristol
Age range: B2–13 G2–11
Fees: Day £11,025–£12,150

Radnor House
Pope's Villa, Cross Deep,
Twickenham, Middlesex TW1 4QG
Tel: 020 8891 6264

Reddiford School
36-38 Cecil Park, Pinner,
Middlesex HA5 5HH
Tel: 020 8866 0660
Headteacher: Mrs J Batt CertEd, NPQH
Age range: 3–11
No. of pupils: 320
Fees: Day £4,860–£11,565

Regent College
Sai House, 167 Imperial Drive,
Harrow, Middlesex HA2 7HD
Tel: 020 8966 9900
Principal: Mrs Tharshiny Pankaj
Age range: 11–19
No. of pupils: 167
Fees: Day £4,100–£15,525

Roxeth Mead School
Buckholt House, 25 Middle Road,
Harrow, Middlesex HA2 0HW
Tel: 020 8422 2092
Headmistress: Mrs A Isaacs
Age range: 3–7
No. of pupils: 54
Fees: Day £4,800–£10,665

ST CATHERINE'S SCHOOL
For further details see p. 120
Cross Deep, Twickenham,
Middlesex TW1 4QJ
Tel: 020 8891 2898
Email: info@stcatherineschool.co.uk
Website:
www.stcatherineschool.co.uk
Headmistress: Mrs Johneen
McPherson MA
Age range: G3–18
No. of pupils: 430
Fees: Day £10,795–£14,910

St Christopher's School
71 Wembley Park Drive,
Wembley, Middlesex HA9 8HE
Tel: 020 8902 5069
Headteacher: Mr G. P. Musetti
Age range: 4–11
Fees: Day £9,006–£9,906

ST HELEN'S COLLEGE
For further details see p. 122
Parkway, Hillingdon, Uxbridge,
Middlesex UB10 9JX
Tel: 01895 234371
Email: info@sthelenscollege.com
Website: www.sthelenscollege.com
Head: Mrs. Shirley Drummond
BA, PGCert, MLDP
Age range: 2–11
No. of pupils: 383
Fees: Day £9,600–£11,850

St Helen's School
Eastbury Road, Northwood,
Middlesex HA6 3AS
Tel: +44 (0)1923 843210
Headmistress: Dr Mary Short BA, PhD
Age range: G3–18
No. of pupils: VIth165

St John's School
Potter Street Hill, Northwood,
Middlesex HA6 3QY
Tel: 020 8866 0067
Headmaster: Mr M S Robinson BSc
Age range: B3–13 years
No. of pupils: 350
Fees: Day £10,420–£15,110

St John's Senior School
North Lodge, The Ridgeway,
Enfield, Middlesex EN2 8BE
Tel: 020 8366 0035
Headmaster: Mr Andrew Tardios
LLB(Hons), BA(Hons), CertEd
Age range: 11–18 years
No. of pupils: 309 VIth95
Fees: Day £13,170

St Martin's School
40 Moor Park Road, Northwood,
Middlesex HA6 2DJ
Tel: 01923 825740
Headmaster: Mr D T
Tidmarsh BSc(Wales)
Age range: B3–13
No. of pupils: 400
Fees: Day £5,775–£15,135

Tashbar of Edgware
47-49 Mowbray Road, Edgware,
Middlesex HA8 8JL
Tel: 020 8958 5162
Headteacher: Mr N Jaffe
Age range: B3–11
No. of pupils: 88

**The Hall Pre-Preparatory
School & Nursery**
The Grange Country House,
Rickmansworth Road, Northwood,
Middlesex HA6 2RB
Tel: 01923 822807
Headmistress: Mrs S M Goodwin
Age range: 1–7
Fees: Day £4,650–£9,900

The John Lyon School
Middle Road, Harrow on the
Hill, Middlesex HA2 0HN
Tel: 020 8515 9400
Head: Miss Katherine Haynes
BA, MEd, NPQH
Age range: B11–18
No. of pupils: 600

The Lady Eleanor Holles School
Hanworth Road, Hampton,
Middlesex TW12 3HF
Tel: 020 8979 1601
Head of School: Mrs Heather Hanbury
Age range: G7–18
No. of pupils: 875
Fees: Day £16,731–£20,196

The Mall School
185 Hampton Road, Twickenham,
Middlesex TW2 5NQ
Tel: 0208 977 2523
Headmaster: Mr D C Price BSc, MA
Age range: B4–13
No. of pupils: 320
Fees: Day £12,240–£13,767

The Noam Primary School
8-10 Forty Avenue, Wembley,
Middlesex HA9 8JW
Tel: 020 8908 9491
Headteacher: Mrs Chaya Posen
Age range: 3–11
No. of pupils: 154

The St Michael Steiner School
Park Road, Hanworth Park,
London, Middlesex TW13 6PN
Tel: 0208 893 1299
Age range: 3–16 (17 from Jul 2014)
No. of pupils: 101
Fees: Day £3,850–£9,500

Twickenham Preparatory School
Beveree, 43 High Street, Hampton,
Middlesex TW12 2SA
Tel: 020 8979 6216
Head: Mr David Malam BA(Hons)
(Southampton), PGCE(Winchester)
Age range: B4–13 G4–11
No. of pupils: 273
Fees: Day £10,470–£11,340

Surrey

Al-Khair School
109-117 Cherry Orchard Road,
Croydon, Surrey CR0 6BE
Tel: 020 8662 8664
Headteacher: Mr Mohammad
R Chaudhry
Age range: 5–16
No. of pupils: 126

Broomfield House School
Broomfield Road, Kew Gardens,
Richmond, Surrey TW9 3HS
Tel: 020 8940 3884
Head Teacher: Mr N O York
BA(Hons), MA, MPhil, FRSA
Age range: 3–11
No. of pupils: 160
Fees: Day £7,104–£14,319

Cambridge Tutors College
Water Tower Hill, Croydon,
Surrey CR0 5SX
Tel: 020 8688 5284/7363
Principal: Dr Chris Drew
Age range: 15–19
No. of pupils: 215 VIth200
Fees: Day £10,400–£22,995

Canbury School
Kingston Hill, Kingston upon
Thames, Surrey KT2 7LN
Tel: 020 8549 8622
Headmistress: Ms Louise Clancy
Age range: 11–18
No. of pupils: 58
Fees: Day £16,401

Collingwood School
3 Springfield Road, Wallington,
Surrey SM6 0BD
Tel: 020 8647 4607
Headmaster: Mr Leigh Hardie
Age range: 3–11
No. of pupils: 120
Fees: Day £4,980–£8,925

Croydon High School GDST
Old Farleigh Road, Selsdon, South
Croydon, Surrey CR2 8YB
Tel: 020 8260 7500
Headmistress: Mrs Emma Pattison
Age range: G3–18
No. of pupils: 565 VIth90

Cumnor House Nursery
91 Pampisford Road, South
Croydon, Surrey CR2 6DH
Tel: +44 (0)2 8660 3445
Manager: Mrs Carole Finch
Age range: 2–4
No. of pupils: 200
Fees: Day £4,980–£10,635

Cumnor House School for Boys
168 Pampisford Road, South
Croydon, Surrey CR2 6DA
Tel: +44 (0)20 8660 3445
Headmaster: Mr Daniel Cummings
Age range: B2–13
No. of pupils: 440
Fees: Day £3,375–£4,250

Cumnor House School for Girls
1 Woodcote Lane, Purley,
Surrey CR8 3HB
Tel: +44 (0)20 8660 3445
Headmistress: Mrs Amanda McShane
Age range: G4–11
No. of pupils: 165
Fees: Day £3,375–£4,250

Date Valley School
Mitcham Court, Cricket Green,
Mitcham, Surrey CR4 4LB
Tel: +44 (0)20 8648 4647
Headteacher: Naheed Mughal
Age range: 3–11
No. of pupils: 110
Fees: Day £4,152–£5,043

Educare Small School
12 Cowleaze Road, Kingston
upon Thames, Surrey KT2 6DZ
Tel: 020 8547 0144
Head Teacher: Mrs E Steinthal
Age range: 3–11
No. of pupils: 46
Fees: Day £6,240

Elmhurst School
44-48 South Park Hill Rd, South
Croydon, Surrey CR2 7DW
Tel: 020 8688 0661
Headmaster: Mr Tony Padfield
Age range: B3–11
No. of pupils: 207
Fees: Day £6,129–£11,403

Holy Cross Preparatory School
George Road, Kingston upon
Thames, Surrey KT2 7NU
Tel: 020 8942 0729
Headteacher: Mrs S Hair BEd(Hons)
Age range: G4–11
No. of pupils: 285
Fees: Day £12,996

Homefield Preparatory School
Western Road, Sutton, Surrey SM1 2TE
Tel: 0208 642 0965
Headmaster: Mr John Towers
Age range: B3–13
No. of pupils: 350
Fees: Day £6,210–£13,320

KEW COLLEGE
For further details see p. 116
24-26 Cumberland Road,
Kew, Surrey TW9 3HQ
Tel: 020 8940 2039
Email: enquiries@kewcollege.com
Website: www.kewcollege.com
Head: Mrs Marianne Austin
BSc(Hons), MA(Hons), ACA, PGCE
Age range: 3–11
No. of pupils: 296

Kew Green Preparatory School
Layton House, Ferry Lane, Kew
Green, Richmond, Surrey TW9 3AF
Tel: 020 8948 5999
Headmaster: Mr J Peck
Age range: 4–11
No. of pupils: 270
Fees: Day £5,626

KING'S HOUSE SCHOOL
For further details see p. 118
68 King's Road, Richmond,
Surrey TW10 6ES
Tel: 020 8940 1878
Email:
schooloffice@kingshouseschool.org
Website: www.kingshouseschool.org
Head: Mr Mark Turner
BA, PGCE, NPQH
Age range: B3–13 G3–4
No. of pupils: 460
Fees: Day £2,370–£5,560

Kingston Grammar School
70 London Rd, Kingston upon
Thames, Surrey KT2 6PY
Tel: 020 8456 5875
Head: Mr Stephen Lehec
Age range: 11–18
No. of pupils: 829
Fees: Day £6,225

Laleham Lea School
29 Peaks Hill, Purley, Surrey CR8 3JJ
Tel: 020 8660 3351
Headteacher: Ms K Barry
Age range: 3–11
Fees: Day £7,110–£7,830

**Marymount International
School London**
George Road, Kingston upon
Thames, Surrey KT2 7PE
Tel: +44 (0)20 8949 0571
Headmistress: Mrs Margaret Frazier
Age range: G11–18
No. of pupils: 250
Fees: Day £23,775 WB
£38,705 FB £40,425

Oakwood Independent School
Godstone Road, Purley,
Surrey CR8 2AN
Tel: 020 8668 8080
Headmaster: Mr Ciro Candia
BA(Hons), PGCE
Age range: 3–11
No. of pupils: 176
Fees: Day £9,030–£9,840

Old Palace of John Whitgift School
Old Palace Road, Croydon,
Surrey CR0 1AX
Tel: 020 8686 7347
Head: Mrs. C Jewell
Age range: B3 months–4 years
G3 months–19 years
No. of pupils: 740 VIth120
Fees: Day £11,316–£15,366

Old Vicarage School
48 Richmond Hill, Richmond,
Surrey TW10 6QX
Tel: 020 8940 0922
Headmistress: Mrs G D Linthwaite
Age range: G4–11
No. of pupils: 200
Fees: Day £4,740

Park Hill School
8 Queens Road, Kingston upon
Thames, Surrey KT2 7SH
Tel: 020 8546 5496
Headmaster: Mr Alistair Bond
Age range: 2–7
No. of pupils: 100
Fees: Day £10,440

Reedham Park School
71A Old Lodge Lane, Purley,
Surrey CR8 4DN
Tel: 020 8660 6357
Headteacher: Mrs Katie Shah
Age range: 4–11
No. of pupils: 122
Fees: Day £5,385

Rokeby School
George Road, Kingston upon
Thames, Surrey KT2 7PB
Tel: 020 8942 2247
Head: Mr J R Peck
Age range: B4–13
No. of pupils: 370
Fees: Day £13,377–£16,656

Royal Russell Junior School
Coombe Lane, Croydon,
Surrey CR9 5BX
Tel: 020 8651 5884
Junior School Headmaster: Mr
James C Thompson
Age range: 3–11
No. of pupils: 300
Fees: Day £11,160–£14,220

Royal Russell School
Coombe Lane, Croydon,
Surrey CR9 5BX
Tel: 020 8657 3669
Headmaster: Christopher Hutchinson
Age range: 11–18
No. of pupils: 590 VIth180
Fees: Day £18,480 FB £36,525

Seaton House School
67 Banstead Road South,
Sutton, Surrey SM2 5LH
Tel: 020 8642 2332
Headmistress: Mrs Debbie Morrison
Higher Diploma in Education (RSA)
Age range: B3–5 G3–11
No. of pupils: 164
Fees: Day £10,188

Shrewsbury House School
107 Ditton Road, Surbiton,
Surrey KT6 6RL
Tel: 020 8399 3066
Headmaster: Mr K Doble
BA, PDM, PGCE
Age range: B7–13
No. of pupils: 320
Fees: Day £18,060

St David's School
23/25 Woodcote Valley Road,
Purley, Surrey CR8 3AL
Tel: 020 8660 0723
Headmistress: Cressida Mardell
Age range: 3–11
No. of pupils: 167
Fees: Day £6,375–£10,650

St James Senior Boys School
Church Road, Ashford, Surrey TW15 3DZ
Tel: 01784 266930
Headmaster: Mr David Brazier
Age range: B11–18
No. of pupils: 403 VIth65
Fees: Day £18,930

Staines Preparatory School
3 Gresham Road, Staines upon
Thames, Surrey TW18 2BT
Tel: 01784 450909
Head of School: Ms Samantha
Sawyer B.Ed (Hons), M.Ed, NPQH
Age range: 3–11
No. of pupils: 367
Fees: Day £9,510–£11,055

Surbiton High School
13-15 Surbiton Crescent, Kingston
upon Thames, Surrey KT1 2JT
Tel: 020 8546 5245
Principal: Mrs Rebecca Glover
Age range: B4–11 G4–18
No. of pupils: 1210 VIth186
Fees: Day £10,857–£17,142

Sutton High School GDST
55 Cheam Road, Sutton,
Surrey SM1 2AX
Tel: 020 8642 0594
Headmistress: Mrs Katharine Crouch
Age range: G3–18
No. of pupils: 600 VIth60
Fees: Day £10,095–£17,043
Ⓐ Ⓔ ⌕ 16

The Cedars School
Coombe Road, Lloyd Park,
Croydon, Surrey CR0 5RD
Tel: 020 8185 7770
Headmaster: Robert Teague Bsc (Hons)
Age range: B11–18

The Falcons Preparatory School for Boys
41 Few Foot Road, Richmond,
Surrey TW9 2SS
Tel: 0844 225 2211
Headmistress: Franciska Bayliss
Age range: B7–13
No. of pupils: 100
Fees: Day £17,835

The Royal Ballet School
White Lodge, Richmond,
Surrey TW10 5HR
Tel: 020 7836 8899
Artistic Director: Christopher Powney
Age range: 11–19
No. of pupils: VIth80
Fees: Day £18,939–£24,885
FB £29,328–£33,567
Ⓐ 🏛 Ⓔ ⌕ 16

The Study School
57 Thetford Road, New
Malden, Surrey KT3 5DP
Tel: 020 8942 0754
Head of School: Mrs Donna
Brackstone-Drake
Age range: 3–11
No. of pupils: 134
Fees: Day £4,860–£11,388

Trinity School
Shirley Park, Croydon, Surrey CR9 7AT
Tel: 020 8656 9541
Head: Alasdair Kennedy MA (Cantab)
Age range: B10–18 G16–18
No. of pupils: 1007
Fees: Day £16,656
Ⓐ Ⓔ ⌕ 16

Unicorn School
238 Kew Road, Richmond,
Surrey TW9 3JX
Tel: 020 8948 3926
Headmaster: Mr Kit Thompson
Age range: 3–11
Fees: Day £6,930–£12,720
Ⓔ ⌕

Westbury House
80 Westbury Road, New
Malden, Surrey KT3 5AS
Tel: 020 8942 5885
Age range: 3–11
Fees: Day £4,860–£11,115

Whitgift School
Haling Park, South Croydon,
Surrey CR2 6YT
Tel: +44 (0)20 8633 9935
Headmaster: Mr Christopher Ramsey
Age range: B10–18
No. of pupils: 1464
Fees: Day £20,136 WB
£32,274 FB £37,866
Ⓐ 🏛 Ⓔ IB ⌕ 16

D330

London

KEY TO SYMBOLS

- Boys' school
- Girls' school
- International school
- Tutorial or sixth form college
- A levels
- Boarding accommodation
- Bursaries
- International Baccalaureate
- Learning support
- Entrance at 16+
- Vocational qualifications
- Independent Association of Preparatory Schools
- The Headmasters' & Headmistresses' Conference
- Independent Schools Association
- Girls' School Association
- Boarding Schools' Association
- Society of Heads

Unless otherwise indicated, all schools are coeducational day schools. Single-sex and boarding schools will be indicated by the relevant icon.

Central London

CATS London
43-45 Bloomsbury Square,
London WC1A 2RA
Tel: 02078 411580
Principal: Mario Di Clemente
Age range: 15–24

Charterhouse Square School
40 Charterhouse Square,
London EC1M 6EA
Tel: 020 7600 3805
Age range: 3–11
No. of pupils: 196
Fees: Day £5,680

CITY OF LONDON SCHOOL
For further details see p. 130
Queen Victoria Street,
London EC4V 3AL
Tel: 020 3680 6300
Email: admissions@
cityoflondonschool.org.uk
Website:
www.cityoflondonschool.org.uk
Head: Mr A R Bird MSc
Age range: B10–18
No. of pupils: 930 VIth250
Fees: Day £17,901

City of London School for Girls
St Giles' Terrace, Barbican,
London EC2Y 8BB
Tel: 020 7847 5500
Headmistress: Mrs E Harrop
Age range: G7–18
No. of pupils: 725

Dallington School
8 Dallington Street, Islington,
London EC1V 0BW
Tel: 020 7251 2284
Headteacher: Mrs M C Hercules MBE
Age range: 3–11
No. of pupils: 134
Fees: Day £9,978–£12,630

École Jeannine Manuel – London
43-45 Bedford Square,
London WC1B 3DN
Tel: 020 3829 5970
Head of School: Pauline Prévot
Age range: 3–18 years
No. of pupils: 360
Fees: Day £17,460

Italia Conti Academy of Theatre Arts
Italia Conti House, 23 Goswell
Road, London EC1M 7AJ
Tel: 020 7608 0047
Director: Chris White
Age range: 10–21

ST PAUL'S CATHEDRAL SCHOOL
For further details see p. 152
2 New Change, London EC4M 9AD
Tel: 020 7248 5156
Email:
admissions@spcs.london.sch.uk
Website: www.spcslondon.com
Headmaster: Simon Larter-
Evans BA (Hons), PGCE, FRSA
Age range: 4–13
No. of pupils: 252
Fees: Day £4,677–£5,035 FB £2,912

The College of Central London
Tower Bridge Business Centre, 46-48
East Smithfield, London E1W 1AW
Tel: +44 (0) 20 3667 7607
Principal: Nicolas Kailides
Fees: Day £3,850

The Lyceum
6 Paul Street, London EC2A 4JH
Tel: 020 7247 1588
Headteacher: Vanessa Bingham
Age range: 4–11
No. of pupils: 100
Fees: Day £16,185

Urdang Academy
The Old Finsbury Town Hall, Rosebery
Avenue, London EC1R 4RP
Tel: 020 7713 7710
Principal: Stephanie Pope
ARAD (dip PDTC)
Age range: 16+

East London

Al-Falah Primary School
48 Kenninghall Road,
Clapton, London E5 8BY
Tel: 020 8985 1059
Headteacher: Mr M A Hussain
Age range: 5–11
No. of pupils: 83
Fees: Day £7,200

Al-Mizan School
46 Whitechapel Road, London E1 1JX
Tel: 020 7650 3070
Head: Mr Askor Ali
Age range: B7–11
No. of pupils: 200 VIth13
Fees: Day £3,400

Azhar Academy
235A Romford Road, Forest
Gate, London E7 9HL
Tel: 020 8534 5959
Headteacher: Mrs R Rehman
Age range: G11–16
No. of pupils: 189

Beis Trana Girls' School
186 Upper Clapton Road,
London E5 9DH
Tel: 020 8815 8003
Age range: G3–16
No. of pupils: 270

Chingford House School
22 Marlborough Road, Waltham
Forest, London E4 9AL
Tel: 020 8527 2902; 07749 899 498
Head teacher: Helen McNulty
Age range: 0–5

Faraday School
Old Gate House, 7 Trinity Buoy
Wharf, London E14 0JW
Tel: 020 8965 7374
Executive Head Teacher: Mrs. S. Gillam
Age range: 4–11
No. of pupils: 105
Fees: Day £3,284

Forest School
College Place, Snaresbrook,
London E17 3PY
Tel: 020 8520 1744
Warden: Mr Cliff Hodges
Age range: 4–18
No. of pupils: 1355 VIth260
Fees: Day £13,095–£18,681

Gatehouse School
Sewardstone Road, Victoria
Park, London E2 9JG
Tel: 020 8980 2978
Acting Headmistress: Sevda Corby
Age range: 3–11
No. of pupils: 320
Fees: Day £11,610–£12,225

Grangewood Independent School
Chester Road, Forest
Gate, London E7 8QT
Tel: 020 8472 3552
Headteacher: Mrs B A Roberts
B.Ed (Hons); PG Cert (SEN)
Age range: 2–11
No. of pupils: 71
Fees: Day £5,157–£6,751.20

Green Gables Montessori School
St George in the East Crypt West, 14
Cannon Street Road, London E1 0BH
Tel: 020 7488 2374
Head: Abeer Al-Baktash
Age range: 0–8
No. of pupils: 45

Hyland House School
Holcombe Road, Tottenham,
London N17 9AD
Tel: 020 8520 4186
Head Teacher: Mrs Gina Abbequaye
Age range: 3–11
Fees: Day £2,520

London East Academy
46-80 Whitechapel Road,
London E1 1JX
Tel: 020 7650 3070
Headteacher: Musleh Faradhi
Age range: B11–18
No. of pupils: VIth18
Fees: Day £3,000

Lubavitch House School (Junior Boys)
135 Clapton Common, London E5 9AE
Tel: 020 8800 1044
Head: Mr R Leach
Age range: B5–11
No. of pupils: 101

Madani Girls School
Myrdle Street, London E1 1HL
Tel: 020 7377 1992
Headteacher: Muhammad S. Rahman
Age range: G11–18
No. of pupils: 248 VIth11
Fees: Day £2,400

Normanhurst School
68-74 Station Road, Chingford,
London E4 7BA
Tel: 020 8529 4307
Headmistress: Mrs Claire Osborn
Age range: 2–16
No. of pupils: 250
Fees: Day £10,350–£13,050

Paragon Christian Academy
233-241 Glyn Road, London E5 0JP
Tel: 020 8985 1119
Headteacher: Mrs Sharon Curry
Age range: 5–16
No. of pupils: 34

Pillar Box Montessori Nursery & Pre-Prep School
107 Bow Road, London E3 2AN
Tel: 020 8980 0700
Director: Lorraine Redknapp
Age range: 0–5
Fees: Day £12,000

PromisedLand Academy
St Cedds Hall, Webb Gardens,
Plaistow, London E13 8SR
Tel: 0207 473 3229
Head: Mr A Coote
Age range: 4–16

Quwwat-ul Islam Girls School
16 Chaucer Road, Forest
Gate, London E7 9NB
Tel: 020 8548 4736
Acting Head: Ms Member
Age range: G4–11
No. of pupils: 150

River House Montessori School
3-4 Shadwell Pierhead, Glamis
Road, London E1W 3TD
Tel: 020 7538 9886
Headmistress: Miss S Greenwood
Age range: 3–16
Fees: Day £3,410–£3,625

Snaresbrook Preparatory School
75 Woodford Road, South
Woodford, London E18 2EA
Tel: 020 8989 2394
Interim Head: Mrs Linda Chiverrell
Age range: 3–11
No. of pupils: 164
Fees: Day £8,922–£11,934

St Joseph's Convent School For Girls
59 Cambridge Park, Wanstead,
London E11 2PR
Tel: 020 8989 4700
Headteacher: Ms C Glover
Age range: G3–11
No. of pupils: 171
Fees: Day £6,780–£8,100

Talmud Torah Machikei Hadass School
96-98 Clapton Common,
London E5 9AL
Tel: 020 8800 6599
Headteacher: Rabbi C Silbiger
Age range: B3–16
No. of pupils: 271

Winston House Preparatory School
140 High Road, London E18 2QS
Tel: 020 8505 6565
Head Teacher: Mrs Marian Kemp
Age range: 3–11

North London

Annemount School
18 Holne Chase, Hampstead
Garden Suburb, London N2 0QN
Tel: 020 8455 2132
Principal: Mrs G Maidment
BA(Hons), MontDip
Age range: 2–7
No. of pupils: 100
Fees: Day £3,275–£6,000

Avenue Nursery & Pre-Preparatory School
2 Highgate Avenue, London N6 5RX
Tel: 020 8348 6815
Principal: Mrs. Mary Fysh
Age range: 2 ½–7 ½
No. of pupils: 79

Beis Chinuch Lebonos Girls School
Woodberry Down Centre,
Woodberry Down, London N4 2SH
Tel: 020 88097 737
Headmistress: Mrs Leah Klein
Age range: G2–16
No. of pupils: 421

Beis Malka Girls School
93 Alkham Road, London N16 6XD
Tel: 020 8806 2070
Headmaster: M Dresdner
Age range: G5–16
No. of pupils: 339

Beis Rochel D'Satmar Girls School
51-57 Amhurst Park, London N16 5DL
Tel: 020 8800 9060
Headmistress: Mrs E Katz
Age range: G2–18
No. of pupils: 788

Bnois Jerusalem School
79-81 Amhurst Park, London N16 5DL
Tel: 020 8802 7470
Head: Mrs Sonnenschein
Age range: G3–16

Channing School
The Bank, Highgate, London N6 5HF
Tel: 020 8340 2328
Head: Mrs B M Elliott
Age range: G4–18
No. of pupils: 746 VIth108
Fees: Day £17,610–£19,410

Dwight School London
6 Friern Barnet Lane, London N11 3LX
Tel: +44 (0)20 8920 0637
Head: Mrs Alison Cobbin
BA, Dip Ed, MBA
Age range: 3–18

Finchley & Acton Yochien School
6 Hendon Avenue, Finchley,
London N3 1UE
Tel: 020 8343 2191
Headteacher: J Tanabe
Age range: 2–6
No. of pupils: 145

Getters Talmud Torah
86 Amhurst Park, London N16 5AR
Tel: 020 8802 2512
Headteacher: Mr David Kahana
Age range: B4–11
No. of pupils: 171

Grange Park Preparatory School
13 The Chine, Grange Park,
Winchmore Hill, London N21 2EA
Tel: 020 8360 1469
Headteacher: Miss F Rizzo
Age range: G4–11
No. of pupils: 90
Fees: Day £10,300–£10,378

Greek Secondary School of London
Avenue Lodge, Bounds Green
Road, London N22 7EU
Tel: 020 8881 9320
Headteacher: Georgia
Dimitrakopoulou
Age range: 13–18
No. of pupils: 200

Highgate
North Road, Highgate, London N6 4AY
Tel: 020 8340 1524
Head Master: Mr A S Pettitt MA
Age range: 3–18
No. of pupils: 1541 VIth312
Fees: Day £18,165–£20,970

Highgate Junior School
Cholmeley House, 3 Bishopswood
Road, London N6 4PL
Tel: 020 8340 9193
Principal: Mr S M James BA
Age range: 7–11
Fees: Day £19,230

Highgate Pre-Preparatory School
7 Bishopswood Road, London N6 4PH
Tel: 020 8340 9196
Principal: Mrs Diane Hecht
Age range: 3–7
No. of pupils: 150
Fees: Day £18,165

Keble Prep
Wades Hill, Winchmore
Hill, London N21 1BG
Tel: 020 8360 3359
Headmaster: Mr M J Mitchell
Age range: B4–13
No. of pupils: 228
Fees: Day £3,850–£4,930

Kerem School
Norrice Lea, London N2 0RE
Tel: 020 8455 0909
Head Teacher: Miss Alyson Burns
Age range: 3–11
Fees: Day £9,435

Lubavitch House School (Senior Girls)
107-115 Stamford Hill, Hackney,
London N16 5RP
Tel: 020 8800 0022
Headmaster: Rabbi Shmuel Lew FRSA
Age range: G11–18
No. of pupils: 102
Fees: Day £3,900

Montessori House
5 Princes Avenue, Muswell
Hill, London N10 3LS
Tel: 020 8444 4399
Head: Paul Jowett
Age range: 6 months–7 years
No. of pupils: 100
Fees: Day £9,216–£12,066

Norfolk House School
10 Muswell Avenue, Muswell
Hill, London N10 2EG
Tel: 020 8883 4584
Head Teacher: Mr Paul Jowett
Age range: 4–11
No. of pupils: 130
Fees: Day £12,066

North London Grammar School
110 Colindeep Lane, Hendon,
London NW9 6HB
Tel: 0208 205 0052
Head Teacher: Hakan Gokce
Age range: 11–18
No. of pupils: VIth20
Fees: Day £10,800–£13,500
FB £18,900–£21,600
Ⓐ Ⓔ

North London Muslim School
131-133 Fore Street, Edmonton,
London N18 2XF
Tel: 020 8345 7008
Headteacher: Mr W Abdulla
Age range: 4–10
No. of pupils: 21

**North London Rudolf
Steiner School**
1-3 The Campsbourne, London N8 7PN
Tel: 020 8341 3770
Age range: 0–7
No. of pupils: 40
✍

Palmers Green High School
Hoppers Road, Winchmore
Hill, London N21 3LJ
Tel: 020 8886 1135
Headmistress: Mrs Wendy Kempster
Age range: G3–16
No. of pupils: 300
Fees: Day £5,880–£15,930
Ⓐ Ⓔ ✍

Pardes House Grammar School
Hendon Lane, Finchley, London N3 1SA
Tel: 020 8349 4222
Headteacher: Rabbi Yitzchok Lev
Age range: B10–16
No. of pupils: 222
Ⓐ

Phoenix Academy
85 Bounces Road, Edmonton,
London N9 8LD
Tel: 020 8887 6888
Headteacher: Mr Paul Kelly
Age range: 5–18
No. of pupils: 19

**Rosemary Works
Independent School**
1 Branch Place, London N1 5PH
Tel: 020 7739 3950
Head: Rob Dell
Age range: 3–11
No. of pupils: 104
Fees: Day £14,097
✍

Salcombe Preparatory School
224-226 Chase Side, Southgate,
London N14 4PL
Tel: 020 8441 5356
Headmistress: Mrs Sarah-Jane
Davies BA(Hons) QTS MEd
Age range: 3–11
No. of pupils: 250
Fees: Day £11,673
Ⓔ

St Paul's Steiner School
1 St Paul's Road, Islington,
London N1 2QH
Tel: 020 7226 4454
College of Teachers: College
of Teachers
Age range: 2–14
No. of pupils: 136
Ⓔ ✍

Sunrise Nursery, Stoke Newington
1 Cazenove Road, Stoke Newington,
Hackney, London N16 6PA
Tel: 020 8806 6279
Principal: Didi Ananda Manika

Sunrise Primary School
55 Coniston Road, Tottenham,
London N17 0EX
Tel: 020 8806 6279 (Office);
020 8885 3354 (School)
Head: Mrs Mary-Anne
Lovage MontDipEd, BA
Age range: 2–11
No. of pupils: 30
Fees: Day £5,550
✍

**Talmud Torah Bobov
Primary School**
87 Egerton Road, London N16 6UE
Tel: 020 8809 1025
Headmaster: Mr Chaim Weissman
Age range: B3–13
No. of pupils: 320
Ⓐ

**Talmud Torah Chaim
Meirim School**
26 Lampard Grove, London N16 6XB
Tel: 020 8806 0017
Principal: Rabbi S Hoffman
Age range: B4–13
Ⓐ

Talmud Torah Yetev Lev School
111-115 Cazenove Road,
London N16 6AX
Tel: 020 8806 3834
Headteacher: Mr J Stauber
Age range: B2–11
No. of pupils: 567

Tawhid Boys School
21 Cazenove Road, London N16 6PA
Tel: 020 8806 2999
Headteacher: Mr Usman Mapara
Age range: B10–15
No. of pupils: 115
Ⓐ

Tayyibah Girls School
88 Filey Avenue, Stamford
Hill, London N16 6JJ
Tel: 020 8880 0085
Headmistress: Mrs N B Qureishi MSc
Age range: G5–18
No. of pupils: 270
Ⓐ Ⓐ

The Children's House Upper School
King Henry's Walk, London N1 4PB
Tel: 020 7249 6273
Headteacher: Kate Orange
Age range: 4–7
No. of pupils: 60
Fees: Day £14,730

**The Gower School
Montessori Nursery**
18 North Road, Islington, London N7 9EY
Tel: 020 7700 2445
Principal: Miss Emma Gowers
Age range: 3 months–5 years
No. of pupils: 237
✍

**The Gower School
Montessori Primary**
10 Cynthia Street, Barnsbury,
London N1 9JF
Tel: 020 7278 2020
Principal: Miss Emma Gowers
Age range: 4–11
No. of pupils: 237
Fees: Day £15,576

TTTYY School
14 Heathland Road, London N16 5NH
Tel: 020 8802 1348
Headmaster: Rabbi A Friesel
Age range: B2–13
No. of pupils: 187
Ⓐ

Vita et Pax School
Priory Close, Southgate,
London N14 4AT
Tel: 020 8449 8336
Headteacher: Miss Gillian Chumbley
Age range: 3–11
Fees: Day £9,360

Yesodey Hatorah School
2-4 Amhurst Park, London N16 5AE
Tel: 020 8826 5500
Headteacher: Rabbi Pinter
Age range: 3–16
No. of pupils: 920

North-West London

Abercorn School
38 Portland Place, London NW8 9XP
Tel: 020 7286 4785
High Mistress: Mrs Andrea
Greystoke BA(Hons)
Age range: 2–13
No. of pupils: 360
Fees: Day £10,020–£20,055

Al-Sadiq & Al-Zahra Schools
134 Salusbury Road, London NW6 6PF
Tel: 020 7372 7706
Headteacher: Dr M Movahedi
Age range: 4–16
No. of pupils: 389

Arnold House School
1 Loudoun Road, St John's
Wood, London NW8 0LH
Tel: 020 7266 4840
Headmaster: Mr Vivian Thomas
Age range: B5–13
No. of pupils: 270
Fees: Day £6,100
Ⓐ Ⓔ ✍

Ayesha Community School
10A Montagu Road, Hendon,
London NW4 3ES
Tel: 02034112660
Headteacher: Mr Shakil Ahmed
Age range: G4–18
Fees: Day £3,000
Ⓐ Ⓐ

Beis Hamedrash Elyon
211 Golders Green Road,
London NW11 9BY
Tel: 020 8201 8668
Headteacher: Mr C Steinhart
Age range: B11–14
No. of pupils: 45
Ⓐ

Beis Soroh Schneirer
Arbiter House, Wilberforce
Road, London NW9 6AT
Tel: 020 8343 1190
Head: Mrs R Weiss
Age range: G2–11
No. of pupils: 150
Ⓐ

**Belmont, Mill Hill
Preparatory School**
The Ridgeway, London NW7 4ED
Tel: 020 8906 7270
Headmaster: Mr Leon Roberts MA
Age range: 7–13
No. of pupils: 490
Fees: Day £18,099
Ⓔ ✍

**Beth Jacob Grammar
School for Girls**
Stratford Road, Hendon,
London NW4 2AT
Tel: 020 8203 4322
Headteacher: Mrs M Gluck
Age range: G11–17
No. of pupils: 264
(symbol)

Brampton College
Lodge House, Lodge Road,
Hendon, London NW4 4DQ
Tel: 020 8203 5025
Principal: B Canetti BA(Hons), MSc
Age range: 15–20
Fees: Day £19,935
(16) (A)

Brondesbury College for Boys
8 Brondesbury Park, London NW6 7BT
Tel: 020 8830 4522
Headteacher: Mr Amzad Ali
Age range: B11–16
No. of pupils: 93
(symbols)

**College Francais
Bilingue De Londres**
87 Holmes Road, Kentish
Town, London NW5 3AX
Tel: +44 (0) 20 7993 7400
Principal: Mr François-Xavier Gabet
Age range: 5–15
No. of pupils: 210
(symbol)

**DEVONSHIRE HOUSE
PREPARATORY SCHOOL**
For further details see p. 132
2 Arkwright Road, Hampstead,
London NW3 6AE
Tel: 020 7435 1916
Email: enquiries@
devonshirehouseprepschool.co.uk
Website:
www.devonshirehouseschool.co.uk
Headmistress: Mrs S. Piper BA(Hons)
Age range: B2½–13 G2½–11
No. of pupils: 650
Fees: Day £10,125–£18,600
(£)

Fine Arts College, Hampstead
Centre Studios, 41-43 England's
Lane, London NW3 4YD
Tel: 020 7586 0312
Head Teacher: Candida Cave MA
Age range: 13–19
No. of pupils: 210
Fees: Day £7,230
(16) (A) (£) (16)

**Francis Holland School,
Regent's Park, NW1**
Clarence Gate, Ivor Place,
Regent's Park, London NW1 6XR
Tel: 020 7723 0176
Head: Mr C B Fillingham MA
(King's College London)
Age range: G11–18
No. of pupils: 495 VIth120
Fees: Day £19,260
(symbols)

Golders Hill School
666 Finchley Road, London NW11 7NT
Tel: 020 8455 2589
Headmistress: Mrs A T Eglash BA(Hons)
Age range: 2–7
No. of pupils: 180
Fees: Day £1,575–£13,827

Goodwyn School
Hammers Lane, Mill Hill,
London NW7 4DB
Tel: 020 8959 3756
Principal: Struan Robertson
Age range: 3–11
No. of pupils: 223
Fees: Day £5,120–£11,042

**Grimsdell, Mill Hill Pre-
Preparatory School**
Winterstoke House, Wills Grove,
Mill Hill, London NW7 1QR
Tel: 020 8959 6884
Head: Mrs Kate Simon BA, PGCE
Age range: 3–7
No. of pupils: 182
Fees: Day £6,852–£14,895
(symbol)

**Hampstead Hill Pre-Prep
& Nursery School**
St Stephen's Hall, Pond Street,
Hampstead, London NW3 2PP
Tel: 020 7435 6262
Principal: Mrs Andrea Taylor
Age range: B2–7+ G2–7+
Fees: Day £10,175–£16,830
(symbol)

HEATHSIDE SCHOOL
For further details see p. 134
84-86 West Heath Road,
London NW3 7UN
Tel: +44 (0)20 3058 4011
Email: admissions@heathside.net
Website: www.heathside.net
Headteacher: Ms Melissa
Remus MSc
Age range: 2–14
No. of pupils: 550
Fees: Day £15,000–£18,300
(symbols)

Hendon Prep School
20 Tenterden Grove, Hendon,
London NW4 1TD
Tel: 020 8203 7727
Age range: 2–13 years
No. of pupils: 165
Fees: Day £6,345–£14,175
(£) (symbol)

Hereward House School
14 Strathray Gardens, London NW3 4NY
Tel: 020 7794 4820
Headmaster: Mr P Evans
Age range: B4–13
No. of pupils: 170
Fees: Day £15,615–£16,065
(symbol)

International Community School
7B Wyndham Place, London NW1 4PT
Tel: +44 (0) 20 7298 8817
Age range: 3–18
No. of pupils: 190
Fees: Day £19,400–£26,000
(symbols)

Islamia Girls' High School
129 Salusbury Road, London NW6 6PE
Tel: 020 7372 3472
Headteacher: Mrs Fawziah Islam
Age range: G11–16 years
Fees: Day £6,900
(symbol)

L'Ile Aux Enfants
22 Vicar's Road, London NW5 4NL
Tel: 020 7267 7119
Headmistress: Mrs Chailleux
Age range: 3–11
No. of pupils: 192
Fees: Day £3,270

London Jewish Girls' High School
18 Raleigh Close, Hendon,
London NW4 2TA
Tel: 020 8203 8618
Headteacher: Mr Joel Rabinowitz
Age range: G11–16
(symbol)

Lyndhurst House Prep School
24 Lyndhurst Gardens, Hampstead,
London NW3 5NW
Tel: 020 7435 4936
Head of School: Mr Andrew
Reid MA (Oxon)
Age range: B4–13
No. of pupils: 165
Fees: Day £5,735–£6,410
(symbols)

Maple Walk School
62A Crownhill Road, London NW10 4EB
Tel: 020 8963 3890
Head Teacher: Mrs S Gillam
Age range: 4–11
No. of pupils: 200
Fees: Day £3,190
(£) (symbol)

Maria Montessori Institute
26 Lyndhurst Gardens, Hampstead,
London NW3 5NW
Tel: 020 7435 3646
Director of Training & School: Mrs Lynne
Lawrence BA, Mont Int Dip(AMI)
Age range: 2–12
No. of pupils: 50
Fees: Day £5,580–£13,560
(16)

**Maria Montessori School
– Hampstead**
26 Lyndhurst Gardens, Hampstead,
London NW3 5NW
Tel: +44 (0)20 7435 3646
Director of School: Miss L Kingston
Age range: 2–12
No. of pupils: 100
Fees: Day £6,270–£13,560

Mill Hill School
The Ridgeway, Mill Hill Village,
London NW7 1QS
Tel: 020 8959 1176
Head: Frances King
Age range: 13–18
No. of pupils: 689 VIth259
Fees: Day £21,141 WB £28,524 FB £33,717
(symbols)

Naima Jewish Preparatory School
21 Andover Place, London NW6 5ED
Tel: 020 7328 2802
Headteacher: Mr Bill Pratt
Age range: 3–11
Fees: Day £7,605–£12,705
£

Nancy Reuben Primary School
Finchley Lane, Hendon,
London NW4 1DJ
Tel: 020 82025646
Head: Anthony Wolfson
Age range: 3–11
No. of pupils: 207

NORTH BRIDGE HOUSE NURSERY AND PRE-PREP SCHOOLS
For further details see p. 144
8 Netherhall Gardens,
London NW3 5RR
Tel: 020 7428 1520
Head of School: Mrs C McLelland
Age range: 2 years 9 months–7 years
No. of pupils: 380
Fees: Day £15,975–£16,575

NORTH BRIDGE HOUSE PREP SCHOOL REGENT'S PARK
For further details see p. 144
1 Gloucester Avenue,
London NW1 7AB
Tel: 020 7428 1520
Head of School: Mr B Bibby
Age range: 7–13 years
No. of pupils: 460
Fees: Day £17,340

NORTH BRIDGE HOUSE SENIOR CANONBURY
For further details see p. 144
6-9 Canonbury Place,
Islington, London N1 2NQ
Tel: 020 7428 1520
Head of School: Mr J. Taylor
Age range: 11–18 years
No. of pupils: 180
Fees: Day £17,295–£18,555

NORTH BRIDGE HOUSE SENIOR HAMPSTEAD
For further details see p. 144
65 Rosslyn Hill, London NW3 5UD
Tel: 020 7428 1520
Email: admissionsenquiries@northbridgehouse.com
Website: www.northbridgehouse.com
Head of Senior Hampstead: Mr Brendan Pavey
Age range: 11–16 years
No. of pupils: 1375

OYH Primary School
Finchley Lane, Hendon,
London NW4 1DJ
Tel: 020 8202 5646
Headteacher: D A David
Age range: 3–11
No. of pupils: 180

Rainbow Montessori School
13 Woodchurch Road,
Hampstead, London NW6 3PL
Tel: 020 7328 8986
Head Mistress: Maggy Miller MontDip
Age range: 5–12
Fees: Day £12,240–£12,417

Saint Christina's School
25 St Edmunds Terrace, Regent's Park, London NW8 7PY
Tel: 020 7722 8784
Headteacher: Miss J Finlayson
Age range: 3–11
No. of pupils: 224
Fees: Day £13,500

Sarum Hall
15 Eton Avenue, London NW3 3EL
Tel: 020 7794 2261
Headmistress: Mrs Christine Smith
Age range: G3–11
No. of pupils: 170
Fees: Day £14,025–£15,180

South Hampstead High School GDST
3 Maresfield Gardens, London NW3 5SS
Tel: 020 7435 2899
Head of School: Mrs V Bingham
Age range: G4–18
No. of pupils: 900
Fees: Day £15,327–£18,654

Southbank International School – Hampstead
16 Netherhall Gardens,
London NW3 5TH
Tel: 020 7243 3803
Principal: Shirley Harwood
Age range: 3–11

St Anthony's School for Boys
90 Fitzjohn's Avenue, Hampstead, London NW3 6NP
Tel: 020 7431 1066
Headmaster: Mr Paul Keyte
Age range: B4–13
No. of pupils: 310

St Christopher's School
32 Belsize Lane, Hampstead,
London NW3 5AE
Tel: 020 7435 1521
Head: Emma Crawford-Nash
Age range: G4–11
No. of pupils: 235
Fees: Day £14,700

St John's Wood Pre-Preparatory School
St Johns Hall, Lords Roundabout,
London NW8 7NE
Tel: 020 7722 7149
Principal: Adrian Ellis
Age range: 3–7

St Margaret's School
18 Kidderpore Gardens,
Hampstead, London NW3 7SR
Tel: 020 7435 2439
Principal: Mr M Webster BSc, PGCE
Age range: G4–16
No. of pupils: 156
Fees: Day £12,591–£14,589

St Martin's School
22 Goodwyn Avenue, Mill Hill, London NW7 3RG
Tel: 020 8959 1965
Head: Dr Jason Walak
Age range: 3–11
No. of pupils: 90
Fees: Day £7,800

St Mary's School Hampstead
47 Fitzjohn's Avenue, Hampstead, London NW3 6PG
Tel: 020 7435 1868
Head Teacher: Mrs Harriet Connor-Earl
Age range: B2 years 9 months–7 years G2 years 9 months–11 years
No. of pupils: 300
Fees: Day £7,305–£13,500

St Nicholas School
22 Salmon Street, London NW9 8PN
Tel: 020 8205 7153
Headmaster: Matt Donaldson
Age range: 3 months–11
No. of pupils: 80
Fees: Day £8,550–£8,850

Swaminarayan School
260 Brentfield Road, Neasden,
London NW10 8HE
Tel: 020 8965 8381
Headteacher: Umesh Raja
Age range: 2–18
No. of pupils: 452 VIth36
Fees: Day £9,948–£13,320

The Academy School
3 Pilgrims Place, Rosslyn Hill,
Hampstead, London NW3 1NG
Tel: 020 7435 6621
Headteacher: Mr Garth Evans
Age range: 6–14

The American School in London
One Waverley Place, London NW8 0NP
Tel: 020 7449 1221
Head: Robin Appleby
Age range: 4–18
No. of pupils: 1350
Fees: Day £27,050–£31,200

The Cavendish School
31 Inverness Street, Camden Town, London NW1 7HB
Tel: 020 7485 1958
Headmistress: Miss Jane Rogers
Age range: G3–11
No. of pupils: 260
Fees: Day £14,700

The Hall School
23 Crossfield Road, Hampstead,
London NW3 4NU
Tel: 020 7722 1700
Headmaster: Mr Chris Godwin
Age range: B4–13
No. of pupils: 440
Fees: Day £17,940–£18,486

The King Alfred School
Manor Wood, North End
Road, London NW11 7HY
Tel: 020 8457 5200
Head: Robert Lobatto MA (Oxon)
Age range: 4–18
No. of pupils: 650 VIth100
Fees: Day £15,531–£18,723

The Mount, Mill Hill International
Milespit Hill, London NW7 2RX
Tel: +44 (0)20 3826 33
Head of School: Ms Sarah Bellotti
Age range: 13–18
No. of pupils: 68
Fees: Day £24,990 WB
£34,461 FB £40,539

The Mulberry House School
7 Minster Road, West Hampstead,
London NW2 3SD
Tel: 020 8452 7340
Headteacher: Ms Victoria Playford
Age range: 2–8
No. of pupils: 184

The School of the Islamic Republic of Iran
100 Carlton Vale, London NW6 5HE
Tel: 020 7372 8051
Headteacher: Mr Seyed Abbas Hosseini
Age range: 6–16
No. of pupils: 53

The Village School
2 Parkhill Road, Belsize Park,
London NW3 2YN
Tel: 020 7485 4673
Headmistress: Miss C E F
Gay BSc(Hons), PGCE
Age range: G3–11
No. of pupils: 106
Fees: Day £15,525

Torah Vodaas
Julian Headon House, West Hendon
Broadway, London NW9 7AL
Tel: 02036704670
Head of School: Rabbi S Klor
Age range: B2–11

Trevor-Roberts School
55-57 Eton Avenue, London NW3 3ET
Tel: 020 7586 1444
Headmaster: Simon Trevor-Roberts BA
Age range: 5–13
Fees: Day £14,700–£16,200

UCS Pre-Prep
36 College Crescent, London NW3 5LF
Tel: 020 7722 4433
Headmistress: Dr Zoe Dunn
Age range: B4–7
No. of pupils: 100

University College School
Frognal, Hampstead, London NW3 6XH
Tel: 020 7435 2215
Headmaster: Mr Mark J Beard MA, MEd
Age range: B11–18 G16–18
No. of pupils: 875 VIth309
Fees: Day £20,328

University College School (Junior)
11 Holly Hill, London NW3 6QN
Tel: 020 7435 3068
Headmaster: Mr Lewis Hayward
MA (Oxon Lit. Hum), MA (OU,
ED. Management), PGCE
Age range: B7–11
No. of pupils: 250
Fees: Day £18,789

Wentworth Tutorial College
6-10 Brentmead Place,
London NW11 9LH
Tel: 020 8458 8524/5
Principal: Manuel Guimaraes
Age range: 14–19
No. of pupils: 115

South-East London

Alleyn's School
Townley Road, Dulwich,
London SE22 8SU
Tel: 020 8557 1500
Headmaster: Dr G Savage
MA, PhD, FRSA
Age range: 4–18
No. of pupils: 1252 VIth302
Fees: Day £17,361–£19,851

Bellerbys College London
Bounty House, Greenwich,
London SE8 3DE
Tel: +44 (0)208 694 7000
Principal: Ms Alison Baines
Age range: 15–19

Blackheath High School GDST
Vanbrugh Park, Blackheath,
London SE3 7AG
Tel: 020 8853 2929
Head: Mrs Carol Chandler-Thompson
BA (Hons) Exeter, PGCE Exeter
Age range: G3–18
No. of pupils: 780

Blackheath Preparatory School
4 St Germans Place, Blackheath,
London SE3 0NJ
Tel: 020 8858 0692
Headmistress: Mrs P J Thompson
Age range: 3–11
No. of pupils: 390
Fees: Day £7,740–£12,930

Colfe's Junior School
Horn Park Lane, Lee, London SE12 8AW
Tel: 020 8463 8240
Head: Ms C Macleod
Age range: 3–11
No. of pupils: 355
Fees: Day £13,230–£13,995

Colfe's School
Horn Park Lane, Lee, London SE12 8AW
Tel: 020 8852 2283
Head: Mr R F Russell MA(Cantab)
Age range: 3–18
No. of pupils: 1120

DLD College London
199 Westminster Bridge
Road, London SE1 7FX
Tel: +44 (0)20 7935 8411
Principal: Irfan H Latif BSc
(Hons) PGCE FRSA FRSC
No. of pupils: 440
Fees: Day £19,000–£23,000
FB £16,500–£24,000

Dulwich College
London SE21 7LD
Tel: 020 8693 3601
Master: Dr J A F Spence
Age range: B0–18
No. of pupils: 1589 VIth470
Fees: Day £20,448 WB
£40,017 FB £42,681

Dulwich College Kindergarten & Infants School
Eller Bank, 87 College Road,
London SE21 7HH
Tel: 020 8693 1538
Head: Mrs Nicky Black
Age range: 3 months–7 years
No. of pupils: 251

Dulwich College Preparatory School
42 Alleyn Park, Dulwich,
London SE21 7AA
Tel: 020 8766 5500
Headmaster: Mr M W
Roulston MBE, MEd
Age range: B3–13 G3–5
No. of pupils: 817
Fees: Day £13,074–£19,314

Eltham College
Grove Park Road, Mottingham,
London SE9 4QF
Tel: 0208 857 1455
Headmaster: Guy Sanderson
Age range: B7–18 G16–18
No. of pupils: 830 VIth220
Fees: Day £15,690–£17,775

Greenwich Steiner School
Woodlands, 90 Mycenae Road,
Blackheath, London SE3 7SE
Tel: 020 8858 4404
Age range: 3–14
No. of pupils: 180
Fees: Day £7,310–£8,100

Heath House Preparatory School
37 Wemyss Road, Blackheath,
London SE3 0TG
Tel: 020 8297 1900
Head Teacher: Mrs Sophia
Laslett CertEd PGDE
Age range: 3–11
No. of pupils: 125
Fees: Day £13,485–£14,985

Herne Hill School
The Old Vicarage, 127 Herne
Hill, London SE24 9LY
Tel: 020 7274 6336
Headteacher: Mrs Ngaire Telford
Age range: 2–7
No. of pupils: 296
Fees: Day £6,225–£14,955

JAMES ALLEN'S GIRLS' SCHOOL
For further details see p. 136
144 East Dulwich Grove,
Dulwich, London SE22 8TE
Tel: 020 8693 1181
Email: enquiries@jags.org.uk
Website: www.jags.org.uk
Head of School: Mrs Sally-
Anne Huang MA, MSc
Age range: G4–18
No. of pupils: 1075

Kings Kids Christian School
New Testament Church of
God, Bawtree Road, New
Cross, London SE14 6ET
Tel: 020 8691 5813
Headteacher: Mrs M Okenwa
Age range: 5–11
No. of pupils: 36

London Christian School
40 Tabard Street, London SE1 4JU
Tel: 020 3130 6430
Headmistress: Miss N Collett-White
Age range: 3–11
No. of pupils: 105
Fees: Day £9,390
£

Marathon Science School
1-9 Evelyn Street, Surrey
Quays, London SE8 5RQ
Tel: +44 (0)20 7231 3232
Headteacher: Mr Uzeyir Onur
Age range: B11–16
No. of pupils: 67

Oakfield Preparatory School
125-128 Thurlow Park Road, West
Dulwich, London SE21 8HP
Tel: 020 8670 4206
Age range: 2–11 years
No. of pupils: 420
Fees: Day £10,785

**Octavia House School,
Kennington**
214b Kennington Road,
London SE11 6AU
Tel: 020 3651 4396 (Option:3)
Executive Head: Mr James Waite

Octavia House School, Vauxhall
Vauxhall Primary School, Vauxhall
Street, London SE11 5LG
Tel: 02036 514396 (Option:1)
Executive Head: Mr James Waite
Age range: 5–14
No. of pupils: 65

Octavia House School, Walworth
Larcom House, Larcom
Street, London SE17 1RT
Tel: 02036 514396 (Option:2)
Executive Head: Mr James Waite

Riverston School
63-69 Eltham Road, Lee
Green, London SE12 8UF
Tel: 020 8318 4327
Headmistress: Mrs S E Salathiel
Age range: 9 months–19 years
No. of pupils: 215
£ ✎ 16 ❀

**Rosemead Preparatory
School & Nursery, Dulwich**
70 Thurlow Park Road, London SE21 8HZ
Tel: 020 8670 5865
Headmaster: Mr Phil Soutar
Age range: 2–11
No. of pupils: 366
Fees: Day £10,272–£11,286
£ ✎

St Dunstan's College
Stanstead Road, London SE6 4TY
Tel: 020 8516 7200
Headmaster: Mr Nicholas Hewlett
Age range: 3–18
No. of pupils: 870
✿ A £ 16

St Olave's Preparatory School
106 Southwood Road, New
Eltham, London SE9 3QS
Tel: 020 8294 8930
Headteacher: Miss Claire
Holloway BEd, QTS
Age range: 3–11
No. of pupils: 220
Fees: Day £10,848–£12,300
✎

Sydenham High School GDST
19 Westwood Hill, London SE26 6BL
Tel: 020 8557 7000
Headmistress: Mrs
Katharine Woodcock
Age range: G4–18
No. of pupils: 600 VIth70
Fees: Day £13,161–£16,737
✿ A £ ✎ 16

The Pointer School
19 Stratheden Road, Blackheath,
London SE3 7TH
Tel: 020 8293 1331
Headmaster: Mr R J S Higgins
MA, BEd, CertEd, FCollP
Age range: 3–11
No. of pupils: 370
Fees: Day £11,415–£13,449
£ ✎

**The Villa Pre-Preparatory
School & Nursery**
54 Lyndhurst Grove, Peckham,
London SE15 5AH
Tel: 020 7703 6216
Head Teacher: Emma Champion
Age range: 2–7
No. of pupils: 210

South-West London

Al-Muntada Islamic School
7 Bridges Place, Parsons
Green, London SW6 4HW
Tel: 020 7471 8283
Headteacher: Amjad Malik
Age range: 4–11
No. of pupils: 165
Fees: Day £3,000–£7,000

Al-Risalah Secondary School
145 Upper Tooting Road,
London SW17 7TJ
Tel: 020 8767 6057
Headteacher: Suhayl Lee
Age range: 3–16
No. of pupils: 250

Beechwood School
55 Leigham Court Road,
Streatham, London SW16 2NJ
Tel: 020 8677 8778
Nursery Director: Ms Bamwo
Age range: 0–5
No. of pupils: 100

Bertrum House School
290 Balham High Road,
London SW17 7AL
Tel: 020 8767 4051
Headteacher: Miss Vicky
Age range: 2–5
No. of pupils: 94
Fees: Day £1,775–£2,140
✎

Broomwood Hall School
68-74 Nightingale Lane,
London SW12 8NR
Tel: 020 8682 8830
Headmistress: Katharine Colquhoun
Age range: B4–8 G4–13
No. of pupils: 670
Fees: Day £16,125–£19,785
✎

CAMERON HOUSE
For further details see p. 128
4 The Vale, Chelsea,
London SW3 6AH
Tel: 020 7352 4040
Email:
laura@cameronhouseschool.org
Website:
www.cameronhouseschool.org
Headmistress: Mrs Dina Mallett
Age range: 4–11
Fees: Day £18,465
£ ✎

Centre Academy London
92 St John's Hill, Battersea,
London SW11 1SH
Tel: 020 7738 2344
Headteacher: Rachel Maddison
Age range: 9–19
Fees: Day £27,600–£40,100
✿ £ ✎ 16

Chelsea Independent College
517-523 Fulham Road, London SW6 1HD
Tel: +44 (0) 20 7610 1114
Principal: Dr Martin Meenagh
Age range: 14–19
No. of pupils: 164
16 ✿

Collingham
23 Collingham Gardens,
London SW5 0HL
Tel: 020 7244 7414
Principal: Sally Powell
Age range: 14–19
No. of pupils: VIth200
Fees: Day £4,260–£22,560
16 A £ ✎

Dolphin School
106 Northcote Road,
London SW11 6QW
Tel: 020 7924 3472
Principal: Mrs. N. Baldwin
Age range: 2–11
No. of pupils: 292
Fees: Day £12,270–£13,485
£ ✎

Donhead
33 Edge Hill, London SW19 4NP
Tel: 020 8946 7000
Headmaster: Mr P J J Barr
Age range: B4–11
No. of pupils: 280
Fees: Day £11,175–£11,622
✿ £ ✎

Eaton House Belgravia
3-5 Eaton Gate, London SW1W 9BA
Tel: 020 7924 6000
Head of School: Mr Huw May
Age range: B3–13
Fees: Day £17,850–£20,700
✿ ✎

**Eaton House The Manor
Girls' School**
58 Clapham Common
Northside, London SW4 9RU
Tel: 020 7924 6000
Head: Mr Oliver Snowball
Age range: G4–11
Fees: Day £16,143
✿ £ ✎

Eaton House The Manor Pre Prep School & Nursery
58 Clapham Common
Northside, London SW4 9RU
Tel: 020 7924 6000
Age range: B3½–8
Fees: Day £16,143
🛉

Eaton House The Manor Prep School
58 Clapham Common
Northside, London SW4 9RU
Tel: 020 7924 6000
Head: Mrs Sarah Segrave
Age range: B8–13
Fees: Day £19,743
🛉 £ ✎

Eaton Square School
79 Eccleston Square, London SW1V 1PP
Tel: 020 7931 9469
Headmaster: Mr Sebastian Hepher BEd(Hons)
Age range: 2–13
No. of pupils: 529
Fees: Day £20,850–£21,900
🏫 £ ✎

Ecole Charles De Gaulle – Wix
Clapham Common North Side, London SW4 0AJ
Tel: +44 20 7738 0287
Headteacher: Mr Blanchard
Age range: 5–11
No. of pupils: 100
🏫

Ecole Marie D'Orliac
60 Clancarty Road, London SW6 3AA
Tel: +44 7736 020 58 63
Principal: Mr Olivier Rauch
Age range: 4–11
No. of pupils: 50
🏫

Emanuel School
Battersea Rise, London SW11 1HS
Tel: 020 8870 4171
Headmaster: Mr Robert Milne
Age range: 10–18
No. of pupils: 930
Fees: Day £18,372
Ⓐ £ ✎ 16+

Eveline Day & Nursery Schools
14 Trinity Crescent, Upper Tooting, London SW17 7AE
Tel: 020 8672 4673
Headmistress: Ms Eveline Drut
Age range: 3 months–11 years
No. of pupils: 80
Fees: Day £13,859
✎

Falkner House
19 Brechin Place, South Kensington, London SW7 4QB
Tel: 020 7373 4501
Headteacher: Mrs Anita Griggs BA(Hons), PGCE
Age range: B3–11 G3–11
🛉 🛉

Finton House School
171 Trinity Road, London SW17 7HL
Tel: 020 8682 0921
Head of School: Mr Ben Freeman
Age range: 4–11
No. of pupils: 300
Fees: Day £15,378–£15,588
£ ✎

Francis Holland School, Sloane Square, SW1
39 Graham Terrace, London SW1W 8JF
Tel: 020 7730 2971
Head: Mrs Lucy Elphinstone MA(Cantab)
Age range: G4–18
No. of pupils: 520 VIth70
Fees: Day £17,760–£20,085
🛉 Ⓐ £ ✎ 16+

Garden House School
Boys' School & Girls' School,
Turk's Row, London SW3 4TW
Tel: 020 7730 1652
Boys' Head: Mr Christian Warland BA(Hons), LLB.
Age range: 3–11
No. of pupils: 490
Fees: Day £17,700–£22,800
£ ✎

Glendower School
86/87 Queen's Gate, London SW7 5JX
Tel: 020 7370 1927
Headmistress: Mrs Sarah Knollys BA, PGCE
Age range: G4–11+
No. of pupils: 206
Fees: Day £19,200
🛉 £ ✎

Hall School Wimbledon
Beavers Holt, Stroud Crescent, Putney Vale, London SW15 3EQ
Tel: 020 8788 2370
Headmaster: Timothy J Hobbs MA
Age range: 4–16
No. of pupils: 520
Fees: Day £13,126–£17,336
✎

Hall School Wimbledon Senior School
17 The Downs, Wimbledon, London SW20 8HF
Tel: 020 8879 9200
Headmaster: Timothy J Hobbs MA
Age range: 11–16
No. of pupils: 520
Fees: Day £17,336
✎

Hill House International Junior School
17 Hans Place, Chelsea, London SW1X 0EP
Tel: 020 7584 1331
Principals: Richard, Janet, William & Edmund Townend
Age range: 4–13
No. of pupils: 740 VIth70
🏫 £ ✎

Hornsby House School
Hearnville Road, Balham, London SW12 8RS
Tel: 020 8673 7573
Headmaster: Mr Edward Rees
Age range: 4–11
Fees: Day £14,280–£15,345
£ ✎

Hurlingham Nursery and Pre-Prep
The Old Methodist Hall, Gwendolen Avenue, London SW15 6EH
Tel: 020 8780 9446
Head: Jane Appleby
Age range: 2–7
No. of pupils: 115
✎

Hurlingham School
122 Putney Bridge Road, Putney, London SW15 2NQ
Tel: 020 8874 7186
Headteacher: Mr Jonathan Brough
Age range: 4–11
No. of pupils: 326
Fees: Day £15,540–£16,185
£ ✎

Hyde Park School, Queen's Gate
24 Elvaston Place, South Kensington, London SW7 5NL
Tel: 020 7225 3131
Age range: 2–11
No. of pupils: 110
Fees: Day £11,280–£16,875
✎

Ibstock Place School
Clarence Lane, London SW15 5PY
Tel: 020 8876 9991
Head: Mrs Anna Sylvester-Johnson BA(Hons), PGCE
Age range: 4–18
No. of pupils: 970
Fees: Day £16,290–£20,880
Ⓐ £ 16+

KENSINGTON PARK SCHOOL
For further details see p. 138
59 Queen's Gate, South Kensington, London SW7 5JP
Tel: +44 (0)20 7225 0577
Email: admissions@kps.co.uk
Website: www.kps.co.uk
Headmaster: Mr Paul Vanni MA
Age range: 11–18
🏛 Ⓐ

Kensington Prep School
596 Fulham Road, London SW6 5PA
Tel: 0207 731 9300
Head: Mrs P Lynch MA (St Andrews) PGCE
Age range: G4–11
No. of pupils: 289
Fees: Day £17,193
🛉

King's College Junior School
Southside, Wimbledon Common, London SW19 4TT
Tel: 020 8255 5335
Headmaster: Dr. G A Silverlock
Age range: B7–13
No. of pupils: 437
🛉 £

King's College School
Southside, Wimbledon Common, London SW19 4TT
Tel: 020 8255 5300
Head Master: A D Halls MA
Age range: B11–18 G16–18
No. of pupils: 967
Fees: Day £19,530–£21,600
🛉 🏫 Ⓐ £ IB 16+

Knightsbridge School
67 Pont Street, Knightsbridge, London SW1X 0BD
Tel: 020 7590 9000
Head: Ms Shona Colaco MA, PGCE, MSB, CBiol
Age range: 3–13
No. of pupils: 400
Fees: Day £18,756–£19,965
£ ✎

L'Ecole de Battersea
Trott Street, Battersea, London SW11 3DS
Tel: 020 7371 8350
Principal: Mrs F Brisset
Age range: 3–11
No. of pupils: 260
Fees: Day £12,150–£12,300

L'Ecole des Petits
2 Hazlebury Road, Fulham,
London SW6 2NB
Tel: 020 7371 8350
Principal: Mrs F Brisset
Age range: 3–6
No. of pupils: 132
Fees: Day £11,895–£11,985

London Steiner School
9 Weir Road, Balham, London SW12 0LT
Tel: 0208 772 3504
Age range: 3–14
£

Lycée Français Charles de Gaulle
35 Cromwell Road, London SW7 2DG
Tel: 020 7584 6322
Head of School: Mr Olivier Rauch
Age range: 5–19
No. of pupils: 4000
A £ 16

Mander Portman Woodward – London
90-92 Queen's Gate, London SW7 5AB
Tel: 020 7835 1355
Principal: Mr John Southworth BSc MSc
Age range: 14–19
No. of pupils: 724
Fees: Day £9,075–£9,833
16 A £

More House School
22-24 Pont Street, Knightsbridge,
London SW1X 0AA
Tel: 020 7235 2855
Co-Heads: Mrs. Amanda Leach
& Mr. Michael Keeley
Age range: G11–18
No. of pupils: 206
Fees: Day £18,930
A £ 16

NEWTON PREP
For further details see p. 142
149 Battersea Park Road,
London SW8 4BX
Tel: 020 7720 4091
Email: enquiries@newtonprep.co.uk
Website:
www.newtonprepschool.co.uk
Headmistress: Mrs Alison
Fleming BA, MA Ed, PGCE
Age range: 3–13
No. of pupils: 632
Fees: Day £9,300–£19,695

£

Northcote Lodge School
26 Bolingbroke Grove, London SW11 6EL
Tel: 020 8682 8888
Headmaster: Mr Peter Clare-Hunt
Age range: B8–13
No. of pupils: 244
Fees: Day £19,785

Oliver House Preparatory School
7 Nightingale Lane, London SW4 9AH
Tel: 020 8772 1911
Headteacher: Mr Rob Farrell
Age range: 3–11
No. of pupils: 144
Fees: Day £6,600–£15,090

Parkgate House School
80 Clapham Common North
Side, London SW4 9SD
Tel: +44 (0)20 7350 2461
Principal: Miss Catherine Shanley
Age range: 2½–11 years
No. of pupils: 220
Fees: Day £5,940–£15,600

Parsons Green Prep School
1 Fulham Park Road, Fulham,
London SW6 4LJ
Tel: 020 7371 9009
Headmaster: Tim Cannell
Age range: 4–11
No. of pupils: 200
Fees: Day £16,857–£18,201

PROSPECT HOUSE SCHOOL
For further details see p. 148
75 Putney Hill, London SW15 3NT
Tel: 020 8246 4897
Email: info@prospecths.org.uk
Website: www.prospecths.org.uk
Headmaster: Mr Michael
Hodge BPED(Rhodes) QTS
Age range: 3–11
No. of pupils: 300
Fees: Day £8,850–£18,450

Putney High School GDST
35 Putney Hill, London SW15 6BH
Tel: 020 8788 4886
Headmistress: Mrs Suzie
Longstaff BA, MA, PGCE
Age range: G4–18
No. of pupils: 976 VIth150
A £ 16

QUEEN'S GATE SCHOOL
For further details see p. 150
133 Queen's Gate, London SW7 5LE
Tel: 020 7589 3587
Email: registrar@queensgate.org.uk
Website: www.queensgate.org.uk
Principal: Mrs R M Kamaryc
BA, MSc, PGCE
Age range: G4–18
No. of pupils: 542 VIth97

A £ 16

Redcliffe School Trust Ltd
47 Redcliffe Gardens, Chelsea,
London SW10 9JH
Tel: 020 7352 9247
Head: Sarah Lemmon
Age range: 3–11
Fees: Day £6,660–£17,730
£

Sinclair House Preparatory School
59 Fulham High Street,
Fulham, London SW6 3JJ
Tel: 0207 736 9182
Principal: Mrs Carlotta T M O'Sullivan
Age range: 2–11
No. of pupils: 120
Fees: Day £5,280–£17,025

St Mary's Summerstown Montessori
46 Wimbledon Road, Tooting,
London SW17 0UQ
Tel: 020 8947 7359
Head: Liz Maitland NNEB, RSH, MontDip
Age range: 18 months–5 years
No. of pupils: 30
Fees: Day £1,300

St Nicholas Preparatory School
23 Princes Gate, Kensington,
London SW7 1PT
Tel: 020 7225 1277
Headmistress: Jill Walker
Age range: 3–11
No. of pupils: 200

St Paul's Juniors
St Paul's School, Lonsdale
Road, London SW13 9JT
Tel: 020 8748 3461
Age range: B7–13
No. of pupils: 436
Fees: Day £20,010
£

St Paul's School
Lonsdale Road, Barnes,
London SW13 9JT
Tel: 020 8748 9162
High Master: Prof Mark Bailey
Age range: B13–18
No. of pupils: 897
Fees: Day £25,032 FB £37,611
A £ 16

St Philip's School
6 Wetherby Place, London SW7 4NE
Tel: 020 7373 3944
Headmaster: Mr Wulffen-Thomas
Age range: B7–13
No. of pupils: 110
Fees: Day £16,200
£

Streatham & Clapham High School GDST
42 Abbotswood Road,
London SW16 1AW
Tel: 020 8677 8400
Headmaster: Dr Millan Sachania
Age range: G3–18
No. of pupils: 603 VIth70
Fees: Day £10,431–£19,743
A £ 16

Sussex House School
68 Cadogan Square, London SW1X 0EA
Tel: 020 7584 1741
Headmaster: Mr N P Kaye
MA(Cantab), ACP, FRSA, FRGS
Age range: B8–13
No. of pupils: 182
Fees: Day £19,770
£

Swedish School
82 Lonsdale Road, London SW13 9JS
Tel: 020 8741 1751
Head of School: Ms. Annika
Simonsson Bergqvist
Age range: 3–18
No. of pupils: 300 VIth145
Fees: Day £8,600–£9,100
16

Thames Christian College
Wye Street, Battersea,
London SW11 2HB
Tel: 020 7228 3933
Executive Head: Stephen
Holsgrove PhD
Age range: 11–16
No. of pupils: 120
Fees: Day £15,780
£

The Falcons School for Girls
11 Woodborough Road,
Putney, London SW15 6PY
Tel: 020 8992 5189
Head of School: Mrs Sophia
Ashworth Jones
Age range: G3–11
No. of pupils: 102
Fees: Day £8,580–£15,705
🧒 £ ✏

The Hampshire School, Chelsea
15 Manresa Road, Chelsea,
London SW3 6NB
Tel: 020 7352 7077
Principal: Mr Donal Brennan
Age range: 3–13
No. of pupils: 300
Fees: Day £16,965–£17,955
£ ✏

The Harrodian School
Lonsdale Road, London SW13 9QN
Tel: 020 8748 6117
Headmaster: James R Hooke
Age range: 4–18
No. of pupils: 890 VIth95
Fees: Day £15,000–£23,040
Ⓐ ✏ ⑯

The Laurels School
126 Atkins Road, Clapham,
London SW12 0AN
Tel: 020 8674 7229
Headmistress: Linda Sanders BA
Hons (Bristol), MA (Madrid)
Age range: G11–18
🧒

The Merlin School
4 Carlton Drive, Putney
Hill, London SW15 2BZ
Tel: 020 8788 2769
Principal: Mrs Kate Prest
Age range: 4–8
No. of pupils: 170

The Moat School
Bishops Avenue, Fulham,
London SW6 6EG
Tel: 020 7610 9018
Head: Ms Clare King
Age range: 9–16
Fees: Day £30,000
✏

The Montessori Pavilion – The Kindergarten School
Vine Road, Barnes, London SW13 0NE
Tel: 020 8878 9695
Headmistress: Ms Georgina Dashwood
Age range: 3–8
No. of pupils: 50
✏

The Norwegian School
28 Arterberry Road, Wimbledon,
London SW20 8AH
Tel: 020 8947 6617
Head: Mr Ivar Chavannes
Age range: 3–16

The Roche School
11 Frogmore, London SW18 1HW
Tel: 020 8877 0823
Headmistress: Mrs V Adams
BA(Hons), PGCE, MA
Age range: 2–11 years
No. of pupils: 305
Fees: Day £14,280–£14,970
£ ✏

The Rowans School
19 Drax Avenue, Wimbledon,
London SW20 0EG
Tel: 020 8946 8220
Head Teacher: Mrs Joanna Hubbard
Age range: 3–8
Fees: Day £7,905–£13,170

The Study Preparatory School
Wilberforce House, Camp
Road, Wimbledon Common,
London SW19 4UN
Tel: 020 8947 6969
Headmistress: Mrs Susan
Pepper MA Oxon, PGCE
Age range: G4–11
No. of pupils: 315
🧒 £ ✏

The White House Preparatory School & Woodentops Kindergarten
24 Thornton Road, London SW12 0LF
Tel: 020 8674 9514
Principal: Mrs. Mary McCahery
Age range: 2–11
Fees: Day £4,436–£4,740
£

Thomas's Preparatory School – Battersea
28-40 Battersea High Street,
London SW11 3JB
Tel: 020 7978 0900
Head: Simon O'Malley
Age range: 4–13
No. of pupils: 547
Fees: Day £18,747–£20,868
✏

Thomas's Preparatory School – Clapham
Broomwood Road, London SW11 6JZ
Tel: 020 7326 9300
Headmaster: Mr Philip Ward BEd(Hons)
Age range: 4–13
No. of pupils: 647
Fees: Day £17,262–£19,518
£ ✏

Thomas's Preparatory School – Fulham
Hugon Road, London SW6 3ES
Tel: 020 7751 8200
Head: Miss Annette Dobson
BEd(Hons), PGCertDys
Age range: 4–11
Fees: Day £17,880–£20,016

Tower House School
188 Sheen Lane, London SW14 8LF
Tel: 020 8876 3323
Head: Mr Gregory Evans
Age range: B4–13
No. of pupils: 180
Fees: Day £13,089–£14,838
🧒 ✏

Ursuline Preparatory School
18 The Downs, London SW20 8HR
Tel: 020 8947 0859
Headmaster: Mr Chris McGrath
Age range: B3–4 G3–11
Fees: Day £6,615–£10,815
£ ✏

Wandsworth Preparatory School
The Old Library, 2 Allfarthing
Lane, London SW18 2PQ
Tel: 0208 870 4133
Head of School: Miss Bridget
Saul BA (Hons), PGCE, MA
Age range: 4–11
No. of pupils: 115
Fees: Day £4,570
🐕 £

Westminster Abbey Choir School
Dean's Yard, London SW1P 3NY
Tel: 0207 654 4918
Headmaster: Jonathan Milton BEd
Age range: B8–13
No. of pupils: 35
Fees: FB £8,571
🧒 ⚓ £

Westminster Cathedral Choir School
Ambrosden Avenue, London SW1P 1QH
Tel: 020 7798 9081
Headmaster: Mr Neil McLaughlan
Age range: B4–13
No. of pupils: 150
Fees: Day £16,350–£19,233 FB £10,086
🧒 ⚓ £ ✏

Westminster School
Little Dean's Yard, Westminster,
London SW1P 3PF
Tel: 020 7963 1003
Headmaster: Mr Patrick Derham
Age range: B13–18 G16–18
No. of pupils: 744
Fees: Day £26,130–£28,566 FB £37,740
🧒 🐕 ⚓ £ ✏ ⑯

Westminster Tutors
86 Old Brompton Road, South
Kensington, London SW7 3LQ
Tel: 020 7584 1288
Principal: Virginia Maguire
BA, MA, MLitt
Age range: 14–mature
No. of pupils: VIth40
Fees: Day £4,000–£25,000
⑯ Ⓐ £ ✏

Westminster Under School
Adrian House, 27 Vincent
Square, London SW1P 2NN
Tel: 020 7821 5788
Headteacher: Mr Mark O'Donnell
Age range: B7–13
No. of pupils: 265
Fees: Day £19,344
🧒 £ ✏

Willington School
Worcester Road, Wimbledon,
London SW19 7QQ
Tel: 020 8944 7020
Acting Headmaster: Mr
Marcus Tattersal
Age range: B4–13
No. of pupils: 250
Fees: Day £12,150–£14,640
🧒 £

Wimbledon Common Preparatory
113 Ridgway, Wimbledon,
London SW19 4TA
Tel: 020 8946 1001
Head Teacher: Mrs Tracey Buck
Age range: B4–8
No. of pupils: 160
Fees: Day £13,185
🧒

Wimbledon High School GDST
Mansel Road, Wimbledon,
London SW19 4AB
Tel: 020 8971 0900
Headmistress: Mrs Jane Lunnon
Age range: G4–18
No. of pupils: 900 VIth155
Fees: Day £14,622–£18,810
🧒 Ⓐ £ ✏ ⑯

West London

Albemarle Independent College
18 Dunraven Street, London W1K 7FE
Tel: 020 7409 7273
Co-Principals: Beverley
Mellon & James Eytle
Age range: 16–19
No. of pupils: 160
Fees: Day £7,000–£24,000
16 A £

Arts Educational Schools London Sixth Form
Cone Ripman House, 14 Bath
Road, Chiswick, London W4 1LY
Tel: 020 8987 6666
Head Teacher: Mr Chris Hocking
Age range: 16–18
No. of pupils: 85
Fees: Day £16,830–£16,990
16

Arts Educational Schools London Years 7-11
Cone Ripman House, 14 Bath
Road, Chiswick, London W4 1LY
Tel: 020 8987 6666
Head Teacher: Mr Chris Hocking
Age range: 11–16
No. of pupils: 141
Fees: Day £15,390–£15,540
A £

Ashbourne Independent Sixth Form College
17 Old Court Place, Kensington,
London W8 4PL
Tel: 020 7937 3858
Principal: M J Kirby MSc, BApSc
Age range: 16–19
No. of pupils: 170
Fees: Day £24,750–£26,250
16 A £

Ashbourne Middle School
17 Old Court Place, Kensington,
London W8 4PL
Tel: 020 7937 3858
Principal: M J Kirby MSc, BApSc
Age range: 13–16
No. of pupils: VIth150
Fees: Day £24,750–£26,250
A £ 16

Avenue House School
70 The Avenue, Ealing, London W13 8LS
Tel: 020 8998 9981
Headteacher: Mr J Sheppard
Age range: 3–11
No. of pupils: 135
Fees: Day £11,250

Bales College
742 Harrow Road, Kensal
Town, London W10 4AA
Tel: 020 8960 5899
Principal: William Moore
Age range: 11–19
No. of pupils: 90
Fees: Day £11,550–£12,750
16 A £

Barbara Speake Stage School
East Acton Lane, East Acton,
London W3 7EG
Tel: 020 8743 1306
Headteacher: Mr David
Speake BA (Hons)
Age range: 3–16
Fees: Day £7,500–£9,000
16

BASSETT HOUSE SCHOOL
For further details see p. 126
60 Bassett Road, London W10 6JP
Tel: 020 8969 0313
Email: info@bassetths.org.uk
Website: www.bassetths.org.uk
Headmistress: Mrs Philippa
Cawthorne MA (Soton)
PGCE Mont Cert
Age range: 3–11
No. of pupils: 190
Fees: Day £8,850–£18,450

Bute House Preparatory School for Girls
Bute House, Luxemburg
Gardens, London W6 7EA
Tel: 020 7603 7381
Head: Mrs Helen Lowe
Age range: G4–11
No. of pupils: 306
Fees: Day £16,458

Chepstow House School
108a Lancaster Road, London W11 1QX
Tel: 0207 243 0243
Headteacher: Angela Barr
Age range: 2½–12 years

Chiswick & Bedford Park Prep School
Priory House, Priory Avenue,
London W4 1TX
Tel: 020 8994 1804
Headmistress: Mrs S Daniell
Age range: B4–7+ G4–11
No. of pupils: 180
Fees: Day £13,275

Clifton Lodge
8 Mattock Lane, Ealing,
London W5 5BG
Tel: 020 8579 3662
Head: Mr. Floyd Steadman
Age range: 3–13
No. of pupils: 140
Fees: Day £12,240–£14,010
£

Connaught House School
47 Connaught Square, London W2 2HL
Tel: 020 7262 8830
Principal: Mrs V Hampton
Age range: 4–11
No. of pupils: 75
Fees: Day £16,650–£18,300
£

David Game College
31 Jewry Street, London EC3N 2ET
Tel: 020 7221 6665
Principal: D T P Game MA, MPhil
Age range: 14–19
No. of pupils: 200 VIth150
Fees: Day £3,680–£30,630
16 A 16

Durston House
12-14 Castlebar Road,
Ealing, London W5 2DR
Tel: 020 8991 6530
Headmaster: Mr Ian Kendrick
MA, BEd(Hons)
Age range: B4–13
No. of pupils: 390
Fees: Day £12,480–£15,180

Ealing Independent College
83 New Broadway, Ealing,
London W5 5AL
Tel: 020 8579 6668
Principal: Dr Ian Moores
Age range: 13–19
No. of pupils: 100 VIth70
Fees: Day £2,910–£18,120
16 A 16

Ecole Francaise Jacques Prevert
59 Brook Green, London W6 7BE
Tel: 020 7602 6871
Headteacher: Delphine Gentil
Age range: 4–11

Fulham Prep School
200 Greyhound Road, London W14 9SD
Tel: 020 7386 2444
Age range: 4–18
No. of pupils: 647
Fees: Day £16,869–£19,749

Great Beginnings Montessori School
The Welsh Church Hall, 82a Chiltern
Street, Marylebone, London W1H 5JE
Tel: 020 7486 2276
Head: Mrs Wendy Innes
Age range: 2–6
Fees: Day £1,095–£1,650

Greek Primary School of London
3 Pierrepoint Road, Acton,
London W3 9JR
Tel: 020 8992 6156
Age range: 1–11

Halcyon London International School
33 Seymour Place, London W1H 5AU
Tel: +44 (0)20 7258 1169
Director: Mr Barry Mansfield
Age range: 11–18
No. of pupils: 160
£ IB

Harvington School
20 Castlebar Road, Ealing,
London W5 2DS
Tel: 020 8997 1583
Headmistress: Mrs Anna Evans
Age range: B3–4 G3–11
No. of pupils: 140
Fees: Day £6,525–£12,615
£

Hawkesdown House School Kensington
27 Edge Street, Kensington,
London W8 7PN
Tel: 020 7727 9090
Headmistress: Mrs. J. A. K.
Mackay B.Ed (Hons)
Age range: 3–11
No. of pupils: 130
Fees: Day £16,020–£18,435

Heathfield House School
Heathfield Gardens, Chiswick,
London W4 4JU
Tel: 020 8994 3385
Headteacher: Mrs Goodsman
Age range: 4–11
No. of pupils: 197
Fees: Day £2,471–£3,676

Holland Park Pre Prep School and Day Nursery
5, Holland Road, Kensington,
London W14 8HJ
Tel: 020 7602 9066/020 7602 9266
Head Mistress: Mrs Kitty Mason
Age range: 3 months–8 years
No. of pupils: 39
Fees: Day £9,180–£18,120

Hyde Park School, Marble Arch
The Long Garden, St George's Fields,
Albion Street, London W2 2AX
Tel: 020 7262 1190
Age range: 2–7
No. of pupils: 74
Fees: Day £11,280–£16,875

Instituto Español Vicente Cañada Blanch
317 Portobello Road, London W10 5SZ
Tel: +44 (0) 20 8969 2664
Principal: Carmen Pinilla Padilla
Age range: 4–19
No. of pupils: 405

International School of London
139 Gunnersbury Avenue,
London W3 8LG
Tel: +44 (0)20 8992 5823
Principal: Richard Parker
Age range: 3–18 years
No. of pupils: 420
Fees: Day £19,000–£26,300

King Fahad Academy
Bromyard Avenue, Acton,
London W3 7HD
Tel: 020 8743 0131
Director General: Dr Abdulghani Alharbi
Age range: 3–19
No. of pupils: 550
Fees: Day £2,500–£4,500

La Petite Ecole Francais
73 Saint Charles Square,
London W10 6EJ
Tel: +44 208 960 1278
Principal: Mme Marjorie Lacassagne
Age range: 3–11

Latymer Prep School
36 Upper Mall, Hammersmith,
London W6 9TA
Tel: 020 7993 0061
Principal: Ms Andrea Rutterford B.Ed (Hons)
Age range: 7–11
No. of pupils: 165
Fees: Day £18,330

Latymer Upper School
King Street, Hammersmith,
London W6 9LR
Tel: 020862 92024
Head: Mr D Goodhew MA(Oxon)
Age range: 11–18
No. of pupils: 1200
Fees: Day £20,130

Le Herisson
River Court Methodist Church, Rover Court Road,
Hammersmith, London W6 9JT
Tel: 020 8563 7664
Director: Maria Frost
Age range: 2–6
Fees: Day £8,730–£8,970

L'Ecole Bilingue
St David's Welsh Church, St Mary's Terrace, London W2 1SJ
Tel: 020 7224 8427
Headteacher: Ms Veronique Ferreira
Age range: 3–11
No. of pupils: 68
Fees: Day £9,960–£10,770

Leiths School of Food & Wine
16-20 Wendell Road, Shepherd's Bush, London W12 9RT
Tel: 020 8749 6400
Managing Director: Camilla Schneideman
Age range: 17–99
No. of pupils: 96

LLOYD WILLIAMSON SCHOOLS
For further details see p. 140
12 Telford Road, London W10 5SH
Tel: 020 8962 0345
Email: admin@lws.org.uk
Website: www.lloydwilliamson.co.uk
Co-Principals: Ms Lucy Meyer & Mr Aaron Williams
Age range: 4 months–14 years (15 in 2019; 16 in 2020)
Fees: Day £14,085

Norland Place School
162-166 Holland Park Avenue,
London W11 4UH
Tel: 020 7603 9103
Headmaster: Mr Patrick Mattar MA
Age range: B4–8 years G4–11 years
Fees: Day £16,107–£18,072

Notting Hill & Ealing High School GDST
2 Cleveland Road, West Ealing, London W13 8AX
Tel: (020) 8799 8400
Headmaster: Mr Matthew Shoults
Age range: G4–18
No. of pupils: 903 VIth150
Fees: Day £14,313–£18,561

Notting Hill Preparatory School
95 Lancaster Road, London W11 1QQ
Tel: 020 7221 0727
Headmistress: Mrs Jane Cameron
Age range: 4–13
No. of pupils: 325
Fees: Day £6,355

One World Montessori Nursery & Pre-Prep
69-71 Brock Green, Hammersmith,
London W6 7BE
Tel: 020 7603 6065
Headteacher: Ms N Greer
Age range: 2–8
No. of pupils: 21

One World Preparatory School
10 Stanley Gardens, Acton,
London W3 7SZ
Tel: 020 87433300
Head: Ms Lisa Manser
Age range: 3–11
No. of pupils: 52
Fees: Day £3,000

ORCHARD HOUSE SCHOOL
For further details see p. 146
16 Newton Grove, Bedford Park, London W4 1LB
Tel: 020 8742 8544
Email: info@orchardhs.org.uk
Website: www.orchardhs.org.uk
Headmistress: Mrs Maria Edwards BEd(Beds) PGCE(Man) Mont Cert
Age range: 3–11
No. of pupils: 290
Fees: Day £8,850–£18,450

Pembridge Hall
18 Pembridge Square, London W2 4EH
Tel: 020 7229 0121
Headteacher: Mr Henry Keighley-Elstub
Age range: G4–11
No. of pupils: 413

Portland Place School
56-58 Portland Place, London W1B 1NJ
Tel: 0207 307 8700
Head: Mr David Bradbury
Age range: 9–18
No. of pupils: 300 VIth50
Fees: Day £21,030

Queen's College
43-49 Harley Street, London W1G 8BT
Tel: 020 7291 7000
Principal: Mr Richard Tillet
Age range: G11–18
No. of pupils: 360 VIth90

Queen's College Preparatory School
61 Portland Place, London W1B 1QP
Tel: 020 7291 0660
Headmistress: Mrs Emma Webb
Age range: G4–11

Ravenscourt Park Preparatory School
16 Ravenscourt Avenue, London W6 0SL
Tel: 020 8846 9153
Headmaster: Mr Carl Howes MA (Cantab), PGCE (Exeter)
Age range: 4–11
No. of pupils: 419
Fees: Day £5,626

Ray Cochrane Beauty School
118 Baker Street, London W1U 6TT
Tel: 02033224738
Principal: Miss Baljeet Suri
Age range: 16–50
No. of pupils: 30
Fees: Day £650–£8,495

**Southbank International
School – Fitzrovia**
17 Conway Street, London W1T 6BN
Tel: +44 2076 312600

**Southbank International
School – Kensington**
36-38 Kensington Park
Road, London W11 3BU
Tel: +44 (0)20 7243 3803
Principal: Siobhan McGrath
Age range: 3–11

**Southbank International
School – Westminster**
63-65 Portland Place, London W1B 1QR
Tel: 020 7243 3803
Principal: Dr Paul Wood
Age range: 11–19

St Augustine's Priory
Hillcrest Road, Ealing, London W5 2JL
Tel: 020 8997 2022
Headteacher: Mrs Sarah
Raffray M.A., N.P.Q.H
Age range: B3–4 G3–18
No. of pupils: 456
Fees: Day £10,656–£15,162

St Benedict's School
54 Eaton Rise, Ealing, London W5 2ES
Tel: 020 8862 2000
Headmaster: Mr A Johnson BA
Age range: 3–18
No. of pupils: 1073 VIth219
Fees: Day £12,500–£16,104

St James Junior School
Earsby Street, London W14 8SH
Tel: 020 7348 1777
Headmistress: Mrs Catherine
Thomlinson BA(Hons)
Age range: B4–11 G4–10
Fees: Day £16,425–£17,910

St James Senior Girls' School
Earsby Street, London W14 8SH
Tel: 020 7348 1777
Headmistress: Mrs Sarah Labram BA
Age range: G11–18
No. of pupils: 295 VIth67
Fees: Day £20,100

St Paul's Girls' School
Brook Green, London W6 7BS
Tel: 020 7603 2288
High Mistress: Mrs Sarah Fletcher
Age range: G11–18 years
No. of pupils: 750 VIth200
Fees: Day £24,891–£26,760

Sylvia Young Theatre School
1 Nutford Place, London W1H 5YZ
Tel: 020 7258 2330
Headteacher: Mrs Frances Chave
Age range: 10–16

Tabernacle School
32 St Anns Villas, Holland
Park, London W11 4RS
Tel: 020 7602 6232
Headteacher: Mrs P Wilson
Age range: 3–16
Fees: Day £6,500–£9,500

The Falcons School for Boys
2 Burnaby Gardens, Chiswick,
London W4 3DT
Tel: 020 8747 8393
**Head of Pre-Preparatory
School:** Mr Andrew Forbes
Age range: B3–13
No. of pupils: 225
Fees: Day £8,475–£17,475

**The Godolphin and
Latymer School**
Iffley Road, Hammersmith,
London W6 0PG
Tel: +44 (0)20 7441 1936
Head Mistress: Dr Frances Ramsey
Age range: G11–18
No. of pupils: 800
Fees: Day £21,615

The Japanese School
87 Creffield Road, Acton,
London W3 9PU
Tel: 020 8993 7145
Headteacher: Mrs Kiyoe Tsuruoka
Age range: 6–16
No. of pupils: 500

**Thomas's Preparatory
School – Kensington**
17-19 Cottesmore Gardens,
London W8 5PR
Tel: 020 7361 6500
Headmistress: Miss Joanna Ebner
MA, BEd(Hons)(Cantab), NPQH
Age range: 4–11
Fees: Day £20,526–£21,789

Wetherby Preparatory School
48 Bryanston Square, London W1H 2EA
Tel: 020 7535 3520
Headteacher: Mr Nick Baker
Age range: B8–13
No. of pupils: 192
Fees: Day £21,660

Wetherby Pre-Preparatory School
11 Pembridge Square, London W2 4ED
Tel: 020 7727 9581
Headmaster: Mr Mark Snell
Age range: B2 ½–8
No. of pupils: 350
Fees: Day £21,600

Wetherby Senior School
100 Marylebone Lane,
London W1U 2QU
Tel: 020 7535 3530
Headmaster: Mr Seth Bolderow
Age range: B11–18
Fees: Day £22,995

Young Dancers Academy
25 Bulwer Street, London W12 8AR
Tel: 020 8743 3856
Head: Mrs K Williams
Age range: 11–16
Fees: Day £12,237–£12,690

**Ysgol Gymraeg Llundain
London Welsh School**
Hanwell Community Centre,
Westcott Crescent, London W7 1PD
Tel: 020 8575 0237
Leadteacher: Miss Sioned Jones
Age range: 3–11
No. of pupils: 30
Fees: Day £3,345

North-East

KEY TO SYMBOLS

- Ⓐ Boys' school
- Ⓐ Girls' school
- Ⓖ International school
- ⑯ Tutorial or sixth form college
- Ⓐ A levels
- Ⓑ Boarding accommodation
- £ Bursaries
- ⒾⒷ International Baccalaureate
- Ⓛ Learning support
- ⑯ Entrance at 16+
- Ⓥ Vocational qualifications
- (IAPS) Independent Association of Preparatory Schools
- (HMC) The Headmasters' & Headmistresses' Conference
- (ISA) Independent Schools Association
- (GSA) Girls' School Association
- (BSA) Boarding Schools' Association
- Ⓢ Society of Heads

Unless otherwise indicated, all schools are coeducational day schools. Single-sex and boarding schools will be indicated by the relevant icon.

Durham

Barnard Castle Preparatory School
Westwick Road, Barnard
Castle, Durham DL12 8UW
Tel: 01833 696032
Headmistress: Mrs Laura Turner
Age range: 4–11
No. of pupils: 180
Fees: Day £6,240–£9,450 FB £18,300

Barnard Castle Senior School
Barnard Castle, Durham DL12 8UN
Tel: 01833 690222
Headmaster: Mr Anthony
C Jackson BA (Hons)
Age range: 11–18
No. of pupils: 570 VIth160
Fees: Day £13,500 FB £24,300

Bow, Durham School
South Road, Durham DH1 3LS
Tel: 0191 384 8233
Headmistress: Mrs Sally Harrod
Age range: 3–11
No. of pupils: 155
Fees: Day £5,676–£11,043

Durham High School for Girls
Farewell Hall, Durham DH1 3TB
Tel: 0191 384 3226
Headmistress: Mrs Lynne Renwick
Age range: G3–18
No. of pupils: 421

Durham School
Durham City, Durham DH1 4SZ
Tel: +44 (0)191 386 4783
Headmaster: Mr K McLaughlin
Age range: 3–18
No. of pupils: 560 VIth156
Fees: Day £2,756–£5,331 WB
£7,347–£8,786 FB £8,460–£9,846

Polam Hall School
Grange Road, Darlington,
Durham DL1 5PA
Tel: 01325 463383
Principal: Mrs Kate Reid
Age range: 4–19
No. of pupils: 182
Fees: WB £10,461 FB £11,100

The Chorister School
The College, Durham DH1 3EL
Tel: 0191 384 2935
Headmaster: Mr Ian Wicks
Age range: 3–13 years
No. of pupils: 214
Fees: Day £9,420–£12,825
FB £11,520–£21,960

**The Independent Grammar
School: Durham**
Claypath, Durham DH1 1RH
Fees: Day £2,700

Northumberland

Longridge Towers School
Longridge Towers, Berwick-upon-
Tweed, Northumberland TD15 2XH
Tel: 01289 307584
Headmaster: Mr Jonathan Lee
Age range: 3–18
No. of pupils: VIth46
Fees: Day £9,300–£13,650 WB
£20,100–£21,600 FB £26,340–£29,400

Mowden Hall School
Newton, Stocksfield,
Northumberland NE43 7TP
Tel: 01661 842147
Headmaster: Mr Neil Bailey
Age range: 3–13
Fees: Day £9,000–£17,160 FB £23,700

Stockton-on-Tees

Red House School
36 The Green, Norton,
Stockton-on-Tees TS20 1DX
Tel: 01642 553370
Headmaster: Mr Ken James LLB
Age range: 3–16
No. of pupils: 363
Fees: Day £4,710–£10,620

Teesside High School
The Avenue, Eaglescliffe,
Stockton-on-Tees TS16 9AT
Tel: 01642 782095
Head of School: Mrs K Mackenzie
Age range: 3–18
No. of pupils: 350 VIth70

Yarm Preparatory School
Grammar School Lane, Yarm,
Stockton-on-Tees TS15 9ES
Tel: 01642 781447
Headteacher: Mr William Sawyer
Age range: 3–11
No. of pupils: 360
Fees: Day £5,232–£10,755

Yarm School
The Friarage, Yarm, Stockton-
on-Tees TS15 9EJ
Tel: 01642 786023
Headmaster: Mr D M Dunn BA
Age range: 3–18
No. of pupils: VIth200
Fees: Day £5,232–£12,888

Tyne & Wear

Argyle House School
19/20 Thornhill Park, Tunstall Road,
Sunderland, Tyne & Wear SR2 7LA
Tel: 0191 510 0726
Headmaster: Mr C Johnson
Age range: 3–16
Fees: Day £6,780–£8,040

Dame Allan Junior School
Hunters Road, Spital Tongues,
Newcastle upon Tyne, Tyne
& Wear NE2 4NG
Tel: 0191 275 0608
Head: Mr A J Edge
Age range: 3–11
No. of pupils: 140
Fees: Day £7,266–£10,419

Dame Allan's Boys' School
Fowberry Crescent, Fenham,
Newcastle upon Tyne,
Tyne & Wear NE4 9YJ
Tel: 0191 275 0608
Head: Mr P Wildsmith
Age range: B11–16
No. of pupils: 304
Fees: Day £12,936–£13,236

Dame Allan's Girls' School
Fowberry Crescent, Fenham,
Newcastle upon Tyne,
Tyne & Wear NE4 9YJ
Tel: 0191 275 0708
Head: Mrs E Fiddaman
Age range: G11–16
No. of pupils: 225
Fees: Day £12,936–£13,236

Dame Allan's Sixth Form
Fowberry Crescent, Fenham,
Newcastle upon Tyne,
Tyne & Wear NE4 9YJ
Tel: 0191 275 0608
Head: Mr D Henry
Age range: 16–18
No. of pupils: 200
Fees: Day £12,936–£13,236
16ᐧ Ⓐ Ⓔ 16ᐧ

Gateshead Jewish Boarding School
10 Rydal Street, Gateshead,
Tyne & Wear NE8 1HG
Tel: 0191 477 1431
Principal: Rabbi Y Ziskind
Age range: B10–16
No. of pupils: 105
⚹

Gateshead Jewish High School for Girls
6 Gladstone Terrace, Gateshead,
Tyne & Wear NE8 4DY
Tel: 0191 4773471
Headteacher: Rabbi D Bowden
Age range: G11–16
No. of pupils: 132
⚹

Gateshead Jewish Primary School
18-20 Gladstone Terrace,
Gateshead, Tyne & Wear NE8 4EA
Tel: 0191 477 2154 / 0191 478 5841
Headmasters: A Hammond & Y Spitzer
Age range: 5–11
No. of pupils: 446
Fees: Day £2,392–£3,016
✎

Newcastle High School for Girls GDST
Tankerville Terrace, Jesmond,
Newcastle upon Tyne,
Tyne & Wear NE2 3BA
Tel: 0191 281 1768
Acting Head: Mr Michael Tippett
Age range: G3–18
No. of pupils: G850 VIth200
Fees: Day £8,409–£13,023
⚹ Ⓐ Ⓔ ✎ 16ᐧ

Newcastle Preparatory School
6 Eslington Road, Jesmond, Newcastle upon Tyne, Tyne & Wear NE2 4RH
Tel: 0191 281 1769
Head Teacher: Mrs Margaret Coates
Age range: 3–11
No. of pupils: 273
Fees: Day £8,742–£11,307
Ⓔ ✎

Newcastle School for Boys
30 West Avenue, Gosforth, Newcastle
upon Tyne, Tyne & Wear NE3 4ES
Tel: 0191 255 9300
Headmaster: Mr David Tickner
Age range: B3–18
No. of pupils: 400
Fees: Day £7,194–£13,848
⚹ Ⓐ Ⓔ ✎ 16ᐧ

Royal Grammar School
Eskdale Terrace, Newcastle upon
Tyne, Tyne & Wear NE2 4DX
Tel: 0191 281 5711
Headmaster: Mr John Fern
Age range: 7–18
No. of pupils: 1325 VIth341
Fees: Day £10,662–£12,657
Ⓐ Ⓔ ✎ 16ᐧ

Westfield School
Oakfield Road, Gosforth, Newcastle
upon Tyne, Tyne & Wear NE3 4HS
Tel: 0191 255 3980
Headmaster: Mr Neil Walker
Age range: G3–18
No. of pupils: 315 VIth50
Fees: Day £7,755–£13,590
⚹ ⚘ Ⓐ 16ᐧ

North-West

KEY TO SYMBOLS

- (♦) Boys' school
- (♦) Girls' school
- (🌐) International school
- (16) Tutorial or sixth form college
- (A) A levels
- (🏛) Boarding accommodation
- (£) Bursaries
- (IB) International Baccalaureate
- (✎) Learning support
- (16) Entrance at 16+
- (🎓) Vocational qualifications
- (IAPS) Independent Association of Preparatory Schools
- (HMC) The Headmasters' & Headmistresses' Conference
- (ISA) Independent Schools Association
- (GSA) Girls' School Association
- (BSA) Boarding Schools' Association
- (S) Society of Heads

Unless otherwise indicated, all schools are coeducational day schools. Single-sex and boarding schools will be indicated by the relevant icon.

Cheshire

Abbey Gate College
Saighton Grange, Saighton,
Chester, Cheshire CH3 6EN
Tel: 01244 332077
Head: Mrs Tracy Pollard
Age range: 4–18
No. of pupils: 468 VIth71
Fees: Day £8,955–£12,840
Ⓐ Ⓔ ✎ ⑯

Alderley Edge School for Girls
Wilmslow Road, Alderley
Edge, Cheshire SK9 7QE
Tel: 01625 583028
Head of School: Mrs Helen Jeys
Age range: G2–18
No. of pupils: 500 VIth60
Fees: Day £8,115–£12,450
🏃 Ⓐ Ⓔ ⒤ⓑ ✎ ⑯

Beech Hall School
Beech Hall Drive, Tytherington,
Macclesfield, Cheshire SK10 2EG
Tel: 01625 422192
Headmaster: Mr James Allen
Age range: 6 months–16 years
No. of pupils: 230
Fees: Day £9,720–£13,020
Ⓔ ✎

Bowdon Preparatory School for Girls
Ashley Road, Altrincham,
Cheshire WA14 2LT
Tel: 0161 928 0678
Headmistress: Mrs Helen Gee
Age range: G3–11
No. of pupils: 200
🏃

Brabyns Preparatory School
34-36 Arkwright Road, Marple,
Stockport, Cheshire SK6 7DB
Tel: 0161 427 2395
Headteacher: Mr Lee Sanders
Age range: 2–11
No. of pupils: 134
Fees: Day £1,900–£2,640
Ⓔ ✎

Cransley School
Belmont Hall, Great Budworth,
Northwich, Cheshire CW9 6HN
Tel: 01606 891747
Head of School: Mr Richard Pollock
LL.B, PGCE, PG Dip (RNCM)
Age range: 4–16
No. of pupils: 150
Fees: Day £7,923–£11,172
Ⓔ ✎

Greater Grace School of Christian Education
Church Lane, Backford,
Chester, Cheshire CH2 4BE
Tel: 01244 851 797
Head Teacher: Mrs A Mulligan
Age range: 5–18
Fees: Day £1,900

Green Meadow Independent Primary School
Robson Way, Lowton, Warrington,
Cheshire WA3 2RD
Tel: 01942 671138
Head: Mrs S Green
Age range: 4–11

Hale Preparatory School
Broomfield Lane, Hale,
Cheshire WA15 9AS
Tel: 0161 928 2386
Headmaster: Mr J F Connor
Age range: 4–11
No. of pupils: 202
Fees: Day £7,650

Lady Barn House School
Schools Hill, Cheadle, Cheshire SK7 1JE
Tel: 0161 428 2912
Age range: 3–11
No. of pupils: 483
Fees: Day £8,640
Ⓔ ✎

Pownall Hall School
Carrwood Road, Pownall Park,
Wilmslow, Cheshire SK9 5DW
Tel: 01625 523141
Headmaster: Mr David Goulbourn
Age range: 2–11
Fees: Day £8,475–£9,975
✎

Terra Nova School
Jodrell Bank, Holmes Chapel,
Crewe, Cheshire CW4 8BT
Tel: 01477 571251
Headmaster: Mr Philip Stewart
Age range: 3–13
No. of pupils: 295
Fees: Day £5,940–£14,697
🏠 Ⓔ ✎

The Firs School
Newton Lane, Upton, Chester,
Cheshire CH2 2HJ
Tel: 01244 322443
Head Teacher: Mrs L Davies
BA (Hons) Durham, PGCE
(Exeter), PGCDL (York), NP+
Age range: 3–11
No. of pupils: 172
Fees: Day £9,147
Ⓔ ✎

The Grange School
Bradburns Lane, Hartford,
Northwich, Cheshire CW8 1LU
Tel: 01606 74007 or 77447
Headmistress: Mrs Deborah Leonard
Age range: 4–18
No. of pupils: 1185 VIth193
Fees: Day £8,340–£11,160
Ⓐ Ⓔ ✎ ⑯

The Hammond School
Mannings Lane, Chester,
Cheshire CH2 4ES
Tel: 01244 305350
Principal: Ms Maggie Evans BA
(Hons) MA, PGCE, NPQH, FRSA
Age range: 6–19
No. of pupils: 280
Fees: Day £8,370–£18,750
FB £20,400–£27,600
🌐 Ⓐ 🏠 Ⓔ ✎ ⑯

The King's School Chester
Wrexham Road, Chester,
Cheshire CH4 7QL
Tel: 01244 689500
Headmaster: G J Hartley MA, MSc
Age range: 4–18
No. of pupils: 1080 VIth218
Fees: Day £9,150–£13,515
Ⓐ Ⓔ ✎ ⑯

The King's School in Macclesfield
Cumberland Street, Macclesfield,
Cheshire SK10 1DA
Tel: 01625 260000
Headmaster: Dr Simon Hyde
Age range: 3–18
No. of pupils: 1200 VIth250
Fees: Day £8,235–£12,990
Ⓐ Ⓔ ✎ ⑯

The Queen's School
City Walls Road, Chester,
Cheshire CH1 2NN
Tel: 01244 312078
Acting Headmistress: Mrs
Joanne Keville
Age range: G4–18
No. of pupils: 610 VIth100
Fees: Day £9,351–£13,341
🏠 Ⓐ Ⓔ ✎ ⑯

The Ryleys School
Ryleys Lane, Alderley Edge,
Cheshire SK9 7UY
Tel: 01625 583241
Headteacher: Mrs Julia Langford
Age range: 2–11
No. of pupils: 251
Fees: Day £10,260–£11,538
Ⓔ ✎

Wilmslow Preparatory School
Grove Avenue, Wilmslow,
Cheshire SK9 5EG
Tel: 01625 524246
Headteacher: Mrs Helen Rigby
Age range: 3–11
No. of pupils: 117
Fees: Day £4,635–£10,365
Ⓔ ✎

Yorston Lodge School
18 St John's Road, Knutsford,
Cheshire WA16 0DP
Tel: 01565 633177
Headmistress: Mrs J
Dallimore BEd(Hons)
Age range: 3–11
Fees: Day £8,250–£8,310

Cumbria

Austin Friars School
Etterby Scaur, Carlisle,
Cumbria CA3 9PB
Tel: 01228 528042
Headmaster: Mr Matt Harris
Age range: 3–18
No. of pupils: 507 VIth70
Fees: Day £7,653–£14,952
Ⓐ Ⓔ ✎ ⑯

Casterton, Sedbergh Preparatory School
Casterton, Carnforth, Cumbria LA6 2SG
Tel: 01524 279200
Headmaster: Mr Will Newman
BA(Ed) Hons MA
Age range: 3–13
No. of pupils: 210
🏠 Ⓔ ✎

Hunter Hall School
Frenchfield, Penrith, Cumbria CA11 8UA
Tel: 01768 891291
Head Teacher: Mrs Donna Vinsome
Age range: 3–11
No. of pupils: 101
Fees: Day £7,749–£8,979
Ⓔ ✎

Lime House School
Holm Hill, Dalston, Carlisle,
Cumbria CA5 7BX
Tel: 01228 710225
Headteacher: Mary Robertson-
Barnett MA(Oxon), PGCE
Age range: 7–18
No. of pupils: 155 VIth35
Fees: Day £9,000–£12,000 WB
£21,000–£27,000 FB £24,000–£27,750
🌐 Ⓐ 🏠 Ⓔ ✎ ⑯

Sedbergh School
Sedbergh, Cumbria LA10 5HG
Tel: 015396 20535
Headmaster: Mr A Fleck MA
Age range: 3–18
No. of pupils: 500 VIth200
Fees: Day £24,915 FB £33,840
🌐 Ⓐ 🏠 Ⓔ ✎ ⑯

Windermere Preparatory School
Ambleside Road, Windermere,
Cumbria LA23 1AP
Tel: 015394 46164
Head: Mrs Rachael Thomas
Age range: 2–11
No. of pupils: 120
🏫 £ 🖊

WINDERMERE SCHOOL
For further details see p. 164
Patterdale Road, Windermere,
Cumbria LA23 1NW
Tel: 015394 46164
Email:
admissions@windermereschool.co.uk
Website:
www.windermereschool.co.uk
Age range: 3–18
No. of pupils: 340
Fees: Day £17,775 WB
£30,150 FB £31,335
🕤 🏫 £ 🆔 16·

Greater Manchester

Abbey College Manchester
5-7 Cheapside, King Street,
Manchester, Greater
Manchester M2 4WG
Tel: 0161 817 2700
Principal: Ms Liz Elam
Age range: 15–19
No. of pupils: 220 VIth175
Fees: Day £12,750
16· Ⓐ £ 🖊 16·

Abbotsford Preparatory School
211 Flixton Road, Urmston, Manchester,
Greater Manchester M41 5PR
Tel: 0161 748 3261
Head Teacher: Catherine Howard
Age range: 3–11
No. of pupils: 106
Fees: Day £7,029–£7,704
£

**Al Jamiah Al Islamiyyah
(Bolton Darul Uloom)**
Willows Lane, Bolton, Greater
Manchester BL3 4HF
Tel: 01204 62622
Headmaster: Maulana Suhail Manya
Age range: B12–18
No. of pupils: 140
Fees: Day £1,500 FB £2,800
🚹 Ⓐ 🏫 16· 🐾

Altrincham Preparatory School
Marlborough Road, Bowdon,
Altrincham, Greater
Manchester WA14 2RR
Tel: 0161 928 3366
Headmaster: Mr Andrew C Potts
Age range: B2–11
No. of pupils: 310
Fees: Day £6,300–£8,340
🚹 🖊

Beech House School
184 Manchester Road, Rochdale,
Greater Manchester OL11 4JQ
Tel: 01706 646309
Principal: Mr A Sartain BSc(Hons),
PGCE, DipSp, CBiol, FIBiol
Age range: 2–16
Fees: Day £5,376–£6,546
🖊

Beis Rochel School
1-7 Seymour Road, Crumpsall,
Manchester, Greater
Manchester M8 5BQ
Tel: 0161 795 1830
Headmistress: Mrs E Krausz
Age range: G3–16
No. of pupils: 200
🚺

Bnos Yisroel School
Foigel Esther Shine House,
Leicester Road, Manchester,
Greater Manchester M7 4DA
Tel: 0161 792 3896
Headmaster: Rabbi R Spitzer
Age range: G2–16
No. of pupils: 489
🚺

Bolton School (Boys' Division)
Chorley New Road, Bolton,
Greater Manchester BL1 4PA
Tel: 01204 840201
Headmaster: Philip J Britton MBE
Age range: B7–18
No. of pupils: VIth210
Fees: Day £9,579–£11,976
🚹 Ⓐ £ 🖊 16·

Bolton School (Girls' Division)
Chorley New Road, Bolton,
Greater Manchester BL1 4PB
Tel: 01204 840201
Headmistress: Miss Sue
Hincks MA(Oxon)
Age range: B0–7 G0–18
No. of pupils: VIth210
Fees: Day £9,579–£11,976
🚺 Ⓐ £ 🖊 16·

Branwood Preparatory School
Stafford Road, Monton,
Eccles, Manchester, Greater
Manchester M30 9HN
Tel: 0161 789 1054
Head of School: Mr Andrew Whittell
Age range: 3–11
No. of pupils: 156
Fees: Day £6,597
🖊

Bridgewater School
Drywood Hall, Worsley Road,
Worsley, Manchester, Greater
Manchester M28 2WQ
Tel: 0161 794 1463
Head Teacher: Mrs J A T Nairn
CertEd(Distinction)
Age range: 3–18
No. of pupils: 467
Fees: Day £8,081–£10,774
Ⓐ £ 16·

Bury Catholic Preparatory School
Arden House, Manchester Road,
Bury, Greater Manchester BL9 9BH
Tel: 0161 764 2346
Acting Headteacher: Mrs C Baumber
Age range: 3–11
Fees: Day £3,800–£6,486
£ 🖊

Bury Grammar School Boys
Tenterden Street, Bury, Greater
Manchester BL9 0HN
Tel: 0161 797 2700
Headmaster: Mr D Cassidy
Age range: B7–18
No. of pupils: 602 VIth92
Fees: Day £7,992–£10,755
🚹 Ⓐ £ 🖊 16·

Bury Grammar School for Girls
Bridge Road, Bury, Greater
Manchester BL9 0HH
Tel: 0161 696 8600
Headmistress: Mrs J Anderson
Age range: B4–7 G4–18
No. of pupils: VIth120
Fees: Day £7,836–£10,755
🚹 Ⓐ £ 🖊 16·

Cheadle Hulme School
Claremont Road, Cheadle Hulme,
Cheadle, Greater Manchester SK8 6EF
Tel: 0161 488 3345
Head: Ms Lucy Pearson B.A. (Oxon)
Age range: 4–18
No. of pupils: 1396 VIth254
Fees: Day £8,950–£11,880
Ⓐ £ 🖊 16·

CHETHAM'S SCHOOL OF MUSIC
For further details see p. 156
Long Millgate, Manchester,
Greater Manchester M3 1SB
Tel: 0161 834 9644
Email: hello@chethams.com
Website: www.chethams.com
Head of School: Mr Alun Jones
Age range: 8–18
No. of pupils: 306
Fees: Day £25,068 FB £32,352
🕤 Ⓐ 🏫 🖊 16·

Clarendon Cottage School
Ivy Bank House, Half Edge Lane,
Eccles, Manchester, Greater
Manchester M30 9BJ
Tel: 0161 950 7868
Headteacher: Mrs A Hartley
Age range: 3–11
No. of pupils: 81
Fees: Day £4,590–£4,740
🖊

Clevelands Preparatory School
425 Chorley New Road, Bolton,
Greater Manchester BL1 5DH
Tel: 01204 843898
Headteacher: Mrs Lesley Parlane
Age range: 2–11
No. of pupils: 141
Fees: Day £7,485
£

Covenant Christian School
The Hawthorns, 48 Heaton
Moor Road, Stockport, Greater
Manchester SK4 4NX
Tel: 0161 432 3782
Head: Dr Roger Slack
Age range: 5–16
No. of pupils: 32

**Darul Uloom Al Arabiya
Al Islamiya**
Holcombe Hall, Holcombe, Bury,
Greater Manchester BL8 4NG
Tel: 01706 826106
Head: Mr Mohammed Atcha
Age range: B12–16
No. of pupils: 326
👤

Etz Chaim School at The Belmont
89 Middleton Road, Crumpsall,
Manchester, Greater
Manchester M8 4JY
Tel: 0161 740 6800
Headteacher: Rabbi Eli Cohen
Age range: B11–16
No. of pupils: 98
👤

**Farrowdale House
Preparatory School**
Farrow Street, Shaw, Oldham,
Greater Manchester OL2 7AD
Tel: 01706 844533
Headteacher: Miss Z. N.
Campbell BA (Hons) PGCE
Age range: 3–11
No. of pupils: 90
Fees: Day £5,790–£6,270

**Firwood Manor
Preparatory School**
Broadway, Chadderton, Oldham,
Greater Manchester OL9 0AD
Tel: 0161 6206570
Headteacher: Mrs Caroline
Greenwood
Age range: 2–11
Fees: Day £6,270
£ 🖊

Forest Park School
Lauriston House, 27 Oakfield, Sale,
Greater Manchester M33 6NB
Tel: 0161 973 4835
Headteacher: Mr Tucker
Age range: 3–11
No. of pupils: 145
Fees: Day £6,690–£7,269
🖊

Forest Preparatory School
Moss Lane, Timperley, Altrincham,
Greater Manchester WA15 6LJ
Tel: 0161 980 4075
Headmaster: Rick Hyde
Age range: 2–11
No. of pupils: 197
Fees: Day £6,549–£7,395

Grafton House Preparatory School
1 Warrington Street, Ashton-under-
Lyne, Greater Manchester OL6 6XB
Tel: 0161 343 3015
Head: Mrs Pamela Oaks
Age range: 2–11
No. of pupils: 110

Greenbank Preparatory School
Heathbank Road, Cheadle Hulme,
Cheadle, Greater Manchester SK8 6HU
Tel: 0161 485 3724
Headmistress: Mrs J L Lowe
Age range: 3–11
Fees: Day £8,400
£ 🖊

Hulme Hall Grammar School
Beech Avenue, Stockport,
Greater Manchester SK3 8HB
Tel: 0161 485 3524
Headteacher: Miss Rachael Allen
Age range: 2–16
No. of pupils: 272
Fees: Day £7,800–£9,057
£ 🖊

**Kassim Darwish Grammar
School for Boys**
Hartley Hall, Alexandra Road
South, Manchester, Greater
Manchester M16 8NH
Tel: 0161 8607676
Headteacher: Mr Akhmed Hussain
Age range: B11–16
No. of pupils: 170
Fees: Day £6,995
👤 Ⓐ

King of Kings School
142 Dantzic Street, Manchester,
Greater Manchester M4 4DN
Tel: 0161 834 4214
Head Teacher: Mrs B Lewis
Age range: 3–18
No. of pupils: 29
🖊

Lord's Independent School
53 Manchester Road, Bolton,
Greater Manchester BL2 1ES
Tel: 01204 523731
Headteacher: Mrs Anne Ainsworth
Age range: 11–16
No. of pupils: 83

Loreto Preparatory School
Dunham Road, Altrincham,
Greater Manchester WA14 4GZ
Tel: 0161 928 8310
Headteacher: Mrs Anne Roberts
Age range: G3–11
No. of pupils: 163
Fees: Day £6,390
👤 🖊

**Madrasatul Imam
Muhammad Zakariya**
Keswick Street, Bolton, Greater
Manchester BL1 8LX
Tel: 01204 384434
Headteacher: Mrs Amena Sader
Age range: G11–19
No. of pupils: 110
👤

Manchester High School for Girls
Grangethorpe Road, Manchester,
Greater Manchester M14 6HS
Tel: 0161 224 0447
Head Mistress: Mrs A C Hewitt
Age range: G4–18
No. of pupils: 936 VIth182
Fees: Day £8,712–£11,874
👤 🌐 Ⓐ £ Ⓘ🅱 🖊 16

**Manchester Islamic
High School for Girls**
55 High Lane, Chorlton Cum
Hardy, Manchester, Greater
Manchester M21 9FA
Tel: 0161 881 2127
Headmistress: Mrs Mona Mohamed
Age range: G11–16
No. of pupils: 235
Fees: Day £5,800
👤

Manchester Junior Girls School
64 Upper Park Road, Salford,
Greater Manchester M7 4JA
Tel: 0161 740 0566
Headmistress: Mrs Lieberman
Age range: G3–11
No. of pupils: 200
👤 🖊

**Manchester Muslim
Preparatory School**
551 Wilmslow Road, Withington,
Manchester, Greater
Manchester M20 4BA
Tel: 0161 445 5452
Head Teacher: Mrs Doris
Ghafori-Kanno
Age range: 3–11
No. of pupils: 186
Fees: Day £5,225–£5,500
🖊

Mechinoh L'Yeshivah
Shenstone House, 13 Upper Park Road,
Salford, Greater Manchester M7 4HY
Tel: 0161 795 9275
The Head: Headmaster
Age range: B11–15
No. of pupils: 49
👤

Monton Village School
Francis Street, Monton,
Eccles, Manchester, Greater
Manchester M30 9PR
Tel: 0161 789 0472
Head: Mrs K S McWilliams
Age range: 1–7
No. of pupils: 109

Moor Allerton School
131 Barlow Moor Road, West
Didsbury, Manchester, Greater
Manchester M20 2PW
Tel: 0161 445 4521
Headmistress: Mrs Adriana Ewart-Jones
Age range: 3–11
Fees: Day £8,310–£8,550
🖊

Oldham Hulme Grammar School
Chamber Road, Oldham,
Greater Manchester OL8 4BX
Tel: 0161 624 4497
Principal: Mr CJD Mairs
Age range: 2–18
No. of pupils: 766
Fees: Day £8,220–£11,235
Ⓐ £ 🖊 16

OYY Lubavitch Girls School
Beis Menachem, Park Lane, Salford,
Greater Manchester M7 4JD
Tel: 0161 795 0002
Headmistress: Mrs J Hanson
Age range: 2–16
No. of pupils: 82

Prestwich Preparatory School
St Margaret's Building, 400 Bury
Old Road, Prestwich, Manchester,
Greater Manchester M25 1PZ
Tel: 0161 773 1223
Headmistress: Miss P Shiels
Age range: 2–11
No. of pupils: 122
Fees: Day £6,300

Ramillies Hall School
Cheadle Hulme, Cheadle,
Greater Manchester SK8 7AJ
Tel: 0161 485 3804
Headmistress: Mrs Denise Anthony
Age range: 0–16
No. of pupils: 166
Fees: Day £6,000–£8,550
(£)(✎)

Rochdale Islamic Academy
Greenbank Road, Rochdale,
Greater Manchester OL12 0HZ
Tel: 01706 710184
Headteacher: Mrs Aishah Akhtar
Age range: G11–16
No. of pupils: 165
Fees: Day £1,600
(�)

Saddleworth School
High Street, Uppermill, Oldham,
Greater Manchester OL3 6BU
Tel: 01457 872072
Headteacher: Mr M Milburn
Age range: 11–16

St Ambrose Preparatory School
Hale Barns, Altrincham, Greater
Manchester WA15 0HE
Tel: 0161 903 9193
Headmaster: F J Driscoll
Age range: B3–11 G3–4
No. of pupils: 150
Fees: Day £7,218
(♟)(£)

St Bede's College
Alexandra Park Road, Manchester,
Greater Manchester M16 8HX
Tel: 0161 226 3323
Headmaster: Dr Richard Robson
Age range: 3–18
Fees: Day £8,076–£11,325
(A)(£)(16+)

Stella Maris Junior School
St Johns Road, Heaton Mersey,
Stockport, Greater Manchester SK4 3BR
Tel: 0161 432 0532
Headteacher: Mrs N Johnson
Age range: 3–11
No. of pupils: 68
Fees: Day £7,713

Stockport Grammar School
Buxton Road, Stockport, Greater
Manchester SK2 7AF
Tel: 0161 456 9000
Headmaster: Dr Paul Owen
Age range: 3–18
No. of pupils: 1439 VIth193
Fees: Day £8,766–£11,700
(A)(£)(✎)(16+)

Tashbar School
20 Upper Park Road, Salford,
Greater Manchester M7 4HL
Tel: 0161 7208254
Headteacher: Mr Pinczewski
Age range: B5–11
No. of pupils: 325
(♟)

The Manchester Grammar School
Old Hall Lane, Fallowfield, Manchester,
Greater Manchester M13 0XT
Tel: 0161 224 7201
High Master: Dr Martin Boulton
Age range: B7–18
Fees: Day £12,570
(♟)(❀)(A)(£)(✎)(16+)

Trinity Christian School
Birbeck Street, Stalybridge,
Greater Manchester SK15 1SH
Tel: 0161 303 0674
Head: Mr Michael Stewart
Age range: 3–16
Fees: Day £4,038–£5,874
(✎)

Withington Girls' School
Wellington Road, Fallowfield,
Manchester, Greater
Manchester M14 6BL
Tel: 0161 224 1077
Headmistress: Mrs S J Haslam BA
Age range: G7–18
No. of pupils: 660 VIth150
Fees: Day £9,195–£12,252
(♟)(A)(£)(✎)(16+)

Yeshivah Ohr Torah School
28 Broom Lane, Salford, Greater
Manchester M7 4FX
Tel: 0161 7921230
Headteacher: Rabbi Y Wind
Age range: B11–16
No. of pupils: 40
(♟)

Isle of Man

King William's College
Castletown, Isle of Man IM9 1TP
Tel: +44 (0)1624 820110
Principal: Mr Joss Buchanan
Age range: 11–18
No. of pupils: 378
Fees: Day £16,800–£22,350
FB £26,886–£32,436
(❀)(⛪)(£)(IB)(✎)(16+)

The Buchan School
West Hill, Castletown, Isle
of Man IM9 1RD
Tel: 01624 820481
Headteacher: Janet Billingsley-Evans
Age range: 4–11
No. of pupils: 195
Fees: Day £9,810–£12,420
(£)

Lancashire

Abrar Academy
56 Garstang Road, Preston,
Lancashire PR1 1NA
Tel: 01772 82 87 32
Head: Mr A Esmail
Age range: 11–16

AKS Lytham
Clifton Drive South, Lytham St
Annes, Lancashire FY8 1DT
Tel: 01253 784100
Headmaster: Mr. Mike Walton
BA, MA (Ed), PGCE, NPQH
Age range: 2–18
No. of pupils: 800 VIth165
Fees: Day £8,895–£11,787
(A)(£)(✎)(16+)

Al-Islah Schools
108 Audley Range, Blackburn,
Lancashire BB1 1TF
Tel: 01254 261573
Headteacher: Nikhat Pardesi
Age range: G11–16
No. of pupils: 192

Ashbridge Independent School
Lindle Lane, Hutton, Preston,
Lancashire PR4 4AQ
Tel: 01772 619900
Headteacher: Karen Mehta
Age range: 0–11
No. of pupils: 315
Fees: Day £7,800
(✎)

Ghausia Girls' High School
1-3 Cross Street, Nelson,
Lancashire BB9 7EN
Tel: 01282 699214
Headteacher: Aneela Masood
Age range: G11–16
No. of pupils: 35
Fees: Day £1,500
(♟)

Heathland School
Broadoak, Sandy Lane, Accrington,
Lancashire BB5 2AN
Tel: 01254 234284
Principal: Mrs J Harrison
BA(Hons), CertEd, FRSA
Age range: 4–16
Fees: Day £6,390–£8,871

Highfield Priory School
58 Fulwood Row, Preston,
Lancashire PR2 5RW
Tel: 01772 709624
Headmaster: Mr Jeremy
Duke BSc (Hons)
Age range: 6 months–11 years
No. of pupils: 276
Fees: Day £7,610
£

Islamiyah School
Willow Street, Blackburn,
Lancashire BB1 5RQ
Tel: 01254 661 259
Headteacher: Mr Yusuf Seedat
Age range: G11–16
No. of pupils: 178

Jamea Al Kauthar
Ashton Road, Lancaster,
Lancashire LA1 5AJ
Tel: 01524 389898
Headteacher: Fazle Haq Wadee
Age range: G11–16
No. of pupils: 392

Jamiatul-Ilm Wal-Huda UK School
15 Moss Street, Blackburn,
Lancashire BB1 5HW
Tel: 01254 673105
Headteacher: Mr A Ahmed
Age range: B11–16
No. of pupils: 348

KIRKHAM GRAMMAR SCHOOL
For further details see p. 158
Ribby Road, Kirkham, Preston,
Lancashire PR4 2BH
Tel: 01772 684264
Email: info@kirkhamgrammar.co.uk
Website: www.kirkhamgrammar.co.uk
Headmaster: Mr. Daniel Berry
Age range: 3–18 years
No. of pupils: 870 VIth180

Lancaster Steiner School
Lune Road, Lancaster,
Lancashire LA1 5QU
Tel: 01524 841351
Headteacher: Mrs Denise Randal
Age range: 0–14

Markazul Uloom
Park Lee Road, Blackburn,
Lancashire BB2 3NY
Tel: 01254 581569
Headteacher: Mr Nu'amaan Limbada
Age range: G11–19
Fees: Day £1,200 FB £2,700

Moorland School
Ribblesdale Avenue, Clitheroe,
Lancashire BB7 2JA
Tel: 01200 423833
Principal: Mr Jonathan Harrison
Age range: 3 months–16 years
Fees: Day £6,996–£9,996 WB
£18,000–£22,800 FB £19,800–£24,900

Oakhill School and Nursery
Wiswell Lane, Whalley, Clitheroe,
Lancashire BB7 9AF
Tel: 01254 823546
Principal: Mrs Carmel Crouch
Age range: 2–16
No. of pupils: 330
Fees: Day £7,440–£11,574

Palm Tree School
Oakenhurst Road, Blackburn,
Lancashire BB2 1SN
Tel: 01254 264254
Headteacher: Mrs N Hameed
Age range: 3–11
Fees: Day £1,200

ROSSALL SCHOOL
For further details see p. 160
Broadway, Fleetwood,
Lancashire FY7 8JW
Tel: +44 (0)1253 774201
Email: admissions@rossall.org.uk
Website: www.rossall.org.uk
Head: Mr Jeremy Quartermain
Age range: 2–18
No. of pupils: 640 VIth180
Fees: Day £8,040–£13,080
FB £20,610–£37,350

Scarisbrick Hall School
Southport Road, Scarisbrisk,
Ormskirk, Lancashire L40 9RQ
Tel: 01704 841151
Headmaster: Mr J Shaw
Age range: 0–18
Fees: Day £7,185–£11,160

St Anne's College Grammar School
293 Clifton Drive South, Lytham
St Annes, Lancashire FY8 1HN
Tel: +44 (0)1253 725815
Principal: Mr S R Welsby
Age range: 2–18
No. of pupils: VIth16
Fees: Day £5,370–£7,320

St Joseph's School, Park Hill
Park Hill, Padiham Road,
Burnley, Lancashire BB12 6TG
Tel: 01282 455622
Headmistress: Mrs Annette Robinson
Age range: 3–11
Fees: Day £6,195

St Pius X Preparatory School
Oak House, 200 Garstang Road,
Fulwood, Preston, Lancashire PR2 8RD
Tel: 01772 719937
Acting Head Teacher: Mrs H Porter
Age range: 2–11
No. of pupils: 260
Fees: Day £7,800

STONYHURST COLLEGE
For further details see p. 162
Stonyhurst, Clitheroe,
Lancashire BB7 9PZ
Tel: 01254 827073
Email: admissions@stonyhurst.ac.uk
Website: www.stonyhurst.ac.uk
Headmaster: Mr John
Browne BA LLB MBA
Age range: 13–18
No. of pupils: 727
Fees: Day £19,950 WB £29,850

Stonyhurst St Mary's Hall
Stonyhurst, Lancashire BB7 9PU
Tel: 01254 827073
Headmaster: Mr Ian Murphy
BA (Hons), PGCE Durham
Age range: 3–13
No. of pupils: 272
Fees: Day £8,370–£15,960
WB £21,330 FB £24,570

The Alternative School
The Old Library, Fern Lea Avenue,
Barnoldswick, Lancashire BB18 5DW
Tel: 01282 851800
Age range: 8–18

Westholme School
Meins Road, Blackburn,
Lancashire BB2 6QU
Tel: 01254 506070
Principal: Mrs Lynne Horner
Age range: 3 months–18 years
No. of pupils: 792 VIth72
Fees: Day £7,890–£10,875

Merseyside

Auckland College
65-67 Parkfield Road, Wavertree,
Liverpool, Merseyside L17 4LE
Tel: 0151 727 0083
Headteacher: Miss Stephanie Boyd
Age range: 0–18
No. of pupils: 172 VIth15
Fees: Day £5,000–£7,500

Avalon Preparatory School
Caldy Road, West Kirby, Wirral,
Merseyside CH48 2HE
Tel: 0151 625 6993
Age range: 2–11
No. of pupils: 178
Fees: Day £4,239–£8,169

Belvedere Preparatory School
23 Belvidere Road, Princes Park,
Aigburth, Liverpool, Merseyside L8 3TF
Tel: 0151 471 1137
Age range: 3–11
No. of pupils: 180

Birkenhead School
The Lodge, 58 Beresford Road,
Birkenhead, Merseyside CH43 2JD
Tel: 0151 652 4014
Headmaster: Mr Paul Vicars
Age range: 3 months–18 years
No. of pupils: VIth103
Fees: Day £8,010–£11,994

Carleton House Preparatory School
145 Menlove Avenue, Liverpool,
Merseyside L18 3EE
Tel: 0151 722 0756
Head of School: Mrs Sandy Coleman
Age range: 3–11
No. of pupils: 179
Fees: Day £7,771

Christian Fellowship School
Overbury Street, Edge Hill,
Liverpool, Merseyside L7 3HL
Tel: 0151 709 1642
Headteacher: Mr Richard Worsley
Age range: 4–16
No. of pupils: 136
Fees: Day £2,628–£5,220
£ ⬭

Kingsmead School
Bertram Drive, Hoylake, Wirral,
Merseyside CH47 0LL
Tel: 0151 632 3156
Headmaster: Mr M G Gibbons
BComm, MSc, QTS
Age range: 2–18
Fees: Day £6,411–£10,800 WB
£14,100–£16,350 FB £19,500–£22,800
🌐 ⬭ £ ⬭

Merchant Taylors' Boys' School
186 Liverpool Road, Crosby,
Liverpool, Merseyside L23 0QP
Tel: 0151 928 3308
Headmaster: Mr Deiniol Williams
Age range: B7–18
No. of pupils: 727
Fees: Day £8,517–£11,394
🧍 Ⓐ £ ⬭ 16

Merchant Taylors' Girls' School
Liverpool Road, Crosby,
Liverpool, Merseyside L23 5SP
Tel: 0151 924 3140
Headmistress: Mrs Claire Tao
Age range: B4–7 G4–18
No. of pupils: 801
Fees: Day £8,517–£11,394
🧍 Ⓐ £ ⬭ 16

Prenton Preparatory School
Mount Pleasant, Oxton, Wirral,
Merseyside CH43 5SY
Tel: 0151 652 3182
Headteacher: Mr M Jones
BSC Hons, PGCE
Age range: 2–11
Fees: Day £800–£8,586
£ ⬭

Redcourt St Anselm's
7 Devonshire Place, Oxton, Prenton,
Wirral, Merseyside CH43 1TX
Tel: 0151 652 5228
Head of School: Miss Rachel Jones
Age range: 3–11
No. of pupils: 140
Fees: Day £6,300

Runnymede St Edward's School
North Drive, Sandfield Park,
Liverpool, Merseyside L12 1LE
Tel: 0151 281 2300
Headmaster: Mr Bradley Slater
Age range: 3–16
No. of pupils: 270
Fees: Day £7,191–£7,584
£ ⬭

St Mary's College
Everest Road, Crosby, Liverpool,
Merseyside L23 5TW
Tel: 0151 924 3926
Principal: Mr Michael Kennedy Bsc, MA
No. of pupils: 880 VIth132
Fees: Day £7,573–£11,161
Ⓐ £ ⬭ 16

Tower College
Mill Lane, Rainhill, Prescot,
Merseyside L35 6NE
Tel: 0151 426 4333
Principal: Miss R J Oxley NNEB, RSH
Age range: 3–16
No. of pupils: 486
Fees: Day £6,972–£8,112
⬭

D356

South-East

Berkshire D358
Buckinghamshire D360
East Sussex D360
Hampshire D362
Isle of Wight D364
Kent D364
Surrey D367
West Sussex D372

KEY TO SYMBOLS

- ⚤ *Boys' school*
- ⚤ *Girls' school*
- 🌐 *International school*
- 16ᵀ *Tutorial or sixth form college*
- Ⓐ *A levels*
- ⬧ *Boarding accommodation*
- £ *Bursaries*
- ⒾⒷ *International Baccalaureate*
- ✎ *Learning support*
- 16⁺ *Entrance at 16+*
- 🎓 *Vocational qualifications*
- ⒾⒶⓅⓈ *Independent Association of Preparatory Schools*
- ⒽⓂⒸ *The Headmasters' & Headmistresses' Conference*
- ⒾⓈⒶ *Independent Schools Association*
- ⒼⓈⒶ *Girls' School Association*
- ⒷⓈⒶ *Boarding Schools' Association*
- Ⓢ *Society of Heads*

Unless otherwise indicated, all schools are coeducational day schools. Single-sex and boarding schools will be indicated by the relevant icon.

Berkshire

Alder Bridge School
Bridge House, Mill Lane, Padworth,
Reading, Berkshire RG7 4JU
Tel: 0118 971 4471
Age range: 0–14 years
No. of pupils: 65
Fees: Day £6,015–£8,880

Bradfield College
Bradfield, Berkshire RG7 6AU
Tel: 0118 964 4516
Headmaster: Dr Christopher Stevens
Age range: 13–18
No. of pupils: 790
Fees: Day £29,925 FB £37,404

Caversham School
16 Peppard Road, Caversham,
Reading, Berkshire RG4 8JZ
Tel: 01189 478 684
Head: Mr Chris Neal
Age range: 4–11
No. of pupils: 60
Fees: Day £9,900

Claires Court Junior Boys
Maidenhead Thicket,
Maidenhead, Berkshire SL6 3QE
Tel: 01628 327700
Head: J M E Spanswick
Age range: B4–11
No. of pupils: 248
Fees: Day £9,270–£15,930

**Claires Court Nursery,
Girls and Sixth Form**
1 College Avenue, Maidenhead,
Berkshire SL6 6AW
Tel: 01628 327700
Head of School: Mrs M Heywood
Age range: B16–18 G3–18
No. of pupils: 495 VIth111
Fees: Day £9,270–£16,740

Claires Court Senior Boys
Ray Mill Road East, Maidenhead,
Berkshire SL6 8TE
Tel: 01628 327700
Headmaster: Mr J M Rayer BSc, PGCE
Age range: B11–16
No. of pupils: 335 VIth112
Fees: Day £15,930–£16,740

Crosfields School
Shinfield, Reading, Berkshire RG2 9BL
Tel: 0118 987 1810
Headmaster: Mr Craig Watson
Age range: 3–13
No. of pupils: 510
Fees: Day £10,314–£15,159

Dolphin School
Waltham Road, Hurst, Reading,
Berkshire RG10 0FR
Tel: 0118 934 1277
Head: Mr Tom Lewis
Age range: 3–13
Fees: Day £10,170–£14,070

EAGLE HOUSE SCHOOL
For further details see p. 182
Sandhurst, Berkshire GU47 8PH
Tel: 01344 772134
Email: info@eaglehouseschool.com
Website:
www.eaglehouseschool.com
Headmaster: Mr A P N
Barnard BA(Hons), PGCE
Age range: 3–13
No. of pupils: 380
Fees: Day £11,580–£18,105 FB £24,330

Elstree School
Woolhampton, Reading,
Berkshire RG7 5TD
Tel: 0118 971 3302
Headmaster: Mr S Inglis
Age range: B3–13 G3–8
No. of pupils: 248
Fees: Day £11,550–£21,000 WB
£26,250–£26,850 FB £26,700–£27,300

Eton College
Windsor, Berkshire SL4 6DW
Tel: 01753 671249
Head Master: Simon Henderson MA
Age range: B13–18
No. of pupils: 1300 VIth520
Fees: FB £40,668

Eton End PNEU School
35 Eton Road, Datchet,
Slough, Berkshire SL3 9AX
Tel: 01753 541075
Headmistress: Sarah Stokes
BA(Hons), PGCE
Age range: B3–7 G3–11
No. of pupils: 245
Fees: Day £9,375–£11,985

Heathfield School
London Road, Ascot, Berkshire SL5 8BQ
Tel: 01344 898342
Head of School: Mrs Marina
Gardiner Legge
Age range: G11–18
No. of pupils: 200

Hemdean House School
Hemdean Road, Caversham,
Reading, Berkshire RG4 7SD
Tel: 0118 947 2590
Head Teacher: Mrs H Chalmers BSc
Age range: B4–11 G4–11
Fees: Day £8,490–£9,300

Herries Preparatory School
Dean Lane, Cookham
Dean, Berkshire SL6 9BD
Tel: 01628 483350
Headmistress: Fiona Long
Age range: 3–11
Fees: Day £9,210–£10,800

Highfield Preparatory School
2 West Road, Maidenhead,
Berkshire SL6 1PD
Tel: 01628 624918
Headteacher: Mrs Joanna Leach
Age range: B3–5 G3–11
Fees: Day £9,225–£12,180

Holme Grange School
Heathlands Road, Wokingham,
Berkshire RG40 3AL
Tel: 0118 978 1566
Headteacher: Mrs Claire Robinson
Age range: 3–16 years
No. of pupils: 476
Fees: Day £9,885–£14,280

Lambrook School
Winkfield Row, Bracknell,
Berkshire RG42 6LU
Tel: 01344 882717
Headmaster: Mr Jonathan Perry
Age range: 3–13
No. of pupils: 440
Fees: Day £11,250–£19,737
WB £22,008–£23,664

Leighton Park School
Shinfield Road, Reading,
Berkshire RG2 7ED
Tel: +44 (0) 118 987 9600
Head: Nigel Williams BA(Bristol),
MA(London), PGCE
Age range: 11–18
No. of pupils: 485
Fees: Day £21,654 WB
£29,301 FB £34,044

Long Close School
Upton Court Road, Upton,
Slough, Berkshire SL3 7LU
Tel: 01753 520095
Headteacher: Melissa McBride
Age range: 2–16
No. of pupils: 350

Luckley House School
Luckley Road, Wokingham,
Berkshire RG40 3EU
Tel: 0118 978 4175
Head: Mrs Jane Tudor
Age range: G11–18
No. of pupils: 230
Fees: Day £16,620 WB
£26,955 FB £29,082

Ludgrove
Wokingham, Berkshire RG40 3AB
Tel: 0118 978 9881
Head of School: Mr Simon Barber
Age range: B8–13
No. of pupils: 190

LVS Ascot
London Road, Ascot, Berkshire SL5 8DR
Tel: 01344 882770
Headmistress: Mrs Christine
Cunniffe BA (Hons), MMus, MBA
Age range: 4–18
No. of pupils: 830
Fees: Day £9,708–£18,609
FB £24,846–£32,694

Meadowbrook Montessori School
Malt Hill Road, Warfield,
Bracknell, Berkshire RG42 6JQ
Tel: 01344 890869
Director of Education: Mrs S Gunn
Age range: 3–11
No. of pupils: 78
Fees: Day £10,044–£11,385

Newbold School
Popeswood Road, Binfield,
Bracknell, Berkshire RG42 4AH
Tel: 01344 421088
Headteacher: Mrs Jaki Crissey
MA, BA, PGCE Primary
Age range: 3–11
Fees: Day £4,500

Our Lady's Preparatory School
The Avenue, Crowthorne,
Wokingham, Berkshire RG45 6PB
Tel: 01344 773394
Headmistress: Mrs Helene Robinson
Age range: 3 months–11 years
No. of pupils: 100
Fees: Day £7,080

Padworth College
Padworth, Reading, Berkshire RG7 4NR
Tel: 0118 983 2644
Acting Principal: Mr Chris Randell
Age range: 13–19
No. of pupils: 116 VIth50
Fees: Day £14,400 FB £29,400

Pangbourne College
Pangbourne, Reading,
Berkshire RG8 8LA
Tel: 0118 984 2101
Headmaster: Thomas J C Garnier
Age range: 11–18
No. of pupils: 426 VIth133
Fees: Day £17,055–£24,036
FB £24,021–£33,996

Papplewick School
Windsor Road, Ascot, Berkshire SL5 7LH
Tel: 01344 621488
Head: Mr T W Bunbury BA, PGCE
Age range: B6–13
No. of pupils: 195

Queen Anne's School
6 Henley Road, Caversham,
Reading, Berkshire RG4 6DX
Tel: 0118 918 7300
Headmistress: Mrs Julia Harrington
BA(Hons), PGCE, NPQH
Age range: G11–18
No. of pupils: 336 VIth100
Fees: Day £24,135 WB
£32,070–£33,810 FB £35,580

Queensmead School
King's Road, Windsor, Berkshire SL4 2AX
Tel: 01753 863779
Head: Mr Simon Larter
Age range: 2–18
No. of pupils: 300
Fees: Day £7,128–£15,318

Reading Blue Coat School
Holme Park, Sonning Lane, Sonning,
Reading, Berkshire RG4 6SU
Tel: 0118 944 1005
Headmaster: Mr Jesse Elzinga
Age range: B11–18 G16–18
No. of pupils: 710 VIth230
Fees: Day £16,695

REDDAM HOUSE BERKSHIRE
For further details see p. 208
Bearwood Road, Sindlesham,
Wokingham, Berkshire RG41 5BG
Tel: 0118 974 8300
Email:
registrar@reddamhouse.org.uk
Website: reddamhouse.org.uk
Principal: Mrs Tammy Howard
Age range: 3 months–18 years
No. of pupils: 570
Fees: Day £10,200–£17,280 WB
£27,075–£31,215 FB £28,665–£32,805

Redroofs School for the Performing Arts (Redroofs Theatre School)
26 Bath Road, Maidenhead,
Berkshire SL6 4JT
Tel: 01628 674092
Principal: June Rose
Age range: 8–18
No. of pupils: 100
Fees: Day £4,882–£5,527

St Andrew's School
Buckhold, Pangbourne,
Reading, Berkshire RG8 8QA
Tel: 0118 974 4276
Headmaster: Mr Jonathan
Bartlett BSc QTS
Age range: 3–13
Fees: Day £5,430–£18,150 WB £3,360

St Bernard's Preparatory School
Hawtrey Close, Slough, Berkshire SL1 1TB
Tel: 01753 521821
Head Teacher: Mr N Cheesman
Age range: 2–11
Fees: Day £8,850–£10,545

St Edward's Prep School
64 Tilehurst Road, Reading,
Berkshire RG30 2JH
Tel: 0118 957 4342
Headmaster: Mr Derek Suttie
Age range: B4–11
No. of pupils: 170
Fees: Day £6,585–£11,025

St George's Ascot
Wells Lane, Ascot, Berkshire SL5 7DZ
Tel: 01344 629920
Headmistress: Mrs Liz Hewer
MA (Hons) (Cantab) PGCE
Age range: G11–18
No. of pupils: 270 VIth70
Fees: Day £22,800 WB
£34,050–£34,680 FB £35,460

St George's School Windsor Castle
Windsor, Berkshire SL4 1QF
Tel: 01753 865553
Head Master: Mr J R Jones
Age range: 3–13
Fees: Day £10,044–£16,674
WB £20,700 FB £21,438

St John's Beaumont Preparatory School
Priest Hill, Old Windsor, Berkshire SL4 2JN
Tel: 01784 432428
Headmaster: Mr G E F Delaney
BA(Hons), PGCE, MSc (Oxon)
Age range: B3–13
No. of pupils: 310
Fees: Day £9,288–£17,772 WB
£17,385–£23,058 FB £21,618–£27,291

St Joseph's College
Upper Redlands Road,
Reading, Berkshire RG1 5JT
Tel: 0118 966 1000
Headmaster: Mr Andrew Colpus
Age range: 3–18
No. of pupils: VIth65
Fees: Day £6,672–£11,406

St Mary's School Ascot
St Mary's Road, Ascot, Berkshire SL5 9JF
Tel: 01344 296614
Headmistress: Mrs Mary Breen BSc, MSc
Age range: G11–18
No. of pupils: 390 VIth120
Fees: Day £26,190 FB £36,780

St Piran's Preparatory School
Gringer Hill, Maidenhead,
Berkshire SL6 7LZ
Tel: 01628 594302
Headmaster: Mr J A Carroll
BA(Hons), BPhilEd, PGCE, NPQH
Age range: 3–11
Fees: Day £10,857–£16,566

Sunningdale School
Dry Arch Road, Sunningdale,
Berkshire SL5 9PY
Tel: 01344 620159
Headmaster: Tom Dawson MA, PGCE
Age range: B7–13
No. of pupils: 90

Teikyo School UK
Framewood Road, Wexham,
Slough, Berkshire SL2 4QS
Tel: 01753 663711
Headmaster: Tadashi Nakayama
Age range: 16–18

The Abbey School
Kendrick Road, Reading,
Berkshire RG1 5DZ
Tel: 0118 987 2256
Head: Mrs Rachel S E Dent
Age range: G3–18
No. of pupils: 1100
Fees: Day £10,410–£17,040

The Deenway Montessori School
3-5 Sidmouth Street, Reading,
Berkshire RG1 4QX
Tel: 0118 9574737
Headteacher: Mr M Karim
Age range: 3–11

The Marist Preparatory School
King's Road, Sunninghill,
Ascot, Berkshire SL5 7PS
Tel: 01344 626137
Vice Principal: Jane Gow
Age range: G2–11
No. of pupils: 225
Fees: Day £9,780–£11,940

The Marist Schools
King's Road, Sunninghill,
Ascot, Berkshire SL5 7PS
Tel: 01344 624291
Head of Secondary
School: Mr K McCloskey
Age range: G2 –18
No. of pupils: 550 VIth60
Fees: Day £9,780–£14,610
(🏊) (A) (16)

The Oratory Preparatory School
Great Oaks, Goring Heath,
Reading, Berkshire RG8 7SF
Tel: 0118 984 4511
Headmaster: Mr Rob Stewart
Age range: 2–13
No. of pupils: 400
Fees: Day £10,266–£16,443
WB £21,153 FB £24,522
(🏫) (£) (✐)

The Oratory School
Woodcote, Reading, Berkshire RG8 0PJ
Tel: 01491 683500
Head Master: Mr J J Smith
BA(Hons), MEd, PGCE
Age range: B11–18
No. of pupils: 380 VIth120
Fees: Day £24,966 FB £34,299
(🏊) (🌐) (A) (£) (16)

The Vine Christian School
SORCF Christian Centre,
Basingstoke Road, Three Mile Cross,
Reading, Berkshire RG7 1AT
Tel: 0118 988 6464
Head of School: Mrs Eve Strike
Age range: 5–13
No. of pupils: 9

Upton House School
115 St Leonard's Road,
Windsor, Berkshire SL4 3DF
Tel: 01753 862610
Headmistress: Rhian Thornton
Age range: B2–7 G2–11
No. of pupils: 280
(£) (✐)

Waverley School
Waverley Way, Finchampstead,
Wokingham, Berkshire RG40 4YD
Tel: 0118 973 1121
Principal: Mr Guy Shore
Age range: 3–11
Fees: Day £8,589–£11,982
(✐)

WELLINGTON COLLEGE
For further details see p. 222
Duke's Ride, Crowthorne,
Berkshire RG45 7PU
Tel: +44 (0)1344 444000
Email:
admissions@wellingtoncollege.org.uk
Website:
www.wellingtoncollege.org.uk
Master: Mr Julian Thomas
Age range: 13–18
No. of pupils: 1040 VIth455
Fees: Day £29,040–
£33,360 FB £39,750
(🌐) (A) (🏫) (£) (IB) (✐) (16)

Buckinghamshire

Gayhurst School
Bull Lane, Gerrards Cross,
Buckinghamshire SL9 8RJ
Tel: 01753 882690
Headmaster: Gareth R A Davies
Age range: 3–11
Fees: Day £12,159–£15,438
(£) (✐)

MALTMAN'S GREEN SCHOOL
For further details see p. 200
Maltman's Lane, Gerrards Cross,
Buckinghamshire SL9 8RR
Tel: 01753 883022
Email:
registrar@maltmansgreen.com
Website: www.maltmansgreen.com
Headmistress: Mrs J Pardon
MA, BSc(Hons), PGCE
Age range: G2–11
No. of pupils: 394
Fees: Day £1,860–£5,090
(🏊) (🏫) (✐)

St Mary's School
94 Packhorse Road, Gerrards
Cross, Buckinghamshire SL9 8JQ
Tel: 01753 883370
Headmistress: Mrs J A Ross
BA(Hons), NPQH
Age range: G3–18
No. of pupils: 350 VIth50
Fees: Day £5,670–£16,980
(🏊) (A) (£) (✐) (16)

Thorpe House School
Oval Way, Gerrards Cross,
Buckinghamshire SL9 8QA
Tel: 01753 882474
Headmaster: Mr Terence Ayres
Age range: B3–16
Fees: Day £10,950–£16,962
(🏊) (£) (✐)

East Sussex

Ashdown House School
Forest Row, East Sussex RH18 5JY
Tel: 01342 822574
Headmaster: Mike Davies
Age range: 4–13
No. of pupils: 141
Fees: Day £8,970–£20,100 FB £27,450
(£) (✐)

Bartholomews Tutorial College
22-23 Prince Albert Street,
Brighton, East Sussex BN1 1HF
Tel: 01273 205965/205141
Director of Studies: Mike Balmer BEd
Age range: 16+
No. of pupils: 40 VIth25
Fees: Day £25,000 WB
£30,000 FB £30,000
(16) (A) (✐)

Battle Abbey School
Battle, East Sussex TN33 0AD
Tel: 01424 772385
Headmaster: Mr D Clark BA(Hons)
Age range: 2–18
No. of pupils: 286 VIth48
Fees: Day £6,939–£16,914
FB £26,649–£31,932
(🌐) (A) (🏫) (£) (✐) (16)

Bede's School
The Dicker, Upper Dicker,
Hailsham, East Sussex BN27 3QH
Tel: +44 (0)1323843252
Head: Mr Peter Goodyer
Age range: 3 months–18
No. of pupils: 800 VIth295
Fees: Day £10,230–£17,400
FB £22,290–£25,650
(🌐) (A) (🏫) (£) (✐) (16) (🏀)

Bellerbys College Brighton
1 Billinton Way, Brighton,
East Sussex BN1 4LF
Tel: +44 (0)1273 339333
Principal: Mr Simon Mower
Age range: 13–18
(🌐) (16) (A) (🏫)

Bricklehurst Manor Preparatory
Bardown Road, Stonegate,
Wadhurst, East Sussex TN5 7EL
Tel: 01580 200448
Principal: Mrs C Flowers
Age range: 3–11
No. of pupils: 117
(£) (✐)

Brighton & Hove High School GDST
Montpelier Road, Brighton,
East Sussex BN1 3AT
Tel: 01273 280280
Head: Jennifer Smith
Age range: G3–18
No. of pupils: 680 VIth70
Fees: Day £7,191–£14,421
(🏊) (A) (£) (✐) (16)

Brighton & Hove Montessori School
67 Stanford Avenue, Brighton,
East Sussex BN1 6FB
Tel: 01273 702485
Headteacher: Mrs Daisy
Cockburn AMI, MontDip
Age range: 2–11

Brighton College
Eastern Road, Brighton,
East Sussex BN2 0AL
Tel: 01273 704200
Head Master: Richard Cairns MA
Age range: 3–18
No. of pupils: 950
Fees: Day £10,050–£24,540 WB
£33,390–£34,410 FB £37,470–£45,210
(🌐) (A) (🏫) (£) (✐) (16)

Brighton Steiner School
John Howard House, Roedean Road,
Brighton, East Sussex BN2 5RA
Tel: 01273 386300
Chair of the College of
Teachers: Carrie Rawle
Age range: 3–16
Fees: Day £7,800–£8,100
(£) (✐)

Buckswood School
Broomham Hall, Rye Road, Guestling,
Hastings, East Sussex TN35 4LT
Tel: 01424 813 813
Headmaster: Mr Giles Sutton
Age range: 10–19
No. of pupils: 420

Buckswood St George's
Westwood House, 7-9 Holmesdale
Gardens, Hastings, East Sussex TN34 1LY
Tel: 01424 813696
College Director: Ian Godfrey
Age range: B16–19 G16–20
No. of pupils: VIth50

Charters Ancaster
Woodgate Place, Gunters Lane,
Bexhill-on-Sea, East Sussex TN39 4EB
Tel: 01424 216670
Nursery Manager: Susannah Crump
Age range: 6 months–5
No. of pupils: 125

**Claremont Preparatory
& Nursery School**
Ebdens Hill, Baldslow, St Leonards-
on-Sea, East Sussex TN37 7PW
Tel: 01424 751555
Headmistress: Abra Stoakley
Age range: 1–13
Fees: Day £6,900–£12,600

**Claremont Senior &
Sixth Form School**
Bodiam, Nr Robertsbridge,
East Sussex TN32 5UJ
Tel: 01580 830396
Headmaster: Mr. Giles Perrin
Age range: 14–18
Fees: Day £17,400

Darvell School
Darvell Bruderhof, Robertsbridge,
East Sussex TN32 5DR
Tel: 01580 883300
Headteacher: Mr Arnold Meier
Age range: 4–16
No. of pupils: 121

Deepdene School
195 New Church Road, Hove,
East Sussex BN3 4ED
Tel: 01273 418984
Heads: Mrs Nicola Gane &
Miss Elizabeth Brown
Age range: 6 months–11 years
Fees: Day £8,349

Dharma School
The White House, Ladies Mile Road,
Patcham, Brighton, East Sussex BN1 8TB
Tel: 01273 502055
Headteacher: Clare Eddison
Age range: 3–11
Fees: Day £8,208

Didac School
16 Trinity Trees, Eastbourne,
East Sussex BN21 3LE
Tel: +44 1323 417276
Age range: 16–18

Eastbourne College
Old Wish Road, Eastbourne,
East Sussex BN21 4JX
Tel: 01323 452323 (Admissions)
Headmaster: Mr Tom
Lawson MA(Oxon)
Age range: 13–18
No. of pupils: 614 VIth284
Fees: Day £23,130–£23,505
FB £35,250–£35,655

**Greenfields Independent
Day & Boarding School**
Priory Road, Forest Row,
East Sussex RH18 5JD
Tel: +44 (0)1342 822189
Executive Head: Mr. Jeff Smith
Age range: 2–19

**Lancing College Preparatory
School at Hove**
The Droveway, Hove,
East Sussex BN3 6LU
Tel: 01273 503452
Headmistress: Mrs Kirsty Keep BEd
Age range: 3–13
No. of pupils: 181
Fees: Day £3,960–£15,975

Lewes Old Grammar School
High Street, Lewes, East Sussex BN7 1XS
Tel: 01273 472634
Headmaster: Mr Robert Blewitt
Age range: 3–18
No. of pupils: 463 VIth50
Fees: Day £8,760–£14,625

Mayfield School
The Old Palace, Mayfield,
East Sussex TN20 6PH
Tel: +44 (0)1435 874600
Head: Ms Antonia Beary MA,
Mphil (Cantab), PGCE
Age range: G11–18
No. of pupils: 365 VIth100
Fees: Day £21,000 FB £33,900

Michael Hall School
Kidbrooke Park, Priory Road, Forest
Row, East Sussex RH18 5BG
Tel: 01342 822275
Age range: 0–18
Fees: Day £9,245–£12,670 FB £8,065

Roedean Moira House
Upper Carlisle Road, Eastbourne,
East Sussex BN20 7TE
Tel: 01323 644144
Headmaster: Mr Andrew Wood
Age range: G0–18
No. of pupils: 289

Roedean School
Roedean Way, Brighton,
East Sussex BN2 5RQ
Tel: 01273 667500
Headmaster: Mr. Oliver Bond
BA(Essex), PGCE, NPQH
Age range: G11–18
No. of pupils: 568 VIth171
Fees: Day £15,960–£20,865 WB
£28,230–£31,470 FB £30,930–£37,440

Sacred Heart School
Mayfield Lane, Durgates,
Wadhurst, East Sussex TN5 6DQ
Tel: 01892 783414
Headteacher: Mrs H Blake
BA(Hons), PGCE
Age range: 2–11
No. of pupils: 121
Fees: Day £8,355

Skippers Hill Manor Prep School
Five Ashes, Mayfield, East
Sussex TN20 6HR
Tel: 01825 830234
Headmaster: Mr M Hammond
MA, BA, PGCE
Age range: 2–13
No. of pupils: 174
Fees: Day £8,400–£13,440

St Andrew's Prep
Meads, Eastbourne, East
Sussex BN20 7RP
Tel: 01323 733203
Headmaster: Gareth Jones
BA(Hons), PGCE
Age range: 9 months–13 years
No. of pupils: 391
Fees: Day £10,050–£17,475
WB £22,110 FB £25,020

St Bede's Preparatory School
Duke's Drive, Eastbourne,
East Sussex BN20 7XL
Tel: 01323 734222
Head: Mr Giles Entwisle
Age range: 3 months–13 years
No. of pupils: 395
Fees: Day £10,230–£17,400
FB £22,290–£25,650

St Christopher's School
33 New Church Road, Hove,
East Sussex BN3 4AD
Tel: 01273 735404
Headmaster: Mr Julian Withers
Age range: 4–13
Fees: Day £8,370–£12,720

The Drive Prep School
101 The Drive, Hove, East Sussex BN3 3JE
Tel: 01273 738444
Head Teacher: Mrs S Parkinson
CertEd, CertPerfArts
Age range: 7–16

Torah Montessori Nursery
29 New Church Road, Hove,
East Sussex BN3 4AD
Tel: 01273 328675
Principal: P Efune
Age range: 1–4

Vinehall School
Robertsbridge, East Sussex TN32 5JL
Tel: 01580 880413
Headmaster: Joff Powis
Age range: 2–13
No. of pupils: 260
Fees: Day £9,555–£17,817 WB
£20,916–£21,360 FB £22,641–£23,208

Windlesham School
190 Dyke Road, Brighton,
East Sussex BN1 5AA
Tel: 01273 553645
Headmaster: Mr John Ingrassia
Age range: 3–11
No. of pupils: 195
Fees: Day £6,015–£8,955

Hampshire

Alton School
Anstey Lane, Alton,
Hampshire GU34 2NG
Tel: 01420 82070
Head: Graham Maher
Age range: 0–18
No. of pupils: 502 VIth53

Ballard School
Fernhill Lane, New Milton,
Hampshire BH25 5SU
Tel: 01425 626900
Headmaster: Mr Andrew McCleave
Age range: 2–16 years
No. of pupils: 400
Fees: Day £8,340–£15,315

Bedales Prep School, Dunhurst
Petersfield, Hampshire GU32 2DP
Tel: 01730 300200
Head of School: Colin Baty
Age range: 8–13
No. of pupils: 200
Fees: Day £16,920–£18,765
FB £22,215–£24,930

Bedales School
Church Road, Steep, Petersfield,
Hampshire GU32 2DG
Tel: 01730 711733
Head of School: Magnus Bashaarat
Age range: 13–18
No. of pupils: 463
Fees: Day £28,515 FB £36,285

Boundary Oak School
Roche Court, Fareham,
Hampshire PO17 5BL
Tel: 01329 280955/820373
Head: Mr James Polansky
Age range: 2–16
No. of pupils: 120
Fees: Day £8,949–£14,487 WB
£15,723–£20,514 FB £17,658–£22,449

Brockwood Park & Inwoods School
Brockwood Park, Bramdean,
Hampshire SO24 0LQ
Tel: +44 (0)1962 771744
Principal: Mr Antonio Autor
Age range: 14–19
No. of pupils: 112 VIth39
Fees: Day £5,630–£6,400 FB £21,400

Brookham School
Highfield Lane, Liphook,
Hampshire GU30 7LQ
Tel: 01428 722005
Headteacher: Mrs Sophie Baber
Age range: 3–8
No. of pupils: 162
Fees: Day £11,100–£15,000

CHURCHER'S COLLEGE
For further details see p. 172
Petersfield, Hampshire GU31 4AS
Tel: 01730 263033
Email:
admissions@churcherscollege.com
Website:
www.churcherscollege.com
Headmaster: Mr Simon
Williams MA, BSc
Age range: 3–18 years
Fees: Day £9,915–£15,420

Daneshill School
Stratfield Turgis, Basingstoke,
Hampshire RG27 0AR
Tel: 01256 882707
Headmaster: Mr David Griffiths
Age range: 3–13
Fees: Day £10,650–£14,000

DITCHAM PARK SCHOOL
For further details see p. 178
Ditcham Park, Petersfield,
Hampshire GU31 5RN
Tel: 01730 825659
Email:
admissions@ditchampark.com
Website: www.ditchampark.com
Headmaster: Mr Graham
Spawforth MA, MEd
Age range: 2½–16
No. of pupils: 379
Fees: Day £2,835–£4,753

DURLSTON COURT
For further details see p. 180
Becton Lane, Barton-on-Sea, New
Milton, Hampshire BH25 7AQ
Tel: 01425 610010
Email:
secretary@durlstoncourt.co.uk
Website: www.durlstoncourt.co.uk
Age range: 2–13
No. of pupils: 296
Fees: Day £3,540–£15,390

Farleigh School
Red Rice, Andover,
Hampshire SP11 7PW
Tel: 01264 710766
Headmaster: Father Simon Everson
Age range: 3–13
Fees: Day £5,385–£19,590
FB £21,675–£25,485

Farnborough Hill
Farnborough Road, Farnborough,
Hampshire GU14 8AT
Tel: 01252 545197
Head: Mrs A Neil BA, MEd, PGCE
Age range: G11–18
No. of pupils: 550 VIth90
Fees: Day £14,796

Forres Sandle Manor
Fordingbridge, Hampshire SP6 1NS
Tel: 01425 653181
Headmaster: Mr M N Hartley BSc(Hons)
Age range: 3–13
No. of pupils: 264

Glenhurst School
16 Beechworth Road, Havant,
Hampshire PO9 1AX
Tel: 023 9248 4054
Principal: Mrs E M Haines
Age range: 3 months–5 years

Hampshire Collegiate School
Embley Park, Romsey,
Hampshire SO51 6ZE
Tel: 01794 512206
Headteacher: Mr Cliff Canning
Age range: 2–18
No. of pupils: 683

Highfield School
Liphook, Hampshire GU30 7LQ
Tel: 01428 728000
Headmaster: Mr Phillip Evitt MA
Age range: 8–13
No. of pupils: 292
Fees: Day £18,975–£21,525
FB £23,850–£26,250

KING EDWARD VI SCHOOL
For further details see p. 192
Wilton Road, Southampton,
Hampshire SO15 5UQ
Tel: 023 8070 4561
Email: registrar@kes.hants.sch.uk
Website: www.kes.hants.sch.uk
Head Master: Mr A J
Thould MA(Oxon)
Age range: 11–18
No. of pupils: 960
Fees: Day £16,050

Kingscourt School
182 Five Heads Road, Catherington,
Hampshire PO8 9NJ
Tel: 023 9259 3251
Head of School: Mr Jamie Lewis
Age range: 3–11
No. of pupils: 210
Fees: Day £2,856

LORD WANDSWORTH COLLEGE
For further details see p. 198
Long Sutton, Hook,
Hampshire RG29 1TB
Tel: 01256 862201
Email:
admissions@lordwandsworth.org
Website: www.lordwandsworth.org
Head of School: Mr Adam Williams
Age range: 11–18 years
No. of pupils: 615
Fees: Day £20,430–£23,460 WB
£28,290–£31,800 FB £29,250–£33,300

Mayville High School
35/37 St Simon's Road, Southsea,
Portsmouth, Hampshire PO5 2PE
Tel: 023 9273 4847
Headteacher: Mrs Rebecca Parkyn
Age range: 6 months–16 years
No. of pupils: 479
Fees: Day £7,635–£11,235

Meoncross School
Burnt House Lane, Stubbington,
Fareham, Hampshire PO14 2EF
Tel: 01329 662182
Headmaster: Mr Mark Cripps
Age range: 2 –16
No. of pupils: 405
Fees: Day £8,736–£12,576

Moyles Court School
Moyles Court, Ringwood,
Hampshire BH24 3NF
Tel: 01425 472856
Headmaster: Mr R Milner-Smith
Age range: 3–16
Fees: Day £2,112–£4,766
FB £6,876–£8,675

New Forest Small School
1 Southampton Road, Lyndhurst,
Hampshire SO43 7BU
Tel: 02380 284 415
Headteacher: Mr Nicholas Alp
Age range: 3–16

Norman Court
West Tytherley, Stockbridge,
Hampshire SP5 1NH
Tel: 01980 322 322

Portsmouth High School GDST
Kent Road, Southsea, Portsmouth,
Hampshire PO5 3EQ
Tel: 023 9282 6714
Headmistress: Mrs Jane
Prescott BSc NPQH
Age range: G3–18
No. of pupils: 500
Fees: Day £2,500–£4,663

PRINCE'S MEAD SCHOOL
For further details see p. 206
Worthy Park House, Kings Worthy,
Winchester, Hampshire SO21 1AN
Tel: 01962 888000
Email:
admin@princesmeadschool.org.uk
Website:
www.princesmeadschool.org.uk
Headmistress: Ms Penelope Kirk
Age range: 4–11

Ringwood Waldorf School
Folly Farm Lane, Ashley, Ringwood,
Hampshire BH24 2NN
Tel: 01425 472664
Age range: 3–18
No. of pupils: 235
Fees: Day £6,240–£9,000

Rookwood School
Weyhill Road, Andover,
Hampshire SP10 3AL
Tel: 01264 325900
Headmaster: Mr A Kirk-Burgess
BSc, PGCE, MSc (Oxon)
Age range: 2–16
Fees: Day £9,360–£15,600
FB £23,250–£27,465

Salesian College
Reading Road, Farnborough,
Hampshire GU14 6PA
Tel: 01252 893000
Headmaster: Mr Gerard Owens
Age range: B11–18 G16–18
No. of pupils: 650 VIth140
Fees: Day £11,961

Sherborne House School
Lakewood Road, Chandlers Ford,
Eastleigh, Hampshire SO53 1EU
Tel: 023 8025 2440
Head Teacher: Mrs Heather Hopson-Hill
Age range: 3–11
No. of pupils: 293
Fees: Day £8,295–£9,675

Sherfield School
Sherfield-on-Loddon, Hook,
Hampshire RG27 0HU
Tel: +44 (0)1256 884 800
Acting Head Master: Mr Christopher
James-Roll BSc (Hons), PGCE
Age range: 3 months–18 years
No. of pupils: 445 VIth16
Fees: Day £9,930–£16,594 WB
£18,408–£25,375 FB £21,474–£29,601

St John's College
Grove Road South, Southsea,
Portsmouth, Hampshire PO5 3QW
Tel: 023 9281 5118
Headmaster: Mr Timothy Bayley
BSc (Hons), MA, PGCE
Age range: 2–18
No. of pupils: 560 VIth86
Fees: Day £9,225–£12,090
FB £25,200–£28,740

ST NEOT'S SCHOOL
For further details see p. 214
St Neot's Road, Eversley,
Hampshire RG27 0PN
Tel: 0118 9739650
Email:
admissions@stneotsprep.co.uk
Website: www.stneotsprep.co.uk
Head of School: Deborah Henderson
Age range: 2–13 years
No. of pupils: 330
Fees: Day £3,655–£15,600

St Nicholas' School
Redfields House, Redfields
Lane, Church Crookham,
Fleet, Hampshire GU52 0RF
Tel: 01252 850121
Headmistress: Dr O Wright
PhD, MA, BA Hons, PGCE
Age range: B3–7 G3–16
No. of pupils: 325

St Swithun's Junior School
Alresford Road, Winchester,
Hampshire SO21 1HA
Tel: 01962 835750
Headmistress: Mrs R Lyons-
Smith BSc, PGCE, MBA
Age range: B3–7 G3–11
No. of pupils: 191
Fees: Day £5,424–£13,971

ST SWITHUN'S SCHOOL
For further details see p. 216
Alresford Road, Winchester,
Hampshire SO21 1HA
Tel: 01962 835700
Email: office@stswithuns.com
Website: www.stswithuns.com
Head of School: Jane
Gandee MA(Cantab)
Age range: G11–18
No. of pupils: 509 VIth136
Fees: Day £20,565 FB £33,600

St. Mary's Independent School
57 Midanbury Lane, Bitterne Park,
Southampton, Hampshire SO18 4DJ
Tel: 023 8067 1267
Executive Head: Mrs C Charlemagne
Age range: 3–16
No. of pupils: 470
Fees: Day £7,620–£9,900

Stockton House School
Stockton Avenue, Fleet,
Hampshire GU51 4NS
Tel: 01252 616323
Early Years Manager: Mrs
Jenny Bounds BA EYPS
Age range: 2–5

**The Children's House and
Grantham Farm Montessori School**
Grantham Farm, Baughurst,
Tadley, Hampshire RG26 5JS
Tel: 0118 981 5821
Head Teacher: Ms Emma Wetherley
Age range: 3–8

The Gregg Prep School
17-19 Winn Road, Southampton,
Hampshire SO17 1EJ
Tel: 023 8055 7352
Head Teacher: Mrs J Caddy
Age range: 3–11
Fees: Day £8,295

The Gregg School
Townhill Park House, Cutbush Lane,
Southampton, Hampshire SO18 2GF
Tel: 023 8047 2133
Headteacher: Mrs S Sellers PGDip,
MSc, BSc(Hons), NPQH, PGCE
Age range: 11–16
No. of pupils: 300
Fees: Day £12,825

The King's School
Lakesmere House, Allington Lane,
Fair Oak, Eastleigh, Southampton,
Hampshire SO50 7DB
Tel: 023 8060 0986
Age range: 3–16
No. of pupils: 256
Fees: Day £4,560–£7,680

The Pilgrims' School
3 The Close, Winchester,
Hampshire SO23 9LT
Tel: 01962 854189
Headmaster: Mr Tom Burden
Age range: B4–13
No. of pupils: 250
Fees: Day £18,150–£19,245 FB £24,330

The Portsmouth Grammar School
High Street, Portsmouth,
Hampshire PO1 2LN
Tel: +44 (0)23 9236 0036
Headmistress: Dr Anne Cotton
Age range: 2–18
No. of pupils: 1556 VIth336
Fees: Day £10,233–£15,951

The Stroud School
Highwood House, Highwood Lane,
Romsey, Hampshire SO51 9ZH
Tel: 01794 513231
Headmaster: Mr Joel Worrall
Age range: 3–13

The Westgate School
Cheriton Road, Winchester,
Hampshire SO22 5AZ
Tel: 01962 854757
Headteacher: Mrs Dean
Age range: 4–16

Twyford School
Twyford, Winchester,
Hampshire SO21 1NW
Tel: 01962 712269
Headmaster: Dr S J Bailey
BEd, PhD, FRSA
Age range: 3–13
Fees: Day £10,953–£19,509 WB £24,552

Walhampton
Walhampton, Lymington,
Hampshire SO41 5ZG
Tel: 01590 613 300
Headmaster: Mr Titus Mills
Age range: 2–13
No. of pupils: 353
Fees: Day £9,000–£17,625
FB £20,250–£24,750

Wessex Tutors
44 Shirley Road, Southampton,
Hampshire SO15 3EU
Tel: 023 8033 4719
Principal: Mrs J E White BA(London)
Age range: 14–21

West Hill Park Preparatory School
Titchfield, Fareham,
Hampshire PO14 4BS
Tel: 01329 842356
Headmaster: A P Ramsay
BEd(Hons), MSc
Age range: 2–13
No. of pupils: 288
Fees: Day £10,800–£18,300
FB £19,500–£22,650

Winchester College
College Street, Winchester,
Hampshire SO23 9NA
Tel: 01962 621247
Headmaster: Dr. T R Hands
Age range: B13–18
No. of pupils: 690 VIth280
Fees: FB £39,912

Woodhill School, Botley
Brook Lane, Botley, Southampton,
Hampshire SO30 2ER
Tel: 01489 781112
Head Teacher: Mrs M Dacombe
Age range: 3–11
No. of pupils: 100
Fees: Day £7,050

Yateley Manor School
51 Reading Road, Yateley,
Hampshire GU46 7UQ
Tel: 01252 405500
Headmaster: Mr Robert Upton
Age range: 3–13
No. of pupils: 453
Fees: Day £11,160–£15,300

Isle of Wight

Priory School
Beatrice Avenue, Whippingham,
Isle of Wight PO32 6LP
Tel: 01983 861222
Principal: Mr E J Matyjaszek
Age range: 4–18
Fees: Day £5,840–£9,900

Ryde School with Upper Chine
Queen's Road, Ryde, Isle
of Wight PO33 3BE
Tel: 01983 617970
Headmaster: Mr M. A. Waldron MA
Age range: 2½–18
No. of pupils: 760
Fees: Day £7,635–£13,230 WB
£26,010 FB £28,725–£29,160

Kent

Ashford School
East Hill, Ashford, Kent TN24 8PB
Tel: 01233 739030
Head: Mr Michael Hall
Age range: 3 months–18 years
No. of pupils: 835 VIth170
Fees: Day £10,500–£16,800
WB £24,000 FB £36,000

Beech Grove School
Beech Grove Bruderhof, Sandwich
Road, Nonington, Dover, Kent CT15 4HH
Tel: 01304 842980
Head: Mr Timothy Maas
Age range: 4–14
No. of pupils: 63

Beechwood Sacred Heart
12 Pembury Road, Tunbridge
Wells, Kent TN2 3QD
Tel: 01892 532747
Acting Head: Mrs Helen Rowe
Age range: 3–18
No. of pupils: 400 VIth70
Fees: Day £8,685–£17,385
WB £26,850 FB £29,850

Benenden School
Cranbrook, Kent TN17 4AA
Tel: 01580 240592
Headmistress: Mrs S Price
Age range: G11–18
No. of pupils: 550
Fees: FB £12,650

BETHANY SCHOOL
For further details see p. 168
Curtisden Green, Goudhurst,
Cranbrook, Kent TN17 1LB
Tel: 01580 211273
Email:
admissions@bethanyschool.org.uk
Website: www.bethanyschool.org.uk
Headmaster: Mr Francie
Healy BSc, HDipEd, NPQH
Age range: 11–18 years
No. of pupils: 313 VIth98
Fees: Day £16,725–£18,465 WB
£25,950–£28,655 FB £27,990–£31,500

Bronte School
Mayfield, 7 Pelham Road,
Gravesend, Kent DA11 0HN
Tel: 01474 533805
Headmistress: Ms Emma Wood
Age range: 3–11
No. of pupils: 120
Fees: Day £9,330

Bryony School
Marshall Road, Rainham,
Gillingham, Kent ME8 0AJ
Tel: 01634 231511
Joint Head: Mr D Edmunds
Age range: 2–11
No. of pupils: 168
Fees: Day £5,978–£6,511

CATS Canterbury
68 New Dover Road,
Canterbury, Kent CT1 3LQ
Tel: +44 (0)1227866540
Principal: Dr Sarah Lockyer
Age range: 14–18
No. of pupils: 400

Chartfield School
45 Minster Road, Westgate
on Sea, Kent CT8 8DA
Tel: 01843 831716
Head & Proprietor: Miss L P Shipley
Age range: 4–11
No. of pupils: 50
Fees: Day £2,700–£3,450

Cobham Hall School
Cobham, Kent DA12 3BL
Tel: 01474 823371
Headmistress: Dr Sandra
Coates-Smith BSc, PhD
Age range: G11–18
No. of pupils: 180

Cranbrook School
Waterloo Road, Cranbrook,
Kent TN17 3JD
Tel: 01580 711800
Head Teacher: Mr John Weeds
Age range: 13–18
No. of pupils: 757 VIth307
Fees: FB £13,362–£16,032

Derwent Lodge School for Girls
Somerhill, Tonbridge, Kent TN11 0NJ
Tel: 01732 352124
Head of School: Mrs Helen Hoffmann
Age range: G7–11
No. of pupils: 134
Fees: Day £15,465

Dover College
Effingham Crescent,
Dover, Kent CT17 9RH
Tel: 01304 205969
Headmaster: Mr Gareth
Doodes MA (Hons)
Age range: 3–18
No. of pupils: 301
Fees: Day £7,725–£16,050 WB
£21,000–£25,500 FB £24,750–£31,500

Dulwich Prep Cranbrook
Coursehorn, Cranbrook, Kent TN17 3NP
Tel: 01580 712179
Headmaster: Mr Paul David BEd(Hons)
Age range: 3–13
No. of pupils: 535
Fees: Day £5,970–£18,390

Elliott Park School
18-20 Marina Drive, Minster,
Sheerness, Kent ME12 2DP
Tel: 01795 873372
Head: Ms Colleen Hiller
Age range: 3–11
No. of pupils: 65
Fees: Day £5,431

Fosse Bank School
Mountains, Noble Tree Road,
Hildenborough, Tonbridge,
Kent TN11 8ND
Tel: 01732 834212
Headmistress: Miss Alison Cordingley
Age range: 3–11
No. of pupils: 124
Fees: Day £10,083–£12,543

Gad's Hill School
Higham, Rochester,
Medway, Kent ME3 7PA
Tel: 01474 822366
Headmaster: Mr Paul Savage
Age range: 3–16
No. of pupils: 370
Fees: Day £8,988–£12,504

Haddon Dene School
57 Gladstone Road,
Broadstairs, Kent CT10 2HY
Tel: 01843 861176
Head: Miss Alison Hatch
Age range: 3–11
No. of pupils: 200
Fees: Day £5,700–£7,230

Hilden Grange School
62 Dry Hill Park Road,
Tonbridge, Kent TN10 3BX
Tel: 01732 352706
Headmaster: Mr J Withers BA(Hons)
Age range: 3–13
No. of pupils: 311

Hilden Oaks School & Nursery
38 Dry Hill Park Road,
Tonbridge, Kent TN10 3BU
Tel: 01732 353941
Head of School: Mrs. K J M Joiner
Age range: 3 months–11
Fees: Day £8,985–£12,450

Holmewood House School
Barrow Lane, Langton Green,
Tunbridge Wells, Kent TN3 0EB
Tel: 01892 860000
Headmaster: Mr Scott Carnochan
Age range: 3–13
No. of pupils: 450

KENT COLLEGE
For further details see p. 190
Whitstable Road, Canterbury,
Kent CT2 9DT
Tel: 01227 763231
Email: enquiries@kentcollege.co.uk
Website: www.kentcollege.com
Executive Head Master: Dr
D J Lamper
Age range: 0–18 years
No. of pupils: 760
Fees: Day £16,464–£18,315
FB £25,236–£34,491

Kent College Junior School
Harbledown, Canterbury,
Kent CT2 9AQ
Tel: 01227 762436
Headmaster: Mr Andrew Carter
Age range: 0–11
No. of pupils: 190
Fees: Day £8,220–£15,621 FB £24,375

Kent College Pembury
Old Church Road, Pembury,
Tunbridge Wells, Kent TN2 4AX
Tel: +44 (0)1892 822006
Headmistress: Ms J Lodrick
Age range: G3–18
No. of pupils: 650 VIth102
Fees: Day £9,459–£20,571 WB
£25,710 FB £25,710–£32,778

**King's Preparatory
School, Rochester**
King Edward Road, Rochester,
Medway, Kent ME1 1UB
Tel: 01634 888577
Headmaster: Mr Tom Morgan
Age range: 8–13
No. of pupils: 220
Fees: Day £13,185–£14,955

**King's Pre-Preparatory
School, Rochester**
Chadlington House, Lockington
Grove, Rochester, Kent ME1 1RH
Tel: 01634 888566
Headmistress: Mrs C Openshaw
Age range: 3–8
No. of pupils: 149
Fees: Day £10,155–£11,010

KING'S ROCHESTER
For further details see p. 194
Satis House, Boley Hill,
Rochester, Kent ME1 1TE
Tel: 01634 888555
Email:
admissions@kings-rochester.co.uk
Website: www.kings-rochester.co.uk
Principal: Mr J Walker
Age range: 13–18
No. of pupils: 625 VIth92
Fees: Day £7,125–£19,320
FB £21,960–£31,590
🌐Ⓐ🏫£⬭16·

Linton Park School
3 Eccleston Road, Tovil,
Maidstone, Kent ME17 4HT
Tel: 01622 740820
Headteacher: Kate Edwards
Age range: 7–18
No. of pupils: 134

Lorenden Preparatory School
Painter's Forstal, Faversham,
Kent ME13 0EN
Tel: 01795 590030
Headmistress: Mrs K Uttley
Age range: 3–11
No. of pupils: 120
Fees: Day £8,640–£12,540
£⬭

Marlborough House School
High Street, Hawkhurst, Kent TN18 4PY
Tel: 01580 753555
Headmaster: Mr Martyn
Ward BEd (Hons)
Age range: 2–13
No. of pupils: 334
Fees: Day £8,730–£18,060
🏫£⬭

**Meredale Independent
Primary School**
Solomon Road, Rainham,
Gillingham, Kent ME8 8EB
Tel: 01634 231405
Headteacher: Mrs Michelle Homer
Age range: 3–11
No. of pupils: 53
Fees: Day £6,945–£7,815
£⬭

NORTHBOURNE PARK SCHOOL
For further details see p. 204
Betteshanger, Deal, Kent CT14 0NW
Tel: 01304 611215/218
Email:
admissions@northbournepark.com
Website:
www.northbournepark.com
Headmaster: Mr Sebastian
Rees BA(Hons), PGCE, NPQH
Age range: 3–13
No. of pupils: 175
Fees: Day £7,632–£16,755
WB £20,985 FB £24,300
🏫£⬭

Radnor House, Sevenoaks
Combe Bank Drive,
Sevenoaks, Kent TN14 6AE
Tel: 01959 563720
Head: Mr David Paton
BComm (Hons) PGCE MA
Age range: 2½–18
No. of pupils: 250
Ⓐ£⬭16·🐾

Rochester Independent College
Star Hill, Rochester, Medway,
Kent ME1 1XF
Tel: 01634 828115
Principals: Alistair Brownlow,
Brian Pain, Pauline Bailey
Age range: 11–19
No. of pupils: 306 VIth233
Fees: Day £12,600–£18,000
WB £12,000 FB £13,500
🌐16·Ⓐ🏫£⬭16·

Rose Hill School
Coniston Avenue, Tunbridge
Wells, Kent TN4 9SY
Tel: 01892 525591
Head: Emma Neville
Age range: 3–13
Fees: Day £11,325–£15,225
£⬭

Russell House School
Station Road, Otford,
Sevenoaks, Kent TN14 5QU
Tel: 01959 522352
Headmaster: Mr Craig McCarthy
Age range: 2–11
No. of pupils: 193

Sackville School
Tonbridge Rd, Hildenborough,
Tonbridge, Kent TN11 9HN
Tel: 01732 838888
Headmaster: Mr Justin Foster-
Gandey BSc (hons)
Age range: 11–18
No. of pupils: 160 VIth29
Fees: Day £15,297

Saint Ronan's School
Water Lane, Hawkhurst, Kent TN18 5DJ
Tel: 01580 752271
Headmaster: William Trelawny-
Vernon BSc(Hons)
Age range: 3–13
No. of pupils: 300
Fees: Day £10,476–£17,952 FB £21,681
🏫£⬭

Sevenoaks Preparatory School
Godden Green, Sevenoaks,
Kent TN15 0JU
Tel: 01732 762336
Headmaster: Mr Luke Harrison
Age range: 2–13
No. of pupils: 388
Fees: Day £10,350–£14,295
£⬭

Sevenoaks School
High Street, Sevenoaks, Kent TN13 1HU
Tel: +44 (0)1732 455133
Head: Dr Katy Ricks MA, DPhil
Age range: 11–18
No. of pupils: 1080
Fees: Day £23,355–£26,523
FB £37,296–£40,464
🌐🏫£ⒾⒷ⬭16·

Shernold School
Hill Place, Queens Avenue,
Maidstone, Kent ME16 0ER
Tel: 01622 752868
Head Teacher: Ms. Sandra Dinsmore
Age range: 3–11
No. of pupils: 142
Fees: Day £6,900–£7,800
£

Solefield School
Solefield Road, Sevenoaks,
Kent TN13 1PH
Tel: 01732 452142
Headmaster: Mr D A Philps BSc(Hons)
Age range: B4–13
No. of pupils: 180
Fees: Day £11,970–£14,580
♂⬭

Somerhill Pre-Prep
Somerhill, Five Oak Green Road,
Tonbridge, Kent TN11 0NJ
Tel: 01732 352124
Headmistress: Miss Zoe Humm
Age range: 3–7
No. of pupils: 245
Fees: Day £10,050–£11,685

Spring Grove School
Harville Road, Wye, Ashford,
Kent TN25 5EZ
Tel: 01233 812337
Headmaster: Mr Bill Jones
Age range: 2–11
No. of pupils: 194
Fees: Day £8,700–£12,600
£⬭

St Andrew's School
24-28 Watts Avenue, Rochester,
Medway, Kent ME1 1SA
Tel: 01634 843479
Principal: Mrs E Steinmann-Gilbert
Age range: 2–11
No. of pupils: 367
Fees: Day £7,464–£7,902
⬭

St Christopher's School
New Dover Road, Canterbury,
Kent CT1 3DT
Tel: 01227 462960
The Master: Mr D Evans
Age range: 3–11
Fees: Day £9,975
£⬭

St Edmund's Junior School
St Thomas Hill, Canterbury,
Kent CT2 8HU
Tel: 01227 475600
Head: Edward O'Connor
Age range: 3–13
No. of pupils: 230
Fees: Day £7,647–£15,594
WB £24,267 FB £26,628
🏫⬭

St Edmund's School
St Thomas' Hill, Canterbury,
Kent CT2 8HU
Tel: 01227 475601
Head: Mr Edward O'Connor
Age range: 3–18
No. of pupils: 535
Fees: Day £7,647–£20,466 WB
£24,267–£32,595 FB £26,628–£34,968
🌐Ⓐ🏫£⬭16·

St Faith's at Ash School
5 The Street, Ash, Canterbury,
Kent CT3 2HH
Tel: 01304 813409
Headmaster: Mr Lawrence Groves
Age range: 2–11
No. of pupils: 225
Fees: Day £5,220–£9,525
£⬭

St Joseph's Convent Prep School
46 Old Road East, Gravesend,
Kent DA12 1NR
Tel: 01474 533012
Head Teacher: Miss D Buckley
Age range: 3–11
No. of pupils: 146
Fees: Day £8,310

St Lawrence College
Ramsgate, Kent CT11 7AE
Tel: 01843 572931
Principal: Mr Antony Spencer
Age range: 3–18
No. of pupils: 640 VIth115
Fees: Day £7,470–£18,495
FB £26,055–£34,635

St Michael's Preparatory School
Otford Court, Otford,
Sevenoaks, Kent TN14 5SA
Tel: 01959 522137
Headteacher: Mrs Jill Aisher
Age range: 2–13
No. of pupils: 472
Fees: Day £11,850–£14,400

Steephill School
Off Castle Hill, Fawkham,
Longfield, Kent DA3 7BG
Tel: 01474 702107
Head: Mrs C Birtwell BSc, MBA, PGCE
Age range: 3–11
No. of pupils: 131
Fees: Day £9,420

SUTTON VALENCE PREPARATORY SCHOOL
For further details see p. 220
Chart Sutton, Maidstone,
Kent ME17 3RF
Tel: 01622 842117
Head: Miss C Corkran
Age range: 3–11
No. of pupils: 320
Fees: Day £3,000–£4,610

SUTTON VALENCE SCHOOL
For further details see p. 220
North Street, Sutton
Valence, Kent ME17 3HL
Tel: 01622 845200
Email: enquiries@svs.org.uk
Website: www.svs.org.uk
Headmaster: Bruce Grindlay MA
Cantab, MusB, FRCO, CHM
Age range: 11–18
No. of pupils: 570

The Granville School
2 Bradbourne Park Road,
Sevenoaks, Kent TN13 3LJ
Tel: 01732 453039
Headmistress: Mrs J Scott BEd(Cantab)
Age range: B3–4 G3–11
No. of pupils: 195
Fees: Day £5,862–£15,111

The Junior King's School, Canterbury
Milner Court, Sturry,
Canterbury, Kent CT2 0AY
Tel: 01227 714000
Head: Emma Károlyi
Age range: 3–13
Fees: Day £11,145–£18,735 FB £25,710

The King's School, Canterbury
The Precincts, Canterbury, Kent CT1 2ES
Tel: 01227 595501
Head: Mr P Roberts
Age range: 13–18
No. of pupils: 858 VIth385
Fees: Day £27,495 FB £37,455

The Mead School
16 Frant Road, Tunbridge
Wells, Kent TN2 5SN
Tel: 01892 525837
Headmaster: Mr Andrew Webster
Age range: 3–11
No. of pupils: 188
Fees: Day £4,236–£10,785

The New Beacon School
Brittains Lane, Sevenoaks,
Kent TN13 2PB
Tel: 01732 452131
Headmaster: Mr M Piercy BA(Hons)
Age range: B4–13
No. of pupils: 400
Fees: Day £11,100–£15,885

Tonbridge School
Tonbridge, Kent TN9 1JP
Tel: 01732 365555
Headmaster: Mr James Priory
Age range: B13–18
No. of pupils: 780

Walthamstow Hall Pre-Prep and Junior School
Sevenoaks, Kent TN13 3LD
Tel: 01732 451334
Headmistress: Miss S Ferro
Age range: G2–11
No. of pupils: 218
Fees: Day £11,775–£14,850

Walthamstow Hall School
Sevenoaks, Kent TN13 3UL
Tel: 01732 451334
Headmistress: Miss S Ferro
Age range: G2–18
No. of pupils: 500 VIth80
Fees: Day £11,775–£20,070

Wellesley House
114 Ramsgate Road,
Broadstairs, Kent CT10 2DG
Tel: 01843 862991
Headmaster: Mr G D Franklin
Age range: 7–13
No. of pupils: 133
Fees: Day £11,961–£19,479 FB £25,752

Yardley Court
Somerhill, Five Oak Green Road,
Tonbridge, Kent TN11 0NJ
Tel: 01732 352124
Headmaster: Duncan Sinclair
Age range: B7–13
No. of pupils: 260
Fees: Day £15,465

Surrey

Aberdour School
Brighton Road, Burgh Heath,
Tadworth, Surrey KT20 6AJ
Tel: 01737 354119
Headmaster: Mr S. D. Collins
Age range: 2–13 years
No. of pupils: 357
Fees: Day £1,350–£4,650

ACS Cobham International School
Heywood, Portsmouth Road,
Cobham, Surrey KT11 1BL
Tel: +44 (0) 1932 867251
Age range: 2–18
No. of pupils: 1460
Fees: Day £11,250–£27,110 WB
£38,810–£41,570 FB £44,170–£46,930

ACS Egham International School
Woodlee, London Road,
Egham, Surrey TW20 0HS
Tel: +44 (0) 1784 430 800
Head of School: Jeremy Lewis
Age range: 4–18
Fees: Day £10,870–£25,360

Aldro School
Shackleford, Godalming,
Surrey GU8 6AS
Tel: 01483 810266
Head: James & Jenny Hanson
Age range: B7–13
No. of pupils: 220
Fees: Day £16,869–£18,729
FB £22,446–£24,309

Amesbury
Hazel Grove, Hindhead,
Surrey GU26 6BL
Tel: 01428 604322
Headmaster: Mr Nigel Taylor MA
Age range: 2–13
No. of pupils: 360

Banstead Preparatory School
Sutton Lane, Banstead, Surrey SM7 3RA
Tel: 01737 363601
Headteacher: Miss Vicky Ellis
Age range: 2–11
No. of pupils: 225

Barfield School
Guildford Road, Runfold,
Farnham, Surrey GU10 1PB
Tel: 01252 782271
Head of School: James Reid
Age range: 2–13 years
No. of pupils: 170
Fees: Day £3,258–£13,980
(£)🖊

Barrow Hills School
Roke Lane, Witley, Godalming,
Surrey GU8 5NY
Tel: +44 (0)1428 683639
Headmaster: Mr Sean Skehan
Age range: 2–13
No. of pupils: 235
Fees: Day £14,985
(£)🖊

Belmont Preparatory School
Feldemore, Holmbury St Mary,
Dorking, Surrey RH5 6LQ
Tel: 01306 730852
Headmistress: Mrs Helen Skrine
BA, PGCE, NPQH, FRSA
Age range: 2–13
No. of pupils: 227
Fees: Day £9,390–£15,930
WB £22,215–£22,695
(🏫)(£)🖊

Bishopsgate School
Bishopsgate Road, Englefield
Green, Egham, Surrey TW20 0YJ
Tel: 01784 432109
Headmaster: Mr R Williams
Age range: 3–13
Fees: Day £5,415–£15,378
(£)🖊

Box Hill School
Old London Road, Mickleham,
Dorking, Surrey RH5 6EA
Tel: 01372 373382
Headmaster: Mr Corydon Lowde
Age range: 11–18
No. of pupils: 425 VIth96
Fees: Day £17,850–£19,710 WB
£27,510–£28,800 FB £33,690–£35,100
(🚌)(🏫)(£)(IB)🖊(16)

Caterham School
Harestone Valley, Caterham,
Surrey CR3 6YA
Tel: 01883 343028
Head: Mr C. W. Jones MA(Cantab)
Age range: 11–18
No. of pupils: VIth321
Fees: Day £18,045 WB
£30,936 FB £34,710
(🚌)(A)(🏫)(£)🖊(16)

Charterhouse
Godalming, Surrey GU7 2DX
Tel: +44 (0)1483 291501
Headmaster: Dr Alex Peterken
Age range: B13–18 G16–18
No. of pupils: 820
(🚌)(A)(🏫)(IB)🖊(16)

Chinthurst School
Tadworth Street, Tadworth,
Surrey KT20 5QZ
Tel: 01737 812011
Head: Miss Catherine Trundle
Age range: B3–11
No. of pupils: 170
Fees: Day £11,010–£14,850
(£)🖊

City of London Freemen's School
Ashtead Park, Ashtead, Surrey KT21 1ET
Tel: 01372 277933
Headmaster: Mr R Martin
Age range: 7–18
No. of pupils: 877 VIth213
Fees: Day £13,398–£18,279 WB
£27,906–£27,957 FB £30,780–£30,816
(🚌)(A)(🏫)(£)🖊(16)

Claremont Fan Court School
Claremont Drive, Esher, Surrey KT10 9LY
Tel: 01372 467841
Head: Mr William Brierly
Age range: 2–18
No. of pupils: 780
Fees: Day £10,680–£17,670
(A)(£)🖊(16)

Coworth Flexlands School
Chertsey Road, Chobham,
Woking, Surrey GU24 8TE
Tel: 01276 855707
Headmistress: Mrs Anne Sweeney
Age range: B2½–7 G2½–11
No. of pupils: 150
Fees: Day £8,490–£13,350
🖊

Cranleigh Preparatory School
Horseshoe Lane, Cranleigh,
Surrey GU6 8QH
Tel: 01483 274199
Headmaster: Mr M T Wilson BSc
Age range: 7–13
No. of pupils: 290
Fees: Day £14,955–£19,395 FB £23,430
(🏫)

CRANLEIGH SCHOOL
For further details see p. 174
Horseshoe Lane, Cranleigh,
Surrey GU6 8QQ
Tel: +44 (0) 1483 273666
Email: admissions@cranleigh.org
Website: www.cranleigh.org
Headmaster: Mr Martin
Reader MA, MPhil, MBA
Age range: 7–18 (including
Prep School)
No. of pupils: 654 VIth240
Fees: Day £31,170 FB £37,905
(🚌)(A)(🏫)(£)🖊(16)

CRANMORE SCHOOL
For further details see p. 176
Epsom Road, West Horsley,
Surrey KT24 6AT
Tel: 01483 280340
Email: office@cranmoreprep.co.uk
Website: www.cranmoreprep.co.uk
Headmaster: Mr Michael
Connolly BSc, BA, MA, MEd
Age range: 2½–13
No. of pupils: 430
Fees: Day £12,375–£14,775
(£)🖊

Danes Hill School
Leatherhead Road, Oxshott,
Surrey KT22 0JG
Tel: 01372 842509
Headmaster: Mr W Murdock BA
Age range: 3–13
No. of pupils: 872
Fees: Day £10,650–£14,400
(£)🖊

Danesfield Manor School
Rydens Avenue, Walton-on-
Thames, Surrey KT12 3JB
Tel: 01932 220930
Principal: Mrs Jo Smith
Age range: 2–11
No. of pupils: 170
Fees: Day £9,135–£9,756
🖊

Downsend School
1 Leatherhead Road,
Leatherhead, Surrey KT22 8TJ
Tel: 01372 372197
Headmaster: Mr Ian Thorpe
Age range: 2–13
No. of pupils: 740
Fees: Day £13,455
🖊

Downsend School (Pre-Prep)
Leatherhead Lodge, Epsom Road,
Leatherhead, Surrey KT22 8ST
Tel: 01372 372123
Headteacher: Mrs Gill Brooks
Age range: 2–6
Fees: Day £11,535

Downsend School Ashtead
Ashtead Lodge, 22 Oakfield
Road, Ashtead, Surrey KT21 2RE
Tel: 01372 385439
Head Teacher: Tessa Roberts
Age range: 2–6
No. of pupils: 66
Fees: Day £11,535

Downsend School Epsom
Epsom Lodge, 6 Norman Avenue,
Epsom, Surrey KT17 3AB
Tel: 01372 385438
Head Teacher: Vanessa Conlan
Age range: 2–6
No. of pupils: 110
Fees: Day £11,535
🖊

**Drayton House Pre-
School and Nursery**
35 Austen Road, Guildford,
Surrey GU1 3NP
Tel: 01483 504707
Headmistress: Mrs J Tyson-Jones
Froebel Cert.Ed. London University
Age range: 6 months–5 years
No. of pupils: 65
Fees: Day £4,420–£12,500
🖊

Duke of Kent School
Peaslake Road, Ewhurst,
Surrey GU6 7NS
Tel: 01483 277313
Head: Mrs Sue Knox
Age range: 3–16
No. of pupils: 234
Fees: Day £6,960–£18,090
(🚌)(🏫)(£)🖊

Dunottar School
High Trees Road, Reigate,
Surrey RH2 7EL
Tel: 01737 761945
Head of School: Mr Mark Tottman
Age range: 11–18
No. of pupils: 319
Fees: Day £16,035
(A)(£)(16)

Edgeborough
Frensham, Farnham, Surrey GU10 3AH
Tel: 01252 792495
Headmaster: Mr Dan Thornburn
Age range: 2–13
No. of pupils: 285
Fees: Day £10,740–£17,535
🏫 £ 🏊

Emberhurst School
94 Ember Lane, Esher, Surrey KT10 8EN
Tel: 020 8398 2933
Headmistress: Mrs P Chadwick BEd
Age range: 2–7
No. of pupils: 70

Epsom College
Epsom, Surrey KT17 4JQ
Tel: 01372 821000
Headmaster: Mr Jay A Piggot MA
Age range: 11–18
No. of pupils: 884
Fees: Day £18,765–£25,266
WB £33,849 FB £37,263
🎓 Ⓐ 🏫 £ 🏊 16

Essendene Lodge School
Essendene Road, Caterham,
Surrey CR3 5PB
Tel: 01883 348349
Head Teacher: Mrs K Ali
Age range: 2–11
No. of pupils: 153
Fees: Day £3,315–£7,305
£ 🏊

Ewell Castle School
Church Street, Ewell, Epsom,
Surrey KT17 2AW
Tel: 020 8393 1413
Principal: Mr Peter Harris
Age range: 3–18
No. of pupils: 557
Fees: Day £4,953–£16,692
Ⓐ £ 🏊 16

FELTONFLEET SCHOOL
For further details see p. 184
Cobham, Surrey KT11 1DR
Tel: 01932 862264
Email: office@feltonfleet.co.uk
Website: www.feltonfleet.co.uk
Head of School: Mrs S Lance
Age range: 3–13
No. of pupils: 398
Fees: Day £11,799–£17,325 WB £21,051
🏫 £ 🏊

Focus School – Hindhead Campus
Tilford Road, Hindhead,
Surrey GU26 6SJ
Tel: 01428 601800
Head: Mr Kristian Still
Age range: 8–18
No. of pupils: 90

Frensham Heights
Rowledge, Farnham, Surrey GU10 4EA
Tel: 01252 792561
Headmaster: Mr Andrew
Fisher BA, MEd, FRSA
Age range: 3–18
No. of pupils: 497 VIth105
Fees: Day £6,900–£20,430
FB £26,370–£30,810
🎓 Ⓐ 🏫 £ 🏊 16

Glenesk School
Ockham Road North, East
Horsley, Surrey KT24 6NS
Tel: 01483 282329
Headmistress: Mrs Sarah Bradley
Age range: 2–7
Fees: Day £11,319–£12,579
£ 🏊

GORDON'S SCHOOL
For further details see p. 186
West End, Woking, Surrey GU24 9PT
Tel: 01276 858084
Email: registrar@gordons.school
Website: www.gordons.school
Head Teacher: Andrew Moss MEd
Age range: 11–18
No. of pupils: 850 VIth250
Fees: Day £5,790 WB
£16,134 FB £17,235
Ⓐ 🏫 £ 🏊 16

Greenfield School
Brooklyn Road, Woking,
Surrey GU22 7TP
Tel: 01483 772525
Headmistress: Mrs Tania Botting BEd
Age range: 3–11
No. of pupils: 179
Fees: Day £5,763–£13,485
£ 🏊

Guildford High School
London Road, Guildford, Surrey GU1 1SJ
Tel: 01483 561440
Headmistress: Mrs F J Boulton BSc, MA
Age range: G4–18
No. of pupils: 980 VIth160
Fees: Day £10,728–£17,214
🏊 Ⓐ £ 16

Hall Grove School
London Road, Bagshot,
Surrey GU19 5HZ
Tel: 01276 473059
Headmaster: Mr Alastair Graham
Age range: 3–13
No. of pupils: 452
Fees: Day £10,455–£13,650
🏫

Halstead Preparatory School
Woodham Rise, Woking,
Surrey GU21 4EE
Tel: 01483 772682
Headmistress: Mrs P Austin
Age range: G3–11
No. of pupils: 220
Fees: Day £10,800–£14,400
🏊 £ 🏊

Hampton Court House
Hampton Court Road, East
Molesey, Surrey KT8 9BS
Tel: 020 8943 0889
Headmaster: Mr Guy Holloway
Age range: 3–18
No. of pupils: 248 VIth30
Fees: Day £13,665–£19,506
Ⓐ

HawleyHurst School
Fernhill Road, Blackwater,
Camberley, Surrey GU17 9HU
Tel: 01276 587190
Principal: Miss V S Smit
Age range: 2–19
£ 🏊

Hazelwood School
Wolf's Hill, Limpsfield, Oxted,
Surrey RH8 0QU
Tel: 01883 712194
Head: Mrs Lindie Louw
Age range: 2–13
No. of pupils: 399
Fees: Day £9,975–£15,900
£ 🏊

HOE BRIDGE SCHOOL
For further details see p. 188
Hoe Place, Old Woking Road,
Woking, Surrey GU22 8JE
Tel: 01483 760018 & 01483 772194
Email: enquiriesprep@
hoebridgeschool.co.uk
Website:
www.hoebridgeschool.co.uk
Head: Mr C Webster MA
BSc (Hons) PGCE
Age range: 3–13
No. of pupils: 460
Fees: Day £5,940–£15,345
£ 🏊

Hurtwood House
Holmbury St Mary, Dorking,
Surrey RH5 6NU
Tel: 01483 279000
Principal: Mr Cosmo Jackson
Age range: 16–18
No. of pupils: 300
Fees: Day £28,950 FB £43,428
16 Ⓐ 🏊

ISL Surrey Primary School
Old Woking Road, Woking,
Surrey GU22 8HY
Tel: +44 (0)1483 750409
Principal: Richard Parker
Age range: 2–11 years
No. of pupils: 100
Fees: Day £10,450–£15,500
🎓 £ 🏊

King Edward's Witley
Godalming, Surrey GU8 5SG
Tel: +44 (0)1428 686700
Headmaster: Mr John Attwater MA
Age range: 11–18
No. of pupils: 410 VIth185
Fees: Day £15,360–£20,460
FB £30,810–£31,995
🎓 Ⓐ 🏫 £ IB 🏊 16

Kingswood House School
56 West Hill, Epsom, Surrey KT19 8LG
Tel: 01372 723590
Headmaster: Mr Duncan Murphy
BA (Hons), MEd, FRSA
Age range: B3–16
No. of pupils: 210
Fees: Day £10,740–£14,850

LANESBOROUGH
For further details see p. 196
Maori Road, Guildford,
Surrey GU1 2EL
Tel: 01483 880489
Email: admissions@
lanesborough.surrey.sch.uk
Website:
www.lanesborough.surrey.sch.uk
Head: Mrs Clare Turnbull
BA(Hons) MEd
Age range: B3–13
No. of pupils: 350
Fees: Day £10,890–£15,270

Lingfield College
Racecourse Road, Lingfield,
Surrey RH7 6PH
Tel: 01342 833176
Headmaster: Mr R Bool
Age range: 2–18
No. of pupils: 935
Fees: Day £11,250–£19,473

Longacre School
Hullbrook Lane, Shamley Green,
Guildford, Surrey GU5 0NQ
Tel: 01483 893225
Head of School: Mr Matthew Bryan
Age range: 2–11
No. of pupils: 260

Lyndhurst School
36 The Avenue, Camberley,
Surrey GU15 3NE
Tel: 01276 22895
Head: Mr A Rudkin BEd(Hons)
Age range: 2–11
Fees: Day £9,300–£12,675

MANOR HOUSE SCHOOL, BOOKHAM
For further details see p. 202
Manor House Lane, Little Bookham,
Leatherhead, Surrey KT23 4EN
Tel: 01372 457077
Email:
admin@manorhouseschool.org
Website:
www.manorhouseschool.org
Headteacher: Ms Tracey Fantham
Age range: B2–4 G2–16
No. of pupils: 300
Fees: Day £9,255–£17,403

Micklefield School
10/12 Somers Road, Reigate,
Surrey RH2 9DU
Tel: 01737 242615
Headmistress: Mrs L Rose
BEd(Hons), CertEd, Dip PC
Age range: 3–11
No. of pupils: 272
Fees: Day £3,360–£11,925

Milbourne Lodge School
Arbrook Lane, Esher, Surrey KT10 9EG
Tel: 01372 462737
Head: Mrs Judy Waite
Age range: 4–13
No. of pupils: 276
Fees: Day £11,760–£14,664

Notre Dame School
Cobham, Surrey KT11 1HA
Tel: 01932 869990
Head of Seniors: Mrs Anna King
MEd, MA (Cantab), PGCE
Age range: 2–18
No. of pupils: 600

Oakhyrst Grange School
160 Stanstead Road,
Caterham, Surrey CR3 6AF
Tel: 01883 343344
Headmaster: Mr Alex Gear
Age range: 4–11 years
No. of pupils: 155

Parkside School
The Manor, Stoke d'Abernon,
Cobham, Surrey KT11 3PX
Tel: 01932 862749
Headmaster: Mr Mark Beach
Age range: B2–13 G2–4
No. of pupils: 382
Fees: Day £12,165–£16,692

Prior's Field
Priorsfield Road, Godalming,
Surrey GU7 2RH
Tel: 01483 810551
Age range: G11–18
No. of pupils: 450
Fees: Day £17,300 FB £29,925

Reed's School
Sandy Lane, Cobham, Surrey KT11 2ES
Tel: 01932 869001
Headmaster: Mr Mark
Hoskins BA MA MSc
Age range: B11–18 G16–18
No. of pupils: 650 VIth230
Fees: Day £19,740–£24,675
FB £26,310–£31,800

Reigate Grammar School
Reigate Road, Reigate, Surrey RH2 0QS
Tel: 01737 222231
Headmaster: Mr Shaun Fenton
MA (Oxon) MEd (Oxon)
Age range: 11–18
No. of pupils: 969 VIth262
Fees: Day £18,600–£18,720

Reigate St Mary's Prep & Choir School
Chart Lane, Reigate, Surrey RH2 7RN
Tel: 01737 244880
Headmaster: Mr Marcus Culverwell MA
Age range: 3–11
No. of pupils: 350

Ripley Court School
Rose Lane, Ripley, Surrey GU23 6NE
Tel: 01483 225217
Headmaster: Mr A J Gough
Age range: 3–13
No. of pupils: 281
Fees: Day £9,300–£14,160

Rowan Preparatory School
6 Fitzalan Road, Claygate,
Surrey KT10 0LX
Tel: 01372 462627
Headmistress: Mrs Susan
Clarke BEd, NPQH
Age range: G2–11
No. of pupils: 317
Fees: Day £11,190–£14,850

Royal Alexandra and Albert School
Gatton Park, Reigate, Surrey RH2 0TD
Tel: 01737 649 000
Headmaster: Mr Mark Dixon
Age range: 7–18 years
No. of pupils: 1000 VIth200
Fees: FB £15,300

Royal Grammar School, Guildford
High Street, Guildford, Surrey GU1 3BB
Tel: 01483 880600
Headmaster: Dr J M Cox BSc, PhD
Age range: B11–18
No. of pupils: 940
Fees: Day £18,285

Rydes Hill Preparatory School
Rydes Hill House, Aldershot Road,
Guildford, Surrey GU2 8BP
Tel: 01483 563160
Headmistress: Mrs Sarah Norville
Age range: B3–7 G3–11
No. of pupils: 180

Shrewsbury Lodge School
22 Milbourne Lane, Esher,
Surrey KT10 9EA
Tel: 01372 462781
Head: Mr James Tilly BA (Hons), QTS
Age range: 3–7
Fees: Day £8,199–£13,080

Sir William Perkins's School
Guildford Road, Chertsey,
Surrey KT16 9BN
Tel: 01932 574900
Head: Mr C Muller
Age range: G11–18 years
No. of pupils: 605 VIth140
Fees: £15,915

ST CATHERINE'S, BRAMLEY
For further details see p. 212
Bramley, Guildford, Surrey GU5 0DF
Tel: 01483 899609
Email: admissions@stcatherines.info
Website: www.stcatherines.info
Headmistress: Mrs A M
Phillips MA(Cantab)
Age range: G4–18
No. of pupils: 900
Fees: Day £8,985–£18,375 FB £30,285

St Christopher's School
6 Downs Road, Epsom, Surrey KT18 5HE
Tel: 01372 721807
Headteacher: Mrs A C
Thackray MA, BA(Hons)
Age range: 3–7
No. of pupils: 137
Fees: Day £10,065
£ ✎

St Edmund's School
Portsmouth Road, Hindhead,
Surrey GU26 6BH
Tel: 01428 604808
Headmaster: Mr A J Walliker
MA(Cantab), MBA, PGCE
Age range: 2–16
No. of pupils: 410
Fees: Day £9,585–£15,945
🏫 £ ✎

St George's College
Weybridge Road, Addlestone,
Weybridge, Surrey KT15 2QS
Tel: 01932 839300
Headmistress: Mrs Rachel Owens
Age range: 11–18
No. of pupils: 909 VIth250
Fees: Day £16,845–£19,185
A ✎ 16

St George's Junior School
Thames Street, Weybridge,
Surrey KT13 8NL
Tel: 01932 839400
Head Master: Mr Antony Hudson
MA (CANTAB), PGCE, NPQH
Age range: 3–11 years
No. of pupils: 644
Fees: Day £5,385–£13,965
£ ✎

St Hilary's School
Holloway Hill, Godalming,
Surrey GU7 1RZ
Tel: 01483 416551
Headmistress: Mrs Jane Whittingham
BEdCert, ProfPracSpLD
Age range: B2–11 G2–11
No. of pupils: 250
Fees: Day £10,092–£14,850
£ ✎

St Ives School
Three Gates Lane, Haslemere,
Surrey GU27 2ES
Tel: 01428 643734
Headteacher: Kay Goldsworthy
Age range: B2–7 G2–11
No. of pupils: 149
Fees: Day £8,850–£13,650
👤 £ ✎

St John's School
Epsom Road, Leatherhead,
Surrey KT22 8SP
Tel: 01372 373000
Head of School: Mrs Rowena Cole
Age range: 11–18
No. of pupils: 761
Fees: Day £19,200–£24,300
WB £24,330–£30,705
🏫 A 🏛 £ ✎ 16

St Teresa's Effingham (Preparatory School)
Effingham, Surrey RH5 6ST
Tel: 01372 453456
Headmaster: Mr. Mike Farmer
Age range: B2–4 G2–11
No. of pupils: 100
Fees: Day £1,185–£13,890
WB £24,300 FB £27,300
👤 🏛 ✎

St Teresa's Effingham (Senior School)
Beech Avenue, Effingham,
Surrey RH5 6ST
Tel: 01372 452037
Head: Mr Mike Farmer
Age range: G11–18
No. of pupils: 640 VIth90
Fees: Day £16,980–£17,595 WB
£27,489–£27,795 FB £29,340–£29,955
👤 🏫 A 🏛 £ ✎ 16

ST. ANDREW'S SCHOOL
For further details see p. 218
Church Hill House, Horsell,
Woking, Surrey GU21 4QW
Tel: 01483 760943
Email:
admin@st-andrews.woking.sch.uk
Website:
www.st-andrews.woking.sch.uk
Headmaster: Mr A Perks
Age range: 3–13
No. of pupils: 300
Fees: Day £3,789–£14,925
£ ✎

Surbiton Preparatory School
3 Avenue Elmers, Surbiton,
Surrey KT6 4SP
Tel: 020 8390 6640
Principal: Mrs Rebecca Glover
Age range: B4–11 G4–11
No. of pupils: 135
Fees: Day £10,857–£13,974
👤 👤 ✎

TASIS The American School in England
Coldharbour Lane, Thorpe,
Surrey TW20 8TE
Tel: +44 (0)1932 582316
Head of School: Mr Bryan Nixon
Age range: 3–18
No. of pupils: 662
Fees: Day £11,230–£23,890 FB £43,550
🏫 🏛 IB 16

The Hawthorns School
Pendell Court, Bletchingley,
Redhill, Surrey RH1 4QJ
Tel: 01883 743048
Headmaster: Mr A E Floyd
BSc(Hons), PGCE
Age range: 2–13
No. of pupils: 535
Fees: Day £2,130–£14,880
£ ✎

The Royal Junior School
Portsmouth Road, Hindhead,
Surrey GU26 6BW
Tel: 01428 607977
Head of School: Mrs Kerrie
Daunter B.Ed (Hons)
Age range: 6 weeks–11 years
Fees: Day £10,200–£11,955
🏫

The Royal School
Farnham Lane, Haslemere,
Surrey GU27 1HQ
Tel: 01428 605805
Principal: Mrs Anne Lynch
BA (Hons), PGCE, FRSA
Age range: 11–18 years
Fees: Day £17,925–£18,144 WB
£26,895–£27,114 FB £30,600–£30,819
🏫 A 🏛 £ ✎ 16

Tormead School
27 Cranley Road, Guildford,
Surrey GU1 2JD
Tel: 01483 575101
Headmistress: Mrs Christina Foord
Age range: G4–18
No. of pupils: 760 VIth120
Fees: Day £8,100–£15,450
👤 🏫 A £ ✎ 16

Warlingham Park School
Chelsham Common,
Warlingham, Surrey CR6 9PB
Tel: 01883 626844
Headmaster: Mr M R Donald BSc
Age range: 2–11
No. of pupils: 96
Fees: Day £4,110–£8,310
✎

Weston Green School
Weston Green Road, Thames
Ditton, Surrey KT7 0JN
Tel: 020 8398 2778
Head: Mrs Sarah Evans
Age range: 4–11
Fees: Day £9,867–£11,094
✎

Westward School
47 Hersham Road, Walton-on-
Thames, Surrey KT12 1LE
Tel: 01932 220911
Headmistress: Mrs Shelley Stevenson
Age range: 3–12
No. of pupils: 140
Fees: Day £7,230–£8,070
£ ✎

Woldingham School
Marden Park, Woldingham,
Surrey CR3 7YA
Tel: 01883 349431
Headmistress: Mrs Alex Hutchinson
Age range: G11–18
No. of pupils: 530 VIth150
Fees: Day £20,580–£22,440
FB £33,570–£36,540
👤 🏫 A 🏛 £ ✎ 16

Woodcote House School
Snows Ride, Windlesham,
Surrey GU20 6PF
Tel: 01276 472115
Headmaster: Mr D.M.K. Paterson
Age range: B7–13
No. of pupils: 100
Fees: Day £17,850 FB £23,850
👤 🏛 £ ✎

Yehudi Menuhin School
Stoke Road, Stoke d'Abernon,
Cobham, Surrey KT11 3QQ
Tel: 01932 864739
Head of School: Kate Clanchy
Age range: 7–19
No. of pupils: 80 VIth36
Fees: FB £34,299
🏫 A 🏛 £ ✎ 16

West Sussex

Ardingly College
College Road, Ardingly, Haywards Heath, West Sussex RH17 6SQ
Tel: +44 (0)1444 893320
Headmaster: Mr Ben Figgis
Age range: 13–18
No. of pupils: 559
Fees: Day £22,995–£23,610
FB £33,405–£35,910

Ardingly College Preparatory School
Haywards Heath, West Sussex RH17 6SQ
Tel: 01444 893200
Headmaster: Mr Harry Hastings
Age range: 2–13
Fees: Day £9,195–£15,750

Ashton Park School
Brinsbury Campus East, Stane Street, North Heath, Pulborough, West Sussex RH20 1DJ
Tel: 01798 875836
Head: Mr G Holding
Age range: 11–16
No. of pupils: 66

Brambletye
Brambletye, East Grinstead, West Sussex RH19 3PD
Tel: 01342 321004
Headmaster: Will Brooks
Age range: 2–13
No. of pupils: 280
Fees: Day £9,615–£20,730
FB £24,705–£25,275

BURGESS HILL GIRLS
For further details see p. 170
Keymer Road, Burgess Hill, West Sussex RH15 0EG
Tel: 01444 241050
Email: registrar@burgesshillgirls.com
Website: www.burgesshillgirls.com
Head of School: Liz Laybourn
Age range: B2½–4 G2½–18
No. of pupils: 505 VIth70
Fees: Day £7,800–£19,200
FB £28,050–£34,200

Christ's Hospital
Horsham, West Sussex RH13 0LJ
Tel: 01403 211293
Headmaster: Mr Simon Reid
Age range: 11–18
No. of pupils: 900
Fees: Day £16,950–£21,330 FB £32,790

Conifers School
Egmont Road, Midhurst, West Sussex GU29 9BG
Tel: 01730 813243
Headmistress: Mrs Emma Smyth
Age range: 2–13
No. of pupils: 104
Fees: Day £7,110–£9,450

Copthorne Prep School
Effingham Lane, Copthorne, West Sussex RH10 3HR
Tel: 01342 712311
Headmaster: Mr Chris Jones
Age range: 2–13
No. of pupils: 340
Fees: Day £9,240–£16,095
WB £17,565 FB £23,985

Cottesmore School
Buchan Hill, Pease Pottage, West Sussex RH11 9AU
Tel: 01293 520648
Head: T F Rogerson
Age range: 4–13
No. of pupils: 170
Fees: Day £3,199–£4,267 FB £9,095

Cumnor House Sussex
London Road, Danehill, Haywards Heath, West Sussex RH17 7HT
Tel: 01825 792 006
Headmaster: Christian Heinrich
Age range: 2–13
No. of pupils: 385
Fees: Day £8,985–£19,530
WB £22,635 FB £23,250

Dorset House School
The Manor, Church Lane, Bury, Pulborough, West Sussex RH20 1PB
Tel: 01798 831456
Headmaster: Matt Thomas
Age range: 3–13
No. of pupils: 135
Fees: Day £8,550–£17,850

Farlington School
Strood Park, Horsham, West Sussex RH12 3PN
Tel: 01403 282573
Headmistress: Ms Louise Higson BSc, PGCE
Age range: G3–18
No. of pupils: 300
Fees: Day £5,400–£17,670 WB £23,205–£28,515 FB £24,540–£29,850

Great Ballard School
Eartham House, Eartham, Nr Chichester, West Sussex PO18 0LR
Tel: 01243 814236
Head: Mr Richard Evans
Age range: 2–13
No. of pupils: 136
Fees: Day £8,580–£15,930 WB £17,010

Great Walstead School
East Mascalls Lane, Lindfield, Haywards Heath, West Sussex RH16 2QL
Tel: 01444 483528
Headmaster: Mr Chris Calvey
Age range: 2½–13
No. of pupils: 465
Fees: Day £11,055–£15,510

Handcross Park School
Handcross, Haywards Heath, West Sussex RH17 6HF
Tel: 01444 400526
Headmaster: Mr Richard Brown
Age range: 2–13
No. of pupils: 339
Fees: Day £3,230–£6,360 WB £5,370–£7,480 FB £6,030–£8,130

Hurstpierpoint College
College Lane, Hurstpierpoint, West Sussex BN6 9JS
Tel: 01273 833636
Headmaster: Mr. T J Manly BA, MSc
Age range: 4–18
No. of pupils: 1156
Fees: Day £8,790–£22,860 WB £28,800

Hurstpierpoint College Prep School
Hurstpierpoint, West Sussex BN6 9JS
Tel: 01273 834975
Head: Mr I D Pattison BSc
Age range: 4–13
No. of pupils: 360

Lancing College
Lancing, West Sussex BN15 0RW
Tel: 01273 465805
Head Master: Mr Dominic T Oliver MPhil
Age range: 13–18
No. of pupils: 550 VIth255
Fees: Day £8,190 FB £11,995

Lancing College Preparatory School at Worthing
Broadwater Road, Worthing, West Sussex BN14 8HU
Tel: 01903 201123
Head: Mrs Heather Beeby
Age range: 2–13
No. of pupils: 165
Fees: Day £8,115–£11,460

Oakwood Preparatory School
Chichester, West Sussex PO18 9AN
Tel: 01243 575209
Headteacher: Mrs Clare Bradbury
Age range: 2½–11
No. of pupils: 260
Fees: Day £1,715–£5,010

Our Lady of Sion School
Gratwicke Road, Worthing, West Sussex BN11 4BL
Tel: 01903 204063
Headmaster: Dr Simon Orchard
Age range: 2–18
No. of pupils: 528 VIth55
Fees: Day £8,310–£13,050

Pennthorpe School
Church Street, Horsham, West Sussex RH12 3HJ
Tel: 01403 822391
Headmistress: Alexia Bolton
Age range: 2–13
No. of pupils: 362
Fees: Day £2,070–£16,605

Rikkyo School in England
Guildford Road, Rudgwick, Horsham, West Sussex RH12 3BE
Tel: 01403 822107
Headmaster: Mr Roger Munechika
Age range: 10–18
No. of pupils: 116
Fees: FB £15,000–£21,600

SEAFORD COLLEGE
For further details see p. 210
Lavington Park, Petworth,
West Sussex GU28 0NB
Tel: 01798 867392
Email: headmasterpa@seaford.org
Website: www.seaford.org
Headmaster: J P Green MA BA
Age range: 7–18
No. of pupils: 732 VIth194
Fees: Day £10,320–£21,390 WB
£21,510–£28,980 FB £33,090

Shoreham College
St Julians Lane, Shoreham-by-
Sea, West Sussex BN43 6YW
Tel: 01273 592681
Headmaster: Mr R Taylor-West
Age range: 3–16 years
No. of pupils: 375
Fees: Day £9,750–£15,150

Slindon College
Slindon House, Slindon, Arundel,
West Sussex BN18 0RH
Tel: 01243 814320
Head Teacher: Mr Mark Birkbeck
Age range: B8–18 years
No. of pupils: 80 VIth17
Fees: Day £21,795 FB £32,280

**Sompting Abbotts Preparatory
School for Boys and Girls**
Church Lane, Sompting,
West Sussex BN15 0AZ
Tel: 01903 235960
Principal: Mrs P M Sinclair
Age range: 2–13
No. of pupils: 185
Fees: Day £9,195–£11,805

Steyning Grammar School
Shooting Field, Steyning,
West Sussex BN44 3RX
Tel: +44 (0)1903 814555
Headteacher: Mr Nick Wergan
Age range: 11–18
No. of pupils: 1975
Fees: WB £9,100 FB £11,100

The Prebendal School
52-55 West Street, Chichester,
West Sussex PO19 1RT
Tel: 01243 772220
Headteacher: Mrs L Salmond Smith
Age range: 3–13
No. of pupils: 181
Fees: Day £8,160–£15,495 WB
£18,975–£20,100 FB £22,290

The Towers Convent School
Convent of the Blessed Sacrement,
Henfield Road, Upper Beeding,
Steyning, West Sussex BN44 3TF
Tel: 01903 812185
Headmistress: Mrs Clare Trelfa
Age range: B4–11 G4–16
No. of pupils: 320
Fees: Day £8,190–£11,550

Westbourne House School
Shopwyke, Chichester,
West Sussex PO20 2BH
Tel: 01243 782739
Headmaster: Mr Martin Barker
Age range: 2½–13 years
No. of pupils: 420
Fees: Day £10,440–£17,985
FB £21,465–£24,105

**Willow Tree Montessori
Kindergarten**
Charlwood House, Charlwood
Road, Lowfield Heath, Crawley,
West Sussex RH11 0QA
Tel: 01293 820721
Headmistress: Mrs G Kerfante MontDip
Age range: 1–8
Fees: Day £2,310–£2,700

Windlesham House School
Washington, Pulborough,
West Sussex RH20 4AY
Tel: 01903 874700
Headmaster: Mr Richard
Foster BEd(Hons)
Age range: 4–13
No. of pupils: 350

Worth School
Paddockhurst Road, Turners Hill,
Crawley, West Sussex RH10 4SD
Tel: +44 (0)1342 710200
Head Master: Stuart McPherson
Age range: 11–18
No. of pupils: 580 VIth222
Fees: Day £15,960–£23,730
FB £21,210–£33,690

D374

South-West

KEY TO SYMBOLS

- Boys' school
- Girls' school
- International school
- Tutorial or sixth form college
- A levels
- Boarding accommodation
- £ Bursaries
- IB International Baccalaureate
- Learning support
- Entrance at 16+
- Vocational qualifications
- IAPS Independent Association of Preparatory Schools
- HMC The Headmasters' & Headmistresses' Conference
- ISA Independent Schools Association
- GSA Girls' School Association
- BSA Boarding Schools' Association
- Society of Heads

Unless otherwise indicated, all schools are coeducational day schools. Single-sex and boarding schools will be indicated by the relevant icon.

Cornwall

Polwhele House School
Truro, Cornwall TR4 9AE
Tel: 01872 273011
Headmaster: Mr Alex McCullough
Age range: 3–13
No. of pupils: 100
Fees: Day £8,820–£13,620

Roselyon School
St Blazey Road, Par, Cornwall PL24 2HZ
Tel: 01726 812110
Head Teacher: Hilary Mann
Age range: 2–11
No. of pupils: 103
Fees: Day £8,880

St Joseph's School
15 St Stephen's Hill, Launceston,
Cornwall PL15 8HN
Tel: 01566 772580
Head Teacher: Mr Oliver Scott
Age range: 4–16
No. of pupils: 215
Fees: Day £5,490–£13,875

St Petroc's School
Ocean View Road, Bude,
Cornwall EX23 8NJ
Tel: 01288 352876
Headmaster: Mr Hilton
Age range: 0–11
Fees: Day £5,850–£8,850

St Piran's School
Trelissick Road, Hayle,
Cornwall TR27 4HY
Tel: 01736 752612
Headteacher: Mrs Carol de
Labat BEd(Hons), CertEd
Age range: 4–16
Fees: Day £2,775–£7,080

The Valley Nursery
Trevowah Road, Crantock,
Newquay, Cornwall TR8 5RU
Tel: 01637 830680
Principal: Kerry Wilson
Age range: 3 months–5 years

Truro High School for Girls
Falmouth Road, Truro, Cornwall TR1 2HU
Tel: 01872 272830
Headmaster: Glenn Moodie
Age range: B3–5 G3–18
No. of pupils: 432 VIth60
Fees: Day £8,001–£13,896 WB
£25,185–£26,040 FB £27,261–£28,182

Truro School
Trennick Lane, Truro, Cornwall TR1 1TH
Tel: 01872 272763
Headmaster: Mr A S Gordon-
Brown BCom, MSc, CA (SA)
Age range: 3–18
No. of pupils: 780 VIth210

Devon

Abbey School
Hampton Court, St Marychurch,
Torquay, Devon TQ1 4PR
Tel: 01803 327868
Principal: Mrs Sylvia Greinig
Age range: 0–11 years
No. of pupils: 78

Blundell's Preparatory School
Milestones House, Blundell's Road,
Tiverton, Devon EX16 4NA
Tel: 01884 252393
Head Master: Mr Andrew
Southgate BA Ed (Hons)
Age range: 2–11
No. of pupils: 220
Fees: Day £5,880–£12,195

Blundell's School
Tiverton, Devon EX16 4DN
Tel: 01884 252543
Head: Mrs Nicola Huggett
Age range: 11–18
No. of pupils: 600 VIth205
Fees: Day £14,130–£22,410 WB
£21,570–£30,660 FB £24,060–£35,205

Bramdean School
Richmond Lodge, Homefield Road,
Heavitree, Exeter, Devon EX1 2QR
Tel: 01392 273387
Head: Miss Diane Stoneman NAHT
Age range: 3–18
No. of pupils: 180 VIth12
Fees: Day £6,204–£11,490

EF ACADEMY TORBAY
For further details see p. 226
Castle Road, Torquay,
Devon TQ1 3BG
Tel: +41 (0) 43 430 4095
Email: iaeurope@ef.com
Website: www.ef.com/academy
Head of School: Mr. Mark Howe
Age range: 14–19
No. of pupils: 300

EXETER CATHEDRAL SCHOOL
For further details see p. 228
The Chantry, Palace Gate,
Exeter, Devon EX1 1HX
Tel: 01392 255298
Email: admissions@exetercs.org
Website: www.exetercs.org
Headmaster: James Featherstone
Age range: 2½–13
No. of pupils: 257
Fees: Day £7,125–£11,877
FB £18,222–£19,287

Exeter School
Victoria Park Road, Exeter,
Devon EX2 4NS
Tel: 01392 273679
Headmaster: Mr James Featherstone
Age range: 7–18
No. of pupils: 923 VIth218
Fees: Day £7,125–£11,877

Exeter Tutorial College
44/46 Magdalen Road,
Exeter, Devon EX2 4TE
Tel: 01392 278101
Principal: K D Jack BA, DipEd
Age range: 16+
No. of pupils: 75

Fletewood School
88 North Road East, Plymouth,
Devon PL4 6AN
Tel: 01752 663782
Headteacher: Mrs R Gray
Age range: 3–11
No. of pupils: 70
Fees: Day £4,425

King's School
Hartley Road, Mannamead,
Plymouth, Devon PL3 5LW
Tel: 01752 771789
Headteacher: Mrs Jane Lee
Age range: 3–11
No. of pupils: 142
Fees: Day £5,895–£7,440

KINGSLEY SCHOOL
For further details see p. 232
Northdown Road, Bideford,
Devon EX39 3LY
Tel: 01237 426200
Email: admissions@
kingsleyschoolbideford.co.uk
Website:
www.kingsleyschoolbideford.co.uk
Headmaster: Mr Pete Last
Age range: 0–18
No. of pupils: 395
Fees: Day £1,950 WB £5,495 FB £7,095

Magdalen Court School
Mulberry House, Victoria Park
Road, Exeter, Devon EX2 4NU
Tel: 01392 494919
Head: Mrs Sarah Wrightson
Age range: 0–18+
No. of pupils: 150 VIth20
Fees: Day £5,670–£10,200

Mount Kelly
Parkwood Road, Tavistock,
Devon PL19 0HZ
Tel: +44 (0)1822 813100
Head Master: Mr. Mark Semmence
Age range: 3–18
No. of pupils: 600
Fees: Day £7,230–£17,520 WB
£16,290–£28,500 FB £18,120–£30,570
(symbols)

Park School
Park Road, Dartington,
Totnes, Devon TQ9 6EQ
Tel: 01803 864588
Teacher-in-charge: Amanda Bellamy
Age range: 3–12
Fees: Day £6,147–£9,654
(symbols)

Plymouth College
Ford Park, Plymouth, Devon PL4 6RN
Tel: +44 (0)1752 505100
Headmaster: Mr. Jonathan Standen
Age range: 3–18
No. of pupils: 501 VIth163
Fees: Day £7,680–£16,290
FB £27,435–£31,440
(symbols)

Plymouth College Preparatory School
St Dunstan's Abbey, The Millfields,
Plymouth, Devon PL1 3JL
Tel: 01752 201352
Headmaster: Chris Gatherer
Age range: 3–11
No. of pupils: 310
Fees: Day £7,680–£10,605
(symbol)

SANDS SCHOOL
For further details see p. 234
Greylands, 48 East Street,
Ashburton, Devon TQ13 7AX
Tel: 01364 653666
Email: enquiry@sands-school.co.uk
Website: www.sands-school.co.uk
Administrator: Sean Bellamy
MA(Cantab), PGCE
Age range: 11–16
Fees: Day £10,710
(symbols)

Shebbear College
Shebbear, Beaworthy, Devon EX21 5HJ
Tel: 01409 282000
Headmaster: Mr S. D. Weale MA (Oxon)
Age range: 3–18
No. of pupils: 350 VIth78
Fees: Day £5,235–£12,975 WB
£14,250–£14,985 FB £18,750–£26,325
(symbols)

South Devon Steiner School
Hood Manor, Buckfastleigh Road,
Dartington, Totnes, Devon TQ9 6AB
Tel: 01803 897 377
Education Manager: Jeff van Zyl
Age range: 3–19
No. of pupils: 307
(symbols)

St Christopher's Preparatory School
Mount Barton, Staverton,
Devon TQ9 6PF
Tel: 01803 762202
Headmistress: Alexandra Cottell
Age range: 3–11
No. of pupils: 100
Fees: Day £7,350–£9,900
(symbols)

St John's International School
Broadway, Sidmouth, Devon EX10 8RG
Tel: 01395 513984
Headmistress: Mrs Caroline Ward
Age range: 2–16
No. of pupils: 200
Fees: Day £6,906–£11,403
FB £19,422–£21,291
(symbols)

St Peter's School
Harefield, Lympstone,
Exmouth, Devon EX8 5AU
Tel: 01395 272148
Headmistress: Mrs Charlotte Johnston
Age range: 3–13
Fees: Day £7,650–£13,065 WB £19,935
(symbols)

St Wilfrid's School
25-29 St David's Hill, Exeter,
Devon EX4 4DA
Tel: 01392 276171
Headmistress: Mrs Alexandra E
M MacDonald-Dent DPhyEd
Age range: 5–16
(symbol)

Stover School
Newton Abbot, Devon TQ12 6QG
Tel: 01626 354505
Headmaster: Mr R W D Notman
Age range: 3–18
No. of pupils: 423 VIth67
Fees: Day £8,220–£12,780 WB
£18,450–£22,200 FB £21,210–£26,190
(symbols)

The Maynard School
Denmark Road, Exeter, Devon EX1 1SJ
Tel: 01392 273417
Headmistress: Miss Sarah Dunn
BSc (Hons) PGCE and NPQH
Age range: G4–18
No. of pupils: VIth80
Fees: Day £6,285–£13,248
(symbols)

The New School
The Avenue, Exminster,
Exeter, Devon EX6 8AT
Tel: 01392 496122
Headmistress: Miss M Taylor
BA(Hons), PGCE
Age range: 3–7
No. of pupils: 61
Fees: Day £7,497
(symbol)

Trinity School
Buckeridge Road, Teignmouth,
Devon TQ14 8LY
Tel: 01626 774138
Headmaster: Mr Lawrence Coen
Age range: 3–18
No. of pupils: 110
Fees: Day £7,755–£12,300 WB
£18,945–£25,590 FB £20,550–£27,750
(symbols)

West Buckland School
Barnstaple, Devon EX32 0SX
Tel: 01598 760281
Headmaster: Mr Phillip Stapleton
Age range: 3–18
No. of pupils: VIth135
Fees: Day £8,070–£15,060
FB £24,345–£30,720
(symbols)

Dorset

Bournemouth Collegiate School
St Osmunds Road, Parkstone,
Poole, Dorset BH14 9JY
Tel: 01202 436 550
Headmaster: Mr Russell Slatford
Age range: 2–18
No. of pupils: 301
Fees: Day £7,800–£14,430
WB £27,180 FB £29,670
(symbol)

Bryanston School
Blandford Forum, Dorset DT11 0PX
Tel: 01258 484633
Head: Ms S J Thomas
Age range: 13–18
No. of pupils: 673
Fees: FB £38,184
(symbols)

Buckholme Towers School & Nursery
18 Commercial Road, Lower
Parkstone, Poole, Dorset BH14 0JW
Tel: 01202 742871
Head of School: Mrs Ruth Darvill
Age range: 3–11
No. of pupils: 85
Fees: Day £6,360–£8,745
(symbol)

Canford School
Canford Magna, Wimborne,
Dorset BH21 3AD
Tel: 01202 841254
Headmaster: B A M Vessey MA, MBA
Age range: 13–18
No. of pupils: 655
Fees: Day £9,241 FB £12,140
(symbols)

Castle Court School
Knoll Lane, Corfe Mullen,
Wimborne, Dorset BH21 3RF
Tel: 01202 694438
Headmaster: Mr Luke Gollings
Age range: 2–13
No. of pupils: 307
Fees: Day £8,790–£15,825
(symbols)

Clayesmore Preparatory School
Iwerne Minster, Blandford
Forum, Dorset DT11 8PH
Tel: 01747 813155
Head of School: Mr William Dunlop
Age range: 3–13
No. of pupils: 230
Fees: Day £13,230–£18,750
FB £17,670–£25,110
♿ £ ✐

Clayesmore School
Iwerne Minster, Blandford
Forum, Dorset DT11 8LL
Tel: 01747 812122
Head of School: Mrs Jo Thomson
Age range: 13–18
No. of pupils: VIth180
Fees: Day £26,220 FB £35,730
🌐 Ⓐ ♿ £ ✐ 16

Dumpton School
Deans Grove House, Deans Grove,
Wimborne, Dorset BH21 7AF
Tel: 01202 883818
Headmaster: Mr A W Browning BSc
(Hons), PGCE, MA(Ed), CChem MRSC
Age range: 2–13
No. of pupils: 328
Fees: Day £8,844–£15,849
£ ✐

Hanford School
Child Okeford, Blandford,
Dorset DT11 8HN
Tel: 01258 860219
Headmaster: Mr Rory Johnston
Age range: G7–13
No. of pupils: 100
Fees: Day £6,250 FB £7,500
♿ ♿ £ ✐

Knighton House School and The Orchard Pre-prep
Durweston, Blandford
Forum, Dorset DT11 0PY
Tel: 01258 452065
Headmaster: Mr Robin Gainher
Age range: B3–7 G3–13
No. of pupils: 140
Fees: Day £2,325–£4,950 FB £7,600
♿ ♿ £ ✐

Leweston Preparatory School
Leweston, Sherborne, Dorset DT9 6EN
Tel: 01963 210790
Headteacher: Alanda Phillips BA
(Hons), MA (Ed), PGCE, PGCE Ed Lead
Age range: 0–11
No. of pupils: 84
Fees: Day £5,925–£11,520 WB
£17,265–£18,240 FB £20,700
♿ £ ✐

Leweston School
Senior School, Sherborne,
Dorset DT9 6EN
Tel: 01963 210691
Head: Mrs K Reynolds MA(Oxon), PGCE
Age range: G11–18
No. of pupils: 240 VIth70
Fees: Day £15,420 WB £21,795–
£25,380 FB £25,050–£27,780
♿ 🌐 Ⓐ ♿ £ ✐ 16

Milton Abbey School
Blandford Forum, Dorset DT11 0BZ
Tel: 01258 880484
Head: Judith Fremont-Barnes
Age range: 13–18
No. of pupils: 229
Fees: Day £20,250–£21,750
FB £38,550–£40,050
🌐 Ⓐ ♿ £ ✐ 16 ♿

Park School
45-49 Queens Park, South Drive,
Bournemouth, Dorset BH8 9BJ
Tel: 01202 396640
Head of School: Mrs Melanie Dowler
Age range: 2–11
No. of pupils: 387
Fees: Day £7,275–£8,805
£ ✐

Port Regis
Motcombe Park, Shaftesbury,
Dorset SP7 9QA
Tel: 01747 857800
Head of School: S L Ilett
Age range: 2–13
No. of pupils: 324
♿ £ ✐

Sherborne Girls
Bradford Road, Sherborne,
Dorset DT9 3QN
Tel: +44 (0)1935 818224
Headmistress: Dr Ruth Sullivan
BSc, PGCE, MSc, PhD
Age range: G11–18
No. of pupils: 485
Fees: Day £21,285 FB £28,920–£35,880
♿ 🌐 Ⓐ ♿ £ IB ✐ 16

Sherborne International
Newell Grange, Newell,
Sherborne, Dorset DT9 4EZ
Tel: 01935 814743
Principal: Mr Tim Waters MA
(Oxon), MSc (Oxon)
Age range: 8–17
No. of pupils: 147
🌐 ♿ ✐

Sherborne Preparatory School
Acreman Street, Sherborne,
Dorset DT9 3NY
Tel: 01935 812097
Headmaster: Mr Nick Folland
Bsc (Hons), MIAPS, MISI
Age range: 2–13
No. of pupils: 258
Fees: Day £9,060–£17,130 WB
£23,445–£24,540 FB £23,445–£24,540
♿ £ ✐

Sherborne School
Abbey Road, Sherborne,
Dorset DT9 3AP
Tel: +44 (0)1935 812249
Headmaster: Dr Dominic
Luckett BA, DPhil, FRSA, FHA
Age range: B13–18
No. of pupils: 596 VIth210
Fees: Day £30,375 FB £37,500
♿ 🌐 Ⓐ ♿ £ 16

St Martin's School
15 Stokewood Road,
Bournemouth, Dorset BH3 7NA
Tel: 01202 292011
Headteacher: Laura Richards
Age range: 4–11 years
No. of pupils: 100
Fees: Day £5,835–£7,533

St Mary's School
Shaftesbury, Dorset SP7 9LP
Tel: 01747 852416
Acting Headmistress: Mrs
Sarah Matthews
Age range: G9–18
No. of pupils: 220
Fees: Day £16,200–£20,850
FB £20,085–£31,470
♿ 🌐 Ⓐ ♿ £ ✐ 16

St Thomas Garnet's School
Parkwood Road, Boscombe,
Bournemouth, Dorset BH5 2BH
Tel: 01202 420172
Headteacher: Mr Craig Lickley
Age range: 3–11
Fees: Day £5,721–£7,995

Sunninghill Preparatory School
South Court, South Walks,
Dorchester, Dorset DT1 1EB
Tel: 01305 262306
Headmaster: Mr John Thorpe
BSc (Hons), PGCE
Age range: 3–13
No. of pupils: 184
Fees: Day £8,850–£15,450
£ ✐

Talbot House Preparatory School
8 Firs Glen Road, Bournemouth,
Dorset BH9 2LR
Tel: 01202 510348
Headteacher: Mrs Emma Haworth
Age range: 3–11
Fees: Day £4,320–£8,097

Yarrells Preparatory School
Yarrells House, Upton, Poole,
Dorset BH16 5EU
Tel: 01202 622229
Headteacher: Mrs Sally Weber-Spokes
Age range: 2–13
No. of pupils: 253
Fees: Day £2,395–£4,250
£ ✐

TALBOT HEATH
For further details see p. 236
Rothesay Road, Bournemouth,
Dorset BH4 9NJ
Tel: 01202 761881
Email: office@talbotheath.org
Website: www.talbotheath.org
Head: Mrs A Holloway MA, PGCE
Age range: G3–18
No. of pupils: 582
Fees: Day £2,201–£4,801
WB £3,305 FB £3,704
♿ 🌐 Ⓐ ♿ £ ✐ 16

Somerset

All Hallows Preparatory School
Cranmore Hall, Shepton
Mallet, Somerset BA4 4SF
Tel: 01749 881600
Head of School: Dr Trevor Richards
Age range: 3–13
No. of pupils: 300

Bruton School for Girls
Sunny Hill, Bruton, Somerset BA10 0NT
Tel: 01749 814400
Headmistress: Mrs Nicola Botterill
Age range: G2–18
No. of pupils: 250
Fees: Day £8,505–£17,805 FB £30,330

Chard School
Fore Street, Chard, Somerset TA20 1QA
Tel: 01460 63234
Head of School: Katie Hill
Age range: 0–11
No. of pupils: 100
Fees: Day £6,450–£7,650

HAZLEGROVE PREP SCHOOL
For further details see p. 230
Hazlegrove House, Sparkford,
Somerset BA22 7JA
Tel: +44 (0)1963 442606
Email: admissions@hazlegrove.co.uk
Website: www.hazlegrove.co.uk
Headmaster: Mr Mark
White MA (Hons)
Age range: 2½–13
No. of pupils: 364
Fees: Day £2,928–£5,937
FB £6,886–£8,787

King's Bruton
The Plox, Bruton, Somerset BA10 0ED
Tel: 01749 814200
Headmaster: Mr I S Wilmshurst MA
Age range: 13–18
No. of pupils: 330

King's College
Taunton, Somerset TA1 3LA
Tel: 01823 328204
Headmaster: Richard Biggs
Age range: 13–18
No. of pupils: 440 VIth180
Fees: Day £22,380 FB £33,165

King's Hall School
Kingston Road, Taunton,
Somerset TA2 8AA
Tel: 01823 285920
Headmaster: Mr Justin Chippendale
Age range: 2–13
Fees: Day £7,725–£16,500
FB £18,450–£23,985

Millfield Preparatory School
Edgarley Hall, Glastonbury,
Somerset BA6 8LD
Tel: 01458 832446
Headmistress: Mrs S Shayler
Age range: 2–13
No. of pupils: 366
Fees: Day £10,815–£18,705
WB £28,380 FB £28,380

Millfield School
Street, Somerset BA16 0YD
Tel: 01458 442291
Headmaster: Gavin Horgan
Age range: 13–18
No. of pupils: 1241
Fees: Day £25,605 FB £38,610

Perrott Hill
North Perrott, Crewkerne,
Somerset TA18 7SL
Tel: 01460 72051
Joint Acting Headteachers: Mr
Bryan Kane & Mr Will Silk
Age range: 3–13
No. of pupils: 183
Fees: Day £6,450–£15,750
WB £19,200 FB £22,740

Queen's College
Trull Road, Taunton, Somerset TA1 4QS
Tel: 01823 272559
Headmistress: Dr Lorraine Earps
Age range: 3–18
No. of pupils: 784 VIth150
Fees: Day £6,450–£18,450
FB £14,655–£31,980

**Springmead Preparatory
School & Nursery**
Castle Corner, Beckington,
Frome, Somerset BA11 6TA
Tel: 01373 831555
Principal: Ms Madeleine Taylor
Age range: 2–11
No. of pupils: 105
Fees: Day £9,390

Sunny Hill Prep School
Sunny Hill, Bruton, Somerset BA10 0NT
Tel: 01749 814 427
Head: Mrs Helen Snow BEd
Age range: B2–7 G2–11
No. of pupils: 68
Fees: Day £8,505–£13,116 WB
£21,300–£21,651 FB £23,529–£23,880

Taunton Preparatory School
Staplegrove Road, Taunton,
Somerset TA2 6AE
Tel: 01823 703305
Headmaster: Andrew Edwards
Age range: 0–13
No. of pupils: 418
Fees: Day £7,350–£15,375
FB £14,685–£25,500

Taunton School
Staplegrove Road, Taunton,
Somerset TA2 6AD
Tel: +44 (0)1823 703703
Headmaster: Mr. Lee Glaser
Age range: 0–18
No. of pupils: 520 VIth240
Fees: Day £7,350–£19,395
FB £14,685–£36,225

The Park School
Chilton Cantelo, Yeovil,
Somerset BA22 8BG
Tel: 01935 850555
Head: Mrs J Huntington ARAM
GRSM LRAM CPSEd
Age range: 4–18+
No. of pupils: 168 VIth24
Fees: Day £6,360–£10,500 WB
£21,600–£23,100 FB £22,500–£26,250

Wellington Prep School
South Street, Wellington,
Somerset TA21 8NT
Tel: 01823 668700
Headmaster: Adam Gibson
Age range: 3–11
Fees: Day £6,330–£11,520

Wellington School
South Street, Wellington,
Somerset TA21 8NT
Tel: 01823 668800
Headmaster: Henry Price MA (Oxon)
Age range: 3–18
No. of pupils: VIth165
Fees: Day £6,330–£15,225 WB
£23,130–£24,105 FB £28,890–£30,810

Wells Cathedral Junior School
8 New Street, Wells, Somerset BA5 2LQ
Tel: 01749 834400
Headteacher: Julie Barrow
Age range: 3–11
No. of pupils: 150
Fees: Day £7,641–£15,375 WB
£20,322–£22,900 FB £23,458–£26,036

Wells Cathedral School
The Liberty, Wells, Somerset BA5 2ST
Tel: 01749 834200
Head: Mr Alastair Tighe
Age range: 3–18
No. of pupils: 750 VIth194
Fees: Day £7,641–£18,801 WB
£20,322–£27,843 FB £23,458–£31,464

D380

West Midlands

KEY TO SYMBOLS

- (♂) *Boys' school*
- (♀) *Girls' school*
- (🌐) *International school*
- (16) *Tutorial or sixth form college*
- (A) *A levels*
- (🏫) *Boarding accommodation*
- (£) *Bursaries*
- (IB) *International Baccalaureate*
- (✎) *Learning support*
- (16) *Entrance at 16+*
- (🎓) *Vocational qualifications*
- (IAPS) *Independent Association of Preparatory Schools*
- (HMC) *The Headmasters' & Headmistresses' Conference*
- (ISA) *Independent Schools Association*
- (GSA) *Girls' School Association*
- (BSA) *Boarding Schools' Association*
- (S) *Society of Heads*

Unless otherwise indicated, all schools are coeducational day schools.
Single-sex and boarding schools will be indicated by the relevant icon.

Herefordshire

Hereford Cathedral Junior School
28 Castle Street, Hereford,
Herefordshire HR1 2NW
Tel: 01432 363511
Headmaster: Mr Chris Wright
Age range: 3–11
Fees: Day £8,028–£10,320
Ⓔ ✍

Hereford Cathedral School
The Old Deanery, The Cathedral Close,
Hereford, Herefordshire HR1 2NG
Tel: 01432 363522
Headmaster: Mr Paul Smith
Age range: 3–18
No. of pupils: 535 VIth130
Ⓐ Ⓔ ✍ ⑯

LUCTON SCHOOL
For further details see p. 246
Lucton, Herefordshire HR6 9PN
Tel: 01568 782000
Email: admissions@luctonschool.org
Website: www.luctonschool.org
Headmistress: Mrs Gill Thorne MA
Age range: 1–18
No. of pupils: 330
Fees: Day £3,300–£4,575 WB
£7,500–£8,825 FB £9,295–£10,625
Ⓐ ⚑ ⚑ Ⓔ ✍ ⑯

Shropshire

Adcote School for Girls
Little Ness, Shrewsbury,
Shropshire SY4 2JY
Tel: 01939 260202
Headmistress: Mrs Diane Browne
Age range: G7–18
No. of pupils: 220
Fees: Day £9,141–£14,838 WB
£17,263–£24,754 FB £19,618–£27,097
⚑ ⚑ Ⓐ ⚑ Ⓔ ✍ ⑯

Bedstone College
Bedstone, Bucknell, Shropshire SY7 0BG
Tel: 01547 530303
Headmaster: Mr David Gajadharsingh
Age range: 4–18
No. of pupils: 230
Fees: Day £5,025–£14,655
FB £17,475–£26,520
⚑ ⚑ Ⓐ ⚑ Ⓔ ✍ ⑯

Birchfield School
Albrighton, Wolverhampton,
Shropshire WV7 3AF
Tel: 01902 372534
Headmaster: Mr Paul Reynolds
Age range: B4–13 G4–12
No. of pupils: 145
Fees: Day £6,825–£14,250
⚑ Ⓔ ✍

Castle House School
Chetwynd End, Newport,
Shropshire TF10 7JE
Tel: 01952 567600
Headmaster: Mr Ian Sterling
Age range: 2–11
No. of pupils: 87
Fees: Day £7,500–£8,850
Ⓔ ✍

Concord College
Acton Burnell Hall, Shrewsbury,
Shropshire SY5 7PF
Tel: 01694 731631
Principal: N G Hawkins
MA(Cantab), PGCE
Age range: 13–19
No. of pupils: 521 VIth343
Fees: Day £14,280 FB £39,900
⚑ Ⓐ ⚑ Ⓔ ✍ ⑯

ELLESMERE COLLEGE
For further details see p. 242
Ellesmere, Shropshire SY12 9AB
Tel: 01691 622321
Email: hmsecretary@ellesmere.com
Website: www.ellesmere.com
Head: Mr B J Wignall
MA, FRSA, MCMI
Age range: 7–18
⚑ Ⓐ ⚑ Ⓔ Ⓘ ✍ ⑯

Moor Park
Richard's Castle, Ludlow,
Shropshire SY8 4DZ
Tel: 01584 777218
Headmaster: Mr Charles
G O'B Minogue
Age range: 3–13 years
No. of pupils: 179
Fees: Day £7,425–£16,575
FB £20,535–£24,600
⚑ Ⓔ ✍

Moreton First
Weston Rhyn, Oswestry,
Shropshire SY11 3EW
Tel: 01691 776028
Head: Mrs Catherine Ford M.A., B.Sc.
Age range: 6 months–11 years
No. of pupils: 181
Fees: Day £9,510–£13,410 FB £21,915
⚑ Ⓐ ⚑ Ⓔ ✍ ⑯ ⚑

Oswestry School
Upper Brook Street, Oswestry,
Shropshire SY11 2TL
Tel: 01691 655711
Headmaster: Mr Julian Noad BEng
Age range: 4–18
No. of pupils: VIth92
Fees: Day £8,700–£15,690 WB
£23,610 FB £26,850–£31,200
⚑ Ⓐ ⚑ Ⓔ ✍ ⑯

PACKWOOD HAUGH SCHOOL
For further details see p. 252
Ruyton XI Towns, Shrewsbury,
Shropshire SY4 1HX
Tel: 01939 260217
Email: hm@packwood-haugh.co.uk
Website:
www.packwood-haugh.co.uk
Headmaster: Clive Smith-
Langridge BA(Hons), PGCE
Age range: 4–13
No. of pupils: 212
Fees: Day £8,805–£18,330
FB £23,430–£26,430
⚑ Ⓔ ✍

Prestfelde Preparatory School
London Road, Shrewsbury,
Shropshire SY2 6NZ
Tel: 01743 245400
Head of School: Mrs F Orchard
Age range: 3–13
No. of pupils: 300
Fees: Day £9,570–£16,140
⚑ Ⓔ ✍

Shrewsbury High School GDST
32 Town Walls, Shrewsbury,
Shropshire SY1 1TN
Tel: 01743 494000
Head: Ms J Sharrock
Age range: B3–13 G3–18
No. of pupils: VIth120
Fees: Day £7,686–£14,481
⚑ ⚑ Ⓐ ⚑ Ⓔ ✍ ⑯

SHREWSBURY SCHOOL
For further details see p. 254
The Schools, Shrewsbury,
Shropshire SY3 7BA
Tel: 01743 280552
Email:
admissions@shrewsbury.org.uk
Website: www.shrewsbury.org.uk
Headmaster: Mr. Leo Winkley
Age range: 13–18
No. of pupils: 792 VIth386
Fees: Day £24,885 FB £36,270
⚑ Ⓐ ⚑ Ⓔ ✍ ⑯

St Winefride's Convent School
Belmont, Shrewsbury, Shropshire SY1 1TE
Tel: 01743 369883
Headmistress: Sister M Felicity
CertEd, BA(Hons)
Age range: 3–11
No. of pupils: 179
Fees: Day £4,355–£4,380
✍

The Old Hall School
Stanley Road, Wellington,
Shropshire TF1 3LB
Tel: 01952 223117
Headmaster: Martin Stott
Age range: 4–11
No. of pupils: 239
Fees: Day £8,310–£13,065
Ⓔ ✍

White House School
Heath Road, Whitchurch,
Shropshire SY13 2AA
Tel: 01948 662730
Headmistress: Mrs H M Clarke
Age range: 3–11
Fees: Day £4,950
✍

Wrekin College
Wellington, Shropshire TF1 3BH
Tel: 01952 265600
Headmaster: Mr Tim Firth
Age range: 11–18
No. of pupils: 415 VIth140
Fees: Day £14,820–£17,925 WB
£21,360–£25,320 FB £27,360–£32,040
Ⓐ Ⓐ ⓐ £ ⤢ ⑯

Staffordshire

Abbots Bromley School
High Street, Abbots Bromley,
Rugeley, Staffordshire WS15 3BW
Tel: 01283 840232
Head: Mr Richard Udy
Age range: B3-11 & 15–18 G3–18
No. of pupils: 198
Fees: Day £4,653–£15,819 WB
£17,550–£22,200 FB £21,531–£26,496
Ⓐ Ⓐ ⓐ £ ⤢ ⑯

Abbotsholme School
Rocester, Uttoxeter,
Staffordshire ST14 5BS
Tel: 01889 590217
Headmaster: Mr Bob Barnes
Age range: 2–18
No. of pupils: 310 VIth55
Fees: Day £8,985–£22,485 WB
£17,985–£26,775 FB £23,985–£32,985
Ⓐ Ⓐ ⓐ £ ⑯ ⓪

Chase Grammar School
Lyncroft House, St John's Road,
Cannock, Staffordshire WS11 0UR
Tel: 01543 501800
Principal: Dr Paul Silverwood
MA(Cantab), MSc, PhD, QTS, CChem
Age range: 2–19
No. of pupils: 300 VIth100
Fees: Day £5,985–£11,685 FB £21,500
Ⓐ Ⓐ ⓐ £ ⑯

Chase Grammar School International Study Centre
Lyncroft House, St John's Road,
Cannock, Staffordshire WS11 0UR
Tel: 01543 501800
Principal: Dr Paul Silverwood
Age range: 2–18
No. of pupils: 102
Fees: Day £5,985–£11,685
FB £21,500–£31,200
Ⓐ ⓐ £ ⑯

Copsewood Primary School
Verulam Road, Stafford,
Staffordshire ST16 3EA
Tel: 01785 258482
Head: Mr J Spicer
Age range: 7–11
No. of pupils: 20

DENSTONE COLLEGE
For further details see p. 240
Uttoxeter, Staffordshire ST14 5HN
Tel: 01889 590484
Email:
admissions@denstonecollege.net
Website: www.denstonecollege.org
Headmaster: Mr Miles
Norris MA (Oxon)
Age range: 11–18
No. of pupils: 616 VIth198
Fees: Day £13,137–£15,879 WB
£19,032–£27,648 FB £18,387–£26,712
Ⓐ Ⓐ ⓐ £ ⤢ ⑯

Denstone College Preparatory School
Smallwood Manor, Uttoxeter,
Staffordshire ST14 8NS
Tel: 01889 562083
Headmaster: Mr Jerry Gear
Age range: 2–11
No. of pupils: 153
Fees: Day £10,185–£12,900
£ ⤢

Edenhurst Preparatory School
Westlands Avenue, Newcastle-
under-Lyme, Staffordshire ST5 2PU
Tel: 01782 619348
Headmaster: Mr Michael Hibbert
Age range: 3 months–11 years
Fees: Day £8,880–£10,749
£ ⤢

Lichfield Cathedral School
The Palace, The Close, Lichfield,
Staffordshire WS13 7LH
Tel: 01543 306170
Head: Mrs Susan E Hannam
BA (Hons) MA PGCE
Age range: 3–18 years
No. of pupils: 426
Fees: Day £8,805–£13,815
Ⓐ £ ⤢

Maple Hayes Dyslexia School
Abnalls Lane, Lichfield,
Staffordshire WS13 8BL
Tel: 01543 264387
Principal: Dr N E Brown MSc, BA, MINS,
MSCMe, AFBPsS, CPsychol, FRSA, CSci
Age range: 7–17
No. of pupils: 118
Fees: Day £15,165–£20,259
£

Newcastle-under-Lyme School
Mount Pleasant, Newcastle-under-
Lyme, Staffordshire ST5 1DB
Tel: 01782 631197
Headmaster: Mr Nick Vernon
Age range: 3–18
No. of pupils: 879 VIth152
Fees: Day £8,550–£11,745
Ⓐ £ ⤢ ⑯

St Bede's School
Bishton Hall, Wolseley Bridge,
Stafford, Staffordshire ST17 0XN
Tel: 01889 881277
Headmaster: Mr Charlie Northcote
Age range: 3–13
No. of pupils: 75
Fees: Day £6,000–£9,900
WB £12,000 FB £12,000
ⓐ £ ⤢

St Dominic's Priory School Stone
21 Station Road, Stone,
Staffordshire ST15 8EN
Tel: +44 (0)1785 814181
Head of School: Mrs Rebecca Harrison
Age range: 3–16
No. of pupils: 163
Fees: Day £7,560–£11,508
Ⓐ Ⓐ £ ⤢ ⑯

St Joseph's Preparatory School
London Road, Trent Vale, Stoke-
on-Trent, Staffordshire ST4 5NT
Tel: 01782 417533
Head: Mrs S D Hutchinson
Age range: 3–11
Fees: Day £7,605–£8,040
£ ⤢

St. Dominic's Brewood
32 Bargate Street, Brewood,
Staffordshire ST19 9BA
Tel: 01902 850248
Headteacher: Mr Peter
McNabb BSc Hons, PGCE
Age range: 2–18 years
No. of pupils: 198 VIth31
Fees: Day £6,834–£13,212
Ⓐ Ⓐ ⓐ £ ⤢ ⑯

Stafford Grammar School
Burton Manor, Stafford,
Staffordshire ST18 9AT
Tel: 01785 249752
Headmaster: Mr M R Darley BA
Age range: 11–18
No. of pupils: 330 VIth96
Fees: Day £12,414
Ⓐ £ ⤢ ⑯

Yarlet School
Yarlet, Stafford, Staffordshire ST18 9SU
Tel: 01785 286568
Headmaster: Mr I Raybould BEd(Hons)
Age range: 2–13
No. of pupils: 169
Fees: Day £7,380–£12,270
ⓐ £ ⤢

Warwickshire

Arnold Lodge School
15-17 Kenilworth Road, Leamington
Spa, Warwickshire CV32 5TW
Tel: 01926 778050
Headmaster: David Preston
Age range: 4–18
No. of pupils: 200
Fees: Day £10,418–£12,592
£ ✏

Bilton Grange
Dunchurch, Rugby,
Warwickshire CV22 6QU
Tel: 01788 810217
Headmaster: Mr Alex
Osiatynski MA Oxon PGCE
Age range: 4–13
No. of pupils: 321
🏛 £ ✏

Crackley Hall School
St Joseph's Park, Kenilworth,
Warwickshire CV8 2FT
Tel: 01926 514444
Headmaster: Mr R Duigan
Age range: 2–11
No. of pupils: 233
Fees: Day £9,288–£9,888
£ ✏

Hijaz College
Watling Street, Nuneaton,
Warwickshire CV11 6BE
Tel: 02476 325 859
Headteacher: Mr Tauqir Ishaq
Age range: B11–21
No. of pupils: 61
Fees: FB £4,550–£5,400
👤 Ⓐ 🏛 ✏

King's High School for Girls
Smith Street, Warwick,
Warwickshire CV34 4HJ
Tel: 01926 494485
Head Master: Mr Richard
Nicholson MA (Oxon)
Age range: G11–18 years
👤 Ⓐ £ ✏ 16+

Milverton House School
Holman Way, Park Street,
Attleborough, Warwickshire CV11 4EL
Tel: 024 7664 1722
Head Teacher: Mr O Pipe
Age range: 0–11
No. of pupils: 275
Fees: Day £4,830–£7,050
✏

Princethorpe College
Leamington Road, Princethorpe,
Rugby, Warwickshire CV23 9PX
Tel: 01926 634200
Headmaster: Mr Ed Hester
Age range: 11–18
No. of pupils: 817 VIth184
Fees: Day £12,693
Ⓐ £ ✏ 16+

Rugby School
Rugby, Warwickshire CV22 5EH
Tel: +44 (0)1788 556274
Headmaster: Peter R.A. Green
Age range: 11–18
No. of pupils: 804 VIth366
Fees: Day £22,437 FB £35,760
👤 Ⓐ 🏛 £ ✏ 16+

Stratford Preparatory School
Church House, Old Town, Stratford-
upon-Avon, Warwickshire CV37 6BG
Tel: 01789 297993
Headmaster: Mr N Musk
MA, BA(Jt Hons), PGCE
Age range: 2–11
Fees: Day £9,600–£11,280
✏

The Crescent School
Bawnmore Road, Bilton, Rugby,
Warwickshire CV22 7QH
Tel: 01788 521595
Headmaster: Mr J.P. Thackway
B.A.Hons, P.G.C.E.
Age range: 4–11
No. of pupils: 137
Fees: Day £8,094–£9,714
£ ✏

The Croft Preparatory School
Alveston Hill, Loxley Road, Stratford-
upon-Avon, Warwickshire CV37 7RL
Tel: 01789 293795
Headmaster: Mr Marcus Cook
Age range: 2–11
No. of pupils: 425
Fees: Day £7,962–£12,213

The Kingsley School
Beauchamp Avenue, Leamington
Spa, Warwickshire CV32 5RD
Tel: 01926 425127
Headteacher: Ms Heather Owens
Age range: B3–11 G3–18
No. of pupils: 333 VIth61
Fees: Day £10,599–£13,254
👤 Ⓐ £ ✏ 16+

Twycross House Pre-Preparatory School
The Hollies, The Green, Atherstone,
Warwickshire CV9 3PQ
Tel: 01827 880725
Joint Heads: Mr S D Assinder
& Mrs R T Assinder
Age range: 4–8
Fees: Day £8,610

Twycross House School
Main Road, Twycross, Atherstone,
Warwickshire CV9 3QA
Tel: 01827 880651
Headmaster: Mr S D Assinder
Age range: 8–18
Fees: Day £9,270–£10,485
Ⓐ 16+

Warwick Preparatory School
Bridge Field, Banbury Road,
Warwick, Warwickshire CV34 6PL
Tel: 01926 491545
Headmistress: Hellen Dodsworth
Age range: B3–7 G3–11
No. of pupils: 438
Fees: Day £7,767–£12,666
✏

Warwick School
Myton Road, Warwick,
Warwickshire CV34 6PP
Tel: 01926 776400
Head Master: Dr D Smith
Age range: B7–18
No. of pupils: 1214 VIth249
Fees: Day £11,181–£13,194
WB £26,883 FB £28,758
👤 🌐 Ⓐ 🏛 £ ✏ 16+

West Midlands

Abu Bakr Girls School
154-160 Wednesbury Road, Palfrey,
Walsall, West Midlands WS1 4JJ
Tel: 01922 626829
Head: Moulana Ramzan
Age range: G11–16
👤

Al Huda Girls School
74-76 Washwood Heath Road, Saltley,
Birmingham, West Midlands B8 1RD
Tel: 0121 328 8999
Headmistress: Mrs Y Jawaid
Age range: G11–17
No. of pupils: 87
👤

Al-Ameen Primary School
Stanfield House, 447 Warwick Way,
Birmingham, West Midlands B11 2JR
Tel: 0121 706 3322
Head: Maulana Mohammed
Aminur Rahman
Age range: 3–11
No. of pupils: 22

Al-Burhan Grammar School
28A George Street, Balsall Heath,
Birmingham, West Midlands B12 9RG
Tel: 0121 4405454
Head: Dr Mohammad Nasrullah
Age range: G11–16
No. of pupils: 80
Fees: Day £11,700
👤

Al-Furqan Community College
Reddings Lane, Tyseley, Birmingham,
West Midlands B11 3EY
Tel: 0121 777 8666
Principal: Mr Amjad Ahmed BSc, PGCE
Age range: G11–16
Fees: Day £6,900
👤 Ⓐ £ ✏ 16+ 🌐

Al-Hijrah School
Cherrywood Centre, Burbidge
Road, Bordesley Green, Birmingham,
West Midlands B9 4US
Tel: 0121 7737979
Headteacher: Arshad Mohammed
Age range: 4–16
No. of pupils: 306

Archway Academy
86 Watery Lane Middleway, Bordesley,
Birmingham, West Midlands B9 4HN
Tel: 0121 772 7772
Executive Managing Director: Jim Ryan
Age range: 14–19

Bablake Junior School
Coundon Road, Coventry,
West Midlands CV1 4AU
Tel: 024 7627 1260
Headmaster: Mr N Price
Age range: 3–11
Fees: Day £8,943

Bablake PrePrep
8 Park Road, Coventry, West
Midlands CV1 2LH
Tel: 024 7622 1677
Head of Pre Prep: Mrs T Horton
Age range: 3–8
Fees: Day £7,128

Bablake School
Coundon Road, Coventry,
West Midlands CV1 4AU
Tel: 024 7627 1200
Headmaster: Mr J W Watson MA
Age range: 11–18
Fees: Day £11,694

Birchfield Independent Girls' School
Beacon House, 30 Beacon Hill, Aston,
Birmingham, West Midlands B6 6JU
Tel: 0121 327 7707
Head: Mrs R Mogra
Age range: G11–17
No. of pupils: 150 VIth100
Fees: Day £5,985

Birmingham Muslim School
Bisley Works, Golden Hillock
Road, Sparkbrook, Birmingham,
West Midlands B11 2PY
Tel: 0121 7668129
Principal: Ms A Abdrabba
Age range: 4–10
No. of pupils: 90

Childfirst Day Nursery Solihull
Cooks Lane, Kingshurst, Solihull,
West Midlands B37 6NZ
Tel: 0121 788 8148

Copsewood School
168-170 Roland Avenue, Holbrooks,
Coventry, West Midlands CV6 4LX
Tel: 024 7668 0680
Headteacher: Mr A R G Shedden
Age range: 11–16
No. of pupils: 77

Darul Uloom Islamic High School
521 Coventry Road, Small Heath,
Birmingham, West Midlands B10 0LL
Tel: 0121 772 6408
Principal: Dr Asm Abdul Rahim
Age range: B11–16
No. of pupils: 70

Edgbaston High School for Girls
Westbourne Road, Edgbaston,
Birmingham, West Midlands B15 3TS
Tel: 0121 454 5831
Headmistress: Dr Ruth A
Weeks BSc, PhD
Age range: G2–18
No. of pupils: 920 VIth112
Fees: Day £8,592–£12,774

Elmfield Rudolf Steiner School
14 Love Lane, Stourbridge,
West Midlands DY8 2EA
Tel: 01384 394633
College of Teachers: Education Admin
Age range: 3–17
No. of pupils: VIth100
Fees: Day £5,220–£8,034

Elmhurst Ballet School
249 Bristol Road, Edgbaston,
Birmingham, West Midlands B5 7UH
Tel: 0121 472 6655
Principal: Jessica Wheeler
BA(Hons), NPQH
Age range: 11–19
No. of pupils: VIth69
Fees: Day £18,564–£19,239
FB £23,793–£25,650

Emmanuel School (Walsall)
36 Wolverhampton Road, Walsall,
West Midlands WS2 8PR
Tel: 01922 635810
Head Teacher: Mr Jonathan
Swain BA PGCE
Age range: 3–16
No. of pupils: 82
Fees: Day £4,044

Eversfield Preparatory School
Warwick Road, Solihull,
West Midlands B91 1AT
Tel: 0121 705 0354
Headmaster: Mr R A Yates
BA, PGCE, LPSH
Age range: 2–11
Fees: Day £9,583–£10,971

Green Heath School
43-51 Whitmore Road, Small Heath,
Birmingham, West Midlands B10 0NR
Tel: 0121 213 1171
Age range: 11–19

Greenfields Primary School
472 Coventry Road, Birmingham,
West Midlands B10 0UG
Tel: 0121 7724567
Headteacher: P. Sa'eed Alam
Age range: 5–11

Hallfield School
Church Road, Edgbaston,
Birmingham, West Midlands B15 3SJ
Tel: 0121 454 1496
Headmaster: Mr Richard J Batchelor
Age range: 3 months–11
No. of pupils: 570

Hamd House Preparatory School
730 Bordesley Green, Birmingham,
West Midlands B9 5PQ
Tel: +44 (0) 121 771 3030
Headteacher: Mr S Ali
Age range: 3–11
No. of pupils: 206

Highclare School
10 Sutton Road, Erdington,
Birmingham, West Midlands B23 6QL
Tel: 0121 373 7400
Head: Dr Richard Luker
Age range: B1–12 G1–18
No. of pupils: 638 VIth28
Fees: Day £5,420–£12,645

Hydesville Tower School
25 Broadway North, Walsall,
West Midlands WS1 2QG
Tel: 01922 624374
Headmaster: Mr Warren Honey
BSc (Hons), PGCE Durham
University, MEd Open Univ+
Age range: 3–16
No. of pupils: 293
Fees: Day £9,432–£13,179

Jamia Islamia Birmingham Islamic College
Fallows Road, Sparkbrook,
Birmingham, West Midlands B11 1PL
Tel: 0121 7726400
Headteacher: Mohammed Govalia
Age range: 11–16
No. of pupils: 111

KING EDWARD VI HIGH SCHOOL FOR GIRLS
For further details see p. 244
Edgbaston Park Road, Birmingham,
West Midlands B15 2UB
Tel: 0121 472 1834
Email: admissions@kehs.co.uk
Website: www.kehs.org.uk
Principal: Ms Ann Clark
Age range: G11–18
No. of pupils: 591
Fees: Day £12,888

King Edward's School
Edgbaston Park Road, Birmingham,
West Midlands B15 2UA
Tel: 0121 472 1672
Chief Master: Dr. Mark Fenton MA MSc
Age range: B11–18
No. of pupils: 877 VIth222
Fees: Day £13,230

King Henry VIII Preparatory School
Kenilworth Road, Coventry,
West Midlands CV3 6PT
Tel: 024 7627 1307
Headteacher: Mrs Gillian Bowser
BA (QTS Hons), NPQH
Age range: 3–11
Fees: Day £8,652–£8,991

King Henry VIII School
Warwick Road, Coventry,
West Midlands CV3 6AQ
Tel: 024 7627 1111
Headmaster: Mr J Slack MA Ed
Age range: 11–18
No. of pupils: 724 VIth210
Fees: Day £11,694

Kingswood School
St James Place, Shirley, Solihull,
West Midlands B90 2BA
Tel: 0121 744 7883
Headmaster: Mr Rob Luckham
BSc(Hons), PGCE
Age range: 3–11
No. of pupils: 89

Lambs Christian School
113 Soho Hill, Hockley, Birmingham,
West Midlands B19 1AY
Tel: 0121 5543790
Headteacher: Mrs Patricia Ekhuenelo
Age range: 3–11
No. of pupils: 43

Lote Tree Primary
643 Foleshill Road, Coventry,
West Midlands CV6 5JQ
Tel: 024 7626 1803
Head: Mrs Ashique
Age range: 2–11
No. of pupils: 97

MANDER PORTMAN WOODWARD – BIRMINGHAM
For further details see p. 250
17-18 Greenfield Crescent,
Edgbaston, Birmingham,
West Midlands B15 3AU
Tel: 0121 454 9637
Email: birmingham@mpw.ac.uk
Website: www.mpw.ac.uk
Principal: Mr Mark Shingleton
Age range: 14–19

Mayfield Preparatory School
Sutton Road, Walsall, West
Midlands WS1 2PD
Tel: 01922 624107
Headmaster: Mr Matthew Draper
Age range: 2–11
No. of pupils: 213
Fees: Day £5,040–£8,400

Newbridge Preparatory School
51 Newbridge Crescent,
Tettenhall, Wolverhampton,
West Midlands WV6 0LH
Tel: 01902 751088
Headmistress: Mrs Sarah Fisher
Age range: B3–4 G3–11
No. of pupils: 148

Norfolk House School
4 Norfolk Road, Edgbaston,
Birmingham, West Midlands B15 3PS
Tel: 0121 454 7021
Headmistress: Mrs Sarah
Morris BA (Hons), PGCE
Age range: 3–11
No. of pupils: 146
Fees: Day £7,176–£10,380

Palfrey Girls School
72 Queen Mary Street, Palfrey,
Walsall, West Midlands WS1 4AB
Tel: 01922 625510
Headteacher: Mrs Jane Collins
Age range: G11–16
No. of pupils: 169
Fees: Day £1,500

Pattison College
86-90 Binley Road, Coventry,
West Midlands CV3 1FQ
Tel: 024 7645 5031
Principal: Mrs E.A.P.
McConnell B.Ed. (Hons)
Age range: 3–16
No. of pupils: 110 VIth16
Fees: Day £6,585–£8,895

Priory School
39 Sir Harry's Road, Edgbaston,
Birmingham, West Midlands B15 2UR
Tel: 0121 440 4103
Headmaster: Mr J Cramb
Age range: 6 months–18 years
No. of pupils: 438 VIth23
Fees: Day £3,275–£4,950

Rosslyn School
1597 Stratford Road, Hall Green,
Birmingham, West Midlands B28 9JB
Tel: 0121 744 2743
Principal: Mrs Jane Scott
Age range: 2–11
Fees: Day £3,588–£6,252

Ruckleigh School
17 Lode Lane, Solihull, West
Midlands B91 2AB
Tel: 0121 705 2773
Headmistress: Mrs Barbara Forster
Age range: 3–11
Fees: Day £8,640–£9,120

Saint Martin's School
Malvern Hall, Brueton Avenue,
Solihull, West Midlands B91 3EN
Tel: 0121 705 1265
Headmistress: Mrs Nicola Smillie
BA (Hons), PGCE, NPQH
Age range: G3–18
No. of pupils: 430 VIth40
Fees: Day £9,900–£12,750

Solihull School
Warwick Road, Solihull,
West Midlands B91 3DJ
Tel: 0121 705 0958
Headmaster: Mr David E J J Lloyd
Age range: 7–18
No. of pupils: 1013 VIth279
Fees: Day £10,491–£12,897

St George's School, Edgbaston
31 Calthorpe Road, Birmingham,
West Midlands B15 1RX
Tel: 0121 625 0398
Head of School: Mr Gary
Neal BEd (Hons)
Age range: 3–18
No. of pupils: 368 VIth48
Fees: Day £6,060–£9,765

Tettenhall College
Wood Road, Tettenhall,
Wolverhampton, West
Midlands WV6 8QX
Tel: 01902 751119
Head: Mr D C Williams
Age range: 2–18
No. of pupils: VIth66
Fees: Day £7,293–£13,881 WB
£26,142–£28,344 FB £29,370–£31,902

The Birmingham Theatre School
The Old Rep Theatre, Station Street,
Birmingham, West Midlands B5 4DY
Tel: 0121 440 1665
Principal: C Rozanski BA(Hons)
Age range: 5–65
Fees: Day £5,400

The Blue Coat School
Somerset Road, Edgbaston,
Birmingham, West Midlands B17 0HR
Tel: 0121 410 6800
Headmaster: Mr N G Neeson
Age range: 2–11
Fees: Day £4,059–£12,714

THE ROYAL SCHOOL WOLVERHAMPTON
For further details see p. 256
Penn Road, Wolverhampton,
West Midlands WV3 0EG
Tel: +44 (0)1902 341230
Email: info@theroyal.school
Website: www.theroyalschool.co.uk
Age range: 4–19
No. of pupils: 1285
Fees: FB £11,900

The Shrubbery School
Walmley Ash Road, Walmley, Sutton
Coldfield, West Midlands B76 1HY
Tel: 0121 351 1582
Head Teacher: Hilary Atkins
Age range: 3–11
Fees: Day £3,765–£8,808

WEST HOUSE SCHOOL
For further details see p. 258
24 St James's Road, Edgbaston,
Birmingham, West Midlands B15 2NX
Tel: 0121 440 4097
Email: secretary@westhouseprep.com
Website: www.westhouseprep.com
Headmaster: Mr Alistair M J
Lyttle BA(Hons), PGCE, NPQH
Age range: B1–11 G1–4
No. of pupils: 350
Fees: Day £1,466–£3,908

WOLVERHAMPTON GRAMMAR SCHOOL
For further details see p. 260
Compton Road, Wolverhampton,
West Midlands WV3 9RB
Tel: 01902 421326
Email: wgs@wgs-sch.net
Website: www.wgs.org.uk
Head: Kathy Crewe-Read BSc
Age range: 7–18
No. of pupils: 738 VIth156
Fees: Day £3,457–£4,554

Woodstock Girls' School
11-15 Woodstock Road, Moseley,
Birmingham, West Midlands B13 9BB
Tel: 0121 4496690
Headteacher: Mrs
Na'zihah Ahmed-Atif
Age range: G11–16
No. of pupils: 123

Worcestershire

Abberley Hall
Abberley Hall, Worcester,
Worcestershire WR6 6DD
Tel: 01299 896275
Headmaster: Mr Will Lockett
Age range: 2–13
Fees: Day £9,120–£19,410 FB £24,375
⊕ £ ✎

Bowbrook House School
Peopleton, Pershore,
Worcestershire WR10 2EE
Tel: 01905 841242
Headteacher: Mr C D Allen BSc(Hons)
Age range: 3–16
Fees: Day £5,775–£11,388
£ ✎

Bromsgrove Preparatory School
Old Station Road, Bromsgrove,
Worcestershire B60 2BU
Tel: 01527 579600
Headmistress: Jacqui Deval-Reed
Age range: 7–13
Fees: Day £11,640–£15,105 WB
£17,685–£21,390 FB £24,240–£29,895
⊕ £ ✎

**Bromsgrove Pre-preparatory
& Nursery School**
Avoncroft House, Hanbury Road,
Bromsgrove, Worcestershire B60 4JS
Tel: 01527 873007
Headmistress: Jacqui Deval-Reed
Age range: 2–7
Fees: Day £5,625–£8,790

Bromsgrove School
Worcester Road, Bromsgrove,
Worcestershire B61 7DU
Tel: +44 (0)1527 579679
Headmaster: Peter Clague
Age range: 13–18
No. of pupils: 1300 VIth374
Fees: Day £16,655 WB
£24,720 FB £37,290
🌐 Ⓐ ⊕ £ Ⓘ🅑 ✎ 16+ 🌐

Cambian New Elizabethan School
Quarry Bank, Hartlebury,
Kidderminster, Worcestershire DY11 7TE
Tel: 0800 138 1184
Headteacher: Craig Moreton
BA (Hons), PGCE, NPQH
Age range: 7–19
No. of pupils: 45
Fees: Day £3,000–£7,500
£ ✎

Dodderhill Independent Girls
Crutch Lane, Droitwich,
Worcestershire WR9 0BE
Tel: 01905 778290
Headmistress: Mrs C Mawston
Age range: G4–16
No. of pupils: 190
Fees: Day £6,870–£11,700
⊕ £ ✎

Heathfield Knoll School
Wolverley Road, Wolverley, Nr.
Kidderminster, Worcestershire DY10 3QE
Tel: 01562 850204
Head of School: Mr. L. G. Collins
B.Sc.(Hons), M.A.,P.G.C.E.
Age range: 3 months–16 years
No. of pupils: 251
Fees: Day £7,800–£12,465
£ ✎

King's College Saint Michaels
Oldwood Road, Tenbury Wells,
Worcestershire WR15 8PH
Tel: +44 (0)1584 811300
Principal: Nicola Walker
BSc, MEd, MBA,NPQH
Age range: 13–18 (academic
programmes)
No. of pupils: 109
Fees: FB £27,600
🌐 Ⓐ ⊕ 16+

King's Hawford
Hawford Lock Lane, Claines,
Worcester, Worcestershire WR3 7SE
Tel: 01905 451292
Headmaster: Mr J Turner
Age range: 2–11
No. of pupils: 330
Fees: Day £7,344–£13,221
£ ✎

King's St Alban's School
Mill Street, Worcester,
Worcestershire WR1 2NJ
Tel: 01905 354906
Headmaster: Mr R Chapman
Age range: 4–11
No. of pupils: 216
Fees: Day £7,008–£12,678
£

King's Worcester
5 College Green, Worcester,
Worcestershire WR1 2LL
Tel: 01905 721700
Headmaster: Mr Matthew
Armstrong MA
Age range: 11–18
No. of pupils: 935 VIth270
Fees: Day £13,989
Ⓐ £ 16+

Madinatul Uloom Islamic College
Butts Lane, Stone, Kidderminster,
Worcestershire DY10 4BH
Tel: 01562 66894
The Head: Head
Age range: B11–24
No. of pupils: 200
⚥ Ⓐ ⊕ 16+

Madresfield Early Years Centre
Hayswood Farm, Madresfield,
Malvern, Worcestershire WR13 5AA
Tel: 01684 574378
Head: Mrs A Bennett M.B.E.
Age range: 1–5
No. of pupils: 216
Fees: Day £5,800–£6,500
£ ✎

Malvern College
College Road, Malvern,
Worcestershire WR14 3DF
Tel: 01684 581500
Headmaster: Antony
Clark MA (Cantab)
Age range: 13–18
No. of pupils: 650
Fees: Day £8,485 FB £12,709–£13,153
🌐 Ⓐ ⊕ £ Ⓘ🅑 ✎ 16+

MALVERN ST JAMES
For further details see p. 248
15 Avenue Road, Great Malvern,
Worcestershire WR14 3BA
Tel: 01684 892288
Email:
admissions@malvernstjames.co.uk
Website: www.malvernstjames.co.uk
Headteacher: Mrs Olivera
Raraty BA PGCE
Age range: G4–18
No. of pupils: 400
Fees: Day £8,445–£19,380 WB
£19,725–£33,285 FB £21,915–£36,720
⚥ 🌐 Ⓐ ⊕ £ ✎ 16+

RGS Springfield
Springfield, Britannia Square,
Worcester, Worcestershire WR1 3DL
Tel: 01905 24999
Headmistress: Mrs Laura Brown
Age range: 2–11
No. of pupils: 140
Fees: Day £8,160–£12,546
£

RGS The Grange
Grange Lane, Claines, Worcester,
Worcestershire WR3 7RR
Tel: 01905 451205
Headmaster: Mr Gareth Hughes
Age range: 2–11
No. of pupils: 350
Fees: Day £8,160–£12,546
✎

River School
Oakfield House, Droitwich Road,
Worcester, Worcestershire WR3 7ST
Tel: 01905 457047
Principal: Mr Adrian Parsonage
Age range: 2–16
Fees: Day £6,600

The Downs Malvern
Colwall, Malvern,
Worcestershire WR13 6EY
Tel: 01684 544100
Headmaster: Mr Alastair Cook
Age range: 3–13
Fees: Day £7,107–£17,076 WB
£12,882–£19,890 FB £14,640–£22,602
⊕ £ ✎

The Elms
Colwall, Malvern,
Worcestershire WR13 6EF
Tel: 01684 540344
Headmaster: Mr Chris Hattam
Age range: 3–13
No. of pupils: 200
Fees: Day £8,085–£19,500
FB £24,000–£24,480
⊕ £ ✎

**The Royal Grammar
School Worcester**
Upper Tything, Worcester,
Worcestershire WR1 1HP
Tel: 01905 613391
Headmaster: Mr John Pitt
Age range: 11–18
No. of pupils: 764
Fees: Day £13,080
Ⓐ £ ✎ 16+

Winterfold House
Chaddesley Corbett, Kidderminster,
Worcestershire DY10 4PW
Tel: 01562 777234
Headmistress: Mrs Denise Toms
Age range: 6 weeks–13 years
£ ✎

Yorkshire & Humberside

KEY TO SYMBOLS

- ⓣ *Boys' school*
- ⓐ *Girls' school*
- 🌐 *International school*
- 16° *Tutorial or sixth form college*
- Ⓐ *A levels*
- ⚐ *Boarding accommodation*
- £ *Bursaries*
- ⒾⒷ *International Baccalaureate*
- ✎ *Learning support*
- 16° *Entrance at 16+*
- ❀ *Vocational qualifications*
- ⒜ⓟⓢ *Independent Association of Preparatory Schools*
- ⒣ⓜⓒ *The Headmasters' & Headmistresses' Conference*
- ⒤ⓢⓐ *Independent Schools Association*
- ⒢ⓢⓐ *Girls' School Association*
- ⒝ⓢⓐ *Boarding Schools' Association*
- Ⓢ *Society of Heads*

Unless otherwise indicated, all schools are coeducational day schools. Single-sex and boarding schools will be indicated by the relevant icon.

East Riding of Yorkshire

**Focus School –
Cottingham Campus**
Old Victorian School, Hallgate,
Cottingham, East Riding of
Yorkshire HU16 4DD
Tel: 01482 840722
Headteacher: Mrs Kimberley Hutton
Age range: 11–16
No. of pupils: 40

Froebel House School
5 Marlborough Avenue, Kingston upon
Hull, East Riding of Yorkshire HU5 3JP
Tel: 01482 342272
Headmaster: Mr A Roberts
M.Ed BA Hons PGCE
Age range: 4–11
No. of pupils: 131
Fees: Day £4,398–£4,623

Hessle Mount School
Jenny Brough Lane, Hessle, East
Riding of Yorkshire HU13 0JZ
Tel: 01482 643371
Headmistress: Miss Sarah Cutting
Age range: 3–8
No. of pupils: 155
Fees: Day £6,000–£6,300

Hull Collegiate School
Tranby Croft, Anlaby, Kingston upon
Hull, East Riding of Yorkshire HU10 7EH
Tel: 01482 657016
Headteacher: Mrs Alex Wilson
Age range: 3–18
No. of pupils: 650
Fees: Day £5,013–£11,796

Hymers College
Hymers Avenue, Kingston upon Hull,
East Riding of Yorkshire HU3 1LW
Tel: 01482 343555
Headmaster: Mr D Elstone
Age range: 8–18
No. of pupils: 977 VIth215
Fees: Day £9,459–£11,358

North Yorkshire

Ampleforth College
York, North Yorkshire YO62 4ER
Tel: 01439 766000
Acting Head: Miss Deirdre Rowe
Age range: 11–18
No. of pupils: VIth255
Fees: Day £24,636 FB £35,424

Ashville College
Green Lane, Harrogate,
North Yorkshire HG2 9JP
Tel: 01423 566358
Headmaster: Mr Richard Marshall
Age range: 3–18
No. of pupils: 870
Fees: Day £8,430–£14,640
FB £18,390–£27,780

Aysgarth School
Newton le Willows, Bedale,
North Yorkshire DL8 1TF
Tel: 01677 450240
No. of pupils: 200
Fees: Day £2,700–£6,630 WB
£995–£1,325 FB £8,630

Belmont Grosvenor School
Swarcliffe Hall, Birstwith, Harrogate,
North Yorkshire HG3 2JG
Tel: 01423 771029
Headteacher: Mrs Jane Merriman
Age range: 3–11

Bootham Junior School
Rawcliffe Lane, York, North
Yorkshire YO30 6NP
Tel: 01904 655021
Head: Mrs Helen Todd
Age range: 3–11
Fees: Day £6,930–£10,365

Bootham School
York, North Yorkshire YO30 7BU
Tel: 01904 623261
Headmaster: Chris Jeffery BA, FRSA
Age range: 11–18
No. of pupils: 480 VIth172
Fees: Day £16,200–£17,865 WB
£18,885–£27,765 FB £18,885–£30,465

Brackenfield School
128 Duchy Road, Harrogate,
North Yorkshire HG1 2HE
Tel: 01423 508558
Headteacher: Ms Patricia Sowa
Age range: 2–11
No. of pupils: 179
Fees: Day £8,235–£8,850

Chapter House Preparatory School
Thorpe Underwood Hall, Ouseburn,
York, North Yorkshire YO26 9SZ
Tel: 01423 333330
Head Teacher: Mrs Karen Kilkenny BSc
Age range: 3–10
No. of pupils: 122
Fees: Day £4,020–£11,100
FB £30,960–£33,270

Clifton School and Nursery
York, North Yorkshire YO30 6AB
Tel: 01904 527361
Head: Philip Hardy BA (Hons) PGCE
Age range: 3–8
No. of pupils: 199
Fees: Day £7,980–£9,240

Cundall Manor School
Helperby, York, North
Yorkshire YO61 2RW
Tel: 01423 360200
Joint Heads: Mrs Amanda Kirby
BA (Hons) PGCE, NPQH & Mr John
Sample BSc (Hons) PGCE
Age range: 2–16
No. of pupils: 350
Fees: Day £9,738–£15,612
WB £20,313–£20,529

Fyling Hall School
Robin Hood's Bay, Whitby,
North Yorkshire YO22 4QD
Tel: 01947 880353
Headmaster: Mr. Steven Allen
Age range: 4–18
No. of pupils: VIth54
Fees: Day £6,684–£9,177 WB
£9,207–£11,778 FB £16,230–£19,995

Giggleswick Junior School
Mill Lane, Giggleswick, Settle,
North Yorkshire BD24 0DG
Tel: 01729 893100
Headmaster: Mr. James Mundell
Age range: 3–11 (boarding from 9)
No. of pupils: 75
Fees: Day £7,965–£12,765 FB £21,240

Giggleswick School
Giggleswick, Settle, North
Yorkshire BD24 0DE
Tel: 01729 893000
Head: Mr Mark Turnbull
Age range: 11–18
No. of pupils: 320 VIth145
Fees: Day £15,585–£20,985
FB £23,550–£33,750

Harrogate Ladies' College
Clarence Drive, Harrogate,
North Yorkshire HG1 2QG
Tel: 01423 504543
Principal: Mrs Sylvia Brett
Age range: G11–18
No. of pupils: 300
Fees: Day £16,035 FB £29,115–£36,510

Highfield Prep School
Clarence Drive, Harrogate,
North Yorkshire HG1 2QG
Tel: 01423 504 543
Head: James Savile
Age range: 4–11
No. of pupils: 216
Fees: Day £9,420–£10,740 FB £23,820

Pocklington Prep School
West Green, Pocklington, York,
North Yorkshire YO42 2NH
Tel: 01759 321228
Headmaster: Mr I D Wright
BSc(Hons), PGCE, NPQH
Age range: 3–11
No. of pupils: 225
Fees: Day £7,812–£12,255 WB
£18,366–£21,393 FB £20,202–£23,046
🏫 £ 🖉

POCKLINGTON SCHOOL
For further details see p. 264
West Green, Pocklington, York,
North Yorkshire YO42 2NJ
Tel: 01759 321200
Email:
enquiry@pocklingtonschool.com
Website:
www.pocklingtonschool.com
Headmaster: Mr Mark
Ronan MA (Cantab)
Age range: 3–18
No. of pupils: 750 VIth162
Fees: Day £14,619 WB
£26,205 FB £28,491

🏇 Ⓐ 🏫 £ 🖉 16⁺

**QUEEN ETHELBURGA'S
COLLEGIATE FOUNDATION**
For further details see p. 266
Thorpe Underwood Hall, Ouseburn,
York, North Yorkshire YO26 9SS
Tel: 01423 33 33 30
Email: info@qe.org
Website: www.qe.org
Principal: Steven Jandrell BA
Age range: 3–19
No. of pupils: 1550 VIth595

🏇 Ⓐ 🏫 £ 🖉 16⁺ 🏐

Queen Margaret's School
Escrick Park, York, North
Yorkshire YO19 6EU
Tel: 01904 727600
Head of School: Mrs Jessica Miles
Age range: G11–18
No. of pupils: 302 VIth120
Fees: Day £21,270 FB £30,400
🏃 🏇 Ⓐ 🏫 £ 🖉 16⁺

Queen Mary's School
Baldersby Park, Topcliffe, Thirsk,
North Yorkshire YO7 3BZ
Tel: 01845 575000
Head: Carole Cameron
Age range: B3–8 G3–16
No. of pupils: 235
Fees: Day £8,265–£18,420
FB £20,475–£24,165
🏃 🏇 🏫 £ 🖉

Scarborough College
Filey Road, Scarborough,
North Yorkshire YO11 3BA
Tel: +44 (0)1723 360620
Headmaster: Mr Charles Ellison
Age range: 3–18
No. of pupils: 418 VIth84
Fees: Day £7,488–£14,694 WB
£17,217–£19,440 FB £22,041–£28,458
🏇 🏫 £ IB 🖉 16⁺

St Martins Ampleforth
Gilling Castle, Gilling East, York,
North Yorkshire YO62 4HP
Tel: 01439 766600
Headmaster: Dr D Moses
Age range: 11–13 years
No. of pupils: 155
Fees: Day £16,401 FB £25,251
🏫 £ 🖉

St Olave's School
Clifton, York, North Yorkshire YO30 6AB
Tel: 01904 527416
The Master: Mr A Falconer
Age range: 8–13
No. of pupils: 355
Fees: Day £12,345–£14,955
FB £23,160–£25,560
🏫 £ 🖉

St Peter's School
Clifton, York, North Yorkshire YO30 6AB
Tel: 01904 527300
Head Master: Mr L Winkley
MA(Oxon), MEd(OU)
Age range: 13–18
No. of pupils: 375 VIth231
Fees: Day £18,075 FB £30,030
🏇 Ⓐ 🏫 £ 🖉 16⁺

Terrington Hall
Terrington, York, North
Yorkshire YO60 6PR
Tel: 01653 648227
Headmaster: Mr. Stephen
Mulryne B.Ed (Hons) Liverpool
Age range: 3–13
No. of pupils: 150
🏫 £ 🖉

The Minster School
Deangate, York, North
Yorkshire YO1 7JA
Tel: 0844 939 0000
Headmaster: Mr A Donaldson
Age range: 3–13
Fees: Day £3,855–£10,398
🖉

The Mount Junior School
Dalton Terrace, York, North
Yorkshire YO24 4DD
Tel: 01904 667513
Head: Mr Martyn Andrews
BSc(Hons), PGCE
Age range: 3–11
Fees: Day £1,710–£2,280
🖉

The Mount School York
Dalton Terrace, York, North
Yorkshire YO24 4DD
Tel: 01904 667500
Principal: Miss Adrienne Richmond
BSc (Hons), PGCE, MA, NPQH
Age range: B2–11 G2–18
No. of pupils: 260 VIth47
Fees: Day £5,850–£16,950 WB
£18,060–£26,253 FB £20,391–£29,691
🏃 🏇 Ⓐ 🏫 £ 🖉 16⁺

The Read School
Drax, Selby, North Yorkshire YO8 8NL
Tel: 01757 618248
Acting Head: M A Voisey
Age range: 3–18
No. of pupils: VIth36
Fees: Day £8,457–£11,970 WB
£21,279–£24,429 FB £22,743–£26,019
🏇 Ⓐ 🏫 £ 🖉 16⁺

Wharfedale Montessori School
Bolton Abbey, Skipton, North
Yorkshire BD23 6AN
Tel: 01756 710452
Headmistress/Principal: Mrs Jane Lord
Age range: 2–12
Fees: Day £7,350
🖉

York Steiner School
Danesmead, Fulford Cross, York,
North Yorkshire YO10 4PB
Tel: 01904 654983
Administrator: Maurice Dobie
Age range: 3–14
No. of pupils: 197
Fees: Day £6,750
🖉

North-East Lincolnshire

Montessori School
Station Road, Stallingborough,
North-East Lincolnshire DN41 8AJ
Tel: 01472 886000
Headteacher: Ms Theresa Ellerby
Age range: 4–11
No. of pupils: 21

St James' School
22 Bargate, Grimsby, North-
East Lincolnshire DN34 4SY
Tel: 01472 503260
Headmaster: Dr J Price
Age range: 2–18
No. of pupils: 238 VIth25
🏇 Ⓐ 🏫 £ 🖉 16⁺

St Martin's Preparatory School
63 Bargate, Grimsby, North-
East Lincolnshire DN34 5AA
Tel: 01472 878907
Headmaster: Mr S Thompson BEd
Age range: 2–11
Fees: Day £5,580–£6,780
🖉

South Yorkshire

Al-Mahad-Al-Islam School
1 Industry Road, Sheffield,
South Yorkshire S9 5FP
Tel: 0114 242 3138
Headteacher: Mrs Juwairiah Khan
Age range: G11–17
No. of pupils: 70

Bethany School
Finlay Street, Sheffield,
South Yorkshire S3 7PS
Tel: 0114 272 6994
Headteacher: Mrs Judith Baxter
Age range: 4–16
No. of pupils: 76

Birkdale School
Oakholme Road, Sheffield,
South Yorkshire S10 3DH
Tel: 0114 2668409
Acting Head: Mr Nicholas Pietrek
Age range: B4–18 G16–18
No. of pupils: VIth200
Fees: Day £8,445–£12,630

Hill House School
6th Avenue, Auckley, Doncaster,
South Yorkshire DN9 3GG
Tel: +44 (0)1302 776300
Principal: David Holland
Age range: 3–18
Fees: Day £8,700–£13,200

**Mylnhurst Preparatory
School & Nursery**
Button Hill, Woodholm Road, Ecclesall,
Sheffield, South Yorkshire S11 9HJ
Tel: 0114 2361411
Headmaster: Christopher
Emmott BSc(Hons), PGCE
Age range: 3–11
No. of pupils: 185
Fees: Day £9,333

Sheffield High School GDST
10 Rutland Park, Sheffield,
South Yorkshire S10 2PE
Tel: 0114 266 0324
Headmistress: Nina Gunson
Age range: G4–18
No. of pupils: 1020
Fees: Day £9,216–£12,975

Sycamore Hall Preparatory School
1 Hall Flat Lane, Balby, Doncaster,
South Yorkshire DN4 8PT
Tel: 01302 856800
Headmistress: Miss J Spencer
Age range: 3–11
Fees: Day £4,890

Westbourne School
Westbourne Road, Sheffield,
South Yorkshire S10 2QT
Tel: 0114 2660374
Headmaster: Mr John B Hicks MEd
Age range: 3–16
No. of pupils: 338
Fees: Day £8,925–£12,750

West Yorkshire

Ackworth School
Pontefract Road, Ackworth, nr.
Pontefract, West Yorkshire WF7 7LT
Tel: 01977 611401
Head: Mr. Anton Maree
BA Rhodes (HDE)
Age range: 3–18
No. of pupils: 490
Fees: Day £8,145–£13,518 FB £29,151

Al Mu'min Primary School
Clifton St, Bradford, West
Yorkshire BD8 7DA
Tel: 01274 488593
Headteacher: Mr M M Azam
Age range: 4–11
No. of pupils: 102

Al-Furqan Preparatory School
Drill Hall House, Bath Street,
Dewsbury, West Yorkshire WF13 2JR
Tel: 01924 453 661
Headteacher: Mr Bilal Aswat
Age range: 3–11
No. of pupils: 139

Bradford Christian School
Livingstone Road, Bolton Woods,
Bradford, West Yorkshire BD2 1BT
Tel: 01274 532649
Headmaster: P J Moon BEd(Hons)
Age range: 4–16
Fees: Day £2,460–£4,440

Bradford Grammar School
Keighley Road, Bradford,
West Yorkshire BD9 4JP
Tel: 01274 542492
Headmaster: Dr Simon Hinchliffe
Age range: 6–18
No. of pupils: VIth266

Bronte House School
Apperley Bridge, Bradford,
West Yorkshire BD10 0NR
Tel: 0113 2502811
Headmaster: Simon W Dunn
Age range: 2–11
No. of pupils: 340
Fees: Day £9,000–£13,575 WB
£26,160–£26,625 FB £27,900–£28,020

Crystal Gardens
38-40 Greaves Street, Bradford,
West Yorkshire BD5 7PE
Tel: 01274 575400
Headteacher: Rashta Bibi
Age range: 4–11
No. of pupils: 20

Dale House Independent School
Ruby Street, Carlinghow, Batley,
West Yorkshire WF17 8HL
Tel: 01924 422215
Headmistress: Mrs S M G
Fletcher BA, CertEd
Age range: 2–11
No. of pupils: 100

Darul Uloom Dawatul Imaan
Harry Street, Off Wakefield Road,
Bradford, West Yorkshire BD4 9PH
Tel: 01274 402233
Principal: Mr Mohamed Bilal Lorgat
Age range: B11–13
No. of pupils: 112

Eternal Light Secondary School
Christopher Street, Off Little Horton
Lane, Bradford, West Yorkshire BD5 9DH
Tel: 01274 501597
Headteacher: Mr Yusuf Collector
Age range: B11–15
No. of pupils: 91

Focus School – York Campus
Bishopthorpe Road, York,
West Yorkshire YO23 2QA
Tel: 01904 663 300
Headteacher: Mr Paul Easton
Age range: 7–18
No. of pupils: 44

Fulneck School
Fulneck, Pudsey, Leeds,
West Yorkshire LS28 8DS
Tel: 0113 257 0235
Principal: Mr Paul Taylor
Age range: 3–18
No. of pupils: 440 VIth67
Fees: Day £8,025–£13,125 WB
£18,450–£23,025 FB £20,040–£25,455

Gateways School
Harewood, Leeds, West
Yorkshire LS17 9LE
Tel: 0113 2886345
Headmistress: Dr Tracy Johnson
Age range: B2–11 G2–18
No. of pupils: 394 VIth48
Fees: Day £8,445–£13,614

Ghyll Royd School and Pre-School
Greystone Manor, Ilkley Road, Burley in
Wharfedale, West Yorkshire LS29 7HW
Tel: 01943 865575
Headteacher: Mr David
Martin BA MA PGCE
Age range: 2–11
No. of pupils: 110
Fees: Day £2,900–£2,990

**Hipperholme Grammar
Junior School**
45 Wakefield Road, Lightcliffe,
Halifax, West Yorkshire HX3 8AQ
Tel: 01422 201330
Headteacher: Mrs S Weller
Age range: 3–11
No. of pupils: 131
Fees: Day £6,600–£8,799

Hipperholme Grammar School
Bramley Lane, Hipperholme,
Halifax, West Yorkshire HX3 8JE
Tel: 01422 202256
Head: Mrs Jackie Griffiths
Age range: 3–18
No. of pupils: VIth30
Fees: Day £8,799–£10,995
(A)(£)(✐)(16)

Huddersfield Grammar School
Royds Mount, Luck Lane, Marsh,
Huddersfield, West Yorkshire HD1 4QX
Tel: 01484 424549
Headmaster: Mr Mike Seaton
Age range: 3–16
No. of pupils: 510
Fees: Day £8,598–£10,602
(£)

Institute of Islamic Education
South Street, Savile Town, Dewsbury,
West Yorkshire WF12 9NG
Tel: 01924 485712/01924 455762
Principal: Mr Mohamed Aswat
Age range: B11–25
No. of pupils: 184
(†)(⌂)

Islamia Girls High School
2 Thornton Lodge Road,
Thornton Lodge, Huddersfield,
West Yorkshire HD1 3JQ
Tel: 01484 518 817
Head: Mrs Samira El-Turabi
Age range: G11–16
Fees: Day £1,300
(†)(✐)

Islamic Tarbiyah Preparatory School
Ambler Street, Bradford,
West Yorkshire BD8 8AW
Tel: 01274 490462
Headteacher: Mr S A Nawaz
Age range: 5–10
No. of pupils: 123

Jaamiatul Imaam Muhammad Zakaria School
Thornton View Road, Clayton,
Bradford, West Yorkshire BD14 6JX
Tel: 01274 882007
Headteacher: Mrs Z Hajee
Age range: G11–16
No. of pupils: 416
(†)

Lady Lane Park School & Nursery
Lady Lane, Bingley, West
Yorkshire BD16 4AP
Tel: 01274 551168
Headmaster: Mr Nigel Saunders
Age range: 2–11
No. of pupils: 150
Fees: Day £8,016
(✐)

Leeds Menorah School
393 Street Lane, Leeds, West
Yorkshire LS17 6HQ
Tel: 0113 268 3390
Headteacher: Rabbi J Refson
Age range: 5–16
No. of pupils: 55

M A Institute
Lumb Lane, Bradford, West
Yorkshire BD8 7RZ
Tel: 01274 395454
Age range: B11–16
No. of pupils: 68
(†)

Madni Muslim Girls High School
Thornie Bank, Off Scarborough
St, Savile Town, Dewsbury,
West Yorkshire WF12 9AX
Tel: 01924 520720
Headmistress: Mrs S A Mirza
Age range: G3–18
No. of pupils: 250
(†)(A)(✿)

Mill Cottage Montessori School
Wakefield Road, Brighouse,
West Yorkshire HD6 4HA
Tel: 01484 400500
Principal: Ailsa Nevile
Age range: 0–11

Moorfield School
Wharfedale Lodge, 11 Ben Rhydding
Road, Ilkley, West Yorkshire LS29 8RL
Tel: 01943 607285
Headmistress: Mrs Jessica Crossley
Age range: 2–11
Fees: Day £9,600
(£)

Moorlands School
Foxhill, Weetwood Lane, Leeds,
West Yorkshire LS16 5PF
Tel: 0113 2785286
Headteacher: Miss J Atkinson
Age range: 2–11
No. of pupils: 149
Fees: Day £8,985–£10,566

Mount School
3 Binham Road, Edgerton,
Huddersfield, West Yorkshire HD2 2AP
Tel: 01484 426432
Headteacher: Janet Brook
Age range: 3–11
Fees: Day £7,095
(✐)

Netherleigh & Rossefield School
Parsons Road, Heaton, Bradford,
West Yorkshire BD9 4AY
Tel: 01274 543162
Headteacher: Miss A Leary
Age range: 2–11
No. of pupils: 141
Fees: Day £6,735
(£)(✐)

New Horizon Community School
Newton Hill House, Newton Hill Road,
Leeds, West Yorkshire LS7 4JE
Tel: 0113 262 4001
Acting Head: Qudisia Butt
Age range: G11–16
No. of pupils: 87
Fees: Day £1,800
(†)(✐)

Olive Secondary School
Byron Street, Bradford, West
Yorkshire BD3 0AD
Tel: +44+ (0)1274 725005 /
+44 (0)1274 725013
Headteacher: Mr Amjad Mohammed
Age range: 11–18
No. of pupils: 115
Fees: Day £2,075

Paradise Primary School
1 Bretton Street, Dewsbury,
West Yorkshire WF12 9BB
Tel: 01924 439803
Headteacher: Mrs Hafsa Patel
Age range: 2–11
No. of pupils: 217

Queen Elizabeth Grammar School (Junior School)
158 Northgate, Wakefield,
West Yorkshire WF1 3QY
Tel: 01924 373821
Head: Mrs L A Gray
Age range: B4–11
No. of pupils: 261
Fees: Day £9,153–£9,987
(†)(£)

Queen Elizabeth Grammar School (Senior School)
154 Northgate, Wakefield,
West Yorkshire WF1 3QY
Tel: 01924 373943
Headmaster: David Craig
Age range: B11–18
No. of pupils: 677
Fees: Day £12,636
(†)(A)(£)(16)

Queenswood School
Queen Street, Morley, Leeds,
West Yorkshire LS27 9EB
Tel: 0113 2534033
Headteacher: Mrs J A Tanner
MMus, BA, FTCL, ARCO
Age range: 4–11
Fees: Day £6,000–£6,447

Rastrick Independent School
Ogden Lane, Rastrick, Brighouse,
West Yorkshire HD6 3HF
Tel: 01484 400344
Headmistress: Mrs S A Vaughey
Age range: 0–16
No. of pupils: 200
Fees: Day £7,680–£9,470
(A)(£)(✐)(16)(✿)

Richmond House School
170 Otley Road, Leeds, West
Yorkshire LS16 5LG
Tel: 0113 2752670
Headteacher: Mrs Helen Stiles
Age range: 3–11
No. of pupils: 219
Fees: Day £5,850–£9,150
(£)(✐)

Rishworth School
Rishworth, Halifax, West
Yorkshire HX6 4QA
Tel: 01422 822217
Headmaster: Mr. A S Gloag
Age range: 3–18
No. of pupils: 600 VIth90
Fees: Day £6,465–£12,660 WB
£24,975–£27,300 FB £27,510–£29,985
(✿)(A)(⌂)(£)(✐)(16)

Silcoates School
Wrenthorpe, Wakefield,
West Yorkshire WF2 0PD
Tel: 01924 291614
Headmaster: Philip Rowe
Age range: 4–18
No. of pupils: 768
Fees: Day £7,530–£13,785
(A)(£)(16)

The Branch Christian School
Dewsbury Revival Centre,
West Park Street, Dewsbury,
West Yorkshire WF13 4LA
Tel: +44 (0)1924 452511
Principal: Pastor Bob Ward
Age range: 3–16
No. of pupils: 26
(✐)

THE FROEBELIAN SCHOOL
For further details see p. 268
Clarence Road, Horsforth,
Leeds, West Yorkshire LS18 4LB
Tel: 0113 2583047
Email: office@froebelian.co.uk
Website: www.froebelian.com
Head Teacher: Mrs Catherine
Dodds BEd (Hons), PGCE
Age range: 3–11
No. of pupils: 189
Fees: Day £5,220–£7,785

(£)(✐)

The Gleddings School
Birdcage Lane, Savile Park,
Halifax, West Yorkshire HX3 0JB
Tel: 01422 354605
School Director: Mrs Jill Wilson CBE
Age range: 3–11
No. of pupils: 191
Fees: Day £3,555–£5,910

(✐)

The Grammar School at Leeds
Alwoodley Gates, Harrogate Road,
Leeds, West Yorkshire LS17 8GS
Tel: 0113 2291552
Principal: Mrs Sue Woodroofe
Age range: 3–18
No. of pupils: 2120 VIth418
Fees: Day £9,441–£13,788

(A)(£)(✐)(16)

**Wakefield Girls' High
School (Junior School)**
2 St John's Square, Wakefield,
West Yorkshire WF1 2QX
Tel: 01924 374577
Headmistress: Mrs Rachel Edwards BEd
Age range: G4–11
No. of pupils: 493
Fees: Day £9,153–£9,987

(♀)(£)(✐)

**Wakefield Girls' High
School (Senior School)**
Wentworth Street, Wakefield,
West Yorkshire WF1 2QS
Tel: 01924 372490
Headmistress: Ms Heidi-
Jayne Boyes BSc
Age range: G11–18
No. of pupils: 715
Fees: Day £12,636

(♀)(A)(£)(✐)(16)

Wakefield Independent School
The Nostell Centre, Doncaster
Road, Nostell, Wakefield,
West Yorkshire WF4 1QG
Tel: 01924 865757
Headmistress: Mrs K E Caryl
Age range: 2½–16
No. of pupils: 190
Fees: Day £5,100–£7,050

(£)(✐)

**West Cliffe Montessori
School & Nursery**
33, Barlow Road, access
Belgrave Road, Keighley,
West Yorkshire BD21 2TA
Tel: 01535 609797
Principal: Mrs T Bisby
Age range: 0–8
No. of pupils: 42

(✐)

**Westville House
Preparatory School**
Carter's Lane, Middleton, Ilkley,
West Yorkshire LS29 0DQ
Tel: 01943 608053
Headteacher: Mrs Nikki
Hammond BA(Hons) PGCE
Age range: 3–11
Fees: Day £5,619–£9,735

(✐)

WOODHOUSE GROVE SCHOOL
For further details see p. 270
Apperley Bridge, Bradford,
West Yorkshire BD10 0NR
Tel: 0113 250 2477
Email:
amos.jl@woodhousegrove.co.uk
Website:
www.woodhousegrove.co.uk
Headmaster: Mr James
Lockwood MA
Age range: 2–18
No. of pupils: 1080
Fees: Day £9,000–£13,575
FB £27,900–£28,020

(✿)(A)(♂)(£)(✐)(16)(✿)

Northern Ireland

KEY TO SYMBOLS

- ⚲ *Boys' school*
- ⚲ *Girls' school*
- 🌐 *International school*
- 16 *Tutorial or sixth form college*
- Ⓐ *A levels*
- ⚐ *Boarding accommodation*
- £ *Bursaries*
- IB *International Baccalaureate*
- ✐ *Learning support*
- 16 *Entrance at 16+*
- ⚒ *Vocational qualifications*
- IAPS *Independent Association of Preparatory Schools*
- HMC *The Headmasters' & Headmistresses' Conference*
- ISA *Independent Schools Association*
- GSA *Girls' School Association*
- BSA *Boarding Schools' Association*
- Ⓢ *Society of Heads*

Unless otherwise indicated, all schools are coeducational day schools.
Single-sex and boarding schools will be indicated by the relevant icon.

County Antrim

Belfast Royal Academy
7 Cliftonville Road, Belfast,
County Antrim BT14 6JL
Tel: 028 9074 0423
Principal: Mrs Hilary Woods
Age range: 11–18
No. of pupils: VIth382
Fees: Day £140
Ⓐ 16+

Campbell College
Belfast, County Antrim BT4 2ND
Tel: 028 9076 3076
Headmaster: Mr Robert Robinson
Age range: B11–18
No. of pupils: 896 VIth200
Fees: Day £2,708–£8,363
FB £14,095–£19,750
♦ 🌐 Ⓐ 🏫 £ ✎ 16+ 🐾

Campbell College Junior School
Belmont Road, Belfast,
County Antrim BT4 2ND
Tel: 028 9076 3076
Head: Miss Andrea Brown
Age range: B3–11 G3–4
Fees: Day £4,145–£4,449
♦ ✎

Hunterhouse College
Finaghy, Belfast, County Antrim BT10 0LE
Tel: 028 9061 2293
Principal: Mr A Gibson MA, DipEd, PQH
Age range: G11–18
No. of pupils: 710 VIth180
Fees: Day £320
♦ Ⓐ ✎ 16+

Inchmarlo
Cranmore Park, Belfast,
County Antrim BT9 6JR
Tel: 028 9038 1454
♦

Methodist College
1 Malone Road, Belfast,
County Antrim BT9 6BY
Tel: 028 9020 5205
Principal: Mr J Scott W Naismith
Age range: 4–19
No. of pupils: 2307 VIth548
🌐 Ⓐ ✎ 16+

Royal Belfast Academical Institution
College Square East, Belfast,
County Antrim BT1 6DL
Tel: 028 9024 0461
Principal: Miss J A Williamson
MA(Oxon), NPQH
Age range: B4–18
No. of pupils: 1290 VIth275
Fees: Day £940–£4,140
♦ Ⓐ 🏫 ✎ 16+

St Mary's Christian Brothers Grammar School
Glen Road, Belfast, County
Antrim BT11 8NR
Tel: 028 9029 4000
Headmaster: Mr. John Martin
Age range: B12–18
No. of pupils: 112
♦ Ⓐ 16+

Victoria College Belfast
Cranmore Park, Belfast,
County Antrim BT9 6JA
Tel: 028 9066 1506
Principal: Ms Patricia Slevin
Age range: G2–18
No. of pupils: 1070 VIth224
Fees: Day £4,825–£7,550
FB £11,100–£18,650
♦ Ⓐ 🏫 ✎ 16+

County Armagh

The Royal School
College Hill, Armagh, County
Armagh BT61 9DH
Tel: 02837 522807
Headmaster: Mr Graham Montgomery
Age range: 11–18
No. of pupils: 654 VIth157
Fees: Day £3,700–£4,415
WB £7,275 FB £10,925
Ⓐ 🏫 16+ 🐾

County Down

Bangor Grammar School
Gransha Road, Bangor,
County Down BT19 7QU
Tel: 028 91 473734
Principal: Mrs E P Huddleson
B.Ed., M.SSc., PQH(NI)
Age range: B3–18
No. of pupils: 900 VIth220
Fees: Day £140–£395
♦ Ⓐ ✎ 16+

Holywood Steiner School
34 Croft Road, Holywood,
County Down BT18 0PR
Tel: 028 9042 8029
**Chairperson of the School
Management Team:** Julie Higgins
Age range: 3–17 years
No. of pupils: 110
Fees: Day £4,008–£4,512
£

Rockport School
Craigavad, Holywood,
County Down BT18 0DD
Tel: 028 9042 8372
Headmaster: Mr George Vance
Age range: 3–18
No. of pupils: 200
Fees: Day £6,540–£15,810 WB
£17,970–£22,770 FB £21,450–£26,160
🌐 Ⓐ 🏫 £ ✎

County Tyrone

The Royal School Dungannon
2 Ranfurly Road, Dungannon,
County Tyrone BT71 6EG
Tel: 028 8772 2710
Headmaster: Dr David Burnett
Age range: 11–18
No. of pupils: 648 VIth105
Fees: Day £70–£150 WB £7,950
FB £10,650–£19,050
🌐 Ⓐ ✎ 16+

Scotland

KEY TO SYMBOLS

- ⚲ *Boys' school*
- ⚲ *Girls' school*
- 🌐 *International school*
- 16: *Tutorial or sixth form college*
- Ⓐ *A levels*
- 🏫 *Boarding accommodation*
- £ *Bursaries*
- (IB) *International Baccalaureate*
- 🖉 *Learning support*
- 16: *Entrance at 16+*
- 🌐 *Vocational qualifications*
- (IAPS) *Independent Association of Preparatory Schools*
- (HMC) *The Headmasters' & Headmistresses' Conference*
- (ISA) *Independent Schools Association*
- (GSA) *Girls' School Association*
- (BSA) *Boarding Schools' Association*
- Ⓢ *Society of Heads*

Unless otherwise indicated, all schools are coeducational day schools. Single-sex and boarding schools will be indicated by the relevant icon.

Aberdeen

Albyn School
17-23 Queen's Road,
Aberdeen AB15 4PB
Tel: 01224 322408
Headmaster: Ian E Long
AKC, PhD, FRGS, FRSA
Age range: 2–18
No. of pupils: 675 VIth57
Fees: Day £8,637–£13,636
WB £27,811 FB £29,948
£ 🖉 16+

Robert Gordon's College
Schoolhill, Aberdeen AB10 1FE
Tel: 01224 646346
Head of College: Mr Simon Mills
Age range: 4–18
No. of pupils: 1573 VIth350
Fees: Day £8,435–£13,130
£ 🖉 16+

St Margaret's School for Girls
17 Albyn Place, Aberdeen AB10 1RU
Tel: 01224 584466
Headmistress: Miss A Tomlinson
MTheol (Hons), PGCE
Age range: B3–5 years G3–18 years
No. of pupils: 380 VIth34
Fees: Day £7,954–£12,600
♣ £ 🖉 16+

**The International School
of Aberdeen**
Pitfodels House, North Deeside Road,
Pitfodels, Cults, Aberdeen AB15 9PN
Tel: 01224 730300
Head of School: Ms Sarah Bruce
Age range: 3–18
No. of pupils: 409 VIth39
Fees: Day £12,830–£14,100
🌐 £ IB 🖉 16+

Angus

Lathallan School
Brotherton Castle, Johnshaven,
Montrose, Angus DD10 0HN
Tel: 01561 362220
Headmaster: Mr R Toley
No. of pupils: 220
Fees: Day £5,031–£6,067
FB £7,281–£8,317
♣ £ 🖉 16+

Argyll & Bute

LOMOND SCHOOL
For further details see p. 276
10 Stafford Street, Helensburgh,
Argyll & Bute G84 9JX
Tel: +44 (0)1436 672476
Email:
admissions@lomondschool.com
Website: www.lomondschool.com
Principal: Mrs Johanna Urquhart
Age range: 3–18
No. of pupils: 360
Fees: Day £8,640–£11,970 FB £27,750
🌐 ♣ £ 🖉 16+

Borders

St Mary's Prep School
Abbey Park, Melrose, Borders TD6 9LN
Tel: 01896 822517
Headmaster: Mr Liam Harvey
Age range: 2–13
Fees: Day £13,200–£16,050 WB £17,982
♣ £ 🖉

Clackmannanshire

Dollar Academy
Dollar, Clackmannanshire FK14 7DU
Tel: 01259 742511
Rector: Mr David Knapman Mphil
Age range: 5–18
No. of pupils: 1200 VIth142
Fees: Day £9,792–£13,095 WB
£25,335–£28,638 FB £27,000–£30,303
🌐 ♣ £ 🖉 16+

Dundee

High School of Dundee
Euclid Crescent, Dundee DD1 1HU
Tel: 01382 202921
Rector: Dr John Halliday
Age range: 3–18
No. of pupils: 1067 VIth102
Fees: Day £9,159–£12,999
£ 🖉 16+

East Lothian

Belhaven Hill
Dunbar, East Lothian EH42 1NN
Tel: 01368 862785
Headmaster: Mr. Henry Knight
Age range: 8–13
No. of pupils: 122
Fees: Day £11,520–£16,875 FB £23,760
♣ £ 🖉

Loretto Junior School
North Esk Lodge, 1 North High Street,
Musselburgh, East Lothian EH21 6JA
Tel: 0131 653 4570
Headmaster: Mr Andrew Dickenson
Age range: 3–12
No. of pupils: 200
Fees: Day £9,180–£15,900 FB £22,335
♣ £ 🖉

Loretto School
Linkfield Road, Musselburgh,
East Lothian EH21 7RE
Tel: 0131 653 4444
Headmaster: Dr Graham
Hawley BSc, PhD
No. of pupils: 629 VIth148
Fees: Day £9,180–£23,325
FB £22,335–£34,260
🌐 A ♣ £ 🖉 16+

The Compass School
West Road, Haddington,
East Lothian EH41 3RD
Tel: 01620 822642
Headmaster: Mr Mark Becher
MA(Hons), PGCE
Age range: 4–12
No. of pupils: 125
Fees: Day £6,450–£9,735
£ 🖉

Edinburgh

Basil Paterson Tutorial College
66 Queen Street, Edinburgh EH2 4NA
Tel: 0131 225 3802
Head of School: Claire Samuel
Age range: 14+
No. of pupils: 40
Fees: Day £3,990–£12,000
16+ A ♣ 🖉

Cargilfield School
45 Gamekeeper's Road,
Edinburgh EH4 6HU
Tel: 0131 336 2207
Headmaster: Mr. Robert Taylor
Age range: 3–13
No. of pupils: 325
Fees: Day £6,051–£15,843 WB £19,443
♣ £ 🖉

Clifton Hall
Newbridge, Edinburgh EH28 8LQ
Tel: 0131 333 1359
Headmaster: Mr R Grant
Age range: 3–18
No. of pupils: 385
Fees: Day £5,100–£12,270
£ 🖉 16+

Edinburgh Steiner School
60 Spylaw Road, Edinburgh EH10 5BR
Tel: 0131 337 3410
**Chair of The College of
Teachers:** Nick Brett
Age range: 3–18
Fees: Day £3,959–£9,262
£ 🖉 16+

Fettes College
Carrington Road, Edinburgh EH4 1QX
Tel: +44 (0)131 332 2281
Headmaster: Mr Geoffrey
Stanford MA (Oxon)
Age range: 7–18
No. of pupils: 760
Fees: Day £15,495–£26,790
FB £24,210–£33,480
🌐 A ♣ £ IB 🖉 16+

Fettes College Preparatory School
East Fettes Avenue, Edinburgh EH4 1QZ
Tel: 0131 332 2976
Headmaster: Mr A A Edwards
Age range: 7–13
No. of pupils: 169
Fees: Day £16,500 FB £24,210
Ⓐ ⛪ £ ⒾⒷ ✎

George Heriot's School
Lauriston Place, Edinburgh EH3 9EQ
Tel: 0131 229 7263
Principal: Mrs Lesley Franklin
Age range: 3–18
No. of pupils: 1641 VIth352
Fees: Day £8,349–£12,522
£ ✎ ⑯ ✿

George Watson's College
Colinton Road, Edinburgh EH10 5EG
Tel: 0131 446 6000
Principal: Mr Melvyn Roffe
Age range: 3–18
No. of pupils: 2362
Fees: Day £8,094–£12,555
🌐 Ⓐ £ ⒾⒷ ✎ ⑯ ✿

Merchiston Castle School
294 Colinton Road, Edinburgh EH13 0PU
Tel: 0131 312 2201
Headmaster: Mr Jonathan Anderson
Age range: B7–18
No. of pupils: 450
Fees: Day £5,010–£8,070
FB £7,030–£10,970
♂ 🌐 Ⓐ ⛪ ✎ ⑯

St George's School for Girls
Garscube Terrace, Edinburgh EH12 6BG
Tel: 0131 311 8000
Head: Mrs Alex Hems BA(Hons) Oxon
Age range: B2–5 years G2–18 years
No. of pupils: 815 VIth170
Fees: Day £8,550–£13,875
FB £26,175–£29,010
♀ 🌐 Ⓐ ⛪ £ ✎ ⑯ ✿

St Mary's Music School
Coates Hall, 25 Grosvenor
Crescent, Edinburgh EH12 5EL
Tel: 0131 538 7766
Headteacher: Dr Kenneth Taylor
BSc Hons, PhD, PGCE, PG Dip
Age range: 9–19
No. of pupils: VIth13
🌐 Ⓐ ⑯

Stewart's Melville College
Queensferry Road, Edinburgh EH4 3EZ
Tel: 0131 311 1000
Principal: Mrs Linda Moule
Age range: B12–18 G16–18
No. of pupils: 864
Fees: Day £11,637 FB £23,349
♂ 🌐 ⛪ £ ✎ ⑯

The Edinburgh Academy
42 Henderson Row, Edinburgh EH3 5BL
Tel: 0131 556 4603
Rector: Barry Welsh
Age range: 2–18
No. of pupils: 992 VIth93
Fees: Day £8,433–£14,121
Ⓐ £ ✎ ⑯

**The Mary Erskine & Stewart's
Melville Junior School**
Queensferry Road, Edinburgh EH4 3EZ
Tel: 0131 311 1111
Headmaster: Mr Bryan Lewis
Age range: 3–11
No. of pupils: 1218
Fees: Day £8,142–£9,123 WB
£20,250 FB £20,835
£

The Mary Erskine School
Ravelston, Edinburgh EH4 3NT
Tel: 0131 347 5700
Headmaster: Mrs Linda Moule
Age range: B16–18 G12–18
Fees: Day £11,637 FB £23,349
♀ 🌐 ⛪ £ ⑯

Wallace College
12 George IV Bridge, Edinburgh EH1 1EE
Tel: 0131 220 3634
Age range: 8–18
Fees: Day £1,410–£6,900
FB £4,070–£9,590
⑯ Ⓐ ⛪

Fife

Osborne House School
Orchard Croft, West Port,
Dysart, Fife KY1 2TD
Tel: 01592 651461
Headteacher: Miss Eunice Cameron
Age range: 10–17
Fees: Day £7,800

St Leonards School
St Andrews, Fife KY16 9QJ
Tel: 01334 472126
Head of School: Dr Michael Carslaw
Age range: 5–18
No. of pupils: 510
Fees: Day £8,700–£14,208
FB £22,746–£34,653
🌐 Ⓐ £ ⒾⒷ ✎ ⑯

Glasgow

Belmont House School
Sandringham Avenue, Newton
Mearns, Glasgow G77 5DU
Tel: 0141 639 2922
Principal: Mr Melvyn D Shanks
BSc, DipEd, MInstP, CPhys, SQH
Age range: 3–18
No. of pupils: 300
Fees: Day £5,841–£13,263
Ⓐ ✎ ⑯ ✿

Craigholme School
72 St Andrews Drive, Pollokshields,
Glasgow G41 4HS
Tel: 0141 427 0375
Principal: June Gilliland
Age range: B3–5 G3–18
No. of pupils: 442 VIth30
Fees: Day £8,265–£10,047
♀ £ ✎ ⑯

Fernhill School
Fernbrae Avenue, Burnside,
Rutherglen, Glasgow G73 4SG
Tel: 0141 634 2674
Headteacher: Dr Laura Murphy
Age range: B4–11 G4–18
No. of pupils: 300 VIth16
Fees: Day £7,580–£11,090
♀ £ ✎ ⑯

Hutchesons' Grammar School
21 Beaton Road, Glasgow G41 4NW
Tel: 0141 423 2933
Rector: Mr Colin Gambles
BSc (Hons) PGCE
Age range: 5–18
No. of pupils: 1242 VIth139
Fees: Day £7,320–£12,168
Ⓐ £ ✎ ⑯

St Aloysius' College
45 Hill Street, Glasgow G3 6RJ
Tel: 0141 332 3190
Head Master: Mr Matthew Bartlett
MA (Cantab), PGCE, NLE, NPQH
Age range: 3–18
No. of pupils: 925 VIth110
Fees: Day £7,263–£12,825
£ ✎ ⑯

The Glasgow Academy
Colebrooke Street, Kelvinbridge,
Glasgow G12 8HE
Tel: 0141 334 8558
Rector: Mr Peter Brodie MA, MA(Ed)
Age range: 3–18
No. of pupils: 1148 VIth221
Fees: Day £5,220–£11,623
£ 16

The Glasgow Academy Dairsie
54 Newlands Road, Newlands,
Glasgow G43 2JG
Tel: 0141 632 0736
Rector: Mr Peter Brodie
Age range: 3–8
No. of pupils: 74
Fees: Day £4,770–£12,029

The Glasgow Academy, Milngavie
Mugdock Road, Milngavie,
Glasgow G62 8NP
Tel: +44 (0)1419 563758
Rector: Mr Peter Brodie
Age range: 3–8
Fees: Day £4,680–£9,861

The High School of Glasgow
637 Crow Road, Glasgow G13 1PL
Tel: 0141 954 9628
Rector: John O'Neill
Age range: 3–18
No. of pupils: 1022 VIth97
Fees: Day £4,419–£12,768
£ 16

The Kelvinside Academy
33 Kirklee Road, Glasgow G12 0SW
Tel: 0141 357 3376
Rector: Mr Ian Munro BSc,
PGCE, MEd(Cantab), FRSB
Age range: 3–18
No. of pupils: 640 VIth73
Fees: Day £7,995–£12,660
A £ 16

Moray

Drumduan School
Clovenside Road, Forres,
Moray IV36 2RD
Tel: + 44 (0)1309 676300
Principal Teacher: Krzysztof
Zajaczkowski
Age range: 3–18

GORDONSTOUN
For further details see p. 274
Elgin, Moray IV30 5RF
Tel: 01343 837829
Email:
admissions@gordonstoun.org.uk
Website: www.gordonstoun.org.uk
Principal: Ms Lisa Kerr BA
Age range: 6–18
No. of pupils: 530 VIth210
Fees: Day £14,361–£28,365 WB
£23,358 FB £23,358–£38,295
A £ 16

Perth & Kinross

Ardvreck School
Gwydyr Road, Crieff, Perth
& Kinross PH7 4EX
Tel: 01764 653112
Headmaster: Mr Dan Davey
Age range: 4–13
Fees: Day £14,961 FB £22,485
£

Craigclowan Preparatory School
Edinburgh Road, Perth,
Perth & Kinross PH2 8PS
Tel: 01738 626310
Head of School: John Gilmour
Age range: 3–13
No. of pupils: 245
Fees: Day £12,660
£

Glenalmond College, Perth
Glenalmond, Perth, Perth
& Kinross PH1 3RY
Tel: 01738 842000
Warden: Elaine Logan
Age range: 12–18
No. of pupils: 400 VIth175
Fees: Day £16,881–£22,503
FB £25,851–£36,510
A £ 16

Kilgraston School
Bridge of Earn, Perth, Perth
& Kinross PH2 9BQ
Tel: 01738 812257
Head: Mrs Dorothy MacGinty
Age range: G5–18
No. of pupils: 260
Fees: Day £10,890–£17,640
FB £23,025–£30,135
A £ 16

Morrison's Academy
Crieff, Perth & Kinross PH7 3AN
Tel: 01764 653885
Principal: Mr Gareth Warren BSc (Hons)
Age range: 3–18
No. of pupils: VIth50
Fees: Day £8,625–£12,996
£ 16

STRATHALLAN SCHOOL
For further details see p. 278
Forgandenny, Perth, Perth
& Kinross PH2 9EG
Tel: 01738 812546
Email: admissions@strathallan.co.uk
Website: www.strathallan.co.uk
Headmaster: Mr Mark
Lauder MA Hons
Age range: 9–18
A £ 16

Perthshire

Queen Victoria School
Dunblane, Perthshire FK15 0JY
Tel: 0131 310 2927
Head: Donald Shaw BSc(Hons) PGCE
Age range: 11–18
No. of pupils: 267 VIth30
Fees: FB £1,403
£ 16

Renfrewshire

Cedars School of Excellence
31 Ardgowan Square, Greenock,
Renfrewshire PA16 8NJ
Tel: 01475 723905
Headteacher: Mrs Alison Speirs
Age range: 5–18
No. of pupils: 95
Fees: Day £5,200–£7,180
£

St Columba's School
Duchal Road, Kilmacolm,
Renfrewshire PA13 4AU
Tel: 01505 872238
Head of School: Mrs
Andrea Y Angus BSc
Age range: 3–18
No. of pupils: 701 VIth125
Fees: Day £3,080–£12,095
£ 16

South Ayrshire

Wellington School
Carleton Turrets, Ayr, South
Ayrshire KA7 2XH
Tel: 01292 269321
Head: Mr S Johnson MA
(Cantab) PGCE
Age range: 3–18
No. of pupils: VIth45
Fees: Day £6,900–£12,900
£ 16

South Lanarkshire

Hamilton College
Bothwell Road, Hamilton,
South Lanarkshire ML3 0AY
Tel: 01698 282700
Principal: Mr Tom McPhail
Age range: 3–18
No. of pupils: VIth49
Fees: Day £7,635–£10,800
£ 16

Wales

KEY TO SYMBOLS

- ⚤ *Boys' school*
- ⚤ *Girls' school*
- 🌐 *International school*
- 16· *Tutorial or sixth form college*
- Ⓐ *A levels*
- 🏛 *Boarding accommodation*
- £ *Bursaries*
- IB *International Baccalaureate*
- ✏ *Learning support*
- 16· *Entrance at 16+*
- 🎓 *Vocational qualifications*
- (IAPS) *Independent Association of Preparatory Schools*
- (HMC) *The Headmasters' & Headmistresses' Conference*
- (ISA) *Independent Schools Association*
- (GSA) *Girls' School Association*
- (BSA) *Boarding Schools' Association*
- S *Society of Heads*

Unless otherwise indicated, all schools are coeducational day schools. Single-sex and boarding schools will be indicated by the relevant icon.

Cardiff

Cardiff Sixth Form College
1-3 Trinity Court, 21-27 Newport
Road, Cardiff CF24 0AA
Tel: +44 (0)29 2049 3121
Principal: Mr Gareth Collier
Age range: 15–19
No. of pupils: 300
Fees: Day £16,600 FB £40,250–£43,750
🌐 (A)

Carmarthenshire

LLANDOVERY COLLEGE
For further details see p. 282
Queensway, Llandovery,
Carmarthenshire SA20 0EE
Tel: +44 (0)1550 723005
Email:
admissions@llandoverycollege.com
Website:
www.llandoverycollege.com
Warden: Guy Ayling MA
Age range: 4–18 years
No. of pupils: 280
Fees: Day £5,985–£17,520
FB £17,880–£26,460
🌐 (A) 🏛 (£) ✎ 16·

St Michael's School
Bryn, Llanelli, Carmarthenshire SA14 9TU
Tel: 01554 820325
Age range: 3–18
No. of pupils: 420 VIth80
Fees: Day £5,064–£12,369
FB £19,722–£22,269
🌐 (A) 🏛 16·

Clwyd

Rydal Penrhos Preparatory School
Pwllycrochan Avenue, Colwyn
Bay, Clwyd LL29 7BP
Tel: 01492 530381
Headmaster: Mr Simon Smith
Age range: 2–11
No. of pupils: 180
Fees: Day £7,452–£9,930
🏛 ✎

St David's College
Gloddaeth Hall, Llandudno,
Clwyd LL30 1RD
Tel: 01492 875974
Headmaster: Mr Andrew Russell
Age range: 9–19
No. of pupils: 254 VIth77
Fees: Day £7,950–£17,550
FB £18,600–£33,000
🌐 (A) 🏛 (£) ✎ 16·

Conwy

Rydal Penrhos School
Pwllycrochan Avenue, Colwyn
Bay, Conwy LL29 7BT
Tel: +44 (0)1492 530155
Headmaster: Mr Simon Smith
Age range: 2–18
No. of pupils: 530
Fees: Day £7,452–£16,785 WB
£20,901–£23,385 FB £27,159–£33,450
🌐 (A) 🏛 (£) IB ✎ 16·

Denbighshire

Fairholme School
The Mount, Mount Road, St
Asaph, Denbighshire LL17 0DH
Tel: 01745 583505
Principal: Mrs E Perkins MA(Oxon)
Age range: 3–11
No. of pupils: 110
Fees: Day £6,300–£8,400

Ruthin School
Ruthin, Denbighshire LL15 1EE
Tel: 01824 702543
Headmaster: Mr T J Belfield
Age range: 3–18
No. of pupils: 240 VIth41
Fees: Day £11,000–£14,000 FB £34,500
🌐 (A) 🏛 (£) 16·

Glamorgan

Cardiff Academy
40-41 The Parade, Cardiff,
Glamorgan CF24 3AB
Tel: 029 2040 9630
Principal: Dr S R Wilson
Age range: 14–18
No. of pupils: 51 VIth44
Fees: Day £12,000–£15,000
(A)

Ffynone House School
36 St James's Crescent, Swansea,
Glamorgan SA1 6DR
Tel: 01792 464967
Headteacher: Mr Michael Boulding
Age range: 11–18
No. of pupils: VIth25
Fees: Day £10,845–£11,010
(A) (£) 16·

Howell's School, Llandaff GDST
Cardiff Road, Llandaff, Cardiff,
Glamorgan CF5 2YD
Tel: 029 2056 2019
Principal: Mrs Sally Davis BSc
Age range: 16–18 G3–18
No. of pupils: 780
Fees: Day £7,755–£14,070
🏃 (A) (£) ✎ 16·

Kings Monkton School
6 West Grove, Cardiff,
Glamorgan CF24 3XL
Tel: 02920 482854
Principal: Mr Paul Norton
Age range: 3–18
No. of pupils: 250
Fees: Day £2,700–£4,068
(A) ✎ 16·

Oakleigh House School
38 Penlan Crescent, Uplands,
Swansea, Glamorgan SA2 0RL
Tel: 01792 298537
Headmistress: Mrs R Ferriman
BA(Hons)Ed, MEd
Age range: 2–11
Fees: Day £6,255–£8,250
(£) ✎

St Clare's School
Newton, Porthcawl,
Glamorgan CF36 5NR
Tel: 01656 782509
Head of School: Helen Hier
Age range: 3–18
No. of pupils: 298 VIth45
Fees: Day £6,753–£11,799
(A) 16·

St John's College, Cardiff
College Green, Old St Mellons,
Cardiff, Glamorgan CF3 5YX
Tel: 029 2077 8936
Headteacher: Mr Shaun
Moody BA (Hons) PGCE
Age range: 3–18
No. of pupils: 548
Fees: Day £7,443–£14,400
(A) (£) ✎ 16·

The Cathedral School, Llandaff
Llandaff, Cardiff, Glamorgan CF5 2YH
Tel: 029 2056 3179
Head: Clare Sherwood
Age range: 3–18
Fees: Day £7,785–£12,714
(£)

Westbourne School
Hickman Road, Penarth,
Glamorgan CF64 2AJ
Tel: 029 2070 5705
Principal: Dr Gerard Griffiths
Age range: 3–18
No. of pupils: 162
Fees: Day £8,100–£13,470
🌐 🏛 (£) IB ✎ 16·

Gwynedd

St Gerard's School
Ffriddoedd Road, Bangor,
Gwynedd LL57 2EL
Tel: 01248 351656
Headteacher: Mr Campbell Harrison
Age range: 3–18
No. of pupils: VIth25
Fees: Day £7,050–£10,695
(A) (£) (16)

Monmouthshire

Haberdashers' Agincourt School
Dixton Lane, Monmouth,
Monmouthshire NP25 3SY
Tel: 01600 713970
Head: Mrs Jennie Phillips
Age range: 3–7
No. of pupils: 124
Fees: Day £4,518–£7,572
(✎)

Monmouth School for Boys
Almshouse Street, Monmouth,
Monmouthshire NP25 3XP
Tel: 01600 713143
Head of School: Dr. Andrew Daniel
Age range: B7–18 years
No. of pupils: 643
Fees: Day £11,091–£15,816
FB £20,280–£32,061
(🧒)(🌐)(A)(🏫)(£)(✎)(16)

Monmouth School for Girls
Hereford Road, Monmouth,
Monmouthshire NP25 5XT
Tel: 01600 711100
Acting Head of School: Mr Tom Arrand
Age range: G7–18 years
No. of pupils: 638
Fees: Day £11,091–£14,778
FB £20,280–£32,061
(🧒)(🌐)(A)(🏫)(£)(✎)(16)

Monmouth Schools Pre-Prep & Nursery
Dixton Lane, Monmouth,
Monmouthshire NP25 3SY
Tel: 01600 713970
Head of School: Mrs Jennie Phillips
Age range: 3–7 years
No. of pupils: 80
Fees: Day £4,518–£7,572

Rougemont School
Llantarnam Hall, Malpas Road,
Newport, Monmouthshire NP20 6QB
Tel: 01633 820800
Headmaster: Mr Robert Carnevale
Age range: 3–18
No. of pupils: 700 VIth111
Fees: Day £7,245–£13,536
(A)(£)(✎)(16)

St John's-on-the-Hill
Tutshill, Chepstow,
Monmouthshire NP16 7LE
Tel: 01291 622045
Head: Mrs Ruth Frett
Age range: 3 months–13 years
No. of pupils: 362
Fees: Day £8,280–£13,632 FB £19,362
(🏫)(£)(✎)

Pembrokeshire

Nant-y-Cwm Steiner School
Llanycefn, Clunderwen,
Pembrokeshire SA66 7QJ
Tel: 01437 563 640
Age range: 0–14

Redhill Preparatory School
The Garth, St David's
Road, Haverfordwest,
Pembrokeshire SA61 2UR
Tel: 01437 762472
Principal: Mrs Lovegrove
Age range: 0–11
Fees: Day £7,650–£7,800
(£)(✎)

Powys

Christ College
Brecon, Powys LD3 8AF
Tel: 01874 615440
Head: Mr Gareth Pearson
Age range: 7–18
No. of pupils: 370
Fees: Day £9,165–£18,536
FB £17,544–£29,043
(🌐)(A)(🏫)(£)(✎)(16)

Vale of Glamorgan

UWC Atlantic College
St Donat's Castle, St Donat's, Llantwit
Major, Vale of Glamorgan CF61 1WF
Tel: +44 (0)1446 799000
Principal: Mr Peter T Howe
Age range: 15–19
No. of pupils: 367
Fees: Day £26,100 FB £42,159–£43,500
(🌐)(🏫)(£)(IB)(16)

D404

Examinations and qualifications

Common Entrance

What is Common Entrance?

The Common Entrance examinations are used in UK independent schools (and some independent schools overseas) for transfer from junior to senior schools at the ages of 11+ and 13+. They were first introduced in 1904 and are internationally recognised as being a rigorous form of assessment following a thorough course of study. The examinations are produced by the Independent Schools Examinations Board and backed by HMC (Headmasters' and Headmistresses' Conference), GSA (Girls' Schools Association), and IAPS (Independent Association of Prep Schools) which together represent the leading independent schools in the UK, and many overseas.

Common Entrance is not a public examination as, for example, GCSE, and candidates may normally be entered only in one of the following circumstances:

a) they have been offered a place at a senior school subject to their passing the examination, or

b) they are entered as a 'trial run', in which case the papers are marked by the junior school concerned

Candidates normally take the examination in their own junior or preparatory schools, either in the UK or overseas.

How does Common Entrance fit into the progression to GCSEs?

Rapid changes in education nationally and internationally have resulted in regular reviews of the syllabuses for all the Common Entrance examinations. Reviews of the National Curriculum, in particular, have brought about a number of changes, with the Board wishing to ensure that it continues to set high standards. It is also a guiding principle that Common Entrance should be part of the natural progression from 11- 16, and not a diversion from it.

Common Entrance at 11+

At 11+, the examination consists of papers in English, mathematics and science. It is designed so that it can be taken by candidates either from independent preparatory schools or by candidates from schools in the maintained sector or overseas who have had no special preparation. The examination is normally taken in January for entrance to senior schools in the following September.

Common Entrance at 13+

At 13+, most candidates come from independent preparatory schools. The compulsory subjects are English, mathematics and science. Papers in French, geography, German, Classical Greek, history, Latin, religious studies and Spanish are also available and candidates usually offer as many subjects as they can. In most subjects, papers are available at more than one level to cater for candidates of different abilities. There are three examination sessions each year, with the majority of candidates sitting in the summer prior to entry to their senior schools in September.

Marking and grading

The papers are set centrally but the answers are marked by the senior school for which a candidate is entered. Mark schemes are provided by the Board but senior schools are free to set their own grade boundaries. Results are available within two weeks of the examinations taking place.

Pre-Testing and the ISEB Common Pre-Tests

A number of senior independent schools 'pre-test' pupils for entry, prior to them taking their main entrance examinations at a later date. Usually, these pre-tests take place when a pupil is in Year 6 or Year 7 of his or her junior school and will then be going on to sit Common Entrance in Year 8. The tests are designed to assess a pupil's academic potential and suitability for a particular senior school so that the child, the parents and the school know well in advance whether he/ she is going to be offered a place at the school, subject to a satisfactory performance in the entrance examinations. The tests enable senior schools which are heavily oversubscribed to manage their lists and help to ensure that pupils are not entered for examinations in which they are unlikely to be successful. In short, it reduces uncertainty for all concerned.

Pre-tests may be written specifically for the senior school for which the candidate is entered but a growing number of schools are choosing to use the Common Pre-Tests provided by the Independent Schools Examinations Board. These online tests are usually taken in the candidate's own junior school and one of their main advantages is that a pupil need sit the tests only once, with the results then made available to any senior school which wishes to use them. The multiple-choice tests cover verbal reasoning, non- verbal reasoning, English and mathematics, with the results standardised according to the pupil's age when they are taken. Further information is available on the ISEB website at www.iseb.co.uk.

Parents are advised to check the entrance requirements for senior schools to see if their child will be required to sit a pre-test.

Further information

Details of the Common Entrance examinations and how to register candidates are available on the ISEB website www.iseb.co.uk. Copies of past papers and a wide range of textbooks and other resources can be purchased from Galore Park Publishing Ltd at www.galorepark.co.uk. Support materials are also available from Hodder Education and other publishers; see the Resources section of the ISEB website for details.

Independent Schools Examinations Board Suite 3,
Endeavour House,
Crow Arch Lane,
Ringwood, Hampshire BH24 1HP

Telephone: 01425 470555
Email: enquiries@iseb.co.uk
Web: www.iseb.co.uk

7+ Entrance Exams

What is the 7+?

The 7+ is the descriptive name given to the entrance exams set by an increasing number of independent schools for pupils wishing to gain admission into their Year 3.

7+ entrance exams may be simply for admission into a selective preparatory school, which will then prepare the child for Common Entrance exams to gain a place at senior school. Alternatively, the 7+ can be a route into a school with both prep and senior departments, therefore often effectively bypassing the 11+ or 13+ Common Entrance exams.

The Independent Schools Examinations Board provides Common Entrance examinations and assessments for pupils seeking entry to independent senior schools at 11+ and 13+, but there is as yet no equivalent for the 7+. The testing is largely undertaken by the individual schools, although some schools might commission test from external agencies. Many schools in the incredibly competitive London area offer entrance exams at 7+ and some, such as Haberdasher's Aske's Boys' School, share specimen papers on their website to clarify what 7+ children will face.

Who sits the 7+?

The 7+ is sat by Year 2 children, who may be moving from a state primary school or a stand-alone pre-prep school to an independent prep school (although many prep schools now have their own pre-prep department, with a cohort of children poised to pass into Year 3 there).

Registration for 7+ entrance exams usually closes in the November of Year 2, with the exams then sat in January or February, for entry that September.

How is the 7+ assessed?

Written exam content will be primarily English and maths based, whilst spelling, dictation, mental arithmetic and more creative skills may be assessed verbally on a one-to-one basis. Group exercises are also sometimes used to look at a child's initiative and their ability to work with others.

Schools will not only be looking for academic potential, but also good citizens and a mixture of personalities to produce a well-rounded year group. For this reason, children are often asked to attend an interview. Some schools interview all candidates, whilst others may call back a limited number with good test results. They will be looking for a child's ability to look an adult in the eye and think on their feet, but also simply to show some spark and personality.

After the assessments, children will be told if they have been successful in gaining a firm place, or a place on a waiting list.

Further Information

As the 7+ is not centrally regulated, it is best for parents to seek accurate admissions and testing information direct from the schools in which they are interested. In addition to a school's facilities and ethos, choosing a school for admission at 7+ will probably also involve whether the school has a senior department and if not, the prep school's record in gaining its students places at target senior schools.

Experienced educational consultants may be able to help parents decide which independent prep school is best suited for their child, based on their personality, senior school ambitions and academic potential. Many parents enlist the help of tutors to prepare children for the 7+, if only to reduce the fear of the unknown in these very young children. This is achieved by teaching them the required curriculum, what to expect on their test and interview days, and giving them the opportunity to practice tackling the type of assessments they will face.

Prep School Baccalaureate

The Prep School Baccalaureate (PSB) is a framework of study for children in junior and preparatory schools that was introduced in 2012, and focuses on the active development and assessment of 6 core skills: Communication, Collaboration, Leadership, Independence, Reviewing and improving and Thinking and Learning. Member schools promote the core skills across all areas of school life, and provide guidance for pupils in progressing these skills, which are seen as essential for developing capable and balanced adults, able to make the most of the opportunities of a fast-changing world. A strong but appropriate knowledge base compliments this, with the use of focused tutoring, pastoral care and Well Being programmes.

Schools do not work to a prescribed curriculum and the emphasis is upon promoting an independent approach which works for each individual school. There are subject INSET days for PSB school staff annually and these are supported by senior school colleagues, to ensure that work done in PSB schools compliments the demands of education at higher levels.

The PSB is a whole school initiative from Early Years to either Year 6 or Year 8, at which point the certificate is awarded at the time of matriculation to senior schools. An additional PSB Year 9 framework is being developed together with international membership.

The development of skills is now recognised as essential by the Independent Schools Inspectorate (ISI), and recent ISI reports on PSB schools highlight the excellent contribution the PSB has in schools achieving excellence.

Assessment

The PSB has a 10 point scale for all subjects studied with a compulsory spine covering: English, Maths, Science, Modern Languages, The Humanities, Art, Design Technology, Music, Sport and PE with each pupil additionally completing a cross curricular project. Optional subjects are agreed with schools but these must be supported by a scheme of work clearly identifying appropriate core skills which are assessed on a 5 point scale. There are distinction levels on both scales and the 10 point scale cross references both ISEB and National Curriculum assessment levels.

Pupils moving on to senior school do so via individual senior school pre-testing arrangements, the award of the PSB certificate, core ISEB papers or a combination of the above.

Membership categories

Partner membership is available to schools developing the PSB with support given from existing schools and the Communications director.

Full membership entitles schools to use the PSB matriculation certificate and join the PSB committee as voting members.

Affiliated membership is for schools that have developed their own skills based approach, in line with PSB principles; staff can participate in all training opportunities and the Heads of Affiliated Schools join committee meetings as non-voting guests.

Membership of the above categories is dependent upon strong ISI reports, the development of a skills based curriculum, with skills clearly identified in schemes of work and excellent teaching.

Associate membership is for senior schools that actively support the PSB in providing staff for subject meetings, hosting meetings, conferences and committee meetings and offer a valuable perspective on the demands of GCSE, A Level and the International Baccalaureate.

Further details

The PSB is an entirely independent charity overseen by a Board of Trustees who have expertise in both primary and secondary education. Details of the PSB can be found on the website – psbacc.org – together with contact details for the Communications Director who can provide further details on request.

General Certificate of Secondary Education (GCSE)

What are the GCSE qualifications?

GCSE qualifications were first introduced in 1986 and are the principal means of assessment at Key Stage 4 across a range of academic subject areas. They command respect and have status not only in the UK but worldwide.

Main features of the GCSE

There are four unitary awarding organisations for GCSEs in England (see 'Awarding organisations and examination dates' section, p425). WJEC and CCEA also offer GCSE qualifications in Wales and Northern Ireland. Each examining group designs its own specifications but they are required to conform to set criteria. For some aspects of the qualification system, the exam boards adopt common ways of working. When the exam boards work together in this way they generally do so through the Joint Council of Qualifications (JCQ). The award of a grade is intended to indicate that a candidate has met the required level of skills, knowledge and understanding.

GCSEs are in the process of reform. New GCSEs in ancient languages (classical Greek, Latin), art and design, biology, chemistry, citizenship studies, combined science (double award), computer science, dance, drama, food preparation and nutrition, geography, history, modern foreign languages (French, German, Spanish), music, physics, physical education and religious studies were first taught in September 2016, with first results in summer 2018. Assessment in these reformed GCSEs consists primarily of formal examinations taken at the end of the student's two-year course. Other types of assessment, non-exam assessment (NEA), is used where there are skills and knowledge which cannot be assessed through exams. Ofqual have set the percentage of the total marks that will come from NEA.

The reformed GCSEs feature new and more demanding content, as required by the government and developed by the exam boards. Courses are designed for two years of study (linear assessment) and no longer divided into different modules.

Exams can only be split into 'foundation tier' and 'higher tier' if one exam paper does not give all students the opportunity to show their knowledge and their abilities. Such tiering is only available in maths, science and modern foreign languages; other subjects do not have tiers. Resit opportunities will only be available each November in English language and maths, and then only for students who have turned 16 by the 31st of August in the year of the November assessment.

New GCSEs taught from September 2017: ancient history, astronomy, business, classical civilisation, design and technology, economics, electronics, engineering, film studies, geology, media studies, psychology, sociology, statistics, other (minority) foreign languages e.g. Italian, Polish.

New GCSEs taught from September 2018: ancient languages (biblical Hebrew) and modern foreign languages (Gujarati, Persian, Portuguese, Turkish).

Grading

The basic principle that exam boards follow when setting grade boundaries is that if the group of students (the cohort) taking a qualification in one year is of similar ability to the cohort in the previous year then the overall results (outcomes) should be comparable.

The reformed exams taken in summer 2017 were the first to show a new grading system, with the A* to G grades being phased out.

The new grading system is 9 to 1, with 9 being the top grade. Ofqual says this allows greater differentiation between students. It expects that broadly the same proportion of students will achieve a grade 4 and above as currently achieve a grade C and above, that broadly the same proportion of students will achieve a grade 7 and above as currently achieve a grade A and above. The bottom of grade 1 will be aligned with the bottom of grade G, grade 5 will be awarded to around the top third of students gaining the equivalent of a grade C and bottom third of a grade B. Grade 9 will be set using the tailored approach formula in the first award.

Grades 2, 3, 5 and 6 will be awarded arithmetically so that the grade boundaries are equally spaced in terms of marks from neighbouring grades.

The government's definition of a 'strong pass' will be set at grade 5 for reformed GCSEs. A grade 4 – or 'standard pass' – will continue to be a level 2 achievement. The DfE does not expect employers, colleges or universities to raise the bar to a grade 5 if a grade 4 would meet their requirements.

Can anyone take GCSE qualifications?

GCSEs are intended mainly for 16-year-old pupils, but are open to anyone of any age, whether studying full-time or part-time at a school, college or privately. There are no formal entry requirements.

Students normally study up to ten subjects over a two-year period. Short course GCSEs are available in some subjects (including PE and religious studies) – these include half the content of a full GCSE, so two short course GCSEs are equivalent to one full GCSE.

The English Baccalaureate

The English Baccalaureate (EBacc) is a school performance measure. It allows people to see how many pupils get a grade C or above (current grading) in the core academic subjects at Key Stage 4 in any government-funded school.

The DfE introduced the EBacc measure in 2010. In June 2015, it announced its intention that all pupils who start year 7 in September 2015 take the EBacc subjects when they reach their GCSEs in 2020.

Progress 8 and Attainment 8

Progress 8 aims to capture the progress a pupil makes from the end of primary school to the end of secondary school. It is a type of value added measure, which means that pupils' results are compared to the actual achievements of other pupils with the same prior attainment.

The new performance measures are designed to encourage schools to offer a broad and balanced curriculum with a focus on an academic core at Key Stage 4, and reward schools for the teaching of all their pupils, measuring performance across 8 qualifications. Every increase in every grade a pupil achieves will attract additional points in the performance tables.

Progress 8 will be calculated for individual pupils solely in order to calculate a school's Progress 8 score, and there will be no need for schools to share individual Progress 8 scores with their pupils. Schools should continue to focus on which qualifications are most suitable for individual pupils, as the grades pupils achieve will help them reach their goals for the next stage of their education or training

Attainment 8 will measure the achievement of a pupil across 8 qualifications including mathematics (double weighted) and English (double weighted), 3 further qualifications that count in the English Baccalaureate (EBacc) measure and 3 further qualifications that can be GCSE qualifications (including EBacc subjects) or any other non-GCSE qualification on the DfE approved list.

General Certificate of Education (GCE) Advanced level (A level)

Typically, A level qualifications are studied over a two-year period. There are no lower or upper age limits. Schools and colleges usually expect students aged 16-18 to have obtained grades A*-C (grade 5 in the new criteria) in five subjects at GCSE level before taking an advanced level course. This requirement may vary between centres and according to which specific subjects are to be studied.

Mature students may be assessed on different criteria as to their suitability to embark on the course.

GCE Qualifications

Over the past few years, AS level and A level qualifications have been in a process of reform. New subjects have been introduced gradually, with the first wave taught from September 2015. Subjects that have not been reformed are no longer be available for teaching from September 2018.

GCE qualifications are available at two levels: the Advanced Subsidiary (AS), which is generally delivered over one year and is seen as half an A level; and the A level (GCE). Nearly 70 titles are available, covering a wide range of subject areas, including humanities, sciences, language, business, arts, mathematics and technology.

One of the major reforms is that AS level results no longer count towards an A level (they previously counted for 50%). The two qualifications are linear, with AS assessments typically taking place after one year and A levels after two.

New-style AS and A levels were first taught from September 2015 for: art and design, biology, business studies, chemistry, computer studies, economics, English language, English language and literature, English literature, history, physics, psychology, and sociology.

Subjects first taught from September 2016 include: ancient languages such as Latin or Greek, dance, drama (theatre studies), geography, modern languages such as Spanish or French, music, physical education, religious studies.

Those introduced for first teaching from September 2017: accounting, design and technology, music technology, history of art, environmental science, philosophy, maths, further maths, archaeology, accounting, electronics, ancient history, law, classical civilisation, film studies, media studies, politics, geology, statistics, Chinese, Italian, Russian. In 2018 Biblical Hebrew, Modern Hebrew & languages such as Bengali, Polish and Urdu will be available for first teaching.

Some GCE AS and A levels, particularly the practical ones, contain a proportion of coursework. All GCE A levels that contain one or more types of assessment will have an element of synoptic assessment that tests students' understanding of the whole specification. GCE AS are graded A-E and A levels are graded A*-E.

Overall the amount of coursework at A level has been reduced in the reforms. In some subjects, such as the sciences, practical work will not contribute to the final A level but will be reported separately in a certificate of endorsement. In the sciences, students will do at least 12 practical activities, covering apparatus and techniques. Exam questions about practical work will make up at least 15% of the total marks for the qualification and students will be assessed on their knowledge, skills and understanding of practical work.

Cambridge International AS & A Level

Cambridge International AS & A Level is an internationally benchmarked qualification, taught in over 130 countries worldwide. It is typically for learners aged 16 to 19 years who need advanced study to prepare for university. It was created specifically for an international audience and the content has been devised to suit the wide variety of schools worldwide and avoid any cultural bias.

Cambridge International A Level is typically a two-year course, and Cambridge International AS Level is typically one year. Some subjects can be started as a Cambridge International AS Level and extended to a Cambridge International A Level. Students can either follow a broad course of study, or specialise in one particular subject area.

Learners use Cambridge International AS & A Levels to gain places at leading universities worldwide, including the UK, Ireland, USA, Canada, Australia, New Zealand, India, Singapore, Egypt, Jordan, South Africa, the Netherlands, Germany and Spain.

In places such as the US and Canada, good grades in carefully chosen Cambridge International A Level subjects can result in up to one year of university course credit.

Assessment options:
Cambridge International AS & A Levels have a linear structure with exams at the end of the course. Students can choose from a range of assessment options:
Option 1: take Cambridge International AS Levels only. The Cambridge International AS Level syllabus content is half a Cambridge International A Level.
Option 2: staged assessment, which means taking the Cambridge International AS Level in one exam session and the Cambridge International A Level at a later session. However, this route is not possible in all subjects.
Option 3: take all Cambridge International A Level papers in the same examination session, usually at the end of the course.

Grades and subjects
Cambridge International A Levels are graded from A* to E. Cambridge International AS Levels are graded from A to E.

Subjects: available in 55 subjects including accounting, Afrikaans, information technology, Arabic, art and design, biology, business, chemistry, Chinese, classical studies, computer science, design and technology, design and textiles, digital media and design, divinity, economics, English general paper, English language, English literature, environmental management, food studies, French, geography, German, Global Perspectives & Research™, Hindi, Hinduism, history, Islamic studies, Japanese, law, marine science, mathematics, further mathematics, media studies, music, physical education, physical science, physics, Portuguese, psychology, sociology, Spanish, Tamil, Telugu, thinking skills, travel and tourism, Urdu.
Website: www.cambridgeinternational.org/aleve

Cambridge International GCSE (IGCSE)

Cambridge IGCSE is the world's most popular international qualification for 14 to16 year olds. It develops skills in creative thinking, enquiry and problem solving, in preparation for the next stage in a student's education. Cambridge IGCSE is taken in over 145 countries, and is widely recognised by employers and higher education institutions worldwide.

Cambridge IGCSE is graded A* to G around the world, however we are introducing the option of 9-1 grading in some countries. Schools in the UK can now choose between A*- G grading or 9-1 grading for our most popular syllabuses. For more information, go to www.cambridgeinternational.org/grading-choice.

In the UK, Cambridge IGCSE is accepted as equivalent to the GCSE. It can be used as preparation for Cambridge International A & AS Levels, UK A and AS levels, IB or AP and in some instances entry into university. Cambridge IGCSE First Language English and Cambridge IGCSE English Language qualifications are recognised by a significant number of UK universities as evidence of competence in the language for university entrance.

Subjects: available in over 70 subjects including accounting, Afrikaans agriculture, Arabic, art and design, Bahasa Indonesia, biology, business studies, chemistry, Chinese, computer science, design and technology, development studies, drama, Dutch, economics, English – first language, English – literature, English – second language, enterprise, environmental management, food and nutrition, French, geography, German, Global Perspectives™, Greek, Hindi, history, Italian, information and communication technology, IsiZulu, Japanese, Korean, Latin, Malay, mathematics, mathematics – additional, international mathematics, music, Pakistan studies, physical education, physical science, physics, Portuguese – first language, Portuguese, religious studies, Russian, sanskrit, science – combined, sciences – co-ordinated (double), sociology,

Spanish, Thai, travel and tourism, Turkish, Urdu, world literature.
Website: www.cambridgeinternational.org/igcse

Cambridge Pre-U

Cambridge Pre-U is a post-16 qualification that equips students with the skills they need to succeed at university. Developed with universities, it was first introduced in UK schools in September 2008. It is now taught in 170 schools, including some schools outside the UK.

Cambridge Pre-U is a linear course, with exams taken at the end of two years. It encourages the development of well-informed, open and independent-minded individuals; promotes deep understanding through subject specialisation, with a depth and rigour appropriate to progression to higher education; and develops skills in independent research valued by universities.

Assessment

Cambridge Pre-U Principal Subjects are examined at the end of two years. Cambridge Pre-U Short Courses are available in some subjects and are typically examined at the end of one year. Students can study a combination of A Levels and Principal Subjects.

In order to gain the Cambridge Pre-U Diploma, students must study at least three Cambridge Pre-U Principal Subjects (up to two A Levels can be substituted for Principal Subjects) and Cambridge Pre-U Global Perspectives & Research (GPR). Cambridge Pre-U GPR includes an extended project in the second year, developing skills in research and critical thinking.

Grades and subjects

Cambridge Pre-U reports achievement on a scale of nine grades, with Distinction 1 being the highest grade and Pass 3 the lowest grade.

Subjects: available in 24 subjects including art and design, art history, biology, business and management, chemistry, drama and theatre, economics, literature in English, French, further mathematics, geography, German, Global Perspectives & Research™, classical Greek, history, Italian, art history, Latin, Mandarin Chinese, mathematics, music, philosophy and theology, physics, psychology, Russian, Spanish.
Website: www.cambridgeinternational.org/preu

Edexcel International GCSEs

Pearson's Edexcel International GCSEs are academic qualifications aimed at learners aged 14 to 16. They're equivalent to a UK General Certificate of Secondary Education (GCSE), and are the main requirement for Level 3 studies, including progression to GCE AS or A levels, BTECs or employment. International GCSEs are linear qualifications, meaning that students take all of the exams at the end of the course. They are available at Level 1 (grades 3-1) and Level 2 (grades 9-4). There are currently more than 100,000 learners studying Edexcel International GCSEs, in countries throughout Asia, Africa, Europe, the Middle East and Latin America. Developed by subject specialists and reviewed regularly, many of Pearson's Edexcel International GCSEs include specific international content to make them relevant to students worldwide.

Pearson's Edexcel International GCSEs were initially developed for international schools. They have since become popular among independent schools in the UK, but are not approved for use in UK state schools. If you're a UK state school, you may be interested in offering Pearson's Edexcel GCSE qualifications. These qualifications are based on the Edexcel International GCSE specifications. They do not count towards national performance measures and are not eligible for funding in UK state schools.

International GCSEs are offered in over 35 subjects. Subject areas include: Business & Economics, Computer Science, English, Humanities, Information and Communication Technology, Languages, Mathematics, Sciences.

Free Standing Maths Qualifications (FSMQ)

Aimed at those students wishing to acquire further qualifications in maths, specifically additional mathematics and foundations of advanced mathematics (MEI).

Further UCAS points can be earned upon completion of the advanced FSMQ in additional mathematics.

For further details see the OCR website.

AQA Certificate in Mathematical Studies (Core Maths)

This new Level 3 qualification has been available from September 2015. It is designed for students who achieved a Grade 4 or above at GCSE and want to continue studying Maths. The qualification carries UCAS points equivalent to an AS level qualification

AQA Certificate in Further Maths

This level 2 qualification has been designed to provide stretch and challenge to the most able mathematicians. This will be best suited to students who either already have, or are expected to achieve the top grades in GCSE Mathematics and are likely to progress to A level Mathematics and Further Mathematics.

Scottish qualifications

Information supplied by Scottish Qualifications Authority

In Scotland, qualifications are awarded by the Scottish Qualifications Authority (SQA), the national accreditation and awarding body. A variety of qualifications are offered, including:

- National Qualifications (National Units, National Courses and Group Awards)
- Wider Achievement Awards
- Skills for Work Courses
- Scottish Baccalaureates

Qualifications in the Scottish qualifications system sit at various levels on the Scottish Credit and Qualifications Framework (SCQF). There are 12 levels on the SCQF and each level represents the difficulty of learning involved. Qualifications in schools span SCQF levels 1 to 7.

National Qualifications (NQ)

SQA designed and developed new National Qualifications to support Curriculum for Excellence (CfE) – the new national curriculum in Scotland for young people aged 3 to 18. They are taught in schools and colleges, and by some training providers.

The National Qualifications are National 1, National 2, National 3, National 4, National 5, Higher and Advanced Higher. They range from SCQF level 1 (National 1) to SCQF level 7 (Advanced Higher).

National 1 to National 5 qualifications have been available since August 2013. The new Higher was introduced in August 2014 and the new Advanced Higher was introduced in August 2015.

National Qualifications help young people to demonstrate the skills, knowledge and understanding they have developed at school or college and enable them to prepare for further learning, training and employment.

National Units

National Units are the building blocks of National Courses and Group Awards. They are also qualifications in their own right and can be done on an individual basis, such as National 1 qualifications, which are standalone units. Units are normally designed to take 40 hours of teaching to complete and each one is assessed by completing a unit assessment. Over 3500 National Units are available, including National Literacy and Numeracy Units, which assess students' literacy and numeracy skills.

National Courses

National Courses are available at National 2, National 3, National 4, National 5, Higher and Advanced Higher levels. There are more than 60 subjects available, at various levels.

National 2, National 3 and National 4 are unit-based courses and they are assessed through internally marked unit assessments. National 4 courses also include an Added Value Unit assessment that assesses the whole course. National 2 to National 4 courses are not graded, but are assessed as pass or fail.

National 5, Higher and Advanced Higher courses are graded A to D or 'no award' and include a course assessment that takes place at the end of the course. For most subjects, the course assessment is a combination of exam(s) and coursework. SQA marks all exams and the majority of coursework.

The assessment of National 5, Higher and Advanced Higher courses is currently undergoing change. Units and unit assessments are being removed from the courses, and the course assessments are being extended to assess more course content. The changes have already been introduced for National 5, and will come into effect for Higher in 2019 and Advanced Higher in 2020.

Skills for Work Courses

Skills for Work courses are designed to introduce school pupils to the demands and expectations of the world of work. They are available in a variety of areas such as construction, hairdressing and hospitality. They involve a strong element of learning through involvement in practical and vocational activities and develop knowledge, skills and experience that are related to employment. They are available at SCQF levels 4 to 6 and are often delivered in partnership with schools and colleges.

Group Awards

National Certificates (NCs) and National Progression Awards (NPAs) are referred to as National Qualification Group Awards. These qualifications provide students preparing for work with opportunities to develop skills that are sought after by employers. They are available at SCQF levels 2 to 6.

NCs prepare students for employment, career development or progression to more advanced study. They are available in a range of subjects, including: Sound Production, Technical Theatre, and Child, Health and Social Care.

NPAs develop specific skills and knowledge in specialist vocational areas, including Journalism, Architecture and Interior Design, and Legal Services. They are taught in partnership between schools, colleges, employers and training providers.

Awards

SQA Awards provide students with opportunities to acquire skills, recognise achievement and promote confidence through independent thinking and positive attitudes, while motivating them to be successful and participate positively in the wider community.

A variety of different awards are offered at a number of levels and cover subjects including leadership, employability and enterprise. These awards are designed to recognise the life, learning and work skills that students gain from taking part in activities such as sports, volunteering and fundraising.

Scottish Baccalaureates

Scottish Baccalaureates consist of a coherent group of Higher and Advanced Higher qualifications and, uniquely, an interdisciplinary project selected by the student in one of four broad topics – languages, science, expressive arts or social studies. The interdisciplinary project is marked at Advanced Higher level and provides students with a platform to apply their knowledge in a realistic context. Aimed at high-achieving sixth year students, the Scottish Baccalaureate encourages personalised, in-depth study and interdisciplinary learning in their final year of secondary school.

For more information on SQA and its portfolio of qualifications, visit www.sqa.org.uk or follow SQA on Twitter @sqanews.

Additional and Alternative

AQA Baccalaureate

The AQA Baccalaureate is awarded to students who achieve at least three A levels (minimum grade E or 2/3), a broader study AS level subject and the EPQ, plus they must undertake a minimum of 100 hours of 'enrichment activities'.

This is a complete curriculum programme, which adds a broader range of study, and includes the Extended Project Qualification (EPQ).

This qualification is built on familiar subjects, so it can be tailored to fit in with existing curricula. It includes extracurricular activities and encourages a series of 'enrichment activities' covering personal qualities, perseverance, leadership, independence, time management, commitment and communication.

The AQA Bacc is accepted by universities; offers are based on the component parts of the baccalaureate, with students receiving their AQA Baccalaureate and enrichment certificates alongside their A level, AS level and EPQ certificates.

Cambridge Primary

Cambridge Primary is typically for learners aged 5 to 11 years. It develops learner skills and understanding through the primary years in English as a first or second language, mathematics, science, Global Perspectives™ and ICT. The flexible curriculum frameworks include optional assessment tools to help schools monitor learners' progress and give detailed feedback to parents. At the end of Cambridge Primary, schools can enter students for Cambridge Primary Checkpoint tests which are marked in Cambridge.
Website: www.cambridgeinternational.org/primary

Cambridge ICT Starters introduces learners, typically aged 5 to 14 years, to the key ICT applications they need to achieve computer literacy and to understand the impact of technology on our daily lives. It can be taught and assessed in English or Spanish.

Cambridge Lower Secondary

Cambridge Lower Secondary is typically for learners aged 11 to 14 years. It develops learner skills and understanding in English as a first or second language, mathematics, science, Global Perspectives™ and ICT for the first three years of secondary education, and includes assessment tools. At the end of Cambridge Lower Secondary, schools can enter students for Cambridge Lower Secondary Checkpoint tests which are marked in Cambridge and provide an external international benchmark for student performance.
Website:www.cambridgeinternational.org/lowersecondary

European Baccalaureate (EB)

Not to be confused with the International Baccalaureate (IB) or the French Baccalaureate, this certificate is available in European schools and recognised in all EU countries.

To obtain the baccalaureate, a student must obtain a minimum score of 60%, which is made up from: coursework, oral participation in class and tests (40%); five written examinations (36%) – mother-tongue, first foreign language and maths are compulsory for all candidates; four oral examinations (24%) – mother tongue and first foreign language are compulsory (history or geography may also be compulsory here, dependant on whether the candidate has taken a written examination in these subjects).

Throughout the EU the syllabus and examinations necessary to achieve the EB are identical. The only exception to this rule is the syllabus for the mother tongue language. The EB has been specifically designed to meet, at the very least, the minimum qualification requirements of each member state.

Study for the EB begins at nursery stage (age 4) and progresses through primary (age six) and on into secondary school (age 12).

Syllabus
Languages: Bulgarian, Czech, Danish, Dutch, English, Estonian, Finnish, Finnish as a second national language, French, German, Greek, Hungarian, Irish, Italian, Latvian, Lithuanian, Maltese, Polish, Portuguese, Romanian, Slovak, Slovenian, Spanish, Swedish, Swedish for Finnish pupils.

Literary: art education, non-confessional ethics, geography, ancient Greek, history, human sciences, Latin, music, philosophy, physical education.

Sciences: biology, chemistry, economics, ICT, integrated science, mathematics, physics.
For more information, contact:
Office of the Secretary-General of the European Schools, c/o European Commission, Rue Joseph II, 30-2ème étage, B-1049 Brussels, Belgium
Tel: +32 2295 3745; Fax: +32 2298 6298
Website: www.eursc.eu

The International Baccalaureate (IB)

TThe International Baccalaureate (IB) offers four challenging and high quality educational programmes for a worldwide community of schools, aiming to develop internationally minded people who, recognizing their common humanity and shared guardianship of the planet, help to create a better, more peaceful world.

The IB works with schools around the world (both state and privately funded) that share the commitment to international education to deliver these programmes.

Schools that have achieved the high standards required for authorization to offer one or more of the IB programmes are known as IB World Schools. There are over half a million students attending more than 4500 IB World Schools in 153 countries and this number is growing annually.

The Primary Years, Middle Years and Diploma Programmes share a common philosophy and common characteristics. They develop the whole student, helping students to grow intellectually, socially, aesthetically and culturally. They provide a broad and balanced education that includes science and the humanities, languages and mathematics, technology and the arts. The programmes teach students to think critically, and encourage them to draw connections between areas of knowledge and to use problem-solving techniques and concepts from many disciplines. They instil in students a sense of responsibility towards others and towards the environment. Lastly, and perhaps most importantly, the programmes give students an awareness and understanding of their own culture and of other cultures, values and ways of life.

A fourth programme called the IB Career Related Certificate (IBCC) became available to IB World Schools from September 2012. All IB programmes include:
- a written curriculum or curriculum framework;
- student assessment appropriate to the age range;
- professional development and networking opportunities for teachers;
- support, authorization and programme evaluation for the school.

The IB Primary Years Programme

The IB Primary Years Programme (PYP), for students aged three to 12, focuses on the development of the whole child as an inquirer, both in the classroom and in the world outside. It is a framework consisting of five essential elements (concepts, knowledge, skills, attitude, action) and guided by six trans-disciplinary themes of global significance, explored using knowledge and skills derived from six subject areas (language, social studies, mathematics, science and technology, arts, and personal, social and physical education) with a powerful emphasis on inquiry-based learning.

The most significant and distinctive feature of the PYP is the six trans-disciplinary themes. These themes are about issues that have meaning for, and are important to, all of us. The programme offers a balance between learning about or through the subject areas, and learning beyond them. The six themes of global significance create a trans-disciplinary framework that allows students to 'step up' beyond the confines of learning within subject areas:
- Who we are.
- Where we are in place and time.
- How we express ourselves.
- How the world works.
- How we organize ourselves.
- Sharing the planet.

The PYP exhibition is the culminating activity of the programme. It requires students to analyse and propose solutions to real-world issues, drawing on what they have learned through the programme. Evidence of student development and records of PYP exhibitions are reviewed by the IB as part of the programme evaluation process.

Assessment is an important part of each unit of inquiry as it both enhances learning and provides opportunities for students to reflect on what they know, understand and can do. The teacher's feedback to the students provides the guidance, the tools and the incentive for them to become more competent, more skilful and better at understanding how to learn.

The IB Middle Years Programme (MYP)

The Middle Years Programme (MYP), for students aged 11 to 16, comprises eight subject groups:
- Language acquisition
- Language and literature
- Individuals and societies
- Sciences
- Mathematics
- Arts
- Physical and health education
- Design

The MYP requires at least 50 hours of teaching time for each subject group in each year of the programme. In years 4 and 5, students have the option to take courses from six of the eight subject groups within certain limits, to provide greater flexibility in meeting local requirements and individual student learning needs.

Each year, students in the MYP also engage in at least one collaboratively planned interdisciplinary unit that involves at least two subject groups.

MYP students also complete a long-term project, where they decide what they want to learn about, identify what they already know, discovering what they will need to know to complete the project, and create a proposal or criteria for completing it

The MYP aims to help students develop their personal understanding, their emerging sense of self and their responsibility in their community.

The MYP allows schools to continue to meet state, provincial or national legal requirements for students with access needs. Schools must develop an inclusion/special educational needs (SEN) policy that explains assessment access arrangements, classroom accommodations and curriculum modification that meet individual student learning needs.

The IB Diploma Programme (IBDP)

The IB Diploma Programme, for students aged 16 to 19, is an academically challenging and motivating curriculum of international education that prepares students for success at university and in life beyond studies.

DP students choose at least one course from six subject groups, thus ensuring depth and breadth of knowledge and experience in languages, social studies, the experimental sciences, mathematics, and the arts. With more than 35 courses to choose from, students have the flexibility to further explore and learn subjects that meet their interest. Out of the six courses required, at least three and not more than four must be taken at higher level (240 teaching hours), the others at standard level (150 teaching hours). Students can take examinations in English, French or Spanish.

In addition, three unique components of the programme – the DP core – aim to broaden students' educational experience and challenge them to apply their knowledge and skills. The DP core – the extended essay (EE), theory of knowledge (TOK) and creativity, activity, service (CAS) – are compulsory and central to the philosophy of the programme.

The IB uses both external and internal assessment to measure student performance in the DP. Student results are determined by performance against set standards, not by each student's position in the overall rank order. DP assessment is unique in the way that it measures the extent to which students have mastered advanced academic skills not what they have memorized. DP assessment also encourages an international outlook and intercultural skills, wherever appropriate.

The IB diploma is awarded to students who gain at least 24 points out of a possible 45 points, subject to certain minimum levels of performance across the whole programme and to satisfactory participation in the creativity, activity, and service requirement.

Recognized and respected by leading universities globally, the DP encourages students to be knowledgeable, inquiring, caring and compassionate, and to develop intercultural understanding, open-mindedness and the attitudes necessary to respect and evaluate a range of viewpoints.

The IB Career Related Programme (IBCP)

The IB Career-related Programme, for students aged 16 to 19, offers an innovative educational framework that combines academic studies with career-related learning. Through the CP, students develop the competencies they need to succeed in the 21st century. More importantly, they have the opportunity to engage with a rigorous study programme that genuinely interests them while gaining transferable and lifelong skills that prepares them to pursue higher education, apprenticeships or direct employment.

CP students complete four core components – language development, personal and professional skills, service learning and a reflective project – in order to receive the International Baccalaureate Career-related Programme Certificate. Designed to enhance critical thinking and intercultural understanding, the CP core helps students develop the communication and personal skills, as well as intellectual habits required for lifelong learning.

Schools that choose to offer the CP can create their own distinctive version of the programme and select career pathways that suit their students and local community needs. The IB works with a variety of CRS providers around the world and schools seeking to develop career pathways with professional communities can benefit from our existing collaborations. All CRS providers undergo a rigorous curriculum evaluation to ensure that their courses align with the CP pedagogy and meet IB quality standards. The flexibility to meet the needs, backgrounds and contexts of learners allows CP schools to offer an education that is relevant and meaningful to their students.

Launched in 2012, there are more than 140 CP schools in over 23 countries to date. Many schools with the IB Diploma Programme (DP) and the Middle Years Programme (MYP) have chosen the CP as an alternative IB pathway to offer students. CP schools often report that the programme has helped them raise student aspiration, increase student engagement and retention and encouraged learners to take responsibility for their own actions, helping them foster high levels of self-esteem through meaningful achievements.

For more information on IB programmes, visit: www.ibo.org

Africa, Europe, Middle East Global Centre, Churchillplein 6, The Hague, 2517JW, The Netherlands
Tel: +31 (0)70 352 6233

Pearson Edexcel Mathematics Awards

Pearson's Edexcel Mathematics Awards are small, stand-alone qualifications designed to help students to develop and demonstrate proficiency in different areas of mathematics. These Awards enable students to focus on understanding key concepts and techniques, and are available across three subjects, including: Number and Measure (Levels 1 and 2), Algebra (Levels 2 and 3) and Statistical Methods (Levels 1, 2 and 3). The level 1 Award in Number and Measure is now also an approved stepping stone qualification for the 16-18 maths condition of funding

Designed to build students' confidence and fluency; the Awards can fit into the existing programme of delivery for mathematics in schools and colleges, prepare students for GCSE and/or GCE Mathematics, and to support further study in other subjects, training or the workplace. They offer a choice of levels to match students' abilities, with clear progression between the levels. These small, 60-70 guided learning hour qualifications are assessed through one written paper per level. Each qualification is funded and approved for pre-16 and 16-18 year old students in England and in schools and colleges in Wales.

Projects

Extended Project Qualification (EPQ)

AQA, OCR, Pearson and WJEC offer the Extended Project Qualification, which is a qualification aimed at developing a student's research and independent learning skills. The EPQ can be taken as a stand-alone qualification, and it is equivalent to half an A level in UCAS points (but only a third of performance points). It is also possible to take the EPQ as part of the AQA Baccalaureate.

Students complete a research based written report and may produce an artefact or a practical science experiment as part of their project

Cambridge International Project Qualification (IPQ)

Cambridge International is offering a new standalone project-based qualification from September 2018, which can be taken alongside Cambridge International AS & A levels. Students complete a 5000-word research project on a topic of their choice. The qualification is assessed by Cambridge International.

For more information, go to www.cambridgeinternational.org/advanced

Entry level and basic skills

Entry Level Qualifications

If you want to take GCSE or NVQ level 1 but have not yet reached the standard required, then entry level qualifications are for you as they are designed to get you started on the qualifications ladder.

Entry level qualifications are available in a wide range of areas. You can take an entry level certificate in most subjects where a similar GCSE exists. There are also vocational entry level qualifications – some in specific areas like retail or catering and others where you can take units in different work-related subjects to get a taster of a number of career areas. There are also entry level certificates in life skills and the basic skills of literacy and numeracy.

Anyone can take an entry level qualification – your school or college will help you decide which qualification is right for you.

Entry level qualifications are flexible programmes so the time it takes to complete will vary according to where you study and how long you need to take the qualification.

Subjects available: art and design, computer science, English, geography, history, Latin, mathematics, physical education and science.

Functional Skills

Functional Skills are qualifications in English, maths and ICT that equip learners with the basic practical skills required in everyday life, education and the workplace. They are available at Entry 1 through to Level 2. Functional Skills are identified as funded 'stepping stone' qualifications to English and maths GCSE for post-16 learners who haven't previously achieved a grade D in these subjects. There are part of apprenticeship completion requirements.

Vocational qualifications

Applied Generals/AQA Level 3 Certificates and Extended Certificates

Applied General qualifications are available in Business and Science and are a practical introduction to these subjects, they are a real alternative to A level support progression to further study or employment aimed at students aged 16 to 19.

Developed together with teachers, schools, colleges and higher education institutions, they help learners to develop knowledge and skills.

A mixture of assessment types means learners can apply their knowledge in a practical way. An integrated approach creates a realistic and relevant qualification for learners.

AQA Technical Awards and Level 1/2 Awards

AQA's new Technical Award and Level 1/2 Awards are practical, vocational level 1/2 qualifications for 14- to 16-year-olds to take alongside GCSEs.

Technical Awards and AQA Level 1/2 Awards provide an introduction to life and work within a range of vocational areas, equipping learners with the practical, transferable skills and core knowledge needed to progress to further general or vocational study, including level 3 qualifications, employment or apprenticeships.

There are nine individual qualifications, one Technical Award in Performing Arts, and nine AQA Level

1/2 awards in: Children's Learning and Development, Fashion and Textiles, Food and Catering, Health and Social Care, IT, Materials Technology, Sport STEM, and Visual Communication.

Learners are assessed on doing rather than knowing through the project-based internal assessments, where they can apply their knowledge to practical tasks. Assignments will vary according to the subject, but activities range from designing and making a working product or prototype; making a short film; planning and putting on a performance, or presenting to others. There are two internally assessed units worth 30% each, and an externally assessed exam worth 40%. The AQA Level 1/2 Awards will not be available beyond 2019.

AQA Tech-levels

Level 3 technical qualifications have been designed in collaboration with employers and professional bodies. They're aimed at learners aged over 16 wanting to progress into a specific sector through apprenticeships, further study or employment. There are 16 individual qualifications within IT, Engineering, Business and Entertainment Technology. These vary in size of qualification.

Transferable skills have been contextualised explicitly within each qualification and are a mandatory part of the qualification outcome.

Learners are assessed through a combination of examinations, internally and externally assessed assignments.

BTECs

BTEC Level 2 First qualifications
ie BTEC Level 2 Diplomas, BTEC Level 2 Extended Certificates, BTEC Level 2 Certificates and BTEC Level 2 Award.

BTEC Firsts are Level 2 introductory work-related programmes covering a wide range of vocational areas including business, engineering, information technology, health and social care, media, travel and tourism, and public services.

Programmes may be taken full or part-time. They are practical programmes that provide a foundation for the knowledge and skills you will need in work. Alternatively, you can progress onto a BTEC National qualification, Applied GCE A level or equivalent.

There are no formal entry requirements and they can be studied alongside GCSEs. Subjects available: agriculture; animal care; applied science; art and design; business; children's care, learning and development; construction; countryside and the environment; engineering; fish husbandry; floristry; health and social care; horse care; horticulture; hospitality; IT; land-based technology; business; creative media production; music; performing arts; public services; sport; travel and tourism; and vehicle technology.

BTEC Foundation Diploma in Art and Design (QCF)
For those students preparing to go on to higher education within the field of art and design. This diploma is recognised as one of the best courses of its type in the UK, and is used in preparation for degree programmes. Units offered include researching, recording and responding in art and design, media experimentation, personal experimental studies, and a final major project.

BTEC Nationals

ie BTEC Level 3 Extended Diplomas (QCF), BTEC Level 3 Diplomas (QCF), BTEC Level 3 Subsidiary Diplomas (QCF), BTEC Level 3 Certificates (QCF)

BTEC National programmes are long-established vocational programmes. They are practical programmes that are highly valued by employers. They enable you to gain the knowledge and skills that you will need in work, or give you the choice to progress on to a BTEC Higher National, a Foundation Degree or a degree programme.

BTEC Nationals, which hold UCAS points cover a range of vocationally specialist sectors including child care, children's play, learning and development, construction, art and design, aeronautical engineering, electrical/electronic engineering, IT, business, creative and media production, performing arts, public services, sport, sport and exercise sciences and applied science. The programmes may be taken full- or part-time, and can be taken in conjunction with NVQs and/or functional skills units at an appropriate level.

There are no formal entry requirements, but if you have any of the following you are likely to be at the right level to study a BTEC national qualification.

- a BTEC Level 2 First qualification
- GCSEs – at grades A* to C in several subjects
- Relevant work experience

There are also very specialist BTEC Nationals, such as pharmaceutical science and blacksmithing and metalworking.

BTEC Higher Nationals

Known as HNDs and HNCs – ie BTEC Level 5 HND Diplomas (QCF) and BTEC Level 4 HNC Diplomas (QCF)

BTEC HNDs and HNCs are further and higher education qualifications that offer a balance of education and vocational training. They are available in a wide range of work-related areas such as graphic design, business, health and social care, computing and systems development, manufacturing engineering, hospitality management, and public services.

Pearson is introducing a new suite of subjects between 2016 and 2018, to match growing demand. For full information on the subjects, visit: www.ocr.org.uk/qualifications/by-type/entry-level/entry-level-2016/

BTEC higher national courses combine study with hands-on work experience during your course. Once completed, you can use the skills you learn to begin your career, or continue on to a related degree course.

HNDs are often taken as a full-time course over two years but can also be followed part-time in some cases.

HNCs are often for people who are working and take two years to complete on a part-time study basis by day release, evenings, or a combination of the two. Some HNC courses are done on a full-time basis.

There are no formal entry requirements, but if you have any of the following you are likely to be at the right academic level:

- at least one A level
- a BTEC Level 3 National qualification
- level 3 NVQ

BTEC specialist and professional qualifications

These qualifications are designed to prepare students for specific and specialist work activities. These are split into two distinct groups:

- Specialist qualifications (entry to level 3)
- Professional qualifications (levels 4 to 7)

Cambridge Nationals

Cambridge Nationals, the updated version of OCR Nationals, are vocationally-related qualifications that take an engaging, practical and inspiring approach to learning and assessment.

They are industry-relevant, geared to key sector requirements and very popular with schools and colleges because they suit such a broad range of learning styles and abilities.

Cambridge Nationals are available in business, child development, engineering, health and social care, ICT, science, sport, and creative iMedia. Available as joint Level 1 and 2 qualifications, the updated Nationals are aimed at students aged 14 to 16 in full-time study.

Cambridge Technicals

OCR's Cambridge Technicals are practical and flexible vocationally-related qualifications, offering students in-depth study in a wide range of subjects, including business, health and social care, IT, sport, art and design, digital media, science, performing arts and engineering.

Cambridge Technicals are aimed at young people aged 16 to 19 who have completed Key Stage 4 of their education and want to study in a more practical, work-related way.

Cambridge Technicals are available at Level 2 and Level 3, and carry UCAS points at Level 3.

NVQs

NVQs reward those who demonstrate skills gained at work. They relate to particular jobs and are usefully taken while you are working. Within reason, NVQs do not have to be completed in a specified amount of time. They can be taken by full-time employees or by school and college students with a work placement or part-time job that enables them to develop the appropriate skills. There are no age limits and no special entry requirements.

NVQs are organised into levels, based on the competencies required. Levels 1-3 are the levels most applicable to learners within the 14-19 phase. Achievement of level 4 within this age group will be rare. See the OCR website for further information.

Occupational Studies (Northern Ireland)

Targeted at learners working towards and at level 1 and 2 in Key Stage 4 within the Northern Ireland curriculum. For further information see the CCEA website.

OCR Vocational Qualifications

These are available at different levels and different sizes. Levels 1-3 are the levels most applicable to learners within the 14-19 phase. The different sizes are indicated with the use of Award, Certificate and Diploma in the qualification title and indicate the number of hours it typically takes to complete the qualification.

Vocational Qualifications are assessed according to each individual specification, but may include practical assessments and/or marked assessments. They are designed to provide evidence of a student's relevant skills and knowledge in their chosen subject. These qualifications can be used for employment or as a path towards further education. See the OCR website for further details.

SVQs (Scotland)

Scottish Vocational Qualifications (SVQs) are based on national standards, which are drawn up by people from industry, commerce and education. They are studied in the workplace, in college or with training providers. Some schools offer them in partnership with colleges and employers. SVQs are available in many subject areas, from forestry to IT, management to catering, and journalism to construction.

Each unit of an SVQ defines one aspect of a job or work role and what it is to be competent in that aspect of the job.

SVQs are available at SCQF levels 4 to 11 and levels 4 to 7 are most applicable to learners aged 16 to 18.

Awarding organisations and examination dates

Awarding organisations and examination dates

In England there are four awarding organisations, each offering GCSEs, AS and A levels (Eduqas offers only reformed qualifications in England, whereas WJEC offers in England, Wales, Northern Ireland and independent regions). There are separate awarding organisations in Wales (WJEC) and Northern Ireland (CCEA). The awarding organisation in Scotland (SQA) offers equivalent qualifications.

This information was supplied by the awarding bodies and was accurate at the time of going to press. It is intended as a general guide only for candidates in the United Kingdom. Dates are subject to variation and should be confirmed with the awarding organisation concerned.

AQA

Qualifications offered:
GCSE
AS and A level
Technical levels
Foundation Certificate of Secondary Education (FCSE)
Free Standing Maths Qualifications (FSMQ)
Entry Level Certificate (ELC)
Foundation and Higher Projects
Extended Project Qualification (EPQ)
AQA Baccalaureate
Applied Generals/AQA Level 3 Certificates and Extended Certificates
Functional Skills
AQA Certificate
Technical Award

Other assessment schemes:
Unit Award Scheme (UAS)
AQA Level 1/2 Tech Awards

Examination dates for summer 2019: 10 May – 25 June

Contact:
Email: eos@aqa.org.uk
Website: www.aqa.org.uk
Tel: 0800 197 7162 (8am–5pm Monday to Friday)
+44 161 696 5995 (Outside the UK)

Devas Street, Manchester M15 6EX
Stag Hill House, Guildford, Surrey GU2 7XJ
31-33 Windsor House, Cornwall Road, Harrogate, HG1 2PW
2nd Floor, Lynton House, 7–12 Tavistock Square, London, WC1H 9LT

CCEA – Council for the Curriculum, Examinations and Assessment

Qualifications offered:
GCSE
GCE AS/A level
Key Skills (Levels 1-4)
Entry Level Qualifications
Essential Skills (Levels 1,2 & Entry Level)
Occupational Studies (Levels 1 & 2)
QCF Qualifications
Applied GCSE, GCE and QCF Level 1 and 2 qualifications

Examination dates for summer 2019: 1 May – 21 June

Contact:
Email: info@ccea.org.uk
Website: www.ccea.org.uk

29 Clarendon Road, Clarendon Dock, Belfast, BT1 3BG
Tel: (028) 9026 1200

Eduqas

Eduqas, part of WJEC, offers Ofqual reformed GCSEs, AS and A levels to secondary schools and colleges. Our qualifications are available in England, Channel Islands, Isle of Man, Northern Ireland and to the independent sector in Wales (restrictions may apply).

Qualifications offered:
GCSE (9-1)
AS
A level
Level 3

Examination dates for summer 2019: 13 May – 26 June

Contact:
Email: info@eduqas.co.uk
Website: www.eduqas.co.uk

Eduqas (WJEC CBAC Ltd),
245 Western Avenue, Cardiff, CF5 2YX
Telephone: 029 2026 5465

IB – International Baccalaureate

Qualification offered:
IB Diploma
IB Career-related Certificate

Contact:
www.ibo.org

Examination dates for summer 2019: 2 –24 May

IB Global Centre, The Hague, Churchillplein 6, 2517 JW, The Hague, The Netherlands

Tel: +31 70 352 60 00

OCR – Oxford Cambridge and RSA Examinations – and Cambridge International*

Qualifications offered by OCR or sister awarding organisation Cambridge Assessment International Education (Cambridge International) include:
GCSE
GCE AS/A level
IGCSE
International AS/A level
Extended Project
Cambridge International Project Qualification
Cambridge Pre-U
Cambridge Nationals
Cambridge Technicals
Functional Skills
FSMQ – Free Standing Maths Qualification
NVQ

Examination dates for summer 2019: 13 May to 25 June

Contact:
Website: www.ocr.org.uk
(or www.cambridgeinternational.org)

OCR Head Office, The Triangle Building, Shaftesbury Road, Cambridge, CB2 8EA
Tel: 01223 553998

Pearson

Qualifications offered:
Pearson's qualifications are offered in the UK but are also available through their international centres across the world. They include:
DiDA, CiDA
GCE A levels
GCSEs
Adult Literacy and Numeracy
Functional Skills
Foundation Learning
International GCSEs
Key Skills
ESOL (Skills for Life)
BTEC Customised Qualifications
BTEC Foundation Diploma in Art & Design
BTEC Nationals
BTEC Higher National Certificates and Higher National Diplomas (HNC/HND)
BTEC Firsts
BTEC Specialist qualifications
BTEC Professional qualifications
BTEC WorkSkills
NVQs
Project qualifications

Examination dates for summer 2019: 13 May – 26 June

Contact:
190 High Holborn, London WC1V 7BH

See website for specific contact details: www.edexcel.com

SQA – Scottish Qualifications Authority

Qualifications offered:
National Qualifications (NQs): National 1 to National 5; Higher; Advanced Higher
Skills for Work
National Certificates (NCs)
National Progression Awards (NPAs)
Scottish Baccalaureate
Awards
Wider Achievement
Core Skills
Scottish Vocational Qualifications (SVQs)
Higher National Certificates and Higher National Diplomas (HNCs/HNDs)*

*SQA offers HNCs and HNDs to centres in Scotland. Outside of Scotland, the equivalent qualifications are the SQA Advanced Certificate and SQA Advanced Diploma.

Examination dates for summer 2019: 25 April – 31 May

Contact:
Email: customer@sqa.org.uk
Website: www.sqa.org.uk

Glasgow – The Optima Building, 58 Robertson Street, Glasgow, G2 8DQ

Dalkeith – Lowden, 24 Wester Shawfair, Dalkeith, Midlothian, EH22 1FD

WJEC

With over 65 years' experience in delivering qualifications, WJEC is the largest provider in Wales and a leading provider in England and Northern Ireland.

Qualifications offered:
GCSE
GCE A/AS
Functional Skills
Entry Level
Welsh Baccalaureate Qualifications
Essential Skills Wales
Wider Key Skills
Project Qualifications Principal Learning
Other general qualifications such as Level 1 and Level 2 Awards and Certificates including English Language, English Literature, Latin Language, Latin Language & Roman Civilisation and Latin Literature
QCF Qualifications

Examination dates for summer 2019: 13 May – 26 June

Contact:
Email: info@wjec.co.uk
Website: www.wjec.co.uk

245 Western Avenue, Cardiff, CF5 2YX
Tel: 029 2026 5000

Educational organisations

Educational organisations

Artsmark

Arts Council England's Artsmark was set up in 2001, and rounds are held annually.
All schools in England can apply for an Artsmark – primary, middle, secondary, special and pupil referral units, maintained and independent – on a voluntary basis. An Artsmark award is made to schools showing commitment to the full range of arts – music, dance, drama and art and design.
Tel: 0845 300 6200/ 0161 934 4317
Email: artsmark@artscouncil.org.uk
Website: www.artsmark.org.uk

Association for the Education and Guardianship of International Students (AEGIS)

AEGIS brings together schools and guardianship organisations to ensure and promote the welfare of international students. AEGIS provides accreditation for all reputable guardianship organisations.
AEGIS, The Wheelhouse, Bond's Mill Estate, Bristol Road, Stonehouse, Gloucestershire GL10 3RF.
Tel: 01453 821293
Email: info@aegisuk.net
Website: www.aegisuk.net

The Association of American Study Abroad Programmes (AASAP)

Established in 1991 to represent American study abroad programmes in the UK.
Contact: Kalyn Franke, AASAP/UK,
University of Maryland in London, Connaught Hall,
36-45 Tavistock Square, London WC1H 9EX
Tel: 020 7756 8350
Email: info@aasapuk.org
Website: www.aasapuk.org

The Association of British Riding Schools (ABRS)

An independent body of proprietors and principals of riding establishments, aiming to look after their interests and those of the riding public and to raise standards of management, instruction and animal welfare.
Association of British Riding Schools, Unit 8, Bramble Hill Farm, Five Oaks Road, Slinfold, Horsham,
West Sussex RH13 0RL. Tel: 01403 790294
Email: office@abrs-info.org
Website: www.abrs-info.org

Association of Colleges (AOC)

Created in 1996 to promote the interest of further education colleges in England and Wales.
2-5 Stedham Place, London WC1A 1HU
Tel: 0207 034 9900
Fax: 0207 034 9950
Email: enquiries@aoc.co.uk
Website: www.aoc.co.uk

Association of Governing Bodies of Independent Schools (AGBIS)

AGBIS supports and advises governing bodies of schools in the independent sector on all aspects of governance. (Registered charity No. 1108756)
Association of Governing Bodies of Independent Schools, 3 Codicote Road, Welwyn, Hertfordshire AL6 9LY
Tel: 01438 840730
Fax: 0560 3432632
Email: admin@agbis.org.uk
Website: www.agbis.org.uk

Association of Employment and Learning Providers (AELP)

AELP's purpose is to influence the education and training agenda. They are the voice of independent learning providers throughout England.
Association of Employment and Learning Providers,
2nd Floor, 9 Apex Court, Bradley Stoke, Bristol, BS32 4JT
Tel: 0117 986 5389
Email: enquiries@aelp.org.uk
Website: www.aelp.org.uk

The Association of School and College Leaders (ASCL)

Formerly the Secondary Heads Association, the ASCL is a professional association for secondary school and college leaders.
130 Regent Road, Leicester LE1 7PG
Tel: 0116 299 1122
Fax: 0116 299 1123
Email: info@ascl.org.uk
Website: www.ascl.org.uk

Boarding Schools' Association (BSA)

For information on the BSA see editorial on page 37

The British Accreditation Council (BAC)

The British Accreditation Council (BAC) has now been the principal accrediting body for the independent further and higher education and training sector for nearly 30 years. BAC-accredited institutions in the UK now number more than 300, offering everything from website design to yoga to equine dentistry, as well as more standard qualifications in subjects such as business, IT, management and law. As well as our accreditation of institutions offering traditional teaching, BAC has developed a new accreditation scheme for providers offering online, distance and blended learning. Some students may also look to study outside the UK at one of the institutions holding BAC international accreditation.
Ground Floor, 14 Devonshire Square, London, EC2M 4YT
Tel: 0300 330 1400
Email: info@the-bac.org
Website: www.the-bac.org

The British Association for Early Childhood Education (BAECE)

Promotes quality provision for all children from birth to eight in whatever setting they are placed. Publishes booklets and organises conferences for those interested in early years education and care. (Registered charity Nos. 313082; SC039472)
54 Clarendon Road, Watford, WD17 1DU
Tel: 01923 438 995
Email: office@early-education.org.uk
Website: www.early-education.org.uk

The Choir Schools' Association (CSA)

Represents 44 schools attached to cathedrals, churches and college chapels, which educate cathedral and collegiate choristers.
CSA Information Officer, Village Farm, The Street, Market Weston, Diss, Norfolk IP22 2NZ
Tel: 01359 221333
Email: info@choirschools.org.uk
Website: www.choirschools.org.uk

CIFE

CIFE is the professional association for independent sixth form and tutorial colleges accredited by the British Accreditation Council (BAC), the Independent Schools Council or the DfE (Ofsted). Member colleges specialise in preparing students for GCSE and A level (AS and A2) in particular and university entrance in general.
The aim of the association is to provide a forum for the exchange of information and ideas, and for the promotion of best practice, and to safeguard adherence to strict standards of professional conduct and ethical propriety.
Further information can be obtained from CIFE:
Tel: 0208 767 8666
Email: enquiries@cife.org.uk
Website: www.cife.org.uk

Council of British International Schools (COBIS)

COBIS is a membership association of British schools of quality worldwide and is committed to a stringent process of quality assurance for all its member schools. COBIS is a member of the Independent Schools Council (ISC) of the United Kingdom.
COBIS, 55–56 Russell Square, Bloomsbury,
London WC1B 4HP
Tel: 020 3826 7190
Email: executive.director@cobis.org.uk*
Website: www.cobis.org.uk

Council of International Schools (CIS)

CIS is a not-for-profit organisation committed to supporting its member schools and colleges in achieving and delivering the highest standards of international education. CIS provides accreditation to schools, teacher and leader recruitment and best practice development. CIS Higher Education assists member colleges and universities in recruiting a diverse profile of qualified international students.
Schipholweg 113, 2316 XC Leiden, The Netherlands.
Tel: +31 71 524 3300
Email: info@cois.org
Website: www.cois.org

Dyslexia Action (DA)

A registered, educational charity (No. 268502), which has established teaching and assessment centres and conducts teacher-training throughout the UK. The aim of the institute is to help people with dyslexia of all ages to overcome their difficulties in learning to read, write and spell and to achieve their potential.
Dyslexia Action Training and Guild, Centurion House, London Road, Staines-upon-Thames TW18 4AX
Tel: 01784 222 304
Website: www.dyslexiaaction.org.uk

European Association for International Education (EAIE)

A not-for-profit organisation aiming for internationalisation in higher education in Europe. It has a membership of over 1800.
PO Box 11189, 1001 GD Amsterdam, The Netherlands
Tel: +31 20 344 5100
Fax: +31 20 344 5119
Email: info@eaie.org
Website: www.eaie.org

ECIS (European Collaborative for International Schools)

ECIS is a membership organisation which provides services to support professional development, good governance and leadership in international schools.
24 Greville Street,
London, EC1N 8SS
Tel: 020 7824 7040
Email: ecis@ecis.org
Website: www.ecis.org

The Girls' Day School Trust (GDST)

The Girls' Day School Trust (GDST) is one of the largest, longest-established and most successful groups of independent schools in the UK, with 4000 staff and over 20,000 students between the ages of 3 and 18. As a charity that owns and runs a family of 26 schools in England and Wales, it reinvests all its income into its schools for the benefit of the pupils. With a long history of pioneering innovation in the education of girls, the GDST now also educates boys in some of its schools, and has two coeducational sixth form colleges. (Registered charity No. 306983)
100 Rochester Row, London SW1P 1JP
Tel: 020 7393 6666
Email: info@wes.gdst.net
Website: www.gdst.net

Girls' Schools Association (GSA)

For information on the GSA see editorial on page 38

The Headmasters' and Headmistresses' Conference (HMC)

For information on the HMC see editorial on page 39

Human Scale Education (HSE)

An educational reform movement aiming for small education communities based on democracy, fairness and respect. (Registered charity No. 1000400)
Email: contact@hse.org.uk
Website: www.hse.org.uk

The Independent Association of Prep Schools (IAPS)

For further information about IAPS see editorial on page 40

The Independent Schools Association (ISA)

For further information about ISA see editorial on page 41

The Independent Schools' Bursars Association (ISBA)

Exists to support and advance financial and operational performance in independent schools. The ISBA is a charitable company limited by guarantee. (Company No. 6410037; registered charity No. 1121757.)
Bluett House, Unit 11–12 Manor Farm, Cliddesden, Basingstoke, Hampshire RG25 2JB
Tel: 01256 330369
Email: office@theisba.org.uk
Website: www.theisba.org.uk

The Independent Schools Council (ISC)

The Independent Schools Council exists to promote choice, diversity and excellence in education; the development of talent at all levels of ability; and the widening of opportunity for children from all backgrounds to achieve their potential. Its 1280 member schools educate more than 500,000 children at all levels of ability and from all socioeconomic classes. Nearly a third of children in ISC schools receive help with fees. The Governing Council of ISC contains representatives from each of the eight ISC constituent associations listed below. See also page 36.

Members:
Association of Governing Bodies of Independent Schools (AGBIS)
Girls' Schools Association (GSA)
Headmasters' and Headmistresses' Conference (HMC)
Independent Association of Prep Schools (IAPS)
Independent Schools Association (ISA)
Independent Schools Bursars' Association (ISBA)
The Society of Heads

The council also has close relations with the BSA, COBIS, SCIS and WISC.

First Floor, 27 Queen Anne's Gate,
London, SW1H 9BU
Tel: 020 7766 7070
Fax: 020 7766 7071
Email: research@isc.co.uk
Website: www.isc.co.uk

The Independent Schools Examinations Board (ISEB)

Details of the Common Entrance examinations are obtainable from:
Independent Schools Examinations Board,
Endeavour House, Crow Arch Lane, Ringwood BH24 1HP
Tel: 01425 470555
Email: enquiries@iseb.co.uk
Website: www.iseb.co.uk
Copies of past papers can be purchased from Galore Park: www.galorepark.co.uk

The Inspiring Futures Foundation (IFF)

The IFF provides careers education and guidance to schools and students. Professional support and training is available to school staff and our Futurewise programme provides individual, web-based, support for students and their parents. Career/subject insight courses, gap-year fairs and an information service are additional elements of the service.
Tel: 01491 820381
Email: helpline@inspiringfutures.org.uk
Website: www.inspiringfutures.org.uk

International Baccalaureate (IB)

For full information about the IB see full entry on page 415.

International Schools Theatre Association (ISTA)

International body of teachers and students of theatre, run by teachers for teachers. Registered charity No. 1050103.
3 Omega Offices, 14 Coinagehall St,
Helston, Cornwall TR13 8EB
Tel: 01326 560398
Email: office@ista.co.uk
Website: www.ista.co.uk

Maria Montessori Institute (MMI)

Authorised by the Association Montessori Internationale (AMI) to run their training course in the UK. Further information is available from:
26 Lyndhurst Gardens, Hampstead, London NW3 5NW
Tel: 020 7435 3646
Email: info@mariamontessori.org
Website: www.mariamontessori.org

The National Association of Independent Schools & Non-Maintained Schools (NASS)

A membership organisation working with and for special schools in the voluntary and private sectors within the UK. Registered charity No. 1083632.
PO Box 705, York YO30 6WW
Tel/Fax: 01904 624446
Email: krippon@nasschools.org.uk
Website: www.nasschools.org.uk

National Day Nurseries Association (NDNA)

A national charity (No. 1078275) that aims to promote quality in early years.
NDNA, National Early Years Enterprise Centre,
Longbow Close, Huddersfield, West Yorkshire HD2 1GQ
Tel: 01484 407070
Fax: 01484 407060
Email: info@ndna.org.uk
Website: www.ndna.org.uk

NDNA Cymru, Office 2, Crown House, 11 Well Street,
Ruthin, Denbighshire LL15 1AE
Tel: 01824 707823;
Fax: 01824 707824;
Email: wales@ndna.org.uk

NDNA Scotland, The Mansfield Traquair Centre,
15 Mansfield Place, Edinburgh EH3 6BB
Tel: 0131 516 6967
Email: scot@ndna.org.uk

National Foundation for Educational Research (NFER)

NFER is the UK's largest independent provider of research, assessment and information services for education, training and children's services. Its clients include UK government departments and agencies at both national and local levels. NFER is a not-for-profit organisation and a registered charity No. 313392.
Head Office, The Mere, Upton Park,
Slough, Berkshire SL1 2DQ
Tel: 01753 574123
Fax: 01753 691632
Email: enquiries@nfer.ac.uk
Website: www.nfer.ac.uk

Potential Plus UK

Potential Plus UK is an independent charity that supports the social, emotional and learning needs of children with high learning potential of all ages and backgrounds. Registered charity No. 313182.
Challenge House, Sherwood Drive, Bletchley, Milton Keynes, Buckinghamshire MK3 6DP
Tel: 01908 646433
Email: amazingchildren@potentialplusuk.org
Website: www.potentialplusuk.org

Round Square

An international group of schools formed in 1967 following the principles of Dr Kurt Hahn, the founder of Salem School in Germany, and Gordonstoun in Scotland. The Round Square, named after Gordonstoun's 17th century circular building in the centre of the school, now has more than 100 member schools. Registered charity No. 327117.
Round Square, Swan House, Madeira Walk, Windsor SL41EU
Tel: 01474 709843
Website: www.roundsquare.org

Royal National Children's SpringBoard Foundation

On 1 July 2017 the Royal National Children's Foundation (RNCF) merged with The SpringBoard Bursary Foundation to create the Royal National Children's SpringBoard Foundation ('Royal SpringBoard'). The newly merged charity gives life-transforming bursaries to disadvantaged and vulnerable children from across the UK.
Buckingham Suite, 7 Grosvenor Gardens,
London SW1W 0BD
Tel: 020 3405 3630
Email: admin@royalspringboard.org.uk
Website: www.royalspringboard.org.uk

School Fees Independent Advice (SFIA)

For further information about SFIA, see editorial page 34

Schools Music Association of Great Britain (SMA)

The SMA is a national 'voice' for music in education. It is now part of the Incorporated Society of Musicians (Registered charity No. 313646)
Website: www.ism.org/sma

Scottish Council of Independent Schools (SCIS)

Representing more than 70 independent, fee-paying schools in Scotland, the Scottish Council of Independent Schools (SCIS) is the foremost authority on independent schools in Scotland and offers impartial information, advice and guidance to parents. Registered charity No. SC018033. They can be contacted at:
61 Dublin Street, Edinburgh EH3 6NL
Tel: 0131 556 2316
Email: info@scis.org.uk
Website: www.scis.org.uk

Society of Education Consultants (SEC)

The Society is a professional membership organisation that supports management consultants who specialise in education and children's services. The society's membership includes consultants who work as individuals, in partnerships or in association with larger consultancies.
SEC, Bellamy House, 13 West Street, Cromer NR27 9HZ
Tel: 0330 323 0457
Email: administration@sec.org.uk
Website: www.sec.org.uk

The Society of Heads

For full information see editorial on page 42

State Boarding Forum (SBF)

For full information about the SBF see editorial on page 37

Steiner Waldorf Schools Fellowship (SWSF)

Representing Steiner education in the UK and Ireland, the SWSF has member schools and early years centres in addition to interest groups and other affiliated organisations. Member schools offer education for children within the normal range of ability, aged 3 to 18. (Registered charity No. 295104)
Steiner Waldorf Schools Fellowship® Ltd, Suite 1, 3rd Floor, Copthall House, 1 New Road, Stourbridge,
West Midlands, DY8 1PH
Tel: 01384 374116
Email: admin@steinerwaldorf.org
Website: www.steinerwaldorf.org.uk

Support and Training in Prep Schools (SATIPS)

SATIPS aims to support teachers in the independent and maintained sectors of education. (Registered charity No. 313688)
West Routengill, Walden, West Burton, Leyburn,
North Yorkshire, DL8 4LF
Tel: 07584 862263
Email: gensec@satips.org
Website: www.satips.org

The Tutors' Association

The Tutors' Association is the professional body for tutoring and wider supplementary education sector in the UK. Launched three years ago it now has over 500 members. Of these 150 are Corporate Members representing some 20,000 tutors throughout the UK.
Tel: 01628 306108
Fax: 01628 890131
Email: info@thetutorsassociation.org.uk
Website: www.thetutorsassociation.org.uk

UCAS (Universities and Colleges Admissions Service)

UCAS is the organisation responsible for managing applications to higher education courses in England, Scotland, Wales and Northern Ireland. (Registered charity Nos. 1024741 and SC038598)
Rosehill, New Barn Lane,
Cheltenham, Gloucestershire GL52 3LZ
Tel: 0371 468 0 468
Website: www.ucas.com

UKCISA – The Council for International Student Affairs

UKCISA is the UK's national advisory body serving the interests of international students and those who work with them. (Registered charity No. 1095294)
Website: www.ukcisa.org.uk

United World Colleges (UWC)

UWC was founded in 1962 and their philosophy is based on the ideas of Dr Kurt Hahn (see Round Square Schools). Registered charity No. 313690.
The United World Colleges (International),
Second Floor, 17–21 Emerald Street,
London WC1N 3QN
Tel: 020 7269 7800
Fax: 020 7405 4374
Email: info@uwcio.uwc.org
Website: www.uwc.org

World-Wide Education Service of CfBT Education Trust (WES)

A leading independent service which provides home education courses worldwide.
Waverley House, Penton,
Carlisle, Cumbria CA6 5QU
Tel: 01228 577123
Email: office@weshome.com
Website: www.weshome.com

Glossary

ACETS	Awards and Certificates in Education	AQA	Assessment and Qualification Alliance/Northern Examinations and Assessment Board	Cantab	Cambridge University
AEA	Advanced Extension Award			CATSC	Catholic Association of Teachers in Schools and Colleges
AEB	Associated Examining Board for the General Certificate of Education	BA	Bachelor of Arts		
		BAC	British Accreditation Council for Independent Further and Higher Education	CCEA	Council for the Curriculum, Examination and Assessment
AEGIS	Association for the Education and Guardianship of International Students				
		BAECE	The British Association for Early Childhood Education	CDT	Craft, Design and Technology
AGBIS	Association of Governing Bodies of Independent Schools			CE	Common Entrance Examination
		BD	Bachelor of Divinity	CEAS	Children's Education Advisory Service
AHIS	Association of Heads of Independent Schools	BEA	Boarding Educational Alliance	CertEd	Certificate of Education
AJIS	Association of Junior Independent Schools	BEd	Bachelor of Education	CIE	Cambridge International Examinations
ALP	Association of Learning Providers	BLitt	Bachelor of Letters	CIFE	Conference for Independent Education
ANTC	The Association of Nursery Training Colleges	BPrimEd	Bachelor of Primary Education	CIS	Council of International Schools
AOC	Association of Colleges	BSA	Boarding Schools' Association	CISC	Catholic Independent Schools' Conference
AP	Advanced Placement	BSc	Bachelor of Science	CLAIT	Computer Literacy and Information Technology
ASCL	Association of School & College Leaders	BTEC	Range of work-related, practical programmes leading to qualifications equivalent to GCSEs and A levels awarded by Edexcel	CNED	Centre National d'enseignement (National Centre of long distance learning)
ASL	Additional and Specialist Learning				
ATI	The Association of Tutors Incorporated			COBIS	Council of British International)

CSA	The Choir Schools' Association	INSET	In service training	PGCE	Post Graduate Certificate in Education
CST	The Christian Schools' Trust	ISA	Independent Schools Association	PhD	Doctor of Philosophy
DfE	Department for Education (formerly DfES and DCFS)	ISBA	Independent Schools' Bursars' Association	PL	Principal Learning
		ISCis	Independent Schools Council information service	PNEU	Parents' National Education Union
DipEd	Diploma of Education	ISC	Independent Schools Council	PYP	Primary Years Programme
DipTchng	Diploma of Teaching	ISEB	Independent Schools Examination Board	QCA	Qualifications and Curriculum Authority
EAIE	European Association for International Education	ISST	International Schools Sports Tournament	QCF	Qualifications and Credit Framework
ECIS	European Council of International Schools	ISTA	International Schools Theatre Association	RSIS	The Round Square Schools
EdD	Doctor of Education	ITEC	International Examination Council	SAT	Scholastic Aptitude Test
Edexcel	GCSE Examining group, incorporating Business and Technology Education Council (BTEC) and University of London Examinations and Assessment Council (ULEAC)	JET	Joint Educational Trust	SATIPS	Support & Training in Prep Schools/Society of Assistant Teachers in Prep Schools
		LA	Local Authority		
		LISA	London International Schools Association	SBSA	State Boarding Schools Association
		MA	Master of Arts	SCE	Service Children's Education
EFL	English as a Foreign Language	MCIL	Member of the Chartered Institute of Linguists	SCIS	Scottish Council of Independent Schools
ELAS	Educational Law Association	MEd	Master of Education	SCQF	Scottish Credit and Qualifications Framework
EPQ	Extended Project qualification	MIoD	Member of the Institute of Directors	SEC	The Society of Educational Consultants
ESL	English as a Second Language	MLitt	Master of Letters	SEN	Special Educational Needs
FCoT	Fellow of the College of Teachers (TESOL)	MSc	Master of Science	SFCF	Sixth Form Colleges' Forum
FEFC	Further Education Funding Council	MusD	Doctor of Music	SFIA	School Fees Insurance Agency Limited
FRSA	Fellow of the Royal Society of Arts	MYP	Middle Years Programme	SFIAET	SFIA Educational Trust
FSMQ	Free-Standing Mathematics Qualification	NABSS	National Association of British Schools in Spain	SMA	Schools Music Association
GCE	General Certificate of Education	NAGC	National Association for Gifted Children	SoH	The Society of Heads
GCSE	General Certificate of Secondary Education	NAHT	National Association of Head Teachers	SQA	Scottish Qualifications Authority
GDST	Girls' Day School Trust	NAIS	National Association of Independent Schools	STEP	Second Term Entrance Paper (Cambridge)
GNVQ	General National Vocational Qualifications	NASS	National Association of Independent Schools & Non-maintained Special Schools	SVQ	Scottish Vocational Qualifications
GOML	Graded Objectives in Modern Languages			SWSF	Steiner Waldorf Schools Fellowship
GSA	Girls' Schools Association	NDNA	National Day Nurseries Association	TABS	The Association of Boarding Schools
GSVQ	General Scottish Vocational Qualifications	NEASC	New England Association of Schools and Colleges	TISCA	The Independent Schools Christian Alliance
HMC	Headmasters' and Headmistresses' Conference			TOEFL	Test of English as a Foreign Language
HMCJ	Headmasters' and Headmistresses' Conference Junior Schools	NFER	National Federation of Educational Research	UCAS	Universities and Colleges Admissions Service for the UK
		NPA	National Progression Award		
HNC	Higher National Certificate	NQ	National Qualification	UCST	United Church Schools Trust
HND	Higher National Diploma	NQF	National Qualifications Framework	UKLA	UK Literacy Association
IAPS	Independent Association of Prep Schools	NQT	Newly Qualified Teacher	UKCISA	The UK Council for International Education
IB	International Baccalaureate	NVQ	National Vocational Qualifications	UWC	United World Colleges
ICT	Information and Communication Technology	OCR	Oxford, Cambridge and RSA Examinations	WISC	World International Studies Committee
IFF	Inspiring Futures Foundation (formerly ISCO)	OLA	Online Language Assessment for Modern Languages	WJEC	Welsh Joint Education Committee
IGCSE	International General Certificate of Secondary Education			WSSA	Welsh Secondary Schools Association
		Oxon	Oxford		

Index

Index

447